Human development
THE SPAN OF LIFE

Human development
THE SPAN OF LIFE

GEORGE KALUGER, Ph.D.
Professor, Department of Psychology,
Shippensburg State College,
Shippensburg, Pennsylvania

MERIEM FAIR KALUGER, Litt. M.
Psycho/Educational Consultant,
Shippensburg, Pennsylvania

SECOND EDITION
with **180** illustrations

The C. V. Mosby Company

ST. LOUIS • TORONTO • LONDON   1979

Cover photo: *Family Group,* an original sculpture by Elisabeth D. Model,
commissioned exclusively by
Collectors' Guild, Ltd., 601 West 26th Street, New York, NY 10001

SECOND EDITION

Copyright © 1979 by The C. V. Mosby Company

Previous edition copyrighted 1974

Printed in the United States of America

The C. V. Mosby Company
11830 Westline Industrial Drive, St. Louis, Missouri 63141

Library of Congress Cataloging in Publication Data

Kaluger, George.
  Human development.

  Includes bibliographical references and index.
  1. Developmental psychology. I. Kaluger, Meriem
Fair, 1921-   joint author. II. Title.
BF713.K34 1979   155   78-12022
ISBN 0-8016-2610-2

CB/CB/B 9 8 7 6 5 4 3 2   02/B/225

To
our parents
who, by precepts and examples,
taught us the joy of living, the goodness
of man, and the love of God.

Preface

The typical young adult students of today are a unique breed. Unlike most of their teachers, they have never known a world that was not subject to the impact of television viewing and computer technology. Does this make a difference in their growth and development? The answer is both yes and no. The advent of computers has expanded the horizons of knowledge in all areas far beyond what the teachers of these students had ever imagined in their own childhood and youth. The information coming forth from computers in the medical field has improved biomedical practice and extended heath care knowledge to the point that survival rates are up and life expectancy is lengthening. As far as television viewing is concerned, many people are exposed to an idea, attitude, or concept at the same moment, making it possible for the thoughts or actions of millions to be influenced. In the United States 27 to 38 million people may be watching a favorite program on a given night. Over a period of time, a commonality of behavioral or attitudinal patterns could evolve. What effects these may have on growth and development are the subject of much research. Certainly some form of social, emotional, cognitive, and/or moral change is possible.

Yet, some aspects of growth and development are fundamental and are not subject to change over the years. The basic physiological growth patterns and needs of ancient cavemen are the same for the people of today. Certain psychological and social developmental characteristics remain constant. The culture can influence certain aspects of growth and development, but innate factors prescribe what changes take place and in what way. A case in point is the advent of puberty. Each man and woman, the world over, will typically have experienced pubertal changes.

This transition from a child's body to an adult's body was bound to take place. However, nutritional factors, health status, and possibly climatic conditions may influence the age and the rate at which the changes were experienced. Environmental and genetic forces interact to influence the total development of an individual. In spite of this interaction, a common thread of development is found in all people, all races, and all cultures. All children must be able to sit up before they can walk, socialization processes are at work throughout an individual's life, the family unit is basic, and love is evident.

The life-span approach to developmental psychology was chosen for this text over the dimensional or topical approach because it tends to show the developing individual as a "whole" person rather than a fragmented individual. Chronological stages make it easier to identify with an age level and to relate developmental characteristics to individuals at the childhood, adolescence, or adulthood phases of growth. On each age level there is a presentation of core topics, such as physical, social, and personality development, which are continued throughout the life span. Developmental tasks are presented for each age division as are age level characteristics of behavior and development, group interaction and influences, and moral or value development. In addition, special emphasis is given to content areas that are particularly pertinent to a specific age level.

Many of the topics included in this text were derived from the questions most frequently asked by our students in undergraduate and graduate level classes. In a sense, the subject matter is directed to what we perceived to be the interests and needs of students studying human development and behavior. Our aim is to stress "continuity with change'' by presenting basic universal principles of growth and development, while indicating the significance of individual differences and recognizing the part that the environment and other factors play in creating those differences.

In this second edition, we have increased our scope of coverage. Chapter 1 in the first edition has been expanded and divided. The "Determinants of Development" constitute Chapter 2. The first chapter now contains eight theoretical views of human development that were not previously presented. The last chapter on old age in the first edition has been expanded and divided into two parts. The extended coverage of the elderly is a major change. Each of the other chapters has at least one important section added as well as a number of minor changes. More content is presented on relevant theories, sex role development, language development, identity and self-concept, the father, the one-parent family, birth order, and the choice to remain single in adulthood. The references have been updated extensively. Many new tables and illustrations, some very different in content, have been added. Although more research studies are cited, the focus is still on processes as a whole and not on isolated research content. The excerpts of the profiles used in this text are taken from our book, *Profiles in Human Development,* published in 1976 by The C. V. Mosby Company. This book of profiles, illustrations, and vignettes can be used as a supplement to this textbook.

We acknowledge and accept the dynamic influence of environmental factors, genetic foundations, psychosocial influences, and personal experiences. If there is any bias, it would be that we tend to emphasize universal principles of growth and development, as seen from a cross-cultural perspective, while recognizing the potent force of individualization and the differences that occur. Seminars with some very great people—and the studies of others—have no doubt influenced our thinking. Jerome Kagan, Jean Piaget, Bernice Neugarten, Carl Rogers, Arnold Gesell, and Jerome Bruner say much to us.

When you love what you are doing, you tend to allow a little of yourself to creep into your work. We have permitted ourselves to do some interpretive writing on research results, and we have included some personal commentaries. We have sought to label all personal observations and opinions as our own thinking so that the reader would not be misled. The intent was to make the text meaningful and thoughtful, as well as informative, for readers who would probably take only one course in developmental psychology.

We express our appreciation to our many students who have been a constant source of inspiration and inquiry to us. Our colleagues have been most supportive. We thank the members of the Unity Hi-Y Club who accepted us as their advisors and enabled us to closely observe thirty-five boys as they grew from preadolescence to manhood and then to the establishment of families of their own. A note of appreciation is extended to Mrs. Gayle Wassell and her third grade students at the Mainsville Elementary School, Shippensburg, Pennsylvania, for their original poetry. We also thank Mrs. Sherry Rollins' fourth grade class at the Central Elementary School, Shippensburg, Pennsylvania, for sharing the newspaper they published based on incidents from fairy tales.

We would like to acknowledge David Strickler of Newville, Pennsylvania and Harold Geyer of Shippensburg, Pennsylvania for their fine photographic contributions to this text. Their pictures truly express a sensitive feeling for people. We were happy to work with them. Special appreciation and thanks go to Norma Strassburger who has now typed manuscripts for six of our seven books and to Sandra Reamer who came through in a pinch to help with the typing chores. To our readers, have a good day and a nicer tomorrow. We invite you to write us if you have any questions or comments. We appreciate the personalized approach.

George Kaluger
Meriem Fair Kaluger

The authors: **Meriem and George Kaluger**

"I am a human being, whatever that may be. I speak for all of us who move and think and feel and whom time consumes. I speak as an individual unique in a universe beyond my understanding, and I speak for man. I am hemmed in by limitations of sense and mind and body, of place and time and circumstances, some of which I know but most of which I do not. I am like a man journeying through a forest, aware of occasional glints of light overhead with recollections of the long trail I have already traveled, and conscious of wider spaces ahead. I want to see more clearly where I have been and where I am going, and above all I want to know why I am where I am and why I am traveling at all."

John Berrill
Man's Emerging Mind
DODD, MEAD & CO.

Contents

Human development
THE SPAN OF LIFE

1 Life-span psychology

An ancient philosopher observed that one of the most significant questions one person can ask of another is "What do you see when you see a man?" The answer to this question will reflect the person's degree of understanding and insight, as well as his faith and acceptance, concerning the dignity of nature and human worthiness.

As a seed develops, changes, and matures into a tree by following a specified pattern of growth, so does an infant change and mature into an adult by following an established pattern of principles relating to growth and development. This maturational sequence is specific enough so that it can be identified, observed, and recorded. The sequence is the same for all individuals. The developmental process is not limited to one aspect of growth, however, since each child grows in five ways—physically, mentally, emotionally, socially, and spiritually. The environment makes an impact on this growth mechanism, but the step-by-step process remains the same. Adults ascribe positive or negative values to this developing personality. The insight that an adult possesses concerning human growth and development largely determines "what he sees when he sees a man."

INDIVIDUALITY AND UNIVERSALITY

A Vermont farmer is quoted as having said "People are mostly alike, but what difference they are can be powerful important." In one statement is the general concept of individuality and universality. "People are mostly alike . . ." reflects a sameness, a "universal likeness" of world man in his development. ". . . but what difference they are can be powerful important" suggests the magnitude and depth of individual differences that can be found in people.

The facts of human individuality are astound-ing. Each one of us is built in a highly distinctive way in every particular—physically, mentally, emotionally, socially, and morally—and these differences form the bases of individuality. It is well known that each individual has distinctive fingerprints and a natural odor, distinctive enough for a bloodhound to follow. It has also been determined that man has distinctive voice prints, lip prints, and footprints. A person can disguise himself in all kinds of wearing apparel and cosmetics, but "you can't fool Mother Nature." More startling are the differences that are inside people. There are variations in the size, shape, and operations of stomachs of normal people. There are also large differences in hearts and endocrine glands. Diversity of structure of the brain and nervous system is as great from man to man as is diversity between related species of animals. Each individual is "extraordinary." Although the illustrations given all pertain to physical growth, they could have been given equally well of any aspect of growth.

Universality refers to the commonality of man. Everyone can give examples of ways in which men and women the world over are alike. Under the facade of cultural influences man is pretty much the same physically, mentally, emotionally, socially, and spiritually. The five ways of growing up are purposely being emphasized so that the total developmental pattern of man can be realized instead of relegating it to just one or two areas of growth. The universality of man is deeply ingrained within the developmental processes. Babies are conceived and born the same way the world over. They go through the same stages in learning to walk and to talk. Children develop their self-concept, their processes of learning, and their adjustive patterns of behavior in much the same way. In other words, there are

1

some basic, fundamental principles of laws governing growth and development to which earthly man is subjected, whether he knows about them or not, whether he agrees with them or not, and whether he is ready for them or not. The scientific laws governing growth are universal and eternal.

The implications of individuality and universality are manifold. For one thing they state that man is like others in some very basic ways. Yet he is different enough in other ways to make him a unique being. The ultimate implication is to recognize the individual worth of each human being, understanding and accepting him, and at the same time understanding and accepting ourselves, seeking to make the most of ourselves with whatever traits we may have.

THE SPAN OF LIFE

The one thing that never changes in the world is the fact that everything changes all the time. Our life is a dizzy succession of changes for which we rarely seem prepared. Like the flowers that bloom and fade, like the grass that sprouts and withers, permanence is at best a dream. Yet, it all works out. Through it all, indeed behind it all, there is an element of stability and structure that serves as a basic foundation upon which a body, a mind, and a life will evolve. There is an essence of universality within the frame of reference called growth and development. In spite of the modifications, reorganizations, and transformations that emerge, there is "continuity with change." Each stage of growth and development has an encompassing relationship to other stages of life, yet it also has its own unique characteristics, needs, and demands. Life-span psychology considers growth and development, in its major components, from the event of conception to the incident of death, and slightly beyond.

The life span

As life advances and experiences increase, both internal and external phases of behavior and growth change constantly. The aim of developmental psychology, of which the study of the span of life is a part, is to learn about the changes that take place. By definition, developmental psychology is the study of the development of activity, growth, and behavior, including both its internal and external phases. Developmental psychologists attempt to determine the characteristic age changes from one developmental period to another. They are interested in learning why these changes come about, when they come about, how they come about, and what factors influence the changes for better or for worse. It is important to learn if the changes are universal and cross-cultural in nature (found in all societies) or if they are found only in certain individuals.

There is also interest in determining the ultimate goal of development and whether or not it is the same for all individuals. Admittedly, speculation on this topic is metaphysical in nature. At this point in time, abstract reasoning has the edge in investigating the nature of the principles and problems of the ultimate reality of the meaning of life and of being. Many psychologists relate to the principle that the goal of development is to enable the individual to adapt to the conditions of his life and to make the most of his human, physical, and psychological potential. Some refer to this goal of development as self-realization. Abraham Maslow[1] refers to this impetus toward "becoming" as self-actualization. He believes that life with a commitment to the highest values that man can envision brings on self-fulfillment and, thus, self-actualization. A different point of view is that of Eric Erikson[2] who believes that the ultimate standard of maturity is the development of a strong ego and a capacity for intimacy. B. F. Skinner[3] says that the concept of man's behavior is determined by external (environmental) factors, so the standard of maturity would be an anxiety-free hierarchy of responses to external stimuli. Different views and theories on development will be presented later in this chapter. But, as you can suspect, it is not easy to get a common consensus of the goal of development nor of the nature of man.

Traditional divisions of the life span include (1) prenatal, (2) infancy, (3) childhood, (4) adolescence, and (5) adulthood. Certainly the stages of life could be grossly delineated along those lines. But, as the amount of research on growth and development increases, psychologists find it desirable to expand some of these stages because within certain divisions, such as adulthood, there is too wide a difference between the adult at 25,

There was never any more inception than there is now,
Nor any more youth or age than there is now;
And will never be any more perfection than there
   is now,
Nor any more heaven or hell than there is now.

Walt Whitman
Leaves of Grass

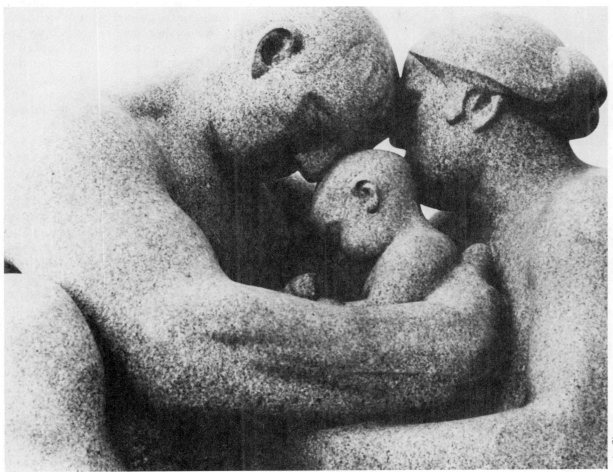

Audun Olsen

55, and 75 years of age. There is also a difference between the early adolescent, just passing
through puberty, and the late adolescent who is
ready for adulthood. What a preschool child of
four can do intellectually and physically is quite
different from that of the child of seven who, in
turn, cannot perform like the child of eleven!

An interesting sidelight on the adolescent stage
is that certain primitive societies, such as the Ma-
sai of East Africa and the natives of the Sepik and
Karawari River areas in Papua, New Guinea, do
not have a distinctive adolescent period. These
individuals move from childhood directly into
adulthood through the practice of puberty rites, a
series of ceremonies that induct the young into
manhood or womanhood. In this text, we separate the stages of growth and development into
stages that are related to more sophisticated
societies and that reflect the broadness of current
research findings.

Harold Geyer

The universality of developmental characteristics makes it possible to understand many cultures, races, and ethnic groups. Mothers care about their children in all parts of the world.

Cultural variations and norms

Although an effort is made to bring in research findings on culturally diverse or different segments of our Western society, there are times when the material will appear to be primarily related to what some call the "white, middle-class" group. There is no bias intended or omission by design. It is just that most of the research has been predicated on the largest and most common segment of the population. It is not exclusively white, nor is it exclusively middle class. It is a conglomerate of people who are mostly white, coming from an upper-lower and a lower-middle socioeconomic group. They do constitute a large majority and, thereby, suggest what the most common practices and levels of development are in Western society. The child-rearing practices, school demands, and adult expectations are made pronounced by the sheer number of people engaged in them. They set somewhat of a norm.

Because of the nature of our diverse population, it will be important for those interested in culturally different populations such as the Appalachian whites, Mexican Americans, Puerto Ricans, rural whites, lower-class milieu, Asian population, migrant workers, Indians, blacks, and other minority groups to recognize that some of the information included is "not the way we experience it." But recognize that most of the material is relevant, regardless of background. If you can distinguish between principles of growth and development that are universal in nature and behavioral or developmental principles that are culturally induced or man-made in nature, then you will be able to gain much from your reading.

It would be interesting to compare and relate man-made differences in behavior and development to the wide diversity of the population that is spread over a continent. As we survey the nation, we find large metropolitan areas with cultural centers, as well as inner cities; agricultural states on the plains; delta and seacoast areas; mountain and desert lands; uncomplicated small villages and towns; lands of forests and lakes; and suburbs that range from the economically sophisticated in nature to those composed of "ticky-tacky boxes" that all look alike. The point to be remembered is that babies, children, adolescents, and adults, in any social or cultural milieu, are more like other babies, children, adolescents, or adults than they are different. They are all to be respected, revered, and esteemed because they are all "children of the universe." We are all born. We live a life in which we seek to survive in as pleasant a manner as we can in our environment. We all eventually die. We come, we go. What we do in between is different only on the surface.

DEVELOPMENTAL PRINCIPLES

The principles of growth and development that follow reflect the universality of the laws by which man grows and develops. The maturational process, the sequential stages of development, and the directions of growth are fundamental to all human life everywhere and at any point in time in history.

Although the physical principles of maturational development unfold naturally because of their innate origin, they are subject to changes in rate of development and often to the extent to which they do develop. For example, under normal conditions, the sequential pattern of development in the prenatal state follows a predictable pattern. However, if the uterine movement of the mother should change due to the introduction of an adverse chemical or drug, such as thalidomide, then the unusual or unexpected change in the environment could affect the typical manner of development of the arms and legs of the embryo. Another example is that of a child raised in an environment that is lacking in sensory-stimulating experiences or is deficient in the proper nutritional values important to neural growth who, as a result, develops an ineffective or inefficient intellectual processing system. Never underestimate the importance of the environment in the developmental process. It is not the only influential factor, but it is quite significant in the part it plays.

Growth gradients

Human growth and development relate to physiological, psychological, and environmental processes that, by nature, are continuous and orderly. They bring about changes in the physical, mental, emotional, social, and moral components of being. Growth refers to organic changes and is basically quantitative in nature. Development generally refers to functional or nonorganic changes and is usually qualitative in nature. Development, therefore, is a life-long process that covers the entire pattern of human existence, whereas some aspects of growth do reach a point of maturity from which no further change is anticipated. The word *development,* however, has several meanings, some of which are not related to the developmental process, and

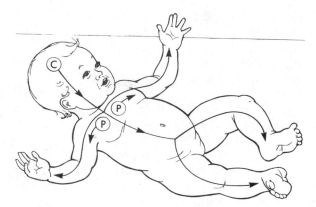

Fig. 1-1. Direction of cephalocaudal sequence, Ⓒ, is from maturation and control of head movement to trunk, to legs, and to feet movements and development. Direction of growth of proximodistal sequence, Ⓟ, is from maturation of the center of the body to development of peripheral parts of the body.

the reader should be aware of these different uses. Since growth and development imply change that is positive in nature, it should be noted that change can also take place in the direction of deterioration. Atrophy, the emaciation or wasting of tissues and organs, also appears. Although atrophy is more predominant in the latter stages of life, it can also be found to occur during the embryonic period when the secondary yolk sac disintegrates.

There are three principles related to directions of growth and development. The first direction of growth is the *cephalocaudal sequence,* which is sometimes referred to as the law of developmental direction. It relates to physical maturation and growth. The cephalocaudal sequence suggests that the direction of growth occurs from the head end to the foot (the tail end). The development of the major aspects of growth takes place in the head first, the trunk next, and the legs last. (See Fig. 1-1.) This direction is vividly illustrated in both prenatal and postnatal stages of development. In the embryonic state the brain and the central nervous system start to develop first, followed by features of the head, then the region of the trunk with its organs. The development of the head proceeds more rapidly than that of any other part of the body because of the importance of the brain and central nervous system to the operation of the rest of the body. At birth the head constitutes 20% of the body length. After the rest of the body grows to maturity the head will be only 8% of the body length. After birth babies first gain control of their head, eyes, mouth, and neck; then they gain control over the trunk. Babies can sit before they can stand, and they can stand before they can walk.

The second direction of growth is the *proximodistal sequence*. It also is related to physical growth. The proximodistal direction of development states that controlled movements proximal to the body axis (the parts of bodily members that lie closest to the center of the body) mature before those that are distal (further away). Progression is from the central parts of the body maturing earlier and functioning before those located nearer the periphery. Babies gain control of their shoulders before their hands. They can control their thighs before they can control their feet. The central nervous system develops more rapidly than the peripheral nervous system.

The third direction of growth is expressed by the principle of *differentiation*. This principle states that the trend of the direction of growth, physical, social, or otherwise, proceeds from mass to specific activities of development. Generalized development will occur before specific or specialized development can occur. In other words, development is from simple operations to more complex performances. It is characterized by increasing differentiation and complex organization. For example, there will be a development of gross muscle usage before fine muscle control can take place. When new babies cry, they seem to cry with their whole body (general); later, they cry only with the upper part of their body, with their shoulders and chests heaving and their faces all red. Even later in development they cry only with their face and eyes. Eventually, only the eyes cry and, perhaps, only a tear escapes without the eyes moving at all. Babies learn to grasp with their whole hand before making use of their thumb and forefinger. They crawl before they creep, and they creep before they walk. Socially, they respond to many people before they decide that they really prefer their mother. Development in all areas—intellectually, socially, emotionally, physically, and morally—proceeds from general to specific.

Specific principles

There are several significant facts about development that are fundamental and predictable and thus important to the understanding of growth and development. The first principle indicates that physical, motor, speech, and cognitive development follow a definite, orderly, sequential, predictable pattern. Growth is a continuous process following an unfolding maturational pattern. It is directional. Normally, each child passes through each stage in the developmental process. Although individual differences exist within the developmental pattern, they do not appreciably influence the general trend of development for the most part. Individual cases may be exceptions, however, because of environmental interference.

A second principle is that development comes from maturation, learning, and influences of the environment. The maturational pattern is genetically programmed so that certain aspects of physiological growth take place innately. The environment provides opportunities for learning that may hinder or aid the maturational process in developing organic elements to their maximum. The maturational process is, in turn, influential in determining when and if certain types of learning are ready to take place. For example, a child will be unable to be toilet trained, walk, read, or respond to conceptual development until the "teachable moment," as established by physiological maturation, has arrived. Parents and teachers should be happy to know that certain undesirable behavior patterns can be changed by maturation and learning, but only if the child learns the new behavior pattern.

A third principle states that although all individuals follow a definite pattern of growth and development, they do so in their own style. Some children develop smoothly, others develop in spurts. Individual differences are partly due to differences in hereditary endowment, to the manner or rate in which the maturational process manifests itself, and to environmental influences and the nature of learning that has taken place. Factors that may be responsible for producing

Harold Geyer

Developmental principles are most evident in early infancy. The cephalocaudal direction of growth can be traced as baby learns to control the head and upper part of the body before being able to control the lower half.

differences in rate of development include innate sex differences (male or female), appropriateness of glandular functions, adequacy of nutrition, genetic endowment, rate of intellectual development, nature of health, amount of fresh air and sunshine, position of the child within the family as regards siblings, incentive and motivational drive, and parental attitudes, interest, and support. The rate of growth is not the same for all children, nor is it consistent for a specific child. There is some correlation between different types of growth, as for example, a heavy child may be a late walker; a child may differ in the rate of growth physically, mentally, socially, emotionally, and morally.

A fourth developmental principle suggests that each phase or stage of life has characteristic traits that are typical of that phase. The phases of life in chronological order are as follows: germinal, embryonic, and fetal before birth, neonatal, infancy (0 to 2 years), early childhood (3 to 5 years), middle childhood (6 to 8 years), late childhood (9 to 11 years), early adolescence (12 to 15 years), middle to late adolescence (16 to 18 years), late adolescence to emerging adulthood (19 to 22 years), early adulthood (23 to 42 years), middle adulthood (43 to 64 years), late adulthood (65 to 74 years), and very old age (75 years and older). Each stage has its own psychology, distinguishing traits and features, and developmental tasks to be achieved.

The fifth principle stresses that it is during infancy and early childhood that basic attitudes, traits, life-styles, behaviors, and patterns of growth are formed. These factors will determine how the individual will develop as he grows older. Different physical and psychological traits have their roots in the earlier stages of life. Basic personality patterns may be set during the first five years of life.[4] The patterns are not irreversible, but they are foundational; future growth builds on them. The role that children play in the family and in the peer group will determine whether they develop into leaders, followers, or nonresponders.[4] Because of the plasticity of the central nervous system of early childhood, children are capable of being molded into a wide variety of developmental patterns by environmental and psychological influences.

A sixth principle is a little less definite in nature because it has not been explained adequately. It is the concept of critical periods in development. The term is used in different ways. It is used to imply a time period in development when an aspect of growth is most susceptible to damage by abnormal conditions. For example, the second to eighth weeks after conception are most critical in terms of being adversely affected by a change in the mother's blood chemistry brought on by a case of rubella (German measles).

A second interpretation of the critical period principle seeks to suggest that there are periods when some forms of development can benefit the most from certain types of training. In other words, there is a point in time when baby can best develop a muscle structure suitable for sports or develop a socialized responsiveness to others; or, more specifically, a time to develop eye and hand motor match or perceptual development. This definition of critical period still needs to be explored.

The third definition relates to the concept of imprinting that is found in animals and birds. It is known that there is a sensitive period when a newly born animal or bird can form a strong social attachment to either the mother or a mother-substitute. The mother-substitute can even be a human being or, for that matter, any moving object. The question is whether or not such a sensitive or critical period exists in human babies. There is a related concept called *mother-infant bonding*. At birth, the newborn is placed on the abdomen of the mother, even before the umbilical cord is cut. Supposedly, a stronger attachment results between baby and mother than would occur otherwise.

BASIC PROCESSES RELATED TO EFFICIENT LIVING

There are many processes at work within the human body, but none of them are as fundamental as homeostasis, motivation, and learning. They are responsible for man's physical and psychological well-being and are instrumental in initiating behavior for a variety of purposes. They are crucial for survival. Many other functions take place as a result of these three processes. For man's body and mind to operate at a high level of efficiency and effectiveness it is necessary for homeostasis, maturation, and learning to function at peak levels of performance.

Homeostasis

In general, the physical scientific laws of the universe operate in precise and specific ways. As long as these laws operate as they were intended to, according to nature, all will be well. However, whenever anything interferes with the effective, efficient operation of these laws, unpleasant, even dire, consequences result. Natural forces then seek to bring about conditions that will restore the initial balance of nature so that the principles once again can operate as they were intended to. To provide an equilibrium, to restore a balance, to be in harmony with the underlying principles and laws by which the universe operates is fundamental to the very essence of life and the universe itself.

Homeostasis is a principle that proclaims that there is a tendency for the body to seek to maintain a relatively stable, constant state of equilibrium of its internal environment, even under changing external or internal circumstances. The purpose of this equilibrium is to maintain a state of constancy of the physiological processes so that all of the "laws" governing the body will "work in harmony" and permit the individual to perform at an efficient and effective level of being. For example, normal body temperature is 98.6° F. It is interesting to note that the body maintains that temperature rather well, whether the air temperature is 120° or 32° F. In general, rapid adjustments are made by the autonomic nervous system to restore or maintain the balance while slower adjustments occur through chemical and hormonal influences.

This demand for a steady, balanced internal constitution, however, does allow for necessary responses of the body to meet the needs of tissues. In some ways it may be said that "Mother Nature," in her wisdom, uses the principle of homeostasis to keep the body in good working order while, at the same time, providing the means by which the person is compelled to do those things that help to keep individual tissues and organisms in good condition. To illustrate, the tissues of the body need to have food to function. A person cannot eat enough food at one

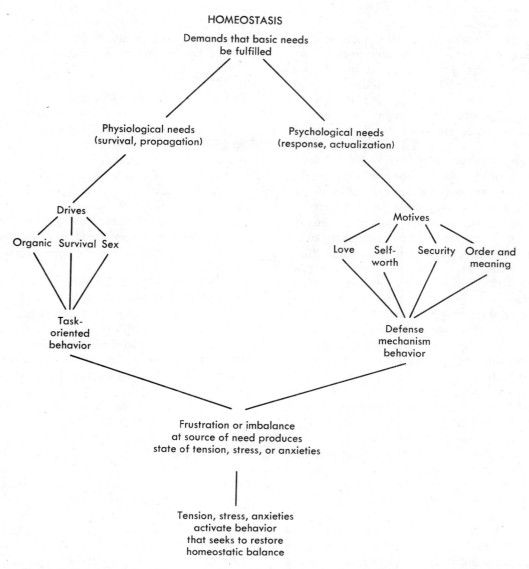

Fig. 1-2. The principle of homeostasis and how it operates to provide a relatively stable, constant state of physiological and psychological balance.

sitting to last him for a lifetime. In fact, he cannot eat enought food to last him for a whole month, or even a whole week. So on the one hand there is a need to maintain a stable, constant balance, and, on the other hand, there is a "built-in" process by which "tissue needs" go out of equilibrium. Means are provided by which behavior that can restore the balance is initiated.

Fig. 1-2 seeks to interpret how the homeostatic principle operates. At the outset it must be said that we are taking some liberties with the technical definition of homeostasis by including psychological processes in its coverage. Actually, there is a seeking of balance in promoting mental well-being, just as there is in achieving physical well-being. Therefore there is a similarity involved when one considers "that which is responsible for initiating behavior." The term *adjustive behavior* is used to indicate the process that sets in motion activities intended to restore mental, or emotional, equilibrium. The difference between homeostatic activity and adjustive behavior is the means by which the action is pursued. Homeostasis uses the autonomic nervous system and some glandular activity; adjustive behavior may use these same elements, but it also uses cognitive (intellectual) and ego functions. Consider Fig. 1-2 as presenting the principle that seeks to explain what it is that initiates the need for some form of behavior to take place.

There are three major aims or goals of the human organism. One is to maintain a physiological well-being for the purpose of survival, a second is the propagation of the species, and the third is to strive for self-actualization and enhancement of one's psychological well-being. The conditions that must be satisfied may be innate, ones with which a person is born, or they may be acquired by learning or experiencing within the environment. Most physiological demands are innate, but the body may learn to crave some things, such as certain drugs, that develop physiological cravings. Innate needs, or genetically programmed behavior, are within themselves a necessary and sufficient condition for the survival of man. Some psychological needs, such as a need for love, security, self-worth, and structure (order and meaning), are considered by many psychologists to be innate. However, many emotional needs are acquired by interacting with people and conditions in the environment as one works his way through the growing-up process. In either area, physical or emotional, when conditions are not as they should be (according to the laws that indicate what is needed to maintain a state of well-being), an imbalance occurs, indicating that there is a deficiency or insufficiency of something needed for an equilibrium to exist. Whenever a disequilibrium occurs, stress or anxieties are created. These, in turn, bring about energy mobilization, which activates the organism to action or behavior. Behavior is actually initiated by the process of motivation.

Motivation

There is a reason or cause responsible for everything that a person does. Behind each action is an explanation, and included in that explanation will be an element of the motivational process. The term *motivation* is used to refer to the process by which behavior is initiated in response to a need, a deficiency, or a lack in the organism or person. Need-instigated behavior is goal-oriented in the sense that the behavior initiated is directed toward a goal or objective that, when attained, will satisfy the need by overcoming the deficiency and restoring the balance (Fig. 1-3). The type of behavior initiated depends on the type of need encountered, physiological or psychological. If the need is physiological, the behavior becomes task-oriented in the sense of "I have a task to fulfill; I must get some food" (or water, sleep, release of bowel or bladder tension, or whatever the biological need may be). If the need is psychological, a defense mechanism is used. Such behavior may be an aggressive action to get what one needs or may be a withdrawal reaction to get away from the problem. Compromise behavior is of the kind that is willing to accept secondary goals if the primary goal is difficult to attain. Defense mechanisms are identifiable forms of normal behavior, utilized to consciously or unconsciously meet psychological needs. If the individual's actions enable him to adjust to the environmental circumstances in order to get something done, then it is considered coping behavior.

In any case if the goal is reached and it is a

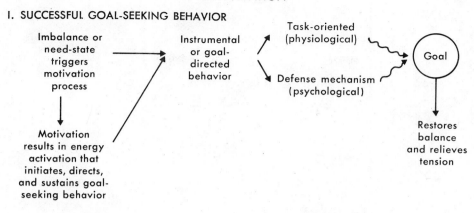

MOTIVATION

I. SUCCESSFUL GOAL-SEEKING BEHAVIOR

II. UNSUCCESSFUL GOAL-SEEKING BEHAVIOR

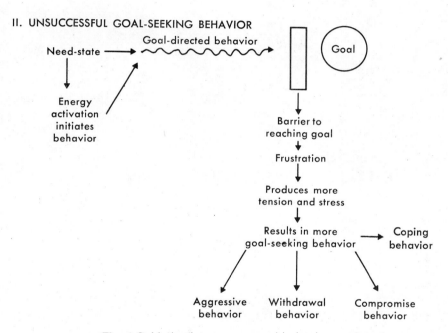

Fig. 1-3. Motivation process and behavior produced.

proper goal (in the sense of providing what it was thought it would provide), the deficiency is overcome, balance is restored, and the individual no longer has any stress or anxiety on that account. If the goal is not appropriate or if the individual is prevented from attaining the goal for some reason, such as use of the wrong behavior, obstacles that have not been overcome, or personal limitations that restrict the use of appropriate behavior, then the inability to gain the needed goal produces a frustration. The frustration, in turn, produces more stress and anxiety, since the need has not been relieved, and more behavior is produced.

Learning

How does a person know what behavior is appropriate for reaching a desired aim? What

Learning by experiences and the use of all of the senses helps to develop a better understanding of the world around us.

would be behavior that would be instrumental in restoring the physiological or psychological balance? An infant is born with some simple behaviors for this purpose, such as the sucking reflex, but most behavior is determined by the reasoning, cognitive process. "I know I have a need for some water, I am thirsty. My mouth is dry, my lips are parched, and I recognize those symptoms from the past as indicating that I am thirsty. Let's see, now, where is there a faucet or a fountain?" This individual has learned what the symptoms of thirst were and what could produce water. An aborigine who has never been out of the wilds of his native bush country could perish from a lack of water if he were trapped in a room in a modern building, even if a drinking fountain were in that room. He may never have learned

what a drinking fountain is or how to operate it to get water. Learning provides man with cognitive and apperceptive materials that enable him to determine appropriate behavior for reaching a desired goal.

Learning is fundamental to the good life. There is a need to learn those things that will help one to survive and to actualize in his culture and environment. The more complex the society or culture within which one lives the more facts and skills one must learn to be able to have a comfortable level of physical and mental balance. The "getting of some goods" may be more difficult or complicated in highly stylized societies. An individual must develop his processes of learning to meet the demands of his culture. The learning processes consist of the perceptual systems, in-

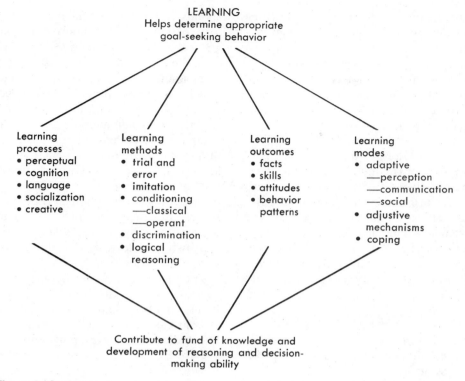

Fig. 1-4. Component parts of learning process that influence quality of goal-seeking behavior.

cluding the visual, auditory, and tactile modalities of learning, language, reasoning or cognitive processes, and creative processes (Fig. 1-4). What a person learns are facts, skills and habits, attitudes or interests (affect), and behavior patterns. He learns these things by the processes of trial and error, conditioning, or associative insight (developed reasoning ability). He makes use of them in adjustive, adaptive, or coping behavior.

Man has a freedom of choice in initiating behavior and in making decisions. He can choose an action that will be correct or one that will be wrong. Perhaps the action will be neutral and produce no results. Once a behavior is initiated, however, its actions are taken over by the cause-and-effect element inherent within all physical and some psychological laws. The outcomes of many actions can be predicted if one could only know all the principles and laws of

nature involved. It behooves an individual to develop a value judgment system, a life philosophy of good and bad, better or worse, desirable or undesirable, to enable him to make decisions in keeping with what he considers to be most important in his life. The environment will contribute, positively or negatively, to the decision-making process. A psychological behaviorist would ask that he learn to stress behavioral controls, how to manipulate factors in the environment to bring about desired results by the use of reinforcement, rewards, or punishment. A psychological existentialist or humanist would suggest that he learn how to achieve self-actualization by looking to the inner self and determining what he feels or values.

Behavior can be learned or innate. Reflexes are an example of unlearned behavior. Most behavior, by far, is learned or initiated on the basis of learned elements. Adaptive behavior is any modification or change in structure or behavior that helps the organism to meet environmental demands. The term is sometimes used more loosely to imply any beneficial change to meet environmental demands. Coping behavior is a learned action that permits an individual to live with extenuating or unwanted circumstances. It enables an individual to adjust to the circumstances so that he can get things done. Adaptive behavior may be behavior in which physiological changes take place for the individual to survive, such as learning to live with contaminated water that is needed for drinking or living with air pollution in larger cities. Coping behavior may be learning to live with a handicap or with the loss of a loved one. All individuals have the capacity and the potential for self-fulfillment. They also have the adaptive power to overcome obstacles of their own or of their environments' making.

VIEWS OF HUMAN DEVELOPMENT

What is the basic nature of human development? There are a number of proponents of different views. None of these views appear to answer all the questions raised concerning growth and development, but all of them offer a rationale that should be considered for the contribution that they make toward a systematic understanding of human development.

Maturational view

A maturational view of development emphasizes the emergence of physical, physiological, and sexual changes under the influence of internal maturational forces, leaving little room for environmental influences. Physical and motor development occur in an almost inevitable, orderly sequential pattern that is universal, regardless of sociocultural environment.

G. Stanley Hall,[5] considered by many to be the father of the child-study movement in America, developed what has come to be called the recapitulation theory. The thesis of his theory is that each individual reenacts or relives each major stage in evolutionary development. He outlined four major stages of development: first, infancy, from birth to age 4, during which the child evolves through the animal stage of development; second, childhood, ages 5 to 7, which corre-

sponds to the hunting-fishing era of human history, playing cowboys and Indians, and hide and go seek; third, youth, ages 8 to 12, the preadolescent period, a savage stage characterized by instinct, but with a predisposition to learn; and fourth, puberty and adolescence, ages 13 to 24, the age of "bud and promise for the race," a time of transition when an individual becomes a more complete and competent organism. Adulthood is the "rational man," the final product of the adolescent period. Hall's works have long been used in the study of adolescence, where he made tremendous contributions. Today, updated research has lessened the influence of Hall's original thinking. Nevertheless, Hall provides a worthwhile historical perspective for human development theory.

The individual who has done much, if not the most, to explore the importance of maturational determinants in shaping human development was Arnold Gesell.[6,7] Gesell did extensive longitudinal studies of the developing human from birth to age 16. He placed great stress on observable behaviors of the child or adolescent and on the role of the environmental variables in adolescent development. He believed that the pattern of human development, particularly physical, followed certain laws of physical maturation that evolved and unfolded in very specific, predetermined ways if they were not interfered with by environmental factors. An individual's behavior resulted from both maturational and environmental factors in the form of conscious rather than unconscious growth. Although Gesell's works are well documented with films and recorded observations and his principles and sequences of physical development are generally well recognized and accepted, a limitation of his work is that he did not stress environmental influences as much as later researchers thought he should.

Interactionistic view

Interactionism recognizes the importance of the relationship between the developing person and the environment. At any one moment the level of total development depends upon the maturation level of development plus the experience and materials encountered in the environment. A simple formula might be: *Maturation +*

Experience = Level of Development. Although development is genetically based in some respects, it is influenced by environmental forces. As a result, it is not a steady, continuous, uninterrupted process; rather it is one that is marked by stages, involving shifts in ways of thinking and behaving that are influenced by the environment. The emphasis is on processes and not on end results. The environment is involved in the extent to which it slows down, speeds up, or contributes to the process of development.

Jean Piaget's theory[8] covers the development of intelligence over the life span. It has influenced much of the research in the fields of perceptual and intellectual growth. All knowledge, according to Piaget, comes from interaction with the environment. The infant has certain reflex behaviors and random movements that can be used in interacting with objects and events in the environment. Knowledge comes as the baby makes a link or connection between his actions and the objects with which he comes into contact. The link becomes a construction of reality, as the baby sees it. With an accumulation of understanding, stages of intellectual development are created. This understanding will filter into other areas, such as social, language, and moral development. If there is a limitation to Piaget's theory, it is in a lack of thorough discussion of physical, motor, and neurological development of the child in the prenatal and postnatal periods of life. Jerome Bruner[9] does relate more to the physical development of the child and to how environmentally produced changes occur in the development of capabilities. Bruner is concerned with a child's thinking process and how knowledge develops out of an interaction between environment and maturational development.

Whereas Piaget and Bruner postulated an interaction between genetic forces and the environment in the development of intelligence, Noam Chomsky[10] postulated an interaction in the development of language. Chomsky is a psychologist who believes that the development of language is based on a maturation of innate potentials for language rather than on the acquiring of language by the process of imitation. His main point is that a child learns a language very rap-idly. Between the ages of 2 and 4, the average child develops from the use of one- or two-word expressions to almost complete command of grammar and syntax. Chomsky does say that language acquisition depends on both the underlying maturation of the brain, whose growth is phenomenal in the first four years of life, and on exposure to a language. Environmental factors are, however, deemphasized, while focus is kept on the supposedly innate, fixed structure common to the use of language.

Genetic-oriented view

The genetic-oriented fields of study of most recent origin are the fields of sociobiology and the new ethologism. Ethology is the study of animal behavior for what it may reveal about humans. In the new ethology animal behavior is studied for the purpose of determining what differences or similarities there are in social behaviors between humans and their nearest primate cognates. Jones[11] believes that there are remarkable likenesses. The implication is that behavior is genetically induced. Man is both the product and the prisoner of his genes. Eibl-Eibesfeldt[12] has studied social behavior in many cultures around the world and has found amazing parallelism in mannerisms, facial expressions, reactions to babies, and the like. The similarities must stem from a biological source.

Sociobiologists, some of whom are ethologists, suggest that genetic factors control our behavior far more than we think. The environment is involved, to be sure, but only as it contributes to the genetically determined outcome. These outcomes are primarily survival in nature. Pursuing survival is basically survival of the species; therefore it is possible for an individual to be altruistic and charitable to others only because of what the individual and/or species gains in return. The production and wide distribution of genes ensures survival, and therefore, is a paramount goal. Writing about survival, Konrad Lorenz,[13] a Nobel-prizewinning ethologist, states that conflict, both in the family and with outsiders, is the essence of life if the right amount of aggression—neither too much nor too little—is used to gain reciprocal altruisms. "I'll do for you, if you will do for me." The environment becomes the arena

The interactionistic view of development implies a strong interplay between genetic aspects of development and environmental forces. Behavior learning theories suggest that overt behavior of children is basically learned behavior, shaped by the environment.

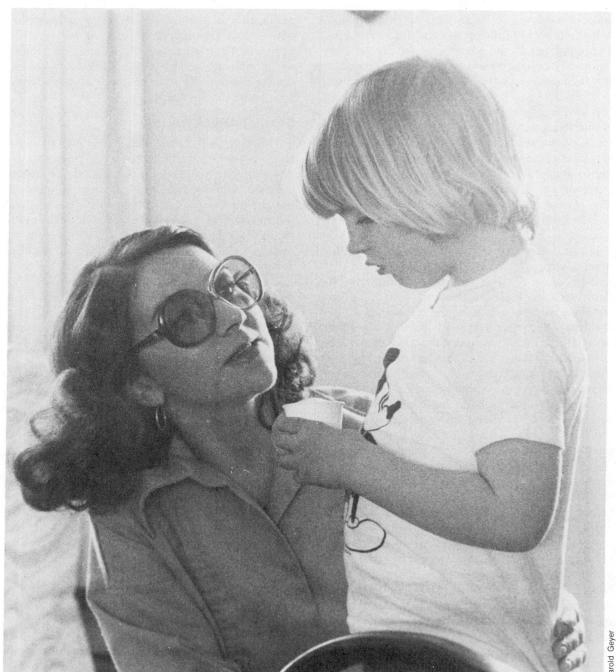

Harold Geyer

where exchanges of favors are made for the purpose of survival. Babies smile and they are picked up and cuddled.

Needless to say, sociobiology and ethology are controversial and have strong opposition. However, the number of scientists who are taking a closer look at these approaches for what they may have to offer in the study of human development is also surprising.

Environmental-oriented view

A point of view opposing ethology is that of mechanistic or behavior-learning theories, where the primary motivator of development and behavior is the environment. It manipulates basic biological and psychological drives and needs by offering rewards for "good" or "correct" behavior and punishment for undesirable behavior. We are what our environment makes us. Changes within the individual are quantitative and therefore are measurable, providing scientists with "proofs" that learning (change in behavior) is taking place. The two basic processes by which learning takes place are classical conditioning and operant or instrumental conditioning. Classical conditioning establishes a relationship between a stimulus and a reward and an accompanying behavior. The stimulus can be the shaking of a box of dry cat food like Friskies. The response is the cat running or coming to be fed. The reward is being given Friskies. Soon the cat responds to the stimulus alone, the shaking of the box, and it will come on signal.

Operant conditioning involves the giving of a reward immediately after obtaining the desired behavior. No stimulus is provided to initiate a behavior. In this case, children (or animals) receive a reward like something to eat or social approval ("good boy") after they have performed the desired behavior. It may be necessary to build by small behavioral steps to the complete desired behavior. Afterwards, the behavior is maintained by reward reinforcement. The procedure is much more complex than presented here. B. F. Skinner[14] has developed elaborate designs whereby all types of animal and human behavior can be instrumentally influenced and changed. Albert Bandura,[15] who has done much work with overt behavior of children, is con-

cerned with complex social behavior, such as skill acquisition, learned aggression, and fear. Behavior modification or behavior therapy are terms used to describe behaviorists who work with people. Behaviorists who work with animals are considered to be in the classical field of experimental psychology.

Psychodynamic view

There are a group of psychoanalytical theories that view the individual as generally seeking to resolve conflicts that arise between internal drives and forces of energy and constraints imposed upon them by a conscience or awareness of values held by society in general and significant persons in the individual's life in particular. The nature of the conflict differs according to the stage of development that the person has attained. Sigmund Freud[16] postulates the major area of conflict, at any stage, to involve psychosexual or pleasure-seeking drives. This conflict may involve periods of anxiety, periods of sexual excitement, and sometimes personality disturbance. Psychosexual development at first involves a close relationship to the parents, especially the mother; then, about the time of puberty, there is a loosening of the emotional ties to the parents.

A sociopsychoanalytical view is presented by Erik Erikson.[17] He modified Freud's theory of psychosexual development and has used modern sociopsychology and anthropology to describe emotional and personality development across the life span. He describes eight stages of an individual's development, each stage with a psychosocial task to master. There is the possibility of a conflict on each stage; the conflict or task must be successfully resolved so that a positive quality can be built into the personality structure and further development take place. The overall task is to acquire a positive ego identity while moving from one stage to the other. The eight stages are discussed in a future chapter.

Not all psychodynamic theories are psychoanalytical in thought. A group of these theories clusters around the terms *humanistic, existential,* or *self-theory psychology*. They tend to emphasize the positive aspects of the human potential. The basic motive for each individual is self-realization, a tendency toward growth and fulfillment as a human being. Carl Rogers[18] speaks of personal growth toward the goal of self-acceptance. He introduces the ideas of the innate goodness of the self, its natural potential, and its desire for knowledge and healthy growth. What is important is that the individual becomes aware of his own potential for growth. Awareness of the various aspects of current external situations is also important.

Abraham Maslow[1] has contributed heavily to the theory of human growth with two concepts. First, he speaks of nested motivation, the idea that human motives are nested in a hierarchical order and that a person is always motivated to higher-order motives as lower-order motives are satisfied. Once the motives of survival (food, water, and so on) are satisfied, the individual seeks higher-order motives such as affiliations, achievement, beauty, creativity, and altruistic motives. The second concept is that of self-actualization, which is attained when individuals make real the breadth and depth of their human potentialities. Complete human beings not only fulfill their needs, but they cope, resolve conflicts, give support to others, and contribute to their societies. The psychoanalyst emphasizes the importance of resolving conflicts originating in the unconscious; the behaviorist stresses interaction with the environment for the purpose of learning desired behaviors; the self-actualization theory concentrates on inner qualities that enhance the personal growth of the individual.

Elastic mind view

There is a group of psychologists who are suggesting that children may not be as vulnerable or irreversibly impressionable in their early years as has generally been assumed. The way children are raised by their parents, whether their homes are happy or not, or how troubled the parents may be really does not matter because these factors have little or nothing to do with the way they turn out as adults. The implications are that people keep remaking their lives all the time and what happens to them later, including what they do for themselves, pretty well compensates for earlier disadvantages in child rearing. Whether this view is just a fleeting, insignificant thought or

a virtual movement still needs to be determined.

An advocate of this view is Jerome Kagan[19] who expanded on this topic in an article "The Baby's Elastic Mind." Kagan concludes that new discoveries about the human infant "imply that his first experiences may be permanently lost. . . . I suspect that it is not until a child is five or six years old . . . that we get a more reliable view of the future. The infant's mind may be more like a sandy beach on a windy day than a reel of recording tape." To some extent, Kagan draws on his research with a tribe of Guatemalan Indians who keep their newborns and infants in virtual isolation for the first two years of life. At first, after this period of isolation, they appeared retarded. However, a study done with the same children ten years later showed them to be as intelligent as other children in a school setting. The point he makes is that some conditions, previously thought to be irreversible, are reversible and changeable. Thus the use of the term, the baby's elastic mind.

There is a suggestion by Arlene Skolnick[20] in her article, "The Myth of the Vulnerable Child," that too frequently poor and disadvantaged parents have been faulted for the inadequate development of their children when the consequences more often than not resulted from the failings of the community at large. Nevertheless, much of what is done to children can be undone if the necessary effort is put forth. There is no necessary connection between a disadvantaged childhood and a troubled adulthood. People can and often do succeed in refashioning their lives. Again, the emphasis is on the point that what happens to children in their infant or early childhood years is not necessarily imprinted on them for life. It is possible for the child's mind and personality to reshape itself to more adjustive forms.

The great concern, if this elastic-mind view of babyhood has any merit, is that attempts to improve the quality of parenting, child-rearing practices, and early childhood development in general may be considered inappropriate and unnecessary. Albert Rosenfeld[21] expresses concern that the more extreme statements of this movement may be taken seriously and that parents, government, and society may rationalize their way out of any responsibility for early childhood education and concerns. Will people care less about the upbringing of the children because what happens in early childhood does not matter? Fortunately, there are a number of studies showing that at least some types of infant and early childhood experiences do matter. Mother-infant bonding research offers impressive evidence that parent-child interaction in the first few hours after birth can affect later emotional life. Many longitudinal studies show relationships between early childhood experiences and emotional development. Work with infants and preschoolers with Down's syndrome (a form of mental deficiency) and blind infants demonstrates the amazing positive growth that can take place. Sensory stimulation in early childhood is essential for intellectual development.

Perhaps the emphasis on the elastic-mind view of development should not be placed on the speculation that early childhood and infancy experiences have no direct influence on later development. Rather, the emphasis should be placed on the point that early childhood and infancy traumas and disadvantages are reversible and can be overcome by personal effort and/or concentrated group effort.

Cultural conditioning view

Cultural anthropologists, such as Margaret Mead[22] and Ruth Benedict,[23] stress the role of culture in personality development and socialization. In their studies, they contrasted primitive cultures with those of Western societies and found distinct cultural differences that influence growth and development patterns. The basic premise of their observations is best illustrated by the principle of continuity versus discontinuity in cultural conditioning. Although the stress in the cultural conditioning view of development is on cultural influences, it should be stated that, in her later writing, Mead showed some recognition of universal aspects of development (incest taboo, for example) and more acknowledgment of the biological role in human development.

Mead and Benedict view growth as a continuous process begun at birth. The more that the culture instills in the children the type of behavior and beliefs that they must exhibit as adults, the

more continuous and less disruptive will be their growth. Mead discovered, for example, that the children of Samoa and the Arapesh of New Guinea follow a relatively continual growth pattern, with no abrupt changes from one age to another. The individuals are not expected to behave one way as a child, another way as an adolescent, and yet another way as an adult. They do not have to change or unlearn as an adult what they learned as a child. There is no sudden change or transition from one pattern of behavior to another. As children, boys play with a bow and arrow at hunting games. As adults, this hunting "play" becomes hunting "work." There is no discontinuity. Social patterns of behavior, such as dominance over younger siblings and sex roles, are also continuous, merging into adult behavior.

By contrast, in Western cultures children have few responsibilities. As they grow up, they must assume drastically different roles. There is a shift from nonresponsible play to responsible work. The child in Western cultures must drop his childhood submissive behavior and adopt its opposite, dominance, as he becomes an adult. In regard to psychosexual development, in Western culture sexuality is denied or deemphasized in childhood and adolescence. When the older adolescent becomes sexually mature, attitudes developed earlier must be changed so the individual can become a sexually responsive adult.

By showing that there is continuity of development in some cultures and not in others, some doubt is cast upon the universality of the concept of stages of growth and development. However, we were interested to note that the continuity versus discontinuity format can exist within the same country. For example, as recently as 1978, we observed the continuity pattern among the primitive cultures of the Sepik and Karawari River areas in Papua New Guinea. There appeared to be no "adolescent" stage of development. The skin-cutting ceremonies and the puberty rites marked the transition from childhood into adulthood, not only with "all the rights and privileges thereof," but also with the skills, knowledge, and responsibilities of adulthood. In the same country, in Port Moresby, their largest city, there was a distinct adolescent group, as

George Kaluger

The family unit is the focal point of all societies. The culture, however, influences the direction of attitudinal growth.

evident by the young people attending high schools and colleges; they exhibited characteristics of individuals in transition from childhood to adulthood. Cultural anthropologists see the continuous growth process as a cultural phenomenon, with individuals reacting to the social expectations of their culture. Only those societies that emphasize discontinuity of behavior—one type of behavior as a child and another as an adult—can be described as "age-grade societies" or as having stages of growth.

Psychosocial view

Robert Havighurst[24] primarily addresses himself to human growth and development in Western societies. As such, he is interested in stages of growth, predicated somewhat on an age basis. At each stage, he presents some major developmental tasks that must be mastered or achieved in order to meet the developmental needs of that age level. His developmental task theory is an eclectic one combining previously developed concepts into one theory. In general, Havighurst

In most Western societies, a developmental task for a 5- or 6-year-old is to enter school and begin formal learning.

seeks to combine the age level needs of the individual with the demands of society—or the culture—for that stage of development. What the individual needs and what society demands comprise the developmental tasks. The tasks are the skills, knowledge, behaviors, and attitudes that an individual has to acquire through physical maturation, social learning, and personal effort.

The developmental tasks may differ from culture to culture, depending on biological, psychological, and cultural expectations of the group. Tasks that are determined primarily by biological factors may be almost universal in nature. Tasks determined by cultural elements may differ greatly, not only from culture to culture, but also according to the demands of socioeconomic classes or "caste" systems existing within a culture. The behavior patterns learned are essential to personal and social adjustment; indeed, some of the tasks to be learned are vital to survival, especially in the earlier years. Each phase or stage of development has a number of tasks or organizational (intellectual) patterns that must be learned if the individual is to achieve the level of maturity expected by the cultural group. The expectations change at each stage of development. These changes, at least for adulthood, have been written in a popularized form by Gail Sheehy in "Passages."[25] Our book, "Profiles of Human Development,"[26] presents human experiences and events extended over the entire span of life.

Havighurst states that "A developmental task is a task which arises at or about a certain period in the life of the individual, successful achievement of which leads to his happiness and to success with later tasks, while failure leads to unhappiness in the individual, disapproval by the society and difficulty with later tasks." Examples of developmental tasks in infancy and early childhood are learning to take solid food, to achieve physiological stability, and to form simple concepts of social and physical reality. In middle childhood some tasks are to learn physical skills necessary for games and to learn appropriate sex roles. In adolescence, tasks include developing new relations with age mates of both sexes and developing intellectual skills necessary for civic competence. Early adulthood tasks may include selecting a mate and getting started in an occupation. Some middle adulthood tasks are establishing and maintaining an economic standard of living and, if married, relating oneself to one's spouse as a person. In later maturity, tasks include adjusting to retirement and reduced income and establishing satisfactory physical living arrangements. In this book developmental tasks will be presented for each age level discussed.

STUDY GUIDE

1. What are the definitions of individuality and universality, and what are their implications for the growth and development of individuals?
2. State the three principles related to directions of growth and development and define them.
3. Six specific developmental principles are mentioned. What are they?
4. Define "developmental task."
5. Look at Fig. 1-2 on homeostasis. Think of the meaning of homeostasis, then follow the diagram to review how homeostasis strives for a balance within the individual.
6. How do motivation and learning influence behavior (Figs. 1-3 and 1-4)?
7. Eight different views of development are presented. Make a chart on which you indicate the following: (a) name of the view, (b) names of major theorists, (c) central thought or message of each theorist, (d) any limitations you detect in each view.
8. The maturational view of development and the genetic-oriented view are both physiological in nature. What do they stress and how do they differ?
9. The interactionistic view is popular because it combines the influences of both nature (heredity) and nurture (environment). Consider the environmental-oriented view of Skinner, the psychodynamic view of Freud, and the cultural conditioning view of Mead. Do these theories fit into interactionism?
10. What meaning does Havighurst's view of developmental tasks have for you?

REFERENCES

1. Maslow, A. *Toward a psychology of being* (2nd ed.). New York: D. Van Nostrand Co., 1968.
2. Erikson, E. *Childhood and society,* New York: W. W. Norton & Co., Inc., 1963.
3. Skinner, B. F. *Beyond freedom and dignity.* New York: Alfred A. Knopf, Inc., 1971.
4. Kagan, J., & Moss, H. A. *Birth to maturity: a study in psychological development.* New York: John Wiley & Sons, Inc., 1962.
5. Hall, G. S. *Adolescence* (Vols. 1 and 2). New York: Appleton-Century-Crofts, 1904.
6. Gesell, A. The ontogenesis of infant behavior. In L. Carmichael (Ed.), *Manual of child psychology* (2nd ed.). New York: John Wiley & Sons, Inc., 1954.
7. Gesell, A., Ilg, F. L., & Ames, L. B. *Youth: the years from 10 to 16.* New York: Harper & Row, Publishers, Inc., 1956.
8. Piaget, J. Piaget's theory. In P. H. Mussen (Ed.), *Carmichael's manual of child psychology* (Vol. I) (3rd ed.). New York: John Wiley & Sons, Inc., 1970.
9. Bruner, J. S. Nature and uses of immaturity. *American Psychologist,* 1972, **27,** 687-708.
10. Chomsky, N. *Language and mind* (Enl. Ed.). New York: Harcourt Brace Jovanovich, Inc., 1972.
11. Jones, N. B. (Ed.) *Ethological studies of child behavior.* London: Cambridge University Press, 1972.
12. Eibl-Eibesfeldt, I. *Ethology: the biology of behavior.* E. Klinghammer (Tr.). New York: Holt, Rinehart & Winston, 1970.
13. Lorenz, K. *On aggression.* New York: Harcourt Brace Jovanovich, Inc., 1966.
14. Skinner, B. F. *About behaviorism.* New York: Alfred A. Knopf, Inc., 1974.
15. Bandura, A. *Aggression: a social learning analysis.* Englewood Cliffs, N.J.: Prentice-Hall, Inc., 1973.
16. Freud, S. A. *A general introduction to psychoanalysis.* J. Riviere (Tr.). New York: Permabooks, 1953.

17. Erikson, E. *Identity: youth and crisis.* New York: W. W. Norton & Co., Inc., 1968.
18. Rogers, C. R. *On becoming a person.* Boston: Houghton-Mifflin Co., 1961.
19. Kagan, J. The baby's elastic mind. *Human Nature,* 1978, **1**, 1.
20. Skolnick, A. The myth of the vulnerable child. *Psychology Today* (February 1978).
21. Rosenfeld, A. The "elastic mind" movement: rationalizing child neglect? *Saturday Review,* 1978, **5**, 26-28.
22. Mead, M. *Culture and commitment: a study of the generation gap.* New York: Doubleday & Co., Inc., 1970.
23. Benedict, B. Continuities and discontinuities in cultural conditioning. In W. Martin, & C. Stendler (Eds.), *Readings in child development.* New York: Harcourt Brace Jovanovich, Inc., 1954, pp. 142-148.
24. Havighurst, R. *Developmental tasks and education* (3rd. ed.). New York: David McKay Co., Inc., 1972.
25. Sheehy, G. *Passages.* New York: E. P. Dutton & Co., Inc., 1976.
26. Kaluger, G., & Kaluger, M. F. *Profiles of human development.* St. Louis: The C. V. Mosby Co., 1976.

2

Determinants of development

The study of life-span development is a complex, multidimensional continuum that requires a multidisciplinary effort. There is a need to examine all the biomedical and psychosocial aspects of human development in the context of a person's total environment. It is necessary to consider the individual's physiology, psychological makeup, family, home, community, culture, education, religion, race, sex, and economic status, as well as those outside events that impinge upon an individual's life. In other words, to study growth and development, you must be concerned with anything and everything that can affect or influence the full spectrum of human life.

FACTORS INFLUENCING DEVELOPMENT

Robert Aldrich[1] made up a diagram listing the broad factors that influence the development of the life-span continuum. Because of the diagram's shape (Fig. 2-1), the concept has been labeled the "watermelon theory." The top half of the "watermelon" acknowledges the biological aspects of development; the bottom half acknowledges the psychosocial aspects. The biomedical aspects are the cardiovascular, central nervous, musculoskeletal, and endocrine systems, and the skin. The psychosocial factors include cognitive, personality, social, and ekistic development. Ekistic refers to a study of human settlements, symbolizing the context of the environment.

The implication of the diagram is that if you want to understand or know a person at any particular point in time, you must slice through the entire "watermelon"—at that moment—to be aware of the many factors that are part of the individual's makeup. By looking at the part of the "watermelon" that has developed since concep-

tion, it is possible to learn a great deal about factors that have influenced the development of the individual. By knowing the present and the past, it is possible to gain a glimpse of future development, although it is recognized that the future is modifiable.

We prefer to speak of the "determinants" of development. The word *determinant* means factors that have an influencing effect on conditions or events; in this case, factors that influence growth, development, and behavior. The categories of determinants are usually two—physiological or biological, and psychosocial, which includes both environmental and psychological factors. For our purpose, we will divide the categories into four groups—physiological, environmental, psychological, and metaphysical. The metaphysical determinant is purely speculative and abstract. We note a number of articles in professional journals dealing with metaphysical questions regarding life, so we feel it is appropriate to call attention to this area of discussion. Fig. 2-2 presents the four major determinants and influential categories or factors in each group.

PHYSIOLOGICAL DETERMINANTS

The physiological basis for growth and development includes the genetic foundation, the neural system, the glandular system, and the maturation process. The presentations given here will be short and slanted toward the way in which they influence growth and development. The mechanics of these influences are discussed in a cursory way. Readers are encouraged to seek other texts dealing specifically with these topics for more detailed information on the mechanics of the processes.

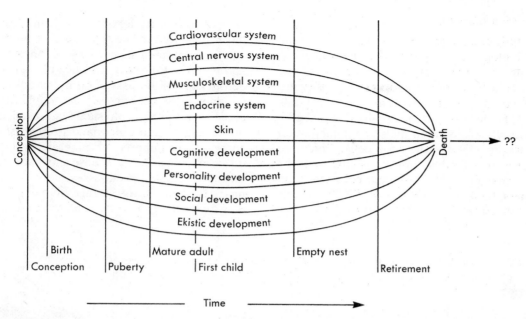

Fig. 2-1. The top half of Robert A. Aldrich's "watermelon model" represents biological factors, and the lower half represents psychosocial factors in the individual's life. The word *ekistic*—coined by the late Constantine Doxiadis—refers to the study of human settlements, here symbolizing the environmental context. Milestones along the way (bottom) indicate possible critical points in the life span. ("Empty nest," for example, refers to that time of life when the children grow up and leave home.) (From Aldrich, R. A. *Major transitions in the human life cycle.* New York: Academy for Educational Development, Inc., 1977.)

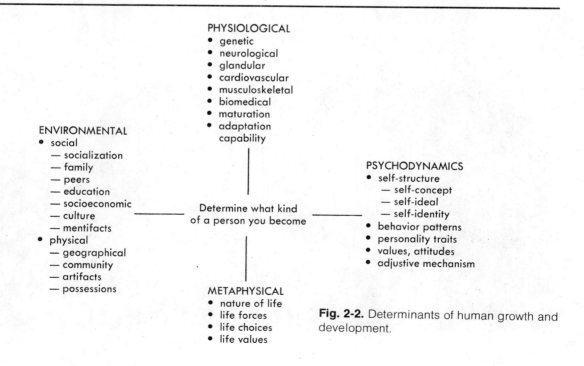

Fig. 2-2. Determinants of human growth and development.

Genetic foundations

The study of genetics (heredity) is a fascinating field of biology in which the causative factors of different characteristics and their means of transmission from one generation to another are introduced. There are two categories of cells found in the body—somatic cells and germ cells. Although all cells contain the same combination of chromosomes, only the germ cells, which are the reproductive cells, are transmitted at the time of conception. The somatic cells make up the organs, the brain, the body itself. These cells are the ones that respond to learning. They de-velop acquired traits. Since the somatic cells are not transmitted in the reproductive process, the acquired learning is not passed on to the off-spring. Only the characteristics contained in the germ cells will be passed on by heredity.

Some of the qualities subject to inheritance in-clude such things as physical features, sensitivity of the sense organs, vigor and strength of tissues, early or late puberty, a vulnerability to certain diseases such as heart disease and diabetes due to inherited bodily weaknesses, level of mainte-nance function in the storage of energy, the rate at which energy can be released and restored,

Similarities of hereditary characteristics are evident in a family group. However, the diversity of genetic combinations allows for some individuality in appearance and development.

Harold Geyer

and the degree of femaleness or maleness that an individual exhibits. Although mental ability, per se, is not inherited, the physical characteristics of the brain and the nervous system that respond to intellectual development are inherited.

DNA and RNA. The elements of heredity constitute a highly complicated process. In humans, each cell of the body contains 23 pairs of chromosomes. Each pair is made up of one chromosome from the mother egg cell and one chromosome from the father sperm cell. A chromosome is a complex structure composed of many chemical packets called genes. They are threaded together to look like a string of beads. A gene is the basic unit of heredity. Each gene contains the chemical substance known as DNA. The DNA makes up the "genetic code." It indicates which hereditary characteristics will be developed in the offspring. DNA guides growth according to its blueprint for every stage of the life cycle. Since there are thousands of genes in each chromosome, there are many possible arrangements of the maternal and paternal chromosomes. As a result, the large variety of combinations make it possible for individuals to develop many unique physical and biomedical characteristics. As McClearn and De-Fries[2] state, "With 4 billion people alive today, this represents an incredible genetic diversity." What is just as interesting is to note that, in spite of the vast array of genetic differences that people have, they all have but one nose, two eyes, two ears, one head, two legs, and two arms.

Deoxyribonucleic acid (DNA) is composed of molecules of sugar, phosphate, and four bases that combine in different sequences within the genes. The bases are the chemicals adenine, guanine, cytosine, and thymine. The DNA molecule is in the shape of a twisted ladder called a *helix*. A sugar molecule alternates with phosphate to form the sides of the ladder. The rungs of the ladder are formed by combinations of either cytosine and guanine or adenine and thymine. The order of the chemical combinations on the rungs of the ladder carry the code for the characteristic to be inherited. Thus a sequence of CG, GC, AT, CG, TA may indicate a color of hair, whereas AT, AT, GC, TA may indicate the shape of eyes. This illustration is an oversimplification, of course. The genetic code for a characteristic may consist of hundreds of "rungs."

When a fertilized egg divides, the DNA genetic code helix (the string of beads in the 23 pairs of chromosomes) unzips like a long zipper. Then, each side of the helix attracts a compatible nitrogen compound that is floating freely in the cell. For example, cytosine and guanine always attract each other and adenine and thymine always go together. Eventually, two new, complete sets of 23 pairs of chromosomes are developed. Each set moves to opposite sides of the cell and the cell divides in half, making two cells, each with a complete set of chromosomes. This special method of cell division or replication of chromosomes is known as *meiosis*. These two cells go through the same process, creating four cells. This division process continues to take place until the fertilized egg attaches itself to the wall of the uterus. At that point, protein and cell development begin to form the shape, organs, and physical characteristics of the new embryo.

DNA is found only within the nucleus of a cell. For development to occur the vital message concerning what tissue or organ is to be built must be delivered to the site of growth. This information is transmitted by ribonucleic acid (RNA). Basically, there are two kinds of RNA molecules that aid in the transfer. One is called the messenger RNA. Produced by DNA, this molecule will eventually move out of the nucleus and into the cytoplasm, carrying with it important instructions for protein synthesis. A second kind of RNA is the transfer RNA. Its function is associated with the regulation of enzymes involved in protein synthesis—the bringing together of types of amino acids in the proper sequence. The building blocks of the protein molecule are amino acids. Transfer RNA delivers amino acids to the templates formed by messenger RNA so that the proper tissues and organs can be built. A change in a characteristic or organ may occur if only one amino acid within the pattern is out of order. For example, sickle cell anemia (characterized by the presence of an abnormal red blood cell of crescent shape) is the result of only one change in the 574 amino acid sequence that makes up the protein hemoglobin. A summary of the protein-building process is presented in Fig. 2-3.

1 DNA code contains genetic instructions in form of four basic control chemicals plus sugar and phosphate.	**2** DNA produces messenger RNA in its nucleus to carry out orders of the DNA blueprint.	**3** Messenger RNAs travel from nucleus to cell where transfer RNAs and twenty different amino acids are found.
4 Transfer RNAs are coded to attract specific kinds of amino acids; messenger RNAs activate appropriate transfer RNAs.	**5** Transfer RNAs with proper amino acids attached approach and match the sequential pattern set up by messenger RNAs.	**6** Amino acids, now in correct sequence, produce proteins at that site as requested by the DNA initially.

Fig. 2-3. How the genetic code produces body cell proteins from amino acids by means of DNA and RNA molecules.

Deviations. In considering genetic characteristics, two terms that often appear are *chromosomal aberration* and *gene mutation*. These processes are responsible for most of the abnormal organic development in humans. Gene mutation refers to a change in the gene's chemical structure. This change can be in the form of being unable to function chemically or of being destroyed or a change in the base coding of DNA. One of the most frequent causes of mutations is exposure to high-energy radiation. A daily bombardment of cosmic rays on the body may cause natural mutations.

Certain chemicals can cause abnormalities in a child's development. Chemicals that produce mutations are formaldehyde, nitrous acid, peroxide, and mustard gas. One particular drug that had a drastic effect on normal development in children was thalidomide. In 1961 and 1962 European physicians were reporting the births of a large number of deformed children. After searching the past records of the mothers, almost all reportedly had taken thalidomide during pregnancy. There were numerous deformities of limbs, absence of fingers, arms, and legs, webbed fingers, undersized ears, dislocation of hips, absence of kidneys or gallbaldders, and abnormal livers.

In chromosomal aberrations there is an altera-tion in the structure of the chromosome or in the number of chromosomes. For example, Down's syndrome, also known as mongolism, is produced when three molecules instead of two get together to form a pair (Fig. 2-4). Down's syndrome is characterized by a short stature, slightly slanted eyes, and mental retardation. It occurs with greater frequency in children born to older women than to younger women, which may be due to the different types of chemical balance and hormonal secretion in older women. According to Nagle,[3] 30% of all Down's syndrome births occur in women over 40 years of age. Other aberrations include Turner's syndrome and Klinefelter's syndrome, each produced by an abnormal number of sex chromosomes. In Turner's syndrome there is only one sex chromosome, whereas in Klinefelter's syndrome there are three instead of the normal two sex chromosomes.

Turner's syndrome is characterized by short stature, infantile sexual development, and variable abnormalities that may include webbing of the neck, low posterior hairline, and cardiac defects. Klinefelter's syndrome is a condition characterized by the presence of small testes, sparse sexual hair, sterility, and sometimes, excessive development of the male mammary glands (breasts), even to the functional state.

There are reasons for knowing more about

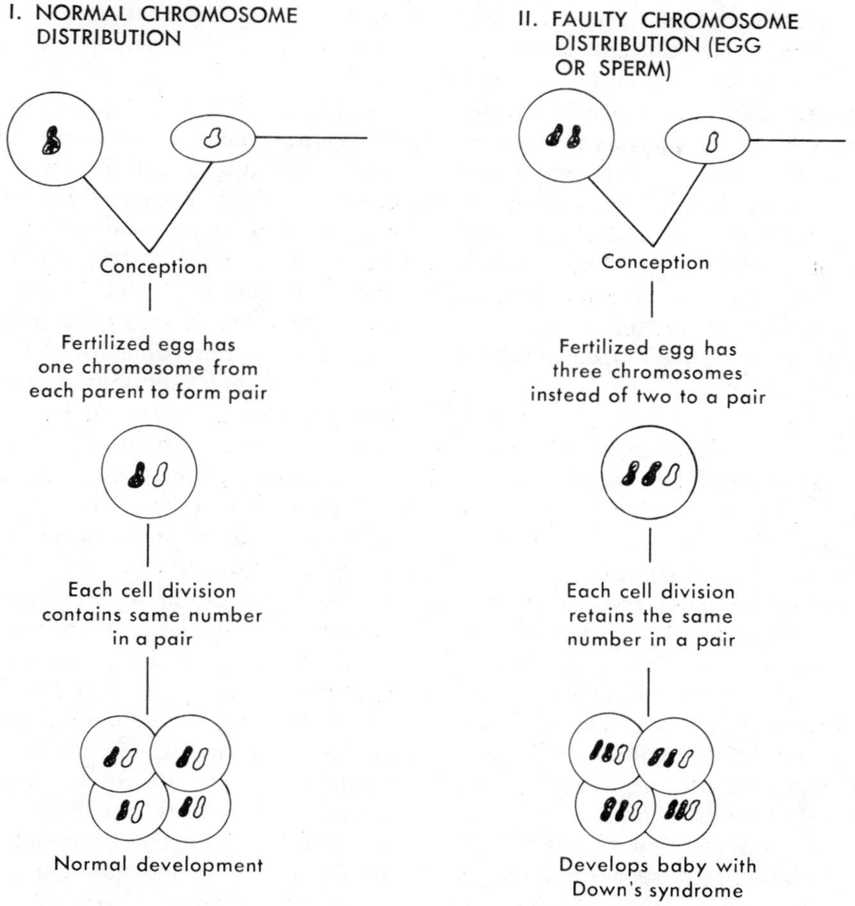

I. NORMAL CHROMOSOME
DISTRIBUTION

II. FAULTY CHROMOSOME
DISTRIBUTION (EGG
OR SPERM)

Conception

Fertilized egg has
one chromosome from
each parent to form pair

Each cell division
contains same number
in a pair

Normal development

Conception

Fertilized egg has
three chromosomes
instead of two to a pair

Each cell division
retains the same
number in a pair

Develops baby with
Down's syndrome

Fig. 2-4. Normal distribution of a set of chromosomes is shown in *I*. Down's syndrome, as caused by a chromosomal aberration, is shown in *II*. The egg in *II* has an extra set of chromosomes and the extra set is transmitted in cell division.

DNA, RNA, and the genetic code. First, DNA, RNA, and enzymes are related in some ways to intelligence and memory. It may be possible some day to determine how to improve intelligence and memory chemically. Second, we should know about chromosomal aberrations and the fact that some of these aberrations are hereditary in nature. If aberrations exist in a family, it may be desirable for the children, at the time of marriage or adulthood, to have genetic counseling to determine if they are carriers of the chromosomal deviation. Third, we should be aware of the genetic code and the social implications of seeking to change, influence, or tamper with it. Changing the genetic code to bring about desirable characteristics and eliminate undesirable ones may be significant, but where and how to draw the line at influencing the genetic code for social or political purposes must be considered.

Nervous system

Of all of the systems of the body the nervous system is one of the most important. Everything that takes place, consciously or unconsciously, voluntarily or automatically, has its primary genesis within the nervous system. Death comes when the brain, not the heart or the lungs, dies. The quality of response is greatly influenced by the quality and capability of the nervous system and the part of the brain related to that response. It is important to know the parts of the nervous system and how they function, but it is equally important to know how the nervous system reacts to stimuli, what it does to interpret those stimuli, and how it gets meaning and makes appropriate responses. This procedure refers to the perceptual-conceptual process and the sensorimotor arc. The arc refers to the mechanical pathway; the perceptual-conceptual process refers to how meaning is derived from impulses traveling along the pathways.

Sensorimotor arc. The sensorimotor arc pertains to the transmission of nerve impulses from receptor tissues or sense organs, to the central nervous system, and to the effector tissues of the muscles and glands. The nerve impulses are triggered by external or internal stimuli.

Receptors such as the ears, eyes, skin, and taste buds are exteroceptors. Nerves in the muscles or tendons, the so-called muscle sense, are proprioceptors. The nerves in the inner membranes, in the body organs, are interoceptors. Receptors merely transmit the stimulus signals to the spinal cord and brain where meanings are attached to them. For a nerve impulse to be activated the stimulus must be powerful enough to overcome the threshold of awareness and trigger the impulse. Not all stimuli are that strong.

If the stimulus has immediate survival or protection value, it may only travel to the spinal cord, where a quick estimate of its value is made. If the situation is harmful, such as the fingers touching something extremely hot, the spinal cord will react with a reflex and jerk the hand from the hot object. If a reflex action is not involved, the nerve impulses are sent to the brain, where they are studied, interpreted, and given meaning. That meaning is scrutinized and a judgment value attached to it. That judgment will determine what action should take place, and the brain will program for the next step.

The programmed information will activate the effectors, the appropriate muscles (motor areas) or glands for a response. The muscles involved may be the striped, or striate, muscles of the skeleton, the cardiac muscles of the heart, or the smooth, internal muscles of the organs. The glands will be either the duct glands (sweat and tears) or the endocrine glands, which constitute a complicated chemical system of hormones that regulate and integrate the whole organism.

Neural divisions. The nervous system has two major divisions, a central nervous system (CNS), consisting of the spinal cord and the brain, and a peripheral nervous system (PNS), made up of (1) the nerves related to the skin and muscles (somatic or voluntary) and (2) the nerves found in the organs and glands (visceral or autonomic). The main subdivisions of the central nervous system and their functions are noted in Table 2-1. Note that some parts, such as the spinal cord, medulla, and cerebellum, are primarily interested in physiological functions, whereas the thalamus, hypothalamus, and cerebrum are concerned with more complex physiological functions and with cognitive processes.

The PNS contains the autonomic nervous system that regulates the normal functioning of the body in such things as rate of heartbeat, breathing, digestion, and so forth. However, when the body or the mind is under great stress or is in physical or psychological danger, the sympathetic division of the autonomic system takes over and tries to help the body and mind to survive as best it can by enabling it to perform better to overcome the emergency threat. Operations unnecessary to survival are slowed down or stopped. Body functions that can help are speeded up. The nostrils of the nose enlarge, and the person breathes more quickly to take in more oxygen. Epinephrine and sugar are secreted into the bloodstream. The heart beats faster to pump blood, with its additional fuel, to all parts of the body. The body is geared to meet the threat. When the emergency is over, the body functions settle down, and the normal, parasympathetic division takes over again. The manner by which the body responds to emergencies is known as the general adaptation syndrome and was hypothesized by Hans Selye.[4]

The general adaptation syndrome, as developed by Selye, states that the body's reaction under stress occurs in three major phases: the alarm reaction, the stage of resistance, and the stage of exhaustion. The alarm reaction or emergency reaction comprises the physiological

Table 2-1. Major structures of the nervous system

I. Central nervous system			
	A. Brain		
Forebrain		1. Cerebrum (Cerebral cortex)	Sense perception; voluntary movements; learning, remembering, thinking; emotion; consciousness; personality integration
		2. Thalamus	Sensory relay station on way to cerebral cortex
		3. Hypothalamus	Control of visceral and somatic function, such as temperature, metabolism, and endocrine balance
Midbrain		4. Corpus callosum	Fibers connecting two cerebral hemispheres
		5. Midbrain	Conduction and switching center; pupillary light reflex, etc.
		6. Reticular formation	Arousal system that activates wide regions of cerebral cortex; involves attention and perceptual discrimination
		7. Limbic system	Active in functions of attention, emotion, motivation, and memory
Hindbrain		8. Cerebellum	Muscle tone; body balance; coordination of voluntary movement, as of fingers and thumb
		9. Medulla	Via cranial nerves exerts important control over breathing, swallowing, digestion, heartbeat
		10. Pons	Fibers connecting two hemispheres of cerebellum
	B. Spinal cord		Conduction paths for motor and sensory impulses; local reflexes
II. Peripheral nervous system			
	A. Autonomic nervous system		Autonomous or self-regulating mechanism
		1. Parasympathetic division	Operates and controls vital life functions at normal level
		2. Sympathetic division	Takes over vital life functions in stress or emergency situation; increases functions of those necessary to meet threat and decreases function of those not necessary for survival
	B. Craniosacral nerves		Control sensory nerves, motor and somatic nerves, and vagus nerve

changes that the body makes initially in response to a stress-provoking situation. These are the functions mentioned in the previous paragraph. If exposure to the stress-producing situation continues, the second phase, the stage of resistance, takes over. Here the organism seems to develop a resistance to the stress agent (stressor) and the physiological functions appear to resume normal functioning. However, there is an increase in the level of secretion of the anterior pituitary and the adrenal cortex. If exposure to the stress situation continues too long, a point is reached where the organism can no longer maintain its resistance and the stage of exhaustion occurs. During this phase, the organism cannot adapt to the continuing stress with the result that physiological dysfunctions, including conditions such as ulcers or hypertension and certain psychosomatic conditions, may occur.

Perceptual process. The perceptual process refers to how the brain deals with the nerve impulses it receives so that it can interpret and give meaning to the stimuli that triggered the impulses (Fig. 2-5). The stimuli are picked up by the sense organ as sensations, and the impulses are transmitted to the central nervous system. The signals are directed to the perceptual areas in the brain for interpretation. The brain may or may not recall having dealt with signals before. A scanning procedure is utilized to bring forth any information that would help the brain to make interpretations. The interpretations would include such things as developing concepts or generalizations, gaining insight, formulation of language, or put-

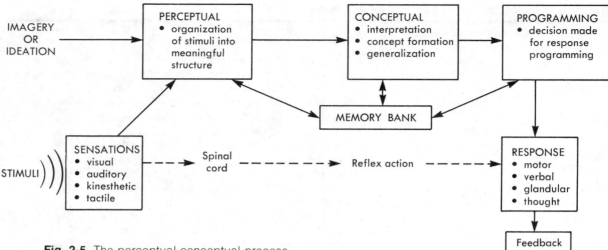

Fig. 2-5. The perceptual-conceptual process.

ting the stimuli sensations into a proper sequence. A decision is made as to what to do with the material, and programming for some form of response is done.

Taking in the pattern of the stimulus would be a receptive action, producing a sensation of some type. Dealing with the sensations and giving meaning to them would be cognitive or perceptive action. Expressive action would be the response. Using computer terms, reception would be input; cognition would first have decoding, then encoding; finally, expressive action would be the output. There is always feedback to indicate the adequacy of the perceptual act. Difficulty in understanding or learning may occur at any point in the perceptual process due to lesions, scars, tumors, poor synaptic transmission, cerebral hemorrhage, or maturational lag in neurological development. Thought does not always have to start with a receptive act; it could begin in the brain in the cognitive part of the perceptual process. In this case the activity is known as ideomotor action, indicating an operational sequence in which a motor response is elicited by an idea. Of course it is possible for thinking to take place without any response in the motor area.

Hemispheric functions. Interesting pioneer work by Roger Sperry and his associates[5,6] has demonstrated that each hemisphere of the brain has cognitive functions in which it specializes. Working with split-brain patients (individuals whose hemispheres were disconnected at the corpus callosum by an accident or the need for drastic surgery), Sperry learned that the right hemisphere and the left hemisphere perform different kinds of functions. For example, the left hemisphere specializes in verbal activities. It is the main language center where speech, writing, and calculations take place. It handles the verbal-intellectual-analytical-symbolic business of life. The right hemisphere is predominantly nonverbal in nature. As Robert Ornstein[7] states, it has a different mode of consciousness. Performing with a mechanical kind of information processing, it excels in spatial construction, perceptual tasks of spatial orientation, recognition of shapes and textures, the use of touch, and musical and artistic ability. It can provide simple language comprehension. It handles the more spontaneous, intuitive, experiential aspects of information processing.

The significance of left hemisphere and right hemisphere specialization becomes more evident when we consider an individual who makes one of the hemispheres dominant over the other in its operations. The capabilities of the dominant hemisphere are enhanced, but the abilities of the other hemisphere are prevented from functioning effectively or efficiently. A person with a split brain has no choice but to use the hemisphere interchangeably according to the needs of the moment. A person with connected hemispheres,

Children must learn to discriminate between letters, remember them, and associate meanings with them. This learning comes with the development of the perceptual-conceptual process.

however, needs to have free interaction between the two modes of consciousness if the highest level of mental potential is to be realized. Neither hemisphere should be so subdominant that it cannot perform adequately.

Endocrine glandular system

Within the human body there exists a group of small capsules of tissue, the endocrine glands. These glands are distributed widely throughout the body; they differ from one another in their structure and in the nature of their secretions. The endocrine glands secrete directly into the bloodstream and are therefore called ductless glands or glands of internal secretion. They include the pituitary, thyroid, parathyroids, adrenals, pancreas, ovaries, testes, thymus, and pineal body.

The endocrine glands are intrinsic regulators of development. They affect health and development through the secretion of complicated chemical substances that are called *hormones*. Hormones are liberated directly into the bloodstream and are carried to all parts of the body, where they have special functions of initiating, regulating, and controlling some of the activities of organs and tissues. Although the amount of the secretions of these glands may be almost imperceptibly small, they have incredible potency.

The functions of these hormones are diversified. They range from influencing the rate and pattern of growth and maturation to regulating the amount of water excreted by the kidneys. They control the processes by which humans digest foods and rebuild them into blood, bone,

Table 2-2. Principle endocrine glands

Gland	Hormones secreted	Function	Oversecretion	Undersecretion
Pituitary				
Anterior lobe	Growth hormone	Growth; regulates other glands; water metabolism	Acromegaly; gigantism	Dwarfism; Simmonds' disease; diabetes insipidus
Posterior lobe	Gonadotrophic Antidiuretic Oxytocin			
Thyroid	Thyroxine	Regulates basal metabolic rate, activity, fatigue, body weight	Toxic goiter; Graves' disease	Cretinism; simple goiter; Gull's disease; myxedema
Parathyroid	Parathormone	Regulates calcium and phosphorus; normal excitability of nervous system	Osteitis fibrosa; sluggishness; loss of weight	Splitting headaches; tetany
Adrenals				
Cortex	Cortisone	Salt, water balance; body changes in emotions; carbohydrate metabolism	Virilism; sexual precocity; Cushing's syndrome	Addison's disease; anemia; low blood pressure
Medulla	Epinephrine			
Pancreas (islets of Langerhans)	Insulin Glucagon	Controls blood sugar level and carbohydrate	Hyperinsulinism stupor	Diabetes mellitus
Gonads				
Ovaries	Androgens	Regulate sexual development and functioning	Menstrual disturbance	Failure of sexual maturation; menopause symptoms
Testes	Estrogens Progesterone			
Pineal	Melatonin Serotonin Noradrenalin	Influences sex hormones; regulates day and night cycles; affects brain chemistry; blanches skin	Delayed sexual development; alters body chemistry	Very early puberty; alters emotions and behavior

muscle, and brain tissue. They largely determine the length of bones, the deposition of fat, and whether an individual shall be short, stout, tall, or thin. They pace the beating of the heart and supervise the working of the liver and kidneys. They time the onset of puberty, control the menstrual cycle, and govern the many staged processes of reproduction, from the first ripening of an egg cell to the final muscle contractions that propel an infant toward independent life.[8] They

even regulate one another. The activity of one gland is affected by the secretion of another, and thus the performance of one gland reflects the activity of another. (See Table 2-2 for their functions.)

When the endocrine glands function in perfect concert, the individual is well and happy. When their delicate balance is upset, the individual may suffer from a host of disease processes or emotional disturbances. They are as indispensable to physical welfare as are food, air, and water. Diseases of the endocrine glands are usually associated with their hyperactivity (oversecretion) or hypoactivity (undersecretion). These changes from normal activity may even exist before the birth of a child. In some cases glandular dysfunction of women during pregnancy may retard fetal development.

The endocrine glands appear to be the bridge between the organic constitution of the body and the mental, moral, and aesthetic capacities of humanity. The importance of these glands as creative forces shaping both the outer form and inner experience of every human individual is becoming ever more manifest and irrefutable.

Physiological maturation

Occasionally students have difficulty understanding the term *maturation*. Maturation always and exclusively, as a principle of growth and development, refers to physiological maturation. Organisms mature through the maturational process. Maturation does not refer to the development of emotional, social, mental, or spiritual maturity. There are several reasons why it is important to know about the physical maturation process. First, it suggests the sequence of physiological maturity and its behavior. By knowing the sequence, the level of development that a child has achieved can be determined. By comparing this level to the proper norms, it is possible to tell if development is at a normal rate or not. Second, knowledge of physiological maturation enables detection if a child is skipping any stages of development or moving through them too quickly or too slowly. These factors are deemed to have some significance in the development of the perceptual learning processes of the child.[9] Third, approximately one fourth of all children ages 5 to 8 years have a maturational lag in neurological development of the perceptual processes. It would behoove parents and teachers to be aware of this lag and its implications.

Maturation is the unfolding of innate organic patterns in an ordered sequence through the growth of the organisms. Prenatal and some postnatal developments of behavior result from the unfolding of potentialities resident within the genes and are thus inherited. However, this growth process results from an integral relation of genes and their constantly changing surroundings. In light of the great amount of work in experimental embryology, development cannot be regarded as potential within the genes alone; neither can it be regarded as essentially determined by environment. It is a product of these two sets of conditions. The universality of the reflex responses is presumptive evidence for the generalization that early fetal behavior is dependent on maturation of sensory, neural, and motor structures. Once the structures have attained a certain degree of functional maturity, exercise may determine some part of further development. Norman Munn[10] states that on the basis of evidence at present available it is difficult to provide a clear-cut distinction between maturation and learning and between heredity and environment. However, as Ashley Montagu[11] has stressed, "Where we control the environment, we to some extent control heredity. Heredity, it has been said, determines what we *can* do, and environment what we *do* do."

There are several implications of the principle of maturation for growth and development. First, implicit in the principle of maturation is the concept of readiness. It is impossible to teach a child, in spite of any amount of practice, any task for which the innate disposition or readiness for learning is not already present. Capacities such as walking, talking, and even doing multiplication depend on natural, innate aptitudes that have reached their "teachable moment" and not on training. The lack of practice in natural functions does not check the development of a maturing pattern, however. Although some capacities are innate and will inevitably emerge irrespective of teaching, practice and training can make all the difference between a skilled or a mediocre or clumsy performance. For some activities there is an optimum time for development that, if it could be determined, is the best time for giving training and practice. For example, it appears that the age for establishing the foundations for a good muscle structure and motor coordination system is about 2½ or 3 years of age.

Environmental conditions play an important part in encouraging or retarding the process of maturation. An environment of some kind is

Unimpeded physiological maturation, at its own pace and in its own time, develops the physical readiness needed to learn to walk, to skip, to ride a bicycle, or to climb to the top of a jungle gym where you can look and see a world to be explored.

Harold Geyer

necessary for the expression of a child's capacities. The environment is the arena in which his potentialities are expressed. The more suitable the environment the better will be the development. The child learns to walk, but he walks "somewhere." What he finds and experiences in the places where he walks will have much to do with the development of his other attributes. The environment determines which of a child's native potentialities are developed and which ones are left undeveloped. It is unlikely that a child born and raised in the Arctic north will ever learn to be a great swimmer.

ENVIRONMENTAL DETERMINANTS

No child is born with a ready-made "human behavior." All children learn to behave like human beings through associating with other humans. All babies are pretty much alike when they are born. They have the same needs, go through the same sequence in developing locomotion and speech, and have a need to relate to people. Chil-

dren become different because of the culture in which they grow, the experiences that they have, the genetic uniqueness of their individual differences, and the physical, geographical, and political conditions under which they live. The process of socialization teaches them how to be like their compatriots.

Socialization

All human beings experience socialization. A child is born in a specific culture and is thus subjected to the socializing forces found in that culture. The brief period of childhood, during which human beings are most malleable, is the period when the whole process of socialization, the shaping of the person into a socially acceptable form, must occur. The perpetuation of a culture requires that each new generation acquire the patterns of living inherent in their culture.

Becoming socialized means that the individual behaves in such a way so as to be acceptable to the social group with which he wishes to identify.

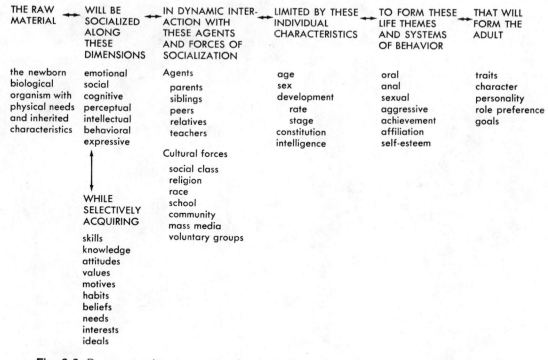

Fig. 2-6. Process and components of socialization. (From McNeil, E. B. *Human socialization.* Copyright 1969 by Wadsworth Publishing Co., Inc. Reprinted by permission of the publisher, Brooks/Cole Publishing Co., Monterey, Calif.)

The family is the primary socializing force in the lives of children. Fortunate is the family that can grow and have fun together, yet respect the individuality of each member.

David Strickler

He develops the social attitudes common to that particular social group and will consciously employ these attitudes so as to regulate and control his behavior.

A social role is a pattern of behavior that is expected of fellow members by the members of a social group. For example, there are roles for teachers, pupils, ministers, and so forth. Their behavior or role is prescribed to them by the other members of their social group, and they must generally act in accordance with these specified patterns of behavior. Every social group has its own recognized patterns of behavior for its members.

Socialization imposes the attitudes, appreciations, social roles, and skills of a culture on the individual. Societies vary in the means used to achieve these goals. Much of the socialization process is implemented by agents—people (or groups) who interpret the culture to the child. They guide and reinforce his learning of the appropriate behavior patterns for his sex, age, and social class, and they inhibit the learning of inappropriate behavior. Fig. 2-6, from McNeill,[12] shows the overall effect that these social agents have on the process of socialization.

Family. The family is the socializing agent most directly responsible for the transmission of the cultural content of the society to the growing child. The socialization process begins in the home. The family passes on its attitudes, prejudices, and points of view to the child. The family also determines the social class, ethnic origin, race, and usually the religion of the child. The family, through the experiences they offer the child, will teach him concepts concerning the world—real and unreal. This information is given to the child through the use of words. Therefore one of the most important roles of the family is to teach the child language.

The parent-child relationship is a factor that has great influence on the social development of the child. The type of discipline used and how the parent reacts to the child is important, as is the life-style of the home. The democratic home life seems to produce an active, aggressive, fearless, and playful child who has leadership characteristics, who tends to be curious and nonconforming. The controlled home, on the other hand,

Table 2-3. Children's personality traits resulting from love or hostility and control or autonomy in the home*

Love and control	Love and autonomy
Submissive, dependent, polite, neat, obedient	Active, socially outgoing, creative, successfully aggressive
Minimal aggression	Minimal rule enforcement, boys
Dependent, not friendly, not creative	Facilitates adult role-taking
Maximal compliance	Minimal self-aggression, boys
Maximum rule enforcement, boys	Independent, friendly, creative, low projective hostility
Hostility and control	**Hostility and autonomy**
"Neurotic" problems	Delinquency
More quarreling and shyness with peers	Noncompliance
Socially withdrawn	Maximal aggression
Low in adult role-taking	
Maximal self-aggression, boys	

*Adapted from Schaefer, E. S. Converging models for maternal behavior and child behavior. In J. Gildewell (Ed.), *Parental attitudes and child behavior,* Springfield, Ill.: Charles C Thomas, Publisher, 1961.

produces a quiet, nonrestricted, well-behaved, and unaggressive child with restricted curiosity, originality, and fancifulness. (See Table 2-3).

The way in which the parent views the child and the circumstances under which the child was born will also affect the parent-child relationship. Such circumstances as, for example, the arrival of a long-awaited baby to older parents, an unwanted child to an unmarried woman, an unwanted child to quarreling parents, or the first child of a young, happy couple will surely have some effect on how the parents feel toward the child, their treatment of the child, and the child's adjustment and social development.

The presence of brothers and sisters within the

family also has an effect on the development of the child. The number of siblings, their ages, and birth order help to determine the socialization practices found in the home. For example, a study done by Elder and Bowerman[13] reveals that in large families the mechanics of managing several children dictates parental authoritarianism. The birth order within the family may have an effect on the social adjustment of the individual. Belmont and Marolla[14] have found that the firstborn child receives more attention, is more likely to be exposed to psychological discipline, and is more anxious and dependent, whereas later-born children are more aggressive and self-confident.

Peer group. The peer group consists of individuals who are approximately of the same age and of the same social class. In childhood the peer group is more like a play group, whereas in adolescence the peer group takes on the appearance of a clique or gang.

The peer group projects a pattern of conformity. The members reinforce responses that conform to their expectations. These responses will be reinforced, adopted, and strengthened by the peer group. Responses that are nonconforming will be discouraged.

The concept of impersonal authority is introduced to the child through the peer group. Even though in the childhood peer group no one child is the leader, there are certain unwritten rules of the game to which the child must conform. Through his peers the child comes in contact with various attitudes toward himself, toward adults, and toward those things that are to be valued or disregarded.

The child soon learns how to secure the recognition of his group, how to participate as one of

Interaction between generations at social gatherings contributes to the understanding of both the young and the old.

David Strickler

its members, and how to avoid the group's displeasure. The child learns patterns of behavior from the peer group that cannot be learned from adults. Concepts of cooperation, sharing, and participation are also transmitted by the peer group to the individual. The child's peer group is one way by which he can become independent of his parents and other authorities. This is particularly apparent during adolescence, when the child identifies with new models and develops new emotional ties.

Society. In the society of today there are numerous opportunities to interact. Mass transportation has provided the ability to reach out and communicate beyond the community. By widening his environment the individual perceives and learns about differences in customs and mores. Society also provides certain rules by which to live, some of which have been written into law and must be adhered to or punishment results.

The community is the first large social structure that provides a framework for socioeconomic life. The community is involved with the individual at every level of development. In comparing one community with another vast differences in their characteristics can be recognized. In many large cities there are communities where the population is constantly on the move. There are few ties between the people. The family receives little assistance in developing a child's civic and interpersonal obligations. The morale of the people is negligible and disorganized; cultural values and expectations appear confused. In more stable communities there is more interaction between the family and school, business people, civic leaders, and clergy, helping to provide a basis for community concern.

The school is the first socializing agent within the community that the child encounters outside of the family. One of the aims of education is to complete the socialization process begun in the family. Educational institutions transmit the knowledge, beliefs, customs, and skills of the society. Organized education is the tool that society employs to civilize its young citizens. The school reaches all the children in the community who are physically and mentally able to attend. The effect of the school on the individual and the community is widespread.

In general, contemporary societies affect individuals across the entire spectrum of the life span. Rapid technological and social changes tend to make the past less relevant and the future less secure. Gaps develop between the generations because their experiences and exposures differ greatly. As a result, communication between the generations is more difficult. Cultural confusion and difficulty in establishing values and beliefs also result when rapid changes take place in a pluralistic society.

Urbanization and bigness make personal relationships more difficult. There is no question but that growing up within an urban complex is very complicated. Bigness is conducive to the creation of alternative life-styles. The observance of a variety of ways of living and the values associated with them can create some confusion as to what is desirable or "best for me." In the last two decades, there has been a semblance of affluence in most societies. Installment buying, the use of credit cards, and an emphasis on consumer buying have made youth more status conscious in terms of possessions. At the same time, a generation of low-income youth has been identified and publicized. As a result, there is an inconsistency within our society in terms of the appearance of affluency on the one hand and pockets of poverty on the other.

Mass communication media have brought all of these conditions to the attention of the public. Ninety-eight percent of all homes in the United States have at least one television set. Not only is the public subjected to instant news but quite often to manipulated or bias news coverage, so that it is difficult at times to put "what's happening" within a proper perspective. The bigness of urban centers makes it almost impossible for a growing child or an adolescent to perceive reality. The hard-sell approach of some mass media even makes it difficult for an adult to know what is "for real."

Physical factors. It would be easy, but dangerous, to surmise generalizations concerning the influence of climatic and geographical features on the growth and development of children. Wide differences do exist. Do children who are raised in rural areas or small villages and towns have the same experiential opportunities for social and

Geographical locations have some influence on living and learning conditions. You would not see this sight in Los Angeles, Chicago, or New York City, but you could see it in the mountains of West Virginia or North Carolina.

David Strickler

educational development as those raised in large urban cities? How are youngsters raised in isolated regions such as mountains, plains, or deserts affected? Think of such areas as they exist around the world. Does it make a difference if a child is raised in a tropical climate where food, such as fruits and vegetables, grows profusely as compared to being raised in a frigid, desolate area where food is difficult to come by? To what extent do physical and geographical factors make a difference in the development of language, cognition, and attitudinal patterns? People do adapt to living in almost any kind of climate or topography, but at what developmental price?

The altoplano of Bolivia, in the area of Lake Titicaca, are at an altitude above 12,000 feet (3,656 meters). Half of all the oxygen in the atmosphere is found below 10,000 feet. How do the thousands of people living in the altoplano survive? Physically, their bodies have adapted to the environmental setting by producing more than the normal amount of red blood cells to transport oxygen to various parts of the body. These people have a "barrel-chest" appearance; the chest and lungs are expanded so that more air and oxygen can be taken in with each breath. We have seen children in this area run and play just as vigorously as do children in the lowlands.

Physical adaptation can take place, but what about language and social development? As with any semi-isolated area, the language and social patterns developed will be affected by whatever restrictive factors are present. This inhibition of development could occur in a large urban area if the child is secluded within a home and not permitted to associate with other children or adults. There are known cases of children who have been isolated in attics or upstairs rooms and never sent to school. Invariably these children are severely restricted in language development. On the other hand, some children living in very isolated areas have good language development because they have access to television and have a supply of books and other reading materials in the home that they are encouraged to use.

What is important to verbal and cognitive development is the nature of the materials present and what use is made of them. A child in a primitive culture plays with materials found in the environment such as sticks, seedpods, and shells. A child in another culture may have toys that can be explored and manipulated, visual materials and books that introduce written language, and access to cultural, social, and educational facilities that can be visited. The child in the primitive culture may become jungle or tribal "wise"; the other child can become book or school "wise." The elastic mind theory of Kagan, however, postulates that the child in a primitive culture need not be forever stymied by impoverished cognitive development because of his early childhood setting. An intellectually enriched environment later in childhood or adolescence can stimulate cognitive growth and improve abstract reasoning ability. Either way, it is somewhat evident that the materials, as well as the people, of the environment can influence growth and development.

Certainly, the quality of nutrition available to the individual influences physical growth and central nervous system development, especially of the brain. Diets do differ according to the locale. In some parts of the world, rice is the staple diet. In other places, diets can be found that consist primarily of fish, sago palm, fruits and vegetables, beef or lamb, or just eggs and dairy products. The lack of a balanced diet can make a difference in total development.

In summary, personal possessions, available artifacts, the ease of making a living and the accessibility of food, the degree of geographical or physical isolation, and the consciousness of the neighborhood, community, or social unit all have an influence on total development. The effects of this influence need not be irreversible, however.

PSYCHODYNAMIC DETERMINANTS

Growth and development is a total process. There is a great interaction of forces that influence the growth process. Intrinsic and extrinsic, internal and external elements are at work contributing their share in manipulating and shaping the individual. Certainly the individual should have something to say about what is happening to him. He cannot control all the forces that are at work on him, but he can make some choices and determine some directions that his life will take through elements that make up his personality. These elements are referred to as "self-determinants," dynamic forces within the individual that make up his "ego," or "conscious self." Ultimately the child will develop a self-structure consisting of a self-concept, a self-ideal and a self-identity, a value judgment system, and a pattern of behavioral response and control. These forces will be instrumental in the development of the personality.

Each individual develops a "self-structure"—a pattern of interacting inner forces that serve as reference points around which experiences are organized and behavior patterns formed. The inner forces are psychophysical systems that will provide dynamics that will influence the direction and the intensity that behavior responses take. Since psychophysical systems differ somewhat from individual to individual, behavioral responses will tend to differ. When a person develops his value judgment system, his value considerations of what is important, good, or interesting will also influence his behavior and the goals he will seek.

There is within the individual at birth a series of primitive impulses and reflexes that are intended to help the newborn child survive. They are responsible for most of the child's behavior in the first 2 years. Although individuals never lose these primitive drives, they do gain control of them and lessen their influence as they become socialized. If survival is ever seriously threatened, the primitive impulses can emerge again to perform their assigned tasks. However, as children grow into adulthood, they develop other means by which they can promote their well-being.

One of the first steps in gaining control of the primitive impulses and drives is when the child develops an image of self and a self-identity. When the child becomes conscious of self, "to know I exist, to know what I am like and who I am," he is taking giant steps toward becoming a conscious being. This stage occurs initially, in a gross manner, about the age of 2 years. It is at this point that children can exert a conscious force to get what they want. However, getting what they want is not always what others in power or authority over them think they should have. The forces of society go to work to make the individual conform to the expectations that society has of the age level of the child.

Children learn. They begin to realize that some behaviors are more acceptable than others. Furthermore, they come to develop some likes and dislikes of their own. They develop a "self-ideal," an image of what they want to be like and of what they need to do to be accepted by those important to them. They can do some of this by 4 years of age. With a self-ideal to guide them and to remind them of what is important to them, they are now in a position to control and direct their behavior in accordance with their intentions and desires, which in turn are acceptable to society. They develop a life-style, a way of living and thinking. In addition, they learn ways of responding to frustrating times when they do not get what they want. As they get older, they modify their action patterns to be in keeping with society's expectations of their new age levels. If they satisfy the demands of society, they feel accepted; if they do not, they feel rejected. The intensity of their needs and the pattern of inner controls that they have developed will determine how they will respond, how well-adjusted they are, and how accepted they feel.

Ultimately, the degree of children's feelings of acceptance or rejection will have something to do with their development. They can develop a negativistic attitude toward those who seek to direct their growth. They may withdraw, lose interest, or seek to escape. They may become belligerent and rebellious so that they cannot be reached to be taught. One way or another their emerging selves and personality styles will largely determine what they will permit to happen to them. They will have something to say about how they develop mentally, socially, emotionally, and spiritually. They may even have something to say about how they will develop physically.

METAPHYSICAL DETERMINANTS

This section is admittedly included for speculative and discussion purposes. The term *metaphysics* refers to the system of principles underlying a particular study or subject. It is a division of philosophy that relates to the nature of being or kinds of existence (ontology) and to the study of the universe as an orderly system (cosmology). Since the particular subject involved in this text is the development of the human being, it would seem reasonable to at least acknowledge the possibility of the existence of principles that underlie the study of the nature of humankind and its place in the universal scheme of things.

Basis of life

What is life? What is humankind? In terms of theories, there are two basic approaches: the human being as a planned genesis designed by the Architect of the universe or the happenstance of a cosmic accident that could bring about another being like itself. The former approach is that of divine creation and the latter is the ultimate consequence of the theory of evolution. The divine creation is set forth in the Book of Genesis: "In the beginning God created the heavens and the earth. . . . And God said, "Let the earth bring forth living creatures, according to their kinds . . ." And God said, "Let us make man in our image, after our likeness . . . "male and female he created them" (Genesis I:1,24,26,27). Evolutionists believe in a slow, gradual process of development of complex organisms from simple predecessors on the basis of mutations that allowed adaptations to hostile environments. Life is a force that culminates in plant life, animal life, and human life. Humans are not plants, but, are they necessarily animals? Is a human being just a little higher than the ape or just a little lower than an angel? Man can act either way. Maybe human beings are something special between animals and angels with the freedom to choose what they prefer to be. Is there an implication here of what they "ought" to be?

For the moment, let us make three points. First, we must recognize that we can approach a study of human development without resolving the question of the basis and significance of life, even though there be a "hidden agenda" involved. Second, the issue of divine creation versus evolutionism need not be an either-or question. Many individuals, scientists and nonscientists, believe that the concept of an evolutionary process in no way rules out belief in the existence of a divine Creator. Of course, if there is such a thing as "truth," then only one answer can be true. What is needed is an expansion of man's mental capacities to see how the two ideas fit

together. Third, there may be other metaphysical considerations that have something more direct to say about human development. We will consider the nature of life forces, life choices, and life values.

Life forces

Life forces refer to innate inner dynamics or motivating drives that impel an individual to certain behaviors. Philosophers have considered this factor down through the ages. Epicurus and Aristippus considered this driving force to be pursuit of pleasure of the senses and of the mind (hedonism). The utilitarians under John Stuart Mill said that the greatest pleasure has as its primary concern the welfare and happiness of others. Arthur Schopenhauer was not so altruistic. He said that the driving force in man was the "will to live," the biological drive inherent in life itself. Friedrich Nietzsche spoke of the "will to power" to conquer and control; William James cited the "will to believe" in something so decisions could be made.

Psychologists have also spoken of the inner driving life forces. Sigmund Freud emphasized the "libido," which is psychic energy in pursuit of pleasure or erotic desire. Alfred Adler stressed the individual's desire to gain "mastery"; Carl Jung spoke of the "collective unconscious," which acts as the background of all human thought and emotion. The "will to love" has been advanced by Rollo May. Carl Rogers considers the central force to be "self-acceptance," and Abraham Maslow makes a case for "self-actualization." In summary, it appears to us that the life force has three thrusts: (1) survival values, for both the individual and the species; (2) social values, in humanization; and (3) self-realization values in the sense of becoming the most that you can be as a total person on the highest level of living and being. If there is such a thing as a life force, or the force of life, might it not have something to say about the direction of human growth and development?

Life choices

Another consideration is the matter of life choices. Does an individual have the freedom to make a free-will decision or are his choices predetermined or predestined? This question is appearing frequently in academic journals in psychology. The answer to the question has much to say about the nature and responsibility of decision making. The basis of behavioral outcomes is involved. We consider three possible positions. First, the position of free-will choices states that an individual determines his own destiny and direction in life by being free to choose and to decide what behavior he wishes to initiate. Regardless of past experiences, or in spite of them, when the moment comes to make a behavioral decision, he can do so on the basis of his own judgment and volition. The second position, determinism, states that what appears to be a free choice is actually predetermined by factors and

You may give them your love
but not your thoughts.
For they have their own thoughts.
You may house their bodies
but not their souls,
For their souls dwell
in the house of tomorrow,
which you cannot visit,
not even in your dreams.

Kahlil Gibran
The Prophet

Harold Geyer

causes beyond the control of the individual. The pattern for life decisions is set, and if you know the pattern, you can even predict what the decision will be.

A third possibility is that both of the previous two conditions exist. The universe is predicated on set principles of governance; these principles have a "cause and effect" element about them. An individual has the freedom to decide what behavior he wishes to initiate, but once the decision is made and the behavior is started, then the "cause and effect" principle takes over and will determine the outcome. Man is free to choose what he wants to do, but he cannot designate what the outcome will be. If he knows the cause and effect principle involved, then, of course, he can choose to initiate the proper behavior to bring about the desired result. The implication for human growth and development is that the more we know about the principles underlying growth and development, the more we can understand what behavior should be instigated and the better we can predict the outcomes.

Life values

Life values or life direction involves decision-making choices. Anytime that an individual makes a choice or expresses a preference, he is indicating a value. "I choose this one because it is better than, or as good as, the other one." The choices made in behavioral matters reflect how the individual considers the nature of values. One view is that values, moral and otherwise, are "relative." They vary for different people, in different circumstances, and in different periods of time. As a result, there is no stabilized "truth" or "good." It changes or "depends upon the situation."

A second view is that values have a universal basis and, as such, are true, correct, or best for all people at all times, under all circumstances, whether they are known, accepted, or not. These values are fundamental and carry a "cause and effect" relationship with them. There is no way you can get around or away from them.

A third view is a combination of the previous two. It states that the nature of values depends upon whether the decision-making topic or sub-

ject is in the realm of man-made values or in the domain of inherent universal values. If the behavior involved is based on superficial or changeable conditions, then a relative-type decision may be in order. However, if the circumstance is basic to humankind, then the universal principle applies. This third view is similar to the admonition to "render unto Caesar what is Caesar's and unto God what is God's."

Metaphysical determinants are interesting speculations. However, their abstract nature makes them difficult to pin down or even to prove their existence. As the horizons of knowledge are extended, however, sooner or later those of us interested in human nature must come to grips with questions that relate to the meaning of life. As of this moment, there is still so much to be learned about the objective facts of life. There is still so much to be discovered about what men, women, children, and their relationships are really like. Principles that we considered as "facts" just a few short years ago are now being demolished by new research, greater perspectives, and deeper insights. Consider the "elastic-mind" concept of Kagan and the "cultural-anthropological" view of Mead and Benedict (Chapter 1). Surely some things that were learned are fundamental. In other matters, however, maybe we have not been as aware or conscious of metaphysical considerations as we should have been.

STUDY GUIDE

1. How do DNA and RNA carry out genetic plans for growth and development?
2. The nervous system is fundamental to all development and behavior. What is the sensorimotor arc? What are the parts and functions of the two major divisions of the nervous system? How is the perceptual system related to the nervous system and the sensorimotor arc?
3. Identify the glands of the endocrine system and give the function of each gland.
4. What is physiological maturation, and what implications does it have for growth and development?
5. Socialization is said to occur through the influences of the family, the peer group, and

society on the developing individual. Which of these three forces do you think is influential in total development? Cite your reasons, even if you conclude that it is difficult or impossible to say which is most important or influential.

6. Describe the emerging self. Can you relate aspects of the emerging self to your own growth and development and behavior? In what ways?

7. Metaphysical determinants is an old, yet a new, concept. What are your opinions on the nature of life, life force, life choices, and life values? Do you agree or disagree that such considerations are significant to a study of human growth and development? Is there any area of application that you can think of where it might be significant?

8. If something cannot be proven, is it worth studying? Precisely how much can science "prove" about life?

REFERENCES

1. Aldrich, R. The watermelon theory: a concept of human life-span development. *Saturday Review,* 1977, **13**(1), 32-33.
2. McClearn, G. E., & DeFries, J. C. *Introduction to behavioral genetics.* San Francisco: W. H. Freeman & Co. Publishers, 1973.
3. Nagle, J. J. *Heredity and human affairs.* St. Louis: The C. V. Mosby Co., 1974.
4. Selye, H. The evolution of the stress concept. *American Scientist,* 1973, **61,** 692-699.
5. Sperry, R. W. Hemisphere deconnection and unity in conscious awareness. *American Psychologist,* 1968, **23,** 723-733.
6. Gazzaniga, M. S. *The bisected brain.* New York: Appleton-Century-Crofts, 1970.
7. Ornstein, R. E. *The psychology of consciousness.* San Francisco: W. H. Freeman & Co., Publishers, 1972.
8. Leukel, F. *Introduction to physiological psychology.* St. Louis: The C. V. Mosby Co., 1976.
9. Kaluger, G., & Kolson, C. J. *Reading and learning disabilities* (2nd ed.). Columbus, Ohio: Charles E. Merrill Publishing Co., 1978.
10. Munn, N. L. *The growth of human behavior* (3rd ed.). Boston: Houghton Mifflin Co., 1974.
11. Montagu, A. *The direction of human development* (Rev. ed.). New York: Hawthorn Books, Inc., 1970.
12. McNeil, E. B. *Human socialization.* Belmont, Calif.: Brooks/Cole Publishing Co., 1969.
13. Elder, G. H., & Bowerman, C. E. Family structure and child-rearing patterns, the effect of family size and sex composition. *American Sociological Review,* 1963, **28,** 891-905.
14. Bellmont, L., & Marolla, F. A. Birth order, family size, and intelligence. *Science,* 1973, **182,** 1096-1101.

3

Prenatal development

The greatest miracle of this age, or of any age, is not the knowledge explosion brought on by electronic technology, or the transplanting of organs from one human being to another, or the landing of men on the moon. The greatest miracle of all is the creation and birth of a new life. When one considers the intricate and complex processes involved in creating, developing, and maintaining life, how a human being is formed from a ball-shaped cell smaller in size than the period at the end of this sentence, and how human development takes place in such an orderly, sequential manner, one has to be impressed by the wonder and marvel of it all.

LIFE BEGINS

Living things have the power to reproduce themselves. The simplest kinds of animals and plants reproduce by the splitting of one cell in half, thus making two separate organisms. Animals and plants that are more complex in development have special cells that are designated for the purpose of reproduction. In human beings, as in other vertebrates, the union of two of these distinctive cells called gametes, the sperm from the male and the egg or ovum from the female, is necessary to create new life.

Sex cells

The sex cells (gametes, or germ cells) are the egg, or *ovum* (plural, ova), in the female and the sperm, or *spermatozoon* (plural, spermatozoa), in the male. The ovum is one of the largest cells in the human body, whereas the spermatozoon is one of the smallest. The spermatozoon is approximately 0.05 mm in diameter or 1/6,000 inch. It has either an oval-shaped head or a smaller, round-shaped head, plus a fine, hairlike tail about ten times as long as its head. The tail lashes back and forth, enabling the spermatozoon to swim through the semen in which it is found. The ovum is a single, ball-shaped cell approximately 0.1 mm or 1/200 inch in diameter and has no means of locomotion within itself. Its movement is dependent on the contractions of the tissues by which it is surrounded. The ovum is a tiny speck barely visible to the naked eye. However, it is still some 85,000 times greater in volume than the sperm.[1]

Female gametes and organs

The human female has in her ovaries at birth over 400,000 rudimentary ova. Many of these will atrophy before she reaches puberty. Of the 150,000 ova remaining at puberty, approximately 400 will mature, one at a time usually, prior to the menopause.[2] The ovum is yellowish in color because it contains yolk that will be used to nourish a new individual should the ovum be fertilized. In its nucleus the ovum contains 46 chromosomes in 23 pairs. Chromosomes direct the cells they occupy to grow in certain ways, perform certain functions, and transmit hereditary traits. When the ovum ripens, the pairs of chromosomes split by a process known as *oogenesis*. Half of the chromosomes remain at the center of the ovum; the other half migrate to the outer portion of the ovum and eventually disappear. When the ovum is fertilized, it will receive 23 chromosomes from the sperm, thus again having a total of 46.

The *uterus* (womb) is a hollow, pear-shaped organ with strong but elastic muscular walls. It is within the uterus that the baby will develop (Fig. 3-1). The lower end of the uterus, which extends into the vagina, is called the *cervix*. The cervix has an opening through which the sperms will make their way from the vagina into the uterus. When the baby is being born, the cervix will di-

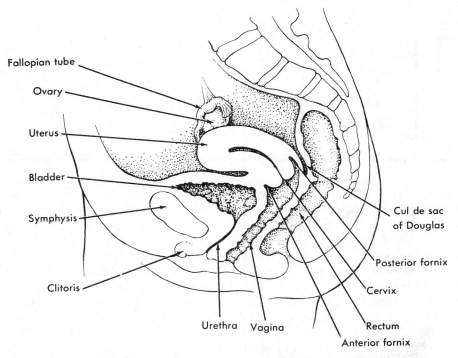

Fig. 3-1. Internal female sex organs. The ovary releases one ovum (egg) a month. The egg travels through the fallopian tube, where fertilization occurs if sperms are present. If the egg is not fertilized, the wall of the uterus breaks down, and blood cells and disintegrated egg are discharged through the vagina by the process of menstruation. The female system prepares itself for motherhood each month. (From Iorio, J. *Childbirth: family-centered nursing* [3rd ed.]. St. Louis: The C. V. Mosby Co., 1975.)

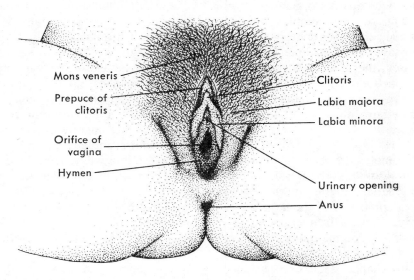

Fig. 3-2. External genitalia of the human female. (From Nagle, J. J. *Heredity and human affairs.* St. Louis: The C. V. Mosby Co., 1974.)

late and the baby will pass through this enlarged opening into the vagina and be discharged into the external world. The external female sex organs are depicted in Fig. 3-2.

During a woman's childbearing years, the uterus is normally prepared each month for fertilization and pregnancy. If no pregnancy occurs, menstruation takes place. The menstrual "cycle" begins with the flow of mucus and blood that had accumulated during the previous cycle. The discharge will continue for four or five days. At the end of this time the uterine wall is relatively thin. In the postmenstrual phase the uterus will come under the influence of an estrogen hormone that seeks to increase sexual excitability—and also influences thickening of the *endometrium* (uterus wall lining). This period is the follicular phase (Fig. 3-3). At the time of ovulation the hormone *progesterone* takes over and prepares the endometrium with thin layers of cells for the reception and development of the fertilized ovum. The lining inside the uterus continues to thicken. If fertilization of the ovum does not take place, the level of progesterone begins to drop about the twenty-fifth day, during the luteal

phase, resulting in a degeneration of the thickened uterine lining. The surface layer of cells passes out with the flow of mucus and blood during the next menstrual phase. The content is normally about 6 to 8 tablespoons. A menstrual cycle lasts for an average of twenty-eight days, paralleling the time of a lunar month.[3]

Ovulation is the process by which a mature ovum is discharged from one of the two ovaries. The ovaries are glands about the size and shape of almonds that lie about 3 inches on either side of the midway point between the vaginal opening and the navel. They are located on each side of the outer uterine wall at the end of the fallopian tubes. There is a tube for each ovary. Generally, the ovaries alternate in releasing one ripe ovum on or about the fourteenth day of the menstrual cycle. The usual cycle is counted from the beginning of one menstrual flow to the beginning of the next. Therefore ovulation—the time when pregnancy can most likely take place in a woman with a normal menstrual cycle—occurs just about midway between the periods of menstrual flow.

The ovum within the ovary is surrounded by a small sac known as a graafian follicle. The follicle

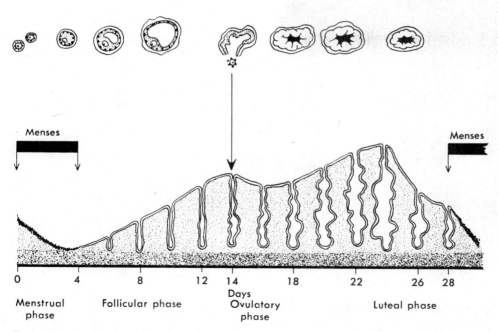

Fig. 3-3. Menstrual cycle. (From Iorio, J. *Childbirth: family-centered nursing* [3rd ed.]. St. Louis: The C. V. Mosby Co., 1975.)

holding the ovum works its way to the surface of the ovary and there forms a blisterlike swelling. This blister, containing estrogen fluid, ruptures and releases the ovum at the open end of the nearest fallopian tube. The tiny round egg finds its way into the tube and is propelled through the tube by hairlike cilia cells on the sides of the tube, by the estrogen fluid, and by rhythmic contractions of the walls of the tube.[4] The fallopian tube is about 4 inches long and connects to the uterus. The ovum will survive for three or four days or longer, although it is fertile only during the first part of that time. If the ovum is not fertilized, it deteriorates, and its remains will then be discharged along with other menstrual materials and blood from the uterine lining.

Male gametes and organs

Whereas only one ovum is ripened every menstrual cycle, several hundred million spermatozoa are developed every four or five days. The implication is that the man is capable of providing sperms for the purpose of conception at almost anytime, whereas the woman produces a mature ovum on the average of only once every twenty-eight days. Furthermore, spermatozoa are formed well into old age, even though the sperms may not always be capable of fertilizing an egg. In the woman, production of the sex cells will cease with the completion of menopause.

Spermatozoa are formed in the two *testes* (testicles or male gonads) suspended in the scrotum, a thin-walled sac of skin (Fig. 3-4). The sperm-making cells within the testicles are extremely sensitive to heat. They must have a temperature several degrees below that of the interior of the body; otherwise, they rapidly degenerate and cease producing the male sex cells. The scrotum has a large area of skin surface for the purpose of heat evaporation. The sac will pull close to the body when cold to get more heat and will hang loose when warm to become cooler.[5]

The process by which sperms are produced is called *spermatogenesis*. Spermatogenesis involves the reduction of the 46 chromosomes by several cell divisions into a sperm that will even-

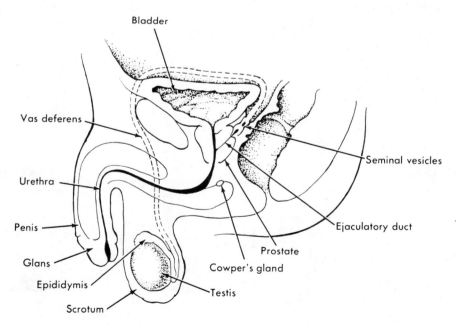

Fig. 3-4. Male sex organs and gamete production. The sperm cells are produced in the testes and are temporarily stored in the seminal vesicles. Male sex organs constantly make and deliver active sperm cells capable of fertilizing the ovum in the body of the female. (From Iorio, J. *Childbirth: family-centered nursing* [3rd ed.]. St. Louis: The C. V. Mosby Co., 1975.)

tually contain only half that number. The mature sperm has 22 chromosomes plus a sex determination chromosome (X or Y). These 23 chromosomes will pair with the 23 chromosomes found in the female sex cell at the time of conception. From the testes the mature spermatozoa will pass through a long, narrow, much coiled tube called the *epididymis,* where they mix with a fluid. The spermatozoa will then move through other long tubes called the *vas deferens* to the seminal vesicles, where the sperm is temporarily stored. Located near the seminal vesicles is the prostate gland. At the time of ejaculation the fluid carrying the sex cells passes the prostate gland, where a milky secretion is added to make semen. Up to the time of ejaculation the spermatozoa have been relatively motionless. With the addition of

the fluids from the prostate gland they become very vigorous. After ejaculation, spermatozoa remain actively mobile in the seminal fluid for as long as 36 to 48 hours in the upper portions of the female reproductive tract.[6] Since spermatozoa can live as long as two or three days within the uterus of the woman, the depositing of sperm in the vagina as much as 72 hours prior to ovulation can lead to pregnancy. Spermatozoa that do not enter the uterus from the vagina usually die within a few hours because of the toxic environment of the vagina.

Fertilization

It is the act of mating, or sexual intercourse, that brings the sperm cells and ovum together. The stimulating effect of intercourse on the penis

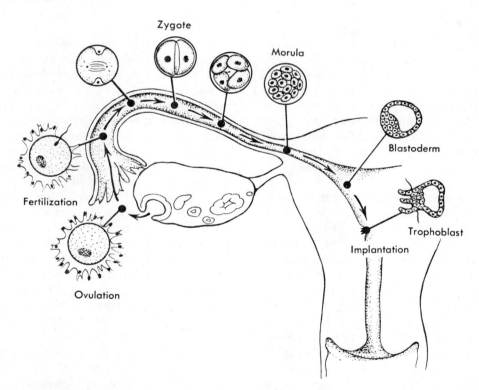

Fig. 3-5. Process of fertilization, cell division, and implantation. Sperm cells enter the uterus and fallopian tube about the time the ovum is released from the ovary and enters the fallopian tube. The sperm and egg cell meet and unite in the tube. The sperm fertilizes the egg by entering its nucleus. The fertilized egg cell begins to divide as it travels to the uterus, where it attaches itself to the uterine wall and begins to form into an embryo. (From Iorio, J. *Childbirth: family-centered nursing* [3rd ed.]. St. Louis: The C. V. Mosby Co., 1975.)

causes the male to ejaculate about a teaspoonful of semen containing about 300 to 400 million spermatozoa into the vagina near the cervix. Only a small number of the spermatozoa succeed in working their way through the cervical opening into the uterus. Even fewer find their way into the fallopian tubes. The journey takes about 1 to 2 hours. If a viable ovum is present in the tube, the spermatozoa that have made their way into the tube will be drawn to the egg and will cover it. Sperm cells make an enzyme that helps to break down the rather tough outer membrane of the egg cell. Once a sperm does pierce the cell wall, it still has to find its way to the nucleus of the egg. Considering that the ovum is 85,000 times larger than the sperm, the little sperm still has a comparatively long way to go. When a sperm does reach the nucleus, the other sperms cease their activities (Fig. 3-5).

The nucleus of the sperm and the nucleus of the ovum will merge, and their contents will combine. The 23 chromosomes of the ovum's nucleus will pair off with the 23 chromosomes from the nucleus of the sperm to make 23 pairs of chromosomes with thousands of genes. In that fraction of a second when the chromosomes form pairs, the sex of the new child will be determined, hereditary characteristics received from each parent will be set, and a new life will have been created.

Infertility. Several conditions might exist that prevent conception from taking place. Some of these conditions are an inability of the male to produce healthy sperm; an inability of the male to transfer the sperm to the genital tract because of injury, psychological trouble, or inability to achieve erection; poor female environment for the fertilized eggs; failure of ovulation due to endocrine or metabolic imbalance; fallopian tubes that are blocked; fear of sex by male or female; or physical obstacles to having children. Out of 600 consecutive private patients investigated for infertility, Payne and Skeels[7] found that major factors were located in both partners in 41% of the cases, in the wife only in 33% of the cases, and in the husband only in 26% of the cases.

Human infertility has struck large areas of Africa. From 20% to 40% of the women in many tribes have become infertile. The countries stricken with infertility include Gabon, Cameroon, Sudan, Uganda, Ghana, Kenya, and Tanzania. They have appealed for help to the World Health Organization. Several reasons have been advanced for the cause. Pinworm infections disturb the lymphatic glands in both male and female and evidently lead to sterility in women. South of the Sahara, the most common cause seems to be gonorrhea, which obstructs the fallopian tubes. A massive penicillin campaign designed to eradicate gonorrhea in New Guinea resulted in an increase in the fertility rate a year later.

Artificial reproduction. There are three major modes of modified reproduction that have eugenic potential; however, there are some ethical questions that must be considered. These are (1) artificial insemination and/or artificial inovulation, (2) in vitro fertilization and embryo transplantation, and (3) asexual reproduction, known as cloning.

Artificial insemination involves the collection of semen, usually through masturbation. It is then introduced directly through the vagina to the cervix of the uterus by a syringe. The semen may be supplied by the husband if he is subfertile and needs more sperms to gain access to the egg. If the husband is infertile, however, then a donor is required. The semen must be used within 30 minutes after it is ejaculated or it can be frozen and placed in a sperm bank. Artificial inovulation is a possibility for women who have blocked oviducts. By means of a simple surgical procedure, eggs can be removed and transferred to lower portions of the oviduct, detouring the blockage. Fertilization can then occur by normal intercourse or artificial insemination.

In vitro fertilization refers to the union of the egg and sperm outside the body in a laboratory. The procedure is more complicated than it may seem. Some successful human fertilizations have occurred but usually for a very short period of cell division. The implication is that if these fertilized cells were to be implanted in a receptive uterus, they may develop normally. Such transplants have been done successfully in mammals such as lambs. On July 26, 1978, a 5-pound, 12-ounce girl believed to be the world's first baby that was conceived in vitro was born in Oldham, England. Mother and child were in excellent

Take twin mounds of clay
Mold them as you may
Shape one after me,
Another after thee.
Then quickly break them both.
Remix, remake them both—
One formed after thee,
The other after me.
Part of my clay is thine;
Part of thy clay is mine.

Kwan Tao-Shing
13th Century

condition. Since then, several other such pregnancies were reported in progress.

Cloning represents a radical departure from traditional reproduction. Cloning is the process of duplicating living things from an individual cell. It has been used to create plants in 1963. Dr. J. B. Gurdon of Oxford University reported the production of cloned frogs in 1966. As far as we know, it has not been attempted on humans. Rumors of such attempts are heard every now and then, even to the point of stating that at least one human was created that way. The problem with human cloning appears to be one of technique. The microsurgical technique used with the cell of the frog to bring about a clone would be totally inadequate to do the same with the more refined, delicate, complex human cell. A cell-fusion technique is said by supporters of the idea to be able to overcome cell damage and offers a better technique of cloning. No scientific evidence has been revealed at this point. The scientific, social, moral, and religious issues involved are overwhelming to both the conscious and the conscience.

PREGNANCY

The moment that a new life is conceived is not immediately evident to the woman. The fertilized egg, however, will probably begin within the hour of conception to divide and to develop into a baby. The woman may not learn of her pregnancy for some days to come.

Diagnosis of pregnancy

A diagnosis of pregnancy can be determined from three types of information: the symptoms of the woman, specific laboratory tests, and certain bodily changes found by the physician on his physical examination of the woman. Failure to menstruate is usually the earliest evidence of pregnancy. However, failure to menstruate may also result from illness or anxiety. Likewise, occasionally a woman may be pregnant and still have signs of menstruation. As a result, laboratory tests for pregnancy provide more definite information. Most laboratory tests seek to determine whether a substance known as chorionic gonadotropic hormone (HCG) is present in the urine. This hormone is secreted by the trophoblasts and is always present nine to ten days after the first missed menstrual period. The HCG reaches a peak between the sixtieth and seventieth days of pregnancy.

Aschheim and Zondek in 1928 did the research that led to the first methods by which pregnancy could be indicated with at least 95% accuracy. A small quantity of the woman's urine is injected into a female mouse or rabbit. If the woman is pregnant, a hormone in her urine will cause changes in the animal's ovaries within 48 to 72 hours. Another test using frogs provides results in 2 to 10 hours. More recently, tests have been devised that can give results within minutes. One test consists of a chemical analysis for color change of the woman's urine when mixed with a special reagent. In another test two preparations are placed on a glass slide, and a drop of urine is put on the preparations. If the preparations do not clump together in particles, the urine contains HCG and the woman is pregnant.[8] Pregnancy frequently can be confirmed as early as three to four weeks after conception, although six weeks is generally required for certainty.

A "do-it-yourself" pregnancy kit became available in 1976 in New England. The E.P.T. In-home Pregnancy Test (E.P.T. stands for Early Pregnancy Test) is now distributed nationally in the United States by Warner-Chilcott. It has been available in Europe since 1970 under the name of "Predictor." The test makes use of the principle that the pregnant body begins to produce HCG on the ninth day after the date that the menstrual period was to begin. Instructions are simple: after the ninth day put three drops of urine into the test tube provided. Add the contents of the plastic vial in the E.P.T kit, shake for 10 seconds, and place the test tube in the holder. It must remain undisturbed for 2 hours. If a dark brown ring is visible in the mirror that comes with the holder after 2 hours, an active pregnancy is indicated. Studies by the company claim that positive readings are 97% accurate. Negative readings indicate that a second test should be taken a week later. If the second test is also negative, then the results are considered to be 91% accurate. E.P.T. information points out that the first sixty days are critical in fetal development and suggests that improper use of cigarettes, alcohol, household medications, or poor nutrition can be harmful to the developing fetus.

The most positive signs of pregnancy include hearing and counting of fetal heart tones after the eighteenth to twentieth week of pregnancy, spontaneous fetal movement as felt by the physician, x-ray evidence after the fifth month, and evidence of fetal bones after the fourth month of pregnancy. Commonly experienced physical signs in a woman include (1) cessation of menstruation, (2) nausea and vomiting (morning sickness) from shortly after the first missed period to the end of the first trimester, (3) fatigue, requiring 10 to 12 hours of sleep, (4) tenderness and gradual enlargement of breasts and deeper color in the area around the nipples about the third month, (5) increased frequency of urination, and (6) the feeling of fetal movements (quickening) about the seventeeth or eighteenth week of pregnancy.[9]

Boy or girl?

Of the 46 chromosomes found in germ cells, two are sex determination chromosomes. In the female these two sex determination chromosomes are identical and so are given the letter designation of X and X. In the male, however, these chromosomes are different and so are designated as X and Y. By the process of *meiosis,* or sex cell production, the ovum will always have 22 non-sex chromosomes (called *autosomes*) plus an X sex determination cell. The sperm will also have 22 autosomes plus a sex determination cell, but that cell may be either an X cell or a Y cell. Should it be an X cell from the male that pairs with the X cell from the female, the result will be a girl. A Y cell from the male that pairs with an X cell from the female will produce a boy. It is from the germ cells of the father that the sex of the child is determined (Fig. 3-6).

There have been numerous theories and methods advocated throughout the ages in an effort to choose the sex of a child. The research of Shettles[10] indicates that some basic principles regarding sex selection may have been found. Using a phase-contrast microscope and carbon dioxide gas to slow down the movement of living sperm cells, Shettles noticed that sperms came in two distinct sizes and shapes. He eventually con-

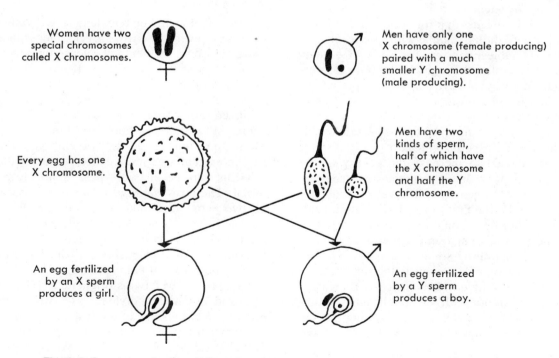

Fig. 3-6. Sex determination. If the X (female producing) sperm of the male unites with the X chromosome from the egg, a girl is produced. If the Y (male producing) sperm unites with the X chromosome from the egg, a boy is created.

cluded that the small, round-headed sperms carry the male-producing Y chromosomes. The larger, oval-shaped type carry the female-producing X chromosomes. The male-producing type he calls *androsperms* and the female-producing type he calls *gynosperms*. He further postulated that the male sperms are weaker and less viable than those carrying the trait for a female. The male sperms are also highly sensitive to the type of acid that is found in the vaginal tract and do not survive long in that environment. In the female, alkaline secretions generally appear only during the 24 hours before ovulation. It also appeared the the relative percentage of androsperms to gynosperms decreases after repeated intercourse and ejaculations.

Based on these findings Shettles and Vande Weile prescribe the following practices for couples who desire a child of a particular sex. One suggestion is to promote a chemical environment favorable to the sperm preferred. Medical advice and examination should be sought before attempting douching for this purpose. Since the male sperms are not strong enough to resist a highly acidic vaginal environment, Shettles and Vande Weile suggest that for couples who desire a boy the wife should douche with a basic alkaline solution (2 tablespoons baking soda to 1 quart water) to neutralize the vaginal acids prior to intercourse. This vaginal environment will permit the male sperm to travel more swiftly as well as to survive better.

For couples desiring a girl a white vinegar douche of 2 tablespoons vinegar to 1 quart water is recommended to increase the acidity of the vagina to destroy or weaken the male sperms. Thus the female sperms will have a greater opportunity to be the first to reach the ovum. Couples desiring a boy should also avoid intercourse until the time of ovulation (as previously determined by temperature studies) to assure a higher concentration of male sperms in the semen. Clinical results show at least 80% success. If the couple is conscientious with the douche and the timing, the researchers claim that choosing the sex of the child is successful 85% to 90% of the time.[11]

It is important to note that the use of a douche to maximize the probability of a certain sex as suggested by Shettles and Vande Weile is still considered highly questionable by many recognized authorities.

Donald and Locky Schuster of Iowa State University hypothesize that the less-stressed parent tends to produce his own or her own gender. Wittels and Bornstein[12] provided support for this idea based on a study of the sex of children born as a result of rape. In such situations, it was reasoned that the mother was probably under greater stress than the father. If the Schusters' hypothesis were true, more than half the children born should be boys. Working with a religious organization, the researchers found ten rape-conceived children out of a total of 349 babies handled by the organization during a 30-month period. Of the 349 babies, 191 were boys and 158 girls. Of the ten rape-caused births, nine were boys. They found that the one rape victim who gave birth to a girl admitted to having a relationship with the alleged father previous to the alleged rape. Further investigation of this theory warrants attention.

More than one

Normally the human female produces only one ripe ovum every menstrual cycle. Occasionally, however, some women will release two or more mature ova at the same time. If more than one ovum are in the fallopian tube at the same time, there is a good chance that more than one will be fertilized. Sometimes only one egg is fertilized in a tube, but certain conditions exist that cause that egg to split, thus producing two embryos. Either way more than one life has been conceived.

Twins may be of two types, identical or fraternal. The term *identical* is misleading because no two people are alike in every way. For this reason geneticists prefer to use terms that refer to the origin of the twin types. Identical twins are referred to as *monozygotic* (MZ), or one-egg twins, and fraternal twins are *dizygotic* (DZ), or two-egg twins. MZ twins originate from a single fertilized ovum that divided into two or more parts at an early stage of development. DZ twins occur when two or more eggs are present in the fallopian tubes (oviducts) and two or more are fertilized by different sperm cells. Since DZ twins originate from different ova as well as different

Harold Geyer

Twins double the love—and the care—needed.

sperm cells, the genetic relationship between the twins is no greater than that of ordinary siblings.[13] Thus DZ twins can be two girls, two boys, or one girl and one boy. MZ twins will always be of the same sex. One third of all twins are MZ twins. Twins occur in one out of eighty-eight births; triplets occur in one out of 7,564 births.[14]

During the development of twins, several factors are present that are not as common in single child pregnancies. Both DZ and MZ conceptions must deal with crowding factors, especially if they have a common placenta. In MZ twins the fertilized egg had enough food stored within it for only one baby. Of course, when the egg splits, the food is divided. Food may be lacking for the zygotes to survive. The chance of a premature birth is greater among multiple births than for single births. Koch[15] studied sixty-two sets of twins and found (1) the incidence of prematurity was about 5% higher for twins, (2) most early births occurred in the lowest class families, (3) prematurity rate is higher for girl twins, (4) prematurity rate is higher for MZ twins, (5) chances for American black mothers to have twins are one-third higher than for whites, but for Japanese and Chinese mothers it is one-third less, and (6) chances for twins increase with the age of the mother and the number of previous births.

Whatever is true about twins applies in extended ways to triplets, quadruplets, and other "twin-plus" sets. These multiple pregnancies are produced by basically the same process as twins.

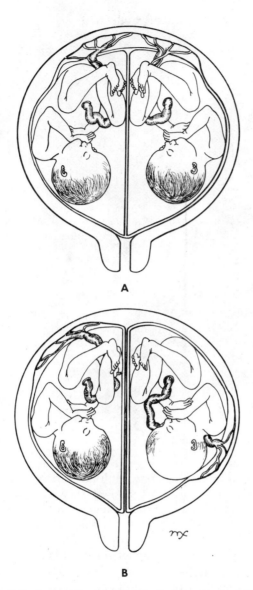

Fig. 3-7. A, Identical twins. **B,** Fraternal twins. Note differences in construction of amniotic sacs. (From Ingalls, J., & Salerno, M. C. *Maternal and child health nursing* [3rd ed.]. St. Louis: The C. V. Mosby Co., 1975.)

Normally, five or six sets of quadruplets are born in the United States every year, but few intact sets manage to survive so that there are probably only about a dozen complete sets in the United States at any one time. Quintuplets are even more rare. The Dionne quintuplets, born in 1934, all of whom survived, were the only all-identical set on record. In 1964 all-surviving quintuplets were born in South Dakota and in Venezuela, but they were mixed sets, combining both identicals and fraternals.

Since the mid-1960s, certain hormones have been administered to previously sterile women to induce ovulation and conception. These procedures often trigger the release of more than one egg at a time and have resulted in twins and "twins plus." Using hormones, four women conceived quadruplets; three sets are surviving and healthy. Two sets of quintuplets were born, with all five surviving in one set but only one surviving in the other.[16] Sextuplets were born in Denver, Colorado, in 1973 and all survived to the time this book was published. In 1971 nine children were born to a woman in South America, but all of them died within ten days. All of these were fraternal fertilizations, since they resulted from more than one egg. The statistics on the number of multiple pregnancies produced may be upset by a wider use of the hormone procedures with sterile women.

PRENATAL DEVELOPMENT AND BEHAVIOR

Once the fertilization of an ovum has taken place, nature appears to be in a fantastic hurry to move on with the developmental processes. Within an hour or two the fertilized egg will divide to form new cells. Cell division continues until the young embryo is implanted in the uterus; then structures begin to appear. By the time the woman misses her first menstrual period the baby's heart, nervous system, and intestines are already developing. The woman, at this point, may not even know that she is pregnant.

Embryologists usually divide prenatal development into three periods. Each period has its own growth characteristics. First is the period of the ovum, also called the period of the zygote or the germinal period, during which the fertilized egg makes its way to the uterus. Second is the embryonic period, at which time the round ball, the fertilized egg, changes to a recognizable human fetus. The third stage is the fetal period, during which the fetus enhances and refines the structures developed during the previous period. The miracle of growth, the wonder of life, and the marvel of the laws of nature are perhaps most perfectly illustrated during these three periods in which a child develops from two minute cells that came together into a baby boy or girl, the newest member of mankind.

Period of the zygote

Once conception has taken place, two things occur simultaneously; the fertilized egg (zygote) begins to divide, and at the same time it makes its way down the fallopian tube to the uterus. The zygote will divide, perhaps within 30 minutes, certainly within an hour or two after conception. Ten hours later these two cells divide to make four cells, then the four to make eight cells, then sixteen cells, and so on. The cells are related to one another in accordance to the master blueprint plan as prescribed for the total organic structure in the DNA molecules. The entire sphere made up of cells is called a *blastocyst,* or a zygote. Although the cells increase in number, they do not increase the overall size of the zygote.

During the first two weeks after fertilization, the important job is not the development of the actual form of the child but the making of clusters of cells that have special functions. Not all of the blastocyst cells become the human being. Imagine a drawing of the fertilized egg. The outer surface of the fertilized egg does not change into the shape of the child but eventually becomes part of the chorion (an extraembryonic membrane) and, later, the placenta.

Cells begin to form within the cell wall of the fertilized egg. The outer layer of cells of the zygote is known as the *trophoblast* (Fig. 3-5). It will develop roots with which to attach itself to the uterus and will eventually become the chorion. An inner mass of cells will develop at one end or side of the interior of the sphere. Within this inner cell mass two hollow areas will be formed with a wall of cells separating the two. The hollow area next to the outer wall will even-

tually become the amnion (water sac), and the other cavity will become the yolk sac. The thick wall of cells between the two cavities is called the embryonic, or germinal, disk. This disk becomes the child.

The journey down the fallopian tube to the uterus takes three to five days. Once in the uterus (womb), the fertilized ovum floats in a fluid for a few days before it attaches itself to the uterus. The uterus, meanwhile, has prepared itself—as it does every month—for the reception of the fertilized egg. At this time its lining is at its thickest state and has considerable nourishment in its cells.

The free zygote begins to attach itself to the uterine wall about the sixth or seventh day after conception. By the tenth day it will usually be completely covered, and implantation will have taken place. Implantation marks the end of the period of the ovum. During this time period the zygote remains at about the size of a pin head.

The trophoblast of the zygote has roots that will act on the uterine lining once the zygote comes to rest. Enzymes enable the trophoblast to digest or liquefy the tissue of the uterus. At implantation it will burrow into the uterine lining and form a nest for the zygote. Now the chorion begins to develop a network of fine roots, called *villi,* which spread into the lining of the uterus. They are important because they contain blood vessels that are connected with the fetus. They are the sole means by which oxygen and nourishment are received from the mother. There is no gross intermingling of the blood of the mother with that of the fetus, however. The placenta will not be completed until the third month of pregnancy.

There are certain hazards to the survival of the fertilized egg during the period of the ovum. The ovum must survive largely on its own food until it is implanted. If it does not receive enough nourishment, either because of the minimal amount of food supply or because the zygote takes too long to become implanted, it dies. It will be shed during the next menstrual period without the woman ever realizing that conception had taken place. Occasionally there will be interference with the migration of the ovum down the fallopian tubes. Again, the ovum will die if it does not reach the uterus in time to become implanted. If the ovum degenerates in the tube, an ectopic pregnancy, which is the implantation of the fertilized ovum outside the uterine cavity, will take place.

Embryonic period

The embryonic period is one of rapid change. It covers that period of pregnancy from the time of implantation of the ball-shaped zygote in the uter-ine wall to the time that the embryo becomes a recognizable human fetus. Embryologists say that this time span extends to the eighth week after conception. It is difficult to be precise about the time span because knowledge of this growth period is limited. The science of human embryology cannot be studied experimentally as is the case with infrahuman embryology. Knowledge of the subject for the most part has been derived from the study of embryos that had to be surgi-

THE FIRST THREE MONTHS

Actual size,
$^3/_{14}$ inch

Heart pulsating and pumping blood. Backbone and spinal canal forming. No eyes, nose or external ears visible. Digestive system beginning to form. Small buds which will eventually become arms and legs are present.

At end of four weeks

At end of eight weeks

About 1 $^1/_8$ inches long.
Weighs about $^1/_{30}$ ounce.
Face and features forming; eyelids fused.
Limbs beginning to show distinct divisions into arms, elbows, forearm and hand, thigh, knee, lower leg, and foot.
Distinct umbilical cord formed.
Long bones and internal organs developing.
Tail-like process disappears.

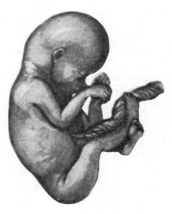

At end of twelve weeks

About 3 inches long.
Weighs about 1 ounce.
Arms, hands, fingers and legs, feet, toes fully formed. Nails on digits beginning to develop.
External ears are present.
Tooth sockets and buds forming in the jawbones.
Eyes almost fully developed, but lids still fused.

Growth of the fetus the first three months. (Original artwork courtesy Carnation Co., Los Angeles, Calif. © Carnation Co., 1962.)

cally removed because the life and health of the mother were endangered.

During the early part of the embryonic period, the placenta, the umbilical cord, and the amniotic sac are developed to the point where they can protect and nourish the embryo until the time of birth. At maturity the pancakelike placenta will measure about 8 inches in diameter and 1 inch in thickness and will weigh about 1 pound. Although the developing placenta is much too small to be seen at the time of implantation, it does begin to alter the hormonal pattern of the mother.

The amniotic sac (amnion) will enclose the embryo in a protective bag of fluid. The fetus will be able to move in this fluid and also to swallow it. This sac will serve to cushion the fetus against possible bumps, shocks, and injuries and will help to regulate its temperature. The yolk sac has a temporary function of making blood cells for the embryo; however, it will soon shrink and gradually disappear when the liver takes over this function. The amniotic sac, the yolk sac, and the embryonic disk will become separated from the outer later of cells by the formation of a short connecting stalk that becomes the umbilical cord.[17]

The umbilical cord is developed from the body stock that connects the placenta to the embryo.

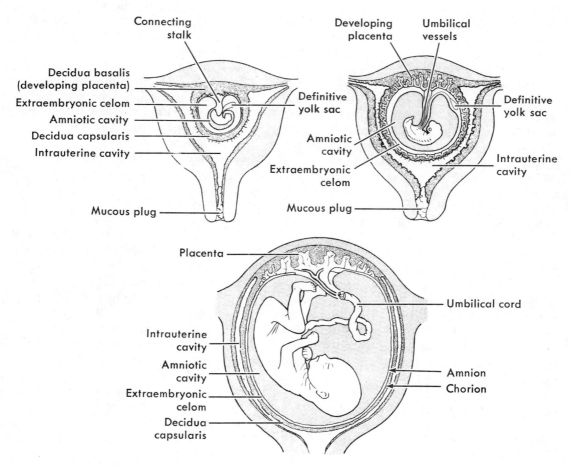

Development of fetal membranes. Note gradual obliteration of uterine cavity as decidua capsularis and decidua vera meet. Also note thinning of uterine wall. Chorionic and amniotic membranes are in apposition to each other but may be peeled apart. (From Jensen, M. D., Benson, R. C., & Bobak, I. M. *Maternity care: the nurse and family.* St. Louis: The C. V. Mosby Co., 1977.)

Nourishment in the form of minerals, proteins, and oxygen from the mother is passed through the placenta to the embryo by way of the umbilical cord, and waste products from the embryo are filtered back. The cord contains two arteries and one vein but no nerves. It eventually becomes abut ¾ inch thick, about 22 inches in length, and looks like a whitish, rubbery tube. It is filled with a substance called Wharton's jelly. The jelly and the pressure of the blood rushing through the blood vessels keep the umbilical cord somewhat stiff, like a soft garden hose. The cord tends to straighten itself automatically when bent. Because of these factors, the danger of the umbilical cord choking a baby are very slim, even though it is not uncommon for it to pass around the baby's neck. The baby is enclosed in the double-walled membrane of the chorion and the amniotic sac. The sac contains a fluid in which the baby floats and moves around, thus giving the umbilical cord a chance to straighten out.

By 2½ weeks the embryo has already begun to take shape. Its head-to-feet and top-to-bottom directions have been determined. The nervous system has begun to develop with the start of a longitudinal neural plate and a groove that will eventually form into a tube with two protrusions for the brain at the upper end. The heart, at first a single tube, may beat haltingly as early as the eighteenth day, even though there is no blood for it to circulate. The heart will pump more confidently by 3½ weeks, but it will not be regular for some weeks to come.

It is during the second and third weeks after conception that the inner mass of cells begins to differentiate into three layers. The outer layer, the ectoderm, will become the skin, hair, nails, sensory and skin glands, and all nerve tissues. From the middle layer, the mesoderm, will come the bones, muscle, and circulatory organs, and part of the excretory organs. From the inner layer, the endoderm, the digestive organs, liver, alimentary tract, lungs, and some of the endocrine glands will develop.

The 28-day embryo still does not look like a baby, but it does have an oval body, a differentiated head region that takes up one third of its length, and at the lower end of the body, a short, slim, tail-like protrusion that will become the last bone in the spine. There is a brain and a primitive spinal cord. The heart is becoming well developed, although it is still only a C-shaped bulge in the body wall. The embryo has developed simple kidneys, a primitive liver, and a simple digestive tract extending from the mouth area to the lower end. The head has rudimentary eyes, ears, and a nose. The first limb buds of the arms and legs appear about this time. Although all these body systems are being developed, the embryo is only about ⅕ inch long—about half the size of a pea. The mother is two weeks overdue for her menstrual cycle. She may not realize she is pregnant as yet because the embryo is so small and causes her no discomfort.

In the beginning the brain and spinal cord grow more quickly than the other structures. Almost all the functions of the body depend on an adequate nervous system. The nervous system develops first so that all the other systems can grow and function as they should. Development starts with the brain and head area and then works down the body, the feet developing last. This progression is the cephalocaudal direction of growth.

During the second month, the main features of the human form rapidly appear. The nose, mouth, and tongue emerge more clearly. The developing eye appears as a dark circle. The black pigment layer of the eye is plainly visible, as is the fainter inner circle that is the lens. What looks like a mouth beneath the eye is actually the ear, still quite low on the head. The limbs grow longer; saddles and ridges appear on the end of them, later forming fingers and toes. The development of the baby teeth begins about six weeks after conception. By the tenth week the rudiments of all twenty teeth are present. The stomach, intestines, pharynx, lungs, and rudiments of the rectum, bladder, and external genital organs all grow from enlargements of the digestive tract. The endocrine system takes shape, the adrenal medulla secretes epinephrine, and the testes in the male begin to secrete androgens.

At the end of the second month the embryo will measure about 1 inch from the top of its head to the buttocks. It will weigh approximately ⅔ ounce. The embryo now represents a miniature individual in its development. The principles in-

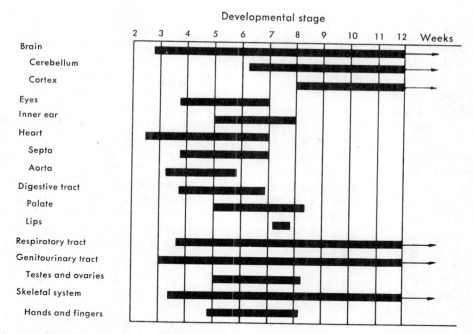

Developmental stage

Approximate periods of critical differentiation for some specific organs. (From Whaley, L. *Understanding inherited disorders.* St. Louis: The C. V. Mosby Co., 1974.)

dicating the completion of the embryonic period are the formation of the first real bone cells that begin to replace the cartilage and the completion of features that resemble a human being. The embryo looks like a human being and not a monkey, a puppy, or a cat. Human likeness is clearly imprinted on it.

The most crucial time when the embryo's development can be most seriously affected is the first eight to nine weeks of pregnancy, which is precisely the time when most women pay little attention to their new condition. There is a sequence of physical development taking place during the embryonic stage that is systematic and regular. There is a particular time for the emergence of each of the organs and their systems. Any disturbance or interruption with this sequence can be disastrous. If the delicate chemical balance of the mother is upset seriously, permanent damage can occur. Rubella (German measles) and certain drugs are especially serious during the first three months of pregnancy, since they can cause damage to what-

ever structures are being formed at the time. The brain, too, is susceptible to damage.

It has been estimated that one out of every ten fertilized ova does not survive, the most critical time being the embryonic period.[18] Miscarriages are nature's way of getting rid of an abnormally developing embryo or fetus. It could also mean that the uterine environment was not conducive to survival. About 75% of all miscarriages occur by the third month. Defective germ plasma, maternal disease, abnormalities of reproductive organs, blood group incompatibilities, malnutrition, and hormone imbalance are among the causes of spontaneous abortion. There are three boy miscarriages for every two girl miscarriages (160 to 100), indicating that in some respects the female has better survival capability than the male. This point will also be noted at other stages in the developmental process.

Period of the fetus

The fetal period of development is from about the eighth week, when the embryo becomes a recognizable human being, to the time of birth. Having passed the critical embryonic stage, the chances of survival for the fetus are greatly increased. The organs, which have all been started by now, continue to develop and become functional. It is about this time that women usually make an appointment with their physician to find out if they are pregnant. Many expectant mothers would be surprised to learn that by the time they first see their physician their child has already been completely formed and is simply growing and preparing for his entrance into this world.

During the ninth week, the eyelids grow rapidly, and their gluey edges soon fuse and seal the eyes shut. The eyes will now be protected during the final, more delicate stages of their formation and will stay shut until the sixth or seventh lunar month. The first muscle movements of the baby probably occur in the mouth and jaw muscles because they are the first ones to develop. As early as the sixth week, a reflex action can be stimulated in these muscles. By the ninth week the muscles of the arms and legs are capable of responding to tactile (touch) stimulation. During the tenth week, the genitals are clearly defined, and it is possible for the first time to determine the sex of the baby by external inspection.

By the end of the third month the buds for the twenty temporary teeth will have appeared. Bones are beginning to replace the cartilage around the cheek, jaw, and nose, giving a more definite shape to the head. Although the fetus gets its oxygen through the umbilical cord from the chorion, it will swallow, inhale, and exhale the fluid in the amniotic sac, as if it were practicing breathing. The fetus becomes more active and vigorous, with much smoother movements than before. It can turn its head, bend its elbows, make a fist, move its hips, and fan its toes. However, these movements are too minute and weak to be felt by the mother. It may even get the hiccups. If it does, the mother will feel every one. For every woman the experience of feeling life for the first time is an unforgettable moment. The fetus is now 3 inches long and weighs ¾ ounce.

The fourth month is a growth month. The fetus will increase its length two or three times and its weight five or six times. By the end of the

month it will be 6 inches long and will weigh about 4 ounces. As a result, the fetus is more crowded than before, and the placenta becomes stretched tightly. The toes and fingers have separated, and fingerprint patterns emerge on the fingertips. Uniqueness and individuality are established at this very early age. The baby gains in strength, and his movements become stronger. About the middle of the month the mother begins to feel the baby stirring. At first it is very soft, like the fluttering of butterfly wings. As the baby develops, the movements become more strenuous, and the mother begins to feel the sharp kicks and thrusts of the arms and legs. Some spontaneous movements of the fetus can be detected by stethoscope by the fourteenth week, although the "quickening" movements felt by the mother are not noticed until the seventeenth week. As the fourth month comes to a close, the mother's abdomen begins to protrude, and she begins to gain weight. Her pregnancy will be noticed by others at about four and a half months, the midpoint of pregnancy. Any morning sickness will probably be past, and she will be in the most comfortable period of pregnancy.

Movements of the fetus continue to get stronger during the fifth month. The baby can turn all the way around from side to side and even turn somersaults. He gives the impression of being an astronaut moving weightlessly in space. He sleeps and wakes at regular times. When sleeping, he has a favorite resting position called a "lie." He may put his thumb in his mouth as if to suck it. The sucking reflex is present. Fingernails reach the tips of the fingers. The heartbeat becomes regular between the fourteenth and sixteenth weeks. By the middle of the fifth month the heartbeat is strong enough for a physician to hear it through a stethoscope placed on the abdomen of the mother, maybe even hearing two beats if there are twins. By the end of the fifth calendar month the fetus weighs over 1 pound and is about 1 foot long.

The sixth month of pregnancy is the time when the skin changes from a thin, transparent layer through which blood vessels can be seen to one that has a layer of fat and some accumulation of hair. In addition, the skin becomes covered with a whitish oily, fatty substance, vernix caseosa,

A fetus will usually assume a head-down attitude or lie (cephalic presentation) within the uterine cavity. At times, the baby will make a breech presentation (buttocks and/or feet first) or a shoulder presentation if there is a transverse lie. **A** and **B** are breech presentations; **C** is a shoulder presentation; **D** is a vertex (head) or occiput presentation, which is the most common; and **E** is a face presentation. (From Iorio, J. *Childbirth: family centered nursing* [3rd ed.]. St. Louis: The C. V. Mosby Co., 1975.)

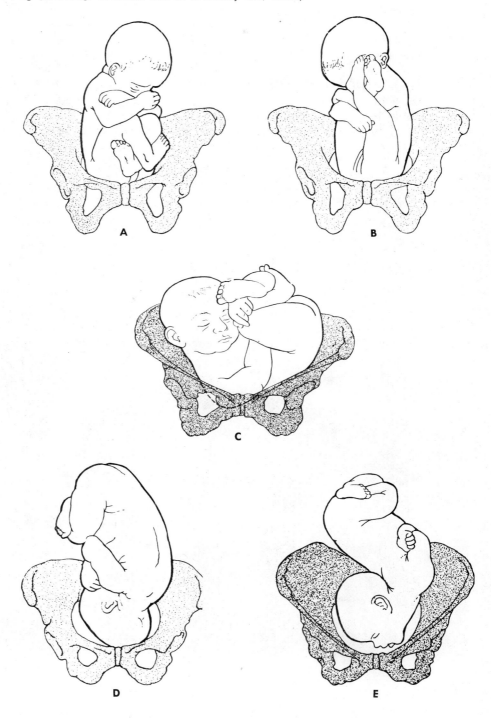

that protects the skin from the long immersion in fluid. During the previous month, a soft, fine hair called *lanugo* began to grow on the body. During the sixth month there is an accumulation of this hair above the eyes and on the upper lip. The vernix caseosa accumulates on the lanugo and gives the fetus an aged appearance. Hair on the scalp begins to grow heavier and longer than in other places. The eyes are developed, and the eyelids may separate so that the fetus can now open and close its eyes. If the baby should be born at the end of this month, he would probably breathe for a few minutes to a few hours, but seldom would he survive. The fetus is now 14 inches long and weighs a little over 2 pounds.

An interesting theory regarding when a conceived zygote is considered to be viable or alive is presented by Dr. Dominick Purpura, a neuroscientist at the Albert Einstein College of Medicine. He says that if "brain life" is used as a determinant, then life begins between the seventh and eighth months of gestation.[19] He defines brain life as the ability of the cerebral cortex, the thinking part of the brain, to develop consciousness, self-awareness, and other functions normally associated with the formation of nerve cell circuits. He says if "brain death" is the chief standard for deciding when a person is dead, then "brain life," when brain waves can be detected, should determine viability. The generally ac-

There is a special thrill that comes from knowing that a new life is kicking and squirming inside the "magic belly."

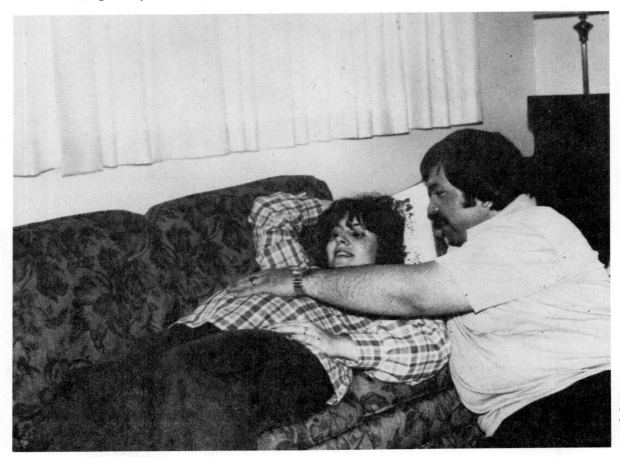

James S. Steck

cepted 24-week standard at which life begins would then have to be lengthened to 28 weeks. Purpura studied the brain wave responses to light of thirty infants delivered prematurely between the twenty-fourth and thirty-second weeks of pregnancy.

The chance for survival of a baby born after twenty-eight weeks of pregnancy is fairly good. It actually depends on the capability of the nervous system to effectively operate the organs and vital functions of the body. If born during the seventh month, the infant will need special care in terms of oxygen, prevention of blindness associated with retrolental fibroplasia (treatment nowadays is good), and protection against infections. Some time will have to be spent in an incubator. The fetus is about 16 inches and weighs about 2½ pounds.

The eighth and ninth months are "fattening-up" months. The fetus gains about ½ pound a week for a total of 5 pounds on the average. The body is becoming more rounded, and fatty layers are developing that will help to nourish the baby and keep him warm after he is born. The rapid growth of the baby may cause stretch marks on the mother's abdomen. The finer lanugo hair is being shed and has largely disappeared. The skin is less reddish looking than before, becoming lighter or pinkish in color even if the baby is black. Fingernails are firm and protrude beyond the end of the fingers. Sometimes nails are so long at birth that the nurse will need to trim them. The baby still moves, but his living quarters are getting more and more crowded. The mother's abdomen stops enlarging about the end of the eighth month, and there is a slowing down of fetal movements. About two weeks before birth the fetus will settle or "drop" into the pelvic cavity.

When the fetus stops its frequent movements and lightening occurs, it will usually take up a more-or-less fixed position. Frequently this position is with the head down, as has been its commonest position during most of the pregnancy. However, the lie assumed could be with feet or bottom downward, or it could be across the opening of the uterus in a traverse lie. Birth through the vagina from a traverse lie is impossible, and the baby's position will need to be changed. The most advantageous presentation is head first.

The total gestation period is 266 days on the average. Since it is difficult, if not impossible, to date conception exactly, pregnancy is generally

"MAGIC BELLY"   **P**erhaps, at this point, I should discuss my wife's "magic belly," as we have come to call it. Most men, I presume, would say that their wives had good figures when they were first married. I am no exception. When we got married, my wife had a figure that would make any woman envious. As the months progressed, things happened and Amy's magic belly began doing magical things. The magic belly made Amy's skin very smooth and silky. The magic belly also made Amy's breasts swell and harden, which is a magic trick that I have thoroughly enjoyed. And the magic belly has even grown itself. Being a woman, Amy is quite upset with her figure these days. But, being her husband, I am quite proud of her physique and still think that she has a beautiful figure. In my estimation, she is the most beautiful pregnant woman in the world.

Meanwhile, back at the ranch . . . or perhaps I should say back in the womb, the little one is doing just fine, kicking about seventy-five to eighty percent of the time. It is such a joyous feeling to place my hand on the magic belly and feel those kicks of life. Amy and I have even obtained a stethoscope with which to hear the little one's heartbeat. Amy is almost seven months pregnant now, and she and I are eagerly looking forward to the next two months.

reckoned from the beginning of the last menstrual period. The normal term is then set at 280 days, or ten lunar months. About 75% of all babies are born within one week, either way, of this date.

Up to this point babies the world over develop the same way. All human beings have this part of their growth processes in common. The stage has now been set. The drama of birth is ready to begin—that magic moment when an unknown entity becomes known.

PREGNANCY AND FAMILY

Having a baby is a family affair. We should really think of a pregnant family rather than of a pregnant woman. The woman has the physical responsibility of pregnancy and labor, but the entire family faces many changes in its way of life.

From the very beginning the support and encouragement given to a woman during her pregnancy are very important to her. The father should attend the clinic or meet the doctor during early pregnancy so both he and the mother can hear what the doctor has to say about the pregnancy and any problems that may be connected with it. Prospective fathers should learn how to help their wives during labor and how to care for newborn babies. Both mother and father are likely to be equally clumsy at changing that first diaper unless thay have attended a "new parents" class.[20]

Pregnancy is rehearsal for family life. The physical change in the mother is related to a baby being created. The psychological change involved in this event actually creates a family. The first trimester is a time of shock. The coming birth is recognized as a cause of major changes; the wife becomes more dependent and the husband gives support "as a father." The second trimester is more peaceful. The most important event is the "quickening"; feeling the movements strengthens the realization that "the baby is human." During the third trimester, there are two themes. First, the couple becomes increasingly aware of obvious sexual differences. It heightens their feelings of femininity and masculinity. Second, there is some worry over the delivery. This concern disappears quickly after the birth and is followed by glee, a feeling of triumph, and a sense of having been creative. (The source

of this idea on the influence of pregnancy on parents is unknown. It was taken from notes in our file.)

TERMINATION OF PREGNANCY

It is interesting to note that abortion is an ancient practice and that it has always provoked differences of opinion. Plato and Aristotle approved of it, under certain conditions. Seneca and Cicero condemned abortions on ethical grounds and the Justinian code prohibited it. Since 1973 when the U.S. Supreme Court ruled that a woman had the right to elect an abortion within 14 weeks after the last menstrual period, provided it was performed by a licensed physician, confirmed abortions have increased dramatically. Legal abortions are replacing self-induced abortion or termination of pregnancy by unskilled persons.

Definitional perspective

The term *abortion* is the termination of pregnancy before viability of the fetus. Viability is considered to be reached at about the twenty-fourth week of gestation when the fetus weighs 600 grams or more. A spontaneous abortion is one that results from natural causes and is usually called a miscarriage. An early spontaneous abortion is one that occurs prior to 16 weeks' gestation, and a late one occurs between 16 and 24 weeks' gestation. About three fourths of abortions occur before the sixteenth week of pregnancy, with the majority of these taking place prior to the eighth week. If a woman has three or more spontaneous abortions, she is considered to be a habitual abortor. (Less than three are said to be incidental.) Habitual abortions are usually due to endocrine imbalance, an abnormality in the reproductive tract, or are psychogenic. Spontaneous abortions may be due to abnormalities of the ovum or sperm or severe maternal disease, infection, or malnutrition. Physical trauma usually does not produce an abortion.

Induced abortion is an intentionally produced loss of pregnancy by the mother or by others. It is considered to be a therapeutic or legal abortion if appropriate interference is used by a licensed practitioner because of a grave or hazardous condition of the mother or any other just cause, such as a genetic defect. A criminal abortion is one that is performed without medical or legal consultation. Indications for induced abortion are chronic hypertension or chronic nephritis, cancer of female organs, advanced diabetes, rubella (German or three-day measles), and psychiatric considerations.

The abortion has different clinical stages. It is classified as threatened if the eventual outcome is uncertain, as implied by slight bleeding or spotting and slight cramping pain. If the cramps become more severe and bleeding increases, the abortion is inevitable. A complete abortion is one in which the uterus empties itself completely of the embryo or fetus and its membranes. If some placental tissue remains within the uterus, the abortion is incomplete. A missed abortion is one where the products of conception are retained within the uterus for about six weeks after the embryo or fetus has died.

Methods of induced abortion

There are four common methods of induced abortion: vacuum aspiration, dilation and curettage (D and C), saline injection, and hysterotomy.

Vacuum aspiration is performed during the first 12 weeks of pregnancy on an outpatient basis. The cervix is dilated and a small hollow tube attached to a suction is inserted into the uterus, resulting in the product of the conception being suctioned. The uterine lining is then curettaged to remove all fetal tissue. Suction abortion done beyond 12 weeks' gestation carries an increased rate of uterine perforation.

Dilation and curettage (D and C) are performed when the pregnancy is of 12 to 14 weeks' duration. A local or general anesthetic is used. The cervix is dilated and a cigar-shaped metal dilator of increasingly-larger diameter is introduced into the uterus. The fetal substance is scraped loose with a curettage and removed with ovum forceps. It is safer for the patient to be admitted to the hospital for an overnight stay.

Saline injection (salting) is done when the pregnancy is from 14 to 24 weeks' duration. An amniocentesis is done after a local anesthetic is administered. Using a large needle, the physician withdraws about 6 ounces of amniotic fluid and replaces it with an equal amount of saline solution. A safer method is to instill the saline via drip infusion since there is better control and placement of the flow. Labor commences within 18 to 36 hours and the patient expels the placenta and the fetus. A short hospital stay is in order.

Hysterotomy is a miniature Caesarean section. A small longitudinal incision is made in the middle of the lower abdomen, the uterus is opened, and the fetus is removed. If sterilization is desired, the fallopian tubes are ligated at the same time. Hysterotomy is performed after 16 weeks' gestation. It requires a few days of hospitalization. It is the type of abortion procedure that is used least.

Personal reactions. A therapeutic abortion will leave women with different kinds of feelings. Most psychiatrists agree that it will not cause lasting psychological damage. In one study mentioned in *Medicine Today,* 22% had moderate guilt feelings and 13% had marked guilt feelings after their abortions. However, these feelings subsided with the passage of time. Most of the women experienced an immediate sense of relief, followed by a period of grief lasting up to six months, followed by adjustment in most cases.

Little is written about how fathers, including unwed fathers, feel about the abortion of their child. A general assumption is that they usually leave the matter up to the mother. Unwed fathers are supposed to "heave a sigh of relief" or indicate they couldn't care less. Not so, say some fathers. Not only do some claim that they care, but they also feel hurt if they are left out of the decision-making process. Of course, there will be all types of reactions. But no one will know for certain how the majority of the fathers feel about abortions until well-designed studies are conducted.

Amniocentesis

The saline injection abortion method requires that an amniocentesis be done. What is an amniocentesis and does it have any other functions? An amniocentesis is a procedure whereby a needle is surgically inserted through the abdomen into the uterus to obtain amniotic fluid. It is done during the second trimester of pregnancy. The fluid contains cells that have been discarded from the fetus. These cells contain the chromosomes of the genetic code and can be analyzed for genetic abnormalities such as Down's syndrome and Tay-Sachs disease. There are 20,000 children in the United States and 700,000 worldwide that are born with detectable abnormalities each year. The test is also useful for women over 40 years of age who have one chance in 50 that the fetus will have Down's syndrome. For the woman who is 44 years of age or older, the chances are one in 20.

Is it safe? Research was done at nine major medical centers by Dr. Aubrey Milunsky.[21] The study compared 1,040 amniocentesis cases to 992 match control cases that did not have it done. There were no significant differences in the rate of fetal deaths, prematurity, infant health, birth defects, or developmental status at 1 year of age. In the 1,040 cases, 34 fetuses had chromosomal metabolic disorders and 11 were in danger of sex-linked diseases. Of the 45 mothers, 35 had abortions. The diagnosis of the 1,040 was 99% accurate, with only six errors in the entire group. Sex determination of the fetus by examination of the sex chromosome was 100% accurate.

STUDY GUIDE

1. Compare the characteristics of female gametes and male gametes.
2. What is the uterus, and what changes occur to it during the menstrual cycle?
3. Describe the ovulation process and the fertilization process.
4. List the various methods or ways by which pregnancy can be diagnosed.
5. What is the difference between monozygotic (MZ) and dizygotic (DZ) twins? What factors are more common for multiple births than for single births?
6. Discuss the growth and development characteristics of the period of the zygote.
7. Discuss the growth and development characteristics of the embryonic period.
8. Discuss the growth and development characteristics of the period of the fetus.
9. List the four types of induced abortions and indicate the characteristics of each type.
10. The question of abortion is an emotional issue. It has sociological, psychological, political, religious, and ethical implications. With so many issues to be considered, how do you think society should approach the resolution of the question of abortion? Is it a personal matter, a state matter, or a universal matter? Or can't the issue be resolved to the satisfaction of most people?

REFERENCES

1. Hellman, L. M., & Pritchard, J. A. *Williams obstetrics* (15th ed.). New York: Appleton-Century-Crofts, 1976.
2. Nagle, J. J. *Heredity and human affairs*. St. Louis: The C. V. Mosby Co., 1974.
3. Willson, J. R., Beecham, C. T., & Carrington, E. R.: *Obstetrics and gynecology* (5th ed.). St. Louis: The C. V. Mosby Co., 1975.
4. Benson, R. *Handbook of obstetrics and gynecology* (5th ed.). Los Altos, Calif.: Lange Medical Publications, 1974.
5. Smith, D. R. *General urology*. Los Altos, Calif.: Lange Medical Publications, 1975.
6. Crouch, J. E. *Functional human anatomy* (2nd ed.). Philadelphia: Lea & Febiger, 1972.
7. Payne, S., & Skeels, R. F. Fertility as evaluated by artificial insemination. *Fertility and Sterility*, 1954, **5**, 32-39.
8. Iorio, J. *Childbirth: family-centered nursing* (3rd ed.). St. Louis: The C. V. Mosby Co., 1975.
9. Jensen, D. J., Benson, R. C., & Bobak, I. M. *Maternity care*. St. Louis: The C. V. Mosby Co., 1977.
10. Shettles, L. B., & Vande Weile, R. L. Can parents choose the sex of their baby? *Birth and Family*, 1974, **1**, 3-5.
11. Roovik, D. M., & Shettles, L. B. *Your baby's sex—now you can choose*. New York: Dodd, Mead & Co., 1970.
12. Wittels, I., & Bornstein, P. A note on stress and sex determination. *Journal of Genetic Psychology*, 1974, **124**, 333-334.
13. Nichols, R. C. The National Merit twin study. In S. G. Vandenberg (Ed.), *Methods and goals in human behavior genetics*. New York: Academic Press, Ltd., 1965.
14. Timras, P. S. *Developmental physiology and aging*. New York: Macmillan, Inc., 1972.
15. Koch, H. *Twins*. Chicago: University of Chicago Press, 1966.
16. Milham, S., Jr. Hormonal induction of human twinning. *Lancet*, 1964, **2**, 566.

17. Moore, K. *Before we are born*. Philadelphia: W. B. Saunders Co., 1974.
18. Willson, Beecham & Carrington, *op. cit.* p. 192.
19. Purpura, D. *Symposium on fetal brain life*. Rose Fitzgerald Kennedy Center, Albert Einstein College of Medicine, New York, May, 1975.
20. Apgar, V. *Be good to your baby before it is born*. New York: The National Foundation—March of Dimes, 1973.
21. Milunsky, A. *How dangerous is amniocentesis?* Paper presented at Annual Meeting, American Academy of Pediatrics, October, 1975.

4 Birth of the baby

**BIRTH:
MY FIRSTBORN**

As we were celebrating our first wedding anniversary, my husband and I were aware of the possibility of my being pregnant. I must admit that this was not a "planned" child. Oh yes, we wanted children, but I did not think that I was ready or prepared to be a mother, not just yet anyway. When the laboratory test showed a positive reaction and the doctor told me that I was very much pregnant, I had mixed emotions. My immediate thought concerned how the baby would affect our lives. Could I ever learn how to properly take care of a baby? I had not been around smaller children like some friends of mine who seemed to know what to do. I suppose part of my deep apprehension was due to a gynecologist who had examined me during my high school days and told me that there was a possibility that, physically, I might never be able to have children. Naturally these thoughts raced through my mind. Yet no doctor had ever cautioned me *not* to have any children. I tried to look at it this way; if this was what God planned for us, then there would be a way and I should have faith and trust.

During my months of pregnancy I had very few complications. In fact, I seemed to enjoy better health during those nine months than I did at other times. I believe this fact is true for most women. What a thrill to have the baby kick me internally at night while I was lying in bed. The baby appeared to kick at one side of my stomach and then jump to the opposite side. We marveled at this experience. So much activity made my husband almost sure it was going to be a boy.

The night I went to the hospital I was more calm than I thought I would be. My husband was very comforting to me in the labor room. We talked and he held my hand. I would squeeze his hand very tightly when an extra hard contraction came. Then wouldn't you know it, he had to leave before the baby came. It was one of those days when his work was such that his presence was practically mandatory. It would not have been fair to delay the work of many other people just because he did not appear. I understood, but I hoped that he could be back at the hospital in time to share our big moment together.

I remember that the delivery room was a large, spotless place full of utensils, an overhead mirror, and beaming with sunlight. As the nurse told me to put on those funny-looking stockings that I thought were very hot and uncomfortable, I began to feel that my baby was on the threshold of being born. The pain increased, and the nurse told me to try to relax and to hold her hand. The problem the gynecologist told me about years before was causing trouble. Then the nurse covered part of my face with a mask and told me to start counting very slowly. I got very sleepy. That is all I remember until in the far distance I heard the doctor say, "You have a baby girl!" My immediate response was, "Are you sure?" Everyone had said I was going to have a baby boy. "Is she all right?" I asked. The answer came loud and clear that she was a healthy baby girl. I said a prayer out loud to thank the Lord for that. The next thing I knew was that they were wheeling me out of the delivery room so that another expectant mother could take my place. I did not get to see my baby! The nurse had taken my baby to bathe her before I could even get a look at her. The delivery room was in great demand that morning. The doctor called the school and told Dale, my husband, that he was a father. Dale came to the hospital within the hour. He saw our baby before I did! I was the one to give birth to her, but he saw her first!

Dale told me that she was a beautiful baby: no redness at all, round, rosy cheeks, little fists, a dimple in her chin, a short, stubby nose like mine, and she looked a lot like him, too! How thrilled we were with our new baby!

Waiting in my room until I could see my baby, I could not get over the "flat" stomach that I now had since the baby was born. When the nurse brought Denise to my bed for the first time, I remember the wonderful feeling I had as I held that tiny 7-pound 9-ounce bundle. I carefully examined her to see if she had developed properly and had the correct number of fingers and toes and that there were no noticeable birthmarks or defects of any kind. Here was truly a bundle from Heaven. This miracle of birth that I had taken part in was a blessing for which I was indeed grateful.

When we came home from the hospital, it suddenly dawned upon me that I and I *alone* would be responsible for taking complete charge of Denise. No more dependence upon the nurse to feed and bathe her. This was my duty now.

I remember the first bath that I gave her. I was worn out by the time I was finished. It took me nearly all morning, counting the time of preparation and cleaning up afterward, to give her the bath. My main problem was in knowing how to hold her. Dale said, "She won't come apart, you know." The way I turned her over I was not so sure that she would not do just that—come apart. I was afraid of hurting her. She seemed so small on the blanket without her clothes on. I was so tired after that venture of the first bath that I had to rest before I could do anything else. Each bath that I gave her went a little better, until finally I got the feel of it and I enjoyed the experience. There is nothing so delightful as a clean, sweet-smelling baby.

As I got Denise on her own self-demand schedule, my husband and I began to relax and enjoy her more and more. Each day there would be something new that she would do that was a little different from the day before. The joy of being parents and watching a child grow is a privilege that we cherish.

The last few weeks before a baby is born are spent by the baby and the mother getting ready for the birth. The baby has assumed its birth position, usually with the head pushing against the cervix. The uterus sinks downward and forward. The mother's profile changes, making her clothes fit differently. The pressure against her upper abdomen is eased, and she breathes more freely. These changes are called the "lightening" by some; others say that the baby has "dropped." The indications are that the baby is getting ready to be born. Lightening may occur as early as four weeks before birth or as late as the onset of labor. The usual time for lightening to occur is ten to fourteen days before delivery. It may be accompanied by some discomfort and intermittent pain. When this occurs, first-time anxious mothers may think that labor has started and call the physician, only to learn later that nothing eventful is about to happen.

BIRTH PROCESS

True labor is characterized by one or more of the following. The most usual sign of real labor is the onset of contractions, which have a definite rhythm, gradually increasing in frequency, duration, and intensity. They may be 10, 15, or 20 minutes apart at first, lasting abut 45 seconds each. Within an hour or two the contractions occur closer together. A characteristic of the true contractions is that they begin in the lower back and then travel to the front of the abdomen. The muscles of the abdomen become stiffer with subsequent contractions. The sharpness of the contractions increases as the uterine muscles prepare to ease the baby out of the uterus. False labor is characterized by contractions that are far apart, with no rhythmic regularity, and with no muscular hardening of the abdomen. Nevertheless, occasionally false labor is difficult to distinguish from real labor. Many a would-be mother has

My mother groan'd! my father wept.
Into the dangerous world I leapt:
Helpless, naked, piping loud:
Like a fiend hid in a cloud.

William Blake
Songs of Experience

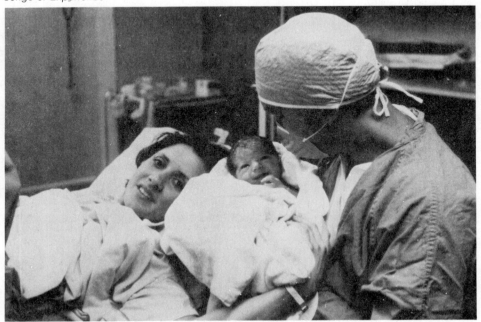

rushed to the hospital only to return home.

A second sign of real labor is the appearance of a blood-tinged mucuslike discharge called *show*. During pregnancy the opening of the uterus is sealed shut by mucus, which acts like a plug. When labor is about to begin, the mucus is eased out and discharged.

A third sign of labor is the "bursting of the water bag." The amniotic fluid that has been cushioning the baby is released before the baby is born, and either a gush of clear fluid or a slow leaking of clear fluid from the vagina may occur. Usually the bag ruptures toward the end of labor. However, it is not unusual for a bag to break a day or more before the child is delivered.

Stages of labor

Obstetricians generally recognize three stages of labor in the birth process. The first and longest phase is the period of rhythmic and regular labor contractions. During this time, the cervix will dilate or "ripen" so that the birth canal can be stretched or widened enough for the baby to pass through. Physicians usually prefer to be called when the contractions are 10 to 15 minutes apart or when the water bag has ruptured, regardless of "show" or contractions. Contractions come closer together as the cervix dilates to its full width of about 4 inches (or 10 centimeters) in diameter. The length of this first stage of labor can vary considerably in time. For a first baby the average length of total labor is about 14 hours. For later babies labor lasts an average of 8 hours. Ideally, the labor should not last too long or take place too quickly, since a slow delivery will exhaust both the mother and the baby and a quick delivery may mean that the baby is unable to make the quick physiological adjustment required. Many such children have marginal perceptual problems in learning when they enter school.

When contractions are about 2 or 3 minutes apart and last 60 to 70 seconds, the second stage of labor begins. The baby is born during this period (Fig. 4-1). The actual birth may take about 20 to 70 minutes. With each contraction the baby moves downward through the cervix, through the vagina, and out. The mother can "bear down" (push) to help these movements once the head

has passed between the bones forming the pelvic outlet. Unless a woman has participated in a natural childbirth education program, she will be given either a local anesthetic, such as a saddle block, a caudal block, or a spinal anesthetic, or a general anesthetic if she requires it. If there is danger of the vaginal or surrounding tissues being torn, the doctor may make a small incision called an *episiotomy* to relieve the strain on the tissues and to make a larger opening. Stitches, which will later dissolve, are made after the delivery.[1]

The "crowning" of the head occurs when the widest diameter of the baby's head is at the mother's vulva, the outer entrance to her vagina. The physician will grasp the emerged head beneath the chin with one hand and gently draw on the baby, helping it out. The rest of the body will usually be delivered with one or two more contractions after the head is out. The baby, as he now appears, has a whitish look from the protective vernix coating with which he was covered while in the amniotic sac. He may also have some blood on him from the mucus and tissues. The head may be a little misshapen because of the contraction pressure exerted on it while in the birth canal, but it is pliable and quickly resumes its normal shape. Nature wisely sees to it that the bones of the head are among the last ones to be formed.

When delivery is completed, a head-downward position is maintained to facilitate drainage of mucus and respiration. Mucus and other amniotic residue are quickly sucked from the mouth and nose. The buttocks or the soles of the baby's feet may be given a mild tap or the back may be rubbed gently to get the baby to inhale enough air to inflate all the tiny air sacs in his lungs, which have never been used before. As the baby exhales, he utters his first audible wail. His crying forces the breath through faster. As the baby takes in oxygen, his body color changes to a pinkish hue. The umbilical cord is tied off, cut, and sterilized to prevent infection. The baby is now completely on his own in terms of bodily functions. Drops are put in each of the baby's eyes to prevent eye infection or blindness, which could be due to a gonorrheal infection of the mother. The baby is cleaned, identified with a name bracelet or band, usually foot-

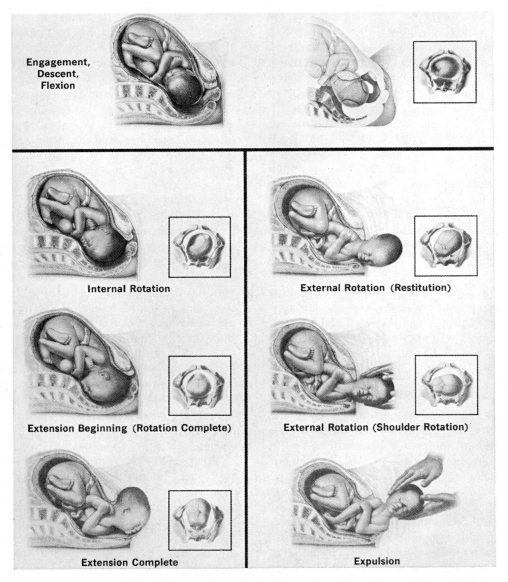

Fig. 4-1. Mechanism of normal labor, L. O. A. position. (From *Nursing education aid,* No. 13, Columbus, Ohio: Ross Laboratories, Publisher, 1964.)

printed or thumbprinted, weighed, measured, and put to bed in a warm blanket. The baby is fine.

The final stage of labor consists of the delivery of the afterbirth—the placenta with the attached amniotic and chorionic membranes and the remainder of the cord. This process takes about 20 minutes and is virtually painless. The physician will quickly examine the mother and the afterbirth to make certain that no abnormalities exist. The mother will lose a pint of blood, more or less, in giving birth. The physician may knead her abdomen to help restore tone to the uterine muscles. For the next ten to fourteen days the uterine lining will disintegrate and will be shed in a process resembling menstruation.

Table 4-1. Apgar score for condition of the newborn baby*

Sign	0	1	2	Score
Heart rate	Absent	Slow, below 100	Over 100	
Respiratory effort	Absent	Slow, irregular	Good, strong cry	
Muscle tone	Limp	Some flexion of extremities	Active motion, well flexed	
Reflex irritability (response to catheter in nostril)	No response	Grimace	Cough, sneeze, or cry	
Color	Blue, pale	Body pink, extremities blue	Completely pink	
			Total score	

*From Apgar, V. The Apgar scoring chart. *Journal of the American Medical Association,* 1958, **168,** 1988.

Kinds of births and deliveries

Ninety-five percent of all babies are born with their heads emerging first in what is called a *vertex presentation.*[2] This type of birth is the normal spontaneous delivery. No instruments are necessary. Things progress according to the plans prescribed by nature in its wonderful wisdom for the birth of a baby.

About 3% of all babies assume a lie just before birth in which the buttocks instead of the head are positioned in the lower pelvic area. As a result, the buttocks and feet emerge first in birth, with the head appearing last. This type of delivery is a *breech presentation.* Such births, which physicians can usually detect before they happen, may require special attention by the physicians because they are generally more difficult. However, in most cases there is a satisfactory delivery.

In cases in which the baby is disproportionately large or where his head is larger than the mother's pelvic opening, the physician may advise a cesarean birth. Such a birth is especially necessary if the fetus has assumed a transverse lie and the position cannot be changed. A cesarean section is a surgical delivery through an incision in the abdominal wall and the uterus. The child is removed through the slits, and then both incisions are carefully sewn. This delivery is considered major surgery, but the risks are minimal with modern medical technique. About one baby in fifty is delivered this way, and the number appears to be increasing. It used to be a common belief that once a woman had a cesarean section, the uterus and abdominal wall were weakened. It is now known that a woman may have several cesarean births satisfactorily.

A forceps or instrument delivery is suggested if the uterine contractions weaken or stop during delivery or when some physiological condition makes it difficult for the baby to push through the birth canal. Forceps are curved, tonglike instruments shaped to fit on each side of the baby's head. As an emergency procedure, a high-forceps delivery may be made during the first stage of labor or early in the second stage. This procedure is somewhat uncertain because an accurate placement of the forceps may be difficult. A low-forceps delivery is made at the stage of actual delivery and involves less risk. The forceps will occasionally make a bluish mark on each side of the infant's head where the tongs touched, but these disappear after several days. Although the technique of using forceps has improved tremendously because of better training, there is a wide variance in the use of forceps from hospital to hospital and physician to physician.

A growing number of obstetricians believe in inducing labor when a woman is at the end of term. The end of term is determined by a drop in the level of progesterone in the mother's blood. Medical indications for induction of labor include: prolonged pregnancy (42 to 43 weeks); prolonged rupture of the membranes; preterm delivery in diabetic mother; severe preeclampsia,

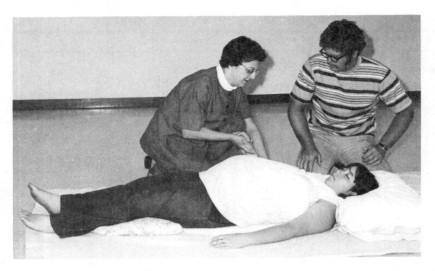

Mother and father learn the Lamaze method of prepared childbirth, giving both a deeper meaning and sense of involvement in the birth process. (From Ingalls, J., & Salerno, M. C. *Maternal and child health nursing.* St. Louis: The C. V. Mosby Co., 1975.)

placenta abruptio, or fetal death; and uterine inertia. Elective indications are multiple pregnancy with a history of precipitate (quick) labor and patients who live long distances from the hospital.

A tiny sensor, in the form of a microballoon, is sometimes inserted between the wall of the uterus and the membranes that surround the baby before birth.[3] The hormone oxytocin is injected intravenously into the patient. The balloon sensor, linked to a pressure recorder, tells the physician the magnitude and character of the uterine contractions and exactly how much oxytocin should be given to create the "ideal" level of labor. Ninety-two percent of the women give birth on the day they receive the oxytocin. The advantage of induced labor is that a woman can have her baby on a chosen day when the hospital is fully staffed.

The normalcy of the baby's condition and survival chances at birth have been systematized in the Apgar score (Table 4-1), developed by Virginia Apgar.[4] The scale gives a sum of ratings, scored from 0 to 10, in five conditions: breathing effort, heart rate, muscle tone, reflex irritability, and skin color. Large-scale research studies show that the scores are good gross predictors in identifying babies who need special care. Scores are given by the physician or anesthetist 60 seconds after complete birth. Nearly all normal infants receive a score of 7 to 9 or 10. A score of 5 to 10 usually indicates no need for treatment; a score of 4 or below indicates need for prompt diagnosis and treatment.

The Lamaze method

The Lamaze technique of "natural childbirth" is more correctly a method of "prepared childbirth." The method, the psychoprophylactic method of childbirth, is a combination course in the education of the physical aspects of childbirth, lessons in neuromuscular control, exercises to help in relaxing certain muscle groups, three breathing techniques to reduce the pain of contractions, and body building and expulsion exercises for use in the delivery room. The technique, developed by the French physician Fernand Lamaze,[5] is taught as a course; it is highly recommended that fathers be part of the entire program. There are six weekly classes, 90 minutes each, during the eighth and ninth months of pregnancy.

Much of the fear felt by mothers-to-be is caused by a lack of knowledge of what is really happening and, as a result, a feeling of helplessness. Fear builds tension and tension eventually

"THE LAMAZE EXPERIENCE"

A number of hours into labor the doctor finally took Meg into the delivery room. I was asked to go with the doctor into the dressing room. There I was supplied with the proper garments for the delivery room. I was asked to scrub and out we went. Once in the delivery room I took my place next to Meg and continued to proceed with the instructions that I had been given for this phase of delivery.

At 5:20 P.M. my first son was born and 13 minutes later my second son arrived. They both were crying before they were completely born. This was the moment when I was most proud. While the doctor was delivering the babies, I felt a real part of the team.

It was the experience of a lifetime to have participated together with my wife in such an important event. It was exciting to see my children right from the start and to have been of moral support and encouragement for my wife. I would have missed a great deal had I been pacing the floor in the waiting room.

When the babies were taken to the incubators, a nurse, mistaking me for a doctor, asked me to come into the nursery to see the boys. I went in but when she asked me to pick up the babies, I was afraid to do so since I had never picked a baby up before. The nurse, noticing my hesitation, asked me if I was a doctor. When I said "No," she sent me packing.

---

produces pain. The program seeks to use relaxation techniques to control pain so that the mother can have a conscious, rewarding experience in the birth of the child. The relaxation technique taught is based on the principle that a new center or focal point of high-level concentration can inhibit the reception of pain. Three techniques of breathing are used for different intensities of pain. The sequence begins with a series of slow deliberate inhalations and exhalations for the relatively mild contractions of the preliminary phase of labor; then sustained bursts of rapid shallow panting for the stronger contractions of the "accelerated" phase; and finally, short bursts of shallow panting interspersed with little explosive exhalations for the very strong contractions of the "traditional" phase, just before the actual expulsion of the baby.

The role of the husband in the Lamaze method is of great importance. A husband and wife team is the best combination at the time of pregnancy. It starts the parents off with a sense of partnership that has long-lasting benefits. By both attending Lamaze classes they develop a common approach in attitudes and expectations. They provide psychological support to each other. The husband can be of help during the daily practice sessions and in the hospital during the actual labor and delivery. Talking together and experiencing together make a relationship that strengthens the husband-wife bond. They are better prepared to handle changes from the delivery and birth pattern that they have been taught to expect. They learn that if things do not happen the way they were told, they should react to their own sensations because every labor is different. If some anesthetic is necessary, such as meperidine (Demerol) to help the mother relax or a paracervical block to relax the cervical area in order to reduce the pain and speed up the dilation, that is acceptable.

The father can be with the expectant mother in the delivery room. He times the interval between the contractions and gives comfort to the mother. He puts on a gown and special sandals and goes into the delivery room with his wife. There, he is by her side as she lies on the delivery table with her legs lifted and spread apart by metal braces. A sterile sheet covers the mother's abdomen and forms a screen. He holds her hand; she grips it hard. The doctor takes over and directs the event to take place. When a contraction starts, she is to bear down with effort and concentration. The doctor gives reassurances and directions, explaining what is happening. "There's the head." "Give me one more good one for the shoulders." "It's a girl!" The baby, still wet from the womb, is held up for the mother and father to see. Mother and father look at each other, their eyes usually brimming with tears. They kiss. "I love you." "I love *you*." Both of them have a sense of pride in the bringing forth of *their* child into the world.*

---

*More information regarding facts about childbirth may be obtained from the American Society for Psychoprophylaxis in Obstetrics, Inc., 36 W. 96th St., New York, NY 10025, or the International Childbirth Education Association, ICEA Secretary, P. O. Box 5852, Milwaukee, Wisconsin 53220.

Research is indicating that the father is more important in the parenting of the newborn infant than was previously believed.

David Strickler

The Leboyer delivery approach

Dr. Frederick Leboyer[6] of France has introduced a different, somewhat controversial, approach to delivery room practices. Whereas Lamaze focuses on the mother, Leboyer focuses on the baby. For instance, Lamaze techniques help to lessen the pain of childbirth for the mother by eliminating the fear of that pain. Leboyer's techniques seek to remove the fear of childbirth for the infant. At least, he believes that the delivery process can be made less traumatic for the baby by making the transition from the uterine environment to the delivery room environment less harsh; this is accomplished by making the differences between the two more similar and less abrupt. Leboyer likes to emphasize that he is seeking to put across an attitude rather than developing a method; the procedures are less important than the feelings behind them. The Lamaze technique of natural childbirth is often used in conjunction with Leboyer's approach.

Leboyer proposes the following procedure to lessen the trauma of normal birth: delivery in a room with soft or subtle lights instead of bright glaring lights; an absolute minimum of sound, with the doctor saying "push, push" in a lowered voice; immediately after birth, placing the baby on the mother's stomach and encouraging her to stroke it; delay in cutting the umbilical cord until it stops pulsating, usually about 6 minutes, unless there is an indication that something might be wrong; and, placing the baby in a body-temperature, warm bath where it becomes weightless again after feeling the new sensation of the weight of its body. The transition from uterine weightlessness, to gravitation pull, back to weightlessness, is reassuring to the infant.

Leboyer is critical of physicians who dangle the baby by its heels and slap it to stimulate breathing. Such tactics may have been necessary when mothers and babies were both anesthetized, but that seldom occurs now that newer

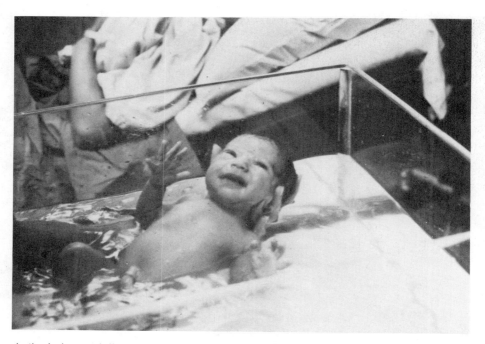

In the Leboyer delivery approach, the baby is placed in body-temperature water soon after birth to reduce the trauma of the transition from uterine weightlessness to the feel of gravitational pull on the body. (From Jensen, M. D., Benson, R. C., & Bobak, I. M. *Maternity care: the nurse and family.* St. Louis: The C. V. Mosby Co., 1977.)

techniques are used. To make certain that the proper perspective is recognized, let it be known that Leboyer is not rigid in insisting on these procedures. The baby's survival and well-being come first. If there is any hint of trouble, he is the first to say, "Turn on the lights, use suction, use oxygen, follow standard medical procedures."

A point made by researchers and observers concerning Leboyer-delivered children is that they are noticeably different in their overall attitude and behavior, in their unusual avid interest in the world around them, in a greater sense of calmness, and in more graceful movements. "They seem to be reaching out instead of protecting themselves." Leboyer feels that a more gentle birth might produce happier children. The report of the Parisian psychologist, Danielle Rapaport, of 120 Leboyer babies, from birth to the age of 3, found them all to be significantly alert,

able to concentrate longer on play, extremely clever with their hands, good in psychomotor tests, and having fewer sleeping and eating problems. Since the babies are more relaxed and agreeable, the mothers are more relaxed, establishing a relationship relatively free of anguish and worry.

BIOMEDICAL INFLUENCES ON PRENATAL DEVELOPMENT

There are a variety of conditions that can affect the normal development of an unborn baby. Some of these influences occur during the prenatal period when the fetus is being developed, whereas others take place at the time of birth or just after. Fortunately, 97% of all babies are born without any serious defect. Of the other 3%, there is a wide range in type and severity of defects. Fig. 4-2 considers morbidity and influential

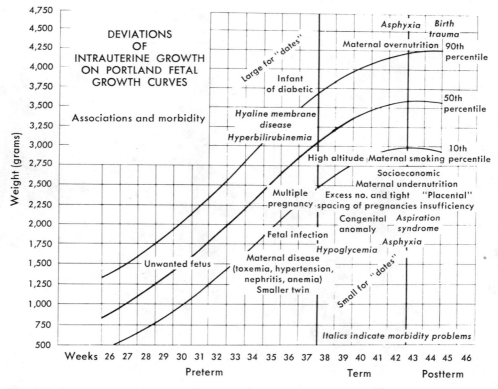

Fig. 4-2. Important associations and morbidity factors of accelerated or reduced fetal growth above 90th percentile for gestational age using Portland curves. Fetal growth data obtained from 40,000 single, white, middle-class infants born near sea level. (From Babson, S. G., Benson, R. C., Pernoll, M. L., & Benda, G. I. *Management of high-risk pregnancy and intensive care of the neonate* [3rd ed.]. St. Louis: The C. V. Mosby Co., 1975.)

factors on prenatal development as compared to fetal growth rate.

Nutrition of the mother

Nutrition has long been considered in prenatal care. However, it is now becoming apparent to an ever-increasing number of health professionals and psychologists that nutrition is not only important, but it is crucial in determining the health of the childbearing woman and her offspring as well as in the development of the cognitive aspects of the brain. The brain develops in two major spurts, the first during the fifteenth and twentieth weeks of pregnancy, the second from late pregnancy to 1 year of life. Shortage of food during either period stunts growth and intelligence.[7]

Mother's milk from birth is basic to normal brain development. Ironically, mothers in low-income groups, for whom breast-feeding recommends itself as economical, are less likely to nurse their babies than are economically secure, better educated mothers. Studies show that inadequate diet is probably the most frequently encountered hazard of intrauterine life. It is awesome to consider the effect of undernourishment on the development of the brain and intellect when one recognizes the worldwide incidence of malnutrition. The "junk food" diets of many Westerners and the inadequate diets of most adolescent mothers suggest that poor nutrition is not limited to the people of poor, developing countries. The incidence of stillbirth, prematurity, rickets, severe anemia, and tuberculosis is somewhat higher for babies whose mothers are malnourished.

It is what the mother eats, not how much, that is crucial to the baby's proper development. The most important foodstuff, so far as mental development is concerned, is protein.[8] In a nationwide study of 50,000 expectant mothers, those who had protein-deficient diets during pregnancy produced children whose IQs at age 4 averaged 16 points below those of children of well-nourished mothers.[9] The average pregnant woman should eat a 2,300 calorie diet every day of foods recommended by her physician. The idea that a woman should not gain more than 10 or 15 pounds during pregnancy has been dispelled.[10] The National Academy of Sciences and the Na-

tional Research Council published a report in 1970 stating that limiting weight gain may be contributing to the high infant mortality rate in the United States. United Nations figures show that many European countries, where women gain up to 25 to 30 pounds, have lower infant death rates. Of course, the extra pounds should result from a sound diet. Weight gains up to 24 pounds are now being recommended in the United States.

Maternal infections

One of the prime functions of the placenta is to safeguard the embryo by keeping out bacteria and bringing in antibodies that produce an immunity to a variety of diseases. The placenta, however, cannot screen out everything that might be injurious. Certain viruses manage to slip through the barrier and cause defects.

German measles, or rubella, if contracted by the mother in the first eight to ten weeks of pregnancy, will cause visual, auditory, mental, or heart abnormalities in one out of three babies.[11] From 1963 to 1965 an epidemic of rubella centered on the eastern seaboard of the United States approached the level of a national disaster. Fifty thousand women were infected during the first trimester of pregnancy. The total result was 30,000 miscarriages and stillbirths. Even more disturbing were the 20,000 children who were born with defects ranging from mental retardation and heart disorders to blindness and deafness. The most common birth defect is a loss of hearing. Affected children may also develop cataracts. Many of these children will be small for their age.

Rubella is characterized by a rash the first few days but no pronounced cold symptoms. Within 24 hours, pink spots appear, which tend to fade and run together. The overall appearance is a flushed effect. Other noticeable symptoms of rubella are swollen lymph glands in the neck, a slight body temperature rise to 100° F., and a scratchy throat. The incubation period is fourteen to twenty-one days, and the disease is contagious. The mother gets over the effects of rubella in three days. Her unborn child, however, may never get over them.

A vaccine has been developed for preventing rubella. Public health officials hope to stamp out rubella by giving the vaccine to the reservoir of susceptible subjects who can spread the infection.[12] Mass inoculation programs have been conducted in many countries. Immunization is usually started in the earliest grades of school, since this age group is the main source of virus dissemination in a community. The main purpose of vaccination, however, is to protect pregnant women for the sake of their unborn children. If a woman wants the vaccine, she should be tested first to be certain she is not pregnant and then she should carefully avoid pregnancy for at least two months following vaccination.

Other viral infections are also suspect. The cold-sore virus herpes simplex can severely damage the fetus, especially if the mother's genital organs are infected, which, in turn, can infect the child during the birth process.[13] Viral diseases such as mumps, polio, smallpox, chickenpox, infectious hepatitis, and regular measles can cause some fetal damage when they occur during pregnancy. There is no evidence, as yet, that the common cold viruses cause any damage, but the influenza virus is suspected of increasing the possibility of some slight damage to the infant. In our study of inefficient learners (children with learning disabilities) we found a larger than usual number of mothers reporting having had the "flu" during early pregnancy. The problems created were not irreversible nor severe, but they did cause some concern for the child during the first three years of schooling.

Undetected syphilis in the mother frequently attacks the nervous system of the fetus and may result in congenital weakness. Syphilis may cause stillbirth, miscarriage, deafness, blindness, or congenital mental deficiency.[14] In some cases the child may not show any signs of syphilitic symptoms until several years later. One known case in which a child was born with syphilis resulted in senility at the age of 14 years because the syphilitic spirochetes had destroyed so many of the brain cells.

Rh factor

Human blood is not interchangeable. Blood from a donor must be matched with the blood of the recipient to ensure that they are compatible. Although the blood of the mother does not mix with that of the fetus, a problem of compatibility could arise if both the mother and the father have a blood type from the Rh blood group. If both parents are Rh negative or if both are Rh positive, there is no problem, because the fetus will inherit a blood type that will be compatible with that of the mother. If the parents differ in their Rh factor and the baby inherits an Rh-positive blood type from the father, there could be a problem if the mother is Rh negative.

In about 10% of the cases some blood from the fetus can be diffused through the placenta into the bloodstream of the mother. Since the blood types are incompatible, the Rh-negative mother will produce antibodies to resist the "invasion of foreign bodies." If the antibodies are passed back to the fetus by diffusion, the antibodies will attack the fetal red cells, causing the fetus to become anemic. Usually the fetus can make red cells fast enough for its needs, but if it cannot, it will either die or be born with a severe anemic condition called *erythroblastosis fetalis*. If the child lives, it is highly susceptible to jaundice, which in severe cases can cause some brain damage.[15] Successive pregnancies of the mother with fetuses having Rh-positive blood will raise the level of antibodies in the mother's blood to a crtical level and will be more dangerous to these fetuses. Only Rh-negative mothers are affected.

The following outline provides the reaction of Rh factors.

1. Rh compatibility
   Father Rh+ and mother Rh+ = baby Rh+
   Father Rh− and mother Rh− = baby Rh−
   Father Rh+ and mother Rh− = baby Rh−
2. Rh incompatibility
   If father Rh+ and mother Rh− = baby Rh+, then Rh− mother and Rh+ baby are incompatible
   a. Blood antigens from Rh+ baby enter mother's Rh− blood.
   b. Mother's Rh− blood produces antibodies to fight off foreign antigens.
   c. Some of mother's antibodies enter baby's blood by diffusion.
   d. Mother's antibodies in baby's blood attack red corpuscles causing anemia, edema, and/or jaundice.
   e. With successive pregnancies mother's supply of antibodies can increase to a level dangerous for the fetus.

How Rh disease develops....

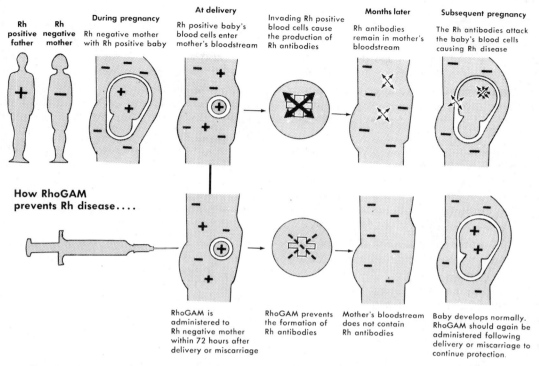

Fig. 4-3. How Rh disease develops. (Reprinted by permission of Ortho Diagnostics, Inc., Raritan, N.J.)

Seventeen percent of mothers in Western societies are Rh negative. Striking advances have taken place in the treatment of Rh incompatibility. A serum, RhoGAM, has been developed to prevent the production of antibodies in mothers who have not already formed antibodies.[16] Fig. 4-3 shows how RhoGAM can be used to prevent Rh disease. If a child with Rh factors is born anemic, an exchange transfusion can be given to remove sensitized blood. In 1963 the first intrauterine transfusion was attempted with considerable success by a New Zealand physician. This treatment is used if the fetus is in danger of death and is too immature to risk premature delivery.

Drugs and medication

The effect of drugs on the unborn baby can be most pronounced. The category "drugs" includes medicines that physicians prescribe such as antibiotics; over-the-counter remedies like aspirin, cold tablets, vitamins, and nose drops; and abused or illegal drugs such as heroin, LSD, cocaine, amphetamines, and marijuana. The full meaning of the influence of medication and drugs on prenatal development is still being investigated. The evidence, however, appears to indicate that women of reproductive age should be cautious about taking medications that are not prescribed.

In the early 1960s a sedative drug named thalidomide appeared on the European market. Not realizing the consequences of its effects on pregnant women, physicians prescribed it for those who were tense due to their new condition. Many babies born to these women had flipperlike arms or no arms or legs at all.[17] Deafness of some children can be traced to the mother's use of quinine.[18]

Addictive narcotics are carried in the bloodstream of the mother and are transmitted to the fetus. Less than a day after birth the baby shows the classic signs of withdrawal, which may be so violent that the infant may die.[19] Premature births are higher among women addicted to narcotics than among the general population.

Although there is still much to be learned about the relationship of drugs and narcotics to birth defects, there is more known about the effects on newborn babies of sedative medication given to mothers during the birth process. These drugs do affect the baby, although only temporarily. The more anesthetic given to the mother, the longer the adjustment period of the newborn baby to postnatal life. Babies of mothers who were heavily medicated showed disorganized behavior for three or four days after birth as compared to one or two days for babies of non-medicated mothers. What is significant in these cases is that at the time of birth, just when a baby's systems have to be at the peak level of performance to make a smooth transition to the outer world, they are in a state of sedation and may not have that extra push needed to overcome difficulties that may arise.

Toxemia of pregnancy

Toxemia refers to a large group of undesirable physical conditions that may occur in the mother after the twenty-fourth week of pregnancy or soon after giving birth. The signs or symptoms that these conditions have in common are (1) edema, a rapid or excessive weight gain during the third trimester owing to an accumulation of fluid in the body; (2) hypertension, a rise in blood pressure; and (3) the presence of albumin, a protein product, in the urine.[20] Acute toxemia is known as preeclampsia. Treatment of preeclampsia is usually effective. If the toxemia becomes severe (eclampsia), convulsions and finally coma will occur. It is estimated that 6% to 10% of all pregnancies are complicated by one of the many toxemias of pregnancy—mostly preeclampsia. With the inception of blood banks and antibiotics, toxemia of pregnancy has replaced hemorrhage and infection as the leading cause of maternal mortality. Infant mortality in all toxemias is about 10% to 25%.

Other factors

The age of the mother when she gives birth to a child appears to have some bearing on the ease of the birth process, the mental ability level of the child, and the physical well-being of the child. Mothers under 18 and over 40 years of age tend

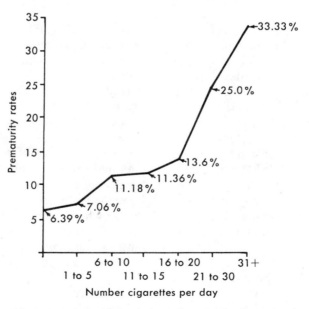

Fig. 4-4. Relationship between number of cigarettes smoked per day by the mother and prematurity rates of infants. (From Simpson, W. J. *American Journal of Obstetrics and Gynecology,* 1957, **73,** 808-815.)

to have a higher proportion of retarded children than do mothers who are between these ages.[21] Women who have their first baby when they are 35 years old or over are more likely than younger women to experience illnesses during pregnancy and have a more difficult labor. The optimum age for childbearing appears to be between 20 and 28 years of age. However, advances in obstetrics have made pregnancy and birth at any age much less dangerous and complicated than previously.

A relationship between the weight of a newborn baby and the amount of smoking done by the mother (Fig. 4-4) is suggested by several studies. The National Institutes of Health report that the size of a newborn baby is affected by the mother's smoking somewhat in proportion to the number of cigarettes she smokes per day. Six or more cigarettes a day was considered very harmful. The heavy cigarette smoker will have smaller babies (on the average, 8 ounces lighter) than a nonsmoker. In addition, there will also be a significantly greater number of premature deliveries among heavy smokers.[22]

The National Institute of Alcohol and Alcoholism reports that at least 9 million Americans are alcoholics and that only about one tenth of these are receiving treatment. The rate of alcoholism in Europe equals or, in most cases, exceeds that of the United States. Alcohol usage among young people is said to have reached epidemic proportions. What effect does alcohol or alcoholism have on pregnancy? To begin with, Iorio[23] points out that alcohol can affect gamete development in an individual even before pregnancy takes place. The use of alcohol (Iorio does not state how much) can produce cadmium (Capsebon) in increased amounts in the kidneys of hypertensive women. In men, it produces busulfan (Myleran) that acts directly on gamete-producing tissue. According to studies done at the University of Washington,[24] alcohol can have serious effects on the fetus or neonate. If the blood level of the fetus or neonate is equal to that of the alcoholic mother, convulsions, withdrawal symptoms, low birth weight, small size for age, poor sucking reflex, poor mental performance, and malformations of various types can occur. If alcohol is used during pregnancy, it should be consumed in small amounts and with moderation.

Alcohol readily passes through the placenta to the developing child. Although it may not be dangerous to the developing child in these quantities, a pregnant woman who drinks to excess increases the likelihood of not eating properly and of possibly injuring herself.

Some anxiety in a pregnant woman is inevitable and seldom harmful. However, excessive emotional stress is known to be transferred to the developing fetus by hormones and chemical factors in the bloodstream. As a result, the infant may be born with a physiological defect or weakness, a slight decrease in bodily weight, or undesirable behavior characteristics. The infant's behavior pattern after birth may take the form of excessive crying, irritability, difficulties in digestion, vomiting, and sometimes diarrhea. Before birth there is increased movement by the fetus whenever the mother is undergoing emotional stress. The longer the period of stress, the greater will be the increase of the baby's activity.[25]

A case illustrating the effect of great emotional stress on prenatal development is that of an 11-year-old girl who developed ulcerative colitis (ulcer of the colon), which is an uncommon condition in persons so young. The prenatal developmental history revealed that during the second month of pregnancy, the girl's mother was subjected to intense emotional stress when both her parents were in a serious accident and were not expected to live. The medical report on the 11-year-old reasoned that this event occurred at the time when the digestive system, including the colon, was being formed. It was assumed that the stress of the moment produced a chemical change in the mother's blood and affected the development of the colon in the fetus, producing a weakness that made it more susceptible to colitis.

In general, if young couples want to conceive bright and healthy children, they should go easy on drinking, smoking, overeating, and worrying.

CONDITIONS AT BIRTH
AFFECTING DEVELOPMENT
Phenylketonuria (PKU)

Phenylketonuria, known as PKU, is a hereditary defect in an enzyme of the liver. The child needs the enzyme to metabolize the common protein food product phenylalanine. If the enzyme abnormality is not found and treated soon after birth, certain substances accumulate in the blood and bring about mental retardation by causing damage to the brain. PKU appears about once in 10,000 births. The condition can often be detected by a simple blood test given before the baby leaves the hospital. The infant's heel is pricked, and a few drops of blood are obtained on filter paper and then tested. A urine test can be done after the infant is 3 weeks old.[26] Treatment consists of a scientifically controlled diet, which is begun within the first few weeks of life. If the diet is continued, the child will grow and develop normally. In some cases PKU children can be given normal diets after a few years.

Anoxia

The ease or difficulty with which the newborn infant starts to breathe after birth is critical to his future development. If breathing is not established soon, enabling oxygen to reach the brain, serious consequences may occur. If oxygen deprivation (anoxia) is severe, the infant may die. Less severe deprivation may result in enough damage to brain cells to cause cerebral palsy or similar conditions. A lesser degree of anoxia may cause disturbances in cognitive functioning, such as in mental processes related to verbal, conceptual, and perceptual development. Visual-motor coordination may be affected.[27] In preschool and early school years special sensory development and teaching techniques may be needed to help the child develop the various cognitive and perceptual processes. The effects of anoxia on learning ability may be temporary or permanent.

Oxygen deprivation may result from a prolonged or difficult birth or by birth in the breech position. Occasionally, infants born by cesarean section will develop a hyaline membrane, a glossylike condition in the lungs, shortly after birth that causes difficulty in breathing and possibly death. Babies born with a congenital heart defect that bars normal circulation of blood can also be oxygen starved. These so-called blue babies are placed in incubators to enable them to survive without producing any damage to the brain. Once their problem has been corrected, they respond adequately.

Also serious in establishing respiration is too rapid a birth. Precipitate labor, which is labor of less than 2 hours duration, may introduce the baby too suddenly to his new environment, with the consequence that he is not yet ready to breathe. Oxygen deprivation occurs in these cases also. The degree of brain damage and the permanence of its effects will depend largely on how quickly the infant can start breathing.

Birth defects

An understandable concern of parents is whether the baby is born free of congenital defects. Fortunately, the large majority of babies are born without serious abnormalities that cause disfigurement or a physical or mental handicap. Yet some children are born with defects, some of which are presented in Table 4-3, which can be found at the end of this chapter. About 20% of birth defects are due to heredity; another 20% are caused by environmental factors, such as drugs, medicine, viral infections, and vitamin deficiencies. The remaining 60% result from an interaction of some environmental factor and a genetic predisposition.[28]

One child in 500 will be born with an open spine (spina bifida). Failure of the spine to close permits some nerves of the spinal cord to protrude. Sometimes surgery in the first three months of the child's life can correct the condition so that other complications do not occur. Clinical cases of mental retardation such as Down's syndrome (mongolism) appear once in 600 births (one in 50 for women over 45 years of age) and as hydrocephaly (water on the brain) in one in 500 births. Mongolism is caused by a chromosomal error, whereas hydrocephaly usually is due to an obstruction of the flow of cerebrospinal fluid. Fibrocystic disease, cystic fibrosis, occurs once in 1,000 births. Children with this condition have chronic respiratory problems and persistent intestinal difficulties. The cause is usually hereditary and involves a metabolic error.

The significant point to be remembered is that most births produce normal, healthy babies. If the mother takes care of herself, especially during the first three months of pregnancy, chances are considerably greater that the baby will be normal.

Prematurity and low birth weight

In the past the term *premature* was applied to the newborn baby who had a gestation age of less than 37 weeks or weighed less than 5½ pounds (2,500 grams) at birth. Several studies have indicated that this "either-or" criterion was inadequate because babies of the same weight spend varied lengths of time within the womb. About 30% of babies born after thirty-seven completed weeks of pregnancy weigh less than 5½ pounds, whereas the truly premature newborn baby of, for example, a diabetic mother, may weigh considerably more. Fig. 4-5 considers zones of mortality and morbidity in relation to fetal development.

The term *premature* relates to the length of the gestation period and applies to an infant born before thirty-seven completed weeks of pregnancy. The term *low birth weight* is applied to any newborn, regardless of gestation age, who weighs less than 2,500 grams at birth. Recognition of the different groups of premature babies is important because they differ greatly in terms of the kind of care they may need.

Premature birth is the biggest single problem facing those responsible for the care of the newborn. Although most body organs can function fairly adequately by the twenty-eighth week, the brain is still insufficiently developed to control behavior. The cerebral cortex has little, if any, control over the behavior patterns of either a 7- or an 8-month-old term baby.[29] Special attention must be given to the physical needs of the newborn infant. The premature infant requires nearly

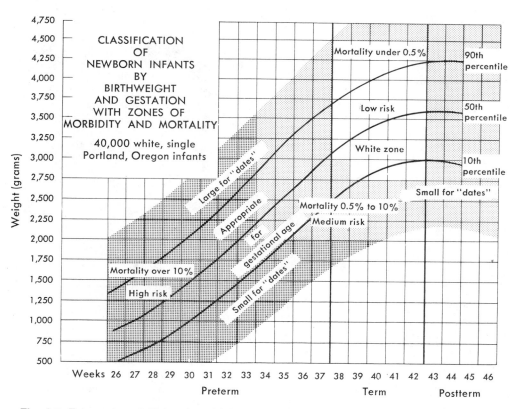

Fig. 4-5. Zones of mortality and morbidity in relation to both weight and gestation. (From Babson, S. G., Benson, R. C., Pernoll, M. L., & Benda, G. I. *Management of high-risk pregnancy and intensive care of the neonate* [3rd ed.]. St. Louis: The C. V. Mosby Co., 1975.)

three times as much oxygen as a full-term infant. He is often anemic and may require a blood transfusion. Furthermore, he is more subject to infection and will require careful medical supervision. The use of an incubator helps with these problems while at the same time providing a temperature and humidity climate that seeks to duplicate conditions of the intrauterine environment.

There are many reasons why a mother may have a baby of low birth weight or a premature delivery. Some of the factors are toxemia, a multiple birth, accidental hemorrhage during pregnancy, a placenta previa (a misplaced placenta covering the opening of the womb instead of lying in the proper place), hypertensive cardiovascular disease, diabetes, glandular disturbance, nutritional deficiency, undue emotional stress, or a number of other reasons. About 7% of all births are premature. Prematurity is more common among first-born babies and among boys than among girls. It is more frequent in the lower socioeconomic class and more frequent among nonwhites than among whites.[30] Of the babies who die within four weeks of birth, over half are born prematurely, which is the greatest cause of

Table 4-2. High-risk infants*

Family history	**Present pregnancy—cont'd**
Presence of mutant genes	Anesthesia
Central nervous system disorders	Maternal rubella in first trimester
Low socioeconomic group	Diabetes
Previous defective sibling	Toxemia
Parental consanguinity	Fetal-maternal blood group incompatibility
Intrafamilial emotional disorder	**Labor and delivery**
Medical history of mother	Absence of prenatal care
Diabetes	Prematurity
Hypertension	Postmaturity or dysmaturity
Radiation	Precipitate, prolonged, or complicated delivery
Cardiovascular or renal disease	Low Apgar score—5 minutes
Thyroid disease	**Placenta**
Idiopathic thrombocytopenic purpura	Massive infarction
Previous obstetrical history of mother	Amnion nodosum
Toxemia	Placentitis
Miscarriage immediately preceding pregnancy	**Neonate**
Size of infants	Single umbilical artery
High parity	Jaundice
Prolonged infertility	Head size
Present pregnancy	Infection
Maternal age <16 or >35	Hypoxia
Multiple births	Severe dehydration, hyperosmolarity, and
Polyhydramnios	hypernatremia
Pyelonephritis	Convulsions
Out-of-wedlock pregnancy	Failure to regain birth weight by 10 days
Oligohydramnios	Manifest congenital defects
Medications	Disproportion between weight or length and
Radiation	gestational age
	Survival following meningitides, encephalopathies, and traumatic intracranial episodes

*Adapted from Proceedings of the White House Conference on Mental Retardation, Washington, D.C., 1963; from the American Medical Association. Mental retardation—a handbook for the primary physician. *Journal of the American Medical Association,* 1965, **191,** 183.

neonatal death in the United States; respiratory distress is second and congenital anomalies are third as causes of death.

Studies of the development of premature children reveal that these infants do differ from the normal, at least up to about the ages of 6, 7, or 8 years. By then most premature children catch up in weight, height, and functional mental ability. At the beginning of school a greater percentage of premature children are distractible and excessively active or restless. They obtain slightly lower scores on tests of motor and cognitive development. More premature children have difficulty in learning to read than do other children. The extent of the lag in maturation and functional ability is related to the degree of deviation in low birth weight or prematurity of birth. Most children, however, have an amazing ability to adapt or compensate for any deficiencies they may have. One should look for positive attributes in children rather than focus or dwell on limitations or deficiencies. Children progress to the degree that they are free to do so, and that includes freedom from overprotectiveness by parents, who frequently underestimate the capabilities of children who are born prematurely.

Apgar and Beck,[31] in their book, *Is My Baby All Right?* make a number of suggestions that could help to prevent birth defects. Some of their suggestions follow:

1. If a close relative has a disorder that might be hereditary, take advantage of genetic counseling.
2. From a statistical point of view, avoid pregnancy before age 18 or after age 40. The ideal age to have children is between 20 and 35 (elsewhere we say 20 to 28).
3. Men should beget their children before they reach the age of 45, although this is not as statistically significant as it is for women.
4. There should be an interval of at least two years between the end of one pregnancy and the beginning of another.
5. After the second birth, statistical chances increase somewhat for stillbirth, congenital malformation, and prematurity.
6. When conceiving, intercourse should be at intervals of no more than 24 hours for

several days, just preceding and during the estimated time of ovulation. The sperms and eggs are fresher and stronger.
7. Have good prenatal care checkups and good obstetrical care and delivery.
8. Be immunized against rubella. Avoid exposure to contagious disease.
9. During pregnancy, avoid eating uncooked meat that might be a source of toxoplasmosis infection. Another source of toxoplasmosis infection is the feces of cats; care should be taken in cleaning litter boxes.
10. Do not take any drugs or medication unless prescribed.
11. Avoid x-ray examinations, especially during the first three months.
12. Do not smoke cigarettes.
13. Eat a nourishing diet, high in proteins, vitamins, and minerals.
14. A prospective mother with Rh-negative blood should have her physician take the necessary steps to protect her and the baby.
15. Take every precaution to prevent a baby from being born prematurely in less than 266 days or under 5½ pounds.

UNWED PARENTS

Although legalized abortion and the widespread use of contraceptives are bringing down the national birth rate (at least until 1977 when it went up 5%), the percentage of illegitimate births has gone up 24% since 1965. Earlier puberty, liberalized social interaction, mass exposure to sex in the media, permissive attitudes concerning sex, and a general uncertainty concerning moral values, self-restraint, and the consequences of sex before marriage have contributed to this increase. Unfortunately, it is the unborn child who is punished because of the trauma, perhaps the lack of care, that is involved.

The unwed mother

Juhasz[32] indicated that the largest number of illegitimate births occur in the 15- to 19-year-old group. Since the birth control pill has become available, it is reasonable to assume that most girls would take some type of precaution in sex-

Text continued on p. 98.

Table 4-3. Types of birth defects, estimates, description, and treatment*

Type of defect	Numbers affected annually	Description	Causes and treatment
Birthmarks	Very common	There are many unimportant birthmarks. The disfiguring ones are reddish or wine-colored patches consisting of numerous small dilated blood vessels. True blood vessel tumors are more rare. These are elevated and may occur on any part of the body.	Cause unknown. Skilled plastic surgeons can remove many marks. Skin grafts are often used. A new technique for large marks is to tattoo normal skin colors right over the purple area.
Cleft lip (harelip)	About 1 in every 1,000 babies in white populations is born with a cleft lip. Seventy percent of these also have cleft palates. The frequency appears higher in Japanese and lower in black populations.	When the embryo is about 6 weeks, swellings that will become the upper lip have not yet met. If they do not fuse at the proper time, the gap will remain and the baby will have a cleft lip.	These conditions are sometimes related to genetic defects. In experiments with animals it appears that the environment in the uterus, such as the position of the embryo or the blood supply, may be a factor, and some drugs given during pregnancy are also under suspicion. There are now many new operative techniques for repairing the defects. Harelip can be repaired in the first few weeks after birth, and cleft palate before the child is 14 months old in most cases.
Cleft palate	About 1 in every 2,500 babies has a cleft palate without a cleft lip. The two conditions are not genetically related.	A cleft palate is a hole in the roof of the mouth. More boys than girls have a harelip, and more girls have a cleft palate.	
Clubfoot	1 in 250	The foot turns inward (usually) or outward and is fixed in a tiptoe position.	Possibly due to the position of the child in the uterus, although maldevelopment of the limb bud may also be the cause. Mild deformities respond well to shoe splints worn at night. Simple braces and corrective shoes may be needed. More serious clubfoot often will be associated with other defects as well. Treatment must begin early and is prolonged because the condition tends to recur. The muscles and ligaments must be stretched and the bones realigned. Plaster casts can often correct the condition. Surgery is sometimes necessary.
Congenital heart disease	1 in 160	There are many known types of congenital heart defects. Some are so slight as to cause little strain on the heart; others are fatal. In some of the abnormalities, the baby appears blue.	Few cases are known, but German measles during pregnancy is one

An ever-increasing number of heart conditions can be repaired by surgery, saving lives and preventing invalidism. |

Congenital urinary tract defects	1 in 250	There are many different types, involving the kidneys, ureters, bladder, and genitalia. Organs may be absent, fused, or obstructed.	Some causes are known, such as certain hormones given during pregnancy. There is some hereditary tendency. Most conditions can be corrected by surgery.
Diabetes	Very common. About 1 in 4 carries the trait. Clinical diabetes, or actual cases, seen in about 1 in 2,500 persons between ages 1 and 20; in 1 in 50 persons over 60 years of age.	Metabolic disorder in which there is a shortage of insulin hormone. Glucose, which comes from carbohydrates, accumulates in the blood and is excreted through the kidneys instead of being stored in the body as glycogen. Possibility of manifestation increases with age. Patient may be susceptible to infection of cuts and bruises. Among older persons serious involvement could lead to hardening of the arteries, gangrene in legs, and blindness.	Cause unknown; possible enzyme defect. Marked hereditary tendency. Persons with family history of diabetes should seek periodic checkups. Physicians can recognize symptoms, make positive diagnosis, and prescribe specific treatment. Special diets, oral medication, and injections of insulin are measures that will usually keep condition under control and permit normal activity.
Erythroblastosis	About 10% of the babies born to Rh-negative mothers married to Rh-positive fathers have this condition. One in 7 of total American population has Rh-negative blood. Among Orientals the figure is 1 in 20.	The baby is often yellow in color soon after birth. Anemia is another symptom. Mental retardation may be severe. Erythroblastosis is a common cause of stillbirth.	Rh blood factor is inherited. Physicians should know Rh factor of both parents. Rh problem exists only if father is Rh positive (baby inherits Rh-positive gene from his father) and mother is Rh negative. Red blood cells of fetus reach mother's blood, causing her blood to form antibodies that pass back through the placenta to the baby and destroy his red cells in varying degrees. First pregnancy is usually uneventful. Cure can now be effected if condition is detected early. Infant mortality used to be 45% but is now 5%. Exchange transfusion, replacing baby's blood with compatible blood right after birth, is the cure. Several transfusions are sometimes necessary.
Extra fingers and toes (polydactyly)	Extra digits are twice as frequent as fused digits. The incidence is 1 in 100 among the black population; 1 in 600 in the white population.	Extra fingers or toes.	Cause unknown; frequently hereditary. Cure is simple amputation of the extra digits. This can often be done at birth or at about 3 years of age.
Fused fingers and toes (syndactyly)	Fused digits do not have such racial variation.	Too few digits.	In syndactyly surgery can improve the function and appearance of the hand or foot. Occasionally artificial limbs are necessary.

Continued.

*From Apgar, V. *With best wishes for a happy birthday.* New York: The National Foundation—March of Dimes, 1963, pp. 4-8.

Table 4-3. Types of birth defects, estimates, description, and treatment—cont'd

Type of defect	Numbers affected annually	Description	Causes and treatment
Fibrocystic disease (cystic fibrosis)	About 1 in 1,000 births. Rare among black populations; found very infrequently in Orientals.	A recently identified disease, now separated from a vast group of conditions producing a sickly, malnourished child with persistent intestinal difficulties. Victims have chronic respiratory problems, and death is usually due to pneumonia or other lung complications. One clue to disease is perspiration with high-salt content.	Hereditary. Due to a metabolic error. Manifests self soon after birth. Mucous material blocks the exit of the digestive juices from the pancreas into the intestinal tract. Excess mucus is also secreted by lungs. Formerly death was expected before age 2. Now antibiotics, chemical substitutions for enzymes, and other treatments have extended life expectancy. Increasing numbers of adults are found to have a mild form of the disease.
Galactosemia	Somewhat more rare than phenylketonuria	A disorder causing eye cataracts and severe damage to the liver and the brain, resulting in mental retardation.	Hereditary. Caused by the absence of an enzyme required to convert galactose to glucose, important in digestion of milk sugar. Formerly led to many early deaths, but experiments now show that early recognition and dietary treatment can arrest the disease. Diagnosis can be made at birth.
Hydrocephaly (water on brain)	1 in 500	Enlargement of the head due to excessive fluid within the brain. Most cases result from obstruction to circulation of cerebrospinal fluid. In others fluid is produced in excess or is not absorbed fast enough. Pressure from fluid often causes compression of the brain with resulting mental retardation.	Obstruction to flow may result from prenatal infection or abnormality in development. Cause of excess fluid not known. Treatment is "shunt" operation to relieve pressure on the brain. A tube with a one-way valve is inserted surgically to lead fluid from the brain directly into the bloodstream or into some other body cavity. Condition frequently fatal if not treated.
Missing limbs	Very rare	Congenital amputees are born with one to four limbs missing or seriously deformed.	Cause unknown. Recently an international outbreak of this defect was traced to the drug thalidomide used by pregnant women. Great strides have been made in prosthetic, or artificial, devices. Emotional problems of the affected parents and children are great but are being overcome to a large extent in many families.

Birth of the baby 97

Condition	Frequency	Description	Causes / Treatment
Mongolism	1 in 600. Women 25 years of age have about 1 chance in 2,000 of producing a mongoloid child. For women of 45 the average expectation is about 1 in 50.	Mongolism, mongoloid idiocy, or the Langdon-Down syndrome is characterized by short stature, slightly slanted eyes, and varying degrees of mental retardation.	All patients have chromosomal error. Causes can be hereditary or environmental. Whereas the normal human cell has 46 chromosomes, cells of those afflicted by this defect have 47 or the equivalent. No known cure, although IQ can be improved by special training.
Open spine (spina bifida)	Approximately 1 in every 500 births. It is more common among white children than among black. About half the patients are also victims of hydrocephaly.	Failure of the spine to close permits the protrusion of spinal cord or nerves. This often leads to total dysfunction of the legs, bladder, and rectum. Often the child has other serious defects.	Cause unknown. In some cases surgery in the first 3 months of child's life can either correct or arrest the condition so that other complications do not occur. In the more serious cases, several new surgical techniques are being used on the bladder, rectum, and spinal cord.
Phenylketonuria (PKU)	Approximately 1 in 10,000	Chemical imbalance, resulting in a form of mental deficiency, inherited from apparently normal parents, each of whom has one defective gene. The child appears normal at birth, but his mind stops developing during the first year of life. Retardation is severe. One-third never learn to walk, and two-thirds never learn to talk. The pigment of skin and hair is decreased.	Caused by a hereditary defect in an enzyme of the liver. In normal metabolism, phenylalanine, a compound making up one twentieth of the weight of proteins in the diet, is changed to tyrosine. In PKU the enzyme responsible for this step is inactive or absent, and phenylalanine accumulates. PKU can be detected between the fifth and seventh days of life. Treatment is dietary; specifically manufactured food with low-phenylalanine content is fed to the infant. The treatment does not cure retardation already present but can prevent it from developing. Therefore treatment should begin soon after birth. Some experiments show that after a few years PKU children can be fed normal diets.
Sickle-cell trait	Low among white populations. Very high (about 40%) in black populations in Africa and high (10%) among American blacks.	When red blood cells of people with the sickle-cell trait are exposed to low-oxygen atmosphere, the cells lose normal form and become crescent or sickle shaped. When accompanied by severe anemia, the condition is usually fatal. The sickle-cell trait carries some immunity to malaria.	Hereditary condition. Severe anemia results if the child receives the abnormal trait from both parents.

ual involvements, but Kantner and Zelnick[33] report that only a relatively small percentage, approximately 20%, of unmarried girls having intercourse have ever used the contraceptive pill to prevent pregnancy. A disturbingly high percentage, between 55% and 75%, have used no contraceptive device whatsoever, at least in their first experience, and only a minority consistently use such a device thereafter. Interestingly, there was only a small difference in percentage of contraceptive use between poor and nonpoor adolescents or between ethnic groups. What is also astonishing is that approximately 29% of all nonvirgin girls report that they have had at least one premarital pregnancy.[34]

A number of factors are related to the incidence of early marriage or illegitimate births. These factors frequently involve family conflicts, willingness to get pregnant to get away from home or out of school, social and economic problems, individual psychological hang-ups, lack of knowledge concerning sexual matters, and/or poor understanding of the responsibilities of sexuality in the family and society. Communities are becoming increasingly aware of the needs of the young unwed parent. In many places the pregnant girl's formal education is permitted to continue. Programs have been initiated for supervised prenatal care; preparations are made for the experiences of pregnancy, labor, and delivery; instruction in mothering skills is given; and assistance with personal and vocational planning is provided. Physicians and nurses, as well as social workers, are learning more about the needs of the teenage obstetrical patient, both in and out of the hospital or agency setting.

The medical profession recognizes that the incidence of toxemia of pregnancy is higher in this age group, especially for girls in their early teens from lower socioeconomic backgrounds.[35] This increased incidence may be related to the poor diets of many young girls. Some overeat because of anxiety and stress; others feel guilty about the pregnancy and use starvation for self-punishment. These patients always have an especially large number of low-weight babies; the incidence of major defects is from two to four times as high for premature as for full-term infants. Poor black women have a starkly high percentage of premature births.

The unwed father

Unwed fathers are also expectant parents. Consideration of both partners is essential for their growth in maturity and self-esteem. Including the father in discussions often provides better planning for the child. It improves the father's behavior and his future relationships. Unwed fathers have about as many problems or concerns as unwed mothers. Pannor and associates[36] have demonstrated that a good counseling relationship must be established and discussions held on attitudes toward sex, mature love, responsibilities of parenthood, and the need for security through family living. In some hospitals, the father is shown the baby to complete the reality of the experience. Both parents are involved in sharing the responsibilities for medical care and living arrangements. Parent participation is usually therapeutic. Pannor learned that (1) most women were willing and able to name the father; (2) the partners were usually close in age and social class; (3) most were from the middle class and had at least completed high school; and (4) ignorance of contraceptive methods was not a factor.

What is interesting is that many unwed fathers want to be involved. The Family Service Association of America, in cooperation with Ladies Home Journal, conducted a study of unwed fathers.[37] A detailed profile of 149 unwed fathers emerged as follows:

1. The men involved were not irresponsible.
2. Usually they were deeply involved with the unwed mothers, the pregnancy, and the child. Sixty-one percent *wanted, and not because of obligation,* to marry the woman. It was the woman who usually rejected the idea.
3. Over 60% of the men visited their babies in the hospital and showed strong paternal feelings.

Recognizing the needs, concerns, and identities of both the unwed mother and the unwed father suggests that there are potentials for growth in unwed parenthood. Marriage is not always the answer. Age, immaturity, personality and social incompatibilities, financial inadequacies, the need for job or career development, or emotional trauma associated with the event may rule out marriage for some couples. More girls are choosing to keep their babies, yet we must recognize that adoption is an option to be considered. What can be gained is a process of support and development for the unwed couple that can increase self-esteem and decrease feelings of guilt. Being able to share the responsibility of deciding about this pregnancy and this infant can be therapeutic. The lives of three people, mother, father, and infant, should be helped. There is a lifetime of living that lies ahead. Making them "pay" for their indiscretion is of dubious value to either society or the individuals involved—and especially to the infant.

STUDY GUIDE

1. Compare the characteristics of true or real labor at the time of birth with those of false labor.
2. What are the three stages of labor?
3. Describe a normal delivery.
4. Rubella, or German measles, is a serious matter when a mother is infected during the first twelve weeks of pregnancy. What are its symptoms, and in what ways can it affect the unborn child?
5. Discuss the implications of incompatible Rh factors and of toxemia in pregnancy.
6. What is anoxia? How can it affect a child?
7. How do premature babies frequently differ from normal term babies?
8. What consideration, care, and cautions should be given to unwed mothers and unwed fathers?
9. Who suffers the most in unwed parenthood, the mother or the father? Should they get married?

REFERENCES

1. Jensen, M. D., Benson, R. C., & Bobak, I. M. *Maternity care: the nurse and the family.* St. Louis: The C. V. Mosby Co., 1977.
2. McLennan, C. E., & Sandberg, E. C. *Synopsis of obstetrics* (9th ed.). St. Louis: The C. V. Mosby Co., 1974.
3. Gabert, H. A., & Stanchever, M. A. Electronic fetal monitoring as a routine practice in an obstetric service: a progress report. *American Journal of Obstetrics and Gynecology,* 1974, **118**, 534.
4. Apgar, V. Perinatal problems and the central nervous system. In United States HEW, *The child with central nervous system deficit,* Washington, D.C.: Government Printing Office, 1967, 75-76.
5. Lemaze, F. Natural childbirth. Explained in D. Tanzer & J. L. Block. *Why natural childbirth?* Garden City, N.Y.: Doubleday & Co., Inc., 1972.
6. Leboyer, F. *Birth without violence.* New York: Alfred A. Knopf, Inc., 1975.
7. Scrimshaw, N. S. Infant malnutrition and adult learning. *Saturday Review,* 1968, **50**, 64 ff.
8. Brewer, T. H. Human maternal-fetal nutrition. *Obstetrics and Gynecology,* 1972, **40**, 868-870.
9. Brody, J. E. How mother affects her unborn child. *Womans Day,* 1970, **12**, 114-115.
10. Ademoware, A. S., Courey, N. G., & Kime, J. S. Relationships of maternal nutrition and weight gain to newborn birthweight. *Obstetrics and Gynecology,* 1972, **39**, 460-464.
11. Behrman, R. E. (Ed.), *Neonatology: disease of the fetus and the infant* (2nd ed.). St. Louis: The C. V. Mosby Co., 1977.
12. Bolognese, R. J. Rubella vaccination: a critical review. *Obstetrics and Gynecology,* 1973, **42**, 4.
13. Neeson, J. D. Herpesvirus genitalis: a nursing perspective. *Nursing Clinics of North America,* 1975, **10**, 599.
14. Bellingham, F. R. Syphilis in pregnancy: transplacental infection. *Medical Journal of Australia,* 1973, **2**, 647.
15. Friedman, C. R. H. *Isoimmunization and erythroblastosis.* New York: Appleton-Century-Crofts, 1969.
16. Keith, L. and others. The multiple use of Rho-GAM. *Journal of the National Medical Association,* 1973, **65**, 1.
17. James, W. H. Teratogenetic properties of thalidomide. *British Medical Journal,* 1965, **5469**, 1064.
18. Dawes, G. The distribution and action of drugs on foetus in utero. *British Journal of Anaesthesia,* 1973, **45**, 766.
19. Pillari, G., & Narus, J. Physical effects of heroin addiction. *American Journal of Nursing,* 1973, **73**, 2105-2108.
20. Ferris, T. Toxemia and hypertension. In G. Burrow, & T. Ferris (Eds.), *Medical complications during pregnancy.* Philadelphia: W. B. Saunders Co., 1975.
21. Anderson, J. M. High risk groups: definitions and identifications. *New England Journal of Medicine,* 1965, **272**, 309.
22. Butler, N. R., & Goldstein, H. Smoking in pregnancy and subsequent child development. *British Medical Journal,* 1973, **4**, 573-575.
23. Iorio, J. *Childbirth: family-centered nursing* (3rd ed.). St. Louis: The C. V. Mosby Co., 1975.
24. Maternal alcoholism and birth defects seen related. *Nursing Care,* 1974, **7**, 34.

25. Ottinger, D. R., & Simons, J. E. Behavior of human neonates and prenatal maternal anxiety. *Psychological Reports,* 1964, **14,** 391-394.

26. Holtzman, N. A., Meck, A. G., & Mellits, E. D. Neonatal screening for phenylketonuria. I. Effectiveness. *Journal of the American Medical Association,* 1974, **229,** 667.

27. Corah, N. L. Perceptual and cognitive deficits in children as related to perinatal anoxia and level of intelligence. *Journal of Consulting Clinical Psychology,* 1966, **30,** 87.

28. Korones, S. B. High-risk newborn infants—the basis for intensive nursing care (2nd ed.). St. Louis: The C. V. Mosby Co., 1976.

29. Bender, S. Problems of prematurity. *Practitioner,* 1970, **204,** 366.

30. Erhardt, C. L. and others. Influence of weight and gestation on perinatal and neonatal mortality by ethnic group. *American Journal of Public Health,* 1964, **54,** 1841.

31. Apgar, V., & Beck, J. *Is my baby all right?* New York: Simon and Schuster, Inc., 1972.

32. Juhasz, A. M. Unmarried adolescent parent. *Adolescence,* 1974, **9,** 263.

33. Kantner, J. F., & Zelnick, M. Contraception and pregnancy: experience of young unmarried women in the United States. *Family Planning Perspectives,* 1973, **5,** 21-35.

34. Sorensen, P. C. *Adolescent sexuality in contemporary America: personal values and sexual behaviors, ages 13-19.* New York: Harry N. Abrams, Inc. 1973.

35. Ingalls, A. J., & Salerno, M. C. *Maternal and child health nursing* (3rd ed.). St. Louis: The C. V. Mosby Co., 1975.

36. Pannor, R., Massarck, F., & Evans, B. *The unmarried father: new approaches for helping unmarried young parents.* New York: Springer Publishing Co., Inc., 1971.

37. Robinson, D. Our surprising moral unwed fathers. *Ladies' Home Journal,* August, 1969, 49-50.

Infant motor and cognitive development

Once upon a time, the world (at least a small part of it) was awaiting a monumental event, when all of a sudden, "All systems go! Countdown! 5-4-3-2-1, hello World! Here I am at last." What a trip for a member of the so-called weaker sex!

This is how it was about thirty-five months ago when I first ventured into the world of Playtex nursers, Johnson's baby powder, Pampers, and Q-Tips. For the next few minutes "this is my world and welcome to it."

The way I figure it, my journey began about nine and one-half months before I made my grand entrance. Someone told me that my trip should have lasted nine months, but either someone miscalculated or else I was a little slow in my development because my anxious mommy was ready two weeks before I was. I finally did reach my destination on August 31 at 11:44 P.M., with the most beautiful set of dimples on my cheeks that you ever saw. Baggage and all, I was weighed in at 8 pounds, which wasn't too bad since I was 21 inches tall.

I worried my mommy and daddy at first because I was placed in an isolette. During my arrival a lot of mucus accumulated to hinder my breathing. Nothing to really worry about, though, but you know how first-time parents are.

After seven days in the hospital I entered the unsterile world of people, machines, and pollution. My trip home was relatively uneventful except for Mother Nature helping me remove certain liquid elements from my body, much to my relief but to my mommy's chagrin.

I don't remember much about the next three or four weeks, but according to my mommy and daddy, nighttime feeding was sometimes hectic when my formula would come up faster than it went down. I wasn't sick or anything dramatic—I was just in a hurry to fill my ever-demanding stomach.

During the next three months I learned to tell the difference between my mommy and daddy and the countless number of visitors to my peaceful abode. Did I ever get the attention! No wonder, I was the first baby around my family in twenty years. Some people said I would be spoiled by all this attention, but the way I look at it—what's a baby for if you can't spoil her?

Within my first nine months I gained nine teeth, 14 pounds, 7 inches and many holes in my posterior because of inoculations for many diseases. I even received a permanent mark, commonly known as a vaccination, on my arm.

My seventh and eighth months were very busy. I learned to sit, I began to crawl and to creep (everywhere to my mommy's dismay), I pulled myself up to a standing position, and I said "Da-Da" and "Mom-Mom." During the ninth month I learned to say, "teddy," "car go," "cow," "doggie," "kitty," and "toe."

I celebrated the month of July (my eleventh month) by asserting my independence by standing without support. When I was about a year old, I began to walk steadily. Since I was chubby (to say the least), I considered this a great feat. I now weighed 25 pounds and was 31½ inches tall.

During my second year I really began to get around. I also improved my talking ability. Because of my association with adults, I suppose my conversation seemed more grown-up than my age would indicate. Once I ran across the road to my neighbor's house. I thought it was a natural thing to do, but nonetheless it must have been frightening to my mommy. I never did it again because my mommy thwarted my adventurous spirit with a swat on my you-know-what.

During my second year I was a big help to my mommy by putting doll clothes in the commode to wash them. My own private washing machine! I also enjoyed sitting on end tables, standing on chairs, and climbing up on tables. Another time I rearranged my mommy's pots and pans in the cupboards. I don't think she appreciated that very much. My favorite friend was an object called a pacifier, or a fooler, which I called a plug. My mommy often said that she wished she would have never given me the plug. I had it since I was 9 days old, so you couldn't expect me to get rid of it just like that. However, I no longer use it any more. My mommy said the vacuum cleaner swallowed it, but I wonder.

Now during my third year I learned a few numbers, some letters, and many colors. I can also tell the difference between the sun and moon, hill and mountain, cow and horse, puppy and dog, and a great variety of other animals. One of my favorite pastimes is talking on my toy telephone to Herman, my imaginary boyfriend. Mommy says I'm too little to have a boyfriend, but she must realize "the times they are a-changing."

When I was 2½ years old, I was potty trained, whatever that means. Mommy used to sit by me in the bathroom and teach me songs while I was being "trained." As a result, I can now sing "How Much Is That Doggie in the Window," "Here Comes Peter Cottontail," "Jesus Loves Me," "Do Lord," and a host of other songs. It took a lot of training!

Right now I want to be like my mommy simply "because I want to be." I help mommy sweep, dust, and wash dishes. Although my mommy praises me for this, I hear her tell others that it takes twice as long now. I am very affectionate and free with my hugs and kisses. I figure it can't hurt me, and some day the experience may come in handy. I like people "little" all the time, and many times I like them "big." (In other words, "little" means some, and "big" means a lot.)

Mommy and daddy are teaching me good manners such as saying "please," "thank you," "you're welcome," and also saying prayers at mealtime and bedtime. One of my greatest verbal accomplishments is reciting the Pledge of Allegiance, but who knows what it means? I learned it from Romper Room. A few weeks ago I said a recitation for Children's Day, which made my mommy and daddy very happy. I got an ice-cream cone for doing such a nice job.

I like playing by myself mainly because I have no little friends nearby to play with. However, when my little cousin, Suzy, and I are together, we really have a good time and don't even fight much. I like to be read to, and I also make up a lot of stories, usually about a bear. For some reason I think a lot about bears. Sometimes I even have to sleep with mommy and daddy because I get awake and am afraid a bear will get after me.

Now that I am almost 3, I weigh 34 pounds and am about 38 inches tall. I guess I'm a pretty big girl because I eat almost anything. I especially like to feed myself with my own spoon and fork.

There are a lot of other things I could tell you about myself, but I'm afraid I don't have any more time right now. I must go out and ride my tricycle and help mommy water the flowers. I would be very glad to finish my story, but you will have to come around a little later. Good-bye.

The newborn baby is not really new at all. By the time the baby's day of birth arrives he is already a distinct and accomplished person with characteristics that are peculiarly his own. He is about 280 days old, and he carries the developmental traits that will influence his future growth characteristics. His birth does not alter the basic patterns of his nervous system. Although his weight has increased 2 billion times from what it was at conception, he is still small enough to curl comfortably in a shoebox. By the time he leaves the hospital he has a name, and his life history is well underway.

During infancy, the baby must accomplish certain developmental tasks that will be important to his overall well-being. As he learns the tasks necessary for his growth and development at his present age level, he makes it easier for himself to learn developmental tasks that he must attain at later stages of life. With each task learned the individual becomes a more competent person, preparing for independent living. According to

Havighurst,[1] the developmental tasks for infancy are (1) to learn to eat solid foods, (2) to walk and to use fine muscles, (3) to gain at least partial control of the processes of elimination, (4) to acquire the foundations of speech and begin to communicate, (5) to achieve reasonable physiological stability, especially in the coordination of eyes, hunger rhythm, and sleep, and (6) to begin to relate emotionally to parents and siblings instead of remaining self-bound.

THE NEWBORN INFANT

Although being born is a natural process, it is not always an easy one. The infant will usually require a few days just to overcome the birth experience. The more difficult the birth, the longer is the period for stabilization or recovery. Since so many features of this stage of life are different from the other stages, a special name is given to the newborn child—he is called a *neonate*. The neonatal period generally lasts for about two weeks but may extend to three or four

HEAD usually strikes you as being too big for the body. (Immediately after birth it may be temporarily out of shape—lopsided or elongated—due to pressure before or during birth.)

ON THE SKULL you will see or feel the two most obvious soft spots, or fontanels. One is above the brow, the other close to crown of head in back.

EYES appear dark blue, have a blank stary gaze. You may catch one or both turning or turned to crossed or wall-eyed position.

A DEEP FLUSH spreads over the entire body if baby cries hard. Veins on head swell and throb. You will notice no tears because tear ducts do not function as yet.

THE FACE will disappoint you unless you expect to see pudgy cheeks, a broad, flat nose with mere hint of a bridge, receding chin, undersized lower jaw.

THE TRUNK may startle you in some normal detail: short neck, small sloping shoulders, swollen breasts, large rounded abdomen, umbilical stump (future navel), slender, narrow pelvis and hips.

THE HANDS, if you open them out flat from their characteristic fist position, have finely lined palms, tissue-paper thin nails, dry, loose-fitting skin, and deep bracelet creases at wrist.

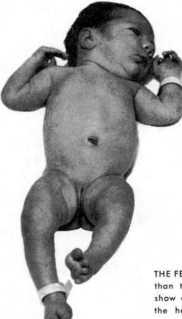

THE LEGS are most often seen drawn up against the abdomen in prebirth position. Extended legs measure shorter than you would expect compared to the arms. The knees stay slightly bent, and legs are more or less bowed.

GENITALS of both sexes will seem large (especially scrotum) in comparison with the scale of, for example, the hands to adult size.

THE FEET look more complete than they are. X-ray would show only one real bone of the heel. Other bones are now cartilage. Skin often loose and wrinkly.

WEIGHT unless well above the average of 6 or 7 pounds will not prepare you for how really tiny newborn is. Top-to-toe measure: anywhere between 18 and 21 inches.

THE SKIN is thin and dry. You may see veins through it. Fair skin may be rosy red temporarily. Downy hair is not unusual.

Fig. 5-1. What a healthy week-old baby looks like. (Photograph from Ingalls, A. J., & Salerno, M. C. *Maternal and child health nursing* [2nd ed.]. St. Louis: The C. V. Mosby Co., 1971; description from Birch, W. G. *A doctor discusses pregnancy.* Chicago: Budlong Press Co., 1963.)

weeks, depending on how much difficulty the child is having adjusting physiologically to his new environment.

Physical characteristics (Fig. 5-1)

Even the fondest of mothers may be somewhat shocked at the sight of her newborn infant, especially if it is her first child. The infant is tiny, his skin is wrinkled or shriveled looking, and his body seems out of proportion. Fat cheeks, a short flat nose, and a receding chin give the newborn a useful facial profile for the purpose of sucking but do not always make the baby attractive initially. The baby's wobbly head is about one fourth the size of his body and may be strangely lopsided due to pressures caused by his passage through the birth canal. The shape of the head will soon become normal in appearance, however. His neck seems to be no more than a fold of skin separating his head from his narrow shoulders. The milky blue eyes that most new arrivals have are about one-half their adult size. Since the body is only about one twentieth of its adult size, the baby appears to have an unusually large head and eyes. The legs are extremely short in relation to the trunk.

The average weight of a newborn is about 7½ pounds, and the average height is 20 to 20½ inches. Girl babies, on the average, weigh slightly less than boy babies and are not quite as tall. During the first four or five days, the neonate may lose 6 to 7 ounces. This loss of weight results from inadequate nutrition while the process of digestion is being established and from the evaporation of moisture from the tissues. Once the body is stabilized, usually in seven to nine days, the child begins to gain weight. The weight will generally double in six months and triple to about 21 pounds in twelve months. The height increases by 30% to 50% to about 30 inches in twelve months.

The newborn baby has a coating or protective layer of vernix over his skin that dries and rubs off in a few days; peeling hands and feet are therefore usual. Rose pink or purplish, mottled skin is common with the new baby. The fingers and toes often look blue and will be cold until the baby's circulation pattern is regulated. The bones are soft and cartilaginous, and the total muscular equipment of the newborn infant weighs less than one fourth of its entire body.[2]

Behavioral characteristics

The most common behavior noted in newborn babies is sleep. For the first few days they seem to exist in a nearly continuous twilight state of being. The neonate sleeps, dozes, or cries approximately 90% of the time. By the fourth week this figure drops to about 79%.[3] Neonatal sleep is broken by short waking periods, which occur every 2 or 3 hours, with fewer and shorter waking periods during the night than during the day. As an infant, the child will sleep as much as is necessary and when necessary. Later he will learn the culturally approved patterns of sleep and wakefulness.

A new baby sleeps best directly after eating.

He quickly becomes used to familiar household noises. He should have a room of his own for sleeping or an undisturbed corner away from family traffic. He sleeps best on a flat firm mattress without a pillow. New babies generally waken once or twice during the night for a feeding, but they grow and mature so quickly that they can soon sleep until breakfast time.

During the neonatal period, stimulation of any part of the body tends to activate the entire body. Stimuli such as pain, hunger, or physical discomfort seem to arouse the greatest activity. A wide-awake, hungry neonate is capable of making as many as fifty movements per mintue.[4] Newborns need exercise to strengthen their muscles. In their brief wakeful periods they will wave their arms and legs, and before a feeding they become exceedingly active.

Although there is little control of the head movements at birth, early movements of the head and shoulders are basic to the later development of manipulation, posture, and perception. Placed on his abdomen on a flat surface, the newborn quickly learns to lift his head and turn it from side to side. Supported in water, he will make swimminglike movements.

The neonate makes throaty sounds, and he can purse his lips. He has an amazing variety of grunts, mews, and sighs. He cries but has no tears at this age. He sneezes to clear his nose of lint, and he yawns when he needs extra oxygen. The accomplished young baby can scowl, grimace with his mouth, and "smile" in a funny uncertain way.

At birth the child has a ready-made capability for learning. This condition is evident in the way an infant can adapt himself to a feeding schedule. The healthy newborn averages seven to eight feedings in 24 hours and takes 20 to 30 minutes to complete his meal. The interrelationship established between the mother and the child during the first weeks after birth will often determine the type of response the child will have toward eating. If an infant feels maternal impatience or hostility, he will have more anxiety than the child whose mother is patient. The newborn who is held lovingly every feeding, and especially if he is breastfed, will have a better psychological and physiological start in life. The satisfactions and

"CHOW TIME"

In the good old days, my meals were ready whenever I acted hungry. The milk was always the right temperature and especially delicious. Any bottle-fed baby will probably tell you that milk was not always this way, particularly at night. Most of us babies awakened during the nights of the first two months of our lives to have our stomachs filled again. The mothers of some of my bottle-fed peers were often too tired from cleaning bottles and washing diapers during the day to give their babies good tasting milk of just the right temperature. True, I have seen in the baby magazines that some makes of prepared formula boast that their milk is good at room temperature, right from the can. But how much thought and love is put into a can of milk? Some of the mothers were even too tired to hold the bottles for their babies.

Do you wonder why my milk was always the correct temperature? I was breast-fed. My mother nursed me almost as soon as I gave my hunger cry. She had no set feeding schedule with me, although I usually became hungry every four hours. I felt pretty important and very loved because my mother was giving of herself to help me feel full and secure.

Let me tell you some benefits of being breast-fed. The milk I received was always fresh, whereas my bottle-fed buddies had older milk that had been heated. Did you know that heat and storage are known to destroy many important nutrients? Mommy's milk digested quickly and easily compared to bottle milk. You have heard about colicky babies. Well, breast-fed babies are less likely to have digestive upsets and disorders. Breast feeding is also a natural method of spacing babies; Mommy had more time to spend with me since she was not preparing for a brother or sister for me. I read all the facts in this paragraph in a LaLeche League reprint from a book written by Niles Newton, *Family Book of Child Care*.

Feeding time brought physical enjoyment to Mommy and me. Both of us wanted and needed each other physically and mentally. The satisfaction of our wants and needs helped to build a secure and loving relationship between Mommy and me. The nursing experience helped us to feel very close to each other, and this did not stop on the day Mommy stopped nursing me. It laid the groundwork for a very good relationship in which I was permitted to grow in independence confidently. Another important result was that Mommy did not feel as if she were simply carrying on her high school baby-sitting jobs with bottle feeding and changing a baby. She felt and still feels like a *real* mother!

pleasures a baby gets from his feeding affect his sense of well-being. Frequent changes in the type of food or manner in which it is given may create problems in learning because the newborn benefits most from some structure, similarity, and routine. It takes the infant two or three weeks to form a hunger rhythm and to adjust to a regular feeding schedule.[5]

Sensory abilities

During the embryonic and fetal stages of life, the sensory mechanisms gradually develop. By the time of birth the senses can function to the extent that they possess survival value. The infant can use the senses to enhance his physiological and cognitive well-being.

Vision. At birth the neonate can see. It is not known, however, how clearly he can see. Researchers had assumed that the newborn could not focus his eyes until he was 3 or 4 weeks old. Until then, the baby would only see things as a blur. Recently, studies on the vision of neonates have discredited this assumption.[6] It is known that soon after birth a baby can respond with his eyes to a moving light. Even on the first day of life a momentary fixation on a near object can be observed. The length of the fixation depends on how alert the infant is. Sustained fixation on a near object, at about 9 inches, is noted by the end of the first week. This is about the same distance the mother's face is from her baby's when she is breast-feeding. There is some suggestion that the baby may be able to look at objects that are between 10 and 20 inches away, but no nearer or farther. By the end of the month the baby can sustain fixation on more distant objects.

Tom Bower of the University of Edinburgh filmed the reactions of babies less than 2 weeks old while an object moved toward them at different speeds. As the objects approached, the babies pulled back their heads and put their hands between themselves and the object.[7] He also found that if the object was moving to one side or away from the baby, he did not react. Another study involved an optical illusion of an object within reach of the infant. An attempt was made to grasp it. Bower concluded that at least one aspect of the coordination between eye and hand is present at birth. The newborn baby ex-

pects to be able to touch the objects he sees. This observation may have important meaning, as noted later, for the development of the cognitive processes.

A major item related to the beginnings of cognition was studied by Robert Fantz of Case Western Reserve University.[8] He showed a series of babies three flat objects the size and shape of a head. On the first, there was a stylized face, on the second a scrambled face, and on the third a half-white, half-black patch (Fig. 5-2). The babies, regardless of age from 4 days to 6 months, looked the most at the real face and the least at the patch.

The very young infant is also sensitive to perceiving color. Peeples and Teller[9] conclude that not only do infants see color but also that brightly colored objects are highly attractive to them. The pupillary reflex, in which the size of the opening of the pupil of the eye reacts to the brightness of light, is well established shortly after birth, as are the protective responses of moving the head, closing the eyelids, and crying. Eye movements generally make use of the gross muscular patterns but not the finer ones. Some children have immature eye muscle development so that one or both eyes may rotate outwardly or inwardly. Eye muscle control is usually gained by 4 weeks of age.

Hearing. While still in the womb, normal babies have been known to respond to musical tones by a speeding up of their heartbeats.[10] Of all the senses at birth, however, hearing is the least functional because the passages of the ear are not completely open. In some infants hearing acuity is completely lacking because the middle ear is filled with amniotic fluid. It may take several hours to several days for the fluid to drain out. Only then can hearing function normally. With normal hearing the neonate can discriminate between loud and soft sounds but does not respond to variations in pitch.[11] The newborn is startled by loud noises but is soothed by a soft, gentle voice or low auditory stimuli.

Eimas[12] has conducted research to assess an infant's ability to perceive sound differentiations that are important in speech. He concluded that infants are able to discriminate important distinctions in speech signals and are receptive to

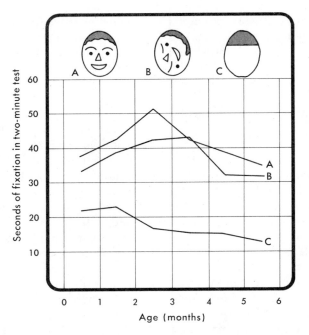

Fig. 5-2. These three stimuli were shown to babies from 2 weeks to 6 months of age. All babies preferred to look at the face, *A,* and scrambled features, *B,* rather than the black-patched oval, *C.* (From Frantz, R. *Scientific American,* 1961, **204,** 66.)

speech. This ability to respond to fine differences in sound is crucial if the infant is going to respond to speech. Mendelson and Haith[13] have attempted to demonstrate a relationship between the visual and auditory capabilities of the newborn infant. They conclude that the infant has the appropriate sensory capabilities and tendencies to begin forming concepts about sight and sound very early in life. They see the infant's tendency to respond to sound by visual scanning as an indication that the early infant is ready to start gathering and processing information from the environment.

Smell, taste, touch. The senses of smell, taste, and touch are all better developed at birth than is sight or hearing. Once the passages of the head are dry, after having been submerged in the prenatal liquid environment, the senses of smell and taste respond fairly well to gross differences in stimuli. Infants can distinguish between different odors such as acetic acid, phenylethyl alcohol, and anise oil and may even try to escape from unpleasant odors by turning their bodies. Five days after birth, they even are capable of spending more time with their heads turned to a pad that had been placed inside the mother's bra so the baby could become familiar with her odor.[14]

Most infants react with a feeling of satisfaction to the taste of milk. A sugar solution will cause a sucking that is maintained. The neonate will usually react negatively to unpleasant taste stimuli such as sour, bitter, and salt solutions.[15] It requires a much greater amount of bitterness or sweetness to elicit a discriminatory response in infants than is the case with adults.

The skin of the newborn infant is sensitive to touch, pressure, temperature, and some pain. At the time of birth, sensitivity to pain is lessened so that the baby will not feel its effects while passing through the birth canal. Responses to pain increase about two days after birth. Certain parts of the body, namely the lips, eyelashes, soles of the feet, skin of the forehead, and the mucous membrane of the nose are more sensitive than are other parts. The neonate can react to differences in temperature, as is shown by differentiated sucking reactions to changes of temperature of its milk. Cold stimuli produce quicker and more pronounced reactions than do heat stimuli.[16] Infants also respond with signs of discomfort to temperatures above or below normal, and especially to extremes of cold.

Body movements and reflexes

Motor development is not a process that begins at the time of birth, but rather, it has its origins in the prenatal period. During the second month of prenatal development, the muscles begin to take shape. By the end of the third month they are developed to the degree that spontaneous movements of arms, legs, shoulders, and fingers are possible. By the fourteenth week the human fetus is capable of producing almost all the reflex responses of a newborn infant. Some reflexes will be vital for survival; other reflexes will function merely as general protective measures. The remainder of the prenatal period is spent in perfecting these movements. Initial diffused mass activities of the organism become more integrated and specific with maturation. Reflexes of the newborn baby are listed in Table 5-1.

Just as in the fetus during prenatal life, the development of the neonate during postnatal life largely follows the cephalocaudal and proximodistal directions of growth. Functions appear and develop earliest in the infant's head and neck, then in the shoulders and upper trunk, and later in the lower trunk and legs. The direction of this sequence is obvious to the observer and is a result of maturation. The newborn baby lacks voluntary coordinated motor control. Neonatal reflex activity is subcortical in origin and so is not voluntary.

Mouth and throat response. From birth the neonate is capable of opening and closing his mouth. One of the earliest of the various lip movements is sucking. The sucking response can be elicited by light pressure on the cheeks or by touching above or below the side of the lips. Swallowing usually follows the sucking movements. Infants less than 2 weeks old show that they are able to discriminate between the intake of milk or air. When sucking milk, the neonate swallows it; when sucking air, there is no swallowing movement.

When the newborn infant cries, there is much mass body activity such as rolling the head, opening the mouth wide, jerking and twisting the body, throwing the arms about, and kicking the legs. Other mouth and throat responses present

Table 5-1. Reflexes of the newborn baby*

Effective stimulus	Reflex
Tap upper lip sharply	Lips protrude
Tap bridge of nose	Eyes close tightly
Show bright light suddenly to eyes	Eyelids close
Clap hands about 18 inches from infant's head	Eyelids close
Touch cornea with light piece of cotton	Eyes close
With baby held on back turn face slowly to right side	Jaw and right arm on side of face extended out; left arm flexes
Extend forearms at elbow	Arms flex briskly
Put fingers into infant's hand and press his palms	Infant's fingers flex and enclose finger
Press thumbs against the ball of infant's feet	Toes flex
Scratch sole of foot starting from toes toward the heels	Big toe bends upward and small toes spread
Prick soles of feet with pin	Infant's knee and foot flex
Tickle area of corner of mouth	Head turns toward side of stimulation
Put index finger into mouth	Sucks
Hold infant in air, stomach down	Infant attempts to lift head and extends legs

*From Mussen, P. H., Conger, J. J., & Kagan, J. *Child development and personality* (4th ed.). New York: Harper & Row, Publishers, 1974, p. 137.

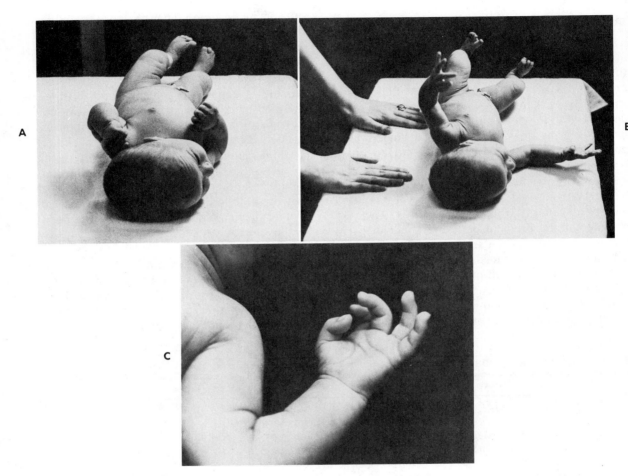

A, Position of rest. **B,** Moro reflex consists predominantly of abduction and extension of arms. **C,** Interesting subtlety of Moro response in newborn infants is C position of fingers: digits extend, except index finger and thumb, which are often semiflexed, forming shape of C. (Courtesy Mead Johnson Laboratories, Evansville, Ind.)

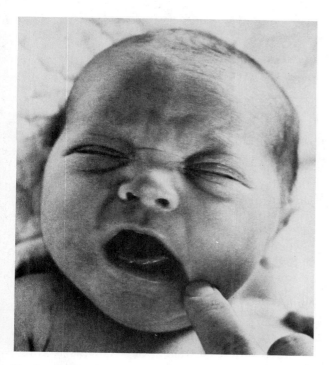

Rooting reflex is apparent when corner of newborn infant's mouth is touched. Bottom lip lowers on same side; tongue moves toward stimulus. (Courtesy Mead Johnson Laboratories, Evansville, Ind.)

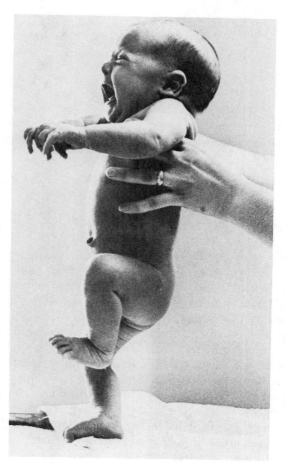

Walking reflex is phase of neuromuscular maturity from which infant normally graduates after 3 or 4 weeks. If infant is held so that sole of foot touches table, reciprocal flexion and extension of leg occur, simulating walking. (Courtesy Mead Johnson Laboratories, Evansville, Ind.)

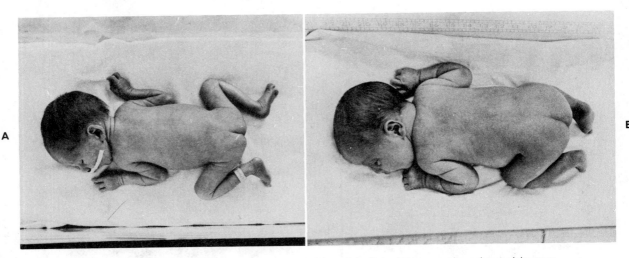

A, In prone position premature infant lies with pelvis flat and legs splayed out sideways like a frog. **B,** Normal infant lies with limbs flexed, pelvis raised, and knees usually drawn under abdomen. (Courtesy Mead Johnson Laboratories, Evansville, Ind.)

in the neonate are sneezing, coughing, yawning, thumb-sucking, hiccoughing, vomiting, holding the breath, and rejecting things from his mouth.

Head and arm movements. A neonate has the ability to move his head up and down as well as to the left and right. He cannot hold the head in midposition, however. He moves his arms a great deal. He flexes them, extends them, randomly moves them about in different directions, throws them over his chest, and moves the hands and fingers. The newborn baby can also grasp a rod or a finger placed in his hand and hold onto it. Many babies are able to support their weight by the grasping reflex when holding onto a rod. This grasping reflex, also known as the Darwinian reflex, later diminishes and is replaced in about three months by the voluntary grasp.

Trunk and leg movements. The newborn baby is only capable of a few trunk movements, since his back is lacking in muscular support. He is able to arch his back and twist his body, but only to a slight degree. The movements in the neonate's legs, feet, and toes are characterized by flexing, extending, kicking, jerking, rotating, rolling, or trembling. The Babinski reflex, the upward and fanning movement of the toes, is observed when the bottoms of the neonate's feet are stroked.

The knee jerk is a characteristic of the newborn. When the infant is in a resting or sleeping position, he will usually have his legs flexed, fists closed, upper arms out straight from his shoulders with the forearms flexed at right angles parallel to the head. When the infant is frightened by a loud noise, such as that caused by someone hitting a table top with his hand, the neonate will throw his arms apart, spread his fingers, extend his legs, and throw his head back. This reaction is the Moro, or startle, reflex. The response is basically symmetrical. It will disappear by the age of 3 or 4 months.[17] Persistence of the entire Moro response beyond 3 or 4 months is considered a sign of delay in neurological development.

A summary* of the responses of a newborn baby follows:

1. Eyelid and pupillary reflexes: opening and closing the eyes. Adequate stimuli for these responses, particularly for closing the eyes, are numerous; for example, blasts of air, bright light, touching

---

*Modified from Dennis, W.: A description and classification of the responses of the newborn infant, *Psychological Bulletin,* **31,** 1934, 5-22.

the face near the eye. The size of the pupil changes in response to variations in intensity of light to which the eyes are exposed.

2. Ocular reflexes: pursuit movements, saccadic movements, coordinated compensatory eye movements. When the head is jerked quickly around, the eyes move in a compensatory direction. This has been observed in infants as early as the second day of life.

3. Facial and mouth responses: opening and closing the mouth, sucking, grimacing, yawning, pushing objects from the mouth, frowning, smiling, upper and lower lip responses to touch.

4. Throat responses: crying, cooing, sobbing, sneezing, coughing, gagging, swallowing, holding breath, hiccoughing, and vomiting.

5. Head movements: upward and downward, turning face to side, balancing in response to change of bodily position (appears at 2 days of age).

6. Hand and arm reflexes: closing hand, arm flexion, rubbing of face, startle response of arms and legs, grasp reflex, and "random" movements.

7. Trunk reactions: arching the back, twisting, drawing in of the stomach (abdominal reflex).

8. Genital organ reflexes: cremasteric reflex (raising the testes), penis erection.

9. Foot and leg reflexes: the knee jerk and the Achilles tendon reflexes have been observed in some infants; flexion and extension of the legs, kicking, fanning the toes in response to stroking the sole, stepping movement when the child is held upright with feet touching a surface.

10. Coordinated responses of many body parts: resting and sleeping position (legs flexed, fists closed, upper arms out straight from shoulder with forearms flexed at right angles parallel to the head), springing position (infant held upright and inclined forward, the arms extend forward and legs are brought up), stretching, shivering, trembling, unrest with crying, creeping, bodily jerk, Moro reflex (throwing arms apart, spreading of fingers, extension of legs, and throwing head back).

SUDDEN INFANT DEATH SYNDROME (SIDS)

Sudden unexpected death in a previously normal 2- to 4-month-old infant constitutes a major health concern, even though it occurs in only 16 out of every 1,000 babies. SIDS or "crib death" is still a mysterious occurrence. Although families at all socioeconomic levels have been affected, several studies point to an increased incidence in the lower strata. It appears more likely to occur in premature babies and babies of teenage mothers who received little or no prenatal care. However, many babies with these characteristics are not affected. Infants who are usually well-nourished and free of any evidence of illness are found dead in their crib or carriage several hours after having been fed.

So far, none of the research has been able to reveal the cause of crib deaths. The most commonly proposed theories are (1) overwhelming infection with an unknown virus, (2) unknown errors in metabolism, (3) abnormalities in the central nervous system that might lead to a spasmodic closure of the larynx or failure of cardiac conduction, and (4) apnea, a cessation of breathing for brief periods during sleep.

A point of interest is the work of pediatricians Harvey Kravitz and Robert G. Scherz reported in the Journal of the American Medical Association.[18] They noted from published reports that crib-death victims almost invariably are found in a horizontal position on their stomachs or backs. They surmised that in this position the baby's air supply might be cut off by a blockage of the lower jaw or tongue, a soft palate, or regurgitated food, milk, or saliva. Of 438 reported victims, the doctors learned that 435 died in a horizontal position. Not one crib-death victim was found in an infant carrier. They offer this advice: (1) Raise the head of the baby's crib up to 2 inches (about a 10-degree angle elevation) by placing a wedge of wood under the mattress. (2) For at least 20 minutes after feeding, put the baby in an infant carrier rather than directly into the crib.

It is important to remember that most of these deaths are not caused by parental negligence. The parents should be supported emotionally to

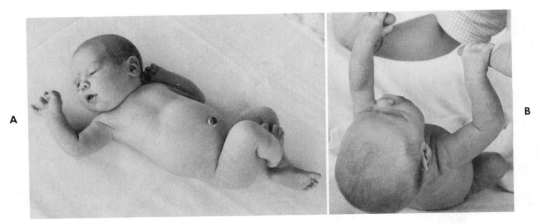

Newborn infant. **A,** Tonic neck posture is readily assumed. **B,** Grasp reflex is strong. (From Ingalls, A. J., & Salerno, M. C. *Maternal and child health nursing* [3rd ed.]. St. Louis: The C. V. Mosby Co., 1975.)

make them feel that they could not in any way have been responsible, that there was nothing they could have done to prevent the event, and that greater care would not have made a difference. There is a society of parents who have had infants die from SIDS; it would be well for parents who lose their baby in this manner to be in touch with this society for supportive and counseling purposes.

MOTOR DEVELOPMENT DURING INFANCY

The period of infancy is one of tremendous motor development. The word *motor* refers to muscular movements. The general mass activity and reflex actions of the neonate gradually change to specific muscle control, permitting voluntary, coordinated motor responses to take place. In addition to muscle development, motor control also makes use of sensory acuity and awareness, perceptual discrimination ability, and adequate sensorimotor integration and coordination. Accurate perception of sensory stimuli is needed to perfect the motor skills.

During the first year of life, maturational forces are of primary importance in the development of motor coordination. Maturation determines the rate, the level of readiness, and the pattern of the early motor responses. Progress in motor devel-opment can be influenced, however, by factors such as a lack of opportunity to practice the motor skills, the child's attitude toward learning the skills, and psychological and physiological inhibitions to learning. The process of development is sequential in nature unless interfered with by abnormal conditions within or outside the infant. Thus movements begun during the prenatal stage are basic to the later development of posture, locomotion, prehension, and cognition.

The following two complex motor tasks must be learned during infancy: (1) upright postural control and locomotion and (2) manipulability and prehension—the ability to reach with the hand, grasp, and manipulate objects.

Postural control and locomotion

There is a basic sequence that leads to walking. This sequence will vary as to time of occurrence from infant to infant, but there is a progressive regularity in the development. The five basic stages are (1) postural control as in sitting with support, (2) postural control as in sitting alone, (3) active efforts toward locomotion, (4) creeping and walking with support, and (5) walking alone.[19]

The newborn infant is normally unable to hold his head erect when lying prone or when being held in a sitting position. At the age of 1 month

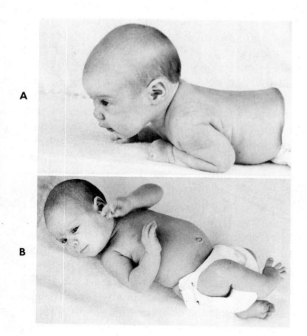

Infant at 1 month. A, Lifts and turns head when supine. **B,** Activity is diffuse and random. (From Ingalls, A. J., & Salerno, M. C. *Maternal and child health nursing* [3rd ed.]. St. Louis: The C. V. Mosby Co., 1975.)

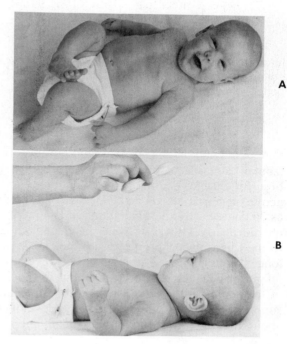

Infant at 2 months. A, A sociable smile appears. **B,** Eyes follow objects. (From Ingalls, A. J., & Salerno, M. C. *Maternal and child health nursing* [3rd ed.]. St. Louis: The C. V. Mosby Co., 1975.)

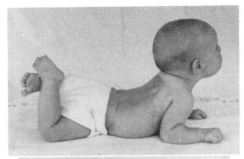

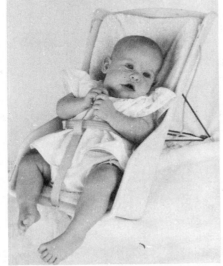

Infant at 3 months. A, Raises head when prone, supported on forearms. **B,** Sits for short period when supported. (From Ingalls, A. J., & Salerno, M. C. *Maternal and child health nursing* [3rd ed.]. St. Louis: The C. V. Mosby Co., 1975.)

the infant can hold his head straight out in a horizontal plane when supported in the prone position. By the age of 2 months he can hold his head above the horizontal plane at an angle of as much as 30 degrees. By the time an infant is 4 months old he nearly always lifts his head and upper trunk when placed prone on a table. He is no longer content to lie on his back. However, the infant must develop a certain amount of rigidity of the spine before he will be able to sit up unsupported. This rigidity is usually developed about the seventh month; then the infant sits alone.

Crawling is attained about the fifth month. Crawling refers to various forms of progression in which the infant does not lift his body from the floor while moving on all fours. In crawling the infant may even move about in a sitting position, using one leg to push himself along. In creeping the infant's body is lifted off the floor and he propels himself on all fours.

Shirley[20] in a classical study has observed the following stages in the development of creeping: (1) lifting the head and chin free when on the stomach, (2) lifting the head and chest free when on the stomach, (3) knee pushing or swimming, (4) rolling, (5) rocking, pivoting, and worming along, (6) scooting backward by using the hands, and (7) creeping forward.

When a child first begins to walk, his movements are awkward. He walks in a stiff-legged manner, with his legs far apart, toes turned outward, and arms close to the body or held out like a tightrope walker. If the infant watches the floor, he cannot maintain balance. To keep from falling he holds his head erect and slightly forward. His steps are high off the floor and uneven. At first he may move one foot forward, shift his weight to it, and then bring the second foot about even with the front foot. Next he may shift his weight back to the second foot and move the first foot forward again. Gradually, as his movements become coordinated, he begins stepping forward by alternating his feet.

By 14 months of age two thirds of the babies can walk without support, and by the age of 18 months the average baby walks like an adult.

The infant will be able to creep up stairs about the thirteenth month. At 18 months he will be able to walk up the stairs if his hand is held, climb into an adult chair, and throw a ball but not with much accuracy. When he reaches the twenty-first month, he will squat while playing, walk upstairs while holding the railing, and kick a large ball. By 24 months of age he can run well without falling and walk up and down the steps alone.

Prehension or grasping

The infant's grasping reflex and his uncoordinated arm movements are the starting points for a sequence that eventually leads to highly skilled manual activities of the adult. Prehension is not merely a function of motor control but, rather, a function of sensorimotor control. Kinesthesis

Text continued on p. 122.

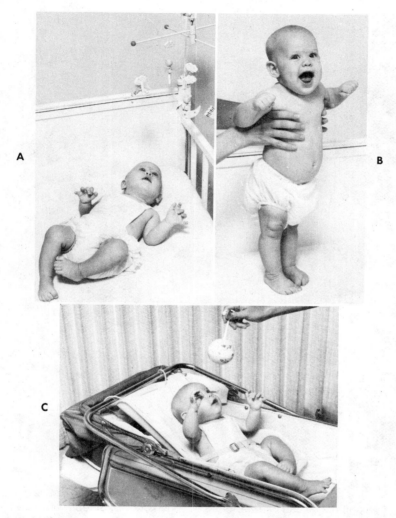

Infant at 4 months. A, Gazes straight up, symmetrical posture predominates. **B,** Pushes with feet when held erect. **C,** Reaches and grasps at objects. (From Ingalls, A. J., & Salerno, M. C. *Maternal and child health nursing* [3rd ed.]. St. Louis: The C. V. Mosby Co., 1975.)

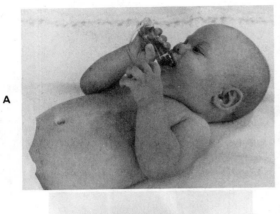

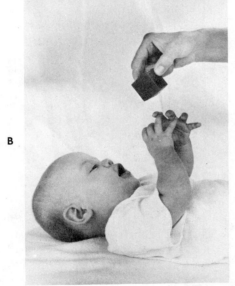

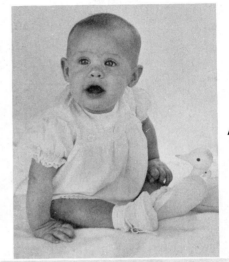

Infant at 5 months. A, Manipulates and chews small objects. **B,** Alert to surroundings. (From Ingalls, A. J., & Salerno, M. C. *Maternal and child health nursing* [3rd ed.]. St. Louis: The C. V. Mosby Co., 1975.)

Infant at 6 months. A, Sits alone, leaning forward on one hand. **B,** Sleeps with favorite blanket and thumb in mouth. (From Ingalls, A. J., & Salerno, M. C. *Maternal and child health nursing* [3rd ed.]. St. Louis: The C. V. Mosby Co., 1975.)

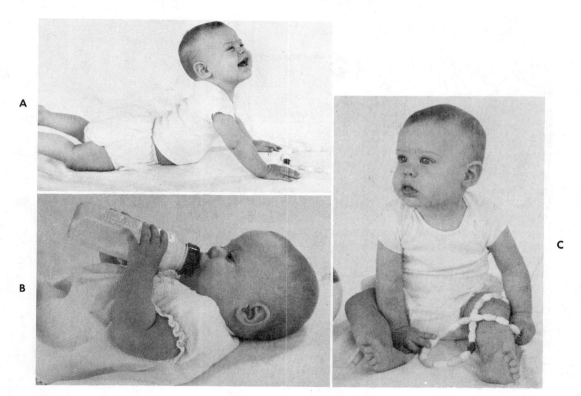

Infant at 7 months. A, Propels self forward on belly (crawling). **B,** Can hold bottle. **C,** Sits alone without support. (From Ingalls, A. J., & Salerno, M. C. *Maternal and child health nursing* [3rd ed.]. St. Louis: The C. V. Mosby Co., 1975.)

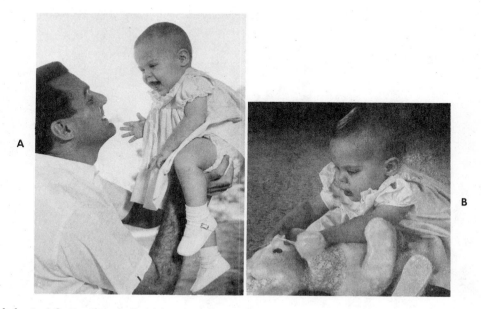

Infant at 8 months. A, Bubbles, gurgles, loves to play with adults. **B,** Can lean forward and straighten up. (From Ingalls, A. J., & Salerno, M. C. *Maternal and child health nursing* [3rd ed.]. St. Louis: The C. V. Mosby Co., 1975.)

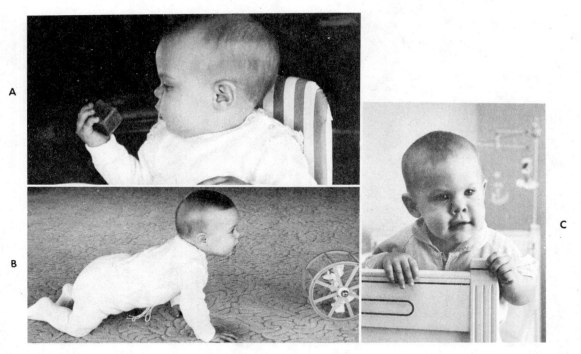

Infant at 9 months. A, Hand preference appears. **B,** Propels self forward on all fours, trunk above and parallel to floor (creeping). **C,** Can pull self to standing position. (From Ingalls, A. J., & Salerno, M. C. *Maternal and child health nursing* [3rd ed.]. St. Louis: The C. V. Mosby Co., 1975.)

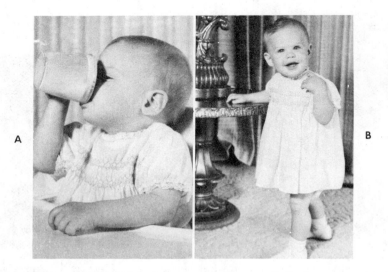

Infant at 10 to 11 months. A, Drinks from a cup with ease. **B,** Cruises around, holding on to furniture. (From Ingalls, A. J., & Salerno, M. C. *Maternal and child health nursing* [3rd ed.]. St. Louis: The C. V. Mosby Co., 1975.)

Table 5-2. Normal development in infancy and childhood*

Age in months†	Motor	Social	Hearing and speech	Eye and hand
1	Head erect for few seconds	Quieted when picked up	Startled by sounds	Follows light with eyes
2	Head up when prone (chin clear)	Smiles	Listens to bell or rattle	Follows ring up, down, and side-ways
3	Kicks well	Follows person with eyes	Searches for sound with eyes	Glances from one object to another
4	Lifts head and chest prone	Returns examiner's smile	Laughs	Clasps and retains cube
5	Holds head erect with no lag	Frolics when played with	Turns head to sound	Pulls paper away from face
6	Rises on to wrists	Turns head to per-son talking	Babbles or coos to voice or music	Takes cube from table
7	Rolls from front to back	Drinks from a cup	Makes four differ-ent sounds	Looks for fallen objects
8	Sits without sup-port	Looks at mirror image	Understands "No" and "Bye-bye"	Passes toy from hand to hand
9	Turns around on floor	Helps to hold cup for drinking	Says "Mama" or "Dada"	Manipulates two ob-jects together
10	Stands when held up	Smiles at mirror image	Imitates playful sounds	Clicks two objects together in imitation
11	Pulls up to stand	Finger feeds	Two words with meaning	Pincer grip
12	Walks or side-steps around pen	Plays pat-a-cake on request	Three words with meaning	Finds toy hidden under cup
13	Stands alone	Holds cup for drinking	Looks at pictures	Preference for one hand
14	Walks alone	Uses spoon	Recognizes own name	Makes marks with pencil
15	Climbs up stairs	Shows shoes	Four to five clear words	Places one object upon another
16	Pushes pram, toy horse, etc.	Tries to turn door knob	Six to seven clear words	Scribbles freely
17	Picks up toy from floor without falling	Manages cup well	Babbled conversa-tion	Pulls (table) cloth to get toy
18	Climbs on to chair	Takes off shoes and socks	Enjoys rhymes and tries to join in	Constructive play with toys
19	Climbs stairs up and down	Knows one part of the body	Nine words	Tower of three bricks
20	Jumps	Bowel control	Twelve words	Tower of four bricks
21	Runs	Bladder control by day	Two-word sen-tences	Circular scribble
22	Walks up stairs	Tries to tell experi-ences	Listens to stories	Tower of five or more bricks
23	Seats self at table	Knows two parts of body	Twenty words or more	Copies perpen-dicular stroke
24	Walks up and down stairs	Knows four parts of body	Names four toys	Copies horizontal stroke

*Reproduced with kind permission from Wood, B. (Ed.). *A pediatric vade-mecum* (8th ed.). London: Lloyd-Luke Medical Books, 1974.

†Conceptual rather than chronological age.

and vision are the two chief sensory activities involved in the coordination of arm-hand movements (Table 5-2).

The reflex grasp that is present at birth is different from the voluntary grasp of later life in that it is a digital grasp rather than a palmar grasp. The thumb is not used in opposition to the forefinger

Table 5-3. Advances in prehension*

Motor performance	Age placement in months
Retains red ring (retains a ring, designed for the test, when placed in his hand)	0.7
Arm thrust in play (when lying in a dorsal position, makes vertical arm thrusts in random play)	1.7
Hands predominantly open (hands predominantly open even though not grasping an object)	3.6
Beginning thumb opposition (beginning evidence of use of thumb in opposed manner in grasping a cube)	4.1
Partial thumb opposition (opposes thumb to fingers in a partial, but not complete, manner, using the palm of the hand, as well as thumb and fingers in picking up the cube)	5.1
Unilateral reaching (tends to reach and manipulate with one hand more often than bimanually)	6.4
Rotates wrist (rotates wrist in manipulating toys)	6.7
Complete thumb opposition (picks up the cube with thumb and fingers completely opposed, and without the use of the palm)	7.6
Partial finger prehension (picks up a small pellet with several fingers opposed to thumb and not with a scooping into the palm with the fingers)	7.8
Fine prehension with pellet (picks up a small pellet precisely with thumb and forefinger)	9.3

*Adapted from Bayley, N. *The development of motor abilities during the first three years.* Monographs of the Society for Research in Child Development, 1935, No. 1.

but, rather, is placed in the palm under the rod. The reflex grasp begins to decline about the second month, and the voluntary grasp, which is well established by the ninth month, begins to develop.

The classical study by Halverson[21] of infant's reaching and grasping behavior illustrated the sequence of development for this type of motor skill. According to his findings, very young infants made no effort to grasp the cube placed before them on the table. At 16 weeks of age the infants looked at the cube for approximately 5 seconds but made no effort to grasp it. By 24 weeks of age one half of the children reached for and touched the cube. The time that the infants spent gazing at the cube also increased.

Infants' grasping movements undergo a series of developmental changes as they grow older. These changes are influenced by maturation and experimentation. Their movements progress from a whole hand closure to a scissors-type of closure and finally to a pincer prehension. Between 4 and 7 months of age a backhand sweep characterizes their grasping. At 5 months of age infants do not grasp the block but, instead, corral it with their hand and press it against their body or other hand. By the seventh month they reach the hand-grasp stage where their fingers encircle the block. The palm grasp, in which position the thumb and fingers cooperate in holding the cube against the palm of the hand, is usually evident by 8 months of age. By 1 year of age the more mature pincer movement is well established. The child grips the cube between the thumb and the ends of the fingers. Children are now able to hold a crayon. In six more months they will be able to scribble with considerable enthusiasm. By 2½ years of age they will be able to copy a vertical or horizontal line.

NEURAL DEVELOPMENT OF COGNITION
Intellect and growth

Consider newborn babies at birth. How much "intelligence" do they have? What is their "intellectual potential"? These questions are difficult to answer because the true nature of intelligence is not yet known. Most of the definitions of intelligence tell what intelligence "does" rather than what intelligence "is." Generally, the

Children are what the mothers are.
No fondest father's fondest care
Can fashion so the infant heart.

Walter Savage Landor
Children

"SHE'S WALKING!" **O**bserving my daughter Audrey learning to walk was a most fascinating experience. The process of "locomotion" actually started when she was in her crib. She would crawl from one end to the other. Soon she yearned for more room and tried to crawl through the posts of the crib. Eventually she was allowed to crawl on the living-room floor. With much struggle and strain she could sometimes traverse the living room in the amazing time of 2 minutes. She started out by using a method that made her look like a frog in water. It was a completely uncoordinated attempt at locomotion. Soon she graudated to kneeling and leaning on her palms, and thus she would creep. This seemed like a most efficacious way to get across the room and pleased her greatly. After each successful venture I tried to give her some kind of reinforcement, be it a kiss or some other type of reinforcer.

Eventually her creeping became a means to an end. Before she was content to creep for the sake of creeping, but now her creeping was goal directed. When she set out on an expedition, her purpose was usually to crawl over to a small coffee table that she could grasp onto. Like an acrobat she would, without hesitation, pull herself up until she was standing. Of course, once she got up she did not know what to do for an encore. She just stood there for a few moments and then realized that she was in trouble. She was too scared to leave the table, but she did not know how to get back down. In a few moments she would beckon our help by a loud wail.

After a few weeks she simply let herself drop to the floor. On hitting the floor, she immediately began to laugh. Often I wanted to stop her, but my wife always intervened. She thought that this was natural and that we should not stop her. Of course there were no injuries, and she soon graudated to her next level of development. Instead of dropping down when she would get adjacent to the table, she would gradually descend. Slowly her knees would bend, and she would lower herself onto the floor.

This up-and-down activity lasted for about a month; then something happened. On certain occasions she would get herself up and then release her grip on the table. With great timidity she would stand about 6 inches away from the table. After about 30 seconds of this she grabbed the table and descended. In no time at all she was taking a step or two away from the table. After a few steps she would lower herself to the floor. The next great achievement occurred when she would take a few additional steps and then fall down. All these precursors of actual walking lasted until about the thirteenth month.

Then it happened! Without any fanfare she just started to walk. It was one of life's greatest moments for me—one that is indelibly marked in my mind. I was talking on the telephone while Audrey was holding onto a chair in the kitchen. Always liking telephones, she apparently wanted to play with the telephone that I was using. Without any hesitation she let go of her support and started to cross the kitchen, a distance of about 20 feet. At first I thought that she would take a few steps and fall to the ground as she had been doing. Holding her hands out for balance, like and acrobat on a high wire, she started to cross the room. Wavering from side to side, but regaining her balance each time, she actually crossed the room. I must have been in a state of shock as I saw her walking for the first time because no words came out of my mouth. The person to whom I was talking on the phone must have thought that I had dropped dead because my silence lasted at least 30 seconds. Finally I was able to shout, "She's walking, Audrey is walking." In about another month she began to walk freely. As walking ability increased, so did her confidence.

definitions speak of (1) the ability to deal effectively with tasks involving abstractions, (2) the ability to learn, and/or (3) the ability to deal with new situations. How much of these three concepts can the newborn or the infant do? Obviously, little or none of them. Would it be correct to say, then, that the newborn babies have no intelligence at all? That does not seem right either. So, newborn babies are said to have a "potential," but they must develop or "mature" into that potential. Something must happen within the neurological system of infants to enable them to make use of cognitive processes that affect their potentialities.

The implications of intellectual growth, as we see them, are as follows: First, the infant must be born with certain innate features and physical characteristics that operate in accordance with principles and laws of nature related to how the intellect is to develop. Second, intellectual attributes will develop only to the extent or limit to which these innate elements have the potentiality to develop. Third, the potentiality of intellectual growth can be influenced by factors or forces outside the child, such as nutritional adequacy, sensory stimulation, perceptual activities, verbal and language development, learning experiences, and opportunity to learn. Each of these factors is of major importance and must not be underestimated.

Fourth, some kind of physical or psychic change must take place within the neurological system when the intellect is developing. Fifth, since the intellect "develops," it must start from

a meager "reflexive-cognitive" beginning and grow to an accumulative, integrated, cognitive, and perceptual pattern or "mental computer" kind of thing that can be used to do abstractions, learning, and problem solving in new situations.

The origins of intelligence are to be found in the central nervous system and in its capability to perceive, retain, recall, integrate, and reorganize cognitive components. Both the maturational process and the functioning of the perceptual processes in a stimulating and responsive environment aid in intellectual development. The word *cognition* and its derivatives refer to any process whereby an organism (the brain) becomes aware or obtains knowledge of an object. It includes perceiving, recognizing, conceiving, judging, reasoning, and sensing.

Piaget's system of cognitive development

Jean Piaget, the noted Swiss child psychologist, has developed a significant theory concerning cognitive development based on his research and observations. Piaget believes that cognitive development is a coherent process whereby the individual develops stages of cognitive structures called *schema* (plural, schemata). Each successive schema is derived logically and inevitably from the processes of assimilation, accommodation, and intellectual adaptation. Assimilation describes the capability of the organism to meet and respond to new situations and new problems with its present mechanisms. In so doing the organism "assimilates" new knowledge, skills, and in-

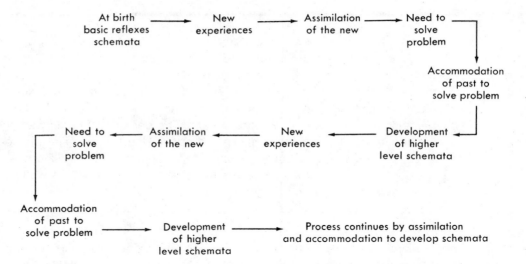

Fig. 5-3. Piaget's development of schemata using assimilation and accommodation.

sights from its interaction with the world. Accommodation describes the process of change through which the organism becomes able to handle situations that were too difficult to handle before. It is a process by which the cognitive process, because of the new material assimilated, has matured to the point that it can now "accommodate" or solve a more difficult task than it could before. (Fig. 5-3.)

Adaptation occurs when the organism has improved its ability to meet new environmental demands. This change is also called coping behavior. One form of adaptation is coping with the environment by organizing and reorganizing thought patterns to the extent that the new cognitive capability becomes a higher level schema. Intelligence, according to Piaget, is a process of adaptation by which higher cognitive levels are attained. Piaget tries to identify the cognitive structures of schemata of each age level and seeks to show how individuals adapt to environmental demands and to one another.[22]

Piaget's theory divides the intellectual development process into four main chronological periods or stages, which are further divided into phases. The order of succession of these steplike patterns is constant, although the ages at which different stages are attained may vary somewhat, depending on the child's maturation, innate capacity, practice, and environmental differences. The four periods are (1) sensorimotor stage covering ages 0 to 2 years, (2) preoperational stage, ages 3 to 7 years, (3) concrete operations stage, 7 to 11 or 12 years of age, and (4) formal operations period, ages 11 to 15 or 16 years. The word *operations* in the foregoing stages refers to intellectual functions or performance. The four stages will be presented separately in the chapters dealing with the appropriate age levels. Only the sensorimotor stage will be presented in this chapter.

Piaget's sensorimotor stage of cognitive development

The sensorimotor stage of development, according to Piaget, encompasses the period in a child's life from birth to about 2 years of age (Table 5-4). This period is essentially preverbal, since children's adaptations to their new environment do not involve extensive use of symbols or language.

Children have several intellectual developmental tasks that they must achieve during this period. They must learn to coordinate and organize simple motor actions and incoming perceptions (sensory) so that they can be converted into adaptive behavior. They must come to realize that information concerning one object or event

Table 5-4. Piaget's sensorimotor period of cognitive development

Stage	Behavior	Examples
1. Reflexive schemata (0 to 1 month)	Use of reflexes	Sucking is most salient reflex
2. Primary circular reactions (1 to 4 months)	Extension of reflexes	Sucks fingers; puts out tongue
3. Secondary circular reactions (4 to 8 months)	Earliest stage at which "intention" is distinguished	Moves in crib to make toys on crib shake
4. Coordination of secondary schemata (8 to 12 months)	Application of familiar means to new situations; "means" differentiated from "ends"	Holds a block in each hand and drops one, picking up a third one just presented to him
5. Tertiary circular reactions (12 to 18 months)	Discovery through active experimentation	Devises different ways of making something fall or slide "to see what happens"
6. Invention of new means through mental combinations (18 to 24 months)	Emergence of capacity to respond to or think about things not immediately observable	Uses a stick to reach out beyond arm length to pull something closer

can be reaching them through different senses and that the information must be coordinated and integrated instead of being considered as unrelated. Infants must also come to think of the world as existing as an independent, permanent place and existing even when they do not perceive it. The same thing is true of the existence of objects in that they must develop an "object reality," which involves learning to differentiate between object and self.[23] Children must learn to combine individual actions into a coordinated effort and sequence to reach a goal. By the end of the sensorimotor period children should be able to use simple tools to obtain what they want by anticipating the consequences of their actions. Although this cause-and-effect principle is not completely comprehended during infancy, its recognition is enhanced by repeating certain actions and observing the results.

Piaget has divided the sensorimotor period into six phases: (1) the use of reflexes, (2) primary circular reactions, (3) secondary circular reactions, (4) coordination of secondary circular reactions, (5) tertiary circular reactions, and (6) invention of new means by mental combinations.

Use of reflexes. The first phase, the use of reflexes, begins at birth and lasts until the end of the first month. Children repeatedly use the reflexes with which they were endowed. The reflex behaviors that Piaget believes are most important are sucking, grasping, eye movements and visual accommodations, and reflexes associated with hearing and phonation. The reflexes mostly used shortly after birth include sucking, tongue movements, swallowing, crying, and gross bodily movements.

Infants do not perceive their accomplishments because they exist in a state of complete bodily egocentrism, unaffected by their contacts with a shadowy, outer reality. There is an absence of genuine intelligent behavior. Nonetheless, this phase is an extremely important one, since it is from behavior established during this period that subsequent intelligence will emerge. The reflexes are the building blocks of the perceptual-motor receptive and expressive patterns.

Primary circular reactions. The second phase, that of primary circular reactions, begins after the first month and lasts until the fourth month. Circular reaction refers to a behavior that provides the stimulus either for its own repetition or for the continuation of the initiating behavior. During this period the neonatal reflexes undergo numerous changes due to the interaction of babies with their environment. Infants are continuously bringing about, prolonging, and repeating some forms of adaptive behavior that have not previously occurred. The simple reflexes are slowly being replaced by systematic, sequential combinations of reflexes and, in some cases, by voluntary movements. For example, sucking is an innate reflex, but systematic thumb and finger sucking is only acquired as infants develop hand-to-mouth coordination.

Infants' vision also becomes more developed during the second and third months. They begin to "look" at objects within their visual field; they learn to focus on stationary objects; then they learn to follow moving objects as well. During this phase, a differentiation is noted in the cries of infants in that they begin to cry in different ways for different needs. They also begin to differentiate other vocalizations and to repeat some sounds for their own sake. Prehension, which requires a coordination of grasping and vision, also develops according to a systematic, sequential pattern. By the end of the second developmental phase children are beginning to lose some of their egocentrism and to respond to the world around them.

Secondary circular reactions. The behavior patterns of the third phase of sensorimotor development, ages 4 to 8 months, consist of secondary circular reactions that are concerned with the external (secondary) environment rather than with the infants' bodies, as in primary reactions. The *beginnings* of "intentional" adaptations are noted; that is, a desire, intention, or a purpose can be associated to the movement. Thus children kick their legs to shake their crib and make a hanging mobile or toy move. They will shake a rattle to produce a sound. They begin to show a greater awareness of the world surrounding them.

Although they are not yet interested in particular objects in their environment, they like to use them and enjoy the resultant actions. They also begin to recognize objects and people that are familiar to them. Their conception of a stable external world has begun. They still do not have an idea of the permanence of objects, nor do they have enough intelligence to reverse a feeding bottle that has been presented to them the wrong way. However, when an object vanishes, they will look for it. Children have attained some idea of the world around them when they look for objects that no longer can be seen.

Coordination of secondary schemata. There are two principal areas of intellectual accomplishment during the fourth developmental phase, from the eighth to the twelfth month. The secondary circular reactions of phase three become coordinated to form new behavior totalities that are now unquestionably intentional. Children also begin to exhibit anticipatory behavior by using signs or signals to anticipate coming events. They indulge in such activities as removing a lid from a box to find a ball inside. They can now reverse a feeding bottle that has been given to them the wrong way. They can use new schemata in different situations to solve problems. For the first time children's actions correspond to a definition of intelligence from a functional point of view. This phase marks the beginning of the permanence of things and of objective spatial groups.

Tertiary circular reactions. The fifth phase, 12 to 18 months of age, deals with tertiary circular reactions and the discovery of new means. These reactions refer to the repetitive behavior that fascinates children of about 1 year of age when they repeat an action many times but do not repeat it in a stereotyped form. Children not only act on the objects in their environment but also vary their action on them or try out new responses to reach the same goal. This is the beginning of trial-and-error experimentation and problem solving. Children also become extremely interested in pursuing new experiences. They try to produce new actions that create a pleasing effect for themselves. Every situation has numerous possibilities that seem to need further exploration, explanation, or modification. The adaptive reactions of this phase have all the characteristics of true intelligence.

Intervention of new means. The final phase begins about the eighteenth month and continues to the twenty-fourth month. The most significant sensorimotor skill developed during this phase involves the children's ability to solve problems without physically exploring their possibilities or solutions as they did in phase five. This is called the invention of new means through deduction or mental combinations. Children are now able, by

David Strickler

During Piaget's tertiary circular reaction phase, an infant will take objects, such as leaves, from the environment and repeat an action with them several times in succession.

use of symbolic or visual imagining, to ''invent'' or ''figure out'' the solutions internally. They can solve some simple problems, can remember, can plan, and can imagine. For example, children playing next to a fence take hold of an object on the other side. The object is too big to be brought in between the slats. At this stage of development they are able to raise the object to the top of the fence (if not too high) and bring it over the top. The children were able to picture the events to themselves and follow them through mentally.

They are doing thinking and primitive problem solving.

DEVELOPMENT OF THE PERCEPTUAL PROCESSES

Although newborn children have about all the brain cells they will ever have, their central nervous systems are not developed or organized to the point that they can provide meaning to stimuli. In fact, the neonate will have only the grossest type of awareness of stimuli that are out-

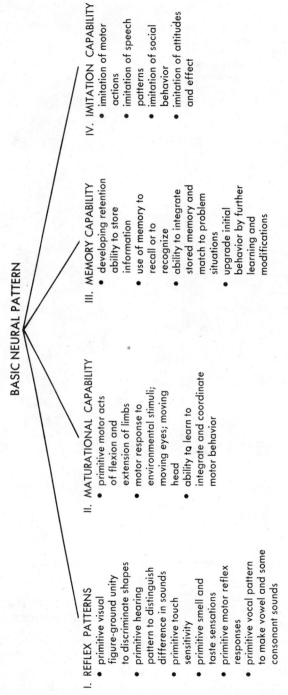

BASIC NEURAL PATTERN

I. REFLEX PATTERNS
- primitive visual figure-ground unity to discriminate shapes
- primitive hearing pattern to distinguish difference in sounds
- primitive touch sensitivity
- primitive smell and taste sensations
- primitive motor reflex responses
- primitive vocal pattern to make vowel and some consonant sounds

II. MATURATIONAL CAPABILITY
- primitive motor acts of flexion and extension of limbs
- motor response to environmental stimuli; moving eyes; moving head
- ability to learn to integrate and coordinate motor behavior

III. MEMORY CAPABILITY
- developing retention ability to store information
- use of memory to recall or to recognize
- ability to integrate stored memory and match to problem situations
- upgrade initial behavior by further learning and modifications

IV. IMITATION CAPABILITY
- imitation of motor actions
- imitation of speech patterns
- imitation of social behavior
- imitation of attitudes and effect

Fig. 5-4. What a baby has at birth to facilitate "learning how to learn." These behaviors are not mature at birth, of course, but the foundations for their development are present.

side of the body. Children need to develop a per-ceptual-conceptual process by which they can receive stimuli, get meaning from them, develop concepts, and make appropriate responses. This sequence approximates the function of the sensorimotor arc, which is basic to the way in which men neurologically come to know their world.

Perception is the cognitive process by which the various senses (1) become aware of stimuli, within or outside the body, and (2) refer the stimuli to the central nervous system (CNS), where some meaningful interpretation is attached to them. The central nervous system then seeks to make an appropriate response. The word *perceptual* pertains to the process and the function of perception. *Conceptual* refers to concept, idea, or general meaning that has evolved from perception. The perceptual-conceptual process refers to the means by which an individual becomes aware of something, attaches meaning to it, and changes the meaning into a ''memory bit'' or apperceptive knowledge that can be used at another time. Learning and the cognitive processes are involved in the perceptual-conceptual process.[24] The development of intelligence, it is believed, hinges on the nature and development of the perceptual-conceptual process.

At birth neonates respond almost completely on the basis of reflexes and primitive reaction behavior. Their perceptual pattern for receptive and expressive behavior is meager. However, they do possess the beginnings of the elements that will make up their perceptual process. Among the things that newborn children can do but do not have to do are (1) observe a very elemental figure on ground perception that will develop into visual perception; (2) perform various motor acts, such as flexing and extending limbs, moving the eyes, turning the head, and grasping objects by reflex; (3) demonstrate a primitive auditory perceptive ability that is aware of loud and soft sounds; (4) produce crying and single noncrying vowels and consonant sounds that will develop into vocal and speech patterns; (5) exhibit a primitive memory ability that can retain impressions gained through simple conditioning acts of learning; and (6) demonstrate the beginning of an ability to integrate and coordinate behavior (Fig. 5-4). All of these fundamental

''beginnings'' or ''primitive patterns'' will be further developed into a viable perceptual-conceptual process by the maturational process and by learning gained through interaction with the environment.

Many authorities working in the realm of intellectual development, including Piaget,[25] Gesell and Ilg,[26] Gibson,[27] and Smith and Henry,[28] suggest that the basis for the development of the cognitive processes is to be found in the perceptual-motor aspects of development at birth or shortly thereafter. Children are able to make use of primitive sensory and motor reactions as well as the reflexes mentioned in the previous paragraph. It is on these basic sensory and motor response patterns that the perceptual-conceptual processes are developed through learning and maturation.

Our work with school-age children who were having difficulty in learning, although they had average or better mental ability, revealed that most of these children lacked the ability to execute basic motor patterns that are normally developed in the first year of life. These children lacked proper body symmetry, posture control, and balance. They were also deficient in the use of one or more of the sensory or perceptual modalities.

The theoretical position of Carolyn L. Heil[29] is that children must develop symmetry in their posture mechanism and adequate weight-shift mechanism for balance before they can develop efficient and effective perceptual and motor skills. The time period in which infants generally learn these body adaptations is from the third to the ninth or tenth month of age, that is, from the time they can lift their chest and hold their head erect at midline position while lying supine to the time they begin to increase their sitting-up or standing activity. This is the period when infants are developing hand-eye coordination because most of the motor activity they are using is from the waist up. They are developing a sensorimotor match by learning to reach to a spot where they are looking. With a symmetrical posture children can better shift their body weight to obtain good balance. With consistent balance children will have a stable base from which they can perceptually move into the outer world. Furthermore, the world will appear the same way to them each time rather than changing because of inconsistent body positions.

An implication of Heil is that babies from the age of 3 months to the time they are sitting unsupported or beginning to walk should be permitted to spend as much of their time as possible in a horizontal prone position. Preferably, they should be placed toward the middle of the room during the time they are awake so they can react to stimuli coming at them from varied directions. If they are lying awake in a crib next to a wall, most of the visual and auditory stimuli will be coming from the same side of the child. Extensive use of infant seats, jump seats, and the like is not recommended for use before a child is ready to sit up unsupported and is capable of crawling and creeping.

STUDY GUIDE

1. Review the developmental tasks of this age level. Do they make sense to you?
2. Who or what is a neonate?
3. List the physical, behavioral, and sensory characteristics of a neonate.
4. Review the summary of motor responses on Tables 5-2 and 5-3 and become aware of the body and limb movements that a baby can make.
5. Trace the basic motor development of locomotion of an infant during the first twelve months of life.
6. How does grasping develop?
7. Jean Piaget is internationally known and accepted for his work on cognition. Answer the following questions according to his theories.
   a. What does he mean by schema or schemata, assimilation, accommodation, and operations?
   b. What are the four periods of cognitive development? Give their age ranges.
   c. At what stage of the sensorimotor period of cognitive development do infants appear to be using their intellect in a manner that can be observed by another person?
   d. Relate the use of the simple reflexes listed in Table 5-1 and the sequence of motor development in Table 5-2 to Piaget's sensorimotor period in cognitive development (Table 5-4).

8. The perceptual process is mentioned in Chapter 2 in the discussion of the nervous system. Combine that information with what is found in Chapter 5. Then look ahead to Chapter 7 for a preview of a more sophisticated interpretation of the function of the perceptual process as it relates to learning. Can you tie all of this information together?

REFERENCES

1. Havighurst, R. *Developmental tasks and education* (3rd ed.). New York: David McKay Co., Inc., 1972.
2. Latham, H. C., Heckel, R. V., Herbert, L. J., & Bennett, E. *Pediatric nursing* (3rd ed.). St. Louis: The C. V. Mosby Co., 1977.
3. Wolff, P. H. Observation on newborn infants. In L. J. Stone, H. T. Smith, & L. B. Murphy (Eds.), *The competent infant, research and commentary.* New York: Basic Books, Inc., Publishers, 1973, 257-268.
4. Tanner, J. M. Physical growth. In P. H. Musser (Ed.), *Carmichael's manual of child psychology* (3rd ed.) (Vol. I). New York: John Wiley & Sons, Inc., 1970.
5. Laupres, W. Feeding of infants. In V. Vaughn, III, & J. R. McKay, *Nelmis textbook of pediatrics* (10th ed.). Philadelphia: W. B. Saunders Co., 1975.
6. Macfarlane, J. A. What a baby knows. *Human Nature,* 1978, **1**(2), 74-81.
7. Bower, T. G. R. *Development in infancy.* San Francisco: W. H. Freeman & Co., Publishers, 1974.
8. Fantz, R. L. Complexity and facial resemblance as determinants of response to facelike stimuli by 5 and 10 week old infants. *Journal of Experimental Child Psychology,* 1974, **18**, 480-487.
9. Peeples, D., & Teller, D. Color vision and brightness discrimination in two-month-old infants. *Science,* 1975, **189**, 1102-1103.
10. Macfarland, J. A. *The psychology of childbirth.* Cambridge, Mass.: Harvard University Press, 1977.
11. Bench, J. Square-wave stimuli and neonatal auditory behavior. *Journal of Experimental Child Psychology,* 1973, **16**, 521-527.
12. Eimas, P. Auditory and linguistic processing of cues for place of articulation by infants. *Perception and Psychophysics,* 1974, **16**, 513-521.
13. Mendelson, M. J., & Haith, M. M. The relation between audition and vision in the human newborn. *Monographs of the Society for Research in Child Development,* 1976, **41**(4), Serial No. 167.

14. Macfarlane, J. A. Olfaction in the development of social preferences in the human neonate. Parent-infant interaction. *CIBA Foundation Symposium No. 33,* New series, ASP, 1975.

15. Engen, T., Lipsitt, L. P., & Peck, M. B. Ability of newborn infants to discriminate sapid substances. *Developmental Psychology,* 1974, **10,** 741-744.

16. Well, G. G., & Bell, R. Q. Basal skin conductance and neonatal state. *Child Development,* 1965, **36,** 647-657.

17. Mingeot, R., & Herbert, M. The functional status of the newborn infant. A study of 5,370 consecutive infants. *American Journal of Obstetrics and Gynecology,* 1973, **115,** 1138.

18. Kravitz, H., & Scherz, R. G. Preventing crib deaths. *Journal of the American Medical Association,* **149**(5), 444-447, 1976.

19. Vaughan, V. C., & McKay, R. J. (Eds.). *Nelson's textbook of pediatrics* (10th ed.). Philadelphia: W. B. Saunders Co., 1975.

20. Shirley, M. *The first two years.* Minneapolis: University of Minnesota Press, 1931.

21. Halverson, H. M. An experimental study of prehension in infants by means of systematic cinema reports. *Genetic Psychology Monographs,* 1931, **10,** 107-286.

22. Piaget, J., & Inhelder, B. *The psychology of the child.* New York: Basic Books, Inc., Publishers, 1969.

23. Inhelder, B., & Piaget, J. *The early growth of logic in a child.* New York: Harper & Row, Publishers, 1964.

24. Kaluger, G., & Kolson, C. J. *Reading and learning disabilities* (2nd ed.). Columbus, Ohio: Charles E. Merrill Publishing Co., 1978.

25. Piaget, J. *The origins of intelligence in children.* New York: International Universities Press, 1952.

26. Gesell, A., & Ilg, F. L. *Child development: an introduction to the study of human development.* New York: Harper & Row, Publishers, 1949.

27. Gibson, J. L. *The senses considered as perceptual systems.* Boston: Houghton Mifflin Co., 1966.

28. Smith, C. V., & Henry, J. P. Cybernetic foundations of rehabilitation. *American Journal of Physical Medicine,* 1967, **46,** 379-467.

29. Kaluger, G., & Heil, C. L. Basic symmetry and balance: their relationship to perceptual-motor development. *Progress in Physical Therapy,* 1970, **1,** 132-137.

Psychosocial development in infancy

The first word, if it was a word, that my daughter learned was "Lordy." One has to wonder how a child would ever learn such a word as her first word. I think it was probably due to the fact that I sang "la, la, la" to her when she was younger. That's the only word she said for quite a while: "Lordy, lordy." I thought for a long time that would be the only word she would ever say. But she was only one year old at the time and had plenty of time to learn other words.

My worries soon came to an end. After learning the motion of waving "bye-bye," she soon formed her lips to roll out the phoneme of "bye." It is interesting to note that she never said "bye-bye" as such. "Hi" was a word that was relatively easy for Stephanie to learn. When I added the motion to the word, however, she seemed to get "hi" and "bye" confused. She would say "hi" when she meant "bye" and vice versa.

Next in her vocabulary came the names of animals. Stephanie learned about animals from her books and from seeing the live animals. The latter seemed to be the more educational. The first animal word Stephanie tried to say was "cow," although it didn't sound like it was supposed to. It came out "keeeee" and sounded that way for nearly a month. I, as a first-time mother, was worried that that was the way she would say cow for the rest of her life.

Soon she came to call all four-legged creatures cows, or in her language, "kees." It wasn't until her grandmother got her a kitten that she learned the correct pronunciation of the word cow. I would say over and over to her: "nice kitty-cat." Soon she came out with "kitty-cat." The kitten had one sound of her own which, as everyone knows, is "meow." When rough treatment of the kitten takes place, naturally the kitten says "meow" and tries to get away. When saying "meow," this kitten really meant "ow!" Soon "meow" was added to the broadening vocabulary of my little one. And it was said as plain as day. Driving into the country one day gave me the opportunity to say to Stephanie: "Look at all the cows." And Stephanie said "cow" just as plain as could be. I was so proud of her that I almost ran off the road. I came to the conclusion that she rhymed "meow" and "cow" and ended with the correct pronunciation.

All parents want their children to learn good manners. Like some, I believe this should be taught while a child is young. So when my daughter wants anything, she has been taught to say "please." Of course, it doesn't quite come out like that; she says "peas." It sounds so cute and innocent that everybody makes a big thing out of it. I even heard an adult saying "peas" back to her. Now the problem is to get her to say "peas" meaning the vegetable and not "please." At the table when she says: "Peas, I want some," I always say: "Some what?" and then follow up with "peas?" Stephanie thinks I want her to say "please" and she says "peas." If only she would say: "Peas, some peas," I would be very happy. Of course, time works everything out. She does say "thank you," but it comes out "tank tu." Thank heavens, there is no homonym for "tank tu"!

Then there are always those expressions I wish my child had never heard. When I once took liver out of the freezer to thaw for supper, my sister-in-law said: "Whew! are you having that for supper?" Of course, my two-year-old echoed: "Whew." I did not reprimand her for saying that word, but an incident soon occurred for her to use it.

We were shopping at the grocery store and one of my selections was a container of liver. Stephanie always places the grocery items in the cart. She put the liver in the cart without saying a word. When I took the liver out of the cart at the check-out counter, Stephanie said as loudly as she could: "Whew." She selected the exact moment when there was a line of customers waiting to be checked out. I was very embarrassed. The lady behind me said: "That's all right; I can't stand liver either."

I guess the word that touches most mothers' hearts is "Mommy" said for the first time. Stephanie says this with no trouble at all. There's one thing that puzzles me, however. I've tried to teach her the word "Grandma"; she always says: "Mom-Mom." I don't know what made her say this, but she calls both of the grandmothers Mom-Mom. So I call them Mom-Mom to her when talking about one or both of them.

No matter what she says, it's always interesting to observe her trying to say different sounds. Sometimes she tries so hard, but they just come out all wrong. I'm sure she thinks they're right. If they're right to her, they're right to me. I know from listening to her she'll soon acquire the correct pronunciation of words.

Although the emergence of motor skills is the most noted and obvious element of development in infancy, there are other aspects of growth that are just as important, if not more so. Psychosocial development is fundamental to the mental well-being of each person throughout life. Speech and language, social and emotional characteristics, and the origins of personality all have their beginnings in infancy.

INFANT SPEECH AND LANGUAGE

The foundations of language development begin as soon as the infant is born. When babies cry and their mothers respond to this cry, the first step in communication has been taken.

Infants make their needs and feelings known by using simple forms of communication consisting of body movements, facial expressions, and emotionally charged vocalizations such as whimpers, urgent screams, gentle coos, attention-seeking calls, and laughter. A mother quickly learns to interpret these prelinguistic communications and reinforces them by responding to their calls. As mother and child interact, speech, language, and thought are developed. Prelinguistic communication reaches a peak at about 16 to

Table 6-1. Development of language in young children*

Age zone	Language
1 month	Impassive face
	Small throaty sounds
4 months	Coos, responds to adult by vocalization
	Laughs aloud
7 months	Squeals
	M-m sound
10 months	Da-Da-Ma-Ma
	One other "word"
12 months	Two other "words"
	Responds to "give it to me"
15 months	Four to six words
18 months	Ten words
	Jargon
24 months	Joins two to three words
	Names three to five pictures
36 months	Sentences
	Gives full name, sex

*Modified from Latham, H. C., & Heckel, R. V. *Pediatric nursing,* (3rd ed.). St. Louis: The C. V. Mosby Co., 1975.

1-6 weeks

20 months of age. As children's spoken language and vocabulary improve, they have less need to communicate in nonverbal ways (Table 6-1).

True language development, that is, interpersonal linguistic communication with understanding, begins when the infant is about 2 years old. Much speech development must have taken place in the meanwhile. According to McClinton and Meier,[1] infants must progress through five essential developmental stages before they can speak conventional, adultlike words. These stages are (1) reflexive vocalization, (2) babbling, (3) lalling, (4) echolalia, and (5) true speech.

Reflexive vocalization

The first sound that a newborn baby makes is the birth cry, which is produced by a reflexive inhalation and exhalation of air across the vocal cords, which were tightened by the trauma associated with air pressure and temperature change of the extrauterine environment. Almost no noncrying vocalization is heard until after

breathing, sucking, and swallowing are well established. The reflexive period of speech development is one of nondescript sounds or speechlessness. It involves undifferentiated crying.

By the end of the first two or three weeks mothers can usually detect differences in the cries of their infants. They have matured enough, physically and mentally, to react with differentiation to varying stimuli and conditions. Babies have one kind of cry that they make when they are hungry, another kind when they have a sharp pain, and still another kind when they have a dull, aching pain or a fever. They have different cries to indicate when they are uncomfortable, wet, tired, or want attention. At this early age children are seeking to communicate to others to make their needs known. Baby now has differentiated crying.

The shrill cries of hunger or discomfort are quite different from sounds made when the baby is comfortable and happy. This is due to the contractions of the facial muscles when a child is experiencing discomfort and to the more relaxed muscle tone when the baby is comfortable. It is with these shrill cries and comfort sounds that the infant begins to form many consonant and vowel sounds. A child makes vowel sounds before making consonant sounds because when the mouth is opened and air is expelled, a vowel-sound is made. To make a consonant sound the lips or the tongue must be used.

Cooing and babbling

6-7 wks

At about 6 or 7 weeks of age infants show by their behavior that they are aware that they are making sounds. Thus reflexive vocalization becomes cooing. They usually make sounds when they are enjoying themselves, and one can tell that they delight in producing or repeating sounds. These sounds are different from the comfort sounds or the discomfort cries. Although they may only be making about seven different phonemes (the smallest unit of speech sounds), the sounds are phonetically diversified. It is usually around the third or fourth month that infants learn to manipulate their tongue and lips along with their throat and voice. At that time they may experiment with the sounds they can make. During the babbling period, which usually lasts until about the sixth month, the sounds produced are still mainly reflexive in nature. As a result, all babies everywhere, the Occidental babies as well as the Oriental babies, make the same sounds. For the same reason babies who are born deaf can babble and make the same sounds that are made by children with normal hearing. For the first 3 months of life the quality of the sounds produced by deaf and hearing children is virtually identical.[2]

The earliest signs of children's response to language are naturally their responses to their mothers' voice. Mothers are the center of children's lives. They satisfy their needs, so their voices become part of the whole experience. As young as 4 or 5 weeks old, infants can be comforted solely by the sound of their mothers' voice. A little later they may smile on hearing her voice, and soon after that they may smile and make comfort sounds and excited bodily movements. At about 4 or 5 months of age infants usually begin to differentiate their responses on the basis of the tone or manner of the voice. They still do not understand specific words, but they can respond to intonation of voice. This is shown by babies who respond differently to the same word spoken in different tones of voice.

Babbling is vocalization that babies make for their own pleasure. While lying in their cribs, they are practicing self-initiated sounds that they will need to use in the more advanced stages of articulation and speech development.

Lalling or imperfect imitation

About the sixth or seventh month it becomes apparent that babies are beginning to repeat sounds that they have picked up from their environment. They are now lalling, which is the repetition of sounds or sound combinations that the child has heard. For the first time hearing and sound production are associated. Hearing comprehension is taking place. Vocalization also becomes more socialized as babies begin making squeals or shouts of delight at the approach of a familiar person.

At about 7 or 8 months of age babies begin to join their vocalized syllables into repetitive sequences, such as ma-ma-ma or ba-ba-ba-ba. It is

usually about this time that the mother or father says that the baby first said "ma-ma" or "da-da." As the parents constantly work with the children to bring about more words, the babies will increasingly use the words of their culture and will drop from their repertoire sounds not used in their environment. Children who are born deaf may increase the number of sound combinations that they make, but these sounds will be mostly of the reflexive type that they were making earlier in life.

Echolalia and imitation of sounds

At about 9 or 10 months of age infants begin to repeat, by imitation, sounds that they have heard around them. There is a definite acoustic awareness of the sounds made by others. Frequently, the sounds just made by the babies are repeated by someone near them. This repetition by others and the consequent echolalia (imitative repetition or "echoing" of sounds or words just spoken by another) by the babies stimulate even more speech activity. In other words language and speech development go along at a faster pace if the parents repeat the baby's sounds. Babies, in turn, will echo the parents' sounds. The feel of their tongue, lips, and throat, the sounds they make and hear, the association of other people's voices with lip and facial movements all play an important part in the development of speech. Soon they will be producing elaborate reduplication of two or more syllable combinations. Although there is no comprehension of the sounds, the babies are developing a repertoire of sounds of the language they are to learn. Children who have a remarkable ability to echo sound combinations and speech inflections may develop an expressive "jargon" that has all the mannerisms of conversational adult speech.

True speech

When the children are 10 to 12 months of age, they begin to pay attention to a few familiar words. They also seem to have more interest in some words than in others. By their first birthday they can stop when told "no" and, sometimes, can follow very simple directions. The infants are demonstrating a passive understanding of the language. The active use of it will come later.

They recognize their name and usually those of their family and household pets. They will turn to look for them if they are mentioned.

True speech takes place when children intentionally and correctly use a conventional sound pattern (a word) and anticipate a response appropriate to the word they have just uttered. Verbal understanding is necessary on the part of children for them to use and to respond to true speech. Average children begin to use true speech between 12 and 18 months of age, although the first word spoken may have been said at the age of 10 or 11 months. By 15 months of age they usually speak four intelligible words even though their understanding vocabulary is much larger.

At about 18 months of age their speaking vocabulary consists of ten spoken words. They can respond to "give me that" and can point to their nose or eyes on command. Children understand the language of others before they are able to use the same words. Average children of 2 years of age use more than fifty words, and they can put two distinct words together into a sentence. Complete speech comes when children can use differentiated speech communication in sentences with grammatical structure.

Language development

It is necessary to point out that the terms *language development* and *speech development* have different meanings to the professional. Language development refers to the words, their pronunciation, and the methods of combining them for use and understanding by others. As a form of communication, language may be verbal, through the use of words or sounds, or it may be nonverbal, as in the use of gestures, motor responses, facial expressions, or "body language." Eventually, language development concerns itself with the length and patterns of sentence structure, grammatical construction, and syntax—the way in which words are put together to form phrases, clauses, or sentences.

Speech development primarily concerns itself with the development of units of speech sounds, the phonemes, and with the maturation and proper articulation of these sounds. In a sense, speech development refers to vocalization, the

earliest vocal form of which is crying. The development of vocalization was described in the last section, indicating how a child goes from reflexive vocalization, to cooing, babbling, lalling, echolalia and jargon, to true speech. True speech is the appropriate usage of a word. At this point, speech and language usage begin to merge.

Language sequence. Language has somewhat of a sequential pattern of development. Language comprehension may occur as early as the third or fourth week when baby responds or attends to a speaking voice, usually that of the mother. Between the third and fourth month baby begins to vocalize in response to social stimulation. During the babbling stage, vocal activity occurs very frequently, especially if a mother talks much to the baby.

By 6 months, an infant can usually discriminate between friendly and angry talking. Between the ninth and tenth months, baby understands gestures and responds to "bye-bye" (if so inclined). It is about this time that babies utter their first word. Response to simple commands occurs between the tenth and twelfth months, when baby begins to understand simple sentences. By 18 months the infant understands and may respond to a simple request, such as "Put your finger on your nose." Baby begins to name animals in a book when about 19 or 20 months of age and, about this time, begins to utter two-word sentences. Full sentences are initiated at about 25 months of age. Prepositions such as "in" and "under" are understood by the 2-year-old. Grammatically correct utterances are common by the age of 3 years. The foundation of language development is now set and giant strides will be made in the next two years.

Social differences. Benedict[3] notes that mothers talk differently to very young children than they do to adults. For example, they use shorter sentences, fewer words, simpler grammar, slower speech, and a lot of repetition. Babies paid much more attention and were more likely to carry out simple commands when the mothers repeated their commands. Strain and Vietze[4] found that infants did much more vocalizing when mothers talked to them; mothers were more likely to continue talking if the infants kept making sounds. Baby would talk to in-

David Strickler

As soon as children learn verbal and nonverbal responses, they seek to communicate with others.

animate objects if mother happened to be out of the room.

According to Tulkin and Kagan,[5] social class differences are evident at a very early age in the way mothers talk to their offspring. Middle-class mothers talk much more to their babies than do working-class or lower socioeconomic class mothers. This difference exists in spite of the fact that both groups of mothers love and care for their babies equally well and spend the same amount of time with them. Working-class mothers apparently do not recognize how early babies can respond to parental involvement with them.

Early intervention. The Milwaukee Project of Richard Heber[6] has special significance concerning the verbal interaction between low socioeconomic-status mothers and their infants. The purpose of the study was to determine if intellectual deficits in "high-risk" infants could be prevented by early intervention. In a fairly well-designed and controlled study, Heber and his associates gathered a group of mothers whose IQs were 80 or lower and brought them into a maternal rehabilitation program. A control group was also part of the study, but they did not participate in the training program. The intent of the program was to provide an environment and a set of experiences that would allow the children to develop normally. For the first year, children were brought to a center on a daily basis. The specific focus of the program was to prevent language, problem-solving, and motivation deficits that are associated with mild mental retardation and severe disadvantagedness.

Although the program was cognitive-language oriented, vocational training, remedial education, and training in homemaking and child-care skills were offered to the mothers. The mothers improved in mother-child interaction. They were encouraged to talk to their babies; they were taught how to initiate problem-solving behavior in the infants by the use of verbal clues or suggestions. The mothers learned to use verbal reinforcement and more verbal responses. The results were exciting! The experimental group of children gained scores of 20 to 30 points higher on standardized IQ tests than the control group. What's more, they maintained that advantage after the third grade in school. The children in the experimental group raised their IQ level from 75-80 to 88-120, with a 20-point IQ advantage over the others, mostly because of better language development, in conjunction with an emphasis on verbal inquiry and discovery.

Nonstandard English. Variations within a language are called dialects; they often result in nonstandard English. The major difference between formal and informal English usage is the carefulness or the casualness of the communication. There are several nonstandard dialects in the United States. A blend of Spanish and English is found in the Southwest, Florida, and New York City. In some areas of the West a mixture of English and American Indian languages has produced a distinctive dialect. The most widespread nonstandard English dialect in the United States is black English.

From a linguistic point of view, the differences between standard English and black English are small. The basic structure of sentences and the formal representation of utterances are very similar.[7] A major difference, however, is that agreement between a subject and verb in person and number is not necessary. Examples are "I gone home now" or "He be coming soon." These differences, plus the dropping of some letter sounds ("bof" for "both") and the merging of some sounds ("gimmedat" for "give me that"), have led some authorities to speculate that academic failure among some black children is due to impoverished or inadequate language development. The sounds for doing phonetic analysis in reading, for example, were not part of the child's everyday vocabulary.

Some school personnel assumed that children from culturally different backgrounds would not have the vocabulary or verbal concepts necessary for traditional school learning. This assumption was especially true for Spanish-speaking children. Teaching English as a second language to both black and Spanish-speaking children seemed to help.[8] In New York City, "downtown English" was taught so the students could get jobs in the stores and offices. They could continue to use their dialect when they were back in their neighborhoods.

Black Americans do emphasize verbal fluency and verbal ability. However, in many cases, their pattern of language does not match standard English, and they have difficulty transferring thoughts from standard to nonstandard so they can understand what they are reading. An interesting experiment was conducted by a teacher in Baltimore in 1976. At Christmas time, he presented to his seventh graders, mostly inner-city blacks, the poem "'Twas the Night Before Christmas." Few could make sense out of the poem. He rewrote the poem in the street language of black English and every child could read and interpret the poem.

Egocentric and socialized speech (Piaget)

Piaget[9] divides the conversation or talk of children into two categories—egocentric speech and socialized speech. In egocentric speech children do not direct their speech to anyone in particular nor do they bother to learn if anyone is listening to them. They talk either for themselves or for the pleasure of associating anyone who happens to be there with their activity of the moment. They are merely talking in the presence of others.

Although the children are not actually speaking to anyone, the speech is related to their own actions and thoughts. This particular kind of egocentricity is a product of the child's intellectual limitations. Egocentric speech aids in the development of their cognitive processes.

Socialized speech is subdivided by Piaget into (1) adapted information, involving an exchange of thought or ideas; (2) criticism of the behavior or work of others; (3) commands, requests, and threats; (4) questions; and (5) answers. At this stage in the development of speech children speak "from the point of view of their audience." They speak now to communicate their thoughts to other people.

EMOTIONAL AND SOCIAL DEVELOPMENT

As with all areas of development in the newborn and infant, the psychosocial aspects of development are either nonexistent at birth or they exist in a primitive form. It is only after infants have adjusted to the "outer" world and survival is more ensured that they begin to differentiate their behavior to develop emotional, social, and personality patterns.

Emotional development

The word *emotion* is sometimes used to describe certain behavior, such as fear, anger, joy, disgust, affection, or pity. It is also used, however, to imply a system of feelings, such as sentiment, instead of a single feeling. Most psychologists agree that (1) emotion is affective and there is a feeling element or awareness present; (2) the central nervous system and the autonomic system are involved in producing characteristic motor, glandular, and visceral activities; (3) emotion is related in some way to motivation as an energizer of behavior; and (4) emotions can be classified into types of phenomena such as fear, anger, and affection. The problem in applying all of these factors of emotions to young infants is in knowing how to determine if they do have such a complex feeling state and, if so, how they manifest this state into a behavior. Because development, in all areas, evolves from mass or general behavior to specific activity, this princi-

ple will be used in the approach to discussing emotional behavior.

A baby's emotional life is relatively simple and spontaneous. Children place no restraint on a free expression of their emotions, which come and go depending on the extent to which their desires and needs are satisfied or frustrated and on the amount of understanding they possess of their relationship to others and to their environmental makeup. The baby's emotions are brief and transitory, although expressed more frequently than in adults.[10] As soon as the emotion is past, it is forgotten and the baby is free from stress and strain until new conditions arise that require an emotional response.

Infants are egocentric little human beings with most of their desires and needs coming from within. There is a definite relationship between emotional states and personal organismic needs. Needs are simple at birth and so are emotions. When babies have a strong need, such as for food, their emotional response will be one of crying and fairly intense physical movements. If children are hungry and their mothers make them wait beyond the point of physical endurance, their whole body will reflect their displeasure. Likewise, when they have been fed and are satisfied, their movements will subside and they appear to no longer have an emotional condition.

The mother is the first emotional climate to which the infant is exposed. The way in which the mother feels about the baby is consequently extremely important. Warmth, softness, and bodily satisfaction become the equivalent of love of the mother for the baby. If the mother is gentle and loving and makes the infant comfortable while being fed, the infant feels physically (and possibly psychologically) secure and develops a positive, friendly response to people.[11]

The reward value of a mother's touch was demonstrated by Harlow[12] in his experimentation with newborn monkeys (Fig. 6-1). He placed each monkey into a booth with two surrogate mothers. One mother substitute was made of wire mesh, which gave it a hard surface. The other surrogate, made of wire mesh also, was covered with foam and terry cloth and made soft. The monkeys consistently preferred the soft mother, even when the only food given to the

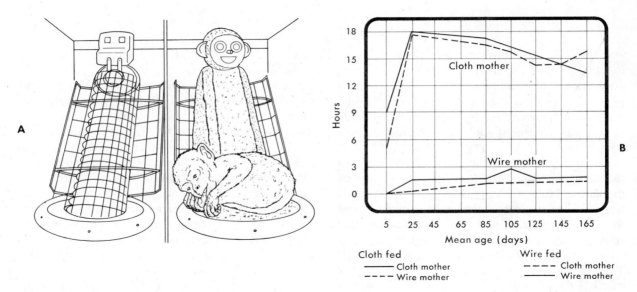

A   B

Fig. 6-1. A, Wire and cloth mother surrogates. **B,** Comparison of time spent on cloth and wire mother surrogates. Long-term effects show that infant monkeys spend their time on the terrycloth mother surrogate no matter which surrogate feeds them—a clear rejection of the reinforcement-theory explanation of infant-mother attachment. (From Harlow, H. F., *American Psychologist,* 1958, **13,** 673-685. Copyright [1958] by the American Psychological Association. Reprinted by permission.)

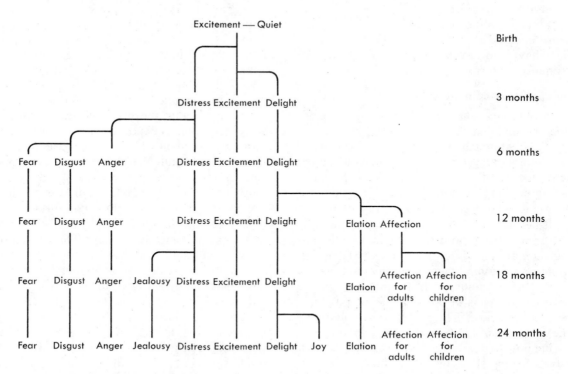

Fig. 6-2. The theory of the development of human emotions. Psychologists assume that a few primitive emotional states become differentiated with age into many human feelings. (From Bridges, K. B. *Child Development,* 1932, **3,** 324.)

Elaine Ward

Self-control is not learned early in life. If you want something, you just reach for it.

monkeys was placed by the hard mother. When frightened, the monkeys would run to the terry cloth mother for security. Similar studies done with babies reflect the same types of preferences. Early mother-child relationships influence both immediate behavior and long-term adjustment.

Considering single emotions, the first emotion that is evident in the newborn is a general, gross, undifferentiated type of response that can best be described by the word *excitement*. This undifferentiated behavior soon changes to some specific types of emotional responses. An oft-quoted study by Bridges,[13] done on the basis of intensive observation of about sixty infants over a period of several months, indicates the ages at which successive differentiations are made (Fig. 6-2). The first emotion to be detected after excitement is distress, which is observed by the end of the first month. By the end of the second month the feeling of delight can be noted. Between the third and sixth months anger, disgust, and fear are reflected. The only two fears that seem to be present at birth are a sudden withdrawal of support of the body and a reaction to loud, harsh noise. All other fears are learned.

Changes that occur in the emotional responses of the infant during middle infancy and the beginning of late infancy are products of complex interactions of maturation and learning. Maturation of the nervous system and muscles provides the potential for differentiated reactions, whereas learning has a determining effect on the manner in which the emotion will be expressed. Learning by conditioning occurs easily during the early years because children lack the reasoning ability and experience to realize how irrational or insignificant many of their emotional experiences are.

By 18 months of age infants show evidence of discrimination among people by smiling at those they know and reacting with fear to strangers, whereas at 6 months of age they would smile indiscriminately in response to a nodding face or mask, regardless of facial expression.[14] This development in perceptual discrimination in the ages from 6 to 18 months demonstrates the role of maturation in emotional and perceptual development.

By the end of the first year the mother should modify her role. She must still provide care but must train the infant according to the demands of her particular society. In the process of this training she should wait until the child is ready before expecting him to take part in processes such as toilet training. With personal emotional participation in learning the infant integrates the experience into his whole being and takes over personal responsibility earlier. The care that the mother provides and the example she sets are of greater influence on the infant than any other in the establishment of temperament, character, and personality traits for later years. Some child psychologists go so far as to say that a child's level of emotional stability is well determined by the end of the first year and that the mother had much to do with this development.

Social development

Every infant, like every adult, depends on other people for existence. Not only is the child dependent on a social group, but the social group also helps to determine what kind of individual the child will become. The first or primary social group of a child is the family. This group plays an important part in establishing the child's attitudes and habits. As the child grows into adolescence, the family is relied on less and friends and other social companions more.

Spock[15] has found that there have been

changes in the overall practice of child rearing and, as a result, so has there been a change of influence on social development. Between the two world wars it was believed that parents had to be extremely rigid in the discipline of their children from the time of birth. In the 1940s a more permissive type of child care was pursued, but in the 1950s the shift went back to more parental restraints on the child. With the 1960s parents sought to follow love and some training in addition to gratifying the child's needs. Parental restraint was less than in the past decade. In the 1970s there was much anxiety and concern, but

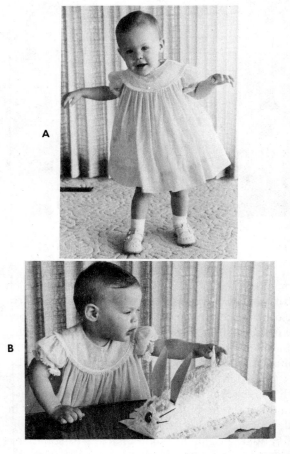

Infant at 12 months. A, Stands alone on wide base. **B,** Good finger-thumb opposition. (From Ingalls, A. J., & Salerno, M. C. *Maternal and child health nursing* [3rd ed.]. St. Louis: The C. V. Mosby Co., 1975.)

there seemed to be no direction except love and hope for the best.

Social development follows a pattern. Every child usually passes through certain phases of becoming socialized at about the same age that other children do. Children must learn social skills and how to make adjustments to others.

At birth babies have a complete lack of interest in people. They do not care for companionship of others as long as their bodily needs are taken care of. They will stop crying when they are lifted or touched.

Social behavior begins when the baby first dis-tinguishes between objects and persons. The first social responses of the baby are to adults. Although at 4 weeks of age the baby is not ready for real social stimulation, behavior patterns are undergoing organization. The baby stares at faces that are close by and seems to enjoy following the movements of objects and people. The baby bab-bles and coos.

In the second month infants give evidence that they are actively aware of adults who care for them but unaware of other babies in the same room. They gradually begin to respond to smiles of those around them and also to differentiate

Meriem Kaluger

Infant at 15 months. A, Climbs up stairs, holding on to the rail; **B,** uses spoon to feed self, but may spill food.

A

Meriem Kaluger

Infant at 18 months. A, Curious but needs supervision. **B,** Loves to pull and push toys.

Meriem Kaluger

Toddler at 24 months. A, Sips juice through a straw. **B,** Begins to emulate a sex role.

Toddler at 30 months. A, Enjoys a swing. **B,** Plays with stuffed animals, imitates social behavior.

among the individuals in their home. They babble and coo.

By the end of the third month babies may turn their head or eyes in response to a voice and may follow their mother's movements. Their social presence is beginning to be felt. A smile can be evoked by an adult exhibiting a smile, an angry face, distorted facial expressions, tones, or gestures. Incidentally, a child born blind knows how to smile. A baby's first response to people is a positive one.

There is an increased demand for sociability at 4 months of age. Infants now like to have people pay attention to them by talking or singing to them or just moving them about. Usually this demand for social attention is stronger toward the end of the day. Beginning at the age of 5 months they may even begin to cry when people leave the room or their presence.

At 5 months of age children smile in reply to another's smile, and they may cry at other social stimuli. Their powers of perception are developing rapidly, and they begin to interact with the various forces of their immediate environment. Their interest in their father and siblings increases.

At 7 months of age children may join in a game of peek-a-boo or "hide your face." They follow any object that is placed in motion and will smile when a person uses his hands to cut off the view from their face. Their interest in people and things is increasing. They can respond to more than one person at a time. They enjoy the attention of others but are becoming a little doubtful of strangers; they prefer familiar faces.

Babies display more aggressive behavior toward adults between the eighth and tenth months. They will pull an adult's hair, grab his

C

Meriem Kaluger

Toddler at 30 months. C, Can put shoes on.

nose, tug at his clothes or other personal features. They are also able to imitate some vocal sounds. They now show an awareness of another child placed close by them, although they are not able to share toys at this point.

At 10 months of age babies will not play by themselves for long periods of time and are quick to show their desire for a shift of company or toys. When shown a mirror, they make a sort of playful response to it. Although they stay in the crib for specific periods of time, they like to be with the family group.

Social give and take is greatly enjoyed at the 1-year-age level. If children have been alone in their playpen during the morning, their sociality occurs in the afternoon. They learn that others besides their family are friendly. Their attention is no longer held by playthings because they now love being chased while they are creeping. They throw things to the floor with the hope that they will be restored to them.

It seems that at the 15-month level children are getting into everything. They seem to enjoy pulling things out of place and, less often, putting them back. At this age children want to be attending to their own business of walking, bending, and stooping, instead of bothering with people. They do, however, cooperate in being dressed.

At 18 months children are still getting into everything, never seeming to stay in one place for any period of time. Now they like to be on their feet to go exploring. They are beginning to know where things are kept because of their interest in the activities of the household, and they know what belongs to different people. At this age they are more responsive to adults and are conscious of social approval.

Moral behavior

The baby is neither moral nor immoral in his actions but nonmoral in the sense that his behavior is not guided by moral standards. Before the baby can behave in a moral way he must learn what the group to which he belongs believes to be right or wrong. He will acquire morals from the teachings, attitudes, and experiences of his parents, peers, teachers, and others.

At first the baby's moral behavior is guided by impulse. He judges right and wrong in relation to the pleasure or pain the act affords him rather than in terms of good or harm done to others. The baby is too young intellectually to realize that an act is wrong unless ill effects follow. He thinks only of his behavior and how it affects him personally, doing what pleases him, regardless of the effect on others. He feels no obligation to modify his behavior because of others unless his behavior is accompanied by unpleasant consequences. A "guilty conscience" from doing wrong is unknown at a young age because it requires the development of definite standards of right and wrong. The baby acts on the basis of his primitive needs, impulses, and the pleasure principle.

No child can be expected to build up a moral code of his own. He must be taught the universal standards of mankind of right and wrong as they are handed down. He must also learn concepts that his social group has found to be useful.

CROSS-CULTURAL DIVERSITY

Cross-cultural analyses help us to see which principles of growth, development, and behavior are universal in nature and which ones are "manmade" or culturally influenced. By cross-cultural analyses, we mean a comparison of the special features, artifacts, and mentifacts of different societies and their groupings of people. All parents, in all societies, want things for and from their children. There appears to be much universality in what parents want for their children. Le Vine[16] has suggested three goals that all parents have for their children:

1. The physical survival and health of the child, including normal development and change during puberty
2. The development of the child's capacity for economic self-maintenance during adulthood (maturity)
3. The development of the child's ability to achieve cultural values and status as considered important by that culture

As noted, physical survival and growth are paramount, followed by providing for self-maintenance, and finally, the perpetuation of the culture and enhancement of one's self within that culture. Le Vine's reviews of studies done in African, Latin American, and Indonesian commu-

A mother in Bolivia nourishes and cherishes her child in very tender ways, always keeping her child near her.

nities with high infant mortality rates show that child-rearing practices in these societies are very responsive to environmental conditions. Our observations in these countries, as well as in primitive societies of New Guinea, the Solomon Islands, and other South Pacific islands, support his conclusions. The more life-threatening an environment is, in terms of food or physical dangers, the more the practice is to leave the baby on or near the mother's body at all times. Whenever the babies cried, the mothers responded quickly by feeding them.

In societies where infant mortality is not high but food and subsistence items are scarce, the emphasis is on the development of behavior that would ensure physical self-maintenance later.[17] The emphasis in subsistence societies is on producing children who are obedient to the task. Obedience produces the self-discipline needed to work at making a living. These, and other cultural factors, influence the nature of the socialization process. Western societies, with their subcultural groups, also produce variations of socialization practices within their countries. Working-class homes have different priorities than do affluent home environments. Liebert, Poulos and Marmor[18] do an excellent job in their text of showing how cross-cultural patterns make a difference in developmental and behavioral practices.

INFANT CARE
Toilet training

Toilet training is a major area of concern for many parents and some psychologists. The toddler is faced with reality when he is asked to give up the pleasure of doing what he wants to gain his mother's approval. The age for beginning this process is a matter of individual growth. However, by the end of the first year, he should be physiologically and psychologically ready. When the child can stand alone, his nerve pathways have developed to the extent that he can physically control his anal and urethral sphincters.[19] However, if the child does not understand what is expected of him, the mother should wait until later to start. Bowel training begins before bladder training, since the number of stools a day is fewer than the number of times the child urinates. Usually it is wise to wait at least a month after bowel training has been established to begin bladder training.

The method of toilet training begins with observing the time of day when the child has bowel movements. He is then placed on a seat that is comfortable for him a little before the time he usually defecates. The child should not be given toys to play with, since he would be distracted from his purpose. After the mother has indicated to the child by some gesture or words what is expected of him, she should keep him on the toilet chair for 10 to 15 minutes. It is good to teach the child an acceptable and easily understood word to use when he must eliminate so that strangers can understand his desire. He should be praised when he succeeds in his task, but disapproval should *not* be shown when he does not. When children are old enough to go to the toilet alone, their clothes should be easy to manage. Bowel control is established by one third of the infants at 18 months of age, daytime bladder control by 2 years of age, and night control by 3 years of age.

Problems in maintaining elimination control are often encountered and should not be upsetting to parents. Sometimes children revert to wetting themselves because they do not want to interrupt their play or do not allow enough time to get to the toilet. Teething, illness, and excessive intake of liquids are reasons for wetting. Any emotional strain or upset may cause a relapse. The arrival of a new baby in the family and going to school are situations that commonly cause strain.

Fecal smearing is a problem that arises with some children. Although this practice is offensive to adults, it is not abnormal for the child. He has not acquired the distaste for his excretions and enjoys the odor, regarding it as a gift from himself. He created it so he may not hesitate to manipulate it and smear it on the floor. The adult should not show strong disapproval, but he should provide a more acceptable means for the child to gratify this desire to smear. Playing with clay or sand are good methods at first. Later, finger painting may be used as a substitute for fecal smearing. Cleaning the child promptly or pinning the diaper securely are ways of preventing access to the feces. Sometimes flushing the toilet can be a helpful diversion by allowing the child to pull the handle.

There have been many evaluations of the effects of toilet training on the child. If training is begun too early before the child can learn to control himself, he can become frustrated and insecure. The child often has ambivalence toward his mother during this period. He loves her but feels antagonistic when she asks him to comply with her wishes. She must have patience and show love and friendliness toward her child. Psychoanalysts traditionally postulate that severe pressure on the child during this period will cause the child to be tight-lipped, stingy, meticulous, and punitive in later life. No pressure at all, however, may cause the child to develop a permissive attitude toward any kind of controls. The modern trend of thought as expressed by many authorities is that there is no significant effect of toilet training itself on the child's personality. Rather, it is the dominating influence of the type of parent who puts pressure on the child that affects his development.

Feeding and eating

There are both advantages and disadvantages to breast-feeding an infant. It is a case where the decision of the parents should be respected. With regard to advantages, breast-feeding is a more convenient method and for most women it provides great emotional satisfaction. Nursing also helps the uterus return to its normal shape more quickly. The composition of breast milk is ideal for most infants' needs; it is superior to a formula, even with vitamin supplements. The protein of human milk is easily digested, aseptic, and delivered at the proper temperature. Holding and cuddling the baby while breast-feeding aids in maternal-infant bonding.[20]

The disadvantages relate more to the restrictive nature of breast-feeding than to any pathology that may occur. Mothers who have to return to work may not want to be involved in the weaning process. Some women and men are repelled by the idea of breast-feeding. If a woman feels strange or unsure of herself concerning the idea, it may be reason enough to begin using a formula. Every care should be taken to help a mother feel comfortable and secure in her child-caring ability. If breast-feeding causes concern, then another approach should be taken.

Information about breast-feeding may be obtained from the La Leche League Information, Inc., 9616 Minneapolis Ave., Franklin Park, Ill. 60131, and the Nursing Mothers Council, 2817 Carlson Circle, Palo Alto, Calif. 94306. Psychological studies done on breast-feeding and infant care can be found in Klaus and Kennell, *Maternal-infant bonding*, listed in the reference section.[11]

The infant's formula or breast milk will be the

Table 6-2. Introduction of solid foods*

3 weeks
Rice cereal: begin with 1 tablespoon of cereal and 1 tablespoon of formula (feed cereal with a baby spoon); increase quantity of cereal as baby needs it; feed it twice a day.
6 weeks
Barley, wheat, oats, etc.: 2 tablespoons twice a day
Fruit (apricots, applesauce, peaches, etc.): ¼ to ½ jar twice a day
2 months
Vegetables (squash, carrots, beets, etc.): ¼ to ½ jar twice a day (Do not give spinach.)
Fruits: ¼ to ½ jar twice a day
Cereals: 2 to 4 tablespoons twice a day
Juices: 2 to 4 ounces twice a day (Do not give orange juice.)
3 to 4 months
Vegetables, meats, cereals, fruits: three solid food meals per day
6 to 8 months
Eggs, meats, vegetables, table food (mashed), junior baby foods, orange juice
8 months
Begin teaching baby to feed self with spoon. Teach baby to drink out of glass.
15 to 18 months
Discontinue bottle feedings.

*From Instructions for the care of your new baby, Baton Rouge, La., 1977, Louisiana State University Pediatric Department, Earl K. Long Memorial Hospital.
NOTE: When starting a new food, give it by itself for 5 to 7 days before beginning another food. If a rash, diarrhea, spitting up, or vomiting occurs, discontinue that specific food and begin another one.

major source of nutrients in the early months of infancy. The formula composition is calculated on the basis of protein, calorie, and fluid needs, which are determined by the infant's body weight. As the infant grows, his stomach capacity increases, and he is able to take a larger amount of formula at each feeding. Supplements to the formula may include some ascorbic acid about the second to the fourth week of life to provide for bone and teeth formation. Some supplements of vitamin D may be needed. Of course, all of this should only be done at the recommendation of the physician. There is some question as to the proper time to begin feeding the infant cereal. Some physicians believe it should not begin before 6 months of age. Others recognize that spoon-feeding cereal to an infant requires learning a new eating technique and time is needed to adjust to it. Their recommendation is to introduce cereal at an early age so that by the time the infant has a need for iron (about the age of 6 months) he will be taking cereal well. Table 6-2 presents one approach to the introduction of solid foods to an infant.

NATURE AND ORIGINS OF PERSONALITY

The distinctness of a human being as a "person" includes the concept of an individual who performs both physiological and psychological functions. This individual, although unique, self-contained, and striving for goals, is also receptive to the world around him and is capable of having experiences. The physiological part of a person is readily observed and accepted. The psychological side is not as easily known or observable. Thus personality, which is basically psychological in nature, is difficult to ascertain with any degree of accuracy or ease.

Nature of personality

The term *personality* embodies two root ideas in definitions. First, it may refer to the outer distinguishing qualities or characteristics of the individual that can be observed by others. Second, personality may also refer to the inner being, which is made up of psychophysical systems and forces that are part of a dynamic intrapersonal organization. The inner self is usually considered to have conscious and unconscious elements of

being. Both outer and inner manifestations of personality must develop.

Many psychologists and psychiatrists believe that, in addition to the individual's organic systems, such as the cardiovascular, neuromuscular, haptic, cerebral, and endocrinal systems, a person also possesses a psyche system. The psyche is that part of a person that is the performer of psychological functions and activities. It is the mind, yet more than the mind—it is the personification of the life principle.

Most psychologists accept a schematization of the psyche, such as the one postulated by Freud and various psychoanalytical theorists. Some believe it neither necessary nor desirable to apply terms to psychological abstractions that are, for all intents and purposes, unknowable and possibly nonexistent. The authors of this text will make use of a schematization because they believe that by this approach the abstract concepts of personality development can be made more understandable.

Theories of personality development

There is no general theory of personality on which psychologists agree. This point alone should make a person careful as to how much stress they place on any one theory as the explanation of personality development. In other words, it would be unwise to proceed on the basis of a theory and to act as if it were fact. Too many wrong notions have been held and too many wrong decisions have been made because someone treated a theoretical concept as a truth.

In general, there are three major contemporary approaches to theories of personality development. These are (1) psychoanalytic theory and its modifications, (2) self-actualization theories, and (3) behavioral theories.

Psychoanalytic theory. Psychoanalytic theory, as developed by Sigmund Freud, was the first of the major contemporary theories on personality development. Although many of Freud's original thoughts have been modified or discarded, he is still highly regarded as the founder of psychoanalysis.[21] His basic principles and views are still strongly supported even though new interpretations or additions have been made by his followers.

Freud's theory includes a schematic representation of a personality structure that is to be developed by each individual. The structure is made up of three major systems—the id, the ego, and the superego. The id consists of all the physiological and psychological drives with which a person is born. It also contains all of the individual's experiences, feelings, and learned behavior. The id operates on the unconscious or subconscious level. The ego is the consciousness of the individual. It comes into existence for two reasons: (1) the individual becomes aware of forces in the environment and (2) behavioral responses must be found by which the individual can satisfy his needs by interacting with the environment. The third major system, the superego, consists of a conscience and an ego ideal. It does not come into being until the child learns to value certain behaviors or objects as being more desirable than others.

According to Freud, behavior is motivated by two basic urges: the life urge and the death urge. The life urge is what is usually emphasized in his theory. The life urge is the libido, the driving force initiating behavior that seeks physical or sensual pleasure through human contact. Psychosexual development is considered to be the genesis of personality development. The major phases of psychosexual development in personality occur in infancy, latency, and puberty. Normal adult personality results from the successful elaboration and expression of these phases. There are three major stages of infancy personality development. These are the oral, the anal, and the phallic stages.

The oral stage (birth to 12 to 18 months) is the period when the mouth is the principal region of dynamic activity. Most of the infant's pleasures during this period come through the mouth as food is eaten while the baby is being held. People with "oral personalities" are ones who were fixated during this period. They may derive much satisfaction from activities involving the mouth, such as kissing, smoking, nailbiting, drinking, or overeating. Fixation, a psychoanalytic term, means the stage or point when an attachment for someone or something develops and persists in an immature form in spite of further growth.

The anal stage (12 to 18 months to 3 years) is when the child derives great pleasure from the movement of his bowels. The manner in which toilet training is handled determines if fixation will occur at this stage. The anal personality may become obsessively clean and neat, obsessively precise and rigidly tied to routines, or defiantly messy. It depends on whether the total training process was too strict and demanding, too lenient and unconcerned, or normal. The key is how the child reacted to the training.

The phallic or early genital stage emerges about the ages of 3 or 4 years when the child becomes interested or conscious of the genital area. It is about the ages of 4 and 5 that the Oedipus complex period (for boys) and the Electra complex period (for girls) emerge. The boy and the girl lavish love and affection on the parent of the opposite sex, competing with the parent of the same sex for the love of the other parent. Conflicting feelings usually emerge during this period, according to the theory. There are feelings of genuine affection for one parent and rivalry and hostility for the other. How these conflicting feelings are resolved is supposed to affect the personality development of the individual. The latency and genital periods occur after infancy.

Other psychoanalytically oriented, post-Freudian psychologists are Alfred Adler, Carl Jung, Eric Erikson (whose theory we will present in the next chapter), Eric Fromm, Karen Horney, and Harry Stack Sullivan. Each makes a contribution to the psychoanalytical theory. You may want to look up their themes and note what differences they propose as compared to Freud.

Self-actualization or holistic theories. The holistic approach is not a systematic theory but more a way of looking at the developing individual as a totality and as what a human being can become. Personality is viewed as the central fact of development and the source of all unity in human behavior. The individual basically does not seek pleasure or the gratification of physical desires (although these are part of his makeup), but rather he seeks the satisfaction that comes from the attainment of wholeness and unity of self.

Abraham Maslow[23] stressed the growth and self-actualizing features of the personality. He conceived personality as the organized striving of a person to be himself. This striving is inhibited by forces of socialization and by needs of survival that are inherent within the physiological being. However, as an individual gains control over the environment to satisfy his basic needs, he is free to move up the hierarchy of values and needs to become the person or gain the potential that is ascribed to all human beings. The highest form of satisfaction, a peak experience, involves a sense of complete fulfillment.

Carl Rogers[24] speaks of self-realization and self-concept. He states that the self exists as it is perceived by the individual in his own perceptual view. The growth and development of the self are influenced by the values of the environment and the persons who constitute it as perceived by the individual. If other people indicate to you that they think you are "bright" or "good," you tend to incorporate into your self-concept the idea that is being expressed. In order to maintain a constant self-concept, we regulate our behavior to match what we perceive to be what we are. Experiences that threaten the self-image, however, may be totally ignored by the self. Rogers believes in the existence of an ideal self that represents the goals and aims of the individual.

Behavioral theories of development suggest that environmental experiences involving reinforcement factors strongly influence social learning.

David Strickler

The individual wants to attain this ideal self in order to become a "fully functioning person."

Behavioral theories. The behavioral approach to personality is based on the psychology of learning. Personality characteristics are learned in much the same manner that other things are learned. Behaviorists concentrate on the environment as a teaching arena. Learning comes as an individual responds to rewards and punishment actions resulting from his own behavior. Learning comes from either classical or operant conditioning situations. Personality is the structure that results from learned behavior.

Dollard and Miller[25] emphasize the role of drives and drive reduction in human behavior. They are interested in learned or acquired drives rather than innate drives. They concentrate on motivation and reinforcement. According to their theory, four childhood situations play a significant role in shaping personality. These are: (1) feeding, (2) cleanliness training, (3) early sex training, and (4) training in the control of anger and aggression. The feeding situation, for example, can be a setting where an infant finds satisfaction and pleasure in the presence of other people, or it can be a time of turmoil and tension if feeding is carried out in a detrimental fashion. Dollard and Miller use the principle of reinforcement to substitute for Freud's concept of the pleasure principle; they also use other principles of behavior modification to explain why a child adopts certain ideas and behavior for himself and rejects others. They relate to some psychoanalytical principles but have different explanations or interpretations than did Freud.

A classical behaviorist, such as B. F. Skinner,[26] does not make a major distinction between behavior and personality. An individual's personality consists of the responses he makes. There is no reference made to concepts such as motivation or drives. The behavior of an individual is made up of functionally unified sets of responses that differ from one situation to another. A person may act one way in front of his peers, another way in front of his parents, and another way in school. It can be said that the

Table 6-3. A comparison of basic concepts in four major approaches to personality*

	Freudian psychoanalytic	Post-Freudian	Self-actualization	Behavioral
Basic unit of study	Life history of individual (based on psychoanalytic interviews)	Life history of individual; emphasizes interpersonal relations	Perception of self	Responses to stimuli
Basic concepts	Unconscious	Inner mental processes	Unawareness, particularly of self	Unawareness; unlabeled behavior
	Libido	Biological needs (rejects libido concept of Freud)	Self-actualization (Maslow also refers to "hierarchy of needs")	Basic drives; also includes acquired drives
	Id	Instinctual aspects of personality	Individual's natural impulses	Principle of reinforcement
	Ego	Mechanisms of perception, memory, thinking; interaction of person with environment	Self	The individual's pattern of learned responses and learned ways of perceiving
	Superego	Acceptance of moral standards; formation of ideals	Guiding principles of conduct; usually conscious	One's moral code, acquired through learning

*From Silverman, R. E. *Psychology* (3rd ed.). Englewood Cliffs, N.J.: Prentice-Hall, 1978, p. 351.

personality "changes according to the specific stimulus context in which the behavior occurs." There is, according to this theory, more than one self.

A social learning theory that recognizes the role of cognition—such as perceiving, thinking, and expecting in the development of personality—is one developed by Rotter.[27] His theory is based on the concept of expectation and the perceived value of rewards. We learn to expect certain consequences as a result of what we do. Some of the consequences are positive; others are negative. They influence us by encouraging or limiting our behavior. The more often we experience positive results, the more likely it is that we will make the behavior that brought about the rewarding experience part of our regular behavior pattern. Whereas Rotter speaks of perceived consequences influencing our behavior, Bandura[28] states that people learn by observing others and that reinforcement helps to determine whether we will do what we have learned. Observation, according to Bandura, is the major factor in learning. In both approaches, however, social learning is involved.

Table 6-3 presents a summary of basic concepts in the major approaches to personality.

Emergence of personality structure

Newborn and very young infants are not considered to have a differentiated conscious awareness of self or even of existence. The stimuli of the external world will force themselves on the infant. As the maturing central nervous system, memory, and perceptual systems absorb and accumulate more and more of these experiences, an organized psychic structure called the ego, or self, is formed.

The ego is the conscious part of the psychic structure. The prime functions of the ego are the perception of reality and the learning to deal rationally and effectively with reality. Eventually, the tasks of the mature ego will include such processes as perception; adaptation to reality; use of the reality principle and the mechanism of anxiety to ensure safety and self-preservation; motor control; reason and making judgments; storing knowledge and solving problems; and overcoming the demands and discharges of the primitive, primary forces and impulses of the self by using the secondary psychic processes of judgment, logic, and intellect to regulate and control them.

The concepts of primary and secondary psychic processes are pertinent to this discussion. All children are born with certain basic, innate processes, drives, and demands that are necessary for self-maintenance and survival. These forces are universal in nature. Babies the world over have the same needs for food, water, air, sleep, comfortable temperature, release of bowel and bladder tension, rest, and avoidance of pain. In addition, they also have certain psychological needs such as those provided for by comfort con-

Table 6-4. Emerging physiological and behavioral characteristics and personality development

Age level	Characteristic phase	Main emphasis
0 to 14 months	Physiological stability	Vital life systems stabilize
	Motor development	Sitting, reaching, locomotion
	Physiological satisfaction	Oral and motor pleasures
15 to 30 months	Attention seeking	Calls attention to self
	Exploration and curiosity	Investigates surroundings
	Verbal imitation	Speech and language development
	Self-assertiveness	Exerts his will
31 to 48 months	Behavior imitation	Copies actions of others
	Suggestibility to feelings	Reflects attitudes and moods
	Identification prone	Personality identification
	Emerging self-ideal	Start of self-judgment

tact, assertiveness, curiosity, affection, and security. Whenever any of the biological or psychological needs is not fulfilled to a satisfactory degree (satisfactory for physical or mental survival), the infant will try in every way it can to make its survival wants known. The behavior pattern that he develops in making his wants known becomes identified as part of his personality. Table 6-4 is a summary.

For the first two years or so of life the primitive biological urges necessary for survival and development emerge. These urges are survival-reaction behavior, egocentric in nature and nonsocial. After the child has learned to do the first developmental tasks necessary for survival, the secondary psychic processes of value judgment and intellect begin to emerge and develop. They will seek to control the intense primitive impulses so that the child can become less egocentric. Development of the ego begins to take place as the cognitive system gains control over the primary forces and permits their expression only in keeping with socially acceptable behavior. The foundations of personality are being formed as the primary and secondary forces compromise and develop behavior patterns. The first two years are spent in permitting the primary psychic forces to express themselves so that these forces can provide survival drive for the child. Then for the next two years or so the secondary psychic processes seek to gain control by developing a behavior control pattern that comes to be recognized as part of the child's unique personality.

The ideas presented here on personality development are theoretical and should not be considered as proven fact. Some of these concepts are based on the modified psychoanalytical teachings of Hadfield,[29] a British child and consultant psychologist, who in turn based much of his thinking on the developmental concepts of Gesell. Hadfield suggested the sequence of personality development described on the following pages.

We believe a substantial part of an infant's personality is related to innate behavioral elements that emerge as part of the unfolding maturational process. These behaviors have physical, psychological, and social survival values. They are the foundation of personality growth. Uniqueness and deviations in personality come from differences in the way these behavioral expressions are treated by persons working with the child and by the artifacts and mentifacts of his environment.

During the first three or four years of life, there are certain behaviors exhibited by the child that appear to be found in children everywhere. These behaviors apparently are universal in the sense that they are part of nature's plan by which human beings mature. Although several types of behaviors can be noted at any one time, there does seem to be one behavior that is emphasized or at least predominates in influence at that period or phase.

The infant and the child, then, do go through phases. Furthermore, each phase has a special learning task, purpose, or function that needs to be accomplished during that phase. If the task is not learned, the demands of that task continue into the next phase and cause some confusion and conflicts. The environment, especially the one involving the parents and siblings, will have a great influence on the nature, direction, and type of personality that a baby develops by determining how well the developmental tasks are accomplished.

Physiological stability. Consider the newborn child. He is born in a state of helplessness. His only responses are reflexes and gross motor reactions. He needs care and help to survive. The first dominant characteristic behavior of the newborn is one of physiological stability and physical dependency. The infant is dependent on others for food, warmth, protection, and security. He is only interested in his own well-being and is so egocentric that he is not even aware at first of the fact that others are tending to him. His self-centered concern is shown during the first month by the fact that he sleeps for 60% of the time and dozes much of the rest of the time. He has a need to have close contact with his mother; he will snuggle close and wants to be nursed and cuddled. This contact gives him a sense of protection and security. He has a cry of distress, and he uses a clinging or embracing movement. This feeling of dependence never completely disappears. It does, however, later in life change its form from physical to psychic, to social dependency, and finally, to interdependency.

Control of body movements. Developing body and motor control is another dominant feature of the first year of life. At about the third month the infant will have sufficiently matured neurologically so that he can now coordinate some of his reflexes and movements; he now has some motor control. His control will start with his eyes, moving down the body from head to foot in sequential order, according to the cephalocaudal direction of growth principle. During the first year he will kick, twist, jerk his head, move his arms, and make many motions that appear to have no purpose. Actually, this period is one of physical preparedness. He is getting ready for the time when he will put his muscles to good use. The maturational process is at work. Motor development, in conjunction with perceptual development, is thought to provide a foundation for the development of the cognitive processes. Certainly personality development in some measure will be related to the ability to have adequate voluntary control of the body. As a person can move, so can he act. When he acts, he makes choices and decisions that reflect his personality pattern.

Physical satisfaction. During the latter half of the first year, the infant appears to be performing several motor actions for the fun he gets out of them. He derives pleasure from shaking things, touching things, and reaching for and trying to grasp objects. And, of course, anything that he can pick up he brings to his mouth, which has been his major source of pleasure. So many of his satisfactions and pleasures up to this time have come to him through his mouth; for instance, consider the number of times he has been fed during the first year alone. Thus it gives him pleasure to suck. He has pleasure in moving his limbs. He is thrilled with his accomplishments in learning to move about. During this phase, he is experiencing pleasure in physiological activities and bodily function. He seeks to enhance those activities that give him pleasure. The child who is permitted to find pleasure in these early physical activities by not being unduly restricted tends to develop a joyous attitude toward life. The happy child is a healthy child, and the healthy child will be a contented child.

Attention seeking. Once the child begins to walk or to get around fairly well, he is now ready to move out of his egocentric shell and take a more active interest in the world around him. He has had a year of protectiveness and close watching. But now he has accomplished some of the personal developmental tasks necessary for his survival, and he is ready to begin emphasizing some of the other primary innate behavioral responses that are necessary for his pursuit of living. He is ready to explore his environment, but he does not have the confidence to feel secure enough to move freely into the environment. So he seeks to call attention to himself to make sure others are watching out after him. This phase of self-display is often brought about because he is left alone in a room more frequently than before. The mother has got used to the baby, and she does have a "million" things to do around the house. The baby, however, wants to make sure that his mother is still near, so he calls out to her. He is reassured when he hears her voice answering. At this age of 12 to 14 months the baby does enjoy being the center of attention. Everybody loves a baby who is socially responsive. The baby of this age can jibber-jabber, wave bye-bye, play peek-a-boo, and enjoy having someone play "this little piggy went to market" with his toes. He is developing social contacts, and he is discovering what behavior pleases people. All of this attention, plus the recognition that his mother is still around even when he cannot see her, helps the infant move from the strong need for direct care and protection of the first year to a freedom to explore in the second year.

Exploration and curiosity. As the baby feels more secure, he begins to use his facilities for moving around. He is now making use of his innate curiosity, exploring at first close to his mother, then allowing himself to move further away. He learns to discriminate between the various objects that he examines. Soon he is going by himself into other rooms and getting into things. This is about the time the baby discovers the bottom cabinets and drawers in the kitchen where his mother keeps her pots and pans. Sooner or later he wants to see what his mother keeps in these cabinets, and so he takes out all the pots and pans and puts them in the middle of the kitchen floor. Soon he wonders how his mother got all of those pots and pans into that

His whole picture of his father's world—the world in which his father moved—as he built it in his brain with all the naive but passionate intensity of childhood was not unlike a Currier and Ives drawing, except that here the canvas was more crowded and the scale more large. It was a world that was drawn in very bright and very innocent and very thrilling colors.

Thomas Wolfe
The Web and the Rock

small cabinet. When she tries to get all of them back into the cabinet, she wonders the same thing! Most parents can recall some similar experience that their child had at this phase of life.

Verbal imitation. Since speech and language are the major adaptive behaviors that are being emphasized during the second year, it is only natural that the innate capacity of imitation should emerge about this time. Imitation, like the reflexes, enables an infant to acquire adaptations to life for which there are no innate or hereditary responses.[25] One of the most valuable acquisitions gained by imitation is speech and language. With speech the child takes a major step in the direction of personal independency and adaptation to life. Verbal communication not only permits the child to make his needs known more readily but it also will serve as a mediator for his thought processes. Thinking usually involves the use of words. Thus the greater the comprehension vocabulary that a child has, the further afield he can go by way of his cognitive processes. As the baby imitates his mother or father, direct learning takes place in behavior, attitudes, and the social graces in addition to language.

Self-assertiveness. By the age of 2 or 2½ years

"TIME-OUT"

It was at this point that we began to notice Sammy's fascination with the knobs and dials on the television set. We felt that the television should be off limits to Sam. We began the discipline process. At first we said in a stern tone of voice: "No, Sammy, you may not touch that!" He persisted, so we picked him up and put him in a different location in the living room. He crawled back over to the television set immediately. Our next step was to say "NO" and give him a paddling. Soon he became immune to the paddling. He would cry and become upset for a few minutes, and then crawl right back to the set.

About this time my husband was taking a class in behavior modification, so we discussed using this technique on Sammy. We decided to institute a "time-out" procedure. One of the few things which Sammy disliked was to be confined and held when there was so much to explore. He would start crying to indicate to us that he had been held long enough and wanted to get down and explore. We decided that each time he touched the television set we would hold him for two minutes or until he stopped crying. The first day he was held about eight times. He looked surprised the first time we initiated our plan. He then began to cry and squirm, trying to get away. He looked confused about the silence on our part. There were no angry words or spankings, just neutral silence. During subsequent holdings he would cry very hard and push our hands, trying to force them open. After the first few times, he gave up the struggling but continued to cry. The second day he touched the television set only four times. The next two days he tried to get the knobs twice a day. The following three days he only attempted his feat once a day. For the next few weeks it was necessary only to hold him once a week. Then about once a month he would test us to see if we were still emphatic about his boundary. We continued to enforce it.

We were happy that our system of "time-out" had worked. It was due to the conscious effort on our part and to the fact that it was consistently enforced, regardless of the inconvenience to us. This was perhaps one of the most efficient and effective ways for extinguishing a particular behavior that we had tried.

the toddler has learned to do the developmental tasks that are basically required of him to survive. He can eat solid food; he can communicate; he can comprehend verbal responses; he can walk and make coordinated movements of all sorts; and he can generally exercise some control of his bodily processes. The primary processes that nature has given him to help him with self-maintenance and self-preservation have served him well. What else is left for him to do but seek to assert his will upon the world? Assertiveness and aggressiveness become the characteristic behavior of this age. The time of the "terrible twos" and temper tantrums has arrived for most children.

As the child pushes to make his wants known, he is not trying to be a "bad" child. He is only emphasizing a concept and behavior pattern that he has learned in the first two years of life. Right or wrong, he has come to believe that the "world revolves around him," and he can pretty much have what he wants. During his first year of life, any time that he ever needed or wanted anything someone provided it for him. The pattern did not change much during the second year. Whenever he wanted anything, he simply cried or asked for it. Sometimes he had to be persistent, but he usually got what he wanted.

However, his parents have now reached the point where they have decided that their child must learn that he cannot always have what he asks for, and certainly he must learn that the crying "has got to stop"! Unfortunately, the parents do not fully realize just how embedded the baby's idea is of how he is supposed to let his parents know when he wants something. He has always cried or made some kind of fuss when he wanted something. This was standard procedure. All of a sudden this approach no longer works because his parents have decided to put a stop to it, but the baby does not know how else he can make his needs known. So he intensifies his crying and fussing. He may even begin to bang his head on the floor or hold his breath until he turns blue to let his parents know how desperately he wants something. He does not realize, as yet, that he is going to have to curb his primary "pleasure-seeking" impulses and that his wishes are not "commands." He will continue his tem-

per-tantrum behavior until he realizes that this approach no longer works. It is at this point that the child is ready to seek new ways of getting what he wants.

Temper tantrums can be considered as ways by which a child is practicing asserting himself. In life there are times when a person must be assertive for his own good. However, one cannot or should not be assertive in all situations. The give and take of social interaction and of compromise must also be learned. Parents can help a child who is having a temper tantrum by diverting his attention from what he is crying about to something else that is interesting, such as looking out a window, or introducing a new object, toy, or idea. The golden rules for the parent are calmness, fairness, firmness, and consistency. A quiet firmness on the part of the parent may enable the child to be quiet and firm with himself. An occasional smack on the bottom is acceptable if it says, "that's enough of that—it's time for you to learn that there are better ways of asking for what you want and also to realize that no one can ever get everything he asks for." In the meanwhile the child should be encouraged to learn more acceptable behavior patterns and control. The parents should set good examples by their actions and attitudes. The child will learn by imitation and identification. The secondary psychic processes are now ready to be developed.

STUDY GUIDE

1. Study Table 6-1. Consider the relationship between language development and speech development.
2. What are the identifying characteristics of the five stages of speech development?
3. According to Piaget, what is the difference between egocentric speech and socialized speech?
4. In terms of emotions and emotional behavior, what are the four points that most psychologists accept as being true?
5. Discuss the implications of Harlow's studies with monkeys for the rearing of infants.
6. Trace social development in infants by citing the types of social behavior manifested at different age levels.
7. Toilet training is said by many psychologists

to have an effect on the child's developing personality characteristics. According to these psychologists, how are toilet training and various aspects of behavior related?

8. What are the two basic categories or root ideas used in defining the term *personality?*

9. Discuss the nature of the ego, or the self, and its relationship to innate, primary psychic processes.

10. What is the main thrust, direction, or purpose of personality development during the first two years?

11. Study Table 6-3 on the theories of personality.

12. Review the phases of personality development as presented in Table 6-4.

REFERENCES

1. McClinton, B. S., & Meier, B. G. *Beginnings: psychology of early childhood.* St. Louis: The C. V. Mosby Co., 1978.

2. Lenneberg, E. H. *Biological functions of language.* New York: John Wiley & Sons, Inc., 1967.

3. Benedict, H. *The role of repetition in early language comprehension.* Paper presented at the annual meeting of the Society for Research in Child Development, Denver, 1975.

4. Strain, B., & Vietze, P. *Early dialogues: the structure of reciprocal infant-mothers vocalization.* Paper presented at the annual meeting of the Society for Research in Child Development, Denver, 1975.

5. Tulkin, S., & Kagan, J. Mother-child interaction in the first year of life. *Child Development,* 1972, **43,** 31-41.

6. Heber, R. The Milwaukee project: early intervention as a technique to prevent mental retardation. Report of second annual Vermont Conference on the Primary Prevention of Psychopathology. *APA Monitor,* September/October, 1976.

7. Munsinger, H. *Fundamentals of child development* (2nd ed.). New York: Holt, Rinehart & Winston, 1975.

8. Coleman, J. S., et al. Equality of educational opportunity. Washington, D. C.: Office of Health, Education & Welfare, 1966.

9. Piaget, J. *Language and thought of the child.* London: Routledge & Kegan Pual, Ltd., 1952.

10. Gesell, A. L., Ilg, F. L., Aimes, L. B., & Rodell, J. L. *Infant and child in the culture of today: the guidance of development in home and nursery school* (Rev. ed.). New York: Harper & Row, Publishers, Inc., 1974.

11. Klaus, M. H., & Kennell, J. H. *Maternal-infant bonding.* St. Louis: The C. V. Mosby Co., 1976.

12. Harlow, H. F. *Learning to love.* San Francisco: Albion Publishing Co., 1971.

13. Bridges, K. M. B. Emotional development in early infancy. *Child Development,* 1932, **3,** 324-241.

14. Morgan, G. A., & Ricciuti, H. N. Infants' responses to strangers during the first year. In L. J. Stone, H. T. Smith, & L. B. Murphy (Eds.) *The competent infant, research and commentary.* New York: Basic Books, Inc., Publishers, 1973.

15. Spock, B. *Baby and child care.* New York: Pocket Books, 1976.

16. Le Vine, R. A. Parental goals: a cross-cultural view. *Teachers College Record,* 1974, **76,** 226-289.

17. Langman, L. *Economic practices and socialization in three societies.* Paper presented at the American Sociological Association meeting, New York, 1973.

18. Liebert, R. M., Poulos, R. W., & Marmor, G. S. *Developmental psychology* (1st ed.). Englewood Cliffs, N.J.: Prentice-Hall, Inc., 1977.

19. Latham, H. C., Heckel, R. V., Herbert, L. J., & Bennett, E. *Pediatric nursing* (3rd ed.). St. Louis: The C. V. Mosby Co., 1977.

20. Jensen, M. D., Benson, R. C., & Bobak, I. M. *Maternity care: the nurse and the family.* St. Louis: The C. V. Mosby Co., 1977.

21. Freud, S. *A general introduction to psychoanalysis* (J. Reviere Trans.). New York: Permabooks, 1953.

22. Lewin, K. *Dynamic theory of personality* (Adams, D. K. and Zener, K., Trans.). New York: McGraw-Hill Book Co., 1935.

23. Maslow, A. H. *Motivation and personality.* New York: Harper & Row, Publishers, Inc., 1954.

24. Rogers, C. R. The concept of the fully functioning person. *Psychotherapy,* 1963, **1,** 17-26.

25. Dollard, J., & Miller, N. E. *Personality and psychotherapy: an analysis in terms of learning, thinking and culture.* New York: McGraw-Hill Book Co., 1950.

26. Skinner, B. F. *Science and human behavior.* New York: The Free Press, 1953.

27. Rotter, J. B. Generalized expectancies for internal versus external control of reinforcement. *Psychological Monographs,* 1966, **80** (1, whole No. 609).

28. Bandura, A. *Aggression: a social learning analysis.* Englewood Cliffs, N.J.: Prentice-Hall, Inc., 1973.

29. Hadfield, J. A. *Childhood and adolescence.* Baltimore: Penguin Books, 1962.

<table>
<tr>
<td>

```
┌─────────┐
│         │
│    7    │
│         │
└─────────┘
```

</td>
<td>

Early childhood

3 to 5 years of age

</td>
</tr>
</table>

IMAGINE THAT

To me, the imagination of a three-and-a-half-year-old boy is limitless. I have a son, Nino, who never ceases to amaze me with his imagination. At about the age of twenty-eight months, Nino was able to talk, using sentences with four to seven words. This was the time when his imagination began to blossom. At first he would carry on conversations between two of his trucks with which he usually played. Sometimes he would have the trucks talking, and sometimes the people who were supposed to be inside the cab talked.

As he grew older, he began to talk to all types of objects as if they were alive. Whenever we would go for a ride out in the country, he would say: "Hi, Mr. Cow." "Hi, Mr. Corn." "What are you doing, Mr. Silo?" The other day my wife bought some blueberries. She gave Nino a few of them to eat. He took one look at them and came running over to me, excitedly shouting: "Look, Daddy, Mr. Blueberry only has one eye. Can't he see?" I told him that Mr. Blueberry doesn't have to see because he just grows big so people can put him in a pie to eat. Nino accepted this explanation but examined each blueberry carefully before putting it into his mouth.

There is also an imaginary friend, a bug, with which he plays. He keeps him in his pocket and takes him out only to pet him, talk to him, or put him in his mouth. I am allowed to pet the bug only if I promise not to eat it.

All of the above experiences are not really out of the ordinary. However, he told me something a few weeks ago that really surprised me. He said he was going to build four buttons on the floor: when he would push a certain one, he would grow big; push another one and I would grow little; push a third one, and Maria, our second child, would grow big; push the last one and Mommy would grow little. I asked him how he was going to make the buttons and he said: "I will go to school with you and learn!"

In early childhood children are complex individuals with important tasks to accomplish. Developmentally, they are about to begin the steepest ascent of their lives. Between the ages of 2½ and 5 years children will be transformed from babies who are just beginning to be aware of the concrete world around them to individuals who are ready to delve into the abstract world of books. Life at this age moves extremely rapidly. Many significant events and achievements take place. The adult of the future is truly being formed.

Infants of the first two years matured and enhanced their physical selves to accomplish the

165

developmental tasks for their age. Preschool children will need to make a more solid contact with the world of people and objects to accomplish their goals. Basically, most of the developmental tasks of early childhood are extensions of tasks that were being learned in infancy. Certain tasks must now be developed to a higher level of proficiency or sophistication. Some new tasks will be added. Life is a combination of continuity and change.

Developmental tasks emphasized during early childhood include the following: (1) achieving integrated motor and perceptual control; (2) completing control of the elimination of bodily wastes; (3) achieving physiological stability; (4) improving ability to communicate and to comprehend what others say; (5) achieving independence in self-care areas such as eating, dressing, and bathing; (6) learning sex differences and sexual modesty; (7) forming simple concepts of social and physical reality and learning how to behave toward persons and things; (8) learning to relate oneself emotionally to parents, siblings, and other people; and (9) learning to distinguish right and wrong and developing a conscience (value judgment system).

PHYSICAL CHARACTERISTICS AND MOTOR SKILLS

Stages of physical maturational development always follow a particular order. Children do not stand before they sit, nor can they draw a square before they can draw a circle. However, this orderly progression of events moves forward at different rates of speed, some children growing and developing at a faster rate than others.

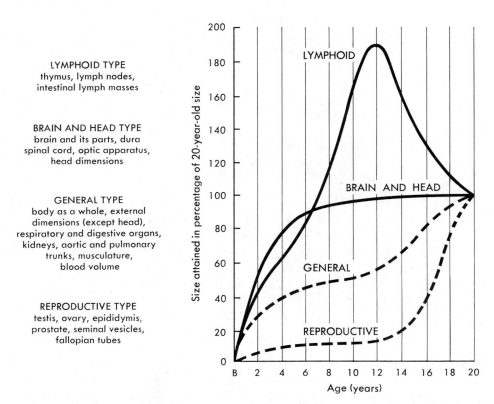

Fig. 7-1. Growth curves of different parts and tissues of the body, showing the four chief types. All curves are of size attained and plotted to that size at age 20, which is 100 on the vertical scale. (From Scammon, R. E. In J. A. Harris et al. *The measurement of man.* Minneapolis: University of Minnesota Press, 1930.)

Therefore some 3-year-olds may be able to do some tasks normally expected of 5-year-olds, and some 5-year-olds can do only the tasks usually expected of 3-year-olds. There is a wide range of individual differences, and each child must be treated as a unique person. It is established, however, that girls pass through the periods of development more rapidly than boys. Adults, as well as the children themselves, should realize that many different patterns of growth are normal.

The plan of physical growth is so well coordinated that the successful emergence and development of each stage is dependent on the level of mastery attained on the previous stage. The growth rates of four major types of organs and tissues, however, do change. General body tissue, including most of the internal organs, muscles, and bones, grows rapidly during the first two years of life. After the third birthday body growth increases at a slow but steady pace until the age of puberty, when a growth spurt takes place. Neural development takes place so rapidly in the early years that by the age of 2 years, neurological development is 60% complete, and by the age of 6 years the brain is close to 90% complete. Nature has provided for this rapid neural growth because it is so important and fundamental to all other aspects of growth. Genital development, however, is slow because reproductive organs need not be functional until after puberty (Fig. 7-1).

Lymphoid development is interesting. It has the second most rapid rate of growth. By the age of 4 years it is 60% complete; by the age of 8 years it is 90% complete. Note the rapid increase in the next three years to a peak, at the age of 11 years, of 195% of what will be total development of the lymphoid masses at maturity. Lymphoid masses fight infections and help ward off illnesses. As compared to any other age level, fewer 11-year-olds die of diseases, and more 11-year-olds die from accidents.

Physical characteristics

The average increase in weight during the second and third years is from 3 to 5 pounds annually. The typical 2-year-old weighs between 25 and 28 pounds. The 3-year-old weighs 3 to 5

pounds more. The average 4-year-old weighs about 36 pounds, and the 5-year-old about 41 pounds. There is no significant difference in weight between boys and girls, although boys do tend to be slightly heavier.[1] The height for a 2-year-old is, on the average, approximately 32 to 36 inches. For a 3-year-old the average height is about 3 inches more. At the age of 4 years the child is about 40 inches tall, and at 5 years the average height is 43 inches. The child's stature at the age of 5 years is a moderately good predictor of his adult height, since the correlation between heights at these two ages is close to .70.

One major change that all children go through is the "lengthening out" process, during which the child's build changes from a baby look to a proportioned "little adult" look. He gradually becomes slimmer, taller, and more solid looking. The protruding abdomen flattens, and the shoulders become broader. These changes in baby proportions are due mainly to an increase in the length of the legs. By the second year the length of the arms and legs has increased 60% to 75% from what they were at birth. The lower part of the head still appears small and underdeveloped, but this appearance is due to the smallness of the baby teeth. However, the set of temporary teeth is generally complete, and the child is equipped to eat solid foods. During early childhood, eyes look oversized. Because of the shape and developmental status of the eyes, most young children are farsighted.

Up to the age of 4 years, growth in the muscular system is roughly proportional to the growth of the body as a whole. Thereafter the muscles develop at a faster pace. During the fifth year, 75% of the child's weight can be attributed to muscular development.[2] Throughout this period the larger muscles remain better developed than the small fine muscles. For this reason the young child is more skillful in activities involving large movements than in those involving fine coordination.

Motor characteristics

Because of their limited physical development, 2-year-olds are still geared to gross motor activity. They like to run and romp, but their coordination is still slow in improving. Their fine

Text continued on p. 174.

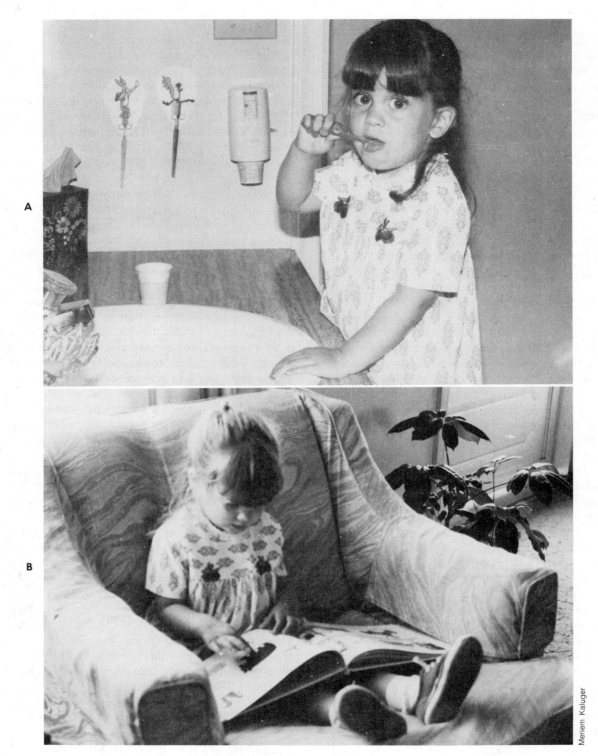

Early childhood at 3 years. A, Can brush teeth and wash hands. **B,** Enjoys hearing stories and looking at picture books.

Meriem Kaluger

Early childhood at 3 years. C, Can use blunt end scissors to cut paper. **D,** Can get drink of water unassisted.

Meriem Kaluger

Early childhood at 4 years. A, Enjoys playing in the sand. **B,** Begins to control crayon for coloring.

Meriem Kaluger

Early childhood at 4 years. C, Can hop on one foot. **D,** Has increased gross motor control.

Meriem Kaluger

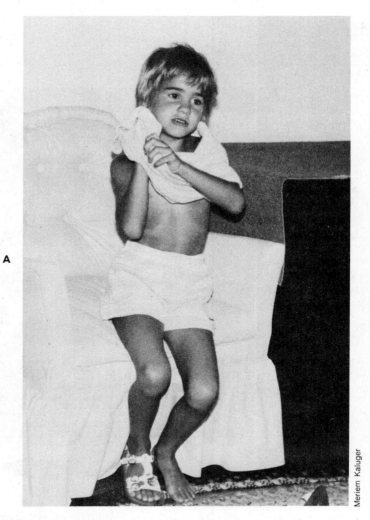

Meriem Kaluger

Early childhood at 5 years. A, Dresses and undresses with minimum help.

Early childhood at 5 years. B, Enjoys sharing in group activities.

motor control is not much better. Two-and-a-half-year-olds are at the crossroads stage in the growth of their action system. Their capacity for determining the proper amount of muscle control to use in a certain action is poor because their nerve cell organization is still immature and incompletely developed. This limitation shows itself in such actions as grasping and releasing. They tend to grasp too strongly and to release with overextension. They have not learned to let go. Limitations of their action system account for their inability to modulate their behavior.

By the time children are 3 years old they have much more motor control. They are more sure on their feet, walk erect, and can stand on one foot. They can go upstairs alternating feet. Their whole motor set is more evenly balanced, and they no longer walk with arms outstretched but, rather, swing them in an alternating pattern somewhat like adults. They like to hurry up and down stairs, but they also enjoy sedentary pastimes that involve finer motor coordination. They can build a block tower of nine or ten blocks. Three-year-olds now have an eye for form, which suggests that the small muscles which operate their eyes are more facile than they were before. This is also the year when sphincter muscles of bladder and bowel come under rather complete voluntary control.

Four-year-olds are able to run smoothly and quickly with confidence. They can swerve to avoid obstacles and turn corners at an angle. They can gallop, but not well. They can steer their tricycle at full speed. The art of learning to catch a ball is gradually developing, and they can now throw the ball overhand. Their eye-hand coordination, which involves the smaller muscles, is developing. They can now pour water from one container to another without spilling it. They can wash their hands and face, brush their teeth (fairly well), dress themselves, button their front buttons, and comb their hair. Although they will work at it, tying their shoelaces is still a difficult task.[3]

Four-year-olds draw objects with few details. They enjoy painting, but they shift their ideas frequently. Their designs and letters are crude. They enjoy having their name put on their drawings. They like to copy their name but usually copy only the first few letters, making marks for the rest of the letters in their name. They attempt to use scissors and can cut a crude straight line.

Five-year-olds are more agile than the 4-year-olds and in greater control of their bodily activities. They are closely knit. Their arms are held near their bodies. Their stance is more narrow. They still have more control over their large muscles than over their small ones. They are beginning to use their hands more in catching a ball, but they still have some trouble catching it. Their

Table 7-1. Schematic sequence of major forms of handedness*

Age zone	Handedness
16 to 20 weeks	Contact unilateral and, in general, tends to be with left hand
24 weeks	Definite shift to bilaterality
28 weeks	Shift to unilaterality; most often right hand is used
32 weeks	Shift again to bilaterality
36 weeks	Bilaterality dropping out; unilaterality coming in; behavior usually characterized "right or left"; left predominates in majority
40 to 44 weeks	Same type of behavior, unilateral, "right or left," but now right predominates in majority
48 weeks	In some a temporary and in many a last shift to use of left hand (as well as use of right), either used unilaterally
52 to 56 weeks	Shift to clear unilateral dominance of right hand
80 weeks	Shift from rather clearcut unilateral behavior to considerable interchangeable confusion; much bilaterality and use of nondominant hand
2 years	Relatively clearcut unilateral use of right hand
2½ to 3½ years	Significant shift to bilaterality
4 years	Unilateral, right-handed behavior predominates

*Modified from Gesell, A., & Ames, L. B. The development of handedness. *Journal of Genetic Psychology*, 1947, **70**, 155-175.

alternating mechanism is put to practice in much of their behavior. They alternate their feet when descending stairs, they can usually skip, and they will try to jump rope. They can march to music with good rhythm. They will experiment with roller skates and perhaps stilts, although they cannot sustain a performance for long. Five-year-olds are active children but without the restlessness that they may have at the age of 4 years. They play in one location for longer periods of time. They respond to their growth needs by en-joying games in which there is plenty of action. Their activity has definite direction.

Handedness is usually established at 4 years of age (Table 7-1); 5-year-olds can identify the hand that they want to use for writing. Their initial approach is with the dominant hand, and they do not transfer the pencil or crayon to the free hand. The hand and eye do not yet work with complete coordination. They may still have difficulty when they try to reach for things beyond arm's length and may sometimes spill or knock them over.

Table 7-2. Clinical signs of nutritional status

	Good	Poor
General appearance	Alert, responsive	Listless, apathetic, cachexic
Hair	Shiny, lustrous; healthy scalp	Stringy, dull, brittle, dry, depigmented
Neck (glands)	No enlargement	Thyroid enlarged
Skin (face and neck)	Smooth, slightly moist; good color, reddish pink mucous membranes	Greasy, discolored, scaly
Eyes	Bright, clear; no fatigue circles beneath	Dryness, signs of infection, increased vascularity, glassiness, thickened conjunctiva
Lips	Good color, moist	Dry, scaly, swollen; angular lesions (stomatitis)
Tongue	Good pink color, surface papillae present, no lesions	Papillary atrophy, smooth appearance; swollen, red, beefy (glossitis)
Gums	Good pink color; no swelling or bleeding, firm	Marginal redness or swelling, receding, spongy
Teeth	Straight, no crowding, well-shaped jaw, clean, no discoloration	Unfilled caries, absent teeth, worn surfaces, mottled, malposition
Skin (general)	Smooth, slightly moist, good color	Rough, dry, scaly, pale, pigmented, irritated, petechiae, bruises
Abdomen	Flat	Swollen
Legs, feet	No tenderness, weakness, or swelling; good color	Edema, tender calf, tingling, weakness
Skeleton	No malformations	Bowlegs, knock-knees, chest deformity at diaphragm, beaded ribs, prominent scapulae
Weight	Normal for height, age, body build	Overweight or underweight
Posture	Erect, arms and legs straight, abdomen in, chest out	Sagging shoulders, sunken chest, humped back
Muscles	Well developed, firm	Flaccid, poor tone; undeveloped, tender
Nervous control	Good attention span for age; does not cry easily, not irritable or restless	Inattentive, irritable
Gastrointestinal function	Good appetite and digestion; normal, regular elimination	Anorexia, indigestion, constipation, or diarrhea
General vitality	Endurance, energetic, sleeps well at night; vigorous	Easily fatigued, no energy, falls asleep in school, looks tired, apathetic

From Williams, S. R. *Nutrition and diet therapy* (3rd ed.). St. Louis: The C. V. Mosby Co., 1977, p. 393.

The drawings of preschoolers may consist only of a series of lines or curves, but this development is the beginning of control for handwriting.

For children to develop normally they must have adequate nutrition, exercise, rest, and sleep. Children inherit their potential for growth from their parents and grandparents, but environmental factors such as physical care, nutritional adequacy, and parents' attitude toward health and safety have a great bearing on the physical growth of the children. Children who are undernourished and lack good sleeping habits are low in energy and will not be mentally alert. Four- or 5-year-olds cannot develop their physical being and motor skills to their fullest potential if they are the victims of poor health.

PERCEPTUAL-MOTOR PROCESSES FOR LEARNING

What happens internally when children are learning to learn? Something has to occur in the neurological processes because it is only there that any kind of cognitive consciousness can take place. As the advertisement used to say, "If it hasn't got it there, it hasn't got it." Young infants are busy maturing their motor areas so they can begin to make coordinated movements that will enhance their survival level. Soon their sensory systems combine with the motor systems to develop the perceptual-motor processes. Eventually children reach a point when they must develop their skills for learning so that they can make better use of their potential intellect.

Although they are born with all the brain cells and nerves that they will ever have, they are not born with an innate, ready-made neurological organization that will automatically begin to "learn" when the time is right. It is true that infants can be "taught" through the use of conditioning techniques and also that they make use of their capacity for imitation and identification to pick up new skills and attitudes. But when it comes to problem-solving ability and cognitive learning, a neurological organization of some type must be developed if children are to attain a high level of functional effectiveness and efficiency in the use of the intellectual processes.

Fig. 7-2 is a representation of the brain and some of its known functional areas and of a schematic representation of the perceptual-conceptual process (PCP). The intent is to coordinate brain functions with the way in which perception takes place. A review of Fig. 2-5 in Chapter 2 will help to illustrate the details of the learning process.

First of all, note that there are circled numbers in the drawing. These represent the four sequences in the perceptual-conceptual process. The smaller numbers in the brain are referred to as Brodmann's areas. They serve as a guide or a map to sites in the brain. The numbers are used universally by neurologists and psychologists to specify locations in the brain. When a researcher identifies a certain portion of the brain as performing a function, the area is usually indicated by numbers. For example, areas 17, 18, and 19 have visual functions; areas 37, 39, 41, and 42 collectively have to do with verbal understanding and reading. Broca's area deals with speech formulation, while area 44 is involved in the motor production of speech. Thought association, reasoning, and idea formation usually take place in the front of the brain in areas 9, 10, and 11. Damage to any of the areas of the brain cited in these examples would affect the intended function(s) of that area.

Rationale

We believe that the perceptual-motor processes must be adequately developed if children are to be able to learn to read, work with symbols, or develop abstract concepts. The only means by which individuals can pick up information from their environment is through their senses (the receptors). The more abstract, intricate, and complex the stimuli, the more efficient must the perceptual processes be in order to perceive complicated stimuli, discriminate differences, and attach meanings to them. The work of developmental specialists and neurologists such as Gesell,[4] Piaget,[5] Penfield and Roberts,[6] Hebb,[7] and Smith and Henry[8] leaves little doubt concerning the importance of combined perceptual and motor experiences in developing a neurological (mental) structure, organization, or pattern (whatever you wish to call it) that can learn, retain, recall, and respond.

It is our theoretical point of view that the basic neural system for learning consists of (1) a pattern of reflexes, including primitive motor, visual, auditory, vocal, and kinesthetic reflexes;

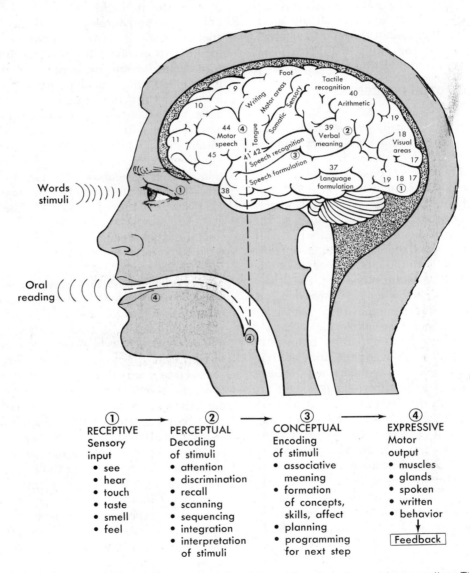

Fig. 7-2. The perceptual pattern for receiving, interpreting, learning, and responding. The drawing illustrates the processes and neural areas involved in oral reading: *1*, receives stimuli and transmits to visual area; *2* and *3*, interpret and prepare responses; *4*, produces the responses.

(2) a motor response capability, including a postural weight-shift mechanism that provides symmetry and balance; (3) a memory endowment to retain and recall bits of information learned; and (4) after a period of maturation, the ability to imitate certain behavior.

Infants are bombarded by stimuli from the world around them. To keep young brains from becoming overloaded nature helps them shut out many of these stimuli by making it possible for them to receive and perceive only the grossest of them. As they become more capable of handling these stimuli (by maturational development and experience), they become aware of finer, more precise stimuli. Soon they are able to reach out into the world of stimuli and select those that are of more significance to themselves. To do this, however, they will need to develop their perceptual processes.

According to Kaluger and Kolson,[9] there are four adaptive processes related to the perceptual pattern for learning that are developing within children during the first six years of life that are germane to this topic. Although all four processes are operating and developing at the same time, they differ as to the degree to which they are emphasized at any age level. These developmental processes related to the perceptual pattern for learning are (1) gross sensorimotor processes, (2) auditory-verbal development, (3) visual perception and fine visual-motor coordination, and (4) the cognitive processes.

Motor and perceptual processes (Table 7-3)

Of all the processes the gross sensorimotor processes receive the most developmental emphasis during the first two years of life. Infants first learn to control their eyes, then to hold their heads in the midline position. The sequential maturation process of motor development soon has them sitting up, reaching out, and grasping as prehension develops. After creeping and crawling infants are walking. These are the more obvious gross perceptual-motor tasks learned.

In a more subtle way infants are actually developing a motor pattern that will enable them eventually to control and to work better with incoming stimuli. The goal of motor development is not only to learn to use all the muscles in a coordinated fashion but also to form a balanced, stable base or body platform; from this base children can perceptually receive stimuli in such a way that they can depend on their accurately perceiving the stimulus as it actually is. What is needed is perceptual constancy and certainty in terms of the perceptual input of symbols. They should reach a point where they can count on their perceptual system telling them every time they look at a "b" that it is a "b" and not a "d," "p," or "q."

If children are to accurately receive and organize information from the world about them, they themselves must be organized or structured internally. Evidence of this internal structure is noted when children can perform integrated motor movements and retain their postural balance in so doing.[10] This ability level may not be reached until the children are 5 years old. Constancy (accurate perception) of sensory input is needed if children are to build an apperceptive mass and mental content that has any degree of efficiency and certainty of its accuracy. In addition, an accurate perceptual-motor match is needed to be able to do the motor movement that they perceptually realize they should do; for example, they should be able to control the movement of their hands and fingers to copy a design accurately with a pencil.

Refer to the two columns to the right in Table 7-3. It is our belief that basic body symmetry in terms of postural control is usually acquired by the age of 6 months. Symmetry and postural weight-shift balance are fundamental to developing an adequate motor base on which perceptual input and information can be structured.

Postural weight shift balance means being able to move the body to one side, out of symmetry, and still maintain a balance. For example, 6-month-old infants lying on their stomach should be able to raise the upper part of their body and support it on one hand, while reaching for an object with the other hand. Another example, for older children, is being able to stand on one foot for several seconds.

Laterality refers to the neurologically preferred sidedness, such as being right handed, right footed, and right eyed. It is an internal preference of handedness, footedness, and eyedness

Table 7-3. Theoretical concept of development of motor and perceptual processes and relationship to each other

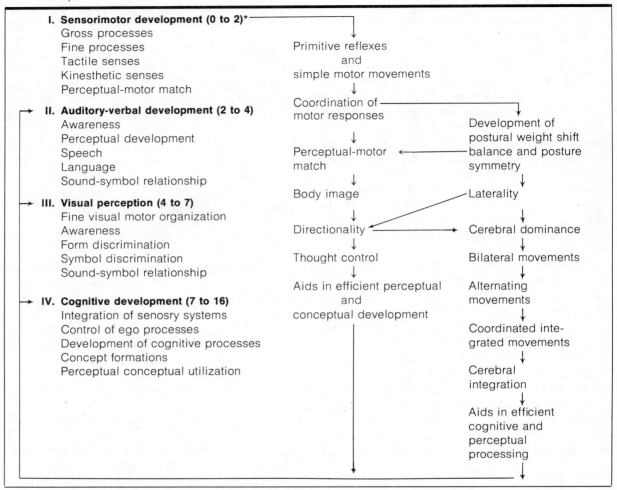

*Numbers refer to mental ages (in years) when development has priority. Left column presents the major process being emphasized for development in each age span. The two columns to the right are interrelated. They show the details of sensorimotor development and how ego control and cerebral integration are cognate to the efficient development of auditory-verbal, visual, and cognitive processes. The two columns to the right indicate progression, but they do not match the age levels indicated in the first column.

and not merely a knowledge of "rights" and "lefts." It entails the preferential use of one side of the body in tasks demanding the use of only one hand, one foot, or one eye. This type of sidedness is thought to be conducive to establishing cerebral dominance, which, in turn, is thought to be needed for an efficient processing of the neural structures related to cognition.

Directionality, or left-right orientation ability, is an inner awareness of outer directional move-

ments and locations in space. It is also the ease with which the individual can project the conscious self into space, relating to rights and lefts and other directional verbalisms. It includes the ability to be able to move one's self in the appropriate direction. For example, it is necessary to develop directionality to keep from reading such words as *was, on,* and *but* backward and saying *saw, no,* and *tub.*

Body image, the identification of size, shape,

Harold Geyer

Sensory stimulation—the seeing, hearing, smelling, tasting, touching, and handling of things—is needed for the preschooler to develop intellectual growth and to encourage intellectual curiosity.

and parts of the body, comes about the age of 2½ years. Laterality continues to develop during the next three years so that handedness is usually well established in a 4-year-old. Directionality stems from good laterality, maturing and increasing in sophisticated use as laterality also matures. Children 6 years of age should be able to tell their left and right sides of the body. Seven-year-olds should be able to cross the midline of their body and perform in the proper manner when directed to "touch your left knee with your right hand."

The first level of gross motor coordination is the bilateral level, where both sides of the body do approximately the same thing at the same time. This movement can be seen in babies who move both arms or both legs at the same time. A more complicated bilateral movement performed by children 3 to 4 years old is the side-straddle hop or jumping jacks exercise. Alternating laterality occurs when the two-sided movement is broken down into the ability to control movement on one side of the body at a time and, also, to alternate or transfer that movement to the other side of the body. Creeping and crawling are alternating lateral movements, as are marching, hopscotch, and hopping games in older children. The integrated laterality level is reached when the two sides of the body can either do different things at the same time or work together and help each other. Skipping is an integrated movement, as are using scissors to cut out a pattern on paper held by the opposite hand, stringing beads, and other manipulatory activities.

As for discerning the right hand from the left, tests have indicated that children are usually able to do this at the age of 5 years. At this age right and left are only names for them; the age of correct orientation for themselves is approximately 6 years. The concept of relativity of left and right in connection with other objects, including lefts and rights of another person, does not emerge until the age of 8 years.

Auditory-verbal development

Infants make distinct vocal sounds early in life, but it is not until they begin to listen to sounds and seek to repeat them that they are ready to get meaning from them. At the age of 1½ to 2 years children can make, understand, and discriminate

between many but not all sounds. More significantly, they say and use words to communicate. Between the ages of 2 and 4 or 5 years language develops at a rapid pace, and vocabulary building is an important activity (Fig. 7-3). Two-year-olds ask, "What is that?" They want to know what do you call that, what is its name? Four-year-olds ask, "Why is that?" They are now seeking to improve their cognition level by gaining more understanding about how things work.

Lack of auditory stimulation or verbal development during this age period will have dire effects on children when they are taught how to read at school. They will have difficulty in dis-

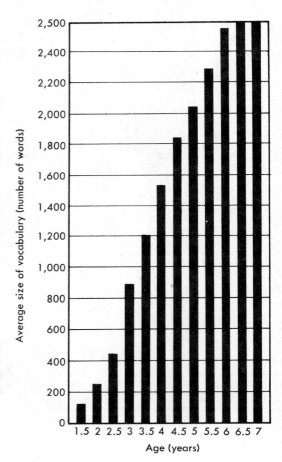

Fig. 7-3. Average vocabulary size at various ages. Ten sample groups of children were used in the study. (Modified from Lenneberg, E. H. *The biological foundations of language.* New York: John Wiley & Sons, Inc., 1967.)

criminating between letter sounds and so will have trouble with phonics. Faulty hearing, even a marginal loss of 15 decibels in the middle and higher frequencies, can also cause a deficiency in learning to read. It is necessary for children to develop auditory awareness (listening), auditory memory to remember what they heard, auditory discrimination to be able to tell differences in sounds, auditory perception to know what the sounds mean, and sound-symbol relationships or auditory-visual integration to be able to relate and connect what they see with what they hear.

Fine visual-motor organization and perception

Neonates are believed to be able visually to discriminate enough to separate what they see into individual objects or figures rather than to consider them as one mass. This ability to perceive figures from ground is especially true if the objects are moving. Infants have this capability even though their eyes do not appear to focus. Gross visual and motor-coordinated movements occur when infants begin to reach out to grasp objects. By the age of 2 years children have fairly

After all, it doesn't amuse me very much to make mudpies, to scribble, to perform my natural functions: in order for these to have value in my eyes, at least one grown-up must go into raptures over my products.

Jean-Paul Sartre
The Words

good gross control, but their finer visual-motor coordination patterns still need to be developed.

Between the ages of 3½ and 7 years children emphasize the development of visual perception and visual-motor coordination and dexterity. Two-year-olds can match a circle, square, and triangle to similar holes in a form board, provided the forms are lined up, such as having the circle next to the cutout hole of the circle in the form board. The average child of 3 years should easily match the forms to the holes, even if the form board has been turned around. The 4-year-old should be able to discriminate among a larger number of shapes, and the 5-year-old should have little difficulty picking out the item that is different in a series of pictures or symbols, such as letters.

Finer visual-motor coordination begins to develop when infants learn to make use of their finger and thumb to pick up a small object that they are observing. They can do this at about 10 months of age. When it comes to controlling and guiding a crayon over paper, however, they still have much maturing to do before they can make

effective use of it. At the age of 18 months the average infant will just make a haphazard line or mark on the paper—there is no rhyme or reason to it. The marking is mostly accidental. By 2 years of age children can control the crayon enough to scribble predominantly in a side-to-side (horizontal) direction. At 2½ years they can scribble in an up-and-down (vertical) direction.

They can copy a single vertical line at the age of 3 years. In fact, the average 3-year-old can control the crayon enough to move it in a circular movement and bring the ends together. It is not until children are 5 years old that they can copy right angles and draw a square. They should be able to stay within narrow lines with a pencil. Average 5-year-olds can print their name, but they usually "draw" each letter instead of writing or printing it smoothly. Average 6-year-olds cannot copy a diamond; it takes a mental age of 7 years before children have enough motor control to make acute angles and reverse directions (Fig. 7-4).

Ocular control is a developmental area that we believe should receive more attention than it

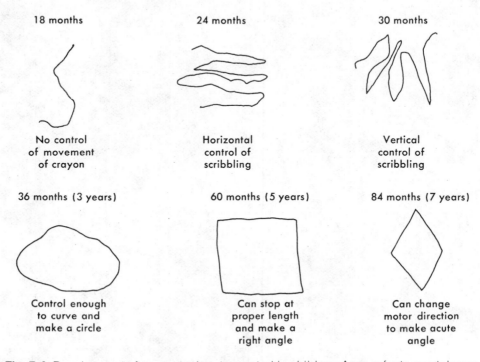

18 months	24 months	30 months
No control of movement of crayon	Horizontal control of scribbling	Vertical control of scribbling

36 months (3 years)	60 months (5 years)	84 months (7 years)
Control enough to curve and make a circle	Can stop at proper length and make a right angle	Can change motor direction to make acute angle

Fig. 7-4. Development of perceptual-motor control in children. Ages refer to mental ages.

does from parents, educators, and psychologists. Complex form perception and discrimination require a high level of coordination because tiny muscles are involved. Eyes (through the brain) must learn to see visual intricacies of form just as legs and body must learn the intricacies of walking. Children who have eyes that are not working together often learn to suppress the vision in one eye so that an image is not double. The problem is that visual input may then become sporadic, since the child intermittently makes use of the suppressed eye and visual perception becomes inconsistent.

Children 6 years of age and under are generally farsighted. As a result, much of what they see at near point, such as reading material, may be seen indistinctly. Five-year-olds should be able to track a moving target, up and down, side to side, in a circle, and diagonally. They should be able to fixate on a target and visually hold on to it as it is moved. If their eyes dart ahead, lag behind, or lose contact completely, they are in visual trouble.

Concluding thought

There can be no cognitive development without sensory input. There can be no efficient, effective perceptual development to provide the sensory input to the brain without a stable, balanced body position from which the senses can pick up stimuli with any degree of accuracy. There can be no stable point of reference within the body from which perceptual constancy can take place without a sound motor structure on which perceptual systems can develop. Gesell points out the sequence by which this development takes place; Hebb suggests what happens neurologically; and Piaget provides the theory that suggests how cognitive development starts with the sensorimotor period. Piaget's ideas are presented in the next section.

PIAGET: PREOPERATIONAL STAGE

The dominant mental activity of children during the sensorimotor period is one of overt actions as evidenced by their outward behavior and their direct interaction with the environment. Apparently little internal intellectualizing is done until close to the end of the sensorimotor period.

During the second stage of cognitive development, the *preoperational period,* it will be noted that the dominant mental activities of the child change from overt actions to perceptions whereby symbols are used to represent the environment. During this preoperational period there will be increasingly differentiating internalization of verbal and nonverbal symbols. The child will be able to make internal responses (mediations) that represent objects or events, even if they are not present.

The second broad stage of cognitive development, preoperational thought, begins at approximately 2 years of age. There are several characteristics of cognitive function noted during this period that Piaget considers to be obstacles to logical thinking. One of these characteristics is egocentrism, which refers to the child's inability to imagine or realize that another person may be viewing the same problem or situation from another perspective or angle. This child thinks, "What I see is what everybody sees." A second characteristic is centered thought, centering, or centration. The child's attention is centered on one detail of an event and is unable to take into account other features that are also important. The child cannot see variations; the focus is on a single, salient part, leading to illogical reasoning. A third characteristic is irreversible thought or irreversibility. The child is unable to change the direction of his thinking to return to its point of origin. If taken on a short walk, the preoperational child would not be able to retrace the walk accurately. If you add three objects to a group, this child would not consider that you can then take three objects away.

Stages of preoperational thought

There are two substages of development during this period. The first two years of this period (until about the age of 4 years) are known as the *preconceptual stage,* or *symbolic thought,* during which children begin to associate certain objects as being representative of other objects. They begin to indulge in symbolic play. They think of their toy gun or even a stick as a real gun and of their tricycle as a racing car or fire engine. They frequently talk to themselves or to their toys, even in the presence of others. Their conversations are associated with their immediate activity, such as asking their truck, "Did you haul in that load of logs that you were supposed to bring?" Physical cause-and-effect relationships or conceptions of the world and nature are of little interest to them at this age.[11]

From approximately 4 to 7 years of age children progress through the next phase of pre-operational thought, which is known as the period of *intuitive thought*. During this time they begin to think more complexly and they elaborate their concepts more. Their egocentrism tends to be replaced by social interaction and social signs.[12] They become more flexible in the use of language and begin to use the word "because" spontaneously, thus making simple associations between ideas. They are now able to group objects together into classes according to their own perception of their aspects of similarity. This cognitive ability is known as classification.

They refrain from talking aloud to themselves to any degree and, instead, resort to covert speech while manipulating an object or a toy. The function of language begins to take on the purpose of communicating their thoughts to other people as they strive to make their hearers listen and contrive to influence them.

As for their perception of the world about them, Piaget noticed that in earlier stages children had no image either of themselves or of the external world as such. However, with the emergence of symbolic thinking, their egocentricity induces them to draw for themselves highly specific images of themselves and of environmental objects.[13] They are likely to ask many questions concerning various phenomena. They begin to have definite perceptions of various situations but can only take into account one idea or dimension at a time. These children cannot cope intellectually with problems concerning time, space, causality, measurement, numbers, quantity, movement, and velocity. They merely understand these things in simple, concrete situations. They are certain that everything is just as it appears.

Preoperational thought tends to be animistic and artificialistic. Consequently, children of this age think of inanimate objects as having human powers such as thinking, feeling with emotion,

and desiring. Their observations are allied somewhat in terms of movement. Hence any object that to them seems to have movement is considered to be conscious or alive. In this respect the sun, moon, stars, clouds, rivers, winds, fire, carts, and so on are all regarded as conscious.[14] The words "because" and "since" increase in their vocabulary. If they are asked to give a reason for a certain happening, they will give some coincidentally occurring characteristic such as "The sun sets because people want to go to bed." This example illustrates *intuitive thought*. The child is becoming aware of the cause-and-effect relationship principle.

Concept formations

According to Piaget's theory of cognitive development, children do not begin to internalize verbal images until sometime after the age of 2 years. After that age their language development provides them with words that will represent objects and events in their environment. At first these words apparently have no other use than merely to provide a means or way of indicating "What is that?" Children are learning the labels (words) by asking, "How do you call that?" Later, about the age of 4 years, they are more interested in "What makes it go?" and "Why?" Thus they indicate that they are beginning to use words as mediators for reasoning. As a result of this gradual development of understanding, many concepts learned by children before the age of 5 years have only "surface" meanings, with no depth of insight or relationships to other concepts.

Concepts of time are rather vague in early childhood. Children cannot tell time by a clock much before the age of 6 or 7 years, and they have no idea of the length of time in terms of minutes, hours, days, weeks, and so forth. By associating specific activities such as "Daddy comes home after my TV program," they can make some estimates if they have been told the time involved. By the age of 4 or 5 years, most children can learn what day of the week it is. They will not know the month, season, or year before the age of 6 years unless they were specifically taught that concept.

Numbers mean little to young children. At

first they learn the concept "one." For a good while afterward any amount or quantity more than one is always "two." A person can usually tell when children have learned "half" because when asked their age, they will often say, "Four and a half" if they are past their fourth birthday. Children ages 3 to 5 years can be taught the meanings of the numbers one to five, but they will have only vague concepts about numbers above that.

Concepts of space and size develop more readily. At a mental age of 3 years children can select the largest and the smallest objects from a group of objects of varying sizes. Selecting middle-sized objects or in-between variations of size in sequential order does not occur until the age of 5 years. When shown two lines of different length, 3-year-olds can also select correctly in answer to, "Which one is shorter?" These children can also answer the question, "Which one has more?" but they cannot do such a simple intellectual task as realizing that the liquid poured from a wide, squatty glass into a narrow tall glass is the same amount. Until children learn that different materials have different weights, they are likely to estimate weight in terms of size. Five-year-olds can make some differentiations.

Classification, seriation, conservation

We would like to mention three concepts that Piaget has studied in the developing cognitive ability of children as they grow from the pre-operational level of thinking and reasoning to concrete operations at the age of 7. These concepts are classification, seriation, and conservation.

Classification is the ability to sort stimuli, such as colors, shapes, or sizes, into categories according to their characteristics. Not only is the sorting important but the ability to verbalize and understand the basis of the categorization is also important. The 2½ to 4½-year-olds make figural designs. They do not sort out the shapes (or whatever the scheme for the classification is). From 4½ to 6 or 7 years, children make quasi-classifications, moving freely from one basis of classification to another, mixing colors or shapes. They work with only one dimension. Children 7 or 8 years and older are able to deal with several dimensions or classes.

Seriation is the ability to arrange objects in a sequence according to one or more relevant dimensions, such as increasing or decreasing size, weight, or volume. Most children can pick the longer and the smallest sticks by ages 4 or 5. However, it took a child of 5 or 6 to put them in sequential order, and then it was usually done only with some degree of difficulty. To be able to insert sticks of varying lengths into a sequence that had empty slots, the child had to be about 7 years of age. Seriation of weight is usually not

Play blocks can introduce differences in size, weight, and shape as well as number concepts and names of letters.

Jack Corn/Image, Inc.

"CONCEPTS OF A 4-YEAR-OLD"

It is about the age of 4 and 5 years that a child no longer completely relies on sensory equipment to learn about things. He can now use his language to satisfy his curiosity by asking question upon question. Sometimes the questions may be asked to get attention, but soon enough he really wants to know.

Questions about life and death are frequent. Although he cannot fully understand the meaning of death, it is necessary to try and answer his questions within his experience and level of understanding. Four-year old Joey accepted the death of his pet goldfish easily because he felt the fish was old and ready to die. When it comes to the thought of himself dying or someone close to him dying, he becomes very disturbed. The sooner he is given short and practical answers that he can understand, the less disturbed he is.

Joey reacts to those things that have meaning for him. However, he needs an experience to develop realistic concepts. Since his experiences are limited, he will create experiences to relate to a realistic concept. Apparently Joey feels the need to create an experience in his imaginary play dealing with birth. He has a toy horse that he can ride and crawl under. He loves to pretend the horse is his mother and that he is the baby horse that came from the mother's belly. While he is trying to provide a realistic experience about birth to gain a realistic concept, he may also be relieving some of the tension he must be feeling because he cannot understand the whole complicated idea of birth. His reasoning tends to explain things by "magical" or mysterious forces.

His spatial relationships are just now beginning to have meaning for him. He understands that adults are taller than he. He knows he cannot reach the sky. He likes to make himself bigger by standing on a chair or sitting on an adult's shoulders. Touching the ceiling is a great feat.

Although he can say his numbers up to nine and recognize their symbols, he still cannot relate a number to a set of objects consisting of that number. He does not understand the sixness of six or the fiveness of five. In fact, he cannot count to nine while touching successive objects up to nine.

Another interesting factor about the 4- and 5-year-old's intellectual development is his sense of time. At this particular age his time sense is just beginning to develop. Joey knows that after he eats lunch he must rest. He knows that during suppertime "Lassie" is on the television. He can tell you that he was born on the eighth of March. He does not know how long he will rest or how long the "Lassie" program will last. He does not make any connection between his birthday and other happenings or holidays in the year. Any important event, such as a tonsillectomy in Joey's case, that occurred in the past week or so may seem ages ago to him. In fact, when we asked him how long ago it was that he was in the hospital, he said it was not a real long time ago, only three months ago. Actually, it was only one week ago.

attained until age 9. Seriation of volume is not arrived at until age 12 or so.

Conservation is the Piagetian term for the awareness that the amount or quantity of a matter remains the same (in substance, weight, length, number, volume, or area) regardless of any changes in shape or position, so long as nothing has been added to or taken away. For example, if we have a row of 8 pennies and we move the pennies farther apart in the row, we still have 8 pennies. A 4- or 5-year old would probably say there are *more* pennies in the row where the pennies are spread out. It isn't until age 6 or 7 that the child learns to conserve numbers. In the conservation of substance, a child is shown two equal balls of clay. If one ball is rolled into a log shape, the child of 4 or 5 will say it has more substance "because it is longer." A child usually cannot conserve substance until they are 6 or 7; at 9 or 10 they can conserve weight; and at 11 or 12 they can conserve volume. The hallmark of preoperational thought is the inability of the child of that age to conserve. The child learns to conserve only when he can decenter his perceptions, reverse operations, and attend to the transformations. In Piaget's developmental theory,

Language development comes as a child is encouraged to ask questions, describe what he sees, and relate experiences that he has had.

Harold Geyer

transformation is the ability to tell how one state or appearance (of a liquid, for example) is changed into another state or appearance.

PRESCHOOL LANGUAGE DEVELOPMENT

During the early childhood years, the development of language and thought is one of the child's most important accomplishments. The development of true language ability (Table 7-4) begins when children are about 2 years old. By the time they are 5 years old they are usually proficient in their speech and are capable of using an amazing number of words. This time of life can be a bit trying for parents, since children seem to ask an inexhaustible number of questions; they want to know "what?" and "why?" about everything. Later development of language is related, almost inseparably, to children's ability to think. Language makes it possible for children to put thoughts and feelings into words. The better their

Table 7-4. Pattern of normal language development in expressive speech and comprehension of speech*

Age	Expression	Comprehension
1 to 2 years	Uses 1 to 3 words at 12 months, 10 to 15 at 15 months, 15 to 20 at 18 months, about 100 to 200 by 2 years. Knows names of most objects he uses. Names few people, uses verbs but not correctly with subjects. Jargon and echolalia. Names 1 to 3 pictures.	Begins to relate symbol and object meaning. Adjusts to comments. Inhibits on command. Responds correctly to "give me that," "sit down," "stand up," with gestures. Puts watch to ear on command. Understands simple questions. Recognizes 120 to 275 words.
2 to 3 years	Vocabulary increases to 300 to 500 words. Says "where kitty" "ball all gone," "want cookie," "go bye bye car." Jargon mostly gone, vocalizing increases. Has fluency trouble. Speech not adequate for communication needs.	Rapid increase in comprehension vocabulary to 400 at 2½ years, 800 at 3 years. Responds to commands using "on," "under," "up," "down," "over there," "bye," "run," "walk," "jump up," "throw," "run fast," "be quiet," and commands containing two related actions.
3 to 4 years	Uses 600 to 1,000 words; becomes conscious of speech. Uses 3 to 4 words per speech response. Personal pronouns, some adjectives, adverbs, and prepositions appear. Mostly simple sentences, but some complex. Speech more useful.	Understands up to 1,500 words by age 4 years. Recognizes plurals, sex difference, pronouns, adjectives. Comprehends complex and compound sentences. Answers simple questions.
4 to 5 years	Increase in vocabulary to 1,100 to 1,600 words. More 3- to 4-syllable words, more adjectives, adverbs, prepositions, and conjunctions. Articles appear. Uses 4-, 5-, and 6-word sentences; syntax quite good. Uses plurals. Fluency improves. Proper nouns decrease, pronouns increase.	Comprehends from 1,500 to 2,000 words. Carries out more complex commands, with 2 to 3 actions. Understands dependent clause, "if," "because," "when," "why."
5 to 6 years	Increase in vocabulary to 1,500 to 2,100 words. Complete 5- to 6-word sentences, compound, complex, with some dependent clauses. Syntax near normal. Quite fluent. More multisyllable words.	Understands vocabulary of 2,500 to 2,800 words. Responds correctly to more complicated sentences but is still confused at times by involved sentences.

*Modified from Miller, G. A. *Language and communication.* New York: McGraw-Hill Book Co., 1951, pp. 140-157.

language ability the better they can make clear to themselves what they know.

By 2 years of age children may know as many as 100 words. By 2½ years most children use twice as many words as they did at 2 years, and by 3 years they can generally use twice as many as at 2½ years. Although this rate of learning does slow down somewhat, children often learn 50 new words a month until they are 4½ years old.[15] Children may spend a good amount of time whispering words to themselves. They seem to do this for the pure enjoyment of making and using the sounds thay have just learned.

By the time they are 3 years of age children start using the vocabulary and language skills that they have been developing. The 3-year-old may often seem to talk continuously with hardly a pause for a breath! This gives the child practice, and usually by 3½ years of age articulation has greatly improved. The mispronunciations used in baby talk are generally gone; however, grammatical constructions still leave much to be desired. A sentence such as, ''I'm busy, I'm the mostest busy'' is typical of this age.[16]

Initially children's vocabulary consists mainly of nouns, although they will use a few verbs, adjectives, or adverbs. In the beginning children hardly ever use pronouns, conjunctions, and prepositions. The relativism of pronouns may cause problems for young children. They may call themselves ''you'' and someone else ''I.'' Much of their vocabulary is learned by hearing words in context. Along with an increase in vocabulary they are also learning grammar and syntax. Their grammar is anything but flawless, however. It is not uncommon to hear them say things like ''I bringed'' or ''I walk homed.''

Children's language is now a social skill. They

Four-year-olds begin to play in small groups. They enjoy simple projects.

Mike Borum/Image, Inc.

learn how to communicate their complex feelings and motivations to others. They use language to solve problems they formerly solved by physical means. They remember, generalize, and reproduce former experiences through words and apply them in the context of the present situation.

Questions at 5 years of age are fewer and more relevant than they were at 4 years. Children now ask questions for information and not merely for practice in the art of speaking. Parents tend to be less annoyed by their questions because they are more meaningful than they were at the age of 4 years.

PSYCHOSOCIAL DEVELOPMENT

As with the other aspects of growth and development in early childhood, social and emotional maturity are still in a beginning budding stage. Two-year-olds receive considerable attention from those around them. However, they

Table 7-5. Developmental sequences of play activities from 15 months to 5 years*

Age	Play activities
15 months	Endless exercise of walking activities Throws and picks up objects Puts objects in and out of receptacles
18 months	Rapid shifts in attention; moves actively and "gets into" everything Pulls toy Carries or hugs doll or teddy bear Imitates many things as reading paper, dusting, and so on Solitary or onlooker play
2 years	Less rapid attention shifts; manipulates play material by patting, pounding Interest in dolls and teddy bears (domestic mimicry), strings beads, transports blocks in wagon Imitates things and events present to senses Parallel play although obviously enjoys being with other children Little social give-and-take Does not ask for help; adult must be constantly watchful and ready to assist without waiting to be asked
3 years	Dramatization and imagination begin to enter into play Interest in combining playthings such as blocks and cars Increasing interest in playing with other children; may play in groups of two or three but these are always shifting in makeup and activity Will put away toys with some supervision
4 years	Considerable increase in constructive use of materials and in manipulation and dramatization of play Has very complicated ideas but is unable to carry them out in detail and has no carry-over from day to day Prefers to play in groups of two or three Suggests turns but is often bossy Puts away toys alone Likes to dress up
5 years	Very fond of cutting out and pasting Likes to work on specific project that is carried over from day to day Plays in groups of two to five Friendships are becoming stronger Spurred on in activity by rivalry

*Modified from Gesell, A., et al. *The first five years of life.* New York: Harper & Row, Publishers, 1940, p. 251.

have been so busy learning how to control their motor processes and how to make their needs known that they have not had time to learn the social and emotional skills necessary for smooth interaction with others.

Social development and play

Two year-old children are egocentric persons. At this stage they take, others give. They are possessive and believe themselves to be the most important person in the universe because that is how they are treated by those close to them. They will become concerned with others, learn their limitations, and develop into socialized persons, but only after they have received some training and have had more social experiences with other children.

Children's companions at this time are usually adults of the family, brothers and sisters, and a few children from the immediate neighborhood. Their social world is that of their immediate environment. Because the first social group for children is their family, that group plays an important role in establishing their attitudes and habits. It also influences their approach to the other groups with which they will come in contact as they grow older. With each succeeding year their interest in playmates of their own age increases, and with this comes a decrease in interest in adult associations.

Negativism is a form of behavior by which children show their resistance to adult authority by being self-assertive and independent. Children are said to be "stubborn and quite difficult to manage." This behavior reaches a peak at 2½ to 3 years. It is so common at this age that it may be regarded as normal. Negativism may result from aggressive use of discipline, intolerant attitudes on the part of adults, or aggressive behavior by children who have not learned to curb their primitive, self-assertive impulses.

Two-year-olds also become increasingly aware of people and at the same time go through a period of being shy with strangers, especially adults. There is the desire to hide from them by burying the head in the mother's lap, hiding behind a piece of furniture, or refusing to speak. How pronounced this will be depends on the opportunities that the children have had to come into contact with different people and environments.

At the beginning of the second year children prefer solitary play to parallel play (playing alongside another child) and seldom play cooperatively. They are in the precooperative stage, watching what others are doing rather than participating. By the age of 2½ years, however, most children enjoy parallel play with another child. They may be together, but each plays or does whatever they like. There is no interaction with other children even when their activity is the same. Two-year-olds have not learned to share or take turns yet, and problems arise when two children want to play with the same toy. This is the period of everything being "mine" and little understanding of "yours." It is a good idea for an adult to stay close by when the children are playing because kicking, pulling hair, and snatching of toys from one another may take place (Table 7-6).

Table. 7-6. Development of social play and concept of possession

Age	Type of social play	Concept of possession
2 years	Isolated or solitary play	"What's mine is mine; what's yours is mine"
3 years	Parallel play alongside	"What's mine is mine; what's yours is yours"
4 years	Begins associative group play (50% to 60%)	"What's mine is mine; but you can play with it sometimes"
5 years	Cooperative socialized play (75% to 80%)	"What's mine is mine; you can have it anytime I don't want it"

Three-year-olds have become a bit more mature in their play activity. There is an increase in social play because these children have increased their ability to control their body movements, to handle objects, and to talk. They are now beginning to understand what it means to take turns and they like to play simple games with others. By the end of this year children begin to impersonate adults near and dear to them.

When children reach 4 years of age, they want to become involved in associative play. They are more mature mentally and physically and can participate in cooperative activities. Furthermore, they are ready to learn social patterns. They get satisfaction from playing with other children and in many cases are rewarded for having friendly and outgoing responses. Four-year-olds will play with others for about half their playtime.

When children encounter frustrating experi-

"FUN AND GAMES" "Pretend" games are Andy's favorite, however, so it's not unusual to see him running and playing in a blue cape. This cape originally made him Robin, Batman's trusted friend; Andy has now advanced to the "big time," so the cape is now Batman's cape and Andy is no longer Robin but Batman himself. Perhaps Andy likes "pretend" games so well because he has such a fine sense of the dramatic. For instance, when he played service station attendant and the older neighborhood children drove their cars (bicycles) into the station for gas, Andy was not satisfied to merely give gas, he asked for credit cards, washed windows, and even gave green stamps.

Another of Andy's great enthusiasms is playing Tarzan. Trouble arose one day this summer when Andy wanted to play Tarzan but was not allowed to take off his shirt. (Whoever heard of playing Tarzan with your shirt on?) He could not comprehend the fact that, even though the season was summer, the weather was not summer weather so he became very angry at having to keep on his shirt. Andy does tend to become angry when he feels he is justified in a certain action but is not permitted to follow his own inclination. He doesn't actually sulk when reprimanded but will become less talkative.

Although Andy definitely avoids the bully type children, he is not otherwise especially particular with whom he plays. His favorite friend with whom to play the silly word games and to work jigsaw puzzles is a seven-year-old girl. On the other hand, I've seen him have a lot of fun playing with a thirteen-month-old baby—just pretending he was a robot and periodically moving (robot fashion, of course) a few feet while the baby tried to catch him. Depending upon which person or age group he is playing with, Andy can be a leader or a follower.

Andy is enthusiastic about many things, both large and small—a bubble machine's "joker" ring, Batman, birch beer (much better than his three-year-old love of orange soda), and visits to the amusement park (in his blue cape, of course). He is curious, wondering about babies, how the garden grows, what different foods taste like, and so on. He watches and imitates (especially his daddy and grandpa) and is rapidly learning as he grows. Andy is a happy, "complete," and alert four-year-old.

ences with one another, they will argue. Boys tend to be more violent and participate in more physical attacks than girls. On the whole, however, 4- and 5-year-olds are more friendly and cooperative than uncooperative. Competitiveness appears around the age of 3 to 4 years. By the time children are 5 years old they are competing vigorously with other children.

Young children who have no real playmates will often create an imaginary playmate or pet. Children derive much pleasure from playing with their imaginary playmates, since this relationship fills a gap in their social development. Parents may have to go along with this imaginary playmate even to the extent of setting an extra plate at the table "for my friend, Charlie." This interest in imaginative playmates can begin as early as 2½ years of age. Imagination and imaginary play reach a peak at about 3½ or 4 years, but it is not unusual for a 5-year-old to have an imaginary playmate. Probably all imaginative life in children satisfies some inner need for companionship, someone to look up to, or someone to boss.[17]

Five-year-olds are very good at playing. It is one of the things they can do best. Their imagination is not used as much as it was previously because their play activity is more practical in nature. They will want to play with others about 80% of the time. Five-year-olds are greatly interested in their home and act out this interest by playing "house," being mother or father, playing "doctor," or "going to the store." Both boys and girls enter into this home-centered dramatic play. A 5-year-old has not yet established his definite sex role and does not mind this type of activity. He will be willing to be mother, baby, or any other character. He, like most 5-year-olds, has an interest in babies and dolls.

The age of 5 years is that delightful stage when one takes life as it comes. Children's life problems are restricted in scope and easy for them to handle. Their parents find them a joy to have around the house. They are extremely helpful; they are usually within earshot; and they keep their parents posted about their activities by asking permission.

Under normal circumstances a 5-year-old boy will display a particularly warm attachment to his mother. He is most concerned if he cannot find her when he comes in from play. He wants a close working relationship with her and constant assurance of her approval. When things go wrong, he wants her physical and spiritual medication. He likes her to talk with him, to explain things, and to tell him about the exciting and mysterious things in life.

All this may be disturbing to a father, but it is only a characteristic of the age. The attachment to the mother will lessen in a year or so. The love of a 5-year-old son for his father can be perfectly normal, and still he will call on his mother when trouble arises. A girl will also depend rather heavily on her mother at this age, but she will also display a warm attachment to her father.

Emotions and behavior

Emotions seen in a simple form in infants change by the age of 2 years, when significant conditioning begins to take place. The infant is egocentric, but the early childhood child shows more responsiveness to the environment. With this involvement comes a change of emphasis from the child's inner world, with its sensations and desires, to an outer world. The eventual outcome is a transfiguration in personality. New contacts and experiences increase children's chances of emotional stimulation. As the children's awareness of their surroundings increases, so does their capacity for emotional response. Not only are children influenced by their immediate environment but also by their anticipation of future events. Even though emotional development of the 3-, 4-, or 5-year-old has extended far beyond infancy, it is important to remember that these children are still babies in many respects. They still depend highly on their parents for emotional support.

At the preschool level children's fears are associated more with imaginary, anticipated, and supernatural dangers rather than with fears of actual objects or unusual stimuli, as is the case in infants. For the most part the frequency and intensity of overt signs of fear decrease with age. Crying reactions diminish, although characteristic facial expressions remain.

Early childhood is the time when personal-social experience, such as the addition of a member to the family, begins to have an influence on

"IMAGINARY MONSTERS"

Fear does strange things to people. Many of our childhood fears are forgotten when we grow up; we look back and laugh at how silly we were. However, these fears will never leave some people. This seems to be my problem.

Many small children imagine seeing things in the dark, especially before falling asleep at night. Well, my imaginary monsters were chickens. Every night as I lay in bed, I remember feeling sure there were chickens all around my bed. The worst part was that I was certain one of them would jump up on the bed and start flapping its wings. Just when I knew one was getting ready to get on the bed, I would scream for my mother. Thinking back now, I realize my mother remained quite patient through this stage. I would explain to her about the chickens surrounding my bed. It was funny that the chickens never seemed to be there when the light was turned on. After a thorough search on all sides of my bed and, of course, under it, I could finally fall asleep.

My grandmother had a pet canary at this time. Often when we went to visit she would let it out of the cage to fly around in the house. This was usually to please my brothers, who were delighted when the bird would land on their heads. At first, I would make excuses to go outside or try to get the boys interested in something else so that my grandmother would put the bird back in the cage. After what seemed an eternity the canary died. To my relief, it was never replaced!

Even walking outside, I remember constantly keeping a lookout for birds that might be nearby. Everywhere I went there seemed to be birds that wanted to fly at me. I even suspected my mother of putting pieces of dead chicken in my food. Chocolate milk was my favorite drink, but for a while I could never finish the whole glass because I thought there was a piece of chicken floating in it.

When I decided to write about this fear, I wanted to find reasons that could possibly be the cause of this fear. There are several incidents that I remember that I'm sure helped to develop it.

One of these is being chased by my brothers with a dead sparrow. We had been outside playing when they found it. The first thing they did was throw it in my direction, and I jumped. This was their cue to have some fun. They picked it up and chased me with it until, sobbing and terrified, I ran to Mother.

Looking back on these things I still remember the thoughts and feelings I had. Even today I don't eat chicken or any other fowl. I try to tell myself that it is because I don't like the taste, although I'm sure it's a carry-over from this fear. The worst part of having this fear was keeping it a secret. I was ashamed and dreaded the ridicule and teasing I would get if I admitted to being afraid of birds. I was a victim of fear that I created in my own mind. How long it took me to allow myself to forget about this, I can't remember. I haven't lost the fear but I now realize how it developed and can understand it. No longer does it completely overshadow everything I do. Perhaps the best part is now I can tell people about it. Will I ever be able to lose this fear entirely? I'm not sure, but I do know I'm better equipped to cope with it.

the child's emotional responses. When a new baby comes, jealousy builds up in preschoolers because they feel deprived of attention and affection. This reaction does not always occur, but it is a common characteristic when the children are the firstborn and have been accustomed to having the full attention of their parents. Because the new baby is showered with so much attention, older children feel neglected. Young children are too immature to comprehend the need for changes in their lives that the arrival of a new baby will bring. It must be realized that a certain amount of jealousy in any child is normal, whether it is jealousy of the baby, older brothers or sisters, or even of the mother or father. Love and affection freely given to the 4- and 5-year-old can go far in counteracting the negative effects of deep-seated jealousy.

Anger is a complex emotion because it takes different forms at different age levels. Children of 4 and 5 outgrow the tantrums of kicking, pounding, and screaming because they can now translate their anger and frustration into words. They often begin to threaten and yell at other children at this age. Four-year-olds usually direct their anger to the object causing the frustration. For example, a boy may blame a chair for causing him to trip and spill his milk rather than put the blame on his own clumsiness. Children of this age tend to remain frustrated and angry for longer periods of time now, but they begin to find ways to keep from showing their anger to other persons. One of the best ways for children to get rid of frustration, fear, anger, and guilty feelings is by creative art work such as painting, using clay, or pounding wood and by playing out the fears that are real and imaginary.

Sex-role identification

Although an individual's biological sexuality is determined at conception by the combination of an ovum and a chance sperm, from that moment on intrauterine and extrauterine environmental influences do much to shape each human's development of a lifetime sex-role pattern of behavior and emotions. Biochemical factors influence the intrauterine environment to the extent that the development of genital organs and the glandular system can be affected. The extrauterine environment, made up of the significant persons in the child's life and the nature of the sex-role pattern prescribed by that culture or society, will influence the individual during many years of life.

Gender labeling begins early in most cases. "Blue" means it's a boy; "pink" means it's a girl. Of course, the babies don't know the significance of the colors, but the adults do. "Look at him. He's all boy. See how tight he can hold on to my finger!" "Isn't she a doll! A real picture-book baby—so dainty and pretty." From the time the infant is viewed in the maternity ward, the infant is exposed to comments such as, "She's such a good girl" and "He is getting to be a big boy." By 2 or 3 years of age, the child can correctly identify her or his own sex. (Did it seem strange to you to read "her or his own sex" instead of "his or her own sex"? Just an example of how we become conditioned to expressing male and female terms.) Gender labeling can help bring about gender identity and sex-role identification, but it can be overdone if stereotyping of the sexes becomes involved in the labeling. Sex-role standards are subject to cultural and societal influences and, as such, are prone to sex-role stereotyping. The question concerning sex-role standards that has to be answered is: At what point do the differences between male and female become artificial and exaggerated? The question, "Is all sex-role stereotyping wrong?" can also be raised. Reasonable answers based on research are difficult to find. To what extent should parental preference be accepted in this matter? Rheingold and Cook[18] found a distinct difference between the contents of boys' and girls' rooms in terms of decorations and toys present, showing that sex-role stereotypes exist in the minds of adults. It is not until school age, and more frequently adolescence, that the socially and parentally defined sex roles are openly questioned.

Maccoby and Jacklin[19] have reviewed many studies on assumed differences between males and females. They stress caution in interpreting their findings because the details of the studies and the variables differed so greatly. In summary, they presented the following findings in regard to beliefs concerning differences between the sexes.

These beliefs are apparently unfounded.

1. Girls are more socially oriented than boys.

Preschool play often centers around household activities. Some sex-role learning is indicated.

2. Girls are more receptive to suggestions.
3. Boys and girls differ in learning ability.
4. Boys are naturally more analytical than girls.

These differences appear to be real.
1. Girls are more proficient at verbal skills.
2. Boys are more capable at making visual-spatial judgments.
3. Boys are better in mathematical areas.
4. Boys are basically more aggressive.

They list the following questions as debatable.
1. Are girls naturally more anxious than boys?
2. Is there an overall difference in activity level?
3. Is one sex more competitive and dominant than the other?
4. Are girls more nurturant and compliant than boys?

Maccoby and Jacklin indicate that some of the differences just mentioned do not appear until middle childhood or adolescence.

ORGANIZATION OF PERSONALITY

Up to the age of 2½ years the personality of infants has been a natural development with the emergence of behavior characteristics that nature provides for children to help them promote their own well-being and survival. Infants developed

"THAT SUBJECT"   It was a pleasant day in June. My five-year-old son, Randy, and I were sitting at the kitchen table having lunch. Randy was chattering away about the things he and the kids across the street had been doing during the hour before lunch. He always talks with great enthusiasm and is very dramatic when describing the events of the day. He makes all kinds of faces and uses his hands to help express his thoughts. While I was listening very carefully and thinking how grown-up he was becoming, Randy suddenly paused, wrinkled up his nose and mouth, and said: "Well, I better not tell you that." I was a little surprised and yet curious, so I tried to be casual and told him that he didn't have to tell me anything he didn't want to but that Mommy was always interested in what he did and would like to know. He paused for a few seconds. I could just see the wheels turning in his mind. He looked right at me. Then, with his hands turned out in a type of shrug: "Well, it's bad. So will you smack me if I tell you?" Still trying to be casual and relaxed and trying to make the right decision, I told him I would not smack him if he was honest with me.

By this time Randy's face had lost some of its brightness, and it was considerably longer. He proceeded to tell me that Sharon had asked him to show her his—he stopped and pointed to his privates, not being able to use the word he always used so naturally before. He then tilted his head a little to the side and, looking at me with a pained expression, waited for me to reply.

Feeling as if someone had just struck me, I tried to think clearly. I asked him if he had shown Sharon and he said he had. I explained to him that he knew that wasn't the thing to do and that just because Sharon had told him to do it, it didn't mean he had to do as she wanted. I reminded him he was getting to be a big boy now and that sometimes he was going to have to decide what to do and what not to do on his own, even if it meant his friends would be mad at him. Randy looked down at his feet and said: "I know, Mommy, but she told me to show her, and then she showed me hers." Feeling terrible and half angry, I replied: "Sharon doesn't have a 'dingy.'" He said: "No, she showed me her hair." Then he stopped, looked at me, made a face, and very pathetically said: "It made me feel sick." I honestly don't know what I said next because Randy began to cry. I do remember him saying he didn't like Sharon and that he wouldn't do it again. After Randy stopped crying, he informed me he didn't want to talk about "that subject" again, and he found something to entertain himself.

through stages where they sequentially emphasized physical dependence, control of body movements, physiological pleasures, self-display, curiosity and exploration, imitation of verbalisms, and by 2½ years, self-assertiveness.

During the phase of self-assertiveness infants are reminded in many ways by their parents that "this is not the way you are supposed to act." Children become amenable and are willing to learn new ways of behaving. Between the ages of 2½ to 4 years or so children learn to control their primary nature forces, drives, and impulses.[20] They also develop a behavior pattern that will reflect the influence of secondary external elements on their personality development. The social and emotional atmosphere and environment of 3- to 5-year-olds are extremely important because both overt and covert aspects of personality are being crystallized.

Duplication of behavior

The temper tantrums of the twos and the general conflict that exists between parents and children at this time give way to children who now say, "Maybe I really wasn't ready to be on my own yet. I guess there is more to be learned." So as they approach being 3-year-olds they revert to a learning technique that they had used earlier. They make use of imitation again. However, this time instead of imitating speech and language, they replicate the behavior and actions of others. In a way they are saying, "If my behavior wasn't correct when I was two, then I'll copy yours so I can learn the right way to behave." They are taking over the behavior of others, especially of their parents. The actions of their parents, for better or worse, will become their actions. They are developing standards of behavior that will be based on the actions of others who are important to them.

Suggestibility of feelings

As children move into the "trusting threes," they allow themselves not only to imitate the behavior of others but also to begin to reflect their moods, attitudes, and ideas. Children are in the phase of suggestibility. In some ways they are becoming dependent on others for the development of their mental and emotional responses. They are unconsciously absorbing their feelings and outlooks. Children tend to copy their mothers or fathers. If their mothers are calm, cheerful, and happy, the children can become the same way; if the children respond more to the fathers, let us hope that he is not irritable, cynical, or selfish. Politeness, friendliness, consideration for others, patience, and moral conduct in general are all suggestible traits.

Children are not aware that they are taking over the moods and feelings of others because suggestibility is an unconscious process. If the suggestions were to be made openly and deliberately taught, children would probably reject

them. To illustrate: At a state park the swimming area was away from the bathhouses where swimmers could change clothes. To get to the lake it was necessary to walk across a road covered with gravel. A father and his boy started barefooted across the road. As he stepped on the small bits of gravel, the boy winced and said, "That hurts." "Yes, it does," replied the father and kept on walking. The little boy made a real effort to be brave like his daddy as he walked across. Another father and his boy started across the graveled road. "That hurts," cried the boy. "Oh, nonsense," said the father, "it doesn't hurt at all." As this boy stepped gingerly over the stones, you could tell by the expression on his face that he was thinking, "That does *so* hurt!" Which father provided a better example for his son? You can imagine the second boy thinking about his father, "He's either lying or else he's some kind of a superman. Either way, can I ever hope to be like him? Can I really trust him to know how I feel?"

Personality identification

The phase of suggestibility gives way to identification, in which children take over the entire personality of another, with all of its strengths and attributes. Personality identification is the process of accepting another person emotionally so completely that his characteristics and abilities are adopted as a person's own. Children no longer are just pretending that they are doing things "like my daddy does," but for all intents and purposes they act as if daddy's traits and abilities are also their own traits and abilities. Children impersonate another so completely that for the moment they are that person.

We know of children who identified so completely with "Superman" or "Batman" in their play that when they received costumes of these characters, the children believed that they could do what Superman and Batman did. Two children, playing in Batman costumes, jumped from the railing of a porch as they pretended to be chasing the "bad guys." Each child broke his right arm. One 4-year-old, pretending he was the "Bionic Man," stepped out into a street and raised his arms as if to stop a truck. Identification is a behavior mechanism used by people of all ages. Have you ever cried during a movie or felt "choked up inside" while reading a story or observing an event? You were identifying with an individual or a situation, and for the moment his or her circumstances were yours.

During the identification phase, children generally respond to people whom they love or who possess some trait or power that they admire. Children gain a sense of security by identifying with an older person whom they love, in whom they have complete confidence and trust. The older person is loved because he is lovable to the child. There is no hesitancy on the part of children to become like that person because "he is so nice to me, and I want to be like him." When children identify with a person or a characterization because of the traits that individual or character possesses, they are beginning to reach out into the world for personal characteristics that they wish to make their own. They like the idea of the power or ability implicit in the brave act or performance of another, and they do not mind becoming that way. With either the identification motive of love or power the children are developing characteristic behaviors or attitudes that can be instrumental in setting the direction that their personality development will take. They are on the threshold of developing their own character, with behavior and attitudes that will have a tremendous influence on all of their future actions.

Beginnings of a value judgment system

As children mature, the impact of the identification process as a motivator of behavior is lessened to the degree that the children will eliminate the personal attachment to the individual as an object of identification, although still retaining the characteristics of that person. It is no longer, "I want to be brave like my daddy." Now it is simply, "I want to be a brave person." The traits and ideals of the person become part of the child's emerging self-ideal. A self-ideal is an integration of the values that one holds for oneself and that one seeks to realize. The self-ideal becomes sort of an inner standard of behavior that is considered important enough to strive for and live by.

The self-ideal is also called the superego, the ego ideal, and the conscience. We like to consider it as a value judgment system that will eventually be highly instrumental in influencing the decisions that an individual makes as well as regulating his behavior. "I want to be brave. Brave boys don't cry, so I'll try very hard not to cry." We can imagine a 4-year-old boy with his eyes filled with tears, biting his lips as he tries so hard not to cry.

As children incorporate a self-ideal into their personality, several things happen. They now have an "other self," which they can consider when they are making decisions about what is good or bad, important or unimportant, of interest or of no interest. They become more conscious and critical of their behavior in terms of its appropriateness and, as a result, seek to control their behavior so it will be more acceptable. This function of self-criticism concerning one's behavior constitutes the essence of a conscience. It should be realized that not all children develop an adequate value system. Some children will identify with adults who have values and ideals that are too strict and severe, others with adults who tend to be too easygoing and undisciplined. Either way, these models can induce unhealthy mental patterns in children who identify with them.

The self-ideal should be such that it (1) can control the innate survival drives and impulses of the early years of life while still enabling use of their energy output and (2) makes use of an integrated, well-developed value judgment system to give direction to one's behavior. It will take many years before individuals will have an effective, competent value system, but when they do develop it, they will be considered "mature persons."

With the beginnings of a self-ideal 4-year-olds develop more self-assurance and independence. They feel more capable because they are acting more like "little adults." After all, they are copying their behavior; they have an organized personality that, along with their budding intellect, is enabling them to ask better questions and to make better decisions than before. They feel more independent. They like to show off, and they ask others to watch them while they demonstrate how capable they are. They are

Value learning is enhanced by exposure to a variety of cultural backgrounds.

Harold Geyer

noisy at times and constantly into something. At Christmas time, several years ago, a mother became aware of an unusual quietness in her house. She decided she had better check on her 4-year-old to see what he was up to. She found him sitting in a chair in the living room. ''What are you doing?'' she asked. ''Nothing,'' he replied. ''What can I do, what with you, God, and Santa Claus watching me all the time!''

CONCEPTS OF MORALITY

At this point a concept regarding the meaning of morality and the development of a moral sense in a child will be introduced. It will be important to realize that the term *morality* has two dramatically different meanings. These meanings stem from what philosophers consider to be the two basic sources of principles, standards, or rules that indicate ''right'' and ''wrong'' in behavior.

One source of right and wrong are the individuals themselves or the group with whom they identify. This source of moral standards states that right and wrong are determined by the people, individually, collectively, or in some combination of the two. Each social structure develops its own moral code. Morality, in this context, implies a conformity to the mores, customs, and rules of the particular group of people if one wants to get along with them. When in Rome, do as the Romans do! Since each group creates or determines its own values of right and wrong, each society can have its own standards of morality. This point of view concerning morality indicates that moral values can change and can differ from group to group and that there is no constant truth. Philosophically, this interpretation of morality is known as relativism.

The other source of morality is believed by some philosophers to be inherent in the very nature of the universe itself. Just as there are physical (scientific) laws that are the same the world over, so are there behavioral (moral) laws that are universal and eternal. All men everywhere are subjected to these laws, whether they agree with them or not, whether they are even aware of them or not, just as they are bound to the cause-and-effect relationships of the scientific laws. Man does not create these laws; he dis-covers them. Just as science reveals physical laws, so do philosophy and theology reveal moral laws. Man's social experiences throughout the ages of history may make him aware of certain standards of conduct that are intrinsically good. This awareness may come in the form of social evolution, but ultimately man learns that these principles always were good for men everywhere, at any time, under any condition. As such, the principles are universal and eternal. Philosophically, this interpretation of morality as universal principles is known as absolutism.

Early moral development

As early as 18 months of age, children will drop and run away from an object that they should not have taken. They are inhibited in their behavior by their mothers' ''no, no.'' At 2 years of age they associate being good with routine duties well performed, and at 3 years of age they try to please and conform by asking, ''Do it this way?'' By the age of 4 years they begin to understand about ''rules,'' although they are not always capable of following them. They may begin to have a considerable interest in God but may ask many inappropriate questions about Him. The 5-year-old often believes that God is responsible for everything, yet the child's sense of goodness and badness is pretty much limited to things the parents permit or forbid.[21]

The development of a moral sense of some sort in the child is inevitable. The elements of imitation, suggestibility, and identification indicate that the child will pick up some kind of a moral consciousness. The nature of that moral sense, whether it be heavily loaded in the direction of relativism or absolutism, will be largely determined by the child's models and environment. Moral insight of an abstract nature will not come to the child for several years yet, however.

It is possible that children may constantly be placed on their own in a highly unstructured situation where they are given no clues as to what they should think in terms of right and wrong. Some parents want their children to ''decide for themselves what they want to believe.'' Such children may eventually develop a morality or identity crisis because they have few or no guidelines to follow.

STUDY GUIDE

1. Review the developmental tasks for this age level. Compare them to the developmental tasks of the infant as mentioned in Chapter 5. What advancements in development and behavior are required?
2. Trace motor development from the age of 2½ to 5 years. Note how gross motor and fine motor skills improve in a relatively few years.
3. The ages of 2 to 5 years are extremely important years for the development of perceptual processes of learning. Consider the following:
   a. Review the information on the perceptual process as it was presented in Chapter 2 in the discussion of the central nervous system and in Chapter 5 in the discussion of cognitive development. Relate all of that information to development of the perceptual pattern for learning as presented in this chapter.
   b. Can you relate any of Piaget's ideas, as presented in Chapter 5 on the sensorimotor operations period, to the sensorimotor processes discussed in this chapter?
   c. Why is auditory-verbal development at this age level so crucial in terms of future learning ability and potential?
   d. Consider a child who is 5 years of age. What would be the child's fine visual-motor capabilities? What would the child normally be able to do?
4. Discuss the characteristics of Piaget's preoperational thought period and its manifestations in concepts formulated during that age bracket.
5. What are the social characteristics of the 3- to 5-year-old?
6. Make a chart showing in one column the stages of personality development found in ages 3 to 5 years, and in a second column, present the features or characteristics of each stage of personality development. When finished, compare your chart to Table 6-4 to note the different emphasis in the type of personality being developed.
7. Define the two basic sources of moral principles or standards. Give illustrations of each type as you note them in today's society and within your age group in particular. What do you think?

REFERENCES

1. Vaughan, V. C. III. Growth and development. In V. C. Vaughan, III, & R. J. McKay, (Eds.), *Nelson's textbook of pediatrics* (10th ed.). Philadelphia: W. B. Saunders Co., 1975.
2. Tanner, J. M. Physical growth. In P. H. Musser (Ed.), *Carmichael's manual of child psychology* (3rd ed.). New York: John Wiley & Sons, Inc., 1970.
3. Lefrancois, G. R. *Of children.* Belmont, Calif.: Wadsworth Publishing Co., Inc., 1973.
4. Gesell, A. The autogenesis of infant behavior. In L. Carmichael (Ed.), *Manual of child psychology* (2nd ed.). New York: John Wiley & Sons, Inc., 1954.
5. Piaget, J. *The origins of intelligence in children.* New York: International Universities Press, 1952.
6. Penfield, W., & Roberts, C. *Speech and brain mechanisms.* Princeton, N.J.: Princeton University Press, 1958.
7. Hebb, D. O. The possibility of a dual type mechanism. In T. D. Landauer (Ed.), *Readings in physiological psychology: the bodily basis of behavior.* New York: McGraw-Hill Book Co., 1967.
8. Smith, O. V., & Henry, J. P. Cybernetic foundations of rehabilitation. *Journal of Physical Medicine,* 1967, **46,** 379-467.
9. Kaluger, G., & Kolson, C. J. *Reading and learning disabilities* (2nd ed.). Columbus, Ohio: Charles E. Merrill Publishing Co., 1978.
10. Kephart, N. C. *The slow learner in the classroom* (2nd ed.). Columbus, Ohio: Charles E. Merrill Publishing Co., 1970.
11. Piaget, J., & Inhelder, B. *The psychology of the child.* (N. Weaver, trans.) New York: Basic Books, Inc., Publishers, 1969.
12. Flavell, J. H. The development of inferences about others. In T. Misebel (Ed.), *Understanding other persons.* Oxford, England: Blackwell & Mott, Ltd., 1973.
13. Phillips, J. L., Jr. *The origins of intellect: Piaget's theory* (2nd ed.). San Francisco: W. H. Freeman & Co., Publishers, 1975.
14. Wadsworth, B. J. *Piaget's theory of cognitive development.* New York: David McKay Co., Inc., 1971.
15. Brown, R. *A first language: the early stages.* Cambridge, Mass.: Harvard University Press, 1973.
16. McNeill, D. *The acquisition of language: the*

study of developmental psycholinguistics. New York: Harper & Row, Publishers, 1970.

17. Manosevitz, M., Prentice, N. M., & Wislon, F. Individual and family correlates of imaginary companions in preschool children. *Developmental Psychology,* 1973, **8** (1), 72-79.

18. Rheingold, H. L., & Cook, K. V. The contrasts of boys and girls room as an index of parents' behavior. *Child Development,* 1975, **46,** 459-463.

19. Maccoby, E. E., & Jacklin, C. M. *The psychology of sex differences.* Stanford, Calif.: Stanford University Press, 1974.

20. Halfield, J. A. *Childhood and adolescence.* Baltimore: Penguin Books, Inc., 1962.

21. Gesell, A., & Ilg, F. L. *Infant and child in the culture today.* New York: Harper & Row, Publishers, 1943.

Middle childhood

6 to 8 years of age

What do you see when you look at a first grader? You may see a front-toothless, squirmy, 5-, 6-, or 7-year-old jumping rope, swinging, or tumbling on the grass. You may see a clean pair of trousers become grass stained before the blink of an eye. You may see imagination and personality bubbling forth as in no other time in life. But to be sure, you will see a group of individuals so unique, and yet so unbelievably alike.

As a first-grade teacher, I never cease to marvel at my "charges." They come to school knowing so little, and they leave, having learned a vast amount of information ranging from reading, to social relationships with others, to a discovery of what school is really all about.

A first grader has usually developed his large muscle movements quite well. Small muscle coordination is another story. A pencil surely is a strange and horrible creation during those first few weeks, and to have to sit still for more than 10 minutes at a time! Unheard of! Often it takes a whole year before some first graders learn to control their small muscles and their huge bursts of energy.

Cognitive development during this age is truly amazing. Imagine looking at all those strange-looking symbols called the alphabet, being told that each symbol is a letter, that each has its own sound, and that combinations of these funny looking things will form something called words. How frightening and overwhelming it must seem in those first few weeks of school. Often I am amazed at how fast these little bundles of energy can learn—not only reading but arithmetic as well. More strange symbols with unique meanings! I feel that in no other grade do the children begin with so little and learn so much. So much progress can be seen in all pupils. Yet for some a sense of frustration is encountered when others begin to pull away, leaving them behind. Learning is harder for some, and these children come to know that "Steve is a good reader," but that "I can't read so good."

Individual differences begin to show through in other areas as well. Social relationships concern every first grader. Whereas some children have companions and best friends, others become isolates and encounter social problems. No one wants to be friends with a child who always wants his own way, who does not play fairly, or who cannot keep up in games because of intellectual or physical limitations. Here children must learn to cope with the "different" children and help them to become accepted and adjusted.

Influence by peers increases greatly in first grade. Previously, ideas fostered at home were supreme. Now the realization begins that other ideas and beliefs might not be so bad after all. Maybe everything Mommy and Daddy say isn't right! "But my friend Jimmy said . . ." becomes a new phrase. First graders want to go to their friends' homes. They want to call them on the telephone. They delight in seeing each other in the grocery store or at the shopping center. They desire to have the toys their friends have and to wear the same types of clothing. One coloring book is shown and is followed by ten more like it the next day. Interests truly are dictated by peer group influence.

Emotional developments are great in 5- to 7-year-olds. Many first graders are quick to cry, whereas others brood and pout. The first day of school is an emotional trauma—the strange bus ride, the new building, meeting a new teacher, and just being taken away from Mommy is enough to set the tears in motion, not to mention being thrown in with twenty-six other children undergoing a similar trauma. But luckily, fears and tears soon disappear as the days go on. Emotional adjustment continues throughout the year, and vast improvements can be seen by the end of school.

First graders love competition. Whether they are racing on the playground or trying to see who will get his work done first, these children are in their glory when competing. They delight in playing games, as long as they do not lose all the time. Spelling bees and arithmetic competitions are a source of enjoyment, even for the slower pupils who manage to win often enough to keep them interested.

A typical day might begin with two children forgetting their lunch money, a common problem. (My Mother forgot to give it to me!) The day continues with a few tattles ("Donnie pulled my hair," "Mark is copying from my paper") and some comments by the teacher: "Michele, put that away," "Robert, don't you ever stop talking?" As an aside, first graders love to talk. They begin when they come in the morning and are still talking as they walk up the hall to their buses when school is over for the day. Recess is enjoyed, since it is a time for running and playing. After lunch the afternoon begins with settling an argument about whose turn it really was to take the ball out at noon recess or determining whose superball Roger really has—his or David's! The afternoon concludes with the usual race of the children riding Bus 51 to see who can get his chair up the fastest and get in line first.

First graders are an interesting and rewarding age group with whom to work. They are dependent, yet independent; serious, yet comical; aggravating, yet satisfying. Their teacher is their mother away from home, their helper, referee, friend, and aid to learning. If one were to look at a first grader, just what *would* he see?

Harold Geyer

Peer association makes group games favorites of 6- and 7-year-olds.

Six- to 8-year-old children are fascinating persons. For the parent they are full of surprises, new and different each day; for their siblings they are someone to love, someone to tolerate, or someone to have nothing to do with; for their teacher they are individuals, eager to learn in any way they can. As children go through these years, different growth characteristics appear. There is no clear-cut line or age, however, where one stage of development ends and the next begins. Generally, children go from one phase to another without any earth-shattering experience to tell people of the change. Most of the time they proceed without any trouble. Parents, teachers, and friends will be able to see differences, however, between children at 6 years of age and at 8 years.

Up to the age of 5 or 6 years children all over the world grow, develop, and act similarly. Throughout the ages, babies everywhere have been much the same. The principles of growth and development are eternal and universal in nature. By the age of 5 or 6 years, however, the distinctive cultures of each society are imprinted on its children. Little Ivan, little Joe, and little Wang-Ti start the same, but the man-made influences of their respective cultures begin to have a different impact on the growth and development of each child, creating differences in attitudes, behavior, and even in certain physical characteristics that are unique to the culture.

The developmental tasks of middle childhood are centered about "three great outward pushes." Socially, children make their way out of their family environs into a peer group society. Physically, they move into a world of games and activities requiring neuromuscular skill. Mentally, there is a thrust into school and the world of concepts, symbols, logics, and communication. Specifically, the developmental tasks are as follows: (1) acquiring social and physical skills necessary for ordinary games, (2) learning to get along with peers, (3) building a wholesome concept of self, (4) learning an appropriate sex role, (5) developing fundamental skills in reading, writing, and arithmetic, (6) breaking family ties and developing a growing independence by entering school, and (7) developing conscience, morality, and a value judgment system.[1] These developmental tasks will be paramount in importance until the child reaches puberty and adolescence.

PHYSICAL DEVELOPMENT

The middle childhood years are characterized by a relatively slow, but steady growth rate as compared to the years of infancy or puberty. This age level is one of the most comfortable periods of physical adjustment. The developmental pace is sufficiently slow so that under normal conditions children can meet the physical and psychological demands made on them.

Body growth

By 6 years of age children have usually lost most of their baby contours. Their legs and arms are lengthening, and they are gaining in height and weight, although growth is less rapid than before. Girls at this age are generally more physically mature than boys in terms of ultimate level of physical development. However, boys do tend to be slightly taller and heavier than girls up to the age of 10 years. The average child of 6 years in North America stands 46 inches tall and weighs about 48 pounds. The annual expected growth is 2 to 3 inches in height and 3 to 6 pounds in

weight.[2] All children have their own growth rate, however, and there are a few 6-year-olds who are as tall and heavy as some 10-year-olds.

There is a change in the structure of the face that is noticeable in comparing a 4- or 5-year-old with a 6-year-old. The face begins to look more slim and lean because the children are beginning to lose their "baby fat." It is during this sixth year, also, that they lose their first tooth. Being more physiologically mature, girls shed their teeth a bit earlier than boys. As permanent teeth replace baby teeth and as new molars come in, the jaw lengthens and the face changes in shape. The "toothless gap era" declines at about the age of 8 years, when the permanent teeth appear, starting at the front and developing to the back. Permanent teeth will continue to arrive until about the age of 11 or 12 years.

The eyes of a 6-year-old are still immature in size and shape. There is a strong tendency to farsightedness, a situation usually corrected naturally between the ages of 8 and 10 years when the child's eyes attain adult size and shape. The younger child should be provided with books that have larger than normal print. At this age it is important for the child to be tested for near-point vision. Most visual screening charts test a child's vision at far point, but it is near-point vision that a child must use in reading.

Motor skills

Children can take fairly good care of themselves at 6 years of age. They can hop, skip, jump, dress and undress, tie a bow, and use scissors. They no longer grasp a pencil with a fist hold but, rather, use a finger hold. The 6-year-olds' larger muscles are more advanced in development than their smaller ones. Because of this condition, their small muscles do not permit them to do precise writing, sewing, or drawing. Tying shoelaces will be an effort for some at this age. They still become frustrated by their lack of fine motor skill development.

Six years is an age of activity. Running, jumping, climbing, bike riding, and "clean-up" jobs at school make use of the child's large muscles. Although they enjoy finer motor activities, they become restless after sitting for a short period of time. They wriggle on a chair and sit on the edge.

Middle childhood at 6 years. A, Has increased interest in games. **B,** Can use knife to spread butter on bread.

Meriem Kaluger

Frequent bangs or thumps can be heard in the classroom—they have fallen off their chairs. Six-year-olds seem to use their whole body in everything they do. There is a good deal of oral activity such as blowing through the lips, extending the tongue, and making all kinds of mouthing noises. When they write, they screw up their faces, bite their lips, and pull themselves back and forth in their chairs. They are easily distracted by the environment.

Although their large muscles are still better developed than their small ones, 7-year-olds are gradually becoming more skillful in using their small muscles in eye-hand coordination activities. Indication of improved small muscle control is shown by the Stanford-Binet test of tying a bowknot. Only 35% of the 6-year-olds could pass this test as compared to 69% of the 7-year-olds and 94% of the 9-year-olds. It is during the second grade in the United States that most children learn to do cursive writing, which requires a different kind of control over their hand motions than was needed for manuscript writing.

Advancing from the gross activities approach of the 6-year-olds, the 7-year-olds combine thought with activity. They are more inclined to "think before jumping." They are more cautious in new performances and show a new awareness of heights. They will play vigorously in one activity but will quickly drop it for another, although they do not change from loud to quiet types of activities as frequently as do the 6-year-olds. Girls have somewhat poorer visual acuity than boys, but their color discrimination is superior on the average to that of boys. Auditory acuity is as good at 7 years of age as it will ever be. The ability to discriminate pitch, however, will continue to improve for the next three or four years.[3] Nervous habits begin to appear in 7-year-olds. The most common habits are nail biting, tongue sucking, or scratching and pulling at the ear. These are more frequently found among girls than among boys. Some of these habits may disappear within a couple of months or years, whereas others, such as nail biting, may persist into adulthood.

Eight-year-olds are continuing to develop steadily and slowly. Active play is most characteristic of this age. Eight-year-olds have achieved equilibrium in body balance and can move freely with fluidity because of improved small muscle development. They do not drop their pencil as frequently as they did when they were 7 years old, nor lose it as often as when they were 6 years old. In writing they space words and sentences well and can control their hand movements so that slanting letters can be achieved easily. Near-sightedness may develop at this age so that visual care must be maintained. They are quicker in their responses, mentally and physically. Their attention span is longer; this is helpful to the teacher since she will not have the multitude of distractions to react to that the first-grade teacher has.

In summary, with the development of large muscles to the point that they can be used effectively in producing alternating movements, the 6- to 8-year-olds now seek to try out a variety of physical skills that they could not do before. They delight in doing the physically unusual or different such as walking on ledges or balancing on fences rather than walking on the sidewalks. A ball becomes an indispensable toy because children can now take aim and make the ball go where or do what they want it to. Kicking skills become important because the repertoire of games in middle childhood includes many involving kicking, running, and jumping. Children in this age group will kick cans, rocks, anything that can be moved. A favorite playground game is kick ball.

A significant developmental point to be noted at this time is that making one's way into the peer group begins to depend on the child's skills for playing the approved games of the group. The importance of these skills increases as the child reaches the ages of 10 to 12 years. This factor is more important for boys than for girls because their sex role includes more physical activities. Many children, boys in particular, become misfits when unfortunate circumstances make them meagerly equipped to play games with their peers. Many delinquent boys have been found to be unskilled in playing games of the group. Most children learn the skills needed for games without help from the school. It is the wise teacher or parent who tries to find ways for children to learn the skills if they do not possess them.

Middle childhood at 7 years. A, Likes to help mother with simple chores. **B,** Rides a bicycle very well.

Middle childhood at 8 years. A, Enjoys a pet. **B,** Relates to younger sibling as an "older" brother or sister.

SOCIAL GROWTH

The ages of 6 to 8 are years when the children's social environment expands rapidly. Children's lives begin to center around the school and the children and activities that are found there. Children now have authority figures other than the mother and father who seek to guide them. Peers take on greater importance, and the group phenomena begin to influence children's behavior and growth. Family influences lessen as the external socialization process makes its impact. Since their whole beings evolve around their

Far from wanting to shine, I laughed in chorus with the others, I repeated their catchwords and phrases, I kept quiet, I obeyed, I imitated my neighbors' gestures, I had only one desire; to be integrated.

Jean-Paul Sartre
The Words

friends and peers, children must learn social skills and communication skills that will enable them to maintain successful relationships. Learning to get along well with others is often difficult, and lack of social experiences or of good teaching models (mothers, fathers, and other acceptable adults) can be handicapping.

Social characteristics

The social behavior of 6-year-olds develops more rapidly than previously because they are away from home more and are with children their own age. Their social maturity and stability are highly inconsistent, however. Their behavior often regresses in maturity, especially when they are tired. Group activities help to develop the social maturity of children. They learn new ascribed roles for their age, develop social interaction and communicative skills, and begin to understand the needs and rights of others. Through maturation and learning children acquire the more refined social behavior of adults.

Six-year-olds are often trying to their parents. One minute they are agreeable and loving, and the next minute they dislike everybody and everything. Six years is just not old enough to be reliable and stable. They crave help but refuse to accept it. They want to play with others, but if things do not go their way, they may threaten to go home or engage in name-calling. Six-year-olds cannot handle a younger brother or sister well without considerable direction and attention on the part of the parent. At times they can be bossy with a younger sibling. Despite all of these problems, there are times when they have a very close relationship with their parents. Six-year-olds are sensitive to parental moods and tensions, and they can be most sympathetic when their mother is sick. Not only may children show anxieties concerning the well-being of the mother and father but of their teacher as well.

A highly important aspect of social development at this age pertains to ethnic identification. Six-year-old white children are unaware of ethnic identification of the children with whom they play. They pick their playmates more on qualities of age and size rather than sex and color. As children mature, they respond more to the prejudice of others, often as a result of the influence

of their home atmosphere. Children view the opinions and ideas of their parents and teachers as most important because to them they are the smartest people in the world.

Comer and Poussaint[4] in their book *Black Child Care* state that ethnic identification for black children is usually different from that of white children. The average 4-year-old black child barely understands racial difference. However, the 7- or 8-year-olds do understand and may respond with anger or hostile racial feelings if they feel rejected or uncertain. This age is the time when children do or do not "sign a contract" with society. They are being exposed to the attitudes, values, and ways of the larger society. These attitudes and values may or may not be what the children's family accepts or believes. Children are mature enough to sense feelings of social conflicts in their parents, and this affects their own attitudes toward society. They may choose not to sign the contract. Comer and Poussaint suggest that black parents teach their children to develop attitudes that will enable them to be prepared to handle the realities of living black in a white-controlled America. Their obligation is to bring about personal skill development in their children that will help them to develop realistic ways of bringing about a better society. The system need not be accepted, but it is necessary to have some obligation to themselves instead of only being against something.

A social concern both at home and at school is manners. Children 6 years of age have considerable difficulty in formal social situations because they have not learned the social skills as yet. They do not know how to speak or act properly. They are not good at shaking hands with strangers and saying "How do you do" or "Goodby"; likewise they have difficulty in responding to "How are you?" They often forget to say "Please," "Thank you," and "Good-by." Children will open the door to people they know and say with enthusiasm "Come in," but it is a different situation with strangers. If parents give children the exact words to use in a social situation, they may be able to repeat them; but on their own they may be at a loss to know what to say or do.

All of the ups and downs of 6-year-olds are a

part of their growing up and their search for autonomy. They thought they were ready for independence when they were 2 years old and had learned all of the developmental tasks that were necessary for their basic survival. Again, when they were 4 years old, they thought that they were ready for the world because they were developing a consciousness of good and bad actions. Now, at 6 years of age they are in a new world; surely they must be ready for independence. Their past experiences and their intellectual insights, however, raise some uncertainties in their minds.

Seven-year-olds are becoming more aware of the social differences around them but not to any great extent that it will change their thinking. The choice of friends at this level is still uninfluenced by the social and economic status of the children or their home. However, the awareness of differences between their home and that of their friends is increasing.

Children of 7 years are learning to be self-critical; they like to do things well. This self-insight is leading toward a state of autonomy. They like to assume some responsibility. Children are also very talkative, often fighting verbally rather than physically. Frequently when they are angry at their parents, they toy with the idea that they are not their child or get a notion about running away from home. Stealing is not unusual at this age.

They can now greet people with "Hello" while looking straight at them, but "Good-by" may not be as easy. They may be able to shake hands but not comfortably. Many 7-year-olds will say "Excuse me" spontaneously if things go wrong. One point difficult for many older people, especially grandparents, to understand is that children may initially behave well when company is present but are likely to withdraw to their own activities before too long. Oftentimes one hears "Why won't Jimmy stay in the room with us when he comes for a visit?" Usually it is because he does not understand what is going on and wants to do something that is of interest to him.

At home 7-year-olds are more cooperative members of the family than they were at 6 years. Although they like to help around the house, their performance does not always match their good

intentions. They do get along better with their mothers and are developing a closer relationship with their fathers. They will play with their younger brothers and sisters and will look after them, although jealousy will still occur at times.

At play 7-year-olds do fairly well with others, but they will spend some time in solitary activity as well. There is less chance that they will use direct physical and verbal attack if things go badly in play. They are more concerned than previously about their place in the group and about being well liked. It is not unusual for 7-year-olds to develop "love affairs." In fact, boys may have more than one girl friend, and girls may like more than one boy. If one friend stops liking you, you simply find another. The loss of a boy or girl friend is usually taken as a matter of course, although some children cannot move this readily from one friend to another. This kind of a child can become upset, and tears may result when they have lost their "one and only." In spite of these relationships, the peer culture is beginning to separate the sexes in play activities.

Most 8-year-olds will have completed the transition to their peer culture. They now accept and prefer the activities, fads, and associations of their peers rather than those of adults. They generally give their allegiance to other children instead of to adults in case of a conflict.

Eight-year-olds gain security from being accepted by the group. They are responsive to group activities, and they hate playing alone. Whatever they do they want to do with other persons. Eight-year-olds are fond of team games, comics, television, movies, adventure stories, and collections. Their best friends are those of the same sex.

They are often careless and argumentative, but at the same time they are alert, friendly, and interested in people. Their self-concept is affected as they learn what other people are like and how they behave. Eight-year-olds are sensitive to criticism. However, they are growing individuals, and their contacts with others will modify their personality for better or for worse.

Eight-year-olds recognize property rights if their training has been sound. There is evidence of increasing modesty and self-control. Social pressures, especially by their peers, are influential in this respect. The children have a new awareness of individual differences and of what to do about them.

The social manners of the 8-year-old are better than they were, but they still need some improvement. Most 8-year-olds verbalize proper greetings and goodbys. Some can carry on excellent social conversations with adults; many have good company and table manners—away from home.[5] Eight-year-olds get along well with their parents, but they get along better with their friends. Their relationship with their mothers can be demanding, complicated, and subtle. They expect her to do certain things and are annoyed when she does not do them. They often demand her complete attention and companionship. Although they express a preference for their mother, father is coming in for an increased share of affection if he is available and reachable. Eight-year-olds can be strict with younger

Unexpected surprises bring spontaneity and enjoyment to childhood play.

David Strickler

"HERE IS A CHEATER"

Since he began kindergarten, T. J. has been an above average student, maintaining all A's and B's on his report card. Until this year he found school life very stimulating, but, due to a very strict teacher and an embarrassing classroom experience, he no longer shows the desire or enthusiasm for school work that he had previously. The unfortunate situation took place in his third grade classroom where the teacher gives speed tests in arithmetic almost daily and always records the grades from the tests. T. J. was caught trying to change an answer after they were supposed to have put their pencils down (in order to obtain a better grade was his excuse). The teacher tore up his paper, gave him a zero, called him in front of the class, and spanked him. She then proceeded to tell the children in the class: "Here is a cheater—we all know you cheat now, T. J. Don't try it again because everyone will be watching you!"

I went to see her about this problem because I was quite shocked at the way the situation was handled. For weeks after this happened, I had to push T. J. out of the door each morning for school. This third grade teacher is basically an excellent teacher of subject matter, but I'm certain she will warp the personalities of young children during her teaching career. This teacher commented recently that T. J. is still doing fine work but he just doesn't seem to have the interest and initiative that he had at the beginning of third grade; well, no wonder!

siblings; they may become upset if forced to follow the same home rules as are required of the younger children, such as the time they have to go to bed. In terms of chores and work around the house they like to be paid for their help; often parents become dismayed by this sudden "money-mad interest."

Peer and play culture

There is something both universal and eternal about the nature, purpose, and semblance of play in children. Children have been playing as long as there has been history. Toys, play materials, and drawings of children playing games have been found in the pyramids of Egypt and in the ruins of Pompeii. Blind-man's bluff, hide-and-seek, and tug-of-war were enjoyed by children in Plato's Greece.[6] Ancient Rome knew the finger-flashing game of paper-scissors-stone, still played around the world and not only by youngsters. We were "taught" the game at a geisha party in Kyoto, Japan, on a visit there. There are drawings in the ancient tombs of noblemen and pharaohs buried in Luxor showing children at play, and on the pavements of old Jerusalem there are stone carvings that were used by the Roman soldiers to play adult games. The interesting observation is the similarity of the types of games played by children throughout the ages in all types of cultures.

The nature, and perhaps the purpose, of play changes as the child gets older (Table 8-1). The center ingredient of play undergoes three separate, although somewhat overlapping, stages of evolution.[7] During the first two or three years of life, the most noticeable feature of play is physical activity involving sensorimotor recognition of objects and happenings. At about the ages of 3 or 4 years to about 6 or 7 years fantasy is added to physical activity, thereby permitting certain gestures, objects, or behavior to indicate or "stand for" other things or situations. Emotions are experienced more intensely at these ages than at any other time in life. The third stage involves much physical activity and fantasy but now includes a greater emphasis on being with children of one's own age group. The children

Table 8-1. General play interests from ages 5 to 10 years*

Age zone	General play interests	Age zone	General play interests
5 years	More independent play Much play centers around a house Plays with dolls Runs, climbs, swings, skips, dances Rides tricycle Uses sand in making roads Imitative play: house, store, hospital Paints, draws, colors, cuts, pastes Copies letters and numbers Builds with blocks	7 years— cont'd	Has "mania" for certain activities Bicycles Puzzles, magic, tricks Collecting and swapping Swimming Rudiments of ball play

6 years	Elaborates and expands 5-year play
	    interests
	Mud, sand, water play
	Games of tag, hide-and-seek
	Ball playing: tossing, bouncing
	Rough-and-tumble play
	Roller skates, ice skates
	Simple carpentry
	Table games with cards
	Paints, colors, draws, uses clay
	Collects odds and ends
	Imaginative play
	Builds with blocks
		8 years	Variety of play interests; prefers
			    companionship in play
			Games of all kinds
			Dramatic play of giving shows
			Collecting and arranging of collections
			Beginning interest in group games
			Unorganized group play of wild run-
			    ning, chasing
			Beginning of secret clubs
			Boys and girls begin to separate in
			    play

7 years	More intense interest in some activi-
	    ties, fewer new ventures
		9 years	Variety of play interests
			Works hard at his play
			Individual differences become
			    stronger
			Baseball, skating, swimming, sports
			Collecting of stamps, minerals, etc.
			Hikes
			Complicated table games

*Modified from Gesell, A., & Ilg, F. *The child from five to ten.* New York: Harper & Row, Publishers, 1946, pp. 367-370.

begin to see the need for rules. They may make up their own rules, and once agreed on, the demand to abide by them is vigorous.

At all age levels the play of children can be divided into four categories: imitative, exploratory, testing, and model-building play.[8] Imitative play reaches a peak when 4- to 6-year-olds play "house," "policeman," "school," or circular group singing and rhythmic games such as "ring-around-the-rosy," "mulberry bush," or "Sally Waters." Exploratory play increases with cognitive development and the discovery of manipulative objects, such as blocks, clay, toy models, and even riddles. Most children 6 to 12 years of age engage in testing play, whereby a child tests his own ability, agility, and capability. Physical contests such as dodge ball or kick ball

become important. Games involving memory, impulse and physical control, choice, or decision are also popular. Five- to six-year-olds play "hide-and-seek" or tag games, which will continue for many years. Seven- to eight-year-olds play "release," "relievo," and "kick the can," which involves some harassment of the person who is "it" (or "he" in Great Britain). On rainy days or in the evenings 8-year-olds and older can be enthusiastic about table games such as Monopoly, Parcheesi, rummy, and hearts. Red rover and run-sheep-run are popular with 9- to 10-year-olds, whereas 11- to 12-year-olds play the more complex game of prisoner's base. Model building in a primitive way becomes explicit by about the age of 4 years and reaches a peak at 10 to 12 years of age. The commercial world of today provides so many model toys such as trains, dolls, cars, and even monsters that they may be interfering with the advantages gained by some of the constructive, solitary play of children who used to make their own models.

As children of 6 years and older grow, individual differences become stronger. Some children read more and enjoy sedentary activities, whereas others head for the out-of-doors at the first chance. The sex role as emphasized by the family, neighborhood, and culture will have some influence on games played and types of interests displayed. A 5-year-old boy will not particularly hesitate to play the part of the mother in playing house; a 9-year-old boy would not be "caught dead" playing that part. Sex differences vary slightly in games and activities for the 5- to 7-year-old, but as the children grow older the more they tend to drift apart in interests and play activities.

At all ages girls generally like to play with boys. Their advanced physical maturity enables them to hold their own in games, but the influence of what it is "to be a man" begins to show in boys. The mores of the peer culture take over, and the gulf between boys and girls begins to widen. As an illustration, at the age of 5 years the girl tells the boy what games they will play and the boy plays them. At 6 years of age the girl tells the boy what games they will play and the boy says "No, I want to play this game," and the girl plays it. At the age of 7 years the boy tells the girl what games they will play, and she plays them. At the age of 8 years the boy says, "I don't know if I want to play with you; you're a girl." The 9-year-old boy is likely to say to the girl "Get out of here!"

INTELLIGENCE, LANGUAGE, AND THOUGHT

Six-year-olds are on the threshold of a new world. They can control their muscle movements so that they can do more precise physical activities than ever before. Socially they are becoming members of a society consisting largely of others of their own age. Intellectually, they are on the verge of answering their own "why" questions. It is important to understand that children are only at the starting point of all of these ven-

tures, but they are at that point, and the school will seek to help them make the most of their newly developed abilities and interests.

For a discussion of Piaget's theory of cognitive development of schemata and of the sensorimotor period, please refer to Chapter 5. Piaget's preoperational thought period is discussed in Chapter 7.

Piaget's stage of concrete operations (ages 7 to 11 or 12 years)

Briefly summarizing the development of cognitive ability from birth to 7 years of age, according to Piaget (Table 8-2), the early months of life consist of disorganized, unrelated, and diffused perceptions. The later months of the sensorimotor period involve egocentric experiences wherein infants become aware of their involvement in actions. During the preoperational thought period, children gradually become aware of their thoughts, although their reasoning is restricted to immediately observable circumstances. They cannot reason beyond the observable. Generalizations and ability to follow through with sustained deductions or successive judgment are lacking. A significant change in intellectual behavior emerges during the preoperational thought period, when children develop symbolic schemata that permit representative or symbolic behavior, in either verbal or nonverbal form. During this stage, children will also progress from making judgments formed from a perceptual basis (what they see) to making judgments from a conceptual basis (what they reason). Decentering is the process by which children develop more than one point of view about a particular subject or by which they can understand the many features or essentials of a group rather than isolated elements. Decentering has its beginning in the preoperational stage, but it becomes a major factor of cognitive functioning in the concrete operations stage.

The period of concrete operations begins at about the age of 7 years and lasts until ages 11 or 12 years. This period is characterized by children's ability to solve concrete problems—problems that they can manipulate or "see" in a concrete fashion. They begin to understand relationships between classes and sizes of objects,

Table 8-2. Piaget's stages of intellectual development*

Stage	Approximate ages	Characterization
I. Sensorimotor period	Birth to 2 years	Infant differentiates himself from objects; seeks stimulation and makes interesting spectacles last; prior to language, meanings defined by manipulations so that object remains "the same object" with changes in location and point of view
II. Preoperational thought period		
Preconceptual phase	2 to 4 years	Child is egocentric, unable to take viewpoint of other people; classifies by single salient features: if A is like B in one respect, then A must be like B in other respects
Intuitive phase	4 to 7 years	Child is now able to think in terms of classes, to see relationships, to handle number concepts, but is "intuitive" because he may be unaware of his classification.
III. Period of concrete operations	7 to 11 years	Child is able now to use logical operations such as *reversibility* (in arithmetic), *classification* (organizing objects into hierarchies of classes), and *seriation* (organizing objects into ordered series, such as increasing size). Gradual development of *conservation* in this order: mass (age 6 or 7), weight (age 9 or 10), and volume (age 11 or 12)
IV. Period of formal operations	11 to 15 years	Final steps toward abstract thinking and conceptualization; capable of hypothesis testing

*Modified from Piaget, J. *The origins of intelligence in children.* New York: International Universities Press, 1952.

something they found difficult to do in their preschool years. They also begin to understand conceptions of time, space, and, eventually, logic. As children grow older, they become more adept at solving concrete problems so that by the end of this period they begin to attack abstract problems.

During the concrete operations period, children reach a level where they understand equality relations, use arithmetic and measurements, understand the notion of right and left as applied to objects in themselves, and understand the concept of number. Piaget hypothesizes that children's conception of numbers goes hand in hand with the development of logic.[9]

It is during this stage that children realize that other people see things differently from the way they do. Through repeated and often frustrating interchanges with their peers they have come to cognitive grips with other viewpoints and perspectives that differ from their own. At the same time the necessity of maintaining an original premise in an argument is also being developed.

During the concrete operations period, children's conception of the world definitely changes. The idea that nature is made by man disappears entirely toward the age of 9 or 10 years. By this time all of nature is imbued with purpose (i.e., the sun has been made for the purpose of giving us warmth and light, and the clouds for the purpose of bringing us rain). As for their conception of physical causality, this third broad stage of cognitive development has produced a new parallelism between logic and the real categories—in other words at approximately the age of 10 years, when logical thought becomes deductive, one's interpretation of reality breaks away from forms of primitive realism, such as "seeing is believing," and becomes a logical or reasoning necessity.[10]

Piaget states that the value system and social interaction of children fit into the nine groupings that make up the concrete operations period. (The nine groups are not presented in this text.) Children must interact socially to grow intellectually because without social life they would never succeed in understanding the reciprocity of viewpoints. Consequently they would not develop adequate perspectives, geometrical or logical.

Mental characteristics

Most 6-year-olds operate on a precausal level of reasoning. These children have not firmly established a concept of "cause and effect" or the idea that a person can sometimes reason what the cause or the result might be. However, children do ask "Why?" and "What for?" and "How?" They begin to realize that objects and events serve certain purposes that they want to know. Six-year-olds are still in the preoperational stage of conceptual development, however. Therefore their reasoning process will be largely governed by the appearance of things, and they can form only rudimentary generalizations.

When given two objects, 6-year-olds can more easily see the differences that exist between the objects than the similarities. Differences can be seen or experienced directly, but similarities must be abstracted from generalizations, an ability not developed until about 9 years of age. Six-year-olds also have difficulty in making decisions, even about such things as what flavor of ice cream they would like to have or what color of a balloon to buy. Their memory is such that they can repeat sentences of ten or twelve words or repeat four digits in order. They know number combinations up to ten.

The experience of school has helped the 7-year-olds in developing their mental powers. Their activities are becoming more specialized; they are not as general as they have been up to

this point. They now have the mental ability that enables them to count by ones, twos, fives, and tens. They now grasp the basic idea of addition and subtraction. However, many times the work done along these lines is the result of memorizing addition and subtraction tables. Modern math seeks to teach how to reason by sets and groups.

Seven-year-olds do little abstract thinking. They learn best in concrete terms and when they can be active while learning. They prefer to participate rather than to be just a spectator. Their speech is no longer egocentric but is now sociocentric—others centered.

They have a rudimentary understanding of time and monetary values. They can tell time and make some small purchases. Allowing children to make these purchases on their own gives them a feeling that their parents trust them to handle money, even if they are standing by and watching them.

At this age curiosity begins to arise as to the difference between the sexes and where babies come from. These ideas show an interest in reality and indicate the importance of giving truthful information. Sex information may well be given at this age—not to be taught in great detail but enough to satisfy the 7-year-old's curiosity.

Seven-year-old children are entering Piaget's stage of concrete operations. They now begin to use elementary logic and to reason about size, space, weight, volume, number, and time. They can group objects according to a given attribute, such as color, and still realize that they can be regrouped according to another attribute, such as size. They can also order things into a series, such as from larger to smaller. They are able to apply the principle of conservation, which states that certain properties remain constant and invariant regardless of changes in their appearance. For example, they understand that the water from a beaker remains the same when poured into a shallow dish.

Almy and associates[11] investigated children's ability to apply the principle of conservation. She used a longitudinal approach to test and retest youngsters on their conservational ability in three tasks, two involving number and one involving quantity of liquid. One of her findings was that 76% of the 7-year-olds from a middle socioeconomic background conserved on all three tasks. This was in agreement with Piaget's theory.

Eight-year-olds show an interest in causal relationships. They are curious about all types of changes and happenings and want to know about cause and effects. This level of thinking represents the scientific dimension of recognition and is proceeding from concrete to abstract and metaphysical relations.

The 8-year-old's memory span is increasing. Their memory span for words will, of course,

Curiosity about all things living, large or small, makes learning a wonder to behold.

David Strickler

Third graders enjoy the opportunity to be creative, especially when given guidelines within which they are permitted to express their ingenuity.

vary greatly according to their familiarity, interest, and meaning for the child. They can answer five out of six simple questions on a story about 100 words long and can repeat without errors a sentence of about sixteen words after hearing it once.

Mentally, 8-year-olds are still developing through experience. They like to take field trips and question all they see. They still see the teacher as the authority. Children are much interested in the past. They like to talk about Indians and their ways. They can now tell the day of the month and the year. Far-off places and ways of communication now have real meaning. As a result of all this experience the children are starting to use some abstract thinking.

Children with learning disabilities

There are some children who, in spite of a good intellect, have difficulties in learning. The children we are referring to are those who have a central nervous system dysfunction and whose condition is called "learning disabilities." They make up about 30% of the 5- and 6-year-olds, about 20% of the 7- and 8-year-olds, and about 10% of those age 9 and older, including adults.

The definition of learning disabilities is still a little tenuous because the field is too new and all the variables have not been worked out. There are, however, four areas of agreement in all the definitions of learning disabilities.[12] They are:

1. Intellectual capacity is average or better.

COLOR ME HAPPY

Five-line poetry written by third graders. The Harper and Row Reading Series book, *Trouble and Turnips,* gives these instructions: The first line of the poem usually has one word and names something. The second line tells in two words what the thing might do. The third line uses three words to describe the thing, and the fourth line is a four-word phrase. The last line names the thing again.

Owl
Sleeping, hooting
Soft, brown, scary
Flying in the night
Owl

by Glenn

Bats
Flies, bites
Ugly, furry, strong
Flies through the sky
Bats

by Stacey

Ducks
Quack, wobble
White, soft, wonderful
Swim in the pond
Ducks

by John

Hermit crabs
Crawl, sleep
Shelled, hard, ugly
Sleeping all the time
Hermit crabs

by Linda

Snakes
Sliver, crawl
Spiney, spring, long
Sneak through the meadow
Snakes

by Donnie

Mouse
Squeaks, scampers
Soft, gray, funny
Squeaking across the floor
Mouse

by Michelle

2. There is a major discrepancy between expected and actual achievement.
3. There is a disorder in one or more of the psychophysical processes involved in using spoken or written language.
4. The deficiencies are not due to visual, hearing, or motor handicaps; to mental retardation; to emotional disturbance; or to environmental disadvantage or differences.

By implication, the problem of the learning disabled children is due to central nervous system dysfunctions in perceptual and conceptual processing. The causes of the dysfunction may be organic or biochemical in nature. The large percentage of 5- and 6-year-olds who are identified as learning disabled have a maturational lag in neurological development of the perceptual-conceptual systems involved in the learning process. They will mature and outgrow their problems.

The largest percentage of LD (learning disabilities) children have mild disturbances. There are, however, some moderate, severe, and profound cases as well. Most LD children have difficulty in learning to read, especially in learning how to use phonetic analysis. Surprisingly, most of the LD children who are poor readers have average to above average achievement in arithmetic and math. About 10% of LD children do very poorly in arithmetic and math but do well in reading. A goodly number of the LD cases, about 35% to 40%, have difficulty with handwriting. The implication is that LD children differ as to the areas of their academic deficiencies because of differences in the location and nature of their central nervous system dysfunction.

According to Kaluger and Kaluger,[13] LD children may have characteristics that can be classified under five headings: (1) difficulties in academic learning, (2) perceptual-motor problems, (3) language and speech disorders, (4) difficulties with thought processes, and (5) behavior and affective characteristics. One of the more common characteristics is distractibility, either visual or auditory, causing the child to have a short attention span. Perceptual processing difficulty, especially of auditory stimuli, is another common symptom. Excessive restlessness, sometimes miscalled as hyperactivity, is

found in about 30% of the children. These factors, plus about fifty other observed characteristics, make these children inefficient learners in some academic areas and, as a result, they get behind in their work.

One contributor to learning disabilities is a central nervous system allergy caused by certain foods that are eaten.[14] Not all individuals are affected; of those that are affected, not all have their problems caused by the same food product. In general, the principle is that LD children appear to be more susceptible than other children to artificial food coloring, artificial food flavoring, food preservatives, and to foods that contain salicylates. Salicylates are salts from salicylic acid. They produce an analgesic action on tissue, but also have irritant qualities. The individual, child or adult, susceptible to salicylates will be more restless, find it difficult to concentrate or settle down, or get physical symptoms such as headaches or a dull feeling. Some adults do not drink coffee at night because it keeps them awake. Some children get "wound up" when they drink artificial colored and artificial flavored fruit punch (usually red in color). In general, "junk food" such as soft drinks, sugar-coated cereals, hot dogs, potato chips, some lunch meats, ice cream, candy, and similar foods are suspect. However, natural salicylates are found in apples, strawberries, tomatoes, cucumbers, and other vegetables and fruits. Remember, not all children are affected by the same foods. One child may be able to eat apples; another may be affected by them.

Language and logical thought

By the time children are 6 years old they have an oral vocabulary of approximately 2,500 words. They use sentences averaging about five words in length, and they make use of all the various parts of speech. They know some of the letters of the alphabet and can give their names on seeing their visual form. They may even be able to recognize the printed form of a few words. During the elementary school years, children refine and extend the language they have developed up to that point. Their speech becomes more socialized. They begin to put their thoughts and feelings into words more easily and soon

Harold Geyer

What makes a pizza? What is mozzarella cheese? Informal learning at its best. You can eat it, too!

begin logical thought. They begin to understand more abstract forms of language such as puns and figures of speech.

Two- to 3-year-olds ask the question "What is that?" They want to increase their vocabulary by asking for a word or a name for an object. Four- to 5-year-olds ask "Who is that . . . ?" "What is he doing . . .?" and "Why does . . .?" and other similar questions. Children are reflecting their awareness of the world around them, especially of the actions of humans. They are

usually satisfied by almost any positive response, as compared to one which merely suggests that they be quiet. The implication is that the children are reflecting their curious and inquisitive natures, but they are not yet aware of logic and reasoning. To some degree their questioning may also indicate the type of communicative skill they have developed for carrying on a conversation with adults. They may not know of any other way by which they can talk to older people. Most 6- to 7-year-olds, however, have reached the precausal level of reasoning, and so their questions of "Why?" and "What for?" and "How?" indicate that they are beginning to know that objects, actions, and events serve certain purposes; they want to know what they are.

During the preschool years, speech is mainly egocentric in the forms of (1) repetition of words, syllables, or rhythmic phrases that children enjoy saying, (2) a monologue whereby children converse with themselves as if they were thinking out loud, or (3) a dual or collective monologue that concerns another person or persons but in which the children do not make a strong effort to communicate with them. By the time children enter school, however, their speech is proceeding toward more socialized speech. Piaget[15] divides socialized speech into (1) adapted information that involves an exchange of information between two or more people; (2) criticism, by which the child is making some sort of a subjective value judgment, not just stating a fact as in adaptive information; (3) commands, requests, and threats, representing the minimum interchange of speech necessary for communication; and (4) questions and answers. Socialization of thought and speech comes to children between their seventh and eighth year, partly because they now have a more extensive social life as they begin to work and play with a larger, more stable peer group.

Verbal understanding increases, and the children can now communicate their own thoughts more objectively. Seven- to 8-year-olds are more likely than younger children to be able to arrange stories of explanations logically. Eight-year-olds' growth in vocabulary is shown not only in an increased number of words but also in their ability to give more precise definitions than previously. Six-year-olds will define an orange as "You eat it," and a puddle as "You step in it." Eight-year-olds respond with "It's a color or a fruit," and "A little pool of water made by rain."

PERSONALITY, SELF-CONCEPT, AND SEX ROLE

A major influence on children's developing personality and self-concept is their entrance into a school situation that stresses learning of the basic academic skills. There is a cultural sig-

nificance attached to "going to school" that may make children see themselves differently in terms of their capabilities (or lack of them) and of what they perceive is expected of them by others.

Personality development

Individual differences in basic personality attributes are fairly well established by the age of 6 years.[16] However, the basic traits are not completely formed by this age, and three significant changes in personal makeup usually occur. First, children learn some degree of self-control. As such, they learn to live and cope with frustrations. They find ways of avoiding trouble and of achieving success through their own decisions. Second, there is an increase in the independence of children between the ages of 6 and 9 years. They make friends away from home, become interested in external events and experiences, and begin to demand decision-making prerogatives in keeping with what they learn other children have. Third, a feeling of self-worth is either enhanced or decreased, depending on the ease with which they acquire the basic skills of reading, writing, and arithmetic. The way in which children react to their specific situation greatly affects their future personality, patterns of adjustment, and degree of self-acceptance.

During middle childhood, children's social and communicative skills must expand rapidly or they risk the possible rejection or aggression of their peers. The teacher becomes a major socializing agent. At least in the initial school environment the teacher assumes the role of the surrogate parent. In this role the teacher is in a position to influence both the social and the personality development of children. She can teach social and communicative skills as they are needed. By her actions, attitudes, and words she is instrumental in shaping the pliable, developing self-image of the children.[17]

For the first time they are away from the constant supervision of their mother. As a result, they are in a position where they can make some value judgments and simple decisions of their own, such as which way to walk home from school and whom to talk and play with in the meanwhile. With this increase in freedom a more realistic self-concept develops. Instead of relying

Self-concept develops as a child compares his own skills and abilities with those of others in the group.

Dave Repp/Image, Inc.

on their parents and family for an appraisal of their behavior, they can now look to their teacher and peers for such impressions. As they get older, more and more will the peer group be influential in determining which personality traits they will develop. The personality of children is affected by people and how they react to them. They are especially vulnerable to labels or characteristics that others apply to them, such as lazy, stupid, happy, friendly, neat, or careless. As children strive for an identity that they can recognize and accept, they will often feel insecure and lonely. Parents and teachers need to show their confidence in children until they gain a satisfactory self-impression.

Self-concept

When children recognize and identify with their ways of growing, behaving, and thinking, they are strengthening their awareness of themselves. This awareness of self-attributes, as they see and believe them to be, constitutes their self-concept. It is their appraisal or evaluation of themselves. The self-concept is developed from comments made by others and from inferences from experiences the children have had in their life space. Only as cognitive ability increases to the stage that children are able to conceptualize will they have a concept of self and their particular physical, social, and emotional characteristics. Their reasoning ability has to develop to the concrete operations stage, as conceived by Piaget, before they have an opportunity to ascertain a more realistic concept of self.

Children reach middle childhood with a self-concept derived through their parents, immediate family, and a limited number of peers. Their self-concept is likely to be distorted or incomplete. As they are subject to the approval or disapproval of teachers, other adults, and peers, they may begin to question the validity of their view of their attributes and abilities. Between the ages of 6 and 9 years children more than once will be concerned about their capability and acceptibility. Negative concerns such as "I'm no good" and "Nobody cares about me" may arise. These thoughts will not be easily dispelled. As children grow more insightful, they are more likely to wonder about themselves. Unfortunately, some children get little or no support or direction from others they consider important to help them keep negative thoughts in proper perspective. In fact

Table 8-3. Relationships between the home and child behavior*

Type of home	Type of child behavior associated with it
Rejective	Submissive, aggressive, adjustment difficulties, feelings of insecurity, sadistic, nervous, shy, stubborn, noncompliant
Overprotective, "babying"	Infantile and withdrawing, submissive, feelings of insecurity, aggressive, jealous, difficult adjustment, nervous
Dominating parent	Dependable, shy, submissive, polite, self-conscious, uncooperative, tense, bold, quarrelsome, disinterested
Submissive parent	Aggressive, careless, disobedient, independent, self-confident, forward in making friends, noncompliant
Inharmonious	Aggressive, neurotic, jealous, delinquent, uncooperative
Defective discipline	Poor adjustment, aggressive, rebellious, jealous, delinquent, neurotic
Harmonious, well adjusted	Submissive, good adjustment
Calm, happy, compatible	Cooperative, superior adjustment, independent
Child accepted	Socially acceptable, faces future confidently
Parents play with child	Security feelings, self-reliant
Logical, scientific approach	Self-reliant, cooperative, responsible
Consistent, strict discipline	Good adjustment
Giving child responsibilities	Good adjustment, self-reliant, security feelings

*From Radke, M. J. *The relation of parental to children's behavior and attitudes*. Child Welfare Monograph No. 22. Minneapolis: University of Minnesota Press. Copyright 1964 by the publisher.

some parents unknowingly nurture a negative self-concept in children by (1) teasing or never being satisfied; (2) usually doing for the children what the children could do for themselves, thus making them feel inadequate and helpless; (3) being so dominant that children feel that they are not being completely trusted and loved; or (4) being more concerned with something other than the children and thus neglecting them. A negative self-concept may also come from a type of discipline by parents or teachers that embarrasses and humiliates (Table 8-3).

A positive self-concept enables a person to feel adequate, likeable, intrinsically worthy, and free.

These feelings lead to self-respect, self-confidence, and eventually, happiness. Children must be considered as individuals with characteristics all their own. They must be brought up in an atmosphere of trust, respect, and good regard if they are to emerge as happy, well-adjusted persons. The middle years is a time when the self-concept needs to be carefully nurtured and developed into a stable, acceptable image.

Sex roles and sex typing

Sex role development refers to the identification of the individual with culturally assigned physiological, sociological, and psychological

Table 8-4. Loevinger's milestones of ego development and extrapolations to sex role development*

Loevinger's milestones of ego development				Sex role development extrapolated
Stage	Impulse control	Interpersonal style	Conscious concerns	Conceptions of sex role
Presocial/symbiotic		Autistic, symbiotic	Self versus nonself	
Impulse ridden	Impulse ridden, fear of retaliation	Exploitive, dependent	Sexual and aggressive bodily feelings	Development of gender identity, self-assertion, self-expression, self-interest
Self-protective (formerly opportunistic)	Expedient, fear of being caught	Exploitive, manipulative, wary	Advantage, control, protection of self	Extension of self, self-extension, self-enhancement
Conformity	Conformity to external rule	Reciprocal, superficial	Things, appearance, reputation, self-acceptance	Conformity to external role, development of sex role stereotypes, bifurcation of sex roles
Conscientious	Internalized rules, guilt	Intensive, responsive	Differentiated inner feelings, motives, self-respect	Examination of self as sex role exemplar vis-à-vis internalized values
Autonomous	Coping with conflict, toleration of differences	Intensive, concern for autonomy	Differentiated inner feelings, role concepts, self-fulfillment	Differentiation of sex role, coping with conflicting masculine–feminine aspects of self
Integrated	Reconciling inner conflicts, renunciation of unattainable	Cherishing of individuality	All of the above plus identity	Achievement of individually defined sex role, integration of both masculine and feminine aspects of self, androgynous sex role definition

*From Block, J. H. Conception of sex role. *American Psychologist*, 1973, **28**, 513-514. Modified from Loevinger, J., & Wessler, R. *Measuring ego development* (Vol. 1). San Francisco: Jossey-Bass, Inc., Publishers, 1970.

characteristics and concepts of what constitutes maleness and femaleness. The implication is that a boy should take on and aspire to the male characteristics and girls to the female characteristics.

Until children reach the middle childhood years, there is no extensive striving or concern for assuming the appropriate sex role. As mentioned previously, at the age of 5 years a boy will play the part of either the father or the mother in a make-believe situation. However, by the age of 9 years the boy would absolutely reject the idea of playing a female part. This change suggests the degree to which sex roles are strengthened during middle childhood. Table 8-4 indicates stages of ego development and conceptions of sex role.

The sex role phenomenon is one that generally takes place in the home and family setting. Boys find it natural to pattern themselves after their fathers and girls after their mothers. The parents find this responsiveness gratifying. When chronic antagonism and disharmony exist between the parents, problems arise. The boy may find it hard to identify with his father because he is afraid of losing his mother's love. Likewise, he is also fearful of identifying with his mother because he may incur his father's anger. However, if emotional circumstances are such that the boy rejects the father completely, he may overidentify with the mother.

A case in point regards a boy in a kindergarten class who was brought to our attention. When the boy was 3 years old, his baby brother died. He witnessed his mother's hysteria and his father's sternness in trying to help his wife gain control of herself by slapping her. Unfortunately, for a long period of time afterward the father showed no love for his wife or for the surviving son. The boy only remembered that his father slapped his mother and that during that period of life his father was rather mean and short-tempered with him. The mother was the child's only adult source of love and protection. He became afraid to go near his father and began to identify with his mother and his two sisters, who were nice to him. The boy became obsessed with the idea of being a girl. He had gone as far as asking the other children to call him Janie. During playtime, he preferred to play house, at times dressing up in women's clothes and pretending to do the shopping or take care of the baby. It was only through skillful handling by his teacher that he began to work at a workbench and finally became interested in working with tools.

If the mother or father is missing from the home and no model is there with whom to identify, the child may identify with the teacher at school. In the case of boys, researchers have concluded that some male teachers are needed in elementary schools. One study of the effects of a man teacher showed an improvement in the behavior of hostile boys, and mothers of boys in the study reported that their sons were easier to handle at home.[18] In another study it was determined that the male elementary school teacher was especially significant in the inner city. The conclusion was that boys from low-income families needed an effective male figure with whom they could associate and identify to learn their appropriate sex role.

In the past, sex roles were rather clearly defined. Today the characteristics of the sex roles are not as readily ascertained; in fact the nature of the roles may be changing. A research study involving 105 white, middle-class, urban children sought to answer the question, "Are children of varying family backgrounds, defined in terms of the modern-type family and the traditional-type family, developing different sex role concepts?" The results showed that 85% of all children chose their own sex as the one they liked better.[19] This result was in keeping with other studies. It was also determined that girls from modern families were the most likely to depart from sex-typed expectations. Traditional families produced the most highly aggressive boys and the most highly dependent girls. The study indicated that sex typing was more the result of family experiences than school experiences.

THE ONE-PARENT FAMILY

So far not enough research has been done to prove that the one-parent family is inherently pathological or is not as good as two parents. The two-parent system has its own pathology—both parents may be equally competent but unable to work together as a team in raising a family; one parent may be more competent than the other but afraid to express this competence for fear of ruining the team effort; one parent may be competent but have his/her efforts overwhelmed by the incompetent parent; the two parents may be in serious conflict as to how their parental roles should be performed, and these may cause the children to be caught in the middle between the two parents.

Parental roles

Identification, defined as the process by which one person tries to become like another, usually with the parent of the same sex, is an important factor in the development of personality in children 6 to 12 years old. If two parents are living at home, it is very rare that a child would identify with only one parent and exclude the other. This identification is not limited to a certain period of time. Children react most to the expectations that the most prominent people in their lives have of them, even though these people do not exhibit the behavior themselves. For example, Billy learns to obey his father because his father expects it, although his father does not obey Billy. Both Billy and his father have expectations of the other and each knows what the other expects of him. Even though Billy has never himself played the father's role, he is learning it through this type of experience.

The roles played by the mother and father are very different and can usually be considered as expressive (being sensitive to the feelings, thoughts, and needs of others) or instrumental (being responsible for solving the problems of the group and making decisions on their behalf). Although both men and women play both expressive and instrumental roles, usually women are the expressive leaders and men the instrumental leaders.

Most sources tended to agree on this description of a two-parent family. Both boys and girls are more closely attached to their mothers than their fathers during infancy through early preschool years. So, children of both sexes first relate to the person playing the expressive role. This is when boys and girls first learn to be expressive, are first exposed to love-oriented discipline, and take basic steps toward internalizing conscience.

The next step is to become attached to the father and outgrow some of the dependence on the mother. The father reacts differently with his sons and daughters. With his daughters he acts very expressively, praising and enjoying their feminine acts, while he is more demanding and applies more discipline to his sons. The father plays boisterously with the boy, stimulating vigorous play, discouraging tears, and acting very casual about bumps and bruises. The father plays with his little girl's hair and tickles her chin. The mother is happy when her son is aggressive, active, and courageous and when her daughter is sensitive, charming, and delightful. The salience of the father in the family was proven to have an important effect on the boy's assumption of his sex role. A boy will be a great deal more masculine the more he interacts with a powerful father, one who does both rewarding and punishing. Sons conformed more to the expectations their fathers had of them when the fathers took part in raising the children.[20]

Every child needs both a mother and father figure to act as models for the child's social and emotional development. When the children are living with only one parent, this parent must play a dual role, that of the mother and father. This dual role is hard to play, but it is especially more difficult when it is only played at intervals—for instance, if the parents are divorced and the children spend time with both parents and see conflicting ideas.

Divorced families

One basic question parents contemplating divorce ask themselves is: Is it better for the children if we remain together in an unhappy marriage, or should we end the marriage and therefore end many personal frustrations? Society in the United States holds two conflicting beliefs. One is that the couple's first concern should be with their parental roles and that they should try to put aside their marital problems, which implies that marriage roles are secondary to parental roles. Yet in a society that places great emphasis on personal ego-need satisfaction in marriage, the placing of marriage in a secondary position may be difficult for the married person to accept.

Within five years of being divorced, three quarters of all divorced people are remarried. There are approximately one million children under 18 years of age living in one-parent homes following the divorce of their parents. Nine times out of ten the mother has custody of the children.[21] As the head of a family, most women will eventually conquer the difficult process of taking over the role of the father. During the time the woman is the head of the family, she no longer has to consult with the other parent or worry about what the other parent thinks. However, if she remarries, she must undertake an even more difficult process of relinquishing the father role that she had previously assumed. Divorced mothers, as well as all other parents without partners, feel that not having to share daily parental decisions with a partner who might not agree with his/her strategy is an advantage. They feel that the parental partner can be a great asset if the two parents agree, but if this is not usually true, one parent can probably do a better job alone.

Mother—only parent

Approximately 13% of American families have only one parent. Since most one-parent families are ones in which the father is absent, it is only natural that mother-only parent families are the ones that are studied most. It is the boys in such families that have been usually researched. Most of the research studies seem to focus on the personality development and cognitive development.

Types. Mothers without husbands fall into five categories: divorced, separated, deserted, widowed, and never married. If the mother has a job outside of the home, there are other factors that create added strain, along with having to fill the role of both parents. Children leave too late for school, get home too early, and have too many vacations to fit into the schedule of the working mother.

Psychologically, desertion may cause more trauma than divorce. This affects both men and women. It is less planned. The parent does not know whether to accept the other parent's role. They are not free to remarry or to go out with other people since they are still technically married. These problems are basically the same for separated parents. Although the widowed mother faces the same problems of being the head of a household, she has one advantage that gives her added emotional support. Her family, friends, and community have a more favorable attitude toward her, as compared to the less desirable attitudes held toward unmarried, separated, deserted, and divorced mothers. The unmarried mother, who keeps her children as opposed to having an abortion or giving her children up for adoption, faces the problems other women as heads of families face, plus one other major one. Society frowns on her status. However, she does know that society disapproves of her, and she does not have to shuffle conflicting public opinion around in her mind.

IQ. Researchers at the Institute for Developmental Studies (IDS) in New York City studied a sample of 543 black and white children who were selected from various socioeconomic levels. For children in first and fifth grades, they found that IQ was definitely related to the presence of a father in the home.[22] Other studies also suggest that IQ as well as academic performance may be negatively affected by father absence. The IDS found that the association between IQ and father absence was higher for fifth graders than for first graders. This finding seems inconsistent with previous research cited, postulating that father influence decreased as the child got older. However, what is clear is that the effect of father absence is definitely interwoven to varying degrees with factors such as community, economics, and family.

Maturity and sex typing. Lacking a father supposedly affects the development of boys mainly because the resolution of the Oedipal situation, as cited in psychoanalytic theory, is supposed to be of major importance in developing emotional maturity and appropriate sex-role identification. Thomes did a study that examined the impact of mother-only families on sons and daughters. She found that the assumption that boys would be more affected than girls by the absence of the father was not true. "On the contrary, the differences that were found between the two groups of children tended to differentiate between girls whose fathers were absent and those whose fathers lived in the home."[23] From this it may be assumed that fathers seem to be more important to their daughters than to their sons.

However, since Thomes' study was the only one giving evidence to the fact that fathers may influence their daughters more than their sons, we should still work on the assumption that fathers serve as the chief model for the development of appropriate sex typing in boys, and if the father is absent, they will develop less appropriate sex typing. Freudian theories imply that if the father is absent from the home, the child will be more mother-identified and is more likely to develop latent or overt homosexual tendencies or feminine characteristics.

Kriesberg[24] showed that the values of education and working hard in school were values that were held by both married and husbandless mothers. The husbandless mothers were even more likely than the married mothers to place high demands on their children. Husbandless mothers may be trying so hard to succeed that they overreact in what they do.

The results of studies done by Mischel[25] suggest that father absence may indicate an overall inadequate home environment, one in which the children may not learn appropriate heterosexual social behavior. This study also included older children between 11 and 14 years of age. For this age group it was found that as the children get more experience outside of the home, their behavior is influenced more by extrafamilial sources. They become less dependent on influences in the home and more dependent on influences from peers.

Masculinity. It is very important that the mother give her son positive descriptions of the father's masculinity in characteristics such as strength, physical ability, and competence for a normal, healthy, masculine development in her boy. This positive action is essential because the mother's interpretation of the father, whether he is absent or present, has a direct influence on the personality development of the children, especially the boys. The mother's feelings about the father, men, and masculinity in general are significant in social relationships. A boy raised in a fatherless home may be unsure about his masculinity and may overcompensate for this in order to prove it to himself and his peers. One

should consider this theory in regard to black children who come from homes where there is a higher ratio of father absence.

Father—only parent

There seems to be little research done on these father-only families, but one must remember that in over 90% of the divorce cases custody of minor children is awarded to the mother. This seems to indicate that most of these father-only families represent either desertion or death of the mother. However, a great number of these fathers remarry, in which case they experience the same problems of role changes as mothers who remarry. Fathers of father-only families experience the same problems as mothers as heads of families. They experience role conflicts with their jobs, their social life, and their parental responsibilities. However, these fathers do feel that it is better for the children to have one parent make the rules and decisions rather than have a conflicting opinion of the other partner.

Black—only parent

Most black families are headed by men as are other American families. However, the proportion of families with female heads is greater at all levels of income among blacks than among whites. This difference among whites and non-whites is greatest among those families in the lowest income bracket—families most likely to live in disadvantaged big-city neighborhoods.

The problem of fatherless families among black families is compounded by the fact that blacks, especially poorer ones, tend to have larger families. "The average poor, urban non-white family contains 4.8 persons, as compared with 3.7 for the average poor, urban white family. This is one of the primary factors in the poverty status of non-white households in large cities." (National Advisory Commission on Civil Disorders, as cited in Glasser, 1970, p. 35.)[26]

Unfortunately, young people in the ghetto are overly conscious of a system that rewards those who exploit others illegally. In such a situation, many people adopt the "hustle" and such exploitation as an acceptable way of life; they forego legitimate work and traditional marriage in favor of casual and temporary relationships.

From generation to generation this pattern reinforces itself, creating a "culture of poverty" and perpetuating a feeling of cynicism about society and its institutions.[27]

How to raise a good child

In some lower-class families, the children grow up in an environment of poverty and deprivation as well as a fatherless situation. This handicap is increased because many mothers are "absent" in the sense that they must go out and work to provide support. If this is the case, many children, without adequate adult supervision at home, spend most of their time roaming the streets. In this environment, one of violence, crime, and poverty, the symbol of success is not one of the "solid citizen," the responsible husband and father, but rather one of the "hustler" who takes care of himself by exploiting others. In this setting the "successful" men are numbers runners, dope sellers, and so on, because their earnings surpass those of men who make a living the honest way.

It is generally assumed that children from father-absent homes are more likely than children from father-present homes to become juvenile delinquents. However, the research also states that there are other factors affecting this relationship. Examples of such factors are that children from broken homes are more likely to be charged and committed for delinquent acts than are children from two-parent homes. The family's socioeconomic status plays an important role because blacks and children from the lower socioeconomic levels are more likely to be tried and convicted for juvenile offenses than are white and middle-class children.[28]

The Juvenile Court of Franklin County, Chambersburg, Pennsylvania published the following set of suggestions on "How to raise a good child." Their recommendations are based on what the judges were observing in working with children, and their families, who were being brought into their courtroom or chambers.

1. Give your child religious and spiritual training; moral backbone. Take him, rather than send him, to Sunday School and Church and other worthwhile places.
2. Setting a good example yourself in all things is the most direct and effective manner of bringing up a child of whom you can always be proud.
3. To prevent untruthfulness in your child, avoid deceptions in your own relations with him or with others. Be frank and honest with your child. If he displays untruthfulness, try to find the real cause and do something to eliminate it.
4. Avoid humiliating your child in the presence of his friends. It lessens his respect for you.
5. Be consistent in giving orders or instructions to your child. If you forbid something today, apply the same rule tomorrow and next week. If you promise him a licking for disobedience, be sure to give it to him. Do not promise or threaten something you do not intend to accomplish.
6. Grave harm results when both parents are not agreed on discipline of the child. It is essential that, outside the child's presence, parents reach agreement on methods of training and that afterward they avoid interfering with each other in requiring obedient conduct on the part of the child. When obedience is not taught in the playpen, it often becomes necessary that it be taught at the federal or state pen.
7. Do your level best to answer the endless "whys" and "hows" of your children.
8. If a conflict of wills arises between you and your child, don't just knock him down . . . try to reason with him, to help him understand. Please note carefully a distinction here. On many occasions, including those when guests are in the home, a child, or any subordinate, should be taught to obey first and to ask reasons some other time.
9. Use constructive discipline, rewarding him for little acts "above and beyond the call of duty." Do not, however, try to buy your child's love, respect, or obedience by means of gifts or privileges. These wholesome attitudes of the child should come as a by-product of your whole manner of living and of all your actions toward him.
10. Keep in mind that his educational and emotional development is first and foremost

a parental responsibility. Schools can neither teach nor apply discipline as well as parents can.

11. Encourage him to discuss plans, problems, or pleasures with you. Never be too busy.
12. In his presence and elsewhere always be respectful of womanhood, of humankind, of law, and of elders.
13. Always speak respectfully of all races, creeds, and color.
14. Open your home to his companions; they won't muss up the place if given a little supervision.
15. If possible, give him a modest allowance. Let him learn early how to save or spend.
16. Keep yourself from being shocked and exploding when he tells you he has done something wrong. Try to understand what motivated him. Think and speak *with* him, not *at* him.
17. Do things *with* him, not *for* him. Let him have a share in earning what he receives.

EMOTIONAL AND MORAL DEVELOPMENT

The innate excitement of the newborn is the beginning of emotions. Gradually, distress and delight appear and eventually other emotions, most of which are learned through experience. During the preschool years children display their emotions rather openly. As they enter school and get older, they tend to use more subtle expressions of emotions. Emotional development is shaped by the experiences of the children and the forms of emotional expression or behavior they have learned to apply to the affective experience. Moral development also partly depends on the types of events, attitudes, and verbal experiences to which children have been exposed. Unlike emotional development that is related to affective responses, moral development depends on cognitive development, knowledge, and awareness.

Emotional characteristics

Although there is a decrease in the number of emotional explosions during the age of 6 years, children are still in a more-or-less constant state of emotional tension and agitation. In some respects 5-year-olds seem to be more emotionally stable than 6-year-olds. The intense activity of 6-year-olds is partly due to new social and scholastic demands and partly to their desire to take a giant step forward in asserting independence, but they are fearful because of their lack of success in doing so at ages 2 and 4 years. In a sense they are now trying to act on their own even though it may be by defiance, and they are beset with uncertainties and fearfulness. Sibling jealousy may still persist, especially if there are younger siblings at home that the children believe may be getting more attention now that they are away at school all day. At 6 years of age children are very fearful, especially of sounds such as are made by thunder, rain, and wind. Man-made noises, such as static, telephone, or flushing of toilet may induce fear until they are identified. There exists some fear of ghosts and witches. Fears of someone hiding under their beds or of someone in the closet are common.

Seven-year-olds are less stubborn, more polite, responsive, and sensitive than they were at 6 years. They show less aggression and have fewer outbursts. Children 7 years of age are their own main concern. They worry that things will be too difficult for them, that second grade may be too hard, that people may not like them, that something might happen to them. These children have a tendency to withdraw from situations or at least are hesitant before acting. They often lack confidence to the point of not wanting even to try. Six-year-olds jump right in only to find they cannot handle the situation. Seven-year-olds are more protective of themselves, possibly because their cognitive development has reached a point where they are just a little more aware of consequences and cause and effect than they were previously. They accept some form of discipline, although grudgingly. They are conscientious and try to take their responsibilities seriously, although they are not old enough to be completely reliable. They are beginning to be able to put themselves in another's place, so much so that they are moved by sad stories. Thus fears can be stimulated by television programs, movies, or reading. They still have fears of ghosts and of "someone hiding in the cellar" but are learning to control some fears such as swimming with their face under water and having their hair washed.

There is a more common understanding regarding fear between children and their peers than between most children and their parents. Parents are likely to recognize and agree with fears related to objective conditions but may be ignorant of subjective situations. For example, some 7-year-olds report a fear of being an adopted child, whereas most mothers are not aware of this fear in their child.

Eight-year-olds are less likely to withdraw than 7-year-olds. In fact they may be full of impatience and wanting to get things done at once. They seek to display courage and often will not admit their fears even to themselves. However, they may still be afraid of fighting, failing in school, or of others finding fault with them. Often they may attack a feared experience, directly or indirectly, or compulsively dwell on it to resolve it. Children who tend to cling to the past and who have difficulty coming smoothly into the future may become worriers. Eight-year-olds cry less than others from inner confusion, but they may burst into tears, especially when tired, for many overt reasons such as having their feelings hurt by being criticized or not receiving or being able to do something that they wanted. Sometimes these children begin to think of themselves as martyrs and rationalize to themselves, "They'll be sorry they treated me so mean when they see how bad I've been hurt (or am gone or when I'm sick in bed because of what they did)." Eight-year-olds are often bossy, rude, and argumentative, even with their mother, but they are also affectionate and friendly. For the first time children think of giving something to their mother and father. They are developing a feeling of being able to create love by initiating an activity on their own.[29]

Moral judgment and character development

Children develop their basic philosophical orientation to life at home. The family is the workshop, where for better or for worse children develop an internal pattern of attitudes and beliefs that shape their character and influence their behavior. The community exerts a major modifying influence, to be sure. However, the home determines the initial strength and nature of the moral character of the children, and this strength, in turn, determines the degree to which the influences of the community can change the character.

Children learn early in childhood that there are some forms of behavior that are acceptable and some that are not. They come to associate "good" with a reward for approved behavior and "bad" with a punishment for unacceptable behavior. Eventually children conceptualize the thought that there are certain rules and regulations that must be followed to receive the acceptance and approval of others (society). By the age of 6 or 7 years children have internalized the concept of rules and the idea of right and wrong. As 6-year-olds enter the classroom world, they become aware of forces outside the home that relate to their concepts of "good," "bad," "right," and "wrong." For the next few years they consider making adjustments to their moral consciousness that they now recognize must be more extensive, insightful, and judgmental than the family-oriented code of conduct that they had developed up to this time. Turner, Peck, and Havighurst, as cited by Rains and Morris,[30] suggest that there is little reason to expect significant changes in a person's basic character after the ages of 9 or 10 years. It could be, then, that the primary teacher may be the last person who could be responsible for or capable of helping to determine the basic character of children.

Six- to 8-year-olds are still egocentric, a characteristic that greatly affects their own concept of moral behavior. As a result, their inclination is to justify their behavior by some rationalization, which to them is perfectly logical and acceptable. If this approach does not work, they may seek to protect themselves by lying or cheating. Seven-year-olds are quick to demand honesty from others and recognize the moral implications of not lying to their friends. Eight-year-olds become conscious of the effect of their wrongdoing on their status among their peers. Older primary children have a strong sense of fair play for themselves. The cry "That's not fair!" is often heard. Children may be right, but sometimes they are trying to avoid the fact that they are in the wrong. By the age of 9 years "being fair" tends to apply to all who are playing the game.

Taking things that belong to others is rather

Young children can learn from older children to be caring and gentle. Together they strengthen each other's value judgment systems.

common among 6- and 7-year-olds. Six-year-olds do this openly and if confronted with the fact, will deny the stealing or will say "But he gave it to me." Seven-year-olds are more subtle, and 8-year-olds are more careful. A conscience, or a moral judgment, is slowly developing in the child. This development started at the age of 4 years, when the child began to develop a self-ideal. By the age of 8 years the conscience will serve as a source of self-control or, if overdeveloped, as a

cause for feelings of guilt. However, the conscience of an 8-year-old will tolerate some stretching of the truth but will have some control over impulses of the moment which suggest that something be stolen. The 8-year-old may become proficient at alibiing or at placing the blame for a misconduct on something or someone else. A third grader who wanted to stay at a friend's house longer to play turned his watch back an hour. When he got home late, he acted surprised, saying that something must be wrong with his watch.

There is an expanding awareness of moral conduct in society as children mature. As they get older, they differentiate between what is acceptable conduct within their peer group and what is acceptable to the adult world. They recognize, but do not necessarily understand, the ambiguities that they observe between what adults tell them is the "right" thing to do and what the adults themselves do under the same circumstances.

Children's spiritual interests appear to develop through experience. The philosopher Kant and some others state that man is born with some basic moral "imperatives" that relate to man's consciousness of what is moral. For example, Kant says that man knows—he does not have to be taught—that it is right "to be good" and that "he ought to be good" (quotation marks are ours). Yet Kant recognizes the influence of the external world on children's "natural morality" and their spiritual growth.

By middle childhood God becomes important to children who have been exposed to the concept of God (or of Buddha, Allah, or Shiva). As children develop reasoning ability, however, they will ask questions such as "How can God be everywhere at one time?" and "How can God see everybody in the world?" Although there is a slight wonderment, if not skepticism, children of these years (who have been exposed to the idea of God) believe that God will help them and may influence what happens to them. They will pray to Him fervently for many things.

Piaget studied the moral development of children and concluded that, in many respects, moral judgment was related to level of cognitive development and to the degree of interaction with other children, especially in learning rules of games. To study children's moral judgments Piaget used pairs of stories in which children were involved in misdeeds of various kinds.[31] The children between 6 and 8 years of age had to decide which story depicted the worst misdeed. In one pair of stories the first was about a boy who broke twelve cups while helping his mother set the table, whereas the second story was about a boy who broke one cup while trying to get some jam that he had been forbidden to have. The children judged the boy who broke the twelve cups to have been most at fault.

Another story involved the telling of falsehoods. A boy came home from school and told his mother, to amuse her, that he had seen an elephant in the street. Another boy tried to deceive his mother and stated that he had received a better grade than he had actually received. In this case the children stated that the boy who told the elephant story was most at fault. Children at this age judge actions on the quantitative basis rather than on intentions.

Piaget studied the games of children to discover their "natural morality." He believed that in simple childhood games the morality or rules are taught by older children to the younger. In this manner the rules are passed down from generation to generation with little or no influence or change by adults. Based on his studies Piaget divides children's morality into (1) the practice of the rules and (2) the consciousness of rules. The practice of the rules evolved through four stages from (1) a purely motor and individual character in which children were learning to play the game, to (2) the egocentric stage in which children play largely by themselves but know that rules exist, to (3) the cooperation on the rules for the games in which children play together, to (4) the codification of the rules, in which the rules are fixed and everyone knows them. Consciousness of the rules develops at the same time that the practice of the rules evolves. Consciousness evolves from the level (1) at which the rules are not coercive in nature or believed to be mandatory, to (2) at which the rules are sacred and must not be broken, to the last stage (3) at which the rules must be respected but may be changed by common consent.

Piaget is challenged by some researchers on his theory concerning development of moral judgment.[32] In general, two observations are made. First, although moral judgment of children is affected somewhat by age, it is more strongly affected by sociocultural influences. Piaget did not place enough emphasis on this point, say the dissident researchers. Second, although Piaget believed that reactions at one given stage tend to be uniform, others found that there seem to be different levels and types of development within a given stage. The researchers challenging Piaget believe that learning experiences are more important than maturational processes in forming character. Significant learning experiences encompass such areas as social class attitudes and learning conditions, cultural and traditional behavior, parental emphasis and attitudes, and type of disciplinary measures to which the child was subjected.

STUDY GUIDE

1. Review the developmental tasks of this age group. Think of a child whom you know who has recently or will soon enter the first or second year of school. Can you see these tasks as being reflected in the needs, behavior, and goals of these children? How?
2. What advancements in motor skills have the 6- to 8-year-olds made as compared to the 3- to 5-year-olds?
3. How does the play culture of the 6- to 8-year-olds relate to their levels of social development? Do you see any carry-over or relationships?
4. Describe Piaget's stage of concrete operations. Compare its level of development in a child with the cognitive developmental features of the preoperational thought stage presented in Chapter 7.
5. How are language, speech development, and logical thought related?
6. It is important that you know the definitions, the details, and the implications of the term *self-concept*. After you study the meaning of self-concept, seek to identify the various aspects and characteristics of your own self-concept. How do you see yourself? How do others see you? Are your notions about yourself correct? Are theirs?
7. The concept of sex roles and sex typing is being challenged by some psychologists and some liberation movement advocates who claim that sex roles are no longer as rigidly defined as they used to be and certainly no longer as applicable and influential as they once were. As you consider growing boys and girls of today, what do you think influences boys to ''act like boys'' and girls to ''act like

girls,'' or do you think there are few directions or influences guiding them into sex roles? Who will do the cooking, the laundry, and care for the baby when you raise your own family?
8. Which age level has a greater sense of morality, the 6-year-old or the 8-year-old? Is it possible to say? Justify your position.
9. How does a one-parent family affect a child? Is a boy affected differently than a girl?

REFERENCES

1. Havighurst, R. *Developmental tasks and education* (3rd ed.). New York: David McKay Co., Inc., 1972.
2. Latham, H. C., Heckel, R. V., Herbert, L. J., & Bennett, E. *Pediatric nursing* (3rd ed.). St. Louis: The C. V. Mosby Co., 1977.
3. Burt, C. L. *Child psychology* (Vol. V). Chicago: Encyclopedia Britannica, Inc., 1969.
4. Comer, J. P., & Puissaint, A. F. *Black child care: how to bring up a healthy black child in America.* New York: Simon & Schuster, 1975.
5. Ilg, F., & Ames, L. *Parents ask.* New York: Harper & Row, Publishers, 1962.
6. Opie, P., & Opie, I. *Children's games in street and playground.* New York: Oxford University Press, 1969.
7. Pickard, P. M. *The activity of children.* London: Longmans, Green & Co., Ltd., 1965.
8. Sutton-Smith, B. *The folkgames of children.* Austin, Texas: The American Folklore Society, 1972.
9. Piaget, J. *The child's conception of number.* New York: W. W. Norton & Co., Inc., 1965.
10. Piaget, J. *The child's conception of physical causality.* London: Routledge & Kegan Paul, Ltd., 1966.
11. Almy, M., Chittenden, E., & Miller, P. *Young children's thinking: studies of some aspects of Piaget's thinking.* New York: Teachers College Press, 1966.
12. Kaluger, G., & Kolson, C. J. *Reading and learning disabilities.* Columbus, Ohio: Charles E. Merrill Publishing Co., 1978.
13. Kaluger, G., & Kaluger, M. Study of characteristics of LD children. In G. Kaluger & C. J. Kolson, *Reading and learning disabilities.* Columbus, Ohio: Charles E. Merrill Publishing Co., 1978, 93-95.
14. Feingold, B. F. *Why your child is hyperactive.* New York: Random House, Inc., 1974.
15. Piaget, J. *The language and thought of the child.* New York: The Humanities Press, Inc., 1959.

16. Emmerick, W. Stability and change in early personality development. *Young Children,* 1966, **21,** 233-243.

17. Hogan, E. O., & Green, R. L. Can teachers modify children's self-concepts? *Teacher's College Record,* 1971, **62,** 423-426.

18. Burtt, M. The effect of a man teacher. *Young Children,* 1965, **21,** 92-97.

19. Minuchin, P. Sex-role concepts and sex-typing in childhood as a function of school and home environments. *Child Development,* 1965, **36,** 1033-1048.

20. Smart, M. S., & Russell, C. *Children:development and relationships.* New York: Macmillan Inc., 1972.

21. Bell, R. R. *Marriage and family interaction.* Homewood, Ill.: Dorsey Press, 1971.

22. Henderson, R. W., & Bergan, J. R. *The cultural context of childhood.* Columbus, Ohio: Charles E. Merrill Publishing Co., 1976.

23. Thomes, M. M. Children with absent fathers. *Journal of Marriage and the Family,* February, 1968.

24. Kriesberg, L. Rearing children for educational achievement in fatherless families. *Journal of Marriage and the Family,* May, 1967.

25. Mischel, W. A social-learning view of sex differences in behavior. In E. E. Maccoby (Ed.), *The development of sex differences.* Stanford, Calif.: Stanford University Press, 1966.

26. Glasser, P. H., & Lois, N. (Eds.). *Families in crisis.* New York: Harper & Row, Publishers, 1970.

27. *Ibid.*

28. Herzog, E., & Leurs, H. Children in poor families: myths and realities. In S. Chess, & A. Thomas (Eds.), *Annual progress in child psychiatry and child development,* New York: Brunner/Mazel, Inc., 1971.

29. Fromm, E. Love between parent and child. *Psychology Today.* **1,** February, 1968.

30. Rains, S., & Morris, R. The role of the primary teacher in character education. *Young Children,* 1969, **25,** 105.

31. Elkind, D. *Children and adolescents: interpretive essays on Jean Piaget.* New York: Oxford University Press, Inc. 1970.

32. Bandura, A., & McDonald, F. J. The influences of social reinforcement and the behavior of models in shaping children's moral judgment. *Journal of Abnormal Psychology,* 1963, **67,** 274-281.

PREADOLESCENCE:
OUR GANG

As I look back over the years when I was 11 and 12 years old, I now wonder how I survived it all! And for my peace of mind I luckily remember many good times but only some of the many traumas I experienced.

Some things I remember were so exciting, especially learning about certain new things. Seventh grade and learning about Greek and Roman mythology and about Norsemen and medieval castles was really interesting. My mind felt like a sponge absorbing all that "good stuff." One particular instance is vivid in my mind. These years were years of isolation—boys stayed away from girls and vice versa, but the competition was for mental achievement. Teams were formed, boys against the girls, of course. We had contests and played the baseball learning game to see who knew more about the geography of Europe. I may be prejudiced, but the girls were usually the champs. Mainly this was because Lonny was the only boy on their team who studied for the contests. That didn't keep the boys from trying to win, but then again that didn't get them to study either.

Top that fact off with the situation that the girls were physically larger than most of the boys. The girls were sometimes larger in two directions, not only taller but wider. I was one of the lucky "chunky" ones, or as my mother kindly put it, "You are solid." I had a horrible nickname to go with my "solidness." The male cafeteria partner I had named me Sixteen Tons, to go along with Ernie Ford's song. All the way to the cafeteria he teased, while a red-faced girl walked beside him.

I may have been chunky, but my physical skill at sports was nothing to tease about. My best—very best—friend, Peggy, and I beat the only boys on our block, Ronnie and his brother, in baseball, hit-the-can, and marbles almost every evening in the summer. Peggy could hit good home runs all the way down the road. I can still see Ronnie hunting for the ball in the high weeds while I cheered for our side. The score? 19 to 4—our favor, of course!

Emotionally it was a trying time. What would I have done if I had not had a best friend to confide in! My mother didn't understand me! Then, too, there were the inevitable discussions about Peggy's heroine, Clara Barton. (Peggy wanted to become a nurse.) My favorite book was *Little Women*. I would sit there and cry for everyone in that family.

Socially, I remember the age of 11 and 12 years as a time of cruelty, according to my adult standards. How inconsiderate we were, but that was our gang.

Our girls' gang had a leader. Meggie had very little going for her academically, but she was one of the biggest girls in our class. She also had red hair, a fiery temper, and could verbalize some of the choicest, vulgar words we girls had ever heard. Of course, we had our home and neighborhood groups, but since we traveled by bus to school, this primary gang was Meggie's private domain. She certainly was cruel to others, but we would not break the solidarity of the gang. Meggie always batted first for her team. If the recess bell rang, all normal sixth graders would go inside the building, but not Meggie. She would stay on the base until everyone was afraid to stay out to tag her out. Then when everyone went tearing in because we were late, Meggie would run to home plate fast and claim another run for her team. She still could run into school fast enough to not be in trouble. How exasperating when you were on the other team!

Meggie also set the intellectual tone for the sixth grade room. If she did a math problem wrong on the chalkboard, most girls would not offer to correct it because Meggie would let words fly at recess and also make faces at you during class. The intellectual corrector could also be sure she would be ostracized from the group at recess—the pressure of the group made conformists of us all. Just to belong to the group was most important.

The nasty notes that Meggie passed to her "enemies" were group pressures, too. The words were overwhelming and the spelling was poor, but no one ever bothered to correct Meggie.

We seldom considered telling an adult about our gang's situation. I can remember going home upset by some of Meggie's antics, but if it had not been for a highly perceptive parent who gave me the option, "You seem upset, want to talk about it?" I think those emotions may have overwhelmed me.

By seventh grade and age 12 years the tone of the group had changed considerably. We formed new gangs, usually excluding Meggie. She was in another homeroom (luckily for us), and she was also separated from her best friend and partner in crime. Divide and conquer seemed to be the best cure for Meggie's actions. At lunch the new gang often sat on a bench and just gossiped about teachers, friends out of the group, and clothes. I still remember the fact that one girl owned fourteen pairs of shoes. Tremendous!

Our notes were now friendlier and sometimes just for fun. Of course we always wrote our notes in pig-Latin code. One dear little teacher intercepted a note of mine en route. Terror! She read it (I guess she could interpret pig Latin), then discreetly tore it up and put it in the paper can.

Even in seventh grade the boys did not bother us much. They played running games a lot; often we just sat on the sidelines and talked. Occasionally, we watched team games.

The most traumatic social experience in seventh grade involved us in a moral issue as well as in pressure of the gang. You might guess that it involved Meggie, and by my standards of today it was quite cruel. One girl in our class was a Jehovah's Witness. No one had ever taken time to explain why she wouldn't salute the flag or participate in some of our group activities, but we weren't bothered about it. Our group accepted Lynda, and things went smoothly. However, Meg's group noticed Lynda's differences and began a campaign for exclusion. Lynda did not give in easily, and since Meggie's power over the group had diminished, the group was on Lynda's side this time. For some time the group was under tremendous pressure, but it ended Meggie's ultimate power over us and helped us to learn about tolerance.

We had our problems, we formed our own solutions, and we tried to go it alone without adult intervention. As I look backward, I see that I gained a great sensitivity to the needs of others from all that cruelty.

The ages of 9 to 12 years are interesting because they depict childhood at its highest form of development. Soon the youngsters will leave childhood and move on to the next major phase of growth and development—adolescence. They will never be children again. There is no universal rule as to when children take on the characteristics of late childhood, or preadolescence. (We use the two terms interchangeably in this text.) Generally, the first psychological signs are detected in 9-year-olds; the signs are clearly evident in the 11- and 12-year-olds.

There are volumes of research material available for the middle childhood years and for adolescence, but research on late childhood is meager by comparison. A major reason for this lack of emphasis in studying late childhood is the overlapping of similarities that exist between middle childhood and late childhood and between late childhood and adolescence. Late childhood is a strong continuation of developmental characteristics started in middle childhood, especially of the 8-year-olds. A study of puberty and early adolescence usually covers the 11- and 12-year-olds of late childhood. However, we submit that the years of 9 to 12 have differences from the middle childhood and adolescent years that are significant and unique enough to deserve special attention.

Preadolescence is a trying period for parents and teachers as well as for the children. The children are trying to grow out of their dependence on their parents for guidance and direction. They enjoy separating themselves from the family in their interests and activities, and so family relationships and interactions change from what they used to be. They may challenge their parents and other authority, although their judgment is often erroneous and immature. The children's interest in acquiring knowledge is a wholesome development, but it also creates problems at times. Children can no longer be "fooled" by their parents or teachers. Yet they do not have enough information and insight to produce good perspectives on their own. Preadolescents are highly competent, as children, but they still lack the development necessary to make them completely reliable, effective, and resourceful.

The developmental tasks of late childhood are somewhat clouded because there is such a strong continuum of life experiences that pass on from middle childhood into the adolescent period. The developmental tasks begun in middle childhood continue to be faced in late childhood. The difference is that in late childhood the tasks require a higher level of proficiency for attainment. The developmental tasks for preadolescence are (1) gaining freedom from a primary identification with adults by learning to become self-reliant, (2) developing social competency in forming and maintaining friendships with peers, (3) learning to live in the adult world by getting a clearer perspective of one's peer group role or place in that world, (4) developing a moral code of conduct based on principles rather than specifics, (5) consolidating the identification made with one's sex role, (6) integrating and refining motor patterns to a higher level of efficiency, (7) learning realistic ways of studying and controlling the physical world, (8) developing appropriate symbol systems and conceptual abilities for learning, communicating, and reasoning, and (9) evolving an understanding of self and the world (society and cosmos).

PHYSICAL GROWTH AND MOTOR DEVELOPMENT

Although the preadolescent is somewhat of a mystery to adults in regard to his internal makeup, external data concerning this age group are available. The preadolescent years are transitional years. For some children, particularly girls, this period is the beginning of pubescence. For others, particularly boys, it is a time of steady growth in height and weight. For all it is the most healthy period of their lives. During these few short years, they will enjoy a pause between childhood diseases and the diseases of adulthood. However, it is important to watch

Motor ability and gracefulness of movement emerge in late childhood as sensorimotor control and coordination are developed.

Kit Luce/Image, Inc.

out for accidents because these are "daring" years.

Physical characteristics

Physical growth during late childhood is characterized by a gradual, steady gain in bodily measurements. The various parts of the body not only increase in size but also become more functional. In other words, physical development improves in quality as well as quantity. The skeletal frame becomes larger, the trunk increases moderately in length, and the extremities become proportionately longer. The trunk broadens and deepens, with shoulders and hips developing similarly in each sex. The muscles accelerate their rate of growth, and the ligamentous structures become firmer and stronger. As a result, body posture is improved over that

Table 9-1. Height and weight gains for boys and girls ages 9 to 12 years*

	Percentiles (boys)				Percentiles (girls)		
	10	50	90		10	50	90
9 years				**9 years**			
Weight in pounds	56.3	66.0	81.0	Weight in pounds	52.6	63.8	79.1
Weight in kilograms	25.54	29.94	36.74	Weight in kilograms	23.86	28.94	35.88
Height in inches	50.5	53.3	56.1	Height in inches	50.0	52.3	55.3
Height in centimeters	128.3	135.5	142.6	Height in centimeters	127.0	132.9	140.4
9½ years				**9½ years**			
Weight in pounds	58.7	69.0	85.5	Weight in pounds	54.9	67.1	84.4
Weight in kilograms	26.63	31.3	38.78	Weight in kilograms	24.9	30.44	38.28
Height in inches	51.4	54.3	57.1	Height in inches	50.9	53.5	56.4
Height in centimeters	130.6	137.9	145.1	Height in centimeters	129.4	135.8	143.2
10 years				**10 years**			
Weight in pounds	61.1	71.9	89.9	Weight in pounds	57.1	70.3	89.7
Weight in kilograms	27.71	32.61	40.78	Weight in kilograms	25.9	31.89	40.69
Height in inches	52.3	55.2	58.1	Height in inches	51.8	54.6	57.5
Height in centimeters	132.8	140.3	147.5	Height in centimeters	131.7	138.6	146.0
10½ years				**10½ years**			
Weight in pounds	63.7	74.8	94.6	Weight in pounds	59.9	74.6	95.1
Weight in kilograms	28.89	33.93	42.91	Weight in kilograms	27.17	33.79	43.14
Height in inches	53.2	56.0	58.9	Height in inches	52.9	55.8	58.9
Height in centimeters	135.1	142.3	149.7	Height in centimeters	134.4	141.7	149.7
11 years				**11 years**			
Weight in pounds	66.3	77.6	99.3	Weight in pounds	62.6	78.8	100.4
Weight in kilograms	30.07	35.2	45.04	Weight in kilograms	28.4	35.74	45.54
Height in inches	54.0	56.8	59.8	Height in inches	53.9	57.0	60.4
Height in centimeters	137.3	144.2	151.8	Height in centimeters	137.0	144.7	153.4
11½ years				**11½ years**			
Weight in pounds	69.2	81.0	104.5	Weight in pounds	66.1	83.2	106.0
Weight in kilograms	31.39	36.74	47.4	Weight in kilograms	29.98	37.74	48.08
Height in kilograms	55.0	57.8	60.9	Height in inches	55.0	58.3	61.8
Height in centimeters	139.8	146.9	154.8	Height in centimeters	139.8	148.1	157.0
12 years				**12 years**			
Weight in pounds	72.0	84.4	109.6	Weight in pounds	69.5	87.6	111.5
Weight in kilograms	32.66	38.28	49.71	Weight in kilograms	31.52	39.74	50.58
Height in inches	56.1	58.9	62.2	Height in inches	56.1	59.8	63.2
Height in centimeters	142.4	149.6	157.9	Height in centimeters	142.6	151.9	160.6

*From Latham, H. C., Heckel, R. V., Herbert, L. J., and Bennett, E. *Pediatric nursing* (3rd ed.). St. Louis: The C. V. Mosby Co., 1977.

found in the young child. Body stance and balance are more appropriate for efficient erectness, for locomotion, and for strength in the use of arms and trunk. At 12 or 13 years of age girls are about a year ahead of boys in the development of the bones of the wrist (carpal bones), which is one of the best single measurements of physical maturity.[1]

Boys at the age of 9 years will have an average height of 53.3 inches and at 11 years, 57 inches. There is an increase in height of 1.1 inch per year. Nine-year-old girls will have an average height of 52.3 inches and 11-year-olds, 58.3 inches (Table 9-1). There is an average increase of 2 inches a year. From third to fifth grade, boys are slightly taller than girls, but in sixth grade the average girl is taller than the boy. Progress in height is closely correlated with approaching sexual maturity. The most rapid growth period in height for girls precedes menarche, usually by two years. Growth in height for boys appears linked to genital development. A positive correlation also exists between tallness in preadolescence and tallness later in adulthood. Children who grow rapidly during this period tend to be taller as adults.

In weight boys at 9 years of age will weigh an average of 66 pounds and at 11 years, 77.2 pounds. Increase in weight for boys per year is 3.7 pounds. Girls will weigh an average of 63.8 pounds at 9 years of age and 78.3 pounds at 11 years. The increase in weight for girls is about 4.8 pounds per year. During late childhood, girls mature faster physically than boys and tend to be larger than boys during the latter part of this developmental stage. Progress in weight tends to be less regular than height, since weight is greatly influenced by environmental factors. Weight, like height, seems related to advent of sexual maturity. The greatest increase in weight for girls occurs about three months before menarche, around 12 years of age (Table 9-1). The greatest growing period for weight for boys is around the age of 14 years.

From birth until the age of 4 years rapid growth development takes place in the heart. There is rather slow growth of the heart during early and middle childhood, but it speeds up during the latter part of preadolescence. The greatest rate of growth of the heart occurs at the time of the child's greatest growth in weight. By 12 years of age the heart has gained seven times in weight as compared to its birth weight, and it will increase its size by twelve times by adulthood. The rate of heart growth during childhood does not seem to keep pace with overall body growth, especially at the ages of 9 and 10 years. The relationship of the size of the arteries and the heart is especially critical. The typical size of the arteries and heart during childhood leads one to question the advisability of extended, intense physical exertion for some children, especially when accompanied by the stress of competition.

Extreme deviations and disturbances in physical growth can affect mental health adjustment of preadolescent children. Very tall girls feel especially self-conscious. Boys are particularly disturbed at being undersized and often worry about whether they will ever grow up. Uneven growth may create problems of awkwardness and self-consciousness. Inappropriate growth, such as a boy who develops feminine features, presents still more problems of adjustment. Personality difficulties and emotional conflicts often arise out of fears of physical inadequacy. Parents and teachers should be particularly understanding of these possibilities and help the child through this period of adjustment.

Late childhood is the time when the permanent teeth appear. Girls are more advanced than boys in dentition at any age in childhood. In the following statements the sequence of the appearance of teeth is more significant than the age at which they are said to appear. Major individual differences occur in the age of appearance. At 8 years of age the first permanent back teeth (first molars) and the center front teeth (central incisors) appear. Between 8 and 9 years of age the eye teeth on the lower jaw (canines) emerge. The upper canines may not appear for at least two more years. Between the ages of 10 and 12 years the two teeth (bicuspids) on the sides behind each canine appear. Most children have all their permanent teeth except wisdom teeth by the age of 12 or 13 years.[2]

Health

The ages from 9 to 12 are usually the healthiest years of a child's life. A major reason is that the lymphoid masses which help to fight infections are at their highest point of development in quantity. Average 11-year-olds have almost twice the lymphoid masses that they will have as adults, and before and after the age of 11 years their bodies will have well above the amount of 20-year-olds. Mother Nature must have known how difficult it would be to keep preadolescents out of the rain and to have them button their coats to keep warm in the winter, so she wisely gave this age group some extra protection to ward off colds and other diseases. A more likely explanation for the extra lymphoid masses is that if the child has survived to this stage in life, nature wanted to do what it could to increase survival potential to adulthood when the individual can help to perpetuate the species, which is one of the basic aims of life.

Another reason for the good health of this age group is that most children have already been exposed to the communicable diseases of childhood or have in some manner become immune. They have an interest in outdoor games that gives them sufficient physical exercise to maintain good muscle tone and good intake of oxygen. For the most part they get 9 to 10 hours of sleep a night. They are not as tempted to stay up late as they will be when they are older. They have enormous appetites so that they generally get enough food. Fresh air, rest, exercise, good nutrition, plus an innate ability to ward off diseases all contribute to a healthy life. However, imaginary illnesses are not uncommon. This youngster soon learns that he is not expected to carry on his usual activities when he is ill. Pressures at school, such as tests or difficulties with his peers, may put him to bed for a day or two. Most, however, miss less school than formerly.

Motor ability and activities

During late childhood, children gain in vigor and balance in sensorimotor control and coordination. They generally improve in manual dexterity, increase their resistance to fatigue, and develop greater muscular strength. These factors allow for finer motor usage of small muscles over longer periods of time, resulting in a rapid improvement in the ability of these children to control their bodies and to manipulate objects with

which they play. They improve in agility, accuracy, and endurance. They run faster, throw and catch much better, and can jump and climb with ease and assurance. By the age of 9 years eye-hand coordination is good. Children are ready for crafts and shop work. Their eyes are almost adult size, and they are ready to do close work with less strain.

This is a period when children have so much energy that they do not know when to stop. Their constant drive, inability to be quiet, and concentration on the game are enough to drive the most understanding adult supervisior to distraction. Parents often become concerned with so much physical play and roughhousing. Popular physical activities at this stage are playing ball, riding a bicycle, jumping rope, ice and roller skating, hiking in the woods, hopscotch, swimming, and running. Team games are popular. Vigorous bodily activities are preferred to finer motor skills. Children usually devote more time to the use of their body than to tools or toys. Unhappy are the youngsters who do not possess the physical skills needed to play the games of their peer group.

At this age children, boys especially, are constantly pushing themselves into new activities that require new skills or courage. "I dare you" is an often-used phrase. Playing "follow the leader" or taking a dare to walk along the top of a narrow fence improves motor skills and balance. Thus children develop more versatility, speed of movement, physical strength, and control of their bodies.

Lack of success is rarely frustrating to the young preschool child. However, elementary grade youngsters become easily frustrated when they fail to grasp immediately the technique of an activity such as dribbling a large rubber ball. They need freedom from overdemanding standards of control while learning simple coordinations. Exposure to fellow classmates and the scrutiny of the teacher when learning a new skill are particularly upsetting. Children are conscious of what they think is a disapproving glance from the teacher and the titters of their classmates. Usually the titters come from the classmates who themselves are inadequate in this particular skill. If at all possible, a teacher should arrange a time

Harold Geyer

Sledding is fun, as you can combine some skills with daring thrills and spills.

or way for the child to experiment and practice motor skills in an accepting atmosphere. It is unwise to push children into a game or test situation until they have an adequate chance to learn the particular skill or skills needed.

Prelude to puberty

The earliest ages at which puberty normally occurs are 10 years for girls and 12 years for boys. As will be noted in the next chapter, there are indications that there is an increase in the number of girls who reach puberty at 9 years of age. In general, the average age of puberty for girls is about 12 years, and for boys it is about 14 years.[3] Before puberty occurs, however, there are some physiological changes that take place in both sexes, in girls before boys.

With the approach of puberty general body proportions change in both sexes. In girls an overall rounding and softening of the body features begins. At 11 years of age noticeable individual differences are apparent between slow and fast physically maturing girls. Heavier, taller girls generally begin the pubertal period before thinner, shorter girls. The pelvic area of the prepubescent girl broadens, whereas the shoulder

"TUB-OF-LARD"   To me, children in the early adolescent stage of development are very cruel. This cruelty can easily be seen at any Little League baseball game.

About one month ago I decided to go see a Little League baseball game in my community. The game was important for both teams because the winner would be in first place.

When the team took the field, I noticed that there was a boy, whom I shall call Joe, who did not seem as excited as the others. Joe's physical appearance was noticeably different. Although he was as tall as or even taller than the other boys, he was fat. As I observed him, he had trouble running or even walking because of his obesity.

When the the inning was over and the team came off the field, some of the boys began moaning at Joe because he was not "hustling" off the field. He did not respond to them verbally but just sat down on the end of the bench. As I suspected, Joe was the last batter, and he struck out. When this happened, the entire team began calling him "stupid," "fat-so," "tub-of-lard," etc.

When his team took the field, there was a fly ball in his direction. Joe tried to get in position to catch the ball, but he fell down in the process. The ball bounded past him, and the other team scored a run. The other eight players all looked disgustedly at Joe but did not really have much to say to him at that time.

At the end of the inning, the captain of the team came over and told Joe that he should quit the team, because he couldn't hit and couldn't even catch a ball. He said this so loudly that everybody in the stands heard what was going on. The coach reprimanded the other boys for yelling at Joe, but they all responded by saying: "We don't need him. He stinks anyway."

The following week, I attended another Little League game between the same teams. When I got there I looked around for Joe, but he was not present. After the game, I asked one of the team members where Joe was, and he answered: "Who cares!"

width remains about the same. An adipose (fatty) tissue is formed on the hips and chest. The face is fuller. The legs become more shapely as they lose their long, thin, toothpick look. The breast buds appear, and the nipples begin to darken. Most 10- to 11-year-old girls are greatly aware of their breast development and may be concerned if there is no evidence of this. Some become concerned because they believe the development is evident to others. The spurt in height growth starts a year or two before the climax of puberty.

For girls the fastest growth in height and weight, on the average, is during the twelfth year. They may gain 2 to 4 inches in height and 8 to 10 pounds in weight during their peak year.

Boys do little sexual maturing until the end of preadolescence, when the genital organs begin to grow. At the age of 10 years a smaller proportion of adult height is achieved than in previous years. Eleven years of age is known as the "fat period" because a general overall adding of fatty tissues occurs. Body proportions of the boys become more solid, and rounding of the contours around the neck and chin becomes noticeable. There is an increase in the bone structure, bringing the skeletal structure into prominence, especially in the chest area. The peak year for gains in height and weight, on the average, is 14 years of age, when boys gain 4 to 5 inches in height and 12 to 14 pounds in weight. At about 11 or 12 years of age boys usually begin to mature sexually. There is rapid development of the primary sex characteristics. Secondary sex characteristics usually do not appear until the ages of 13 or 14 years.

There is a change in body chemistry in prepubescence. The pituitary gland pours hormones into the bloodstream that have potent effects on growth. Other hormones produce emotional effects on the children. In some cases personality traits change or behavior patterns become different. Children may withdraw temporarily from their family, they may react with irritation over little things that never bothered them before, and they have some strong rebellious feelings that manifest themselves in unexpected ways. They have a growing awareness of sex and sex differences. They are concerned about the appearance of their changing bodies. Not all children mature at the same rate—physical growth proceeds unevenly. Natural developments may alarm some youngsters if they do not understand what is happening. They need information and reassurance from a competent adult they can trust.

SEXUAL AWARENESS AND SEX INFORMATION

One of the characteristics of the so-called permissive society of recent years has been a liberal, less restricted, uninhibited social and cultural mass media approach to sex and sexuality. The availability of pictorial and printed material on the topic of sex, the open display of nudity and sexual behavior in films, innuendos on television, and the loose, sometimes completely lacking, moral considerations of such matters have subjected individuals of all ages to behaviors, suggestions, and attitudes that in the past were treated, at least in the open marketplaces of society, with more restraint. What effect this

exposure has or will have on today's children is open to speculation. Characteristics related to sex and sexuality in children and adults in the world of tomorrow are yet to be determined because of life-space influences of today. As far as we are concerned, we can only report the results of research on this topic as they are available at this time.

Psychosexual development and awareness

Sexual awareness begins long before puberty. In a general way it may be said that in earliest infancy children are exposed to environmental stimuli that affect the development of sexuality. Babies' bodies are washed, examined, dressed, and caressed. They are picked up, fed, and rocked. Almost all their feelings of pleasure and security come from some form of physical contact. It is reasonable to assume that infants will soon associate contentment, well-being, and love with the pleasant physical and sensory stimulations provided by the persons taking care of them. Before long infants enjoy physical stimulation that they provide for themselves. They play with their hands, explore their feet and toes, move their arms and legs, and eventually put almost everything they pick up into their mouths. Love, pleasure, and physical stimulation go together. The importance of the quality of physical contact provided by mothers is indicated by the studies of Harlow[4] with infant monkeys. Monkeys exposed to a "hard-surface" surrogate mother made of chicken wire did not develop as healthy a sexuality in adulthood as did the monkeys exposed to a soft mother.

In early childhood, between the ages of 3 and 5 years, there is a growing concept in children that their physical sexual characteristics differ from those of some other people. The degree and appearance of this awareness depend on the age and the sex of the children, the presence or absence of brothers and sisters, and the bathroom and dressing practices of the home in which they are reared. Physical responses between preschool children are not unusual. They will hug and kiss each other without giving any indication that one sex is preferred over another. Sexual awareness enters the life of a preschool or school child when a new arrival is expected in the family. Depending on the age of the child, questions concerning the physical change in the mother are asked, and curiosity is expressed regarding preparations being made for the arrival of the new baby.

It is when the child enters school that he learns the true meaning of sex differences and sex roles. The boys belong to one group, and the girls belong to another. A number of activities and situations, such as separate lavatory facilities, increase the awareness of differences. Feelings of modesty develop in earnest. The child from 5 to 8 years of age has many questions that are related to sex. Questions such as "How does a baby get inside the mother?" and "Does the mother's egg ever go into the father?" and "How does the baby breathe inside the mother?" are often asked. Six-year-olds are usually satisfied with a simple explanation, but an 8-year-old may need a more detailed answer. Mild forms of sex play between members of the same sex or with the opposite sex are not unusual because they are curious and interested in each other's bodies. By 8 years of age there is some interest in peeping, provocative giggling, and in writing or whispering words dealing with sex or elimination functions. This interest and activity increases during late childhood.

The late childhood youngster socializes with his or her own sex. This is a period when emotional identification is with the peers of one's own sex and the opposite sex is rejected. Just because there is little connection between the two sexes at this time, it does not mean that they are not aware of each other. It is during the preadolescent years that boys draw the female anatomy, look through mail-order catalogues in the section showing pictures of women modeling panties, brassieres, and lingerie, and try hard to get their hands on pornographic literature. Girls are not all innocent. Some of them also draw pictures, read and write notes with sexual implications, and engage in double-meaning talk among themselves.

Preadolescent girls show an absorbed interest in their new physical developments, not only of their own but also of other girls their age. Many look ahead to the day when their breasts will be advanced enough to wear a brassiere. Fortu-

nately, manufacturers have recognized the desire and need for a very small brassiere so that even small-breasted girls can qualify when contemporaries check on which ones are wearing brassieres. Not all girls, however, are pleased or proud of their breast development. Some are embarrassed and hunch their shoulders in an effort to hide their development. For most girls, however, this initial embarrassment will be alleviated by 12 or 13 years of age, and they will exchange their loose blouses for sweaters and T-shirts. By 11 years of age most girls have some knowledge about menstruation, intercourse, and reproduction.

Most preadolescent boys, especially at the age of 9 or 10 years, do not feel free to discuss sex matters with their parents. If they do ask questions, they do so at inopportune times for discussion, indicating their immaturity in such matters. Some 10-year-olds will still think that being married is essential for having babies. They still have to learn about the functions of marriage and the importance of the family for the birth and rearing of a baby.[5] An 11-year-old is starting to realize that marriage involves personal relationships which go beyond mating and that someone does not have to be married to have a baby. Spontaneous erections occur among some 11-year-olds, caused by such things as physical movements, conversations, pictures, daydreams, and general excitement of any kind, not necessarily sexual in nature. As at all ages, boys are more likely than girls to tell smutty jokes and write four-letter words in public places. They do not completely understand why these words and jokes are emotionally loaded, but they do know that "it sure gets adults."

Sexuality and sexual learning

There is evidence to support the claim that many children experience some type of sex play during or before the preadolescent years. Children are experimentalists and curious. The sex play is incidental and transitory in nature. It is not due to love relationships or to a sex urge, since organic development has not yet begun. It is play and not lovemaking. Whether or not emotional scars or guilt feelings result depends a great deal on how the behavior is handled by the parents if such play has been discovered or if the children view their actions as something wrong in the eyes of their parents or God.

Elias and Gebhard[6] did a study on sex and sexuality in 1969 with a sample population of 305 boys and 127 girls, ages 8 to 12 years, grouped by occupational class of the parents. Part of the research was related to sex play engaged in before reaching puberty. The study reported that sex play before puberty involving more than oneself had been experienced by 52% of the boys with other boys and 34% of the boys with girls. In the sample of girls 35% had sex play with other girls, and 37% had heterosexual experiences. The average age for some sex play among boys was 9.2 years and for heterosexual play was 8.8 years. The same study revealed that although boys and girls from blue-collar homes learn at an earlier age about intercourse, abortions, and prostitution (average age range 8 to 10 years), children from white-collar homes (middle-class socioeconomic status) surpass the others in total knowledge in all categories of sex information surveyed. The girls from the lower-class homes were pathetically lacking about some extremely vital information. For example, more of these girls knew more about coitus than they did about the cause of pregnancy; many were unaware of "where babies come from."

Schofield[7] cites a study of 934 boys and 939 girls designed to determine when they first found out about the facts of life. The research indicated that 67% of the boys and 76% of the girls had such information by the age of 12 or 13 years. The implication is that the time for giving sex information should be no later than late childhood, since after that age period there would be a need for reeducation because of incomplete facts or misinformation learned previously. Most sex learning during this period comes from the peer group and often brings with it many misconceptions. Eighty-eight percent of the boys in the blue-collar group and 70% of the boys in the middle-class group received their sex knowledge from their peer group.[8]

SOCIAL BEHAVIOR

By the age of 9 years most children will have made the change from being family oriented in activities and control to being members of their own age group. The group begins to have a tremendous influence on the attitudes, desires, and behavior of the child—an influence that increases as the child grows older and becomes an adolescent. Late childhood is a transitional period, during which the social patterns and behavioral characteristics of childhood change to those that are considered more typical of adolescence. Specifically, the social behavior characteristics of preadolescence stem from three basic attitudes. First, there is strong desire to be with age mates of one's own sex. Second, there is a loyalty to a gang or group composed of other children similar in age, sex, size, and interests. Third, there is a change in regard to authority, expressed largely by a seeming rejection of adult standards.

Social structure in preadolescence

Social development and change take place rapidly in late childhood. Children no longer want to play at home alone or do things with members of the family. One or two friends are not enough. They want to be with the "gang," their play group. The gang gives them a feeling of belonging and of being liked. Learning to live in the social world, however, is hard for children, especially if they have not received preparatory training for it at home during their earlier years. The gang members will work it out and help each other. Unfortunately, there is a survival element in the give-and-take of group interaction, and some "hurts" will be encountered. Some children will not make the grade and will have to go into adolescence socially unprepared or as misfits.

During late childhood, boys tend to develop a social structure separate from that of girls. Boys are more interested in developing and asserting their masculinity than they are in being friendly with girls. To be a "he-man" means to be tough, strong, and daring. Nicknames may crop up among the boys, such as Rocky, Speedy, or Alligator. Their toughness and adventurousness are expressed by the television programs they watch, the books they read, and the "I dare you" schemes they concoct.

This period is also the secret club age, where

David Strickler

Common interests, intellectual curiosity, and physical skills draw boys into a social structure that frequently overlooks girls.

boys seek to have their own hideaway. Their retreat may be a tree house, a garage, an abandoned shack, or an outdoor spot difficult to get to or find. It is their way of saying to others, "I belong here and you belong elsewhere." In spite of all this atmosphere of mystery and intrigue, the gang is rather loosely knit with no strong organizational structure and probably even without a recognized leader, except for special activities. As the boys approach the ages of 11 and 12 years, their relationships take on a more organized appearance and become more activity oriented, such as organizing a sports team or joining the Boy Scouts or the YMCA. Boys have an interest in the gang stage longer than do girls.

In late childhood the boys set the social pace, and girls have little choice but to form their own groups. Girls' groups tend to be more tightly knit than are those of boys. They are also more exclusive and autocratic about who can belong and who cannot. They place more demands on themselves as to how to act toward each other and what to do in certain situations. They keep in touch with each other by incessantly writing notes in school; note writing is one of their favorite pastimes. Girls usually meet in the home of a member where there is a minimum of interference.

Girls and boys do travel different social routes during late childhood. Furthermore, there is some bickering or antagonism toward each other. Boys seem to work harder at this with their aloofness and teasing than do girls. Boys and girls set up differing values and standards, too. The most admired qualities in boys at 11 and 12 years of age are competence in group games, ability to lead or keep a game going, and fearlessness and readiness to take a chance. It is much more desirable for a boy to be rough, tough, and a degree unkempt than to be quiet, withdrawn, and too clean.

In girls, aggressive behavior is strongly disapproved, unless it might be in a game against the boys. Some girls, however, do become tomboys and try to imitate the boys' sex role. Disturbances in the classroom are frowned on by girls. For girls, prestige demands such qualities as being friendly, attractive, tidy, quietly gracious and considerate, and more "grown up." They are taught to control aggression, including assertion and extension, while being encouraged to regard the familial world as the proper sphere of their interest.[9] Differing value patterns for boys and girls can, in part, be attributed to an earlier maturity status in girls during these years of growth.

Friendships in later childhood

In addition to the gang or group phenomenon personal friendships are important to preadolescents. The behavior of "friends" might seem strange to onlookers. The more boys like one another the more frequently they seem to get into fights. Actually, they are developing loyalty and the capacity to stand up for each other. Girls tend to have an on-again off-again relationship. They get angry at each other over little things and then make up again. Both boys and girls have long

talks on the telephone, calling each other often. To fathers it sometimes seems as if their daughters are forever on the telephone. The youngsters are mostly seeking support and security from each other while going through the growing-up process. Children choose friends who are much like themselves. The reasons given for choosing friends are primarily personal. They choose friends who are cheerful, kind, agreeable, even tempered, and loyal. As children grow older, they show a preference for responsibility in their friends and for children of their own socioeconomic and racial groups.[10] Frequent associations, such as the same grade in school or the same neighborhood, and similarity of interest, age, and social maturity are other factors frequently found among friends.

A statement should be made concerning boy-girl relationships in fifth and sixth grades. Not all prepubertal boys and girls reject members of the opposite sex. In some communities and subcultures there are children of these grades or ages who are interested in the opposite sex because it seems to be the fashionable thing to do. Some are even dating before entering junior high school. Cultural and social influences have been stressing boy-girl relationships, albeit on an older age level, through television, movies, comics dealing with romance, and books. Some parents consider boy-girl relationships a sign of growing up and often will push their children into early dating before the youngsters really want it or are ready for it. If dating and pairing off are encouraged during preadolescence, it is our belief that many children will be deprived of time needed to develop social and communicative skills necessary for social adequacy in junior high school. We also believe that early dating patterns will promote a faster pace and a greater diversity of social life in adolescence. The outcome will result in social experiences and behavior that could be inappropriate and possibly harmful to children in terms of what their adolescent level of social and emotional maturity can accept.

Emerging social independence and the family

Even though the home and family will continue to be a major emotional focus for years to come,

Becoming members of an organized group not only leads to expanded social development and the learning of social skills but is also a step toward social independence.

Harold Geyer

the preadolescent child is taking increasing interest in people outside the home. Consequently, contacts with family members become fewer, less influential, and less meaningful than contacts with persons outside the family unit.

As early as the age of 6 years, when they enter school, children become more independent than previously by virtue of being on their own and by making more independent decisions. By the age of 8 years they make an important discovery—they suddenly realize that adults can make mistakes, that they do not know everything, and that they can be criticized. This knowledge provides a giant step toward self-autonomy. Because of increasing intellectual development, 9- to 12-year-olds reach a point where they can see more clearly the shortcomings of adults. They challenge the thinking and decisions of persons in positions of authority. Soon they reject or question many of the standards of their parents and of adults in general. This characteristic does not imply that the children become discipline and behavior problems, but it does mean that they are not as ready to accept rules and standards unquestioningly as they did at an earlier age. Clashes may result, overtly or covertly.

Children from 8 through 11 years tend to be irritable toward adults, willful, critical, easily discouraged, and rejecting of rules and standards that they previously respected.[11] They begin to wonder about adult intellectual and behavioral competency. A sixth grader was asked to write an essay for his English lesson on the subject of "Parents." His comment: "We get our parents when they are so old it is very hard to change their habits or to educate them." Piaget,[12] in discussing the moral judgment of children, suggests that a change takes place in children's relationship to authority at ages 9 or 10 years. He suggests that at the age of 8 or 9 years children begin to respond to the standards of their peers. It is at that age that Piaget finds children beginning to reject adult standards.

Although friction within family relationships is on an increase, families are still a most significant part of the children's social life. Members of the family can help or hinder the children in their social adjustment process by the way in which they are treated, respected, trusted, loved,

and permitted to grow. Personality and adjustment of the parents, parental expectations, methods of child training used, socioeconomic status, parental occupations, and solidarity of the family are all factors that influence the type of relationship preadolescent children have with different family members. These are critical years in adult-child relationships. If children break away from their families, they will have only the judgment and influence of their gang to guide them. Rejecting attitudes of this period will only become more intensified during the adolescent years.

Children's perspective of their parents changes at this age. Whereas their concept of "mother" is still primarily in terms of what she does for them, they recognize that she has less authority in the world than they thought she did when they were younger. The concept of "father" depends on how the father has been relating to his children. If he has delegated the job of raising the children to the mother and has been more-or-less an outsider providing for the material needs of the family, the children may never develop a close relationship with him because of the distance between them in past years. In fact, he may even be rejected if the children had an image of what the ideal father should be like and their father failed to live up to it. On the other hand, if the father has been responsive to his children during their developing years, he may now assume a greater role of importance in their eyes.[13] Father, to the children of this age, represents the "outside world" —the world they associate with independence. He does all the things they want to do some day. He becomes a model that they want to copy. To both boys and girls the father can now become an important influence.

BIRTH ORDER AND DEVELOPMENT

No two children living in the same family, however, not even twins, have exactly the same environment. Each has a different combination of brothers and sisters as well as a different length of time for being the only or the youngest child. Each develops a unique self-concept and personality. Each has a different position in the family and different roles to play. Generally there is agreement that the order of birth does influence a child's development, although this varies with the nature and the sex of the child, the number, age, and spacing of siblings, and favorable or unfavorable parental attitudes.

Studies that have been made correlating achievement with birth order reveal some interesting information.[14] The five U.S. Presidents at or near the top in virtually every ranking—George Washington, Abraham Lincoln, Thomas Jefferson, Woodrow Wilson, and Franklin D. Roosevelt—were all firstborns. Of the first 23 astronauts to go on U.S. space missions, 21 were either the eldest or only children. Nearly 60% of the finalists for National Merit Scholarships are firstborns. There is no reliable evidence that firstborns have more intellect.[15] Rather, the way they are raised makes them more achievement-oriented. Let's take a look at how children tend to be treated according to their ordinal position in a family.

The firstborn child

It can be generalized that firstborn children are usually much more responsive to their parents than are their brothers and sisters. They try hard to conform to parental expectations and to the adult world. They show more zeal, perseverance, and drive than their siblings. They seem to have a higher achievement motive as well as a higher degree of responsibility.

Several studies have sought to delineate these effects and to postulate causes for them. Typical among these studies is that of Harris and Howard.[16] They found that firstborn children internalize parental expectations with a resulting sense of stronger moral responsibility. They feel that this sense of responsibility is due primarily to parental fatigue—the oldest children must fulfill parental surrogate functions for their siblings, thus inculcating a high degree of responsibility in later childhood. This same dilution of parental attention, however, may lessen the sense of responsibility of the younger siblings and heighten their peer orientation.

Lichtenwalner and Maxwell[17] found that firstborn children are considerably more creative than later-born children. They feel that this effect is caused by the parental relationships with their initial children. The parents tend to be anxious

and overprotective. These children receive more verbal and physical stimulation than do successive children. Their achievement of each developmental stage in growth is appreciated and reinforced by their parents. When other children are born, they tend to look to the first child as a leader for ideas. This factor stimulates the firstborns' creative production and reduces that of their siblings, who learn to rely on others for their creative needs.

Schacter has observed a marked association between firstborn children and attending college. Firstborn children predominate in college life; the effects are even more noticeable in graduate school. Grade point averages tend to be higher for firstborns. Schacter feels that this latter effect is caused by a higher degree of achievement motive, rather than by any significant advantages in intelligence possessed by firstborn children as opposed to later-born children.[18]

With the arrival of the second child, firstborns must make adjustments. Eventually they resolve their feelings of jealousy and become the leaders for their siblings. In a sense, they could be called the trailblazers for their brothers and sisters. They tend to have a high level of responsibility, since it is their job to care for their siblings. As the eldest, they are often held responsible for the actions of their younger followers. These factors all seem to indicate definite trends in the development of firstborn children.

The middle child

Middle children have a difficult position within the family. Their parents have a different attitude toward their second and subsequent children, since they now feel experienced. They are more relaxed and employ trial-and-error less frequently. Middle children are permanently faced with the problem of comparison with their older sibling. They usually receive hand-me-down clothes and toys. These effects may induce feelings of hostility and inferiority. Not only must they compete with their older sibling, but there are younger children who steal their status as the babies of the family.

Middle children are allowed more freedom to be themselves and to explore their surroundings with less restrictions. Their displacement is usually not as severe as that of the firstborn when another baby arrives since they have always shared their parents. However, they may still feel a little pushed aside and lacking in their due of affection and attention. Sometimes they may exhibit hostility toward their older and younger siblings, regretting the authority of the firstborn and the helplessness of the baby.

These factors have particular consequences depending on whether middle children identify with their older sibling or their younger siblings. Konig[19] feels that the second-borns tend to be calm and relaxed persons. They make the best out of life and seek pleasure. Conversely, third-borns do not resolve their difficulties as middle children. They tend to be restrained and have difficulty getting along with others.

The last-born child

Last-born children grow up in a complicated family situation, since they must interact with their parents and all their siblings. There is a tendency on the part of the parents to prolong the babyhood of these children. The parents are older and usually have a stronger financial position. Thus the parents tend to indulge these children, and discipline may even break down completely. Their siblings also tend to intercede for these children and make contacts for them. Life is a relatively easy matter for the youngest children. Although these conclusions may be over-generalized, they do show the basic trend of sibling interactions for last-born children.

Tomeh[20] found a tendency for last-born girls to visit with friends more often than for other girls. She concluded that this result shows that last-born children have a greater affinity toward their peers than firstborn children. She attributes this outcome to the fact that parents relax their expectations for their last child. While the firstborn is adult-oriented, the last child is free to establish contacts outside of the family. Thus the youngest children seem to be somewhat other-directed in their search for social contacts and approval.

Last-born children, then, have greater freedom than their siblings. They are raised in a more permissive environment and tend to be less oriented to adult expectations than their brothers and sisters. These factors all have significance for

Table 9-2. Personality characteristics of oldest/only, middle, and youngest children*

Oldest/only	Middle	Youngest
Scholarly	Optimistic	Uncomplicated
Apprehensive	Rebellious	Narcissistic
Conforming	Sociable	Personable
Conservative	Aggressive	Precocious
Conscientious	Self-confident	Affectionate
Sensitive	Manipulative	Outgoing
Serious	Competitive	Demanding
Achieving	Self-reliant	Forward-think-ing

*Adapted from Rockower, I. Why no two children in a family are ever alike. *Woman's Day,* January, 1969, p. 82.

the personality development of last-born children.

The only child

One couple out of six, of all married couples who have children, have only one child. One child in eighteen children has no brothers or sisters. The absence of siblings can have an effect on the only child's personality development.

The advantages only children realize are the effects of having parents who, in the absence of other children, have more time to devote to their supervision and to a better economic position in life. Most only children receive better medical care, food, and clothing, have their own playthings and room, and later on receive a good education. As a group, firstborn and only children hold a favored educational position. More are listed in *Who's Who in America,* and research has shown that these two groups are more destined to become good readers than middle or youngest children.[21] Perhaps the greatest asset of being an only child is the feeling of security in being the sole object of the parents' affection.

On the other hand, only children lack the comradeship and social support of having brothers and sisters who could accustom them to being with others of similar age and interests. All is not lost, however, if parents encourage outside-the-family friendships and open their home to potential playmates. School will provide an automatic opportunity for making friends. In middle and later childhood, dancing classes, camp, and playground activities all provide prior situations in which only children can seek out and respond to others, and in doing so can profit by the associations. The great majority of only children grow up to become well-adjusted adult members of society.

Sex and spacing of siblings

Most of the evidence concerning the sex of and spacing between siblings as influences on development are reported by Janis.[22] The studies show that the sex of an older sibling affects the sex-typed behavior of a younger child. Girls with older brothers tend to be more masculine; boys with older sisters seem less masculine. This finding goes along with the assumption that younger children, to some degree, identify with older siblings and imitate their desirable behavior.

The effects of birth order were found to be influenced by both factors of sex and spacing. When siblings were of the same sex and less than two years apart in age, few behavioral differences were found. When the spacing in age was increased to four years in siblings of opposite sexes, the behavioral differences became greater. The most threatening situation to the older child occurs when the age difference is between two and four years. This condition results from the anxiety that 2- to 4-year old children have over the potential loss of their mothers to new babies and to their as yet undeveloped self-image.

COGNITIVE DEVELOPMENT AND SCHOOL LEARNING

As children grow from the ages of 9 to 12 years there is major improvement in their ability to do more complicated intellectual tasks. According to Bruner,[23] this cognitive development is illustrated (1) by an increased ability to see significant details in a situation and to detect absurdities, (2) by more sensible answers to questions, (3) by using words more correctly and defining abstract words more precisely, (4) by making generalizations from verbal and mathematical relationships, and (5) by exhibiting a larger fund of general information. They are better able to use information they already know to make judgments or deductions in areas that are only indi-

rectly related to the information. Development of cognitive abilities during the concrete operations stage (ages 7 to 12 years) of Piaget was presented in Chapter 8. The reader is referred to that chapter for a theoretical interpretation of cognitive development for this age level.

Mental characteristics

Nine-year-olds are fairly responsible and dependable. They understand explanations and try to do things well. They have some original ideas and interests and are capable of carrying them out, although not always. They do have many interests and will often drop a project when their attention wanes. They may go on to another project or activity, never finishing the original project. However, their attention is somewhat longer than that of 8-year-olds, and they are capable of concentrating on a particular subject for a longer period of time. Girls may spend longer on a task than do boys. At 9 years of age children are becoming critical of their performance and may work hard to perfect a skill. They want and need to be good at physical and mental skills so that they can get the admiration of other children.

Ten-year-olds are less enthusiastic about rote learning and drill exercises as compared to 9-year-olds. At 10 years children are developing a growing capacity for abstract thinking. They ask many searching questions and want thoughtful answers. They are now aware that people have many varying opinions and that different adults, even among those they admire, have different standards of right and wrong, good and bad. They are sensitive to lying, cheating, and unfairness and may turn on anyone with indignation if they suspect this kind of behavior. They are becoming aware of differences among people and of social problems. Their ideas are broadening, and their attitudes and prejudices are being formed. They cannot understand why there are hungry people and criminals. Why doesn't somebody do something about it? In an elementary way they are interested in discussing social concerns.

Eleven- and 12-year-olds are rounding out their childhood years and are alert to what it means to grow up. They often seem to be looking curiously and eagerly, but with some apprehen-

Intellectual curiosity is great in later childhood. Sex stereotyping should not hamper children from learning all they can about the world around them.

sion, to adulthood. They are concerned about their own physical and mental development as they approach puberty. These preadolescents are intensely realistic—even imaginative activities are applied in concrete ways. It is a time for eager absorption of information and accumulation of ideas. They ask many questions. Almost two fifths of their questions are scientific in nature, dealing with the physical world. About half their questions concern social studies, an area into which they are just now beginning to gain some insight. They understand the significance of the natural laws of science, but they are just beginning to feel their way with the social realm.

School learning

Children of this age are seeking reality in social and physical relationships. Not only are they interested in the immediate but also in matters well removed from them in time and place. Their sense of time and space has developed sufficiently so that their thinking reaches backward into ancient lands and times and forward into the world of tomorrow. They are fascinated by faraway places and distant times. They are collectors of facts as well as of baseball pictures, international dolls, and seashells.

Children's oral or spoken vocabularies are about 3,600 words at the age of 8 years, 5,400

Harold Geyer

Hands-on experiences, learning to design and construct, do much to bring out creative ability and an appreciation for productive endeavors.

words at 10 years, and 7,200 words at 12 years. By sixth grade their reading vocabulary will average 50,000 words.[24] Words with special meaning and limited use, such as a science, social studies, or health vocabulary, are learned at this time. Sixth graders should know how to use a dictionary, an encyclopedia, a card catalogue, and an atlas. They should understand the use of footnotes and index. Slang and swear words become part of the vocabulary, more so for boys than for girls. A new form of language, a secret language, may be developed at this time for use in communication with intimate friends. The language may be in written form using a code, in verbal form using ''pig Latin'' or clicking tongue sounds, or in kinetic form using fingers or gestures.

Girls as a group are superior to boys in word building, sentence completion tests, and rote memory. They write longer compositions and use longer sentences. Generally, girls make higher marks in language arts. Boys and girls, as

The Daily Tale

WEATHER

It will rain cats and dogs today.

LOCAL ROBBERY

Tom, the piper's son allegedly stole a pig last night. He was last seen fleeing the scene of the crime.

CAT COMES BACK

Be on the lookout for a strange talking cat who keeps returning to the area. He can be identified by his hat. He always wears the same one. See photo below.

Staff Photo

Wanted

Six inch brass bed. Call T. Thumb at 555-6753.

★   ★   ★

Wanted

Twenty bedroom house with ten bathrooms and very large kitchen. Call old woman tired of shoe.

★   ★   ★

Lost

Three pairs of mittens. Three flealined furries crying at home. If found call 555-6739.

Fourth graders published a newspaper with "news" stories based on incidents from children's stories and fairy tales.

RECENT U F O SIGHTINGS

Witnesses across the state reported several sightings of unidentified flying objects this week.

The first report involved an object that looked like a cow jumping over the moon. Also seen in the area were a cat playing a fiddle and a dish and spoon were seen in nearby skies.

In another part of the state, residents described a boy-shaped object wearing a green hat, green panty hose, and a green suit.

Accident

At 3:30 A.M. today Humpty Dumpty had a great fall. He was rushed to General Hospital. He may need open shell surgery.

Staff Photo

HEALTH DEPARTMENT INSPECTS RESTAURANT

A customer reported that he went into a local restaurant and ordered a piece of pie. When he took a bite, 24 blackbirds flew up in his face. He immediately reported the incident to the County Health Inspector. Investigation will begin this morning.

★　　★　　★

Guinness World Record Broken

The record for having the longest nose has been broken this week. The new record holder explained that his nose grows each time he tells a lie.

Staff Photo

THOUGHT FOR THE DAY:
Don't talk to chickens — they use fowl language!

a group, like to read books about travel, biography, science, nature, home, and school. Girls specifically like books about heroines and some romance. Boys like books about adventure, explorations, science fiction, mysteries, and tall tales. There is a great range of reading ability in late childhood. A range of reading achievement of two years above and two years below the grade level is usual within the class. In a heterogeneous classroom of sixth graders the reading ability can range from third to tenth grade.

Boys excel in abilities involving number manipulation and in arithmetical reasoning. A boy's ability to reason in the fourth, fifth, and sixth grades seems to be better than that of girls. Numbers take on new meaning. Schoolwork in math helps this age level to formulate more definite ideas of space and distance. Children can estimate short intervals of time more accurately at the age of 12 than at 6 years; in childhood boys do better than girls in this sort of perception.

Most children show the onset of permanent memory by 4 years of age. For some, however, it comes as late as the eighth year. Memory span for digits increases to six digits between fourth and sixth grade. Children remember longer what they see than what they hear. Words need to be reinforced by pictures. Memorizing is impeded by boredom, worry, a scolding, or daydreaming. It is not unusual for a boy in this age bracket to remember batting averages, completed passes, or the make, model, and year of most cars on the road, but it is difficult for him to remember how much is eight times nine.

Power of attention gradually increases. Many of an adult's complaints about children's inability to give attention is a wrong appraisal. Children are probably not interested in the thing they are asked to learn or attend to. They are more interested in learning what they want to know than in what the teacher may want to teach. A boy is curious and loves to manipulate objects. He is a creative thinker. He is a questioner. A girl is more likely to remember the details of such things as a presidential campaign. A boy is more likely to question its purpose. Boys outclass girls in mathematics, science, and creative thinking.

Between 7 and 11 years of age children are still not capable of formal logical thought. They try to justify their judgments, yet they are often unable to share the point of view of the person with whom they are conversing. By the age of 12 years this special condition of childhood has faded. Children are now able to see the point of view of the person with whom they are talking. No longer do they ask questions as if answers are always possible and as if unforeseen circumstances never intervene in the course of events.

AFFECTIVE AND MORAL DEVELOPMENT

The affective and moral development of children is closely integrated with cognitive and social development. Children at this stage are greatly influenced by the way others react to them. They have the basic emotional needs of love, belonging, security, success, new experiences, and independence. Although they exhibit less open expression of love to their parents, they still are greatly concerned about the amount of love their parents have for them. They want to be independent and express their desires in the form of rebellion, back talk, disobedience, and discourtesy. Many parents at this stage feel they must have brought their children up wrongly.

Preadolescents often daydream of wild conquests or adventures they will undertake and often engage in a fantasy life. By contrast they often go through long periods of empty daydreaming or staring into space. When asked what they are thinking about, they reply, "Nothing." And nothing may be actually what they are thinking about. Occasionally, a child of this age may revert to an infantile form of behavior such as bedwetting, constant moving of legs, arms, and head, or fingernail biting. It is all too frustrating to adults. Although these types of actions are irritating to parents, what angers and troubles them most is the seeming breakdown of the solid relationship they enjoyed with their child during earlier childhood.

One reason given for the resurfacing of regressive or infantile characteristics is that the childhood personality is becoming disorganized and loose to permit the child to develop a new personality for adolescence and adulthood. It is essential that children leave behind many of their childhood attitudes, behaviors, and habits. Internal emotional and personality changes are taking place, resulting in conflict and stress. These emotional factors, in turn, express themselves in fears, suspicion, and a withdrawal from parents and other adults. Peer standards take on significant meaning and importance for prepubescent children.

Emotional characteristics

The emotional characteristics of late childhood are both pleasant and unpleasant. They are pleasant to the children when they are releasing pent-up spirits by giggling, squirming, and general body activity. They are unpleasant when they involve tempers, anxiety, and feelings of frustration. The emotions found at this age are the same as those found in early childhood. The only difference is in the circumstances that give rise to the emotions and in the form of expression. Experiences and learning are responsible for the changes. Girls cry and have temper outbursts, and boys are sullen and sulky, but they both learn that violent expressions of unpleasant emotions are not acceptable to their contemporaries so they try to control their outward expression of emotions. There is an increase in the fear of imaginary, fanciful, or supernatural things. This age group is afraid of being "different" or of being called "chicken" or "'fraidy cat." The most common worries are about the family, school, personal and social adjustment, and health. School worries are more common than out-of-school worries. Girls worry more about school and safety than boys do. Generalized anxiety is more common than any one specific worry. This anxiety is greater in the child who is unpopular and, as a rule, is greater in girls. It increases in intensity for girls as they grow older. Anxiety can be strong enough in late childhood to handicap a child in learning, especially in reading and arithmetic. Errors tend to increase their feelings of insecurity and, as a result, the level of anxiety is increased, causing more errors or else inhibiting responses or attempts to learn.

Ten-year-olds are easygoing and balanced. They seldom cry and do not anger easily. When they get angry, it is physically and emotionally violent and immediate, but it soon becomes re-solved. They may plot revenge, but they seldom remember to carry it out. They seem to enjoy noise—at least they make enough of it. They have fewer worries than they do fears. Their worries center around school, such as homework, grades, and being late. They are scared of blood, ghosts, dead bodies of animals, criminals, wild animals, high places, and the dark. During the fourth and fifth grades, children may have the feeling that no one—teachers, friends, or parents—likes them, and this may result in crying sessions with the mother. No matter how much is said to allay these fears, the children remain or pretend to be adamant on the subject. They need their ego nurtured and bolstered.

The age of 11 years is one of the most worried and fearful ages for children. They worry about school, money, their parents' welfare, and their own health. Some children even worry about their father's driving, family relations, and world conditions. Some of these concerns may be due to an advanced level of cognitive development but with no knowledge or insight to back up the interpretations of what is seen or experienced. Strange animals are feared most, although the child still has a great fear of being in the dark and of high places. Anger is aroused more frequently than at the age of 10 years. Physical violence is the most common response, although violent verbal retorts are also common. By this time, however, children have developed enough behavior control so that they can suppress laughter where it is inappropriate, such as in church or on a solemn occasion. Instead of laughing, they express their joviality by a twinkle of the eye, a smile through tightly compressed lips, or a meaningful clearing of the throat.

Twelve-year-olds have fewer worries than they did at 11 years. School is still the main source of worries, but social and personal worries are on an increase. They fear being alone, being in the dark, snakes, crowds, and high places. Twelve years is the last age when immediate physical violence is more common than verbal responses to anger. Children of this age level gossip, make disparaging remarks, use retaliatory behavior, and get jealous over prestige in games, achievement in school, honors, and family reputation. Feats of strength and skills give boys great

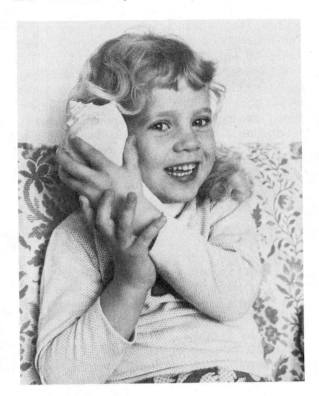

I have seen
A curious child, who dwelt upon a tract
Of inland ground, applying to his ear
The convolutions of a smooth-lipped shell,
To which, in silence hushed, his very soul
Listened intensely; and his countenance soon
Brightened with joy, for from within were heard
Murmurings, whereby the monitor expressed
Mysterious union with its native sea.

William Wordsworth
The Excursion

satisfaction. Although they have reached an age when they can be reasoned with, 12-year-olds can be overcritical, changeable, and uncooperative. However, they can also be decisive, responsible, and dependable when they feel more secure and confident. Also, they either love or hate—there is no middle ground.

Moral and spiritual development

Children in late childhood make substantial gains in their understanding of and feelings toward right and wrong. They do have conflicts, however, between the morality of adult authority, including the home, and that of the gang. Although preteen children assert themselves against authority, this is a period when conscience develops more fully. The home will have the most influence in religion, racial attitudes, and general ideology. The gang will have the most influence in manners, speech, and general behavior. They will make all kinds of rules of conduct for themselves, for what to wear, for the way to talk and act, and for playing games.

Children of 11 and 12 years commonly believe in justice and fair play. To this point in age the key to moral development in individuals has been their interaction with others in their environment. Intellectual speculating about right and wrong has been minimal up to now due to an inability to do much abstract reasoning. Now children are on the verge of being able to do formal logic and reasoning, and the next few years will bring about some pointed questions concerning morality and spiritual concerns.

The growth of spiritual and ethical concepts is related to cognitive development, experience, and social interaction. The following sequence of spiritual and ethical growth was determined by Gesell and his co-workers.[25] Twelve-month-olds may be inhibited by "no, no"; 18-month-olds drop an object they should not have taken and run away when they hear someone coming. Two-year-olds associate "good boy or girl" with routine duties well performed. Three-year-olds try to please and ask "Do it this way?" Four-year-olds begin to understand about rules and show a considerable interest in God if they are taken to Sunday School or church by their parents, although they will ask inappropriate questions about God. Five-year-olds think of God being a man like their father; they may believe that God is responsible for everything, including pushing them when they fall.

At the age of 6 years children grasp the idea of God as Creator of the world, the animals, and nature. Prayers are important, and they expect them to be answered. Seven-year-olds ask more appropriate questions about God, have continued interest in Sunday School and Bible stories, but they have a slight skepticism when they distinguish what they now know from what they were told in the past. For 8-year-olds good and bad are no longer only what parents permit or forbid. They are interested in the information that the soul only, and not the body, goes to heaven.

Nine-year-olds do not have a strong interest in God and religious matters, but they may pray spontaneously on occasion if in great need or danger. Bible story interest shifts to portions of the Old Testament. They may begin an interest in "fairness." Ten-year-olds may think of God as an invisible man. They may seek God's help to find something and do not always blame Him for misfortunes. At 11 years of age they may regard God as spirit. They vaguely begin to feel that what happens to you is determined by your acts. Twelve-year-olds do a lot of thinking about God and religion. Belief in God becomes more important than attending Sunday School or church. God is defined as "half spirit and half man."

Thirteen-year-olds may be more skeptical about the existence of God than at any other age. They may be shocked at their own disbelief. However, the practice of religion is important to them, and they may pray every night. At the age of 14 years they have more definite beliefs, and for many this is a peak year of enthusiasm for religious youth program activities. God is more abstract, such as a "power over us." Fifteen-year-olds are more searching rather than reaching. At this age they are uncertain about ideas of the Deity—"kind of hard to say." Church service may be preferred, but often they do not want to sit with their parents. Sixteen-year-olds show more belief in God than at any preceding age but still have not built up a continuing personal relationship with God. They think of God as a divine power or guiding ruler. A mental age of 17 years is needed before deeper meanings of God can be recognized, and a mental age of 20 years is needed to perceive profound spiritual insights.

STUDY GUIDE

1. Review the developmental tasks of late childhood. Compare these tasks to those of middle childhood and of early adolescence. What common threads do you find connecting these three stages of growth?
2. Compare height and weight gain of boys and girls by consulting Table 9-1. How do extreme deviations in physical growth affect the mental health of preadolescents?
3. What physical changes take place in the period preceding the peak of pubertal development? Why do you suppose most girls reach puberty before boys?
4. Read the section on psychosexual development and awareness. Think of when you were 6 to 10 years old. How did you and your young friends learn about sex? You are not being asked to share this personal information with others.
5. What does the research say about the source of sex information and the age at which it was obtained?
6. In what ways do girls and boys differ in their social patterns during preadolescence? To your knowledge, do the groups of boys and girls of this age with whom you are familiar act this way? Does a boy act differently when he is by himself than when he is with a group?
7. What steps do many children of late childhood years take toward independence or self-autonomy?
8. What meaning does birth order have to you? Which child were you? How does the description for your particular level fit you?
9. What are the major characteristics of cognitive development during late adolescence?

How are these characteristics manifested in school?

10. Late childhood children have their emotional problems. What do they worry about? What are they anxious about?

11. The moral consciousness of many preadolescents is highly pragmatic, concrete, and narrow in expression and related strongly to the situation at hand. Is this point of view much different from that held by adults with whom you are acquainted? How? Do you find it difficult to identify the moral beliefs of others? How about identifying your own beliefs?

REFERENCES

1. Latham, H. C., Heckel, R. V., Herbert, L. J., & Bennett, E. *Pediatric nursing* (3rd ed.). St. Louis: The C. V. Mosby Co., 1977.

2. *Ibid.* p. 151-152.

3. Tanner, J. M. Growing up. *Scientific American*, 1973, **229**(3), 35-43.

4. Harlow, H. F., & Suomi, S. J. The nature of love—simplified. *American Psychologist*, 1970, **25**, 161-168.

5. Calderone, M. How parents should teach their children about sex. *Today's Health*, December, 1973, 68-70.

6. Elias, J., & Gebbard, P. Sexuality and sexual learning in childhood. *Phi Delta Kappa*, 1969, **50**, 401-405.

7. Schofield, M. *The sexual behavior of young people*. Boston: Little, Brown, & Co., 1965.

8. Athamasiou, R. A review of public attitudes on sexual issues. In J. Zubic, & J. Money (Eds.), *Contemporary sexual behavior: critical issues in the 1970's*. Baltimore: Johns Hopkins University Press, 1973.

9. Black, J. H. Conceptions of sex roles: some cross-cultural and logitudinal perspectives, *American Psychologist*, 1973, **25**, 512-526.

10. Munsinger, H. *Fundamentals of child develop-ment* (2nd ed.). New York: Holt, Rinehart, & Winston, 1975.

11. Bossard, J. H., & Boll, E. S. *The sociology of child development* (4th ed.). New York: Harper & Row, Publishers, 1966.

12. Piaget, J. *The moral judgment of the child*. New York: Macmillan, Inc., 1955.

13. Lynn, D. *The father: his role in child development*. Monterey, Calif.: Brooks/Cole Publishing Co., 1974.

14. Schachter, S. Birth order, eminence and higher education. *American Sociological Review*, 1963, **28**, 764-767.

15. McCall, J. N., & Johnson, O. G. The independence of intelligence from family size and birth orders. *Journal of Genetic Psychology*, 1972, **121**, 207-213.

16. Harris, I. D., & Howard, K. J. Birth order and responsibility. *Journal of Marriage and the Family*, 1968, **30**, 431.

17. Lichtenwalner, J. S., & Maxwell, J. W. The relationship of birth order and socioeconomic status to the creativity of preschool children. *Child Development*, 1969, **40**, 1241-1246.

18. Schacter, *op. cit.* p. 766.

19. Konig, K. *Brothers and sisters: a study in child psychology*. New York: St. George Books, 1963.

20. Tomeh, A. K. Birth order and friendship associations, *Journal of Marriage and the Family*, 1970, **32**, 361-362.

21. Otto, W. Family position and success in reading. *Reading Teacher*, November, 1965.

22. Janis, I. L. (Ed.), *Personality: dynamics, development and assessment*. New York: Harcourt Brace Janovich, Inc., 1969.

23. Bruner, J. Course of cognitive development, *American Psychologist*, 1964, **19**, 8.

24. Wolman, R. D., & Barker, E. N. A developmental study of word definitions, *Journal of Genetic Psychology*, 1965, **107**, 119-166.

25. Gesell, A, Ilg, F. L., & Ames, L. P. *Youth—the years from ten to sixteen*. New York: Harper & Row, Publishers, 1956.

10 Puberty and early adolescence

12 to 14 years of age

A MOTHER'S THOUGHTS

Dear Son,

In a few minutes you will be coming home from your last day in sixth grade. Next month you will be twelve years old and ready to begin junior high school. Do you find it as difficult to believe as I do that you are now half way through your public school days?

You and your bedroom—what bridges from the past to the future you both are! Each is anchored in yesteryear and reaches for a destination planned for, yet not clearly visible. Your bedroom has a firm foundation—sturdy steel beams in the basement, a sturdy floor, rising walls, two sparkling windows, and a brightly lit ceiling. Within it are your treasures, your delights, your fears, and your aspirations.

Yes, you are very much like your bedroom. Dad and I have supplied the foundation by giving you life, guiding, loving, and nourishing you so that you are becoming more firm. Together, we have all laid the sturdy floor. A few boards were difficult to nail down, but most seemed to fit easily into place when we all worked together.

Your eyes are your windows—clear, revealing, allowing the light of knowledge to enter, and occasionally needing the sprinkle of tears to be blotted away.

Your body, "growing into your legs," rises as do your bedroom walls. And what a bright light your mind is—perhaps not brilliant, but certainly illuminating your world and ours.

Your room has changed as you have. Where your crib used to be, there is a new full-sized bed. Remember how hard you tried to stretch out to reach from one end to the other? I'm glad you reach out, son, and are eager to be a man.

Your closet no longer contains snowsuits and diapers. Instead, I see your Boy Scout and Little League uniforms. Next to them is your old yellow slicker and rain hat. I remember the day I said you looked like a little yellow duckling and off you went, quacking, to kindergarten. Beside that I see a pair of bell bottoms, just like your older brother's. In many ways he has become more of a model for you than Dad. Also on the floor are the socks I told you three times to pick up!

Your rocking horse has been replaced by a drum set. With the former I worried for your safety; with the latter, I'm concerned for *my* sanity. Your record collection, here, is a "now" thing, but I think your interest in music will last. How proud I was of you at your band concert, your head barely visible above the others, but your "flam taps" coming through loud and clear.

Your bookcase and desk reflect your whole life. Your very first books are there, including several well-worn ones by Dr. Seuss. How you loved to "read" before you started to school! You have always been a great one for classifying things. Here is your third grade bird scrapbook, and, next to it, a notebook you kept on states and birds you counted when we went to California four years ago. Baseball cards, again classified by league and position, will soon need a larger box. Beside the books on baseball are a few mysteries you enjoyed. I think you must have every "Happy Hollister" book ever written. You quickly outgrew these and room was made for history books and encyclopedias. Do you still want to be an historian? With your love of searching for answers, I know you'd be a good one. Maybe your reluctance to part with things from the past reflects your love of history?

On the edge of the unmade bed is your newspaper bag. I never thought anything would get you up that early! I had reservations about your taking a paper route but I recognize your need to earn some money on your own besides what you earn mowing the lawn for Dad.

On the wall, almost as good as new, is the .410 you got for Christmas. Again, I think this was your brother's influence. Your compassion for animals and love of nature prevent you from enjoying hunting. Grandma was so pleased when I told her how you had rescued a bird from the creek and had used the first aid methods you learned in school. You checked its breathing, looked for broken bones or bleeding—but how do you give a bird artificial respiration?

Life will always be interesting and challenging to you. You make learning relevant by applying what you have learned to everyday situations. Remember using fractions to make fudge the other night?

You have also learned early in life that you can't excel in everything. Track was a disappointment to you. Because of your size, you weren't able to keep up to the larger boys. So, you competed with yourself and were pleased when each day you were able to run a few seconds faster than you could the day before.

Size is only one thing you've had to compensate for. Being left-handed has never seemed to be a drawback because you haven't allowed it to be. You seem to take pride in the accomplishments of other left-handers. Playing the drums was more difficult because the major parts are written for the right hand. But look how that has helped in baseball. You're a switch hitter. You've said you're not a big hitter, but the team can always count on you to steal when you do get on base. This is perhaps the greatest thing I admire about you. You recognize your limitations and your capabilities. You are always able to rechannel your efforts and to think positively.

Some children find it a disadvantage in school if their parents are teachers. You have not yet reached the point where you are embarrassed or ashamed of them, as some are. You love to learn, and you dislike a situation where no learning takes place. You prefer a strict teacher with high standards. Remember how proud you were that you could spell so well when you were in first grade? We used to take long walks and you'd spell any word I'd give you. I'm proud of your scholastic record and the fact that you can appreciate learning for its own sake. You have always been so highly self-motivated that we never had to prod you.

Being a younger child can also present problems, but you seem to have taken it in stride. You are naturally envious because your brother is bigger and can do more things than you can. The other day I saw you trying on his old sixth grade gym suit to see if you are as big as he was. You seemed quite disappointed that the suit was too large. But we talked this over, and I think you understand now that all children don't grow at the same rate. You laugh now and seem so disgusted over the fact that he has a girl friend. I hope you will be able to laugh about it when you get to be his age and become interested in girls.

As I turn to leave your room, the last thing I see is the bureau with pictures of your best friends on it. They have become quite an influence on your life and I'm pleased to see you've made wise choices. I would put some things away but I know you have a "private drawer," and I wouldn't destroy the trust you have placed in me.

I hear the school bus coming, so I'll close the door. It's almost like closing the door to elementary school and waiting to see what awaits as it again opens— this time to junior high school, puberty, and, sadly, probably a very, very different boy.

Early adolescence is a time of growing, learning, adventuring, scorning, and dreaming. It is a time of anxieties and problems, but these are outweighed by joy, innocence, excitement, and gladness. The term *adolescence* comes from the Latin verb *adolescere,* meaning "to grow into maturity." As such it is a transitional period—a time of physical, social, and emotional metamorphosis. As someone has said, it is a time when the individual is "neither man nor child, nor fish nor fowl." In some ways adolescents are like squirming, wiggling caterpillars engaged in the agonizing fight to escape childhood's cocoon and enter into adulthood's full flight. All adolescents view the adult world as full of beautiful butterflies free of everything restrictive. They cannot wait to break out and fly. Unfortunately, nature prefers that this be done in an orderly, maturing fashion.

Early adolescents are no longer children, yet they are not adults. They are at an in-between stage, when it is difficult to know how they should be considered. If they are treated as children, they resent it bitterly. If they are treated as adults, their lack of maturity becomes evident and they are embarrassed. What should be recognized is that adolescence is more than a period, or stage, of human development. It is a way of life with its own culture, values, characteristics, activities, demands, situations, and problems. In a complex society, adults must not be too quick to make the child a man or woman. In a primitive society in a less intricate world it might be possible to move from childhood to adulthood with a minimum of complications.

Today's world with its computerized systems approach to the business of life requires more cognitive, communicative, and collective competencies on the part of individuals before they can become independent, self-supporting adults. A longer period of time is required to learn the skills needed for competent adult living. This extended length of time makes it possible for the

Puberty is when you're fixing to kiss a girl for the first time and don't know who's supposed to make the smacking noise

Puberty is when you kiss a girl for the first time and neither one of you makes the smacking noise

Puberty is when all the other girls in class have bras whether they need them or not but *your* mom says you're going to wait until you have a reason

Puberty is when you write a love letter to the girl you're crazy about and she starts passing it around

Puberty is when the boy you're crazy about calls and your mom gets to the phone first and starts asking questions

adolescents of today to reveal their uniqueness and to develop and demonstrate characteristics that are typically adolescent in nature but that in another day and age would not have had the time to be expressed. In a less complex society youth went about doing the work of an adult world soon after they left the period of childhood. Youth of today have the time to be adolescents.

No sharp age lines separate the stages of growth at any level. Especially is this statement true when one works with narrow developmental divisions as in this text. As long as we talk about the characteristics of the group, we are reasonably accurate. If we think in terms of an individual, then we must definitely keep in mind the broad range of normal differences that exist within the group. The reader must make allowances for these individual differences when making application of characteristics mentioned in this book to a specific person. In addition, one must recognize and accept the fact that there will always be an overlapping of characteristics of successive developmental stages in individuals.

During the total span of adolescence, the individual is working harder than ever before on two primary developmental tasks: (1) to establish independence from adults, and parents in particular, in self-identification and emotional independence, and (2) to develop social, intellectual, language, and motor skills that are essential for individual and group participation in heterosexual activities. Other developmental tasks include (1) accepting changes taking place in one's body and physical appearance and learning good grooming practices, (2) achieving appropriate relationships with age mates of both sexes, (3) accepting a masculine or feminine role that is appropriate for the age level, and (4) acquiring moral concepts, values, and attitudes that contribute something to life in family, school, church, and peer group activities. Adolescents see this period as beset with problems, but they generally enjoy themselves as they make their way to adulthood.

PUBERTAL AND PHYSICAL DEVELOPMENT

Early adolescence is a time of physical growth and change. Many physiological changes occur rather suddenly and are frequently a striking contrast to characteristics that existed earlier. Such changes are disquieting to the young person, but adults often think of them as humorous, if not wonderful. Physical changes, as at any age, mean that the fairly well-formulated body image of the preadolescent must now be changed. The new bodily form at least must be reconciled to the existing self-concept. Neither alternative is easy. Many individuals find that adjusting to the realities of their new physical selves is an exceedingly difficult thing to do. This adjustment must be made by the teenager, the middle-aged person, and the individual in senescence. The teenager is confronted with the problem more quickly because changes occur in such a short span of time, almost "overnight."

Onset of puberty

The early stage of adolescent development is referred to as the pubertal period. The term *puberty* is derived from the Latin word *pubertos,* which means "the age of manhood." The implication is that a person who has gone through the pubertal period has entered adulthood and is now physically able to participate in the reproduction of the human species. Manhood or womanhood is not achieved suddenly or completely at puberty. The changes taking place at this stage are part of a developing process that began early in the life of the individual and that will continue to be active for some years to come.

The pubertal stage consists of three periods of development: pubescence, puberty, and post-pubescence. The entire stage usually lasts about four years. Pubescence, called *prepuberty,* or *preadolescence,* by some writers, refers to the period of about two years before puberty when the child is developing preliminary characteristics of sexual maturity. It is characterized by a spurt in physical growth, changes in body proportion, and the beginning of primary and secondary sex characteristics. The peak, or climax, of the pubertal stage is called puberty, the period during which the generative (reproductive) organs become capable of functioning and the secondary sex characteristics become highly evident. The initial appearance of these characteristics does not mean that the boy or girl is immediately capable of reproduction, however. In the postpubescence period there is a one- to two-year span of adolescent sterility. During this time, most of the skeletal growth is completed and the new biological functions become fairly well established. The age of nubility or fertility has now arrived. It should be noted that in England the term *puberty* is sometimes used in a legal rather than a biological sense. In the eyes of British law, girls reach puberty at the age of 12 years and boys at 14 years.

Sex characteristics. At this point it would be well to define the terms *primary sex characteristics* and *secondary sex characteristics*. The external and internal organs that carry on the reproductive functions are known as the primary sex organs. During infancy and childhood, the sex organs are small and do not produce cells for reproduction. The pubescent stage, when functional maturity takes place in these organs, is the dividing line between the sexually immature and sexually mature person. The primary sex organs were discussed in an earlier chapter on prenatal development (Fig. 10-1).

The secondary sex characteristics are those that distinguish the sexes from each other but play no direct part in reproduction. In boys these include pubic hair, which becomes curly, darker, and coarser with adolescent age; facial hair, first above the upper lip, then on other parts of the face, necessitating shaving at about the age of 16 years; body hair on the arms, chest, legs, and armpits; coarser skin with enlarged pores; changes in voice; increased length of the shoulders, depth of the chest, and size of the neck; and slight enlargements or breast knots around the mammary glands, lasting only a few weeks.

Secondary sex characteristics in girls include an increase in the width and roundness of the hips; more shapely legs and arms; menarche; thicker, coarser skin with enlarged glands; the appearance of facial hair on the upper lip and cheeks; development of breasts through four stages, starting with the papilla stage (nipple of early childhood), the bud stage about 10 or 11 years of age when there is an elevation of the nipple and surrounding areola, the primary breast stage where fatty tissue develops under and

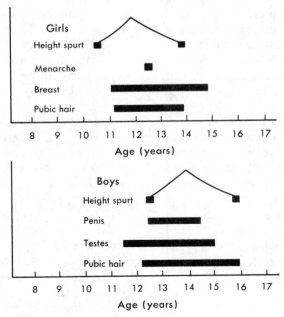

Fig. 10-1. Sequence of events of puberty for girls and boys and predictable patterns of development of the secondary sex characteristics. (Adapted from Marshall, W. A., & Tanner, J. M. *Archives of Disease in Childhood,* 1970, **45,** 13-23.)

around nipple and areola, and the secondary breast stage of maturity; appearance of pubic hair, first as straight, then as kinky hair (pubic hair appears in a large amount only after the breasts develop); and changes of voice from a high-pitched tone to a more mature tone because of a slight growth of the larynx (Table 10-1).

Signs of puberty. Several criteria are used to determine the climax of puberty. Menarche (pronounced "men-AR-kee"), which is the occurrence of the first menstruation, is usually a valid sign of puberty in girls. At the same time the secondary sex characteristics appear. The average age at which most North American girls experience their first menses is 12.5 years old. The normal age range is considered to be 10 to 16 years. About 3% to 4% of all girls have menarche before the age of 10 years. Some school nurses report an increase in this percentage in their districts. Few begin menses after the age of 16½ years.[1] Evidence from many parts of the world indicates that the average age of menarche has dropped by at least two years and perhaps by as many as five years in the last century.[2] In 1820 working girls in Manchester, England, reached menarche on the average at 15.7 years. Studies done in the late sixties in England and in many

other parts of the world show averages at about midway between 12 and 13 years (Fig. 10-2). In New York City in 1934 the average age of menarche was 13.5 years; in 1964 it was 12.5 years. Better nutrition and better living conditions are

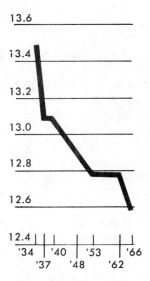

Fig. 10-2. Lowering age of first menses in American girls.

Table 10-1. Normal maturation sequence in girls*

Phase	Appearance of sexual characteristics	Average age	Age range
Childhood through preadolescence	No pubic hair; breasts are flat; growth in height is constant		
Early adolescence	Rounding of hips; breasts and nipples are elevated to form bud stage; no true pubic hair	10 to 11 years	9 to 14 years
Middle adolescence	Appearance of pubic hair; increment in height to 18 months before menarche; with menarche, labia become enlarged, vaginal secretions become acid, areola and nipple elevate to form "primary breast"	11 to 14 years	10 to 16 years
Late adolescence	Pubic hair fully developed; breast fills out to adult form; menstruation is well established; growth in height decelerates between 16¼ and 17¼ years	14 to 16 years	13 to 18 years
Post-adolescence	Breasts fully developed; height increases stop	16 to 18 years	15 to 19 years

*From Caplan, G., & Lebovici, S. (Eds.), *Adolescence: psychosocial perspectives.* New York: Basic Books, Inc., Publishers, 1969, p. 33.

generally cited as the reasons for the lowering age of first menses. There is some indication, however, that the drop in the age of menarche may be leveling off in the more affluent populations.[3]

The classic view that menarche occurs earlier in hot, humid climates has been largely discredited. The mean age of menarche for girls in Nigeria has been found to be 14.22 years, and for Alaskan Eskimos it is 14.42 years. Tanner reports that Chinese girls in Hong Kong and Cuban girls experience menarche as early as European girls on the highest living standard.[4] Girls who are city dwellers, live in low altitudes, or are totally blind appear to reach menarche earlier than their counterparts. An interesting effect of altitude on menarche has been found in the high Andes of Peru by Jean McClung of the Harvard Medical School. Menarche is reported so delayed there that it is difficult to find a girl in the high Andes who has borne children before the age of 18 years.[5]

In boys there is no striking change to indicate puberty. One of the more reliable indicators of

puberty in boys is the presence of live spermatozoa in their urine. The presence of the gonadotrophic hormone, or androgen, in the urine is also an indication of puberty. An overt sign in boys is the beginning of nocturnal emissions. When the boy is sleeping, the penis becomes erect, and semen, which is fluid with sperms, spurts out or is released. Spontaneous nocturnal emissions will persist into adulthood and will occur whenever the reproductive organ has an excess of semen. After puberty this action is frequently accompanied by a dream of short duration whose content has sexual connotations. At puberty the male gonadal hormones also stimulate the growth of the male sexual apparatus, including the penis, the prostate gland, seminal vesicles, and scrotum. These hormones bring about the development of male secondary sexual characteristics (Table 10-2). The average age at which boys reach puberty is 14.0 years. Two thirds of all boys attain puberty between 12.5 and 16.5 years of age. We have not been able to find research since 1935 indicating that the average

Table 10-2. Normal maturation sequence in boys*

Phase	Appearance of sexual characteristics	Average age	Age range
Childhood through preadolescence	No pubic hair; no growth in testes and penis since infancy; growth in height constant		
Early adolescence	Testes increase in size; scrotum grows; penis follows with growth in length and circumference; no true pubic hair	12 to 13 years	10 to 15 years
Middle adolescence	Pubic hair becomes apparent; penis, testes, and scrotum continue growing and become larger; significant spurt of growth in height; prostate seminal vesicles mature; spontaneous or induced emissions occur; voice begins to change as larynx thickens	13 to 16 years	11 to 18 years
Late adolescence	Facial and body hair appear and spread; pubic hair becomes denser; voice deepens; testes and penis continue to grow; growth in height decreases; 98% of mature stature between 17¾ and 18½ years; indentation of frontal hair line	16 to 18 years	14 to 20 years
Post-adolescence	Mature and full development of primary and secondary sex characteristics; muscles may continue increasing	Onset 18 to 21 years	Onset 16 to 21 years

*From Caplan, G., & Lebovici, S. (Eds.), *Adolescence: psychosocial perspectives.* New York: Basic Books, Inc., Publishers, 1969, p. 30.

age of puberty in boys has lowered the same as it has for girls.

Physical changes at puberty

Growth spurt. Among the earliest physical signs of puberty are obvious gains in weight and height. The growth spurt begins one to two years before the child becomes sexually mature and continues for six months to a year afterward. The growth spurt in girls begins at between 8.5 and 11.5 years of age and reaches a peak between 11 and 13 years of age. After the spurt, growth continues until the age of 17 or 18 years, when height is fairly well established. Some girls continue to grow until about 21 years of age. As indicated in the last chapter, girls will grow 2 to 4 inches a year during the growth spurt and gain 8 to 10 pounds or so. Gains of 5 or 6 inches are not unusual. Boys begin the accelerated growth pattern between 10.5 and 14.5 years of age and reach a peak between 13.0 and 15.5 years. This period is followed by a gradual decline until about 21 years of age, although some continue to grow until 25 years of age.[6] On the average, boys gain 12 to 14 pounds and grow 4 to 5 inches in the peak year.

As a teacher of ninth graders, whose average age was 14 years, one of the authors had his homeroom group of thirty-eight pupils mark their height on a wallboard during their first week of school in September and again during the last week in May at the end of school. Every youngster in that room grew at least 2 inches during the school year; most grew 3 to 4 inches. One boy grew 7 inches in nine months! Increases in height and weight in either sex generally result in a greater intake of food. Appetite becomes ravenous and will be so for three or four years, necessitating frequent and more costly trips to the supermarket.

Statistical studies show a worldwide tendency in the last century toward an increase of stature.[7] The average 14-year-old boy in the United States is 5 inches taller than a boy of the same age in 1880. This increase is proportional for most other countries in the world. The average height at maturity for American women today is 65 to 66 inches. The average American boy at 18 years of age is 69.5 inches with little growth beyond that age. Including all adults, the average American woman today weighs 135 pounds, whereas the average American man weighs 165 pounds. American adults weigh more than those of twenty-five years ago. Women weigh, on the average, 6 pounds more and men 10 pounds more than the preceding generation.[8]

Body changes. There are sex differences in the distribution of fat during puberty due to hormonal changes and an increase in appetite. About half of all boys and girls go through this fat period. The thickness of the skin in the neck,

Adolescent fat is a natural part of growth after puberty. A stocky-built body, however, may be the result of genetic influence.

Harold Geyer

THE UGLY DUMPLING

In this society much emphasis is placed upon the appearance of the female. A female must be pretty and have a stunning figure. Fashions are designed for the woman who has the hip size of a teenage boy. Television and motion picture screens emphasize facial beauty. The mass media rarely suggest that the "Plain Jane" exists, and if they do suggest such existence they never picture a successful one.

This paper is being written to describe a girl named Cindy who is between twelve and thirteen years of age. She has a problem suffered by many people in America; she is overweight. She is not the beautiful woman shown on the television screen. She has plain, ordinary brown hair. Her eyes are hazel and are functional. They do not, however, glow in the dark or seduce helpless men. As a matter of fact, she resembles her father, who definitely does not resemble Elizabeth Taylor.

More of her appearance will be described in the pages that follow, but it will be described by Cindy—in her own words—from her diary.

• • •

Dear Diary,

I'm glad you cannot see me when I write in you. Otherwise you would probably lose your key so I couldn't open you. I would understand, though. I looked into the mirror and saw that horror my parents say they love. How can they? I've disappointed them. My sister is so pretty, and my parents can be proud of her, but me! Just look at me. Why do *I* have to look this way? I do not have a waist. I think if I could be about eight inches taller I'd be fine. Then all of the fat would stretch out.

The school nurse said not to eat bread and potatoes for a while. She measured and weighed us yesterday. I am four feet, eight inches tall and weigh 142 pounds. At least I'm not like my friends Carol and Nancy. Carol weighs 175 and Nancy weighs 190. What does that nurse know anyway? I have starved myself, and still nothing happened.

Dear Diary,

Tonight at the school dance the kids started to call me the "vitamin pill." At least that's not as bad as "the ugly dumpling." I'll never go to a school dance again. I was so insulted that I cried. I might go see a doctor without my Mom knowing about it. But how would I pay?

Dear Diary,

I don't know if you feel this way, but every time I go out I feel like everyone is saying something about me or looking at me and laughing. I don't know why I can't be accepted for myself rather than the way I look. That's what we talked about in history class today. I really like my teacher. I really cannot understand why people don't like me. I can't help it if I'm fat. The boys can't stand me. They don't like other girls either, but they hate me.

Dear Diary,

I've started a new hobby after school. I'm reading all the books I can. I love Nancy Drew, but my favorite is Trixie Belden. Trixie is just who I want to be. She's pretty and skinny, but she is nice. If I read after school, then I do not have to go out with the rest of the kids and play games.

---

thorax, and abdomen increases more in boys than in girls. Just before puberty in boys there is an increase in fat around the nipples and over the stomach, hips, and thighs. Fatty tissue in boys decreases after puberty. With the beginning of puberty girls develop fat over the abdomen and hips. The adolescent fat in girls will be present for about two years or so until their bodies gain some physical stability. The way girls react to their chubby appearance varies according to their past experiences of behaving under stress. Some girls withdraw to their room, away from people. Other girls resort to wearing loose-fitting, matronly clothing. Some girls go on "crash" or starvation diets, often encouraged by well-meaning mothers, whereas other girls go to a "fat camp," where a prescribed routine for losing weight is followed. Some accept their weight gain as being normal.

Significant changes in body proportions and contours are characteristic of this age group. The early adolescent boy's form usually is characterized by straight leg lines, slender hips, wide shoulders, broadened chest, and accentuated muscle development in shoulders, arms, and thighs. The girl's leg lines become curved, her breasts fill, and her hips become wider. There is a deposit of fat in the buttocks, thighs, and upper arms. Disproportionate facial features are noticeable in either sex when the face lengthens. The forehead becomes higher and wider. The nose looks large because it grows before puberty and is nearly completed at puberty. Later the mouth and lips become fuller. The jaw is the last part to reach adult size. A high waistline develops in early adolescence as the trunk lengthens, but it drops as adult proportions are reached. Just before puberty the legs become longer than the trunk, and the arms increase in length. Hands and feet look disproportionate because they reach their mature size before the arms and legs.

Most children will have some obvious, uneven features during these years (Fig. 10-3).

Motor awkwardness in early adolescence is often partly caused by uneven growth of muscles and bones. If the bones grow faster than the muscles, the muscles become taut on the bones, making them respond with a quick, jerky motion. If the muscles grow faster than the bones, the muscles become loose and sluggish. The brain has been programmed during late childhood to provide the muscles with a certain amount of energy to move the limbs of the body to a certain position in space. In early adolescence the ratio of the bones and muscles changes, but the brain still operates on the programming pattern of an earlier age; it will continue to do so until it has been reprogrammed. As a result, when a certain movement is needed, such as reaching out with the arm and hand to catch a ball, the brain sends the same amount of energy to the muscles as it did for the bone-muscle ratio of the younger age. The energy applied now to taut muscles causes the arm to move too fast to catch the ball; applied to loose muscles, the energy is not enough to get the hand up in time to catch the ball. A clumsy-appearing performance results. This awkwardness in arm and leg movements will continue until the growth of bones and muscles reaches a stable condition and the brain can be reprogrammed for the new bone-muscle ratio. It must also be stated that the emotional response of the early adolescent to various motor activities may also have something to do with the degree of awkward motor responses that a child may make.

Psychological reactions. It is almost certain that the physical changes that occur at puberty will have psychological implications. Boys who are awkward in motor skills necessary to play sports or the games of their peers will believe that they are not acceptable. Embarrassment among boys is often caused by their changing, uncon-

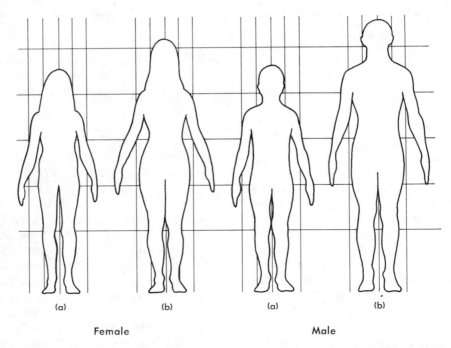

(a)	(b)	(a)	(b)
Female		Male	

Fig. 10-3. Changes in body proportions of boys and girls, *(a)*, before and, *(b)*, after puberty changes have been completed. (Adapted from Tanner, J. M. *Scientific American*, 1973, **229**(3), 35-43.)

trollable voices. The growth of hair, especially on the face, may create emotional concern. A boy may be as sensitive about his first shaving experience as a girl is about wearing her first brassiere. Some girls attempt to hide their developing breasts, whereas others are delighted with their bust development and wear tight-fitting sweaters to accentuate it. In cultures where breasts are considered sexually attractive—and they are not considered so in all cultures—a flat-chested female may feel inferior. Menstruation can be a traumatic experience because of its sudden onset, especially if the girl was not taught what to expect. The way in which a girl accepts menstruation depends a great deal on the strength of her female identity and her acceptance of the inevitable. Boys may be concerned about the size of their genitalia and may be upset about having to shower and change clothes for gym class. Skin eruptions, clogged pores, perspiration, and body odors bother most teenagers. Learning good grooming habits becomes a major task.

Psychological reactions to being too tall or too short are prevalent among early adolescents. It is no problem for the boy if he is taller than his classmates and is coordinated enough to use the height to his advantage, especially in sports. Shortness in boys, however, is incompatible with their ideal of maleness. Short boys often seek to compensate for their lack of height by swearing, smoking, boisterousness, or being overdaring. Being tall may be a problem for the early adolescent girl, however, because she dreads being different from the other girls. Furthermore, few boys want to date or go with a girl who is much taller than themselves. Many women vividly recall the embarrassment they felt as shy teenagers as they towered over their partner's head on the dance floor at a school party. Many postures have suffered as a consequence. In late childhood boys are taller and huskier than girls. From ages 11 to 14 years girls have the advantage. Thereafter boys are again physically taller and heavier than girls.

Some psychological reactions, such as changes in interests and attitudes, are desirable and mentally healthy. Other reactions, such as fear, guilt, and shame brought about by the development of the sex organs, should be avoided. The extent and depth of psychological responses to puberty are predicated partly on the adequacy of the preparations for these changes that the early adolescent has received. If youngsters have been adequately prepared or if the changes occur slowly, the transition may take place without psychological disturbance. One way or another teenagers will have to accept the changes that have occurred in their bodies. Their parents can do much to help them develop pride in their new status.

PERSONAL CHARACTERISTICS

The change in physical appearance brought on by puberty is accompanied by a change in emotional control and response. In late childhood youngsters were rather stable individuals. They had reached the peak of childhood development. They knew and understood what their bodies could do. They were satisfied with their peer and family relationships. Their pattern of behavior was acceptable to them, they knew what they could get away with and how to manipulate situations to their advantage. In short, they were in control of their life pattern. All of a sudden puberty comes along and upsets their well-structured approach to the world. Their bodies change rapidly, and they are bewildered. They no longer look like children, but they are not ready for adulthood and its demands. Their emotional approach to handling frustrating or conflicting situations is undermined and no longer appropriate. They are uncertain as to how to act, what to do, or what to think. It looks like they are going to have to start all over again, building new self-images, adapting to new social patterns, and developing new emotional responses and mental health mechanisms. In addition to all these changes, the instability of the chemical balance in their bloodstreams hinders them from making quick adjustments simply because their hormones will not permit them to do so.

In the early years of adolescence feelings and emotions vary considerably. The origins of most of these feelings are within teenagers rather than their environment.[9] There is a great increase in moods and sentiments. Emotions vacillate up and down; one moment they are up on cloud nine, and the next moment they are down in pit five. Ambivalent feelings are prevalent. Control or balance of affective experiences seems lost; emotions frequently get out of proportion. Little things can cause an emotional upheaval and can mean a lot, depending on how the teenagers interpret what they encounter.

Emotional responses and feelings, such as enthusiasm for a project, cannot be counted on from day to day. Heightened emotionality often causes overreaction of response. Transfer of affection and love from parents to peers and eventually to members of the opposite sex is a major change. New mental defense mechanisms must be developed. In the meanwhile the mechanisms that are used may be taken to extremes. Daydreaming may be so intense that adolescents may not hear a person talking to them (withdrawal mechanism), or they become hostile and ready to fight, complain, or resist everything (aggressive mechanisms). And when an adult seeks to be compassionate, they may get the reply, "Just because I'm a teenager you don't have to be so understanding!"

Age characteristics

Twelve-year-olds are happy most of the time because the majority are not well into the puberty period. They can still use their preadolescent behavior in acceptable ways. They are becoming funnier from an adult point of view, but their humor is biting, and they use it to criticize actions of their parents and to insult their friends. "If I couldn't do better than that, I'd go and hide my head in the sand." "Oh yeah, you think you're smart—how about the time you . . ." And so it goes. Twelve-year-olds try to keep moods and feelings a secret. However, when their feelings are hurt, they will react with talking back, name calling, or saying something mean rather than leaving the scene.

Although 13-year-olds are moderately calm, they will sulk and cry and make faces at people. Generally, they will simply ignore the situation

A love of food is typical of most early adolescents. Their appetites do vary, how-ever—sometimes large, sometimes none at all. Mothers need to recognize this incon-sistency.

David Strickler

or the person who hurt their feelings. They will confide in certain friends while hiding their hurts from others. This is an age when many youngsters worry about their schoolwork. It can be particularly upsetting for some if they have to take a course from a teacher who has a reputation for being tough and strict, but a good teacher. One eighth grade teacher, a big hulk of a woman with such a reputation, told us of a telephone call she received from a parent: "I think you should know that my son is learning a lot in your class, but he is petrified every day he goes to your room. If he ever does anything wrong in your class, instead of bawling him out, pick on the child next to him. This will frighten my child so much that he'll stop whatever he shouldn't be doing. If you pick on him, he'll collapse and be a nervous wreck!"

Fourteen-year-olds are more adept at controlling their anger in front of people. They may lock themselves in their room and occasionally slam doors or make harsh verbal responses later on to show their discontent. Humor, mostly of the insulting or teasing variety, is often used against teachers and parents. They are practical jokers, which can make them rather irritating at times. Generally, they are more happy than not. They do not cry much and when they do, it is usually caused by anger.[10]

Psychological needs

Early adolescents need to develop ego strength and to experience acceptance and love. They need to be able to give as well as to receive these qualities. It is important that they be able to display tenderness, admiration, and appreciation. Deprivation only leads to exaggerated, often unacceptable, behavior. The following excerpt is from a nun who was a student in one of our classes in human development.

The lack of love and the inability to express love can lead to the saddest of consequences. This I have observed while working in a protectory, a home for boys staffed by our sisters. The need to be deeply and uniquely loved and accepted was of paramount importance to these boys. The lack of these responses worked havoc with most of them. Yet, more detrimental to them was the fact that they were not able to display any beautiful emotions. They had already ex-

perienced deep rejection at home and did not want to be rejected by the boys with whom they were now living. In order to be accepted, they had to conform to the standards set by the other boys. The first standard was to refuse to be emotional, appreciative or affectionate toward anyone. They developed an almost hostile reaction toward adults when they were in the presence of the other boys. However, when they were in their own cubicle at bedtime, and I went to say good night to them, they responded beautifully to a pat on the head or a touch on their shoulder. On occasion they would try to display their affection by saying small simple phrases, such as "You're O.K." or "You really understand." It hurt to see the boys looking in all four directions to make sure that no one could see them saying "thanks." Even more painful was the experience of watching the difficulty these boys had trying to understand how anyone could really care for them. How often have I heard them say, "How can you really love me when even my own parents don't?" Sad to say, they were convinced that this rejection by their parents was due not to parental neglect or indifference, but rather to their own imagined unlovableness.

Even under the best of family conditions there is anxiety, uneasiness, and uncertainty in early adolescents. There is a great discrepancy between what they are and what they know they have to become. But how do you get there? "There is so much to learn, and I don't even know where or how to begin." Fears of ridicule, of personal failure, and of inadequacy persist. Becoming an adolescent does not alleviate personal concerns and fears, many of which were started in childhood.

SOCIAL DEVELOPMENT

Just as physical changes at puberty have an effect on emotions, so do they have an effect on social development and relationships. There is no chemical factor involved to influence social development as there is to modify emotional development, but the changes in physical characteristics are great enough to create attitudes and concerns regarding social relationships. Early-maturing children feel different from the others and may want to withdraw. However, the other children may look to early-maturing individuals for leadership and direction. Late maturers have social problems because they seem to be "too

Organized sports have many advantages because they provide supervised play. However, a disadvantage results when emphasis is placed on winning at all costs.

far behind'' everybody else and are not ''grown-up'' enough.

On another point the appearance of adult physical characteristics often brings a demand from adults for the teenager to be more responsible and to act more ''grown-up.'' Early teenagers do not possess the social and cognitive skills necessary to be competent as adults. Their physical maturity belies their social maturity. Finally, the physical discrepancies in weight and height between girls and boys,

especially at the age of 13 years, is enough to make some boys cringe. There is a gap to be bridged. Can the girls wait for the boys to catch up?

Peer group influence

Although early adolescents are struggling for independence, strong dependency needs arise as they attempt to find themselves and identify their role in society. Peer groups play a major part in the gratification of these needs. Through

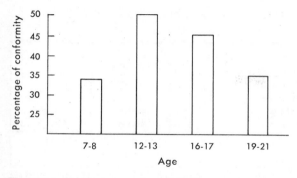

Fig. 10-4. Percentages of conformity as a function of age level (n=36 per age level). (Adapted from Costanzo, P. R. *Journal of Personality and Social Psychology,* 1970, **14,** 366-374.)

frequent contacts with their peers plus an increasing absence of parents from the home—or at least fewer hours of contact with parents—the peer group becomes the important socializing agent. Group pressures are beginning to have tremendous effects on behavior (Fig. 10-4). Values and attitudes are being created and reinforced by the group phenomena. Conformity demanded by the group may discourage individualism and self-assertion. However, as adolescents mature, they tend to regain their individual characteristics.[11]

Adolescents measure their whole being by the reaction of their peers. It is they who accept them and encourage them to keep on behaving as they are. If they are ignored or criticized by their peers, they may develop feelings of inferiority, inadequacy, and incompetency. The peer group is greatly responsible for the modification of behavior and for providing a forum by which teenagers see themselves for better or for worse.

Teaching how to get along with others is a socializing value of the peer group. Within the group they must learn to be considerate of the feelings of others and must be able to listen to their views. The first groups in early adolescence are usually made up of one sex. This situation is merely a continuation of the group makeup in late childhood. Girls congregate in the intimacy of someone's bedroom to talk about boys, clothes, boys, makeup, and boys. The activities of boys revolve around sports, hobby activities, and rough games. There is some comfort and advantage in being with one's own kind at this time. Give and take are more acceptable. There is more freedom to discuss any and all subjects. They can give each other support in learning about themselves and, eventually, about the opposite sex. Ego development, increased self-reliance, and establishing self-esteem through contributions made to the group are all possible by group association.

By the age of 13 years girls have begun to form definite cliques based on personal likes, dislikes, interests, similarities in socioeconomic background, and proximity of residence. They exclude others on the basis of irrelevant factors. The peer group may begin to shift from one sex to both, often in imitation of older teens. It must be kept in mind that early adolescents are less concerned with expressing heterosexual feelings than with the questions of growing up, their social status in the group, and their comparative standing with others of their own sex.[12] Here is an opportunity to associate with others having similar growing problems.

Although early adolescence is a gregarious, social stage, it is also one in which youngsters tend to select a "best" friend of the same sex with whom confidences are exchanged.[13] Some parents become concerned when they note such a strong relationship between their child and another. Parents wonder if good heterosexual relationships with others will ever develop. Parents need not worry about this type of association. As children grow older, they tend to widen their circle of acquaintances and may eventually drift apart from earlier friends. People often talk about this happening by saying "When they were in junior high school, they were as close as two peas in a pod. No one ever thought that anything could separate them. Now they hardly ever see each other."

Parent-teenager relationships

A major developmental task in early adolescence is the attempt to achieve emancipation from the home. As a result, early adolescence emerges as a period of antagonism toward adults, and especially toward parents. This reaction is not consistent, however, because it varies from

Table 10-3. Parental happiness, child-rearing practices, and adolescent rebellion*
(Figures indicate percent who are rebellious.)

Parental happiness	Total sample	Child-rearing practices		Authority		
		Very re-strictive or very permissive	Slightly re-strictive or slightly permissive	Average	Non-patri-archal	Patri-archal
Unhappy	29	49	23	22	23	31
Happy	19	23	21	10	22	17

*Adapted from Balswick, J. O., & Macrides, C. Parental stimulus for adolescent rebellion. *Adolescence,* 1975, **10,** 256. Used by permission.

mood to mood of the teenager. Sometimes young people feel highly competent and demand their "rights." At other times, after they have been hurt in their battles with the world, they become compliant and accept parental guidance. Adolescents issue their "declaration of independence," but the problem is that they need to be independent in a dependent type of way. Children who come from families in which the mother and father have helped the child in the growing-up process by providing opportunities to learn responsibility, self-reliance, necessary skills, and self-respect make a much smoother transition from childhood dependency to adulthood competency. Parents who have been liberal, overly permissive, or uninterested about their children's behavior may have more difficulty with their children because they lack a structure or system of standards or values by which they can determine whether their behavior is suitable and their decisions appropriate.[14] Overprotective parents never give their child an opportunity to learn how to make important decisions and how to assume responsibilities (Table 10-3).

Many parents have ambivalent feelings about their growing children. Some parents are among the last to accept the fact that they are growing. It is alarming, to some fathers in particular, to learn that their "little girl" is going out on her first date with a boy. When teenagers assert their right to be more grown-up, they often create tensions within the home. They resist family control; they resent being treated like a child. This is the age of "You don't understand me" and "You

always treat me like a baby." If really pressed, the child may think, if not say, "It's not my fault I was born. You have to put up with me."

Parents sometimes feel hurt at this lack of gratitude or appreciation. "This is the kind of thanks I get for staying up late at night with you when you were sick? This is the way you treat me after all I have sacrificed for you so that you could have nice things to wear and good food to eat?" It is necessary to recognize that it is difficult for parents to change as quickly as the child is changing at puberty. For the past twelve or thirteen years the parents have been making decisions for their child; the child was dependent on them. How can parents change these relationships overnight, especially when they are struggling with their own problems and life? The most important thing for parents to keep in mind, at any time or any age of the child, is not to do or say anything that will break down or cut off the lines of communication between parent and child. All teenagers need help, even if they do not recognize this need or seem grateful for it. They must feel comfortable and free to seek that help from their parents or loved ones. If teenagers cannot talk to their parents or to other acceptable adults, they have only their peers and friends to turn to. How much good advice and information on serious matters can one 13-year-old or 15-year-old give to another?

Conflict areas between parents and children include use of the telephone, use of time, homework, performing chores, hours for coming in from activities or for going to bed, readiness for

Table 10-4. Summary of conflicts between parents and youths*

Sources of conflict	Frequency mentioned
Performing home chores	134
Use of time	104
Attitude toward studies	76
Expenditures of money	72
Morals and manners	48
Choice of friends	43
Selection of clothes	42
Use of phone	36
Dating practices	33
Use of car	27
Total	615

*Adapted from Schvaneveldt, J. D. Mormon adolescents' likes and dislikes toward parents and home. *Adolescence,* 1973, **8,** 171. Used by permission.

Harold Geyer

The telephone is frequently a source of conflict between parent and teenager. Restraint and understanding is needed on both sides. The teenager's mind is bubbling over with thoughts and must give impulsive response to them by calling friends. The parents need the occasional use of the telephone.

adult responsibilities, money, grooming habits, and dress (Table 10-4). The teenager's room and its cleanliness are always a source of friction, especially if it's a girl's room. Concerning good grooming and dress, conflict in these areas is high before the age of 14 years. According to current indications, this conflict may be continuing throughout later adolescence—either that or the parents simply say "I give up!" Parental disapproval is often based on a rationale of "It isn't right." More likely, parental objections are really related to tradition, status quo, or the sin of disobedience toward one who has their best interest at heart. Adolescence is a period of experimentation during which identity is sought. Since manner of dress usually means conformity to the peer group, adolescents are willing to defy parental authority, sometimes in a nice way and sometimes more violently, to be acceptable to their group.[15]

Teenagers want to complain or talk about schools, but they do not want their parents to fight their battles for them, to visit the school, or to attend the parent-teacher organization (secondary level). In fact, teenagers often are embarrassed by being seen with their parents, especially by their friends. Some say that when children become adolescents, they no longer want to sit with their parents in church or go to the movies with them. When they return to sit voluntarily with their parents, they have outgrown their early adolescent stage.

Developing heterosexuality

Early adolescence begins with gangs or groups made up of members of the same sex and ends with a coming together of the two sexes in crowd activities and possibly with some dating (Fig. 10-5). There is a gradual mixing together of the sexes, starting with parties in sixth and seventh grades. By the ninth grade most boys are willing to tolerate or seek girls just for the fun they get from being around them.

As social development takes place in early adolescence, teenagers begin to reconstruct their value systems and interest patterns regarding the opposite sex. They change according to their

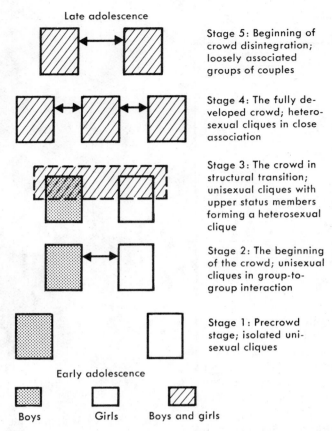

Late adolescence

Stage 5: Beginning of crowd disintegration; loosely associated groups of couples

Stage 4: The fully developed crowd; heterosexual cliques in close association

Stage 3: The crowd in structural transition; unisexual cliques with upper status members forming a heterosexual clique

Stage 2: The beginning of the crowd; unisexual cliques in group-to-group interaction

Stage 1: Precrowd stage; isolated unisexual cliques

Early adolescence

Boys   Girls   Boys and girls

Fig. 10-5. Stages of group development in adolescence. (From Dunphy, D. C. *Sociometry*, 1963, **26,** 236.)

interpretation of what are considered by their peers, parents, and community to be accepted heterosexual practices and activities. The age at which heterosexual interests begin is largely determined by these forces. If there is a conflict of thinking among these forces, teenagers respond to the force that has the greatest meaning and influence to them personally.

In some areas heterosexual activities begin on a noticeable scale among 11- and 12-year-olds. In other communities heterosexual involvements are not widely noted until the ages of 14 or 15 years. Two points relevant to our statements concerning age level heterosexual interests and practices will be emphasized. First, there are age level differences in social practices in various communities, social groups, and subcultures.

Children in different communal areas are exposed to differences in accepted mores, customs, roles, and degrees of permissiveness in social relationships. In some communities it is proper for a 13-year-old girl to go out on a single date. In other communities this action is deeply frowned on, and all kinds of social restrictions are imposed to hinder such dating. Second, regardless of the community, there will always be individuals who do not follow the generally accepted practices. People do not fit neat, rigid categories, and some persons will not abide by the customs. These statements are intended to refer to "commonly observed practices" and not to "the exception to the rule" or to the few who are the forerunners of a change in social behavior.

Early adolescent years include a considerable number of heterosexual contacts, most of which are related to school affairs or to community activities provided for young people. Group contacts are desirable because they give opportunities to practice social skills, such as conversation, courtesy, and cooperation. Usually the first heterosexual activities are "group" or "crowd" affairs. Pairing off by couples is not the usual relationship. A group or the "crowd" is invited to a party. The girls will dance together while the boys watch. Some special activity, such as a mixer game, will be needed to bring the two sexes together. However, at a party in a home, it would not be unusual for the group to play kissing games such as "post office" or "spin the bottle."[16] Boys go along with such games because the products of the games are "daring"—something like "forbidden fruit." Boys get a feeling of pleasant amazement "to think that someone likes me well enough to call *my* number to go to the post office for a stamp!" It is not that the kiss means so much; it is the idea that "someone likes me enough to ask for a kiss."

There is less antagonism toward the opposite sex, an ever widening circle of friends of both sexes, and a broader range of social experiences in early adolescence. The barriers set up by the same sex groups are tumbling down. There will be a few holdouts, especially among the boys. As far as unwillingness to engage in heterosexual activities is concerned, these cases will be rare by the age of 14 years. Dating activities will begin when shyness, timidity, and antipathy toward the opposite sex decrease and a desire to be like older teenagers increases.

In sixth grade most boys are still embarrassed enough around girls to consider it a major threat to their self-esteem to be seated between two girls. Girls at this age tend to be more mature, and they do not mind boys. If given a chance at a party or school dance, girls will seek to dance with boys even though the boys are usually shorter. By the seventh grade boys are more interested in girls than before, and fewer would feel threatened by being placed between two girls. In fact, some boys would be highly pleased to be forced to sit next to a girl, but they would try not to show it. They may protest loud and

long but don't try to change their places! They are still unsure of themselves but do mingle more freely.

Eighth grade girls tend to be more aggressive and more openly "boy crazy" than at any other age. The problem they have, however, is that they have not learned the subtle, social skills necessary to know how to show an interest in boys without appearing too eager, too forward, or too bold. One eighth grade girl was asked by a teasing adult, "Jack McDonald says he likes you, do you like him?" "Yes," replied the girl. "Who is he?" "You mean you don't know him and you say you like him?" "Sure," replied the quick-thinking girl, "if he likes me, he has good taste, and that's all that matters!"

The summer between the eighth and ninth grades seems to bring about unbelievable changes in heterosexual development as a number of boy-girl relationships blossom and begin to be longer lasting. Many boys are now taller than their girl classmates. They are more sure of themselves and less embarrassed about seeking female companionship. Ninth grade girls are definitely interested in male companions. The more mature girls may be dating fellows who are several years older than themselves.

Observation on early heterosexuality

There may be a risk in having too many older or adult-type social experiences at too young an age. An emphasis placed on "earliness" in developing social relationships, especially involving dating, could be undesirable. A rationale for such beliefs is not proven scientifically, but our associations and work with young people lead us to certain premises and hypotheses.

The first premise is that many young people do not develop the social stability, judgment, and emotional control necessary to overcome the dominant influence of peer demands, attitudes, and pressures concerning social relationships and activities until they are about 19 or 20 years old. Up to this age adolescents respond to group domination. Their dress, talk, attitudes, and actions are determined largely by their peer group or the prevalent social moods and thoughts of the time. They are unsure of themselves and too inexperienced to know what decisions to make or what behavior to pursue. The world knows best, and they are willing to follow the world. As a result, they will continue to be group oriented and to involve themselves in a variety of interpersonal experiences. Not until they reach a point of social stability or maturity will they feel competent enough to break away from group thought and emphasis and to judge and decide for themselves what behavior is important to their well-being.

A second premise is that each society has within its social framework a body of skills and knowledge that is learned by most of the adolescents of that culture as part of their heterosexual development. This core is somewhat sequential in nature, going from global social activities at first to more mature, individualized activities later on. Movement in social development is step by step; young people move from one level of competency to another. There is a point in development, however, at which they are considered to have attained the information and skills necessary to operate effectively in everyday adult behavior. The rapidity with which individuals acquire this level depends on (1) the initial age at which the needed experiences were encountered, (2) the amount of practice they had in developing the social skills related to those experiences, and (3) the degree to which they assimilated or internalized the lessons and emotions of those experiences. Some individuals go through these basic social learnings much sooner than others. For example, some girls begin to date when they are 12 or 13 years old. Some may have their first cigarette, drink, or sex involvement at that age. Other girls may have none of these experiences until they are much older. The basic point of the second premise is that there is a hierarchy of skills and information, learned by different activities and experiences, culminating in an acceptable level of social competency. Earliness of social experiences within the hierarchy is a crucial factor in determining the age at which that level of competency is reached.

A third and last premise is that adolescents who have not attained personal dominance in social judgment and control will continue to place a great emphasis on social experiences and activities in their daily lives, even though they have learned all the skills they need to know.

Once a certain skill has been mastered or a desired activity has been experienced to a satisfying degree, adolescents rarely want to stay on that level of development. They will seek new social experiences. They still have a great need for social contact, participation, and acceptance. This need is a major dominating force in their rational life. It is at this stage that they are most susceptible to involvement in a wide range of unusual, unacceptable, and often dangerous experiences. They have already had the usual social experiences. They want something different. Not until they place a different value on the importance of social acceptance or on social activities in their life will they change their focus of emphasis in daily behavior. Social maturity will not be reached until the individual is no longer "group-dominated" in judgment making decisions. Our experience seems to indicate that most individuals do not reach this level of personal control and change of philosophy until they are 19 to 20 years old.

The conclusion would seem to be that too much social sophistication too soon makes it easier for adolescents to engage in practices that they would have rejected or avoided had they not had the more typical social activities too early in life. Emotional growth cannot take place as rapidly in early adolescence as can social growth. Even though a 12-year-old may be superior in worldly social know-how, he still has only the natural emotional needs of a 12-year-old. This level of emotional development is hardly adequate for an adult world.

Sexual awareness

The typical preadolescent appears to be relatively unconfused about sexuality. However, with the onset of puberty and adolescence, even the most well-adjusted child will have some uncertainties and confusion. Even when children have received most of their sex education at home in an anxiety-free atmosphere, they may still be perplexed. They are at an age when adult authority is not respected and accepted as it once was. The parents of 12-year-olds may find their children far more inclined to believe in the teaching of their peers (Table 10-5). Discrepancies between what the peers say and what the

Table 10-5. Adolescent sex information sources*

Source	Male N–392 (%)	Female N–566 (%)	Total N–958 (%)
Peers	45.7	32.4	38.7
Literature	16.7	23.8	20.9
School	18.3	20.4	19.5
Mother	5.6	18.7	13.4
Father	4.1	.7	2.1
Experiences	8.0	2.8	5.0
Minister	1.0	.6	.7
Physician	.6	.6	.6
	100.0	100.0	100.0

*From H. D. Thornberg. *Contemporary adolescence: readings* (2nd ed.). Copyright 1975 by Wadsworth Publishing Company, Inc. Reprinted by permission of the publisher, Brooks/Cole Publishing Company, Monterey, California.

parents say add to the uncertainty. If the peers provide a more extensive, in-depth discussion concerning sex, children may wonder whether the parents may be hiding some facts from them and "treating them like babies." They begin to look for answers of their own. The parents applaud their desire to look for information relating to a history project but may show no enthusiasm when they seek answers to sex questions. The youngsters are further confused by this inconsistency.

Television and magazine advertisements bombard young teenagers during their free moments. The glowing reports of what happens when you use a certain mouthwash, hair cream, toothpaste, or underarm deodorant make heterosexual activities of a romantic nature seem so possible. Girls tend to be more influenced by these pressures than boys, but boys are definitely influenced by the glamorous portrayal of the virile male. They may begin smoking under the impression that "it is manly." At about 14 years of age, boys appear to begin worrying about their own ability to perform the sex act. They do not usually seek to experiment to find out, but they do show a greater curiosity about the sex act. Their interests are no longer just in their own maleness but in their ability to become part of a heterosexual society.

Adolescents show some concern about their secondary sex characteristics. Boys are conscious of the formation of their sex structure and concerned if they believe there are any deviations. They are troubled by nocturnal emissions and wonder if anyone, especially their mother who usually washes the pajamas and bed sheets, might find out. Girls are concerned mostly with breast development and whether or not anyone can tell when they are having their monthly periods. Most adolescents of this age level experience something akin to masturbation, boys more so than girls. There are questions such as why is there an erection, what causes it, why does it feel different to "do it," will it hurt anything, is it sinful or bad, does it mean that I'm oversexed, and does anyone else do this too? Most adolescents probably engage in self-stimulation because of sexual responses that are stirred and the emotional tone experience that is felt.[17] Sex attraction begins in the middle adolescent years. The sensory experience of just looking at or touching that certain person, or their picture, is enough to bring about a sexual response. Boys may be extremely upset over trying to hide the fact that they are having an erection in daylight, in public, and often for no apparent reason.

Petting, attachments to others of the opposite sex, and masturbation are the most frequent methods of sexual release during this period. Our counseling work with young teenagers has indicated that there is more sexual involvement taking place among girls of this age than most adults realize. The involvement is generally of the initial necking and petting variety. Almost always this activity involves an older boy. Our counseling experiences indicate that whenever a 13- or 14-year-old girl goes steady for at least three months with a boy who is two or three years older, there is invariably some extensive petting taking place (not necessarily the sex act). Petting takes place sooner if an automobile is used extensively by the couple. Among junior high school couples who go steady for more than a three-month period, there may be necking and some light petting taking place but seldom much heavy petting. We are less concerned about a junior high school girl if she is going steady with a boy of her own age than if she is a steady dater of a boy two or three years older than herself.

TEEN CULTURE AND INTERESTS

The development of interests during early adolescence can offer many positive rewards. Interests open gateways to the mind and usually make a person more receptive and eager to learn. Interests help to establish channels of communication with others. Sharing ideas on the professional football players and exchanging records provide a bond of mutuality among teenagers. The development of interests can lead to constructive use of leisure time and may help to crystallize a vocational pattern for later years.

Interests

Boys like to spend a great deal of time in active outdoor sports and just ''going out with the guys.'' They also spend time on hobbies of a mechanical nature. Watching television comprises a good bit of their time. Being with girls does not constitute a large part of their leisure activity, although it does occupy more time as they enter the freshman year of high school.

Girls' leisure activities show a sharp contrast. Their activities include fewer outdoor pursuits than those of boys. More time is spent in ''just

Early adolescents are the largest consumers of records, tapes, and pop music items. Music serves as an outlet for pent-up energy, provides for freedom of movement, and allows for the harmless expression of emotions.

Harold Geyer

being with the girls," listening to records, and experimenting with makeup. Due to their increased awareness of the feminine role, they now are highly conscious of their personal appearance. Exploration of the female world seems to be a natural inclination. Lipstick and makeup may appear on girls as early as the age of 9 years. Clothing of the latest style is a must for them. They like to go shopping for clothes, but they seldom agree with mother on fads and colors.

Other interests include listening to new records and loud music. Being able to recite the most popular hit records is part of this pattern. Watching movies or television programs is another pastime. Any movie, book, or television program dealing with romance will be of interest to girls at this level. Also typical for this stage is keeping a diary. Daydreams, events, and emotions that cannot be shared with real people are confessed to a diary. The diary affords role playing and fantasy without involving action in reality.

The young adolescent and preadolescent may become an active community participant as a member of Girl Scouts, Boy Scouts, Boys' Clubs, or Campfire Girls because it is at this time that the young person is greatly interested in forming groups and joining social clubs. For boys, gangs are a spontaneous effort to create a society for themselves and get the thrill of participating in common interests, fishing, hunting, and the like. Girls may be even more organizationally oriented than boys. They are more mature in seeking friendships with others and are more interested in social activities. Girls' club activities include more participation on an organized team than formerly. Young adolescents may watch television because it is something they can do together. Reading may satisfy their demands for adventure, boys preferring stories about animals, adventure, and sports of all kinds, girls enjoying biographies about women, mysteries, stories of home life, and love stories. In early adolescence there is usually a great interest in movies for the same reason adolescents have an interest in television—because they can go together. Movies catering to youth, often relating to differences in generations, draw many junior high students on weekends. Girls prefer

movies over athletics, whereas boys do not. Boys who go to the movies would prefer to see a sports, mystery, or adventure story or a movie with excitement, realism, humor, or violence.

Whereas a movie is not something a junior high student can enjoy all the time, a radio is. Many young adolescents carry around transistor radios and combine the music with studying, walking, and many other activities. In study halls it is not uncommon to see a boy or girl with a transistor radio hidden in his lap and a listener's plug in his ear. Rock and roll or popular music is preferred at all grade levels. Girls at early adolescence prefer music on television or the radio to a greater degree than boys. Rock and roll is one of the surest ways to the heart and wallet of the adolescent, creating a ritualized world of dances, slang, the charts, and fan magazines.[18]

When young adolescents are not going to the movies, reading, or listening to music, they are probably talking. They find it easy and desirable to talk to their friends in "rap sessions," which is their main out-of-school activity. Boys may spend hours talking about sports figures, athletics, and cars; girls talk about parties, dates, clothes, and social happenings at school. These conversations may take place on the telephone, exasperating parents and the person on the party line alike. However, this conversation with friends is helpful to the young adolescent, building up his self-confidence and ability to converse with others.

Fads and fashion

A form of interest that seems most characteristic of early adolescence is the "fad." A fad is a short-term fashion or practice pursued with exaggerated zeal and bordering on a cult. It is usually temporary and unpredictable. Young adolescents are extremely concerned with being accepted by their peers. This intense desire for acceptance is part of the reason why fads catch on so quickly during adolescent years. They help to give each individual a feeling of belonging while saying to adults "We're different from you." It seems that junior high schools can expect at least one major fad to hit the school each year. Teachers often wonder, "What will they

To be part of a group, to be able to display skills, and to achieve recognition for a good performance, all contribute to the total development of a teenager.

Harold Geyer

think of next!'' A perennial fad in some areas is the use of water pistols by the boys.

One junior high school teacher writes concerning her experiences with fads in her school:

One group of our junior high girls went around for days braless in tee-shirts and jeans. The fellows all wore headbands. Girls used curling irons so their hair was in ringlets. (Two years ago I spent hours trying to straighten mine.) When I was in junior high we wore sneakers in the spring to be ''in.'' When my sister reached her junior high school years, a dime in each loafer was the thing to do. I also spent hours making a chain with gum wrappers as tall as my boyfriend at the time, then burning it; if it burned all the way to the end, our ''love'' would last. Strange as it may seem, none of mine ever made it to the end. Fads, of course, can change overnight as do the interests of early adolescents; but they allow the adolescent to feel he is truly like his peer group.

Other fads include the wearing of certain clothing or certain colors, usually wild. Stockings and socks have gone the route from white ankle socks, to ribbed white socks half-way up the calf and knee socks, to flesh-colored nylon hose, to colored hose, to textured or patterned hose, to hose and long-line girdles, to colored panty hose and leotards. Hair styles among boys have included crew cuts, skin heads, Mohawk Indian cuts, flat tops, duck style, brush cuts, shaggy hair, and no cuts. Girls would bleach streaks of their hair, use food dye to color their hair green, blue, or red, or let their hair grow stringy and long, giving them an ''intellectual, unwashed look.'' In some schools students would speak in an imitation ''Chinese language'' by beginning the words with the ''y'' sound. A recent fad was the use of psychedelic-colored flower posters and stickers on textbooks, clothing, or bedroom walls. Can you recall what fads were popular in your crowd when you were 13 to 15 years old?

Various attempts have been made to explain the reason why adolescents' fads take hold. The strongest motive appears to be a combination of the desire to receive attention, the desire to assert independence from adults, and the desire to be one of the gang. Rejected by adults, adolescents feel a comfort in being like others their age. Apparently the most important factor in understanding teen fads is recognizing the ''herd'' instinct, to look alike, to feel part of a group by wearing the same clothes, using the same language, or developing the same mannerisms.

At the same time fads permit adolescents to express their individuality by wearing more and crazier charms on their bracelets or by being the first to hear and use a new slang phrase. Fads may compensate for boredom and low morale—especially for the adolescent who is patiently waiting for the time until he becomes an adult. They can represent a pioneer spirit and a yearning for freedom from regimentation. In fact, food fads and idiosyncrasies in language, manner, and clothes may be subtle expressions of the rebellion typical of this age.

Another related and familiar phenomenon is simply fashion—the very latest in dressing, writing, behaving, etc. This usually involves a socially approved variation of dress, furniture, music, art, speech, and other areas of culture. Each age group has its own varieties of fashion, reflecting certain characteristics of that age. At times, being in fashion is a question of keeping tabs on changing sizes; knowing, for example, that sunglasses are growing larger, hair lengths are changing, and the width of neckties is different. Whatever their cause or result, fads and fashions are a part of modern society.

PERSONAL PROBLEMS AND CONCERNS

The personal problems of adolescents are fairly well documented. At this point, we merely wish to present some personal statements written in a free-response, permissive situation by junior high school pupils. The intent of personalizing the problems of teenagers is to show the degree of intensification these young people have concerning their problems and the implications of these problems for a need on the part of the adolescent to reconstruct and reorganize his personality from what it was in childhood. The child of 9, 10, or 11 years was a fairly stable individual. With the coming of puberty every single avenue of growth and development undergoes extensive changes, making the personality of the younger child inadequate for the emerging new individual.

Problems of adolescents can be grouped under the following categories: (1) physical problems, such as facial problems, uneven growth, late maturing, early maturing, and sex problems; (2) personal problems involving self-identity, self-concept, and personality; (3) social problems relating to home and family, peer group, and social status; (4) scholastic problems of the school, including study, tests, homework, and teachers; (5) religion, moral values, and development of a personal philosophy; and (6) future problems concerning vocations and alienation from society.

The following personal concerns were written by seventh, eighth, and ninth graders in response to the query: "What problems or difficulties do you have for which you would like help? In other words, what is bothering you in relation to people, your family, money, friends, or any other part of your life? (Your name is not needed.)" The problems are presented as they were written. They are some of the more common problems and concerns.

Girl, 12 years, seventh grade
I don't have any problems other than not getting enough allowance and having pimples. My pimples are getting better, thank goodness.

Girl, 12 years, seventh grade
Do you think I am old enough to let a boy kiss me? He tried to do it a few times, but I covered my face. He asked me to go to the football game, but my mother would not let me go; she said I was too young. I know he will ask me to go some place else. How can I get my mother to let me go? The trouble is I want to go but I would rather pay my own way.

Boy, 12 years, seventh grade
How will I know what to say to a girl so I won't get my head knocked off?

Boy, 13 years, eighth grade
My father left my mother, my sister, and me when I was 12 years old. If I were younger, it wouldn't have meant much to me, but I wasn't and I have felt strong resentment toward him. It bothers me in school and in other places. If I could overcome my resentment toward him, I could get along better with other people.

Boy, 13 years, eighth grade
I don't know when I have time to study, since I work to help support the family because my father is sick. I do not get very much sleep in the evenings. So, when I don't have any written work in class, I sort of doze off.

Girl, 13 years, eighth grade
I have learned to be happy most of the time, and I am very contented with my life. But, when I act happy, people think I am nuts.

Boy, 13 years, eighth grade
Parents are pests. They're always nagging me and will not let me outside past 8 o'clock.

Girl, 13 years, eighth grade
How old do you think I should be before I should be allowed to date? Some of the girls my age are already dating. Do you think this is the right age or should I wait till I'm older?

Girl, 13 years, eighth grade
Last week in geography class I had to collect the homework papers. As I went to collect one of the girl's papers, she told me not to tell the teacher because she didn't have her homework finished. As I went up to tell the teacher I just couldn't figure out whether to tell the teacher or leave it go because I was afraid the girl would be mad at me. Would you please tell me if I should have told the teacher?

Girl, 14 years, eighth grade
I am worried about someone grabbing me in a car coming home after dark.

Boy, 13 years, eighth grade
What should you do when your parents always seem to be arguing and you don't even want to go home? It seems I'm always trying to figure out a different excuse for going somewhere. The family seems to be growing further apart.

Girl, 14 years, ninth grade
My father is under the impression that no boys are good enough for me, and therefore I'm not permitted to associate with them. But this is not true. It's just that I may not be good enough for the boys and they do not seem interested in me.

Boy, 14 years, ninth grade
The school—it stinks! I hate school. I like young teachers, not old, grouchy teachers. School is all right if you don't have too many lessons.

Girl, 14 years, ninth grade
I don't know what course to take in high school. It is hard for me to make up my mind as to what I want to do and what subjects to take.

Boy, 14 years, ninth grade
The main question in my mind is sex education. I wouldn't want anybody to think I am immoral or

indecent but rather just trying to receive a good education. When you receive any advice on this matter from another guy, you never get it straight. It is always told to you the wrong way. I have gathered that sex is a thing to be hidden and whispered about. The movies and magazines play it up but that is not sex information. I cannot help but think that educated people should take this open-mindedly and straightforwardly. I would like some advice or help on this question. Maybe I'm too young; I don't know. But if I am, I wish someone that is qualified to say would tell me.

Boy, 14 years, ninth grade

My father and I aren't together enough. I would like to get closer acquainted with him and have more activities together when he is not working.

Boy, 15 years, ninth grade

I live 13 miles from high school. I have to get up at 5 o'clock in the morning so I can do my barn work. Then I leave for school at 7:30 to catch a bus. I don't get home until 5:30 in the evening. After I get my barn work done and eat supper it is time to go to bed. And the teachers want us to work at least two hours at home on our lessons. We should have shorter school days or fewer unimportant subjects.

Girl, 15 years, ninth grade

How can I learn to study at home with a lot of kids playing in the hallways, television sets blaring out all over the apartment house, and people yelling at the top of their voices?

Girl, 14 years, ninth grade

I would like to get along with my sisters and brothers, but they don't seem to like me for some reason.

Girl, 16 years, special education class

I don't have much interest in school. But my parents want me to go to school. I try to get my work but can't get it too well. I would like to know of a way that might interest me in school. I feel so self-conscious because I am only in eighth grade (special education). I was thinking about quitting school, but then I took the second thought about it. What can you do without an education? My parents don't want me to quit, but I don't seem to have any interest in school.

It was difficult to pick out representative problems as they were written by early adolescents because there were so many good ones from which to choose. We have conducted this study over a five-year period and have over a thousand papers. The first time I (G. K.) collected papers from the students I could not wait to read what they had written. So I read a number of the papers before I left school to go home. I will never forget the depressed, heavy feeling that overcame me. My shoulders and head actually felt the weight of the burden of their problems. I thought that they were such happy-go-lucky kids, but, instead, they were immersed in deep, often unresolvable problems. Here were children worrying about their mothers and fathers separating, about when they would get something decent to eat, or how to avoid the clutches of criminal elements and drugs, and we teachers were trying to teach them something about ancient Rome, binomial theorems, and dangling participles! Categories of students' problems in 1977 are indicated in Table 10-6.

AWAKENING OF REASONING

Approximately one year after the beginning of puberty individuals begin to feel confident in their intellectual abilities. There is a growing insistence on submitting all things to the test of

Table 10-6. Percentage of free-response problems stated by 231 junior high school students (eastern town, population 18,000)

	7th grade	8th grade	9th grade	Total
Problems related to school	18	39	36	31
Parents and home	23	18	21	21
Personal; self-concern	11	11	10	11
Peer relationships	10	6	14	10
Sibling relationships	8	6	4	6
Boy-girl relationships	5	8	3	5
No response or inadequate	25	12	12	16

David Strickler

Early adolescence is the first time that a youngster can apply abstract reasoning in satisfying intellectual curiosity.

one's own reason. It is at this time that they think they know everything. Despite this attitude, which certainly may get them into trouble with adults, they are beginning to show interest in thinking, experimenting, and generalizing. Often these interests are directed to science. The act of formulating a hypothesis and actually testing it gives them great satisfaction. Prior to this time they have used the method of trial and error to reach their learning goals. They will now spend some of their time thinking of a solution rather than immediately acting and then having to make corrections. Piaget's explanation of this stage will be given in Chapter 11.

A tendency to insist on one's own judgment and reason increases throughout early and middle adolescence. In childhood many things were accepted on the authoritative statement of parents or teachers, but in adolescence all authority may be questioned and criticized. Childhood was generally marked by unquestioning belief and acceptance of what was said by parent or teacher or Bible or textbook, but adolescence is an age of doubt.

Many parents and teachers are disturbed by this natural appearance of a tendency to question matters that are accepted implicitly by children and considered authoritative by adults. There is, however, a kind of good fortune in this adolescent trait. Were it not for the adolescent tendency to criticize and doubt, they would all come to adulthood with a fixed confidence in the status quo, and progress would not exist.

Since the mental functions grow in an orderly sequence, memory, reasoning, imagination, and interpreting ability develop to their highest peak during late adolescence. Mental growth curves show an increase in mental development from childhood through early adolescence to a gradual increase in late adolescence. Social interaction gives adolescents many experiences and opportunities to help develop their mental functions fully while in the adolescent stage of life.

Daydreaming

Early adolescence is marked by an exuberant imagination that is not yet under control. The mind is awakening to a deeper intuition of the meaning of things but has not yet learned how to regulate by use of reason this unraveling of insight.

Early adolescence is the period of daydreams and extravagant imagination and hence is peculiarly exasperating to the unsympathetic adult whose youthful visions have long faded. The boy or girl who goes through the day sluggishly and absentmindedly may be lost in a world of daydreams. Of course, such a person must be recalled to realities of life, but it should be done with sympathy and understanding. Many boys and girls who have been harshly treated on this score, their youthful ideals meeting no sympathetic response from older people, have built a wall of defensive reserve and behind this have lived a dream life that is quite isolated from everyday experiences.

Socioeconomic influence on intelligence

Functional intelligence is traditionally measured by an "intelligence" test. Items on such tests generally include measurements of general information, vocabulary or word usage, the ability to reason, arithmetical reasoning, memory, common sense judgment, and aspects of visual-motor performance. Many of these items are related to or influenced by life-space culture.

Social class has been found to be related to mental ability. Dielman[19] has found correlations between family socioeconomic variables and mental test scores of children and adolescents. At the adolescent level, the mental test scores of boys showed a higher correlation with the father's occupation than with any other socioeconomic variable. Girls' test scores showed the highest correlation with the mother's and father's education. It has been noted by Hansen[20] that a global environmental variable, such as social class, should not be used in studying the relationship between the environment and the adolescent's performance. Variables such as emphasis on school achievement, freedom to engage in verbal expression, and parental involvement with the child were significantly related to the youngster's IQ.

Socioeconomic relationships play an important part in the mental development of the early adolescent. On intelligence tests Billy, who comes from a middle-class white home, as an example, often outscores Harvey, who comes from an economically deprived black home. We dare not conclude that Harvey is less intelligent than Billy, however. Billy perhaps has had more verbal and sensory experiences than Harvey. Also important in this situation is the adolescent's relationship with his parents and the motivating atmosphere of the home environment. Harvey has learned to put value on immediate, extrinsic results that he can partake of today rather than on something of an elusive, intellectual nature because the latter is not tangible to him. Billy, on the other hand, thinks about his future, his learning, and further education because he has been guided by parents and siblings and has been influenced by the accepted thinking of his immediate environment, which stresses the future.

Moral awakening

Early adolescents' moral development depends on their parents, their peer group, and their own experiences of resolving right from wrong. They usually adopt the accepted behavior of the group that is most significant to them. They must feel a relatedness to someone or some group to feel free to accept and develop a strong moral code. Right and wrong must be presented in tangible terms. Groups set norms for their members, and enforcement of the norms results in conforming behavior. Groups also relate to other groups. As a result, group behavior can be influenced in directions that involve status-earning achievements. The influence may be positive, as in the case of a group seeking to excel in sports or some other form of healthy competition, or it may be negative, as in the case of aggressive behavior, gang wars, or disruptive activities.

Children entering adolescence have no difficulty in being able to identify the truth. They have developed the power to reason and easily recognize the truthful manner. However, they are also governed by their peers, and this calls for ability to know when to and when not to lie in preservation of the self.

Adolescents soon discover that what people say and what they do may be two entirely different things in certain situations. This inconsistency results in much misunderstanding and questioning in their minds. At this stage in life teenagers are highly idealistic, and when these ideals are shattered by adult hypocrisy, detrimental effects may result if they are not strong enough to accept the fact of fallacy.

As adolescents gain experience, they also gain responsibility. They want to follow common sense on issues that require a decision of right or wrong, and they are always ready to take a stand on what they believe. Drinking, smoking, cheating, stealing, and drugs are very tangible issues in the life of adolescents. Not being fully committed to such practices, adolescents may casually attempt these activities, or they may decide to participate fully in one or more of them. The dominant alter influence in their lives will determine if they will accept or reject these behaviors.

ERIKSON: EGO IDENTITY

Eric Erikson modified Freud's psychoanalytic theory in order to include a greater emphasis on social context in the development of personality. Erikson[21] has developed an elaborate stage theory that describes emotional and personality development across the life span. The central theme of his theory is that life is constant change. He has emphasized the development of "ego identity" in adolescence and youth. It is for that reason that his theory is included at this point in the text.

Erikson's theory of psychosocial development, including ego identity, describes eight stages of human development. Each stage has a psychosocial task to be mastered. The overall purpose for the individual is to acquire a positive ego identity as he or she moves from one stage to the next. Confronting and learning to solve the problems at one stage of life, however, does not guarantee that they will not reappear and have to be solved again. Nevertheless, contrary to Freud's theory, adolescent or adult crises need not be traced to childhood frustrations as the basic cause of failure.

Infancy and childhood

Identity formation neither begins nor ends with adolescence. Its roots go back in childhood to the experience of mothering and being mothered. For the various stages, study Table 10-4. The initial psychosocial task to be achieved is that of trust; failure to achieve it leads to mistrust. Trust of people and of the world depends on the quality of care and love the infant receives. The issue is not entirely resolved at this time, but a beginning toward learning trust can be made. During the second stage, children are to gain a sense of autonomy, implying that they learn that they can do some things for themselves. Children build on new motor and mental skills and must learn to feel capable of being in control. Overprotective parents, ones who do too much for their children, can induce failure to get the feeling of autonomy. Complete autonomy is not gained at this time, but children should, at least, not have a fear of going beyond their present capabilities.

From the third through the fifth year of life, children are exposed to environmental invitations and even demands to assume some responsibilities and to master certain tasks. The psychosocial task situation is one of initiative versus guilt. Parents must reinforce intellectual and motor initiatives rather than making children feel like nuisances. Freedom to pursue initiatives without a feeling of guilt is very important. From six to the onset of puberty, children are to learn how things are made and how they work. They should be encouraged by their family and school to do so, and they should receive praise for their industry. The neighborhood and the school can encourage or discourage their work. If their efforts are viewed as mischief, they can develop feelings of inferiority.

Adolescence

Adolescence is a time for the integration of the roles that an individual follows. For example, a boy may see himself in the roles of a son, a student, a scout, and an aspiring athlete. He should be able to integrate these various views he sees of himself into an ego identity. Having learned trust, autonomy, initiative, and industry in the past will help toward the development and integration of identity roles. The peer group and models of leadership, the social milieu, help or hurt the continuity of development of ego identity. Role confusion (identity diffusion) leads to a fragmented ego or to negative or oppositional identity. The identity formed now is not the final identity of an individual; it will be challenged by changes that occur later in life.

Erikson[22] emphasizes that adolescence is a normal phase of increased conflict, characterized by a fluctuation of ego strength. To establish identity requires individual effort in evaluating personal assets and liabilities and learning how to use them to achieve a clearer concept of who he or she is and what the individual wants to be and to become. There are converging identity elements at this point that can be divided into seven major parts.

1. Temporal perspective versus time confusion—Erikson is referring to gaining a sense of time and the continuity of life so that some concept of how long it will take to achieve one's life plans can be gained.
2. Self-certainty versus self-consciousness—adolescents go through a period of increasing self-awareness, but self-confidence must be developed so that there is a reasonable chance of accomplishing future aims.
3. Role experimentation versus role fixation—adolescents have an opportunity to try out different roles and identities with different personality characteristics, with different ways of talking and ideas, and with different philosophies and goals.
4. Apprenticeship versus work paralysis—there is also an opportunity to try out different occupations and career studies before deciding on a vocation.
5. Sexual polarization versus bisexual confusion—Erikson feels it is important that adolescents develop a clear identification with one sex or the other as a basis for future heterosexual intimacy and identity. Some people question Erikson's position on the need for sexual polarization.
6. Leadership and fellowship versus authority confusion—as social contacts and horizons are expanded, adolescents begin to learn to

I think I could turn and live with animals, they're so placid and self-contain'd . . .

Walt Whitman
Song of Myself

Table 10-7. Eight stages of psychosocial development*

Stages (ages are approximate)	Psychosocial crises	Radius of significant relations	Psychosocial modalities	Favorable outcomes
Birth through first year	Trust versus mistrust	Maternal person	To get To give in return	Drive and hope
Second year	Autonomy versus shame, doubt	Parental persons	To hold on To let go	Self-control and willpower
Third year through fifth year	Initiative versus guilt	Basic family	To make (going after) To "make like" (playing)	Direction and purpose
Sixth year to onset of puberty	Industry versus inferiority	Neighborhood; school	To make things (competing) To make things together	Method and competence
Adolescence	Identity and repudiation versus identity diffusion	Peer groups and outgroups, models of leadership	To be oneself (or not to be) To share being oneself	Devotion and fidelity
Early adulthood	Intimacy and solidarity versus isolation	Partners in friendships, sex, competition, cooperation	To lose and find oneself in another	Affiliation and love
Young and middle adulthood	Generativity versus self-absorption	Divided labor and shared household	To make be To take care of	Production and care
Later adulthood	Integrity versus despair	"Mankind" "My kind"	To be, through having been To face not being	Renunciation and wisdom

*Modified from Erikson, E. H. *Childhood and society* (2nd ed.). New York: W. W. Norton & Co., Inc., 1963.

take leadership responsibilities as well as to follow others. There may be some authority confusion develop as the adolescent wonders who to listen to, what to believe, and whom to follow.

7. Ideological commitment versus confusion of values—this conflict is closely related to a resolution of the other six areas. This struggle as the "search for fidelity" ceases when the adolescent no longer has to question his or her own identity and when childhood identity has been changed into a new self-identification.

Adulthood

Early adulthood is the period of courtship and early family life. Intimacy and solidarity refer to the ability to share and to care about others.

Young adulthood changes to middle adulthood and concern for others beyond the family must be extended to future generations and worlds. The children must be raised as a contribution to humankind and to society. Generativity is a concern with productivity in work and with the welfare and care of others. Self-absorption merely leads to stagnation. In later adulthood, the major efforts of life are nearing completion, with the result that the time becomes one of reflection. Integrity is being able to look back on life with some satisfaction. A person at this stage who feels despair fears death in an ironic way that those with ego integrity do not. Although the despairing person expresses disgust over his life, he yearns for another chance. The person with integrity accepts death as another step in a meaningful life.

STUDY GUIDE

1. Review the developmental tasks of early adolescence. Can you recognize how they are heading down the pathway leading to adulthood?
2. Define the terms *primary sex characteristics* and *secondary sex characteristics.*
3. What is considered to be evidence of the climax of puberty in boys and in girls?
4. Physical changes are abundant during the pubertal and early adolescent period. Make a list of what you would consider to be the more dramatic or outstanding changes in boys and in girls.
5. Most early adolescents lack emotional control. Why is this so?
6. Parent-teenager relationships often become strained during early and middle adolescence. What are some of the more common sources of conflict? When you were an early adolescent, did you have any adjustment problems with your parents? Did the problems seem insurmountable or all-important then? As you look back, were the problems of that moment as demanding and as gigantic as you thought them to be? How were they finally resolved?
7. When you were 12 to 15 years of age, what were some of the fads or fashions that you or your classmates followed? Consider clothing, activities, slang expressions, or food. What fads or fashions are you responding to now that you are older?
8. Study the Erikson chart on psychosocial development (Table 10-4).

REFERENCES

1. MacMahon, B. Age at menarche: United States, vital health statistics. *Science 11,* **133,** Washington, D.C.: U.S. Dept. of Health, Education and Welfare, 1974.
2. Sullivan, W. Boys and girls are maturing earlier. *The New York Times,* January 24, 1971, p. 36.
3. Zacharias, L., Rand, W. M., & Wiestman, R. J. A prospective study of sexual development and growth in American girls: the statistics of menarche. *Obstetrical and Gynecological Survey,* 1976, **31**(4), 323-337.
4. Tarrer, J. M. Growing up. *Scientific American,* 1973, **229**(3), 35-43.
5. McClung, J. (quoted in Alexander, W. M.) *The emergent middle school.* New York: Holt, Rinehart & Winston, 1969, p. 76.
6. Roche, A. F., & Dairla, G. H. Late adolescent growth in stature. *Pediatrics,* 1972, **50**(6), 874-880.
7. Muuss, R. E. Adolescent development and the secular trend. *Adolescence,* 1970, **5,** 267-284.
8. Tanner, J. M. Earlier maturation in man. *Scientific American,* 1968, **218,** 21-27.
9. Offer, D., & Offer, J. L. *The psychological world of the teen-ager.* New York: Basic Books Publishers, Inc., 1969.
10. Gesell, A., Ilg, F. L., & Ames, L. B. *Youth: the years ten to sixteen.* New York: Harper & Row, Publishers, 1956, 339-352.
11. Wagner, H. Increasing impact of the peer group during adolescence. *Adolescence,* 1971, **2,** 52-53.
12. Jersild, A. T., Brook, J. S., & Brook, D. W. *The psychology of adolescence* (3rd ed.), New York: Macmillan Inc., 1978.
13. Maccoby, E. E., & Jacklin, C. N. *The psychology of sex differences.* Stanford, Calif.: Stanford University Press, 1974.
14. Scheck, D., et. al. Adolescents' perceptions of parent-child relations and the development of internal-external control operation. *Journal of Marriage and Family,* 1973, **35,** 643-654.
15. Weimberger, M. J. Dress codes—we forget our own advice, *Clearing House,* 1970, **44,** 471-475.
16. Kanter, J. F., & Zelnick, M. Three-fourths of teenage first pregnancies are premaritally conceived. *Family Planning Digest,* 1974, **3**(4), 14-15.
17. Mondy, J., & Ehrhardt, A. A. *Man and woman, boy and girl: the differentiation and dimorphism of gender identity from conception to maturity.* Baltimore: John Hopkins University Press, 1972.
18. Lyndon, M. Rock for sale. *Ramparts,* 1969, **137,** 19-20.
19. Dielman, T. E., Barton, K., & Cattell, R. B. Adolescent personality and intelligence scores as related to family demography. *Journal of Genetic Psychology,* 1974, **124,** 151-154.
20. Hansen, R. A. Consistency and stability of home environmental measures related to IQ. *Child Development Quarterly,* 1975, **46,** 470-480.
21. Erikson, E. H. Eight ages of man. In C. S. Lavatelli, & F. Stendler (Eds.), *Readings in child behavior and child development.* New York: Harcourt Brace Janovich, Inc., 1972.
22. Erikson, E. H. *Identity youth and crises.* New York: W. W. Norton & Co., 1968.

Middle and later adolescence

15 to 18 years of age

Stan is 16 years old. He is the elder of two boys belonging to an upper middle-class family. In appearance he is handsome, slim, 5 feet 8 inches tall, has beautiful white teeth, and is very tan from his job as a lifeguard. Since hair is often a bone of contention between some parents and sons, I feel I should mention that Stan's hair is fashionably long, but he keeps it carefully trimmed so that neither teachers nor parents could object.

As typical of most boys his age, he is concerned about his appearance. He had the beginnings of an acne problem about two years ago. This was expected because both of his parents had bad acne problems when they were teenagers. Stan, however, watched his diet meticulously and would not eat anything that could possibly cause a bad complexion. He exercised the same self-control when he was on his high school wrestling team and needed to maintain a particular weight.

Stan's grades are high average. His grades in algebra, science, and physical education have always been "A," but he has had some trouble in the past in English and geography. At one time he was in an accelerated class, but he did not believe that it was important enough to do the necessary extra work to maintain the standards. He will be a senior this year and has already been accepted at the college of his choice. He will be a liberal arts major because his career decision has not been made. Neither of his parents had any college education.

Stan was not allowed to date until the tenth grade, even though girls were calling him on the telephone a couple of years before that. His dating pattern now is to date one girl exclusively for several weeks and then switch to another partner. His parents always know where he is going and with whom. Over Memorial Day weekend he took a carload of his friends to the all-night drive-in movies. His parents were not too happy about this but did not think that it was a legitimate battleground.

Stan's parents bought him a car this summer primarily to let him drive back and forth to work. He is a cautious driver. Stan never seemed to have to learn how to drive. As a very young child, he would go everywhere with his father, and driving seemed like a natural thing for him to do. Most of his summer's earnings are going for dates, car upkeep, records, and some clothes. His parents were more concerned with his having a constructive way of spending his summer than with his making much money.

The one time that Stan really upset his parents, primarily his father, was when he seemed to be searching for answers, as teenagers will, and decided to investigate another religion. He had been brought up as a Protestant and attended church every Sunday with both of his parents. Stan's parents had a mixed marriage. His mother was Jewish, and he had been exposed to Judaism through her family. Completely on his own, Stan began attending a Conservative Jewish Temple every Friday night and had private talks with the Rabbi. This continued for several months and then abruptly stopped. Whether or not Stan found his answers in his original church or whether he decided the answers he was looking for were not to be found at all is uncertain. I believe that the interesting aspect was that he sought answers not through drugs, the use of which is prevalent at his high school, but, rather, through religion. This is indicative that at this point in his life he is seeking answers and values in a healthy manner, at least so far. The fact that college contacts will shortly be exposing him to different moral and value judgments cannot help but make us wonder how much longer he can maintain his conservatism. It will be interesting to note in two or three years what going away to college can do to an unsophisticated young man.

Stan is a well-mannered person and has good rapport with his parents. He compliments his mother when appropriate, but recently he drove her "up a tree" until she gave up her nineteen-year habit of smoking a pack of cigarettes a day. He explained to her that she could not expect him to respect all her wishes unless she also would listen to reason about something as hazardous to her and thus to her family as smoking. Quite a guy!

It is more appropriate to title this chapter "middle adolescence" rather than "late adolescence" because the ages it intends to cover do not extend to the ages of 20 or 21 years, which are usually cited as the ages at which full maturity and development are attained.

In recent years it has seemed unrealistic to speak of a 19- or 20-year-old as an adolescent, even though there is still some "growing-up" to be done. The level of worldly sophistication of 18- to 21-year-olds is so much higher than that of the same age group of recent generations. Their behavior patterns are more adultlike. To further negate the label of *adolescent* for this older age group, the age at which an individual is legally considered an adult has been changed in most states from the age of 21 to 18 years. Voting privileges in federal elections have been granted to 18-year-olds. However, there are still disquiet-ing questions that ask, "Is an individual matured, in all ways, to adulthood before the age of 21?" "Does a change in laws necessarily produce a change in developmental characteristics?"

People recognize that 18- to 21-year-olds of today are different in many social ways from individuals of the same ages of two or three decades ago. But are they different physically, emotionally, or even morally? Do they make better value judgments? There is no common consensus on these points. Therefore we consider "middle adolescence" in this chapter as dealing with high school youth. Chapter 12 will discuss post–high school youth, or emerging adulthood. There is an overlapping of characteristics of these two groups, even though their behavior patterns may differ. We want to stress the need to consider both chapters as discussing final adolescence.

The developmental tasks of this age group are basically an extension of the tasks of early adolescence. Although the physical changes brought about by puberty are now fairly well established, there is still a need to develop a feeling of physical adequacy and acceptability. A greater degree of social and emotional independence must be attained. Heterosexuality must be established on a higher level than previously, and a regard and respect for others in general must become part of one's attitudinal pattern. Progressive growth in the development of a value judgment system is important for middle adolescents, as is the development of ego identity in personality and character structures. The initial skills, interests, and information related to such matters as civic competency, choice of a vocation, post–high school living, and preparation for marriage and family life must be garnered at this time. The ultimate goal of adolescence is that of "identity" as an adult.

ADOLESCENCE AND THE COMING OF AGE

In simple, less complex societies a young person had no difficulty in knowing when he passed from childhood to adulthood. There was an event or ceremony that marked his or her coming of age. In primitive tribal societies the transition was and still is marked by initiation or puberty rites. In ancient Rome this changeover was signaled by the wearing of a toga; in medieval times it occurred when the boy of 14 years, who was not a serf, became a squire and began his apprenticeship for knighthood. All of the ceremonies and status symbols stress the passing from the capricious behavior of childhood to the serious accountability of adulthood.

Puberty rites still exist among people such as the Mende of Sierra Leone in Africa, the Hopi Indians of Arizona, the aborigines of Australia, and the Sevaray tribe in the Sahara. The Duna tribe, the Porgaiga tribe, the Arapesh tribe from the Highlands, and the "mudmen" from the Asaro Valley, all from New Guinea, as well as the Amaaiura Indians, also practice puberty rites. The ceremonies of these groups are all different, but a common theme underlies the rites in whatever kind of society they may occur. The theme is that having learned the traditions and the behavior patterns of the tribe, having passed the tests of adulthood, young people now leave their childhood behind them forever and socially are accepted as adults by the other tribal members.

Western societies do not provide a symbolic event, signal, or custom by which young people know for sure that they have entered adulthood and are accepted by adults as such. There are ceremonies such as Confirmation, the first Communion, and the celebration of Bar Mitzvah that give a child a sense of identity with an adult group, but these events do not signal a general acceptance of the child into the social world of adults. Western societies of today have increased the amount of knowledge and preparation needed before an individual can be considered ready for adulthood. More education and training is required before an individual is ready for an advanced, technological society. Children no longer go into the job market at the ages of 14 or 16 years. They "are not ready for it." The result has been to extend the period between childhood and adulthood, giving the adolescent stage greater visibility.

Adolescence, as a stage of development, has only received an identity of its own within our society in the last thirty years or so. The term *teenager* has only gained wide usage in that same time span. It was after World War II that adolescence was recognized and treated by adults as a separate developmental period with needs and characteristics of its own. Times were changing. For the first time these young people did not drop out of school in large numbers at the end of ninth grade to enter the adult job market.

At that time this identifiable group began to emerge as a significant element of society. First were the bobby-soxers of the prewar and wartime era who were popularized by the news media. No doubt the "zoot suits" of the late forties gave the boys a sense of "being different" from younger children and the more conservative adults. Manufacturers of women's clothing found a ready market for "clothes for teens." Terms such as *junior miss, debutante, teens, preteens,* and others appeared on clothing for girls. Department stores added a "teen" section of clothing in addition to their traditional Misses and Children's sections. The news media of the 1950s popularized the term *teenager.* Unfortunately, it did so in connection with the term *juvenile delin-*

quency. The late 1950s saw an emphasis in the news media on the "beat generation" with its beatniks; the 1960s had their hippies; and Pepsi-Cola created a whole new emphasis on youth with its "generation" advertising campaign. Today adolescence is accepted as a stage of growth with an identity of its own. A recognition of young adults or the 18- to 21-year-old group has also been achieved. The lines between the various groups never have been clear-cut, but there are enough characteristics particular to each developmental group—childhood, adolescence, young adult, adulthood—to permit separate categories and classifications of each.

The principal characteristics of adolescence, however, are universal and timeless. Adolescents the world over exhibit the same type of needs. The ways in which these needs are expressed differ, but their implications are the same. Teenagers have to accomplish the developmental tasks that will prepare them for adulthood in their society. In some societies the transition runs smoothly; in others, with more effort. There is always that criterion of adult maturity, which time alone does not ensure. The demands of the particular society set the standards. If the requirements are meager, such as in primitive societies, there are few problems. If the criteria of maturity are too high, such as in more complex societies, youth will have time to assert itself by revealing its own standards and probably exhibiting immature, inexperienced, and often unwarranted behavior as compared to adult expectations.

Here are three quotations of interest. "I see no hope for the future of our people if they are dependent on the frivolous youth of today, for certainly all youth are reckless beyond words. . . When I was a boy, we were taught to be discreet and respectful of elders, but the present youth are exceedingly wise and impatient of restraint." A second quotation is as follows, "Our youth now love luxury. They have bad manners, contempt for authority, disrespect for older people. Children nowadays are tyrants. They no longer rise when their elders enter the room. They contradict their parents, chatter before company, gobble their food and tyrannize their teachers." A third quotation: "Could you but take a view of this part of town on a Sunday, you would be shocked indeed for then the streets are filled with multitudes of these wretches who spend their time in riot and noise, cursing and swearing in a manner so horrid as to convey to any serious mind an idea of hell rather than of any other place. Their parents have no idea of instilling into the minds of their children principles to which they themselves are entire strangers." The first quotation was written by Hesiod in the eighth century B.C.; the second quotation is from Socrates, written 2,300 years ago in Plato's *Republic;* and the third quotation is by Robert Raikes, founder of the Sunday School movement, in Gloucester, England, 1783. The least that can be said is that adolescence appears to be consistent throughout the years in the sense that "this generation is going to the dogs."

Adolescence bridges the gap between dependency and adulthood. It is usually an uncertain period for the adolescent because it is a time when parents relax their hold and shift responsibilities to a young person who has not learned how to handle them. This is a time of trials, experimentation, and learning. Three major types of changes are taking place—physical, social, and emotional changes. They constitute growth that is continuous rather than periodic, and more gradual than abrupt. To survive, every society must train its young for responsible adult roles if it wishes to avoid an unsettledness that comes from the uncertainty of youth trying to find its place in the adult world.

PHYSICAL GROWTH AND DEVELOPMENT

Increase in height and weight during middle and later adolescence gradually lessens. This slowdown permits the older adolescent to stabilize the organization and functions of the different muscular patterns. As a result, the awkwardness that was characteristic of early adolescence gradually corrects itself.

The ultimate weight and height of adolescents when their growth is completed will depend on such factors as hereditary endowment, prenatal and postnatal feeding and health, race, environmental conditions, exercise during infancy and childhood, and general health. The age at which pubertal maturing occurs influences the ultimate size of the individual, with late maturers tending

David Strickler

The world of women in sports is developing rapidly. Physical growth is ready for training programs to develop agility, speed, and accuracy.

to be somewhat taller than early maturers. According to national averages the average American male is 69½ inches tall and weighs 153 pounds, whereas the average woman is 66 inches tall and weighs 135 pounds.[1] Girls reach mature physical development around the age of 18 years and boys approximately one year later. Differences in height are less noticeable than are differences in weight. No predictable evidence has been discovered which would show that the age of maturing has any permanent effect on weight. The increases in weight during late adolescence are usually found in areas of the body that did not fill out during early adolescence.

The problem of a disproportioned body, which causes great anxiety in the young adolescent, slowly changes as the youngster's body takes on the form of an adult. The oversized nose of early adolescence now assumes a correct adult proportion. The lower jaw grows larger in late adolescence, and the lips become fuller. The trunk elongates and the chest broadens. The "gawky" look of the early adolescent disappears. The breasts and hips of a girl are fully developed by late adolescence so that her body now has the smooth curves of an adult female. Studies show that late-maturing individuals, girls and boys, tend to have thin legs, whereas early-maturing individuals have stocky legs.

Bone measurements show that the skeleton, on

the average, stops growing at the age of 18 years. The wisdom teeth usually do not emerge until late adolescence. Despite the fact that secondary sex characteristics are usually mature in size and are functioning late in adolescence, the primary sex organs may not be mature until a year or two after puberty. The oiliness of hair and skin, characteristic of early adolescence, gradually stops, and skin problems like acne usually subside with the onset of late adolescence. The growth of the digestive system also slows, and girls and boys tend to eat less during this growth period than during early adolescence. However, they may have unwise appetites and erratic habits of food consumption.[2]

A healthy childhood generally indicates that adolescence will be a healthy period. Menstruation during late adolescence is usually much less uncomfortable than during the previous stage of adolescence. Girls have generally adjusted to the menstrual cycle and can continue with their active daily routines.

Imaginary illness is a curious "disease" that occurs in early and late adolescence. Both age groups frequently use illness as an excuse for escaping from unpleasant duties or responsibilities. Small upsets are frequently exaggerated to the point where the youth feels that he is too ill to face his problems. Girls have more imaginary illnesses than boys. Social situations are usually the cause of girls' frustrations.

ACHIEVING INDEPENDENCE FROM HOME

By the age of 16 years most teenagers will have learned to accept adults in their lives. Parents, if they had been relegated to a minor role during the previous two years, are usually reinstated to their position of prominence within the thinking of the adolescent. If adolescents are treated with respect and positive regard and if they have been permitted to grow responsibly without undue restraint, they will begin to assume their adult roles and to be comfortable with them. They will think it less necessary to assert their independence with exaggerated, extravagant behavior. Understandings between parent and child still have to be "hammered out," however, but these can be accomplished with less conflict and fewer hurt feelings than previously. Arguments

with adolescents should not be interpreted as an indication of an unhappy home. Rather, they are indications that the children are growing up naturally. The time to be concerned is when the child is unusually acquiescent or amenable and does not seek to achieve a spot outside the family.

Problems in seeking independence

The need for a sense of independence from family domination is a requirement for adolescents if they are to achieve full maturity. There are barriers to be overcome, and there are skills to be attained. Reasons for parent-child conflicts during adolescence tend to fall into two main categories: (1) issues involving greater demands for independence by the adolescent than the parents are willing to grant, and (2) issues involving more dependent or childish behavior on the part of the adolescent than the parents feel able to tolerate.

A cause of conflict may be due to a need for experiences by adolescents to mature their thinking and the refusal by the parents to grant the adolescents ample experimental opportunity to prepare for adulthood. The young people may feel psychologically ready to assert themselves as grown-ups, but their efforts to act as one may be thwarted by a lack of money to carry out their plans or by the parents ignoring their wishes or ideas. Depriving adolescents of their attempt to enter or to contribute to adult society may frustrate them into retaliatory action. Dejected, the adolescents may sever communications with their parents and set out on their own to prove they are independent individuals (Table 11-1).

Frequently adolescents will aggressively demand adult prerogatives but strenuously resist the rights of others to control or limit their use of them. The fact that they appear to be uncompromising in their determination to impose their terms on the adult culture leaves the parent in a quandary. A conflict of interests or wishes between the parents and the youth leads to an unfortunate struggle for domination.[3]

It is difficult for parents to know when they are overprotective or overrestrictive with their children. Children have different limits of tolerance due to differences in their personalities. They also have different degrees of need for

Achieving independence from the home involves both emotional and social growth. Cultural customs within the family influence the ease with which adolescents can make the transition to adulthood.

David Strickler

Table 11-1. Middle-aged adult and adolescent personalities*

Middle-aged adult generation	Adolescent generation
1. Cautious, based upon experience	1. Daring, willing to try new things, but lacks judgment based upon experience
2. Oriented to past, compares present with way things used to be	2. Present is only reality; past is irrelevant, future is dim, uncertain
3. Realistic, sometimes cynical about life, people	3. Idealistic, optimistic
4. Conservative in manners, morals, mores	4. Liberal, challenges traditional codes, ethics, experiments with new ideas, life-styles
5. Generally contented, satisfied, resigned to status quo	5. Critical, restless, unhappy with things as they are
6. Wants to keep young, fears age	6. Wants to be grown-up, but never wants to become old; contempt for aged

*Adapted from Andersen, W. J. *Design for family living.* Minneapolis: T. S. Denison & Co., 1964, p. 256. Used by permission.

security. Independence does not come overnight for any child. It is a gradual process, taking place over a number of years. Wise parents and teachers will provide opportunities to learn responsibilities at a rate that can be tolerated by the adolescent and will not be too demanding, too restrictive, or too permissive during the learning process. Some semblance of direction, structure, and limits is needed. Communication channels must also be kept open at all costs.

Conflicts within the family

Rice[4] lists five areas of conflicts with parents: social life and customs, responsibility, school, family relationships, and values and morals.

The telephone is frequently a source of irritation between parents and adolescents in the home. Teenagers spend a great deal of their time talking to friends and neighbors on the telephone, discussing dates, experiences, school—just about anything. Since their social relationships have greatly increased with adolescence, it is understandable why so much time is consumed conversing on the telephone. Parents, unfortunately, do not always view the problem sympathetically. To some parents it seems that the son or daughter is always tying up the telephone. Thus restrictions and rules regarding its use must be made and enforced, much to the protests of the youngsters.

Some parents demand to know the thoughts and activities of their teenagers. They want to

know where they are going, where they have been, whom they are with, and why they are late. Parents have great concern about the use of drugs, alcohol, and sex. These kinds of parents may also go through their child's possessions and then justify this action by saying that they were only trying to find out what their son or daughter was doing, since they never talk about themselves. Parents will establish trust only when they show an honest and sincere interest in what the adolescent believes and feels. In their quest for privacy adolescents may ask for their own bedroom and telephone.

Another sensitive area of conflict centers around use of the family automobile. This is primarily a problem with boys, usually at the age of 16 years, when they have received their driver's license. Heated arguments often result over the amount of time teenagers use the car, where they plan to go, when they will return, and why they need a car in the first place! A car is a sign of security and independence to adolescents; it may also serve as a status element among their peers. A deeper understanding of adolescents' needs, a concern for them as individuals, and a sense of sharing the family items can do much to eliminate such stress.

Some adolescents lack respect for and trust in their parents. They have been taught to believe in their mother and father and to honor them, yet they often have difficulty in explaining inconsistencies that they see between what their par-

Adam was but human—this explains it all. He did not want the apple for the apple's sake, he wanted it only because it was forbidden.
Mark Twain
Pudd'nhead Wilson

ents say is the right thing to do and the behavior their parents exhibit. At a time when so many values, judgments, and adjustments have overwhelmed adolescents' thinking, their struggle for an understanding of themselves is further complicated by a breakdown in regard for parental sanctification. A disinterested adult society also adds to the bewilderment. Who can you trust? What can you believe?

Conflicts between parents and adolescents over the young persons' social activities reach a peak in middle adolescence. Disagreements are usually centered around dating and choice of friends. Often parents are guilty of a superficial ''popularity status'' in which they involve their children. This status is measured not only in terms of the number of friends the youngster has but also of the social status they hold in the community and the type of prominent social activities in which they engage. A popular son or daughter is often a source of social prestige for some parents—something to talk about over the telephone or to brag about over the bridge table. Adolescents in this situation will question their own value as well as the true meaning of friendship. In addition, they may see themselves as objects being used by their parents for their own gratification and not as persons of intrinsic worth.

Control versus autonomy in parent-child relationships

A study by Baumrind[5] on the topic of parental variations in child-rearing techniques revealed several parental structures along a continuum of authority and control as opposed to freedom and autonomy. These parental types, including variations, are as follows: (1) autocratic—youths are not permitted to express their views on decisions related to themselves; sometimes this position is considered to be authoritarian—youth may express views, but parents make decisions based on their judgment; (2) democratic—youth contributes freely and may make a decision, but parents reserve the right to approve the decision or change it; or equalitarian—parents and child are involved to an equal degree in decision making; (3) permissive—adolescent is more active and influential than parents in making decisions; or laissez-faire—youth is in a posi-

tion to either accept or reject parental wishes in making decisions; and (4) ignoring—parents do not involve themselves at all in directing the adolescent's behavior or decision making; or erratic—parents who are inconsistent in their approach to their children.

Results of a study by Elder[6] indicate that autocratic or authoritarian parents tend to suppress the orderly development in the adolescent of independence from the domination of the parents. Laissez-faire, ignoring, and completely permissive parents may fail to encourage the development of responsibility. The parents who retain an interest in and some responsibility for adolescents' decisions, whereas encouraging autonomy as they grow, are likely to develop both responsibility and independence in youths. The study, involving 7,400 adolescents, also revealed that (1) children exposed to democratic practices consider their parents more fair (85%) as compared to autocratic parents (50%), (2) fathers are more likely to be considered autocratic (35%) than are mothers (22%), (3) parents of larger families tend to be more autocratic regardless of social class, (4) fathers are considered more fair if they at least listen, even though they make all the final decisions, (5) permissiveness is considered a more acceptable role for mothers than for fathers, and (6) by far, the largest percentage of adolescents who felt unwanted were those with autocratic (40%) or laissez-faire or ignoring parents (58%), as compared to democratic parents (8%).

It appears that a feeling of independence occurs more frequently among adolescents whose parents listen, who frequently explain their reasons for decisions and expectations, and who are less autocratic in their exercise of parental powers.

ESTABLISHING HETEROSEXUAL RELATIONSHIPS

Fifteen- to 18-years-olds have developed rather specific perceptions of their sex roles. Now they are seeking opportunities to play out their roles in adult ways. Boys become more interested in social activities, although sports remain a close second in their interests. A gathering place, possibly a school setting, usually becomes a focal point where young people gather to practice their social skills and to engage in heterosexual activities. Adolescents are sensitive to social approval, acceptance, and demands. No other problem seems to them as important as the establishment of themselves in their own society.

Peer acceptance

Adolescents have a need to be recognized and accepted by someone. This is most readily done through friends and acquaintances who are their peer mates. Being of the same age, they share their feelings, experiences, goals, and doubts in a way that their parents cannot do. In a peer group situation adolescents can find belonging, affiliation, acceptance, and status as the independent persons that they so strongly desire to be.

Most adolescents are not sufficiently secure or confident so that they can tolerate differences between themselves and their colleagues. As a result, sameness becomes a rule within the primary group of friends. This conformity extends to appearance, dress, fads, fashion, hair style, makeup, activities, and attitudes. As a result, adolescents often find that their personal values clash with those of their friends in such matters, for example, as drugs, starting to smoke, drink, or engage in questionable behavior. Threatened by a possible loss of friends, adolescents, will generally give in rather than stand by their beliefs. The fear of losing friends is too powerful a threat. This action, in turn, may cause mental anxieties and concerns, since they are not being true to themselves. This is one conflict that can only be resolved by adopting the behavior of their group or else by leaving these friends and seeking new ones. Group pressures are hard to overcome.

There are several reasons for lack of acceptance by a group. Being retiring is one of the causes of not finding social acceptance. If individuals do not have confidence in themselves, the group has none in them. Social ineptness may be a stumbling block, since the social skills that provide access to the group have never been learned. A person who seems emotionally unstable is actively rejected by the group because they cannot afford to have such a person identified with their group. Social distance, the degree of intimacy to which an individual is willing to accept a certain person, is a relative matter for many individuals. However, in certain localities ethnic, racial, and social differences are magnified and are causes for exclusion, rejection, or ignoring.

Sequential pattern of dating

The sequence by which the dating pattern emerges is fairly certain; the time and rapidity with which it emerges are dependent on many cultural variables. The general attitude and philosophy of the community (or locale), the general wishes of the parents of the children involved, the customs, traditions, and folkways of the area, and the thinking of the young people themselves have a great influence on the age at which different levels of the dating sequence take place. Some communities may be two or three years ahead of others in the time at which girls and boys begin to date. In some communities, steps within the dating sequence are compressed within a short time span, whereas other steps persist for a long period. There are differences in dating practices. The time sequence presented here is typical of the country as a whole rather than of specific regions. Large cosmopolitan areas usually have an earlier beginning of the sequential pattern.

The 11- or 12-year-old boy and girl are still in a period of social development in which they cling to friends of their own sex. There may be some mixed group activities and heterosexual interests as early as the fifth grade, but these are not the typically sought-after activities or choices of the youngsters. The nature of most school programs and organizations, including the middle school and junior high school grades, is such that there are more opportunities for mixed group activities than previously. Sports and music programs of the school, club organizations, and exposure to more classes and teachers broaden social possibilities.

Dating sequence. The more typical dating activities, the first in the dating sequence, are "crowd" dates, usually at organized school functions in the seventh grade. A group of girls just happens to be around a certain group of boys at a football or basketball game. What is interesting

Harold Geyer

Dating interests and dating patterns vary from one locality to another, but the end result is the same—boy and girl get together!

is that the same group of girls seems to be around the same group of boys at most of the activities. Seldom is there any pairing off within the groups until the eighth grade. By the ninth grade crowd dates are still popular, but now there is a noticeable pairing off of couples. It is not unusual in the seventh grade to notice a few boys and girls who are seeing each other frequently on a paired-off basis. It will be obvious that some eighth grade couples are going steady, but as we said earlier, this is not typical or expected of the majority of the seventh and eighth graders. Steady couples are more common in the ninth grade than in earlier grades. In most places, going steady takes a big jump in tenth grade.[7]

In the tenth grade there will be paired crowd dates for special social functions. Some boys and girls will come to the activity as a couple and join the crowd. Four, five, or more couples will make up the crowd, although there may still be some unattached friends within the group. It is not uncommon in some cities for single dating to start in ninth grade and increase in popularity. Double dating is a common practice in eleventh grade and twelfth grade.

By the end of the freshman year about half of the freshman boys in socially oriented urban or suburban areas will have dated a girl. By the end of the junior year about three fourths will have dated, and by their senior year 95% are dating to some degree. Might there be some single dates in seventh or even sixth grade? Yes, but it probably would not be the common practice. Each community and social group has its own features. What was typical of dating practices when you were 12 to 16 years old?

The median age at which young people begin dating has decreased by about three years since 1920. The age for girls beginning to date in 1924 was 16 years, in 1958 it was 13.3 years, and in 1968 it was 13.2 years of age. Our recent study indicated that in 1978 the age was slightly below 13 years. A study by Place[8] indicates that, in a northeast Texas community, the median age for the first date for whites remained relatively stable over a ten-year period, but the median age for blacks decreased from 14.9 years in 1964 to 13.9 in 1974. Fig. 11-1 shows the distribution. In that study, 4% of the whites and 5% of the blacks never had a date.

Dating differs in types and degrees of seriousness. The first stage of dating, during early adolescence, is of a noncommittal nature. It is extremely mobile in style in that there are few if any deep romantic attachments. The nervous excitement of a novel experience is sufficient to interest a person in another. Playing the field does not produce lasting relationships, and there is a minimum of emotional stress involved. The amount of time spent in this type of dating varies from individual to individual. Interests in love, courtship, and marriage do not reach a peak until late adolescence.

Personal comment. We would like to illustrate

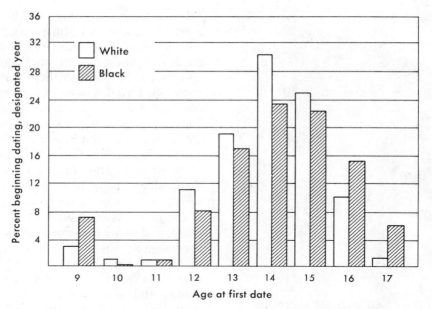

Fig. 11-1. Frequency distribution (in percentages) of age at first date in 1974, by race. (Adapted from Dickinson, G. E. *Journal of Marriage and the Family,* 1975, **37,** 604. In Rice, *The adolescent* [2nd ed.]. p. 332, Allyn and Bacon.)

boy-girl relationships from our experiences. We had the extraordinary opportunity of being with the same group of boys from the time they were in seventh grade until they graduated from high school. Of twenty-nine boys who started with us in a seventh grade Junior Hi-Y, twenty-four boys were still with us when they graduated. This was a most unusual group of boys—service minded and extremely active. They adopted an 84-year-old man and kept him in food, tobacco, and company for over three years. They collected two panel truck loads of comic books, while in eighth grade, and gave them to be used at a veterans' hospital nearby.

In ninth grade they sponsored a "Have-a-Heart Week" during the week of St. Valentine's Day as a campaign to improve courtesy within the school. Any young persons seen by a teacher or club member doing a courteous act or a good deed had their name turned in to a central point that evening. The next morning when the pupils returned to school, they found a small paper heart on their desk for each time their names were turned in. The students proudly wore these hearts. At the end of the week a prize was given

to the boy and girl with the biggest (most) heart, the homeroom with the biggest heart, and several other prizes for "hearts." No one ever saw a group of 12- to 14-year-olds in a school of 900 pupils who were so courteous, not only for that week but for the rest of the year.

Every boy in the club went on to some type of post–high school education (not all college). From that group there are now six engineers, four electronics specialists, three lawyers, several merchants, one physician, one teacher, one YMCA secretary, a Roman Catholic priest who studied at the Vatican for four years, a boy who studied for the Lutheran ministry, a Greek Orthodox priest, and a Jewish Rabbi, who among other things was arrested in one of the early civil rights marches in the South.

Now for the development of the dating pattern. In seventh grade the boys decided they would like to have a hayride. For six weeks they planned whom to contact for the wagons, how to get there, and what to eat. They went on the hayride and had a marvelous time. Nobody mentioned girls, and no one brought a girl. In eighth grade they voted to have another hayride. Some-

Table 11-2. Personality traits liked or disliked*

Liked	Disliked
Personal appearance	**Personal appearance**
Good-looking	Homely, unattractive
Feminine, nice figure (girls)	Boyish figure, or too fat or skinny (girls)
Masculine, good build (boys)	Sissy, skinny, fat (boys)
Neat, clean, well groomed	Sloppy, dirty, unkempt
Appropriate clothes	Clothes out of style, don't fit, not appropriate, dirty
	Greaser (boys)
	Physical handicap
Social behavior	**Social behavior**
Outgoing, friendly	Shy, timid, withdrawn, quiet
Active, energetic	Lethargic, listless, passive
Participant in activities	Nonjoiner, recluse
Social skills: good manners, conversationalist, courteous, poised, natural, tactful, can dance, play many games, sports	Loud, boisterous, ill- mannered, disrespectful, braggart, show-off, not "cool," giggles, rude, crude, tongue-tied, doesn't know how to do or play anything
Lots of fun, good sport	Real drip, poor sport
Acts age, mature	Childish, immature
Good reputation	Bad reputation
Personal qualities of character	**Personal qualities of character**
Kind, sympathetic, understanding	Cruel, hostile, disinterested
Cooperative, gets along well, even tempered, stable	Quarrelsome, bully, bad tempered, domineering, sorehead
Unselfish, generous, helpful	Inconsiderate, selfish, stingy
Cheerful, optimistic, happy	Pessimistic, complaining person
Responsible, dependable	Irresponsible, not reliable
Honest, truthful, fair	Liar, cheat, unfair
Good sense of humor	Can't take a joke, no sense of humor
High ideals	Dirty minded
Self-confident, self-accepting but modest	Conceited, vain

*Composite from Rice, F. P. The adolescent (2nd ed.). Boston: Allyn and Bacon, Inc., 1978, p. 324.

one said, "Let's bring girls." Everyone laughed, but no one brought a girl. In ninth grade they again decided on a hayride. Someone said, "Let's bring girls." Someone else said, "Let's not." They voted, and the girls lost out by two votes. That same night, in early October, they voted to bring girls to their Christmas Party. Anyone who did not want to bring a girl could be on the refreshment and clean-up committee. Three boys ended up on that committee, two of whom were the first of the group to get married later on. The hayride was a "so-so" affair that year. Everyone was looking forward to the Christmas Party.

While in tenth grade they agreed to have another hayride. The topic of girls was brought up again. Someone said, "Let's vote." The girls won out by a good margin. In the junior year they decided on a hayride. Someone asked, "Are we bringing girls?" Someone replied, "What else?" To continue the tradition of hayrides in twelfth grade they decided to have a final hayride. All the plans for the activity were completed within a half hour. No one mentioned girls, but everyone brought a girl. That was the most eerie hayride by moonlight my wife and I ever went on. For much of the ride we were the only ones who could be seen on the wagons. Laughter, giggling, and singing seemed to be coming from underneath the straw on the wagons. After the hayride we had the biggest problem ever getting the couples off the wagons and out of the haystacks on the farm so they could get back to town by midnight!

Personality traits. Within Western culture it has been the responsibility of the male to select the dating partner. Girls must make sure that they are attractive enough to become selected. There are various ways of doing this. External attributes that many girls consider essential for entry into the dating game are being dressed in the latest fashions, whether they be sweaters and skirts or blue jeans, and good looks. The nonmaterial, idealist point of view of many of today's youth is slowly lessening the emphasis on money, clothes, and social prestige. What a boy seeks are personality, concern for others, looks, and dependability. According to Place,[8] girls, on the other hand, seem to want good personality, good looks, acceptable social actions of the boy, and one who dresses well, in addition to manners, neatness, and an ability to carry on a conversation. Table 11-2 indicates those personality traits that are liked and disliked. These are not the only qualifications, but they provide some idea of what a later adolescent looks for in a dating partner. Similarity in characteristics is also an important factor in date selection. The tendency is to choose someone with similar rather than opposite interests, needs, and appearance. What might be noted is that the qualities being sought are of the type needed for a good life mate. This could indicate the seriousness of dating during this period. Late adolescents are beginning to search for that certain person with whom to spend the rest of their lives.

Parental concerns. Early dating and steady dating of adolescents are chief concerns of parents. Parents fear that pairing off on a steady basis leads young adolescents into sexual and emotional intimacies long before they are ready for marriage. Adolescents, on the other hand, believe that steady dating, even as early as 12 or 13 years of age, provides security and acceptance by the group. They cannot understand their parents' reasoning. Many a household is filled with turmoil resulting from conflicting views on dating. The teenager who is denied dating privileges

Table 11-3. Adolescent sexual activity*

	Percent having sexual intercourse	
	Before age 16	By age 19
Males		
1948	39	72
1973	44	72
Females		
1953	3	20
1973	30	57

*From *Adolescent sexuality in contemporary America.* Copyright 1972, 1973 by Robert C. Sorenson (World Pub. Co.). Reprinted by permission of Harper & Row, Publishers, Inc.

may feel rejected, resentful, and deceived. He may increase the friction by sneaking out on dates; some will exceed sexual behavioral limits simply to spite their parents.

Dating problems. Problems related to dating are of two types: namely, "I can't get a date," or else, "Now that I'm dating, how far should I go?" Individuals who have not had the opportunity to develop social skills will have trouble knowing what to do to get to know the opposite sex better. This may also leave them isolated in other group activities. Concerning the second problem, girls are upset by the aggressive behavior of boys who try to see how far they can go. Boys dislike the way girls flaunt their sexuality.[9] Even a nice girl can give the wrong impression. As to "How far should I go in kissing, necking, and petting?" usually the boy tries to get as much as possible, and the girl yields as little as possible. The girl is expected to set the limits, and the boy is expected to conform. Girls may be the aggressors, but that is not considered to be their role. These questions cause considerable anxiety and tension for adolescents. There are a number of girls who are questioning and resisting the implications of a "double standard" system (Table 11-3).

LOVE RELATIONSHIPS

Early adolescence, marked by the advent of heterosexual relationships, is a critical period in the life of 13-, 14-, or 15-year-olds. They are placed in closer social contact with the opposite sex, thus offering them more opportunity to establish feelings of affection for particular mem-

A COMMITMENT? It finally happened. After seventeen years, eleven months, and eighteen days of guarding my virginity, I had lost it.

He was tall, dark, and handsome, as the saying goes. I had been wild about him since our sophomore year in high school. He hadn't paid much attention to me until now, our senior year.

We had been dating for about four months. I was going steady with him. I suspected that he was not going steady with me. But that didn't matter. I was just happy to be with him. I was content to look at him and to feel him near me.

When he held me and kissed me, I felt such peace and comfort and, yet, excitement. We did a lot of necking in the beginning. Then we started to have petting sessions. I always managed to call a halt to these sessions before things got out of hand.

My stepmother placed great value on virginity. She was constantly telling me of the dangers of necking and petting. I felt that she knew what she was talking about, since she and my father had gotten carried away. She got pregnant and they had to get married. At the same time, I felt that she should understand how hard it is to control one's emotions. At any rate, whenever the big moment loomed near, her preachings would come to mind and I would again be saved.

So I kept resisting. He kept insisting. He even started insisting that he loved me. He hinted at marriage. And finally came the old argument: "If you love me, prove it."

And because I felt I loved him more than life itself, I proved it!

When I think back on it, it's not a very pleasant memory. Being had in the front seat of a car in a cemetery is not at all romantic. But, at the time, I was very happy. I had pleased him. I had committed myself and felt that he had also committed himself. I was sure that I, as in the fairy tales, would live happily ever after.

Afterward, he was very gentle, reassuring me that he loved me more than ever before. And I believed him. He took me home, walked me to the door, kissed me gently and lovingly, made a date for the following evening, got into his car, and left.

I was deliriously happy. I spent the night dreaming of wedding bells and booties.

The following evening came but my intended did not. I didn't try to make excuses. Somehow I knew I was being stood up. Not only for one night but for the rest of my life.

I had been rejected again. First by my mother in favor of her new lover. Then by my father in favor of his new wife. And now by him in favor of what? I did not know.

I did know that he had gotten what he wanted—and I had lost far more than my virginity!

bers of the opposite sex. They might very well consider themselves in love with a person, yet their strong feelings are too often dismissed by adults as "puppy love," nonsense, or simply a game all teenagers play. Closer observation reveals this stage to be a trying one for adolescents, since they have never before felt this way about the opposite sex. In later adolescence the relationships become more involved, hence the problems become more complicated.

A common phase that many adolescents go through is the "crush" stage, in which an adult individual or individuals are the center of the adolescent's affection. This particular phenomenon is also known as hero worshipping. Crushes occur in situations where some important or well-liked person in the youngster's life, perhaps a teacher or friend, embodies the qualities that the youngster regards as being important or desirable. This leads to strong feelings of attachment and a reaction that the adolescent usually interprets as love. Crushes seem to occur most between 15 and 19 years of age in boys and between 13 and 18 years in girls. Most of them last from one to six months, some longer. Boys base the attraction on physical and/or mental abilities, whereas girls concentrate mainly on mental and personality qualities.

The crush itself is common and not a problem. The difficulty arises, however, when adolescents become too involved emotionally with the "love object," perhaps to the point where sex interests are implicit in their affection. If the love object fails to recognize the amorous intentions of the adolescent, deeper frustrations resulting in more extreme behavior may set in. It is at this point that many youngsters are torn between their "love" for the individual and their "hatred" at his or her failure to see it and respond to it effectively. Such tensions may cause erratic behavior in school and at home. Girls with such problems are embarrassed to discuss them at home, fearing being labeled childish or immature.

One cannot ignore the fact that there is substantial evidence supporting the fact that many adolescent love relationships, crushes and otherwise, are legitimate. They necessitate careful consideration and understanding to avoid severe emotional harm to the adolescents involved.

A problem arising from being in love and going

steady is early marriage. Many adolescents get married within a couple of years after graduation from high school. Marriage between college students or living together is increasing at a surprising rate. Prolonged association with one person leads to sexual exploration. Sex "with a commitment" or "for love" is usually considered by young people to be justification for having sex. Many couples who are going steady end up getting married so that their child will have a name or making arrangements for the girl to have an abortion. Marriages on this basis are not solid and are a major cause for divorce among those who married during the adolescent years.

Although the healthy child has always realized that love and sexuality are related, adolescence is a time when this realization is brought most sharply into focus. Most older teenage boys believe that love and sex can be separated—an attitude that is carried often into adulthood. But middle teenagers, boys and girls alike, believe that one cannot exist without the other. They get crushes on each other. They are certain that they feel real love for each other. They feel strong desires to touch and excite one another.

The feelings of a teenage girl are further confused by the fact that society gives to her the responsibility of stopping the boy's advances; however, conformity and popularity are key reasons for girls conceding. Boys, even in the so-called "enlightened era," still have a tendency to distinguish between "good" and "bad" girls and to prefer "good" girls for marrying and "bad" girls for satisfying loneliness or lust. Thus no matter how strong the girl's love and desire may be, she has to face a barrage of fears. She has the fear of pregnancy, of being designated as "bad," of venereal disease, and of being considered everybody's pet but no-one's girl. She has, on the other hand, to face the fear of unpopularity if she is a "prude." The boy's fears are much the same. He may fear hurting the girl or causing her to become pregnant. He often fears his own sexual inadequacy or that the girl may expect him to go "farther" than he does.

CHILDBEARING IN ADOLESCENCE
Contributing factors

Speaking at a Symposium on Childbearing in Adolescence, Frederick Green, M.D.,[10] identi-

THE LAST PARTY   **M**y senior year of high school was my big year for friends and good times. Since we seniors had been together in high school for three years, we were fairly secure in our friendships and in our position in the school.

Of course, all good things must come to an end, and graduation ushered in the end for the group as a whole. Summer parties and Winston's swimming pool kept us together for a few final occasions. Jo Alice threw the last party at the end of the summer. A lot of drinking went on, and almost everyone there was drunk. Some of us managed to refrain from becoming inebriated and acted as baby-sitters for those who needed them. Both Randy and Winston were drunk and asleep on the floor. The others were scattered about the room talking or sleeping. Marvin was pretty drunk and his behavior became rather uninhibited. Usually he was careful about his actions and guarded himself against expressing any deep-seated feelings. He let himself go that night and shocked everyone when he made implicit passes at Randy and Winston and tried to get them into the back rooms. He didn't stop his advances until Jo Alice and I tore him away and asked him what he was trying to prove. At that point I guess he didn't care what he said. Marvin told us he was "different"; he didn't know why; all he knew was that he's always felt this way. He admitted he was a homosexual and that he was in love with Winston. He liked Randy but felt he wasn't his type, but that Winston was.

Randy and Winston were both too drunk to react one way or another to Marvin's advances, and they really did not realize what he was doing at the time. It wasn't until the next day that Randy and Winston shocked themselves into the realization that a good friend of theirs had actually made passes at them and was a real homosexual.

I was shocked and surprised, to say the least, since I had no clue of his being that type at all. But I was more angry by the entire group's reaction to Marvin's behavior. He was "queer" to them, and it was disgusting. No one wanted anything to do with Marvin because he was sick and abnormal. Now he had no friends to speak of. All of his activities and interests had been centered around the gang, and his friends were only those in our group. Marvin went from being a "big man"—popular, well-liked, and admired—to a sick, grotesque person no one wanted anything to do with.

---

fied factors contributing to the high risk of pregnancy for some adolescents. These include the collective preoccupation with sexuality in our society, familial patterns of adolescent parenthood, membership in a dysfunctional family, and the inadequate knowledge of or an inaccessibility to contraceptive measures. He noted exclusion from peers, unhappy teenage marriages, inescapable dependency on parents, unresolved sexual conflicts, increased medical risk, and limited parental competence in caring for the child as a few of the consequences of teenage parenthood. The effect of the termination of a pregnancy on the ability of adolescents to accomplish many of the developmental tasks is of increasing interest to researchers since many teenagers are using abortion as a method of birth control.

Virginia Abernethy[11] identifies psychological factors that underlie the predisposition to risk unwanted pregnancy. Factors such as self-esteem, feelings about each parent, and the parents' marriage appear to be related to the variables of sexual and contraceptive behavior. The absence of a feminine identification with a well-regarded mother is associated with low self-esteem. In keeping with her alienation from her mother, the high-risk individual is unlikely to have satisfying friendships with other women. A marriage in which parents are affectionate and close appears to facilitate the daughter's making a satisfactory identification with the mother, probably because the latter is seen as loved and loving and can thus be esteemed. An exceptionally disastrous parental marriage also appears to decrease the daughter's risk of unwanted pregnancy.

Percentages

Research by Zelnick and Kantner[12] indicates that the percentage of white teenage girls having premarital intercourse and getting pregnant has increased by one-third over a five-year period. The figures indicate that 37.2% of white teenage girls between 15 and 19 years of age in 1976 had engaged in premarital sex and about 10% of them got pregnant. In 1971, 26.3% of the girls in this category had premarital sex and a little over 6% got pregnant. The increase in pregnancy was in spite of "impressive improvement in contraceptive use." The percentage of black teenage girls between 15 and 19 having premarital intercourse was 64.3% in 1976 compared to 54.1% in 1971. The percentage getting pregnant remained rather stable at 25.4%. The percentage of white girls who had abortions rose from 33% to 45%. For black girls it rose from 5% to 8%. The study also revealed that four out of five pregnancies among teenagers were conceived out of wedlock. All but 7% of the babies born out of wedlock lived with their teenage mothers despite increasing emphasis to put them up for adoption or foster placement. If they had the baby, they kept it.

Use of contraceptives

The vast majority of pregnant unmarried teenagers use no method of contraception to prevent pregnancy. In a study of 502 patients aged 17 years or younger, unwed, never pregnant, and seeking birth control for the first time, Settlage

Baroff, and Cooper[13] indicated that most of the girls became sexually active by 15 or 16 years of age and three out of five had been having intercourse for more than a year. The decision to have intercourse was unrelated to contraception. A majority of teenagers in the study never used even those methods of birth control obtainable without medical assistance. The data suggest that contraceptive information and educational programs directed at minors will not be a significant factor in the decision to become sexually active. It has been our observation that when a teenager requests contraception, she is in great need of it, both in terms of prior onset of coital activity and the length of time she has been exposed to the risk of pregnancy. Access to effective medically supervised contraception and legal abortion is no more likely to encourage teenage promiscuity than the denial of access has been to discourage sexual activity.

Deliverers and aborters

Dr. Susan H. Fischman[14] states that an increasing number of teenagers in the United States are ignoring the availability of contraceptive services and legal abortion and are instead choosing to bear their illegitimate children. In Baltimore City, where illegitimate births account for nearly half of all deliveries, a study was undertaken to determine what characteristics distinguished teenage girls who chose to deliver from those who elected to abort. Of the 229 black unwed adolescents in the study group, 66% chose to have their baby. All were experiencing their first pregnancy.

The differences found between the deliverers and aborters challenged many generalizations that have been made in the past about girls pregnant out of wedlock. Contrary to expectations, the majority of the delivery group claimed to have satisfactory relationships with their mother and father, and revealed a high or medium self-esteem. The girl who had an abortion was more likely to reveal interpersonal difficulties with family members, and to score low on the self-esteem scale. Whereas many studies have frequently linked the absent father with the teenage childbearer, this study showed that half of both groups of girls reported their father out of the home. The deliverer's father, however, tended to be alive and living nearby, while the aborter claimed that her father was dead.

Distinct differences were noted between the two groups in schooling and relationships with boyfriends. In general, the deliverers had either discontinued school or were not on the appropriate grade level for their age, whereas the aborters were apt to be attending school and on grade level. The deliverers' boyfriends, who on the average were older than the boyfriends of the aborters, tended to be school dropouts, currently employed full time or seeking work, while the aborters' boyfriends were attending school either full or part time. In addition, most of the deliverers had longer, more stable relationships with their boyfriend and indicated that he would help to support the baby. The deliverers reported a significantly lower socioeconomic status, in that nearly half of the deliverers were supported by welfare compared to one out of four aborters. The mothers of the deliverers had completed less schooling than the aborters' mothers and, if employed, held a lower paying job.

In summary, compared to the aborter, the deliverer emerged as one with higher self-esteem, satisfactory family and boyfriend relationships, a poorer school record, and a lower socioeconomic household. These facts suggest that, within the milieu of poverty and inadequate education, childbearing may be deliberately sought by some girls as one of the few acceptable roles available to them. The findings of this study, although not generalizable to diverse populations, suggest that the prevention of adolescent pregnancy and childbearing requires a variety of health, educational, and social services. Foremost, however, it appears that keeping young girls and boys in school could effect a reduction in illegitimate births to teenagers.

The adolescent

It is evident that childbearing in adolescence has a great effect on the teenage girl's ability to achieve the developmental tasks of the period. A similar effect could be postulated for teenage boys, particularly those who assume responsibility for their part in the pregnancy. An adolescent father must work to support his growing family, necessitating absence from school. This results in the acceptance of unskilled jobs with little opportunity for development intellectually, economically, or socially. The necessity of parental financial and emotional assistance may be devastating for the teenager desiring independence. At best, childbearing and parenting in adolescence can be considered a maturing experience.

Preventing the crisis of childbearing in adolescence and dealing with the situation when it arises are interwoven processes. The latter may require changing the life-styles of individuals in certain groups—a monumental task not undertaken lightly. Adolescent parents have a great need for adequate health care. There is no typical childbearing adolescent. Adolescence is such a rapid period of transition that the individual maturity of each teenager must be considered. All persons requiring health services need understandable answers to their concerns and questions. They need to be educated so they can become full-fledged members of a team effort to assist them through their illness or crisis. They need to be treated with concern and respect. This is particularly true of the childbearing adolescent.

MATURING INTELLECTUAL OPERATIONS

Middle and late adolescence is a period of steady development in learning how to use the various intellectual functions. These include mental operations such as (1) cognitive thinking, involving discovery, recognition, or awareness of knowledge; (2) memory or the retention of what was cognized; (3) divergent thinking, the ability to produce a large variety of responses by moving apart from the usual opinions, attitudes, and thinking and to come up with new ideas; (4) convergent thinking, the ability to reason or use logic to arrive at the one best answer; and (5) evaluation, or assessment, of how adequate one's reasoning or conclusion is at that moment.[15] The capability to use abstract reasoning starts about the ages of 11 or 12 years. Early adolescence is a time when this capability emerges to a functional level. Middle adolescence is the period when this capability matures to its highest potentiality.

Harold Geyer

Maturing intellectual and perceptual abilities make it possible for late adolescents to do very intricate artistic or mechanical work.

Hopefully, the late adolescent learns how to use this potentiality.

Typical 15-year-olds can do rational, realistic thinking about themselves. They are mainly interested in the present, but they begin to think more about their future. After this age they become increasingly open-minded and liberal in their attitudes. They are largely responsible for determining their own behavior and are willing to assume responsibility for their actions. When necessary, they are able to compromise their intellectual behavior according to the challenges and demands of their life situation. However,

their collective cognitive ability to make good judgments and to have deep intellectual insights is limited by an inexperienced, underdeveloped, apperceptive mass of knowledge from which they can establish an adequate perspective concerning the problem they are seeking to solve. Their idealistic and pseudo-optimistic nature also distorts their perspective.

Mental characteristics

In any large group of adolescents there will be a wide distribution of mental ages. Among the general population of 15-year-olds, for example, almost 23% are likely to have a mental age between 14-6 and 15-11 years; 23%, a mental age between 13-8 and 14-6 years; 18%, a mental age between 16-0 and 17-6 years. About 2% would have a mental age under 10 years, and a little over 4%, a mental age above 19 years, with the rest of the group being distributed between these extremes.[16] Intellectual differences increase during adolescence as the experiences and environments of individuals become more diversified. Individual differences within any group of late adolescents, boys, girls, blacks, whites, Spanish-speaking, high or low socioeconomic level, are much greater than differences between groups.

At one time it was believed that young people stopped growing mentally at about 16 years of age. Now many authorities believe that individuals grow in certain aspects of intelligence beyond the age of 16 years. Intellectual growth is more a horizontal growth of potential ability than a vertical growth. Some kinds of mental ability increase more than others during the late adolescent years. For example, both boys and girls may be expected to increase in vocabulary. Boys generally show a greater increase in arithmetical scores than do girls. Both sexes show little or no increase in scores on items that primarily involve memory. By the age of 20 years the rate of growth on oral directions, dissected sentences, and arithmetic problems reaches a peak and does not decline until later. On common sense items, analogies, and numerical completions the peak of performance is reached before 20 years of age, whereas growth in vocabulary and general information continues to a slight degree well into the adult years.

Growth in mental abilities as measured by various intelligence tests is influenced by the kind and amount of schooling individuals have received, the nature of their work and other experiences, and the cultural content and reading level of the test. Those who leave school often lose the intellectual stimulation necessary for the full development of their mental ability, whereas those who continue their education in high school and college may realize undeveloped capacities.

Piaget's period of formal operations

Piaget's theory divides the intellectual development process into four main chronological periods, which are further divided into phases or stages. The order of succession of these steplike patterns is constant, although the ages at which different stages are attained may vary somewhat depending on the child's motivation, practice, and cultural differences. Also, as the child progresses from one stage to the next, early structures become integrated with later ones—they are interdependent and interactive. The first three periods were presented in earlier chapters.

The fourth broad period of cognitive development, known as the period of formal operations, begins early in adolescence (11 to 15 years of age) and it is during this period of development that Piaget characterizes individuals as living in both the present and the nonpresent. They are no longer merely concerned with the real but also are concerned with the possible. In committing themselves to possible outcomes of a situation, they think beyond the present. In other words "the adolescent begins to build systems or theories, whereas the child does not theorize or build systems."

It is during this period of development that they become capable of scientific reasoning and of formal logic in verbal argument; moreover, they reflect about, evaluate and criticize the logic and quality of their own thinking. They do not need to center their attention on the immediate situation. They can imagine what might be possible and can consider hypotheses that may or may not be true; they can consider also what would follow if they were true. As they approach 15 years of age, they are able to use formal logic in an adult manner, and when this is possible, Piaget asserts that they have reached the critical stage of intellectual development. From now on learning how to use the tools of logic and frequent practice in their usage will be necessary to enable individuals to function well within their level of potentiality. Use of the tool provides horizontal growth of intellect.

EMOTIONALITY

If children received abundant love and patient understanding during infancy and early childhood, if the imposition of societal demands reflected an understanding by parents of individual patterns of readiness, and if occasional regressions were accepted as merely a part of growing

Baking cakes and making fudge with friends allows for social interaction while developing cognitive skills, especially if imagination and creativity are used.

David Strickler

up and as inevitable, at adolescence there is usually a minimal amount of difficulty and strain in coping with the problems and conflicts of this stage. On the other hand, children who have been the object of parental rejection, overdominance, or overindulgence are likely to experience an unusually stormy adolescence. Achievement of independence and emotional maturity is hampered by excesses in parental domination, friction between the parents, sibling rivalry, and an unwillingness on the part of the parents to allow adolescents to share in decisions that affect the family.[17]

Emotional characteristics

The older adolescent experiences similar emotions as the child and early adolescent. The differences deal with the amount, intensity, types of responses, and types of stimuli that create the emotions of the late adolescent.

Anger. Anger is the major disruptive emotion found in later adolescence. Moodiness is the most common nondisruptive emotion. The most common causes of anger are restraints on the adolescent's desire to do something and interruption of activities that have become routine for the adolescent. Environment is the major stimulus for anger. If the environment of later adolescents prohibits their desires, anger will usually result. Girls respond more often and more violently to social situations than do boys.

The childish responses to anger of hurting, biting, and throwing objects are no longer found. Name calling and verbal responses are the most common responses of anger in later adolescence.[18] The duration of anger is longer because older adolescents attempt to conceal their anger, thus making it last longer.

Jealousy. Jealousy displays itself in heterosexual situations in later adolescence more than in any other way. Toward the end of adolescence, interests change from a general regard for members of the opposite sex to one specific person of the opposite sex. In this situation jealousy arises when one member, or both, feels that the other is cheating in their relationship.

Envy. Material possessions and social status have a strong appeal to the later adolescent. Leadership and social status are closely related,

and the older adolescent is envious of persons who possess these two items. Most adolescents seek jobs to acquire material goods, but some resort to shoplifting and stealing as their means of achieving social equality with others. The cause of much juvenile delinquency is envy of the possessions of others more fortunate than the delinquent.

Happiness. Happiness comes from four situations. If the adolescent is able to feel at ease in a situation, contentment will usually follow. The adolescent must also be able to understand the comic parts, the humorous aspects of a situation. When the later adolescent has achieved superiority over others, happiness and pride are the result. Finally, situations are needed where the adolescent can release stored-up emotional energy.

Affection. Later adolescence is a period of intense affection because the individuals are concentrating their affection on one member of the opposite sex or on a small group of friends. Generally, if the individuals are well adjusted, this display of affection will be directed toward a member of the opposite sex.

Fear and worry. Fear is less recognizable in later adolescence than it was in the previous period. Fear of social situations, environment, and people is no longer a problem. Adolescents are capable of avoiding embarrassing situations by planning activities that will enable them to avoid these situations.

In later adolescence worries take the form of imaginary fears. Feelings of inadequacy are an extremely common occurrence. Problems related to money, jobs, the use of the automobile, physical appearance, social acceptability, sex, and marriage are also causes of worry.

Emotional maturity. Individuals have achieved emotional maturity when they are capable of controlling their emotions until a socially proper time and place are available for them to "let off" their feelings. Emotionally mature individuals are capable of ignoring stimuli that as children they would have reacted to emotionally. Heightened emotionality, when expressed, reflects itself through feelings of insecurity, tension, indecision, and exaggerated or sometimes irrational behavior.

Self-identity

Early in the adolescent period growing children begin to realize that they are individuals and not simply extensions of their parents. It is at this point that they want to know "Who am I?" This drive for self-assertion becomes one of the prime motivating forces during this period.[19] It is a struggle against "getting lost" and feeling like a stranger to oneself. By the time individuals are ready to leave later adolescence they have probably developed their sense of personal identity and now know who they are. The struggle to find this identity can be a difficult one.

Adolescents achieve their self-identity through their self-concept. The self-concept is developed as they confront the world and gain an impression of it. They must relate the world to themselves and themselves to it. At this time they are greatly concerned with their own personal worth. In their struggle to find themselves they are afraid that they cannot live up to their own expectations. They may ask "Am I good enough, smart enough, or popular enough?"

NEED FOR A VALUE JUDGMENT SYSTEM

Changing times bring changes in attitudes and in people's beliefs as to what is and what is not important. An activity or a point of view acceptable to one generation may not be equally acceptable to another. It is often difficult for one generation to appreciate the point of view of another generation. It is important for young people to know the effect of given attitudes or values on themselves and on others. It is also important to know ways and means of developing "good" attitudes and of discouraging "bad" ones. The development of a value judgment system is basic not only because of its moral and ethical implications but also because of its influence on the decision-making process.

Value judgment system

A value judgment system consists of individuals' beliefs, values, and attitudes that reflect their views and opinions of what is good or bad, desirable or undesirable, important or unimportant, right or wrong, valuable or not valuable, and that influence their emotional and rational thought processes in the making of decisions and choices. The development of a value judgment system begins when children learn to inhibit or to direct their behavior according to the wishes of others. It does not become mature until, as adults, they have overcome external domination of their behavioral and judgmental processes.

Environmental factors such as the peer group, parents, institutions, vicarious experiences, and prevailing social attitudes as revealed by communications media are important in shaping an adolescent's attitudes. Of these, peer group and parental influences and dominant social beliefs are the most significant. In general, adolescents will tend to be readily influenced by those individuals they like or love and by those who possess some attributes or skills that they admire.

Moral and spiritual growth

During adolescence a serious questioning of the moral code begins. Often these codes are questioned as a result of discovering that adults, frequently parents, verbally ascribe to a code but do not adhere to it.

One aspect of morality involves a recognition of the consequences of behavior and the way it affects others. At this stage adolescents begin to do logic and reasoning. They search themselves and their beliefs. They decide which part of society's moral code is applicable to them in their relationship to others. There is always concern by adults about the lack of morality among the young. There is no need for excessive alarm. Many of the problems of moral behavior in adolescents come from developmental changes in perception and insight. Most, although not all, adolescents recognize their inept behavior and seek to make adjustments. Many will need a point of reference from which they can begin to restructure their moral thinking.

There is a lack of attendance at church. This may be due to their questioning of all authority, including church, to the beginning of a period of investigating religion anew as a possible source of emotional and intellectual satisfaction, to hesitancy of being associated with any pious group or members of the "establishment," or to their busy social calendar.

However, most adolescents are idealistic and basically good. Informal prayer is used frequently by adolescents. The modern adolescent wants to find meaning in life. In spite of a small minority of highly verbal cynics, religion continues to play a part in human existence and is of special value during the adolescent years in formulating ideals and standards of conduct. All churches and moral groups must attempt to meet the needs of the young who really seek a philosophy of life.

In general, adolescents acquire religious attitudes and ideas much as they acquire other types of attitudes and ideas. If the importance of religion and morality is stressed in the daily environment and if it is presented in such a manner that it meets adolescents' needs, religion and morality are likely to be important forces in their lives. If, on the other hand, religion and morality are presented in such a manner that they are foreign to the needs and aspirations of adolescents, if they are harsh and unreasonable, or if they are ignored by the parents, individuals are likely to reject them or to set them aside as much as they possibly can.

Adolescents who have accepted the religious and moral beliefs of their parents in early years may face fear and guilt feelings if they find their beliefs and attitudes changing. It becomes particularly difficult for adolescents to make an adjustment when they first encounter conflicting points of view toward religion and moral behavior, unless they have been so completely indoctrinated that they are unwilling to consider varying points of view. The longer children have retained their beliefs in religion and morality, the less likely they are to change. A completely new environment providing points of view that are entirely different from those that they had in the past may bring about changes in the individual.

Colleges have been pointed to as a source of changes in religious attitudes. The evidence indicating that students become more liberal in their beliefs and attitudes about religion is inconclusive when related to all colleges, however. It is not possible to evaluate the contributions of schools, churches, and other forces outside the home on the moral development of adolescents, but each contact may contribute to their moral development. A religious worker told us recently, "My own experience with adolescents and church has seemed to indicate that young people admit they need God, as we all do, but they are not so certain that they can find Him in formal public worship. It is our task to make them feel a part of our religious community and to make morality meaningful to them especially through our example."

PROBLEMS OF MIDDLE ADOLESCENCE

Middle and later adolescents are still in the process of establishing a new life-style and of learning the basic skills and information related to their new pattern of living. Problems, worries, and concerns are to be expected. The intensity of the concerns will be in keeping with the adequacy of the adjustment pattern that the adolescent will have developed in the past. Problem areas include home and family relations, peer status and social development in general, educational planning, adjustment and achievement, emotional stability and personality factors, physical adjustment and sexual maturity, and self-identity, value judgment, and life existence concerns. Inasmuch as some of these problem areas have been discussed in other sections in this chapter, more attention will be given to related areas (Table 11-4).

Delinquency and youth

Aggressive, destructive, and antisocial behavior is characteristically a behavior of youth rather than adulthood. The incidence of delinquency rises slowly during the early teens. It gathers momentum at the ages of 14 and 15 years and climbs precipitously until the age of 19 years. During the early twenties the rate of delinquency still increases but at a slower rate. The peak of delinquent and criminal incidence is reached by the age of 25 years and declines rapidly thereafter.[20] To view the problem of adolescent delinquency in its proper perspective one must keep in mind that only a small percentage, perhaps less than 5% of all adolescents, ever are legally classified as delinquents. Few aggressive or destructive acts result in apprehension, formal arrest, and prosecution. Some forms of antisocial behavior violate no existing statutes. The actual

Table 11-4. Person whom adolescent would rely upon for advice and guidance*

Type of problem	Person relied upon							
	Friends (%)	Mother (%)	Father (%)	Siblings (%)	Teacher (%)	Guidance counselor (%)	Other (%)	Total N
School grades								
U.S.	3	15	5	2	43	31	1	(1,057)
Denmark	6	25	19	3	42		5	(955)
Career plans								
U.S.	4	23	17	3	3	46	4	(1,053)
Denmark	4	23	53	2	8		10	(947)
College								
U.S.	3	15	15	2	10	52	3	(994)
Denmark	8	18	28	2	38		6	(846)
Personal problems with parents								
U.S.	25	20	7	16	2	6	24	(1,042)
Denmark	28	26	9	30	3		4	(912)
Personal problems not involving parents								
U.S.	33	32	10	10	2	3	10	(1,032)
Denmark	49	26	7	13	2		3	(923)
Morals and values								
U.S.	17	39	12	6	3	2	21	(1,008)
Denmark	49	22	12	9	5		3	(911)
Dating								
U.S.	35	36	13	11		1	4	(1,027)
Denmark	47	33	7	9			4	(926)
What clothing to buy								
U.S.	30	51	6	9			4	(1,018)
Denmark	20	61	6	8			5	(936)
Choice of friends								
U.S.	30	40	10	10	1	1	8	(972)
Denmark	31	27	11	25			6	(861)
What books to read								
U.S.	27	10	4	5	48	3	3	(999)
Denmark	52	7	15	10	14		2	(904)

Note: All differences between United States and Denmark for each problem significant at .001 level (chi-square test).
*From Kandel, D. B., & Lesser, G. S. *Youth in two worlds.* San Francisco: Jossey-Bass, 1972, p. 119. Reprinted by permission.

amount of delinquency among adolescents may never be completely known.

The probability of delinquency occurring during adolescence is much greater if there is a childhood history of antisocial behavior. In fact, approximately two thirds of adolescent delinquents begin their delinquent careers in preadolescence.[21] The adolescent period is characteristically associated with a more regular, serious, and organized kind of delinquency. Greater freedom of movement and less adult supervision during adolescence also make delinquent behavior more possible.

More important perhaps than greater opportunity and capacity for executing delinquent acts are the developmental task pressures, antiauthority responses, aggressive attitudes, and peer group sanctions that exist during adolescence.

Table 11-5. Comparison between street gang members and nonmembers regarding antisocial and illegal acts they were forced to commit by gangs*

Item	Gang (%)	Non-gang (%)
Stay out all night long	17	16
Cause trouble in neighborhood	21	13
Call police names	22	14
Get drunk	32	16
Bother grown-ups	15	10
Fight	44	21
Get a weapon or hide a weapon	29	12
Stab someone or injure someone with a weapon	22	10
Shoot at someone	25	9
Take heroin, "scag," or "smack"	7	8
Have sex with a girl	38	14
Have sex with other guys	4	3
Steal	27	13
Fight at school	38	18
Skip homework	25	9
Take pot, grass, reefers, hash, or marijuana	20	15
Stay away from school	24	13
"Shake down" other guys	24	33
Take speed or meth or methedrine	7	6
Break up parties	26	9
Destroy public property	20	12
Mark or spray paint on walls	30	15

*Adapted from Friedman, C. J., et al. Juvenile street gangs: the victimization of youth. *Adolescence*, 1976, **11,** 527-533.

Prolonged status deprivation superimposed on other psychosocial and psychobiological problems increases emotional instability and lowers the threshold for aggressive behavior.

Important differences exist between boys and girls in the incidence, age of onset, etiology, and kind of delinquency practiced. Four to seven times as many boys as girls become delinquent, but the ratio of boys to girls has shown a steady decline over the past fifty years.[22] Boys also become involved in delinquency at an earlier age than girls. This difference is partly due to the greater supervision to which younger adolescent girls are subjected and partly to the fact that sex offenses, which constitute the most frequent category of delinquency among girls, do not occur until an older age. However, if these differences between boys and girls are environmentally determined and reflect cultural attitudes toward male and female sex roles, the difference in age of onset of delinquency can be expected to become increasingly less pronounced in the future.

Sex differences in the kinds of offenses committed are striking. Stealing, mischief, traffic violations, truancy, auto thefts, and running away from home are the major misdemeanors of adolescent boys. Delinquent girls, on the other hand, are most frequently charged with ungovernability, sex offenses, and leaving home.[23] Table 11-5 presents some activities of gangs.

Personal problems of adolescents

The following statements are taken from unpublished research conducted by the authors in which over 1,000 adolescents between 15 and 18 years were sampled.

Male, 15 years, ninth grade

I have trouble with algebra. I don't see why anyone has to take algebra unless they want to be a doctor or an engineer. It's just silly junk. My mother took algebra and it didn't help her. I think I should learn more about how to write a check, how to use interest, and other useful studies.

Female, 15 years, tenth grade

My home is my problem, especially my father. I had to leave my home last year because he beat me and was always threatening me. He has always abused me.

Female, 15 years, eleventh grade

I'm in love! It's real, too! The boy I'm in love with loves me just as much. He's in the service. Every once in a while he gets a weekend pass and comes home. We don't see each other very often and that's really hard when you're in love. We always try to squeeze so much into one evening that things start to happen. We're neither one that kind of person. We just can't help ourselves. So far

Adolescence is a time of uncertainty, with many questions to be answered and many problems to be solved.

David Strickler

we've been able to stop before it goes too far. What can we do to keep even this little bit from taking place? It's not what we want, it just happens.

Male, 16 years, eleventh grade

My trouble is money. I have a job and work five nights a week, 4 to 12 o'clock. My parents have very little money so I don't like to ask them for any. But my parents don't want me to work so long. They'd rather I spend more time on my schoolwork.

Male, 16 years, eleventh grade

I seem to find it very hard to get my parents to understand that I have somewhat of a life of my own. They can't understand that I have also grown in age and maturity. They still want me to abide by the privileges they granted me at age 13.

Female, 16 years, eleventh grade

My problem is that I have a very bad inferiority complex. I feel that people are talking about me. When I'm with a group, I hardly know what to say. When I leave the group I get the feeling that they talk about me and don't want me.

Male, 16 years, eleventh grade

I have a slight amount of trouble with my mother. It bothers me because I don't want to make her unhappy. I realize she has done many things for me and I want to repay her.

Male, 17 years, twelfth grade

Although my parents treat me exceptionally well as far as material things are concerned, I would sooner have a little less of these things and a little more understanding.

Female, 17 years, twelfth grade

My parents object to my marriage to a boy of a different race. Why should they object when the boy and girl are willing to give up certain things for each other and are sure they can make it work?

Female, 17 years, twelfth grade

Right now I have the problem that I have applied for admission to a very fine college to further my education. However, I wonder sometimes if I really want to go to college. My parents say it is up to me.

Female, 17 years, twelfth grade

I have gone with a fellow for about two years but we have just recently broken up. I can see him going deeper and deeper on drugs and he won't stop. I still want him, but not that way.

Female, 17 years, twelfth grade

I have been planning to be married in July but the boy is of a different religion than me and is quite a few years older. He is in the Army. My parents don't think it would be good to marry him. I don't agree because he can be depended upon; he is thoughtful and kind and loves me a lot. I'm looking forward to marriage. But there's going to be some trouble because a boy I haven't seen for two years who has been in Germany is coming back. He knows I'm to be married but he says he still loves me.

Female, 18 years, twelfth grade

I have a problem. My mother and father are separated and getting a divorce. I don't know who to go with if I were asked to pick my home.

Male, 18 years, twelfth grade

Do you think it is right to always ask Mom or Dad for some cash to spend if you never stay home in evenings to be with them? I usually come in at all hours of the night and a word has never been said. Do you think that your parents should worry?

Male, 18 years, twelfth grade

With my senior year drawing to a close it won't be long until I will be going away to college. It bothers me to realize that I will be leaving my family and that I will have to depend upon myself.

ADOLESCENCE IN DISADVANTAGED ENVIRONMENTS
Poverty

Between 15% and 20% of the population of the United States is classified, by federal definition, to be living on the poverty level. Often they are members of a minority group or immigrants who have recently migrated to large northern metropolitan areas. The majority of the urban poor live in highly concentrated depressed areas within large cities. However, there is a large segment of economic and socially disadvantaged families who live in rural areas, geographically isolated parts of the country, such as mountain land or on reservations. For the most part the disadvantaged comprise the economic underworld of American life, including the unemployed, the underemployed, the blue collar workers, the minorities, and the aged. This is the segment of the American population that has been isolated and removed from the mainstream of American life by various processes, not the least of which is the mass exodus of the middle class to the sanctity of suburbia. Although not as obvious as in previous decades, this hidden portion of American society still suffers the ravages of poor housing, inadequate nutrition, overcrowding, lack of sanitation, and other forms of social and cultural deprivation.

Because the large majority of the disadvantaged class is made up of sporadic laborers, crop followers, and reliefers, there is a tendency for the mainstream of society to look down on these people. Parents in this group are likely to be passive and fatalistic about their status. In general, they work sporadically, move frequently, and live in the poorest dwellings. Because of the meager and often nonexistent earnings of the fathers, the mothers often work as domestics to supplement the family income. Although there is an average of five children per mother, more than half of the homes are broken by separation, desertion, or death. Due to the instability of marriage, common-law marriages and mutual agreement living situations are increasing in number—the poor cannot afford the cost of a divorce.

Family structure

Perhaps an extreme but realistic study of the lower class social structure is characterized by the deterioration of the black family. The statistical data surrounding the family structure of black society is overwhelming. Nearly one third of the black women living in large metropolitan areas who have ever been married are divorced, separated, or living apart from their husbands. In 1964 over one fourth of all black births were illegitimate. An offshoot of this disproportionately high divorce, separation, and desertion rate is the fact that only a minority of black children reach the age of 18 years having lived all their lives with both parents.[24]

In general terms the black family has the largest number of children and the lowest net income; consequently, many black fathers cannot support their families. The only solutions rest in either the mother going to work or the family applying for welfare assistance. Should the mother choose to work, the dependence on her income tends to undermine the position of the father and deprives the children of maternal attention and care. Should the family apply for welfare assistance, in most cases the father will undergo serious feelings of inadequacy. Also, in view of current welfare rulings, the family can obtain increased aid if the father is not in the home but is receiving separate aid. Thus the family structure is torn apart for the family to seek out a meager subsistence.

Perhaps the individual who suffers the most severe consequences of this disorganization of the basic family structure is the child. Since the discipline and authority of the father figure is lacking in over one third of the families of the lower echelon of society, the process of young males identifying with their fathers as strong figures so necessary in sex typing is forestalled. Often the mother, who heads the family, is forced to neglect the children, since she must earn their living.

Growing up in a family lacking strong traditions and consistent discipline will often produce a child who lacks strong goals for himself and may be characterized as aimless and unambitious. Often the child who has not learned consistent standards of behavior in the home will turn to the streets because there he can find meaning that appears to be consistent and obviously related to his way of life. Since disorganized families tend to be concentrated in the least desirable sections of any city, the codes of conduct that are offered to the child by the street-corner gang are likely to be at best socially disapproved and at worst blatantly antisocial.

Social groups

During adolescence, social groups such as cliques, crowds, or gangs will be formed. Cliques are small, closely knit groups based on clannishness and exclusion. Crowds are looser, somewhat less personal groups. Gangs, however, have a membership that is highly organized and usually arise out of conflict and outside pressures that bring the members together for mutual assistance and support. They are most frequently found among immigrant groups and in neighborhoods where there are racial or ethnic tensions.

Although some gangs are benign, a number

appear to be breeding grounds for juvenile de-linquency. The gang member finds the gang a proving ground, a need-fulfilling but fear-inspiring stage on which to strut his nascent manhood and prove his emancipation. The gang sets tasks and standards which he must meet, and there is always the fear that he may not meet these standards, that he may fail the test of gang membership and acceptance. This is especially significant with the disadvantaged adolescent. The motivation to pursue the delinquent act is bolstered by pressure to achieve those things that are of greatest value to the peer or reference groups of the delinquent, rather than by rebellious elements within his personality organization. The compelling elements of gang motivation appear to be adherence to group standards of excitement, toughness, and smartness.

Dropouts

Another segment of disadvantaged adolescents is the school dropout, or as the case may be, the "shove out." But who are the dropouts? They are more frequently males than females. They are young people who have usually endured environmental, social, and personal liabilities that affected their chances to compete equally with others in most phases of life. Most dropouts quit in the tenth grade because this is the transition grade from junior high school to senior high school, and they generally have reached the age whereby they can legally separate from school. Some of the major factors involved in the dropout problem are reading retardation, grade retention, low intelligence, negative self-images, and poor family attitudes. It should be emphasized that the dropout is not synonymous with the juvenile delinquent.

Several generalizations may be made concerning the disadvantaged adolescent. In general he has received inadequate nurturing during his early childhood. He is likely to lack ego skills, to have an extremely poor self-image, and to see the world as a pervasively hostile, inconsistent environment. Although disadvantaged individuals share many of the dominant or conventional values of society, they also show more acceptance of certain unconventional or different values. The value structure of the lower class

differs in many ways from that of the middle class, and the child will be affected by these differences. Immediate, extrinsic values such as a big car or flashy clothes are frequently more sought after than are delayed, intrinsic values such as those that are brought about by schooling or long effort.

THE YOUTH MARKET

The youth market has emerged as a powerful influence on national economy in the United States. The purchasing power of young people is felt not only through their direct purchases but also through a significant influence on family purchases.

Significance of youth market

Recognition that teenagers constitute a separate market segment has occurred during the last twenty-five years. Prior to this time there was a children's market and an adult market; youth was not recognized as a separate market. Even the word, *teenager,* was not in the dictionary. The marketers classified teenagers either as children or as adults, using some age, such as 15 or 16 years, as the dividing line. By the early 1950s most marketers realized that teenagers were a distinct market segment and that they had their own social rules and their own patterns of buying behavior, as well as product and brand preferences. Furthermore, the teenage peer group exerted strong influences on individual buying decisions.[25]

The growth of the youth market is significant. It was estimated that during 1959 there were 18 million teenagers who spent an average of $555 a year each for goods and services, not including the necessities normally supplied by their families. In 1965 there were approximately 20 million teenagers who spent $10 billion. Girls averaged $9.53 per week, and boys averaged $10.25 per week. In 1967 the teenage population was still increasing, and the annual income of boys and girls in the 13- to 19-year-old group was estimated at around $600 overall. In 1968 there were 28 million teenagers who spent $20 billion for an average of $714 each for the year. In 1969 teenagers spent about $22 billion.[26] One marketer estimates that the population for the age group of 10

Everybody wants to be "number one." Group reaction and peer fashions make the youth market a lucrative one.

to 19 years will increase to over 53 million by 1990. This group includes the teenagers plus what many people call the preteen group.

Teenage purchases

The teenager buys many items and services, but the most common purchases are records, cameras, cosmetics, cars, soft drinks, wristwatches, and clothing. *Sponsor*[27] magazine said that some of the teenage buying statistics were as follows:

Teens account for 81 percent of all phonograph records, 55 percent of all soft drinks, 53 percent of all movie tickets and 20 percent of all potato chip consumption. Teenage girls account for 23 percent of all cosmetic expenditures and 22 percent of all women's apparel sales. Teenage boys account for 40 percent of all men's slacks and 33 percent of all men's sweater sales.*

It is also estimated that teenagers buy 24% of the nation's wristwatches, 30% of its low-priced cameras, 45% of its soft drinks, and have a significant say in another $30 billion in family purchases.

In addition to the preceding items, teenagers have been buying more and more appliances such as tape recorders, radios, television sets, and hairsetters. Housewares have also taken on increasing importance because many teenagers are becoming engaged or married. In 1966 it was estimated that 800,000 girls would be engaged and over half of the women under the age of 20 years would become housewives before reaching that age.[28]

STUDY GUIDE

1. Review the developmental tasks of middle and later adolescence.
2. Physical development is nearly complete during this period. Give a thumbnail sketch of the physical characteristics of late adolescents.
3. Study the section discussing control as opposed to autonomy in parent-child relationships. What do you think this study says as to how parents should treat, raise, or consider their adolescent children?
4. Remember the first time you became inter-

ested in someone of the opposite sex? The second time you did? The third time . . . ? How did your experiences fit in with peer group heterosexual behavior and the sequential pattern of dating as presented in this book?
5. Do the statistics and information on child-bearing adolescents seem realistic to you?
6. What are some of the mental characteristics of this age level? How do they reflect the cognitive characteristics of Piaget's period of normal operations?
7. Define "self-identity." Has this ever been a problem for you? Is it a problem now? Will self-identity ever be recognized and defined to a point where the individual will never have to change his self-concept or identity again?
8. In your opinion is the need for the development of a value judgment system by late adolescents as crucial as the authors seem to be suggesting? Could this value judgment system be developed later with no harm done? Need it be developed at all?
9. There have been some changes for the better occurring in many so-called disadvantaged neighborhoods and communities. From your vantage point in time, what do you see happening to the ghetto black, the poor white, the rural poor, the Chicano, the Spanish-speaking Easterners, and the migrant workers? Have conditions changed "all that much" since the civil rights movement started in the middle 1950s? Does each generation require a new effort, bringing with it new problems?
10. What was your allowance when you were a kid? Did you even have one? What did you buy with your money?

REFERENCES

1. Latham, H. C., Heckel, R. V., Herbert, L. J., & Bennett, E. *Pediatric nursing* (3rd ed.). St. Louis: The C. V. Mosby Co., 1977.
2. Ingalls, A. J., & Salerno, M. C. *Maternal and child health nursing* (3rd ed.). St. Louis: The C. V. Mosby Co., 1975.
3. Conger, J. J. *Adolescence and youth: psychological development in a changing world* (2nd ed.). New York: Harper & Row, Publishers, 1977.
4. Rice, F. P. *The adolescent: development relation-*

*From The U.S. teen market, *Sponsor*, 1968, **22**, 25-26.

ships and culture (2nd ed.). Boston: Allyn & Bacon, Inc., 1978.

5. Baumrind, D. Current patterns of parental authority. *Developmental Psychology Monograph,* 1971, **4** (i, pt. 2).

6. Elder, G. H. Jr. Parent-youth relations in cross-national perspective. *Social Science Quarterly,* 1968, **49,** 216-228.

7. Kaluger, G. *Dating practices of 152 adolescents from communities of varying populations.* Shippensburg, Pa.: Unpublished research, April, 1978.

8. Place, D. M. The dating experience for adolescent girls. *Adolescence,* 1975, **10,** 157-174.

9. Leidy, T. R. & Starry, A. P. The American adolescent: a bewildering amalgam. *National Education Association Journal,* 1967, **5,** 11.

10. Green, F. Factors contributing to the high risk of pregnancy for adolescents. *Symposium on Childbearing in Adolescence,* Washington, D.C., 1974.

11. Abernethy, V. Illegitimate conception among teenagers. *American Journal of Public Health,* 1974, **64**(7), 662-665.

12. Zelnick, M., & Kantner, J. Teenage sex and pregnancy, *Family Planning Perspectives,* 1977, **9,** 102-116.

13. Settlage, C. F., Baroff, R., & Cooper, A. Adolescence and social change. *Journal of the American Academy of Child Psychiatry,* 1970, **9,** 205-215.

14. Fischman, S. H. Characteristics associated with pregnancy resolution decisions of unwed adolescents. *Symposium on Childbearing in Adolescence,* Washington, D.C., 1974.

15. Guilford, J. P. *The nature of intelligence.* New York: McGraw-Hill Book Co., 1967.

16. Terman, L. M., & Merrill, M. A. *Standford-Binet intelligence scale: manual* (3rd ed.). Boston: Houghton Mifflin Co., 1960.

17. Balswick, J. O., & Macrides, C. Parental stimulus for adolescent rebellion. *Adolescence,* 1975, **10,** 253-266.

18. Miller, D. *Adolescence.* New York: Jason Aronson, 1974.

19. Wittenberg, R. M. *The troubled generation.* New York: Association Press, 1967, p. 89.

20. Conger, J. J., & Miller, W. E. *Personality, social class and delinquency.* New York: John Wiley & Sons, Inc., 1966, p. 4.

21. Kvaraceus, W. C. *Anxious youth: dynamics of delinquency.* Columbus, Ohio: Charles E. Merrill Publishing Co., 1966.

22. Glaser, D. Social disorganization and delinquent subcultures. In H. C. Quay (Ed.), *Juvenile delinquency.* New York: D. Van Nostrand Co., Inc., 1965, pp. 30-36.

23. Gold, M. Juvenile delinquency as a symptom of alienation. *Journal of Social Issues,* 1969, **25,** 130.

24. United States Department of Labor. *The case for national action; the Negro family.* Washington, D.C.: Office of Planning and Research, Government Printing Office, 1965, pp. 5-27.

25. Cundeff, E. W., & Still, R. R. *Basic marketing: concepts, environment and decisions.* Englewood Cliffs, N.J.: Prentice-Hall, Inc., 1964, p. 28.

26. Teen spending still soaring, Rand Bureau says: per capita youth cigarette spending wanes. *Advertising Age,* 1970, **41,** 67.

27. The U.S. teen market. *Sponsor,* 1968, **22,** 25-26.

28. MacLoed, A. I am curious (teen-ager) should be the marketer's motto. *Media/Scope,* 1969, **13,** 33-34.

12 Emerging adulthood

The awakening years

IDENTITY CRISIS

A teenager who rebels against his parents and the establishment and ventures out to find his own values is a familiar story. That is, it seems familiar and run-of-the-mill until it happens to someone you know well. Then all at once the little pat answers and simple solutions that should work fall apart.

When I first met Paul, he was a typical fifteen-year-old high school student. He was popular with both boys and girls; he was interested in sports and was an active participant. He didn't particularly enjoy school. Thinking back, I believe he was about the same as I was when I was in school. But I was to see differences occur only two years later.

Most adolescents, as they mature, begin to think about their future. But this is where Paul differed. He did nothing to prepare for his future. He was not thinking of an occupation, considering colleges, or doing any of those things that one normally expects of a high school senior. He also refused to assume any responsibilities at home. He made little contribution to the family and took for granted everything that was done or given to him. He did not try very hard to find a job to help earn spending money. His grades, instead of improving, became steadily worse.

He assumed that he would get to go to college, although he didn't know what his major would be. He could decide that later. As for getting accepted, there was no problem. He was quite good in track—he had even gone to the state championships. Paul figured this would be enough to have a college grab him.

To his dismay, Paul soon learned that more was needed for college than to be good in track and have a recommendation from the coach. He did not get accepted to the schools he had wanted. This unexpected rejection disturbed him and affected his behavior. During his last semester in high school he began to display an open, defiant "I don't care" attitude. He gave up many of his interests and values at this time, even to the extent of quitting the track team. Because the establishment had hurt Paul by saying, in effect, that he wasn't good enough, he took refuge in deviant behavior and ideas. He let his hair grow longer, wore wild clothes, and subscribed to the philosophy of "Peace, Love, and Brotherhood." He began to associate with like-minded individuals.

As his new friends became all-important, his family became increasingly less so. Although he was extremely concerned with showing love for his fellow man, the sincerity of this belief was not apparent from his actions toward his family. He treated them with actions that ranged from indifference to contempt.

Paul claimed to be finding himself as an "individual"; instead, he was becoming more like his friends. He was still too confused and insecure to be actually on his own. He needed others who were like himself to give him a feeling of security and acceptance. So, although he was different from the "establishment," he was just conforming to the ways of his friends.

But even as confused and dejected as he was, the summer after he graduated from high school he decided that he would go to college. Apparently, he still had the desire to do something and to succeed. He also got a summer job, a sports car, and seemed to be becoming a working member of the establishment. Soon, however, he began thinking of working and going to school every day as a "real drag." He changed his mind about attending college. He also thought of his living at home as being unbearable to his independence, although very few restrictions were forced upon him. He made plans to move in with some of his friends.

Also showing his confusion were the many contradictions to his "back-to-nature" philosophy. He kept saying he wanted to do away with luxuries and go back to the simple things. But, on the other hand, he bought a little yellow Triumph sports car, electric guitars and amplifiers, and a good stereo system. When he decided to go to a dance, he bought a flashy knit jump suit.

I don't believe Paul is intentionally being different or difficult, but he is confused. This confusion is manifested in many young people. Most of them have been brought up on traditional values, concepts, and goals, but they cannot see how they can work in today's world. So they claim to disown them while still trying to attain them, although in a different way and under different titles. This, I believe, is what has happened in Paul's case. He has not found himself or a value system he can accept. To keep from having to face this identity problem, he has taken shelter in a new look that seemingly rejects the values of the past while claiming to expound the true "basics" of life.

Paul is still lost.

Society in America changed its concept of "when a person becomes an adult" when legislation was passed granting 18-year-olds the right to vote. Before that time the age of 21 years was considered to be the time when a person "legally" became an adult. Laws, however, cannot dictate or change developmental patterns decreed by nature. The question still remains, "Developmentally, when does a person become an adult?"

THE AGE LEVEL

The terms late adolescence, postadolescence, and young adulthood are used by developmental psychologists to indicate the age range of 18 to 21 or 22 years of age. Labels (terms) as they are applied to human beings are seldom satisfactory categorical descriptive devices because there are so many exceptions to the rule. In adulthood, in particular, it is better to describe developmental stages by a criterion rather than by a label, phrase, or certain age.

The late adolescent is in the final stages of making the transition from being a teenager to being an adult. This individual will have some adultlike characteristics but not all of them. There will also be some characteristics that are peculiar to the 18- to 22-year age level. A general criterion for suggesting when an individual is more of an adult than a late adolescent would be that point in time when an individual assumes the role of an adult by taking on the responsibilities, obligations, and characteristics of adulthood.

Specifically, adulthood is attained when an individual achieves a competent level of emotional, social, and economic independence, establishes a career or family pattern, and maintains a degree of personal, behavioral, and conceptual maturity that enables him to live with some measure of satisfaction within a social milieu. Late adolescence is a stage of transition wherein the individual is approaching the attainment of several developmental goals related to adulthood but has not yet completed them.

Attitudinal and behavioral characteristics common in late adolescence generally result from (1) an idealistic view of the world, its people, and the means by which progress is accomplished, (2) a recently developed ability to do abstract reasoning about ways of men, the course of things, and life in general, and (3) a tendency to intensify on a problem or issue to a degree beyond its worth. Since this postadolescent period generally provides some time free from the all-encompassing responsibility of making one's living and providing for one's family, individuals at this stage of growth will think about those things in which they are interested and find important. They may be swept up in the current issues and social fads of the times. If so, they generally bring their idealism and power of reasoning and self-answering to bear on these issues. They are influenced by statements or clichés that to them seem so obviously true. Assertions such as, ''There are answers and solutions for the problems of the world

if you look at them in their simplest details, devoid of the encumbrances imposed on them by the past, and study them,'' and, ''All things are possible through love, hard work, and smart thinking if only you can separate yourself from traditional ideas that have you trapped.''

In recent years emphasis on the social issues of the times has led many young adults to the conclusion that there is much about governmental, social, and institutional structures that is inadequate, incompetent, and inappropriate; that the adult world and its pattern of living is inept, indifferent, and not at all what it could or should be; and that ''the system'' has things bound in such a way that freedom of thought, choice, and movement are unduly and unnecessarily restricted. Not all young people have these ideas, of course. Some individuals are not particularly interested in the social issues, some are less aggressive by nature and prefer a spectator role rather than a participant role, some have their own concerns and problems to worry about, and some have insights and guidance that make them less susceptible to group domination of their thoughts and behavior.

What is not recognized or fully realized by this age group is that their capacity to make good, valid judgments is restricted because they are limited in the effective use of their reasoning powers by their limited experiences, depth and breadth of knowledge, and inadequately developed foresight. Their idealism further influences their decision-making processes. As a result, their perspective concerning total reality is extremely narrow, restricted, and sometimes even distorted. There is no question that they do have a glimpse of the truth of reality, but often they are unprepared to see the whole picture. There is an old proverb that says, ''He who has seen little, amazes much.'' One might add, ''He who makes major pronouncements based on the little he has seen will find himself at odds with those who have been around a lot longer.''

There is a universal timeless characteristic typical of those who are at the stage of emerging adulthood. Young people seek to assert themselves in different ways to let others know (and perhaps to convince themselves) that they are of age, that they know something too, and that they

Table 12-1. The 36 contemporary topics questionnaire (CTQ) items and mean responses for the two generational groups (Members of each group were asked to [1] rate themselves [on an attitude scale of 1-7] and to [2] estimate how members of the other group would rate themselves on the same issue.)

CTQ item	Mean adolescent ratings		Mean parent ratings	
	Self	Parents	Self	Children
1. My conscience would bother me if I killed a man in war.	2.5	3.1	3.2	2.1
2. Premarital intercourse is acceptable for men but not for women.	5.7	4.7	5.9	5.0
3. In respect to youth, shoplifting is of greater moral concern than is premarital sex.	3.7	4.8	4.4	3.5
4. Racial equality deserves more attention in America than does curtailing obscenity.	1.6	3.7	2.9	2.3
5. Laws dealing with drugs, such as marijuana, are in dire need of revision.	2.0	4.1	2.8	2.2
6. A home setting for healthy adolescent development is best described as having consistent restrictions.	3.3	2.4	2.1	2.3
7. All war is immoral.	3.8	4.4	3.6	2.2
8. Authority of the police must be increased rather than decreased.	4.4	2.5	2.0	3.3
9. Marijuana should be legalized.	3.3	6.2	5.7	3.7
10. A person's appearance is his own concern, and others should tolerate whatever that person wears.	2.2	5.5	4.1	2.0
11. Disappointment or concern would overshadow approval if a close friend admitted smoking marijuana.	5.0	2.0	2.2	3.4
12. Universities should not oppose radical groups but should provide them with the protection that others have.	3.0	5.4	4.8	3.0
13. All organizations should be afforded equal and adequate police protection, if necessary, at meetings.	2.5	3.3	3.0	2.1
14. Political power of the United States military establishment is reaching a dangerous level.	2.6	3.7	3.8	2.6
15. As a parent, I would be concerned if my child of 18 years attended a lecture given by an advocate of the use of LSD.	4.2	2.3	2.9	3.7
16. Suspension from high school for smoking should be enforced, rather than allowing this behavior to exist.	5.5	2.9	4.1	5.5

NOTE: 1 = "strongly agree," 2 = "moderately agree," 3 = "slightly agree," 4 = "neutral," 5 = "slightly disagree," 6 = "moderately disagree," and 7 = "strongly disagree."

*From Lerner, R. Showdown at generation gap: attitudes of adolescents and their parents toward contemporary issues. In H. D. Thornburg (Ed.), *Contemporary adolescence: readings* (2nd ed.). Copyright © 1971, 1975 by Wadsworth Publishing Company, Inc. Reprinted by permission of the publisher, Brooks/Cole Publishing Company, Monterey, California.

Table 12-1. The 36 contemporary topics questionnaire (CTQ) items and mean responses for the two generational groups (Members of each group were asked to [1] rate themselves [on an attitude scale of 1-7] and to [2] estimate how members of the other group would rate themselves on the same issue.)—cont'd

CTQ item	Mean adolescent ratings		Mean parent ratings	
	Self	Parents	Self	Children
17. Need for strict law enforcement by the police has been justified and generated by the action of troublemakers.	4.1	2.0	1.6	3.4
18. Birth-control devices and information should be made available to all who desire them.	1.5	3.8	1.9	1.7
19. Black people have many just grievances, but they expect too much too soon.	4.4	2.2	2.8	3.6
20. A woman's place is in the home.	5.0	3.6	4.7	4.8
21. A school's dress code is a reasonable demand that students should abide by.	5.1	2.2	1.9	4.1
22. In civil disorders, the police do their job as well as can be expected.	4.5	2.5	3.1	3.8
23. The Church is playing an active role in shaping people's moral character.	5.5	3.4	3.5	4.4
24. Black revolutionaries are harmful to the advancement of their race.	4.1	2.1	2.1	2.8
25. Anti-abortion laws are absurd; the woman, and not the government, should have control over her reproductive functions.	2.0	3.9	2.6	2.4
26. Premarital sexual activities have no place in our present society.	6.3	3.2	4.0	4.7
27. Sex education in the public schools is immoral.	6.7	5.6	6.2	6.3
28. It is moral to flee to Canada to escape the draft.	3.0	5.2	5.5	3.9
29. Revision of America's legal system could help bridge the "generation gap."	3.2	3.9	3.7	2.9
30. I would not hesitate to experiment with marijuana.	3.4	6.6	6.5	4.7
31. Premarital sexual activities are and always should be considered immoral.	6.1	3.4	3.7	4.6
32. LSD is a dangerous drug that requires strict, prohibitive law enforcement.	2.8	1.5	1.3	1.9
33. Those who use drugs are usually careless about their personal appearance.	5.3	2.2	2.6	3.6
34. Laws dealing with drug conviction are too harsh.	2.7	5.0	4.7	3.3
35. The "New Left" (society's radical element) has no valid reasons for its positions.	5.4	3.0	3.9	4.4
36. A home setting for healthy adolescent development should be highly permissive.	4.6	5.1	6.1	5.5

possess an intellectual and social power that must be recognized and accepted. The world over, youth at this age show agitation and confusion that they reveal by their protests. In America the "establishment" was attacked. In Japan, where there was a national commitment to peace and antimilitarism, the students were among the most determined of all young radicals. French students had none of the American causes to protest against and none of the Japanese causes, yet protests occurred. Even in Venezuela student behavior followed the same pattern, and their protests were perhaps the most violent of all. There appears to be a universal tendency for young people to want to change or reject the life-style imposed on them by their elders. They want to "improve things." They must find some issue or authority against which they can protest. The "protest" is the characteristic; the issue is secondary. Table 12-1 indicates some of the differences of opinions that they have with their parents.

Consider the statement: "Youth is disintegrating. The youngsters of the land have a disrespect for authority of every form. Vandalism is rife, and crime of all kinds is rampant among our youth. The nation is in peril!" This quotation was not written by an adult of this generation. It was written by an Egyptian priest about 4,000 years ago when his country was undergoing one of its periodic transitions.

DEVELOPMENTAL SELF

The gradual emergence of adolescents' independence from the family and the confrontation with new responsibilities, new abilities, new values, and new freedoms make it necessary for postadolescents to restructure their images of self and their potential and worth for the world. There are new things to be learned at this new stage of life; there are new dimensions to be added to one's personality and value judgment system.[1]

Developmental tasks

Primarily, late adolescents define their values in terms of relationships with age mates. Together they display a high degree of conformity to the norms of that particular peer group. In spite of a high degree of conformity to peer norms,

adolescents are aware of adult expectations at this developmental stage. Most realize that they are expected to "settle down" and make many adjustments and decisions about the future. Such decisions as choice of vocation, choice of post–high school education, and personal code of conduct are imminent, and the adolescent responds to societal demands by conforming or withdrawing.

The idealism that characterizes this period results in a closer evaluation of principles in terms of "real" behavior–their own and others. Often the result is disillusionment because people fail to live up to their expressed ideals. Negative reactions to this feeling result in maladaptive behavior, at times, and are observable in such ways as social or political unrest, withdrawal from the social order, and the drug-laden or alcohol-saturated culture.

Positive reactions might be expressed in a desire to change the culture by becoming involved in pursuits that serve mankind such as service as a volunteer in Vista, the Peace Corps, or social agencies. At worst an inability to correlate ideals with life tasks may result in a feeling of meaninglessness, currently called "the existential vacuum," which is expressed in apathy or in extreme manifestations of exaggerated behavior. The existence of such attitudes appears to be characteristic of times of great social and technological change, when the culture fails to "provide definitive models for identification."[2] Moreover, lacking models who base conduct on inner convictions, young people may require a longer period of experimentation to consolidate an adult system of values. The nature of the task demands that it be resolved by the individuals themselves. It has been suggested that a mature acceptance of spiritual values may provide an organizing principle for this whole process, since it identifies the goals and relationships of the individual during the present life and relates them to a life of happiness hereafter.[3]

Specifically, the developmental tasks of emerging adulthood are (1) selecting and preparing for an initial occupation or career pattern; (2) desiring and achieving socially responsible behavior; (3) developing concepts for civic competency in terms of moral, ethical, social, economic, and

In a complex, technical-oriented society, career development that stressed the need for post–high school education in the past maintains that emphasis and frequently increases the demand for further education.

David Strickler

political aspects of life; (4) building sound personality traits, social and communications skills, and healthy attitudes in preparation for marriage and family life; and (5) acquiring a set of values by the formation of an identity and a concept of one's place in the world as a human being.

Physical and intellectual self

Although social development in the youth stage is transitional, physical and intellectual growth is essentially coming to a state of completion.

The height of the late adolescent has reached its peak for adult life and will remain stable until a person reaches old age. The weight spurts of the adolescent years level off near the end of the second decade of life, increasing gradually until the middle fifties, much to the dismay of many individuals. By the age of 17 years muscle growth has reached adult proportions, but muscular strength continues to grow, reaching its peak in the late twenties.

The brain has reached full size by the age of 16 years, but the adolescent has not developed suf-

Mass media communication is a vocational area in which sex bias has been greatly diminished. Many young people are attracted to this field by its creative possibilities.

David Strickler

ficiently neurologically to use all brain parts adequately. Brain waves reach adult patterns in all cortical areas around the ages of 19 or 20 years, although this range of maturity may extend to 30 years of age.[4]

Most of the glandular development in the youth stage has reached its peak. The glandular processes level off for adulthood, although certain glands continue to develop. From puberty to the age of 17 to 18 years the heart size doubles, primarily because of the increase in muscular development around the heart. Blood pressure reaches a normal level for adults. The heartbeat stabilizes at about 72 beats per minute. At about the age of 17 years the lung capacity of girls has reached adult proportions; male lung capacity is reached several years later.

Bone growth ends when bone fusion takes place. The ossification of bone parts begins in the hands at the age of 17 years with girls and 19 years with boys. Continual bone fusion takes place over the next few years. In general, there is modification of body proportions between the ages of 18 and 22 years, changing the appearance of the oversized limbs and facial features of earlier adolescence.

The development of intellectual potentials is also reaching its peak when a person is 18 to 22 years old. As was noted previously, full brain use occurs around the age of 19 to 20 years, which may well account for the mental aggressiveness displayed during this period.

Individuals of this age have approximately 85% of their logical reasoning abilities developed. Studies done by Welford[5] on subjects ranging in age from approximately 6 to 60 years investigated a person's capacity to understand and to apply a fresh method of thinking. He concluded that between 15 and 25 years of age the person tends to draw logical deductions based strictly on the statements as given in the test, whereas older adults sought to introduce supplementary premises based on their broader backgrounds or to confine themselves to comments on statements. Younger persons confine their logical reasoning to the question and knowledge at hand, whereas older persons operate from a broader perspective. On the other hand, young subjects can easily shift their thinking processes if they have

additional problems to solve, whereas the older group has difficulty with mental flexibility.

Emotional self

The prolonged task of achieving emotional independence actually begins many years before adolescence when children enter school, expand their contacts with peers, and widen their sphere of autonomous activities. Unless the importance and difficulty of the task are realized by parents, some young people will be facing problems of achieving emotional independence from parents. The task of achieving emotional independence is made particularly difficult in American society by prolonged education, which forces young people to be financially dependent on their parents for many years, by delay in work opportunities brought about by child labor laws, by mechanization and automation, and by continuous family contacts, which render it difficult for parents to perceive the growth changes that are slowly but steadily pushing the young person toward maturity.

The growth and development of the child in adolescence are accompanied by glandular changes that are closely related to emotional control. The heightened emotional states during this period of life have been recognized as a part of the nature of adolescents. However, there is also an expansion of the emotions into the social realm. Fears and angers related to social situations become important. Self-conscious feelings about one's own inadequacy appear. Adolescents are concerned over the approval of their peers. This increased fear is observed in connection with classroom situations. Fear of reciting in class, fear of failure, and fear of ridicule are common, although less common than at 14 to 16 years of age.

One of the most noticeable characteristics of late adolescence is an increase in stability and control. Interests, friendships, career choices, and relations with parents are all more stable and predictable than they were in early adolescence. Opinions tend to be based on fact and are less liable to be affected by the generalities of propaganda than they were during the more "impressionable" period of adolescence. Their opinions can and do change under planned study and from

"I HURT ALL OVER"

He came into my life when, as the axiom states, I least expected it. I was happily going about my own business, just having a good time; then he walked into my life and took over completely. I didn't know I could be so happy. I had somebody besides my family to share with. Every day when we talked, he'd ask me how my day had gone. If I had a problem, he'd listen and advise. I seldom took his advice, but it was comforting knowing that he cared.

Then, on Valentine's Day, we had our first and, as a matter of fact, our only major argument. This happened on Friday. That weekend was miserable. He didn't call to break our date on Saturday; when I called him and realized that I was being "stood up," I was quite upset. I cried. Sunday was just as bad. Monday was worse! I could hardly wait to get home from the office so I could let myself "feel." I sobbed.

That night I went to a movie. Really, I only went to get out of the house. Brian called after I got home. I don't remember the conversation, but I do know that he apologized and that we talked it out. He asked me how I felt and I said: "I felt like you dropped me from the third floor, watched me splatter, and laughed." He said: "I wasn't laughing." Everything, I thought, was back to normal.

From that time on, however, we saw each other less and less.

I began to question myself and my situation. I tried to talk it out with him, but all he managed to do was to criticize me. I wanted to say: "Okay, don't bother me anymore." But I couldn't do it. I didn't want to lose him.

One time when we'd had a minor disagreement, I very coolly stated our problem as I saw it. We happened "to like each other" in spite of everything. This should be a problem? It was for us because neither of us wanted to hurt the other—or ourselves.

Through April and May, Brian called less and less frequently. By the end of May he wasn't calling at all. How did I feel? I hurt all over. It was especially bad, too, because I'd moved into my own apartment on May 19, and I was not yet used to living alone. I felt absolutely empty. I was lonely, unsure, bereft. All I had to do with my time was to fill it with thinking. Finally he called. He made a date for the next day, and I was elated. He never came. From the heights of ecstasy to the depths of despair in twenty-four hours—that was me! There it was, all over again. All the fresh, new hurt. He called later that week and acted as if nothing at all had happened. He asked about every member of my family, about everything that I was doing. But no date!

So now I'm concentrating on falling out of love. But I find myself daydreaming about him constantly. I have long, involved, imaginary conversations with him that are filled with questions and explanations. Sometimes I quarrel with him. I remember our good times and I become depressed. When I'm shopping and I see a cute greeting card, I have to remind myself that I can't send it to him. I catch myself thinking: "I'll have to remember to tell Brian that joke . . . or this story . . . or that comment." When I buy a dress, I wonder if he will like it—then I remember that it doesn't really matter any more. I find his name creeping into conversations that shouldn't relate to him at all. I jump when the phone rings, and I'm sad when it doesn't. Until very recently I've had no desire to see other people socially, and I've turned down more dates than I've accepted. I have so much energy that I don't know what to do with it all—and yet I have no ambition to do anything. I get violently jealous when I see couples our age having a good time with each other. I get angry with myself for feeling this way. Knowing that others have had the same experience is no consolation at all. Even the realization that I am better off without him doesn't help. Logic has absolutely nothing to do with my feelings.

So what is it like to fall out of love? It is hard. It is lonely. It is depressing. It is necessary. I keep telling myself that it gets easier every day, and most days it does. I just hope that I never have to do it again.

---

the impact of interpersonal relationships. Current experiences still have an impact on the responses of the late adolescent, however.

IDENTITY AND SELF-IMAGE

The question of identity has two aspects. On one hand it is a question of self-image, "Who am I?" on the other hand it is a plea, "Don't lose my individuality in the mass of technology and over-population." Until the end of formal schooling individuals have been "role playing" the image of adolescents. They are not sure how they should act or what they should be so they act out their role as they perceive it from watching their peers. Postadolescents realize that role playing is no longer adequate. They must accept the fact that they are making some decisions that will affect their lives for years to come. They are also taking on some characteristics that will identify them with certain values and life-styles. Self-image conflicts pervade the transition between adolescence and adulthood and seldom permit the individual to be at rest emotionally.

Self-image

Postadolescents must have a positive self-image if they are to function properly. This is a large part of their search during postadolescence. They are looking for a stable, balanced self-image, a reliable view of themselves that remains more or less steady throughout life. This image may come about through the values of community, family, or from conflicting groups among their contemporaries. In earlier adolescence the self-image was not much of a problem. The adolescents could do as their parents told them or do the opposite. They could live with their self-image by doing either of these because either form of behavior was expected and accepted.

In today's society it is becoming increasingly difficult for young adults to find their self-image. They stand rather alone in an unstructured moral climate. They are not given guidelines or standards to contemplate and by which to pattern their life. Emphasis is on being free and "doing your own thing." With a lack of background, how can they know what is most desirable for them? They proceed, timidly, by trial and error or by imitating those who seem to know what they are doing. Some writers believe that a counterculture is needed to provide a climate of intimacy in which the individual can come to a sufficient sense of self so that the process of self-image integration can begin.[6]

Identity

The struggle for an identity is like a struggle against getting lost. Often it is a feeling of depersonalization, frequently brought on by some distinct change in the life of the postadolescent from a known, familiar environment to an unknown, impersonal world. It may be starting a job, entering college and living in a dormitory, or joining the armed forces. There is an uncertainty as to how one fits into the new world. Then there is a fear that the new world might not recognize and appreciate the individual's uniqueness and competencies. There may be serious questions raised as to whether the individual is as capable or as ready as he thought he was. "What am I

The quality of self-identity is important at any age. In emerging adulthood, it begins to be more definite in construct, with individuals seeking what is most relevant to the image they want to portray.

Harold Geyer

doing here?'' ''Is this really what I want?'' ''Save me from getting lost in this maze of life!'' Much of adolescents' anger results from frustrations encountered in defining goals and being accepted for what they can produce.[7]

Identities are easily lost to students at big universities, where they are dehumanized to the extent that they begin to think of themselves as numbers on a class card or anonymous units in a statistics population. At a large university, for example, students are bound to feel like a nonentity when they pick up the undergraduate catalogue and read the impressive list of emeriti assigned to teach their courses and then report to class to find it being taught by a succession of underqualified graduate students, filling in for the Big Name while he does research or takes sabbaticals. Treatment of this sort can easily cause a

Cultural variations exist in identity development. If individuals are from a culture that is in a minority, they usually seek to develop responsible skills that will enable them to survive.

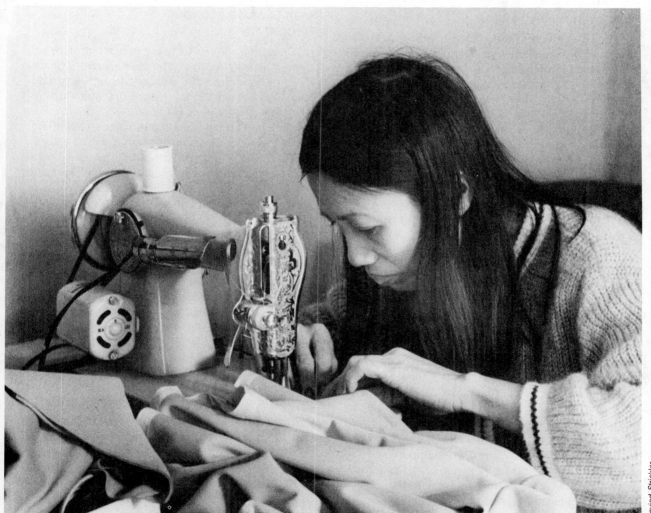

Daviod Strickler

student to question the system and even to grow hostile toward the institution itself.

The mass media, another sprawling institution so influential in American culture, provide young people with multiple and often conflicting reflections of their identity. The individuals see student activists and at the same time they see their contemporaries cleaning up the environment. They are faced with making decisions about their own identity while being bombarded with many images of what they could be like. The mass media have kept them so well informed that, unlike any previous generation, they have a myriad of choices at their disposal but no clues as to which image is better for them.

Identity in minority groups

Perhaps the most difficult of all identity crises are endured by members of minority groups and disadvantaged youth from poverty pockets. The tendency is for such young people to cling fiercely to their minority status, claiming pride in their origins, and to lash out in violent resentment against those in authority on whom they blame their present plight. They feel trapped by their situation and react aggressively. The city street becomes the medium of expression for these young people. It is the common ground and liaison between all minorities in a poverty area, lending them a sense of belonging and unity. It gives birth to gangs of young people who because of class, society's ostracism, or perhaps a police record, have been snubbed or discriminated against. Gangs offer youngsters an escape from the boredom that stalks impoverished areas. They provide a certain amount of security, as do most groups, and a sense of importance when intimidating a rival gang. Young people involved in gangs find heroes among themselves to emulate, generally the gang leaders, and these become a sort of father figure to the boys. Gang dynamics have been extensively analyzed as an extremely important facet of minority and poverty culture.[4] They provide a kind of instant identity for underprivileged young people.

Responsibility is a key word in today's identity crisis. Young people long to be able to respect themselves as adults, and self-respect is generally a product of learning to handle responsibility ca-

pably. Today's young people want to take credit for their successes; *just as much* they want to pay the penalty for their own mistakes. These youngsters know they have done wrong and are ready to atone for it. When they do not get the discipline they need, they feel frustrated and resentful. Young people are ready for responsibility well before their twenty-first birthdays. They are ready to prove that they can pay the price, both in successes and in failures, for this load. Perhaps the current legislation lowering the voting age nationwide in America will allow postadolescents all the privileges and penalties of adulthood at an earlier age and thus take some of the edge off the identity crisis.

MORAL AND RELIGIOUS UNCERTAINTY

Accepting values to live by is a major developmental task for the later adolescent. The behavioral guidelines of childhood and early adolescence are no longer tenable as standards of behavior, and neither is a value system based on a concept of rewards or punishment adequate, nor a moral code structured on a list of "do's" and "don'ts" or the "either-or" criteria. Adolescents realize that the system that enabled them to make judgments in the past is not applicable to their newly acquired growth status in society. Unfortunately, society of today does not seem to have a frame of reference concerning right or wrong, good or bad, whereby youth can begin to build a more adequate value judgment system for themselves. Too much uncertainty, too much hesitancy, and the lack of positive guidance seem to exist in all nations of the world, wherein the individual rather than society is placed in the exalted position of having a freedom of choice in the determination of physical, social, and cognitive behavior.

Commentary on moral uncertainty

In the United States the history of the 1930s and 1940s seems to provide some insight into the problem. What we are about to present is all speculative, of course. Consider the adults of the late 1970s. They are the children and the young adolescents of the depression years of the 1930s —hard times when jobs, money, food, and adequate clothing were scarce. During the 1940s they were personally involved in wartime activities and its aftermath. The 1950s were years of personal building and of getting one's feet on the ground. An entire generation grew into adulthood from a background that stressed security and survival. As adults, this generation concentrated on supplying the material goods that were missing in their youth and on advancing technology, which it believed to be the key to future survival. As a result, the world experienced a knowledge and technological explosion such as had never been experienced before in the history of mankind. One of its most laudable achievements was the landing of man on the moon. Unfortunately, the technological sciences far surpassed advancements in the social sciences, with the result that man did not learn how to live in his new world of computers, electronics, and instant communication. A balanced life was lacking. Youth of today are faced with the moral and cultural vacuum that was permitted to develop during the past thirty to forty years.

A second factor instrumental in creating an image of moral uncertainty has been the inconsistent, ambiguous, indefinite, sometimes lacking responses by adults to the social and moral issues of the day. The abundance of pornographic-type literature for sale on the magazine stands and the wide distribution of films featuring nudity, sex, and violence make young people ask, "If you don't believe it is right or good, why don't you do something about it?" There is a great outcry concerning crime in the streets, and the country has witnessed three assassinations of national figures. A gun control law was passed, only to be watered-down to the point of making it meaningless. Young people have keen minds and time in which to use them. They have time to examine what is taking place, and they conclude that adults have much uncertainty in the realms of morality and religion. Adults offer little in these areas that young people can hold on to.

A third factor contributing to a moral uncertainty has been the attitudes and acceptance of adults concerning the need for changes in society. As young adults, they saw and were revolted by violations of civil rights in various parts of the country. They could not understand acts of prejudice against different religious and major political groups within the nation. They were the ones who pleaded with educational leaders to "make education more practical (relevant)." The pressures of the times, however, demanded that the young people of those years devote their energies to the business of making a living and making up for lost years. In turn, however, they did create an affluent society that gave more time and money to its youth. Young people could now afford to devote more time to right the wrongs of society. Adults were predisposed to permit changes to take place, and they were permissive with their children when they sought to do something about it. Some activities got out of hand because young people lack a social and political perspective, but many good changes were brought about.

Religious uncertainty

Religious uncertainty developed much in the same way. Mothers and fathers placed great stress on producing and gathering the material goods of life. Moral development was left to the church and school. There was one brief flare-up during the 1950s wherein attention was paid to the importance of spiritual, moral, and patriotic development. The movement quickly subsided, however, because of a lack of knowledge of how to promote spiritual and moral values. Regardless, the time had come to enter the race for space. The emphasis on science and mathematics overshadowed all else in the schools. Parents somehow hoped that spiritual values would be absorbed by their children.

For a period of time church membership soared from 30% of the prewar population to 65% in the late 1950s. Increased church membership, however, was not the answer. The church could not seem to meet the social problems of racial prejudice, poverty, and war in the 1960s. The church failed, the schools failed, and the parents failed. Young people grew up in a spiritual vacuum with no guidelines, no structure, no pressures "to conform." The stage was set for a "permissive point of view." Much of the mass communications media began to emphasize "the new morality" and "the permissive society." The United States Supreme Court at one time seemed to promote permissiveness by its rulings on obscenity, pornography, and criminal actions. Of course, the Supreme Court sought to stress "due process" and "the rights and freedom of the individual." But the public read the other side of the coin, which said, "permissiveness"!

In the late 1960s there was a strong movement among young people that had religious overtones. Having gone through unrest, violence, sex, drugs, flowers, and hippie communes, young people began to seek something more meaningful and more permanent than these things. Many were beginning to say "I believe in God, but not in the church."

In a survey of 2,000 youths in 1969, Bienvenu[9] found that most of them believed in God, that they wanted more religious activities involving the family, and, most important, that they wanted better lines of communication. It seems that most parents were upset at the young people rebelling against childhood practices such as attending Sunday School or church services. The young people said that they still believed but wanted to do it their way. The time had come for the church once again, as it had done periodically throughout the centuries, to upgrade its level of thinking and restructure its program to meet the demands of a more sophisticated society.

As far as religion is concerned, it should be noted that Americans remain one of the world's most religious-oriented people—in purpose, if not always in practice. A global survey in 1976 by the Gallup Poll (see reference 3) found that 56% of Americans regard religion as "very important" in their lives. The same was true of only 36% of the population in Italy and Canada, 23% in the United Kingdom, and 17% in West Germany, the Scandinavian countries, and Japan. A belief in God was expressed by 94% of those questioned in the United States, 88% in Italy, 76% in the United Kingdom, and 65% in Scandinavia. With figures like these latter ones, one wonders what has become of the central force of religion in shaping the conscience and behavior of people.

KOHLBERG: MORAL DEVELOPMENT

A look at the various developmental stages of moral judgment in individuals may give some in-

sight into the levels of moral judgment pursued by societies. Kohlberg[10] has formulated and validated a conception of moral development based on the core assumptions of the "cognitive-developmental" theory of moral education (Table 12-2). A key assumption of this theory is that the stimulation of moral development rests on the stimulation of thinking and problem solving by the child. The theory claims that morality represents a set of rational principles of judgment concerning human welfare and justice which are valid for every culture. Individuals acquire and refine the sense of justice through a sequence of invariant developmental stages as follows:

1. Orientation to punishment and reward and to physical and material power. Social power is diffused. Moral thought is based largely on doing good to avoid punishment.
2. Right action consists of that which satisfies one's own needs and occasionally the needs of others. Beginning notions of reciprocity. "You be nice to me and I'll be nice to you."
3. Moral behavior is that which is approved by others. There is much conformity to stereotypical images of what is "majority behavior." Morality is defined by individual ties of relationships.
4. Orientation toward authority, fixed rules, duty, and maintenance of the social order. "Law and order" is important. Whether the order is social or religious depends on which is considered of primary value.
5. Right action tends to be defined in terms of (a) general individual rights and (b) standards such as the American Constitution, that have been examined and agreed on. This is a "social-contract" orientation with emphasis on equality and mutual obligation.
6. Morality consists of self-chosen abstract ethical principles that have logical comprehensiveness, universality, and consistency. These are principles of justice and equality of human rights and of respect for the dignity of human beings as individual persons. Life is inherently worthwhile in itself.

The stages are not defined by opinions or judgments but by ways of thinking about moral matters and bases of choice. Stages 1 and 2, which are typical of children and delinquents, are

Table 12-2. Stages of moral development according to Kohlberg*

I. Preconventional level	Behavior abides by cultural rules because of punishment or reward consequences.
Stage 1: The punishment and obedience orientation	Good and bad and right and wrong are thought of in terms of consequences of action. Avoidance of punishment.
Stage 2: The instrumental realistic orientation	Right action is whatever satisfies one's own needs and occasionally the needs of others. Exchange of favors. "Do for me and I do for you."
II. Conventional level	Behavior is self-controlled due to expectations of others and desire to conform and accept social expectations.
Stage 3: Interpersonal acceptance of "good boy, nice girl" social concept	Good behavior is what pleases and is approved by others. Response to stereotype; social units are loose and flexible.
Stage 4: The "law and order" orientation	Right behavior accepts and shows respect for authority. Doing one's duty for the good of the social order; laws are permanent and not likely to change.
III. Postconventional, autonomous, or principled level	Effort to define moral values and principles that are valid beyond the authority of the group and even beyond the self.
Stage 5: The social contract, utilitarian orientation	Adherence to legal rights commonly agreed upon by society but with laws subject to interpretation and change in terms of rational consideration for the rights of the individual while maintaining respect of self and others.
Stage 6: The universal ethical principle orientation	Right behavior is defined in terms of ethical principles based on logical comprehensiveness, universality, and consistency, and respects the inherent dignity of human beings as individuals.

*Based on data from Kohlberg, L.: Stage and sequence: the cognitive-development approach to socialization. In D. Goslin (Ed.), *Handbook of socialization: theory and research,* Chicago: Rand McNally & Co., 1969.

described as "premoral," since moral decisions are based on self-interest and material considerations. The group-oriented stages 3 and 4 are the conventional ones at which most of the adult population operates. Stages 5 and 6 are "principles" stages, with only 5% to 10% of the population ever reaching stage 6.

Why do some people reach higher levels of moral development than others? Much depends on the value judgment system and philosophy developed by the individual. That development depends on the type of reasoning and problem-solving experience individuals have had and the type of knowledge and information they use in their thinking. Individuals who receive little or no information develop moral and religious uncer-

tainty because they have to work out so many answers for themselves. In addition to suffering from a "kindergarten theology," which is of no use in solving problems in an "adult world of reality," people also suffer from being too busy making a living and just getting along in the daily world to be able to take time to deal with weighty moral problems. Some help is needed.

YOUTH AND SOCIETY

The appearance and actions of youth are often so dramatic that it is easy for adults to be diverted or misled from the universal principles that truly interpret this age group. To emphasize such things as hair styles, daily behavior, language usage, the "natural look," or the whole area of

Music is a thread that transcends all generations; different styles are fashionable at different times.

fads and fashions that we group under the heading of the "blue jeans syndrome" (named after a widely accepted dress style) is to overlook the true nature of this age group. Fads and fashions change. Popular social behavior, music, and clothing styles change, But the basic needs of youth are universal and eternal. This point must not be forgotten when adults look at today's youth.

Continuity with change

A study of the culture of emerging adulthood is a lesson in bewilderment, especially if an attempt is made to pinpoint specifics. The individual of the early and middle 60s did not look, act, or think like his counterpart of the middle and late 50s. The picture of the young adult in the late 60s and early 70s is not like the individual of the early and middle 60s. The middle and late 70s saw another change in this age group when compared with those of the early 70s. Patterns of behavior, attitudes, and goals have constantly been changing. Yet underneath this flow of change there remains a thread of continuity that exemplifies emerging adulthood. That thread is the desire to get started about the business of adulthood, to make things happen, and to become part of the world as it is envisioned by them.

A personal illustration might be in order. We were in the process of writing the first edition of this text in 1972 and 1973. We had a file drawer full of folders on "emerging adults." When it came time to write this chapter, we could use very little of the material because we could see a major change taking place. No longer was there campus unrest and civil violence; the hippie culture had disappeared. The so-called "generation gap" had shrunk. Activism was changing its style. The material on the "rebellious generation" had, almost overnight, become outdated and irrelevant to that point in time.

We find ourselves in almost the same situation as we write this version. Much of the material we've collected recently is becoming outdated. The statistics of "then" are not a reflection of "now." A five-year time span isn't all that long in a lifetime. In part, it shows the narrow perspective of time and conditions that this age group holds. It is not uncommon to hear a girl or a guy of 19 or 20 speak of the "tremendous" difference between "how things are in high school as compared to when we were there." It is not unusual for college juniors to speak of how different the freshmen are—and only two years have gone by since they were freshmen. Is there really that much of a change or has time and experience made a difference in values, expectations, and goals?

Nevertheless, over a five- or six-year span there have been major differences taking place. The drug culture has, by and large, given way to an alcohol splurge; the small conversational group has changed to "partying"; sex "with a commitment" has increased unbelievably; attending college for career reasons has replaced a search for "naturalism"; hair styles, clothing, fashions, and involvement in physical activities have changed. The search for self-fulfillment, while a member of the organized society, has broadened. The identity for cultural minorities has developed a dichotomy between those who have made it to the middle class and those who have not. It is no longer a unified struggle.

Changes in views

Research by Yankelovich and his associates[11] reflected the changing times. They found that college students were beginning to emphasize work ethics. As a group, they were also more content with their circumstances. College students were moving away from the social reform movements of a few years earlier and were focusing on the self and the changes that had to be made in pursuing traditional career-oriented programs.[12]

Noncollege students were more dissatisfied than previously. Noncollege youth were now placing stress on finding "interesting work" as well as work that provides a good salary. They tend to take for granted the extrinsic rewards of work—good pay, a mounting standard of living, and economic security. They have taken up the quest for a new definition of success that stresses personal self-fulfillment and quality of working life as much as it does economic security. Earlier the emphasis was on the idea that "hard work always pays off." The emphasis now is on self-directed self-expression, creativity, self-development, physical well-being, self-fulfillment both on and off the job. Saving the world, saving the environment, saving minority groups no longer hold the appeal they did just a few short years ago.

Both groups in the Yankelovich study of 1973 and 1974 have moved in the direction of permissiveness in matters of sex.[13] They question marriage as an institution, support population control, abortions, and sexual freedom, and look to themselves rather than to family, spouse, or children for fulfillment and meaning in life. However, a study by Yankelovich, Skelly, and White[14] in 1977 is finding different trends, suggesting that the "sexual revolution" may be experiencing a counterrevolution. (Social issues that are difficult to settle frequently operate on a pendulum principle, jumping from one extreme to the other.) This controlled study by Yankelovich supported the concept of "moral uncertainty" and moral confusion; this was admitted by 65% of those over 50 and, surprisingly, 66% of those under the age of 25! Extramarital sex was disapproved by three fourths of those surveyed. Two thirds of the group were against premarital sex, although 3 out of 5 under 25 accepted the idea. The parents had no illusions, however, that it did not take place.

Although a very slim majority (51%) made up mostly of men and the young did not think it was morally wrong for couples who are not married to live together, a resounding 70% disapproved of having children without marriage. The majority also found these behaviors unacceptable: nude bathing beaches (61%), massage parlors (60%), male nudity in movies (59%), and female nudity in movies (54%). Fully 64% said that pornographic movies are morally wrong. Casual sex and instant sex are suffering a backlash because a lot of people were hurt. There is a strong reaction against situations where sex is being widely commercialized and where people's emotional needs are manipulated and exploited.

It is interesting to note that a substantial majority of Americans cling to a belief in many of the values of family life. Whatever the future brings, the idealism of young adults concerning the world and their place in it will prevail, even if their attitudes and behaviors change from time to time.

The social dropout

From a society that has a long-standing commitment to a stress on individualism and on an intellective mode of consciousness, the young are moving toward a sense of identity that is communal and nonintellective in nature. Youth's very desire to experiment with drugs, sex, and alcohol has had a prominent and provocative effect on society. Their actions seem appalling and rebellious to older members of society. A gap of acceptability was created between the generations. This dissent in young people began in the late 1950s, when they began to question the American ideal of the "self-made" man and the importance of "material success."

Basic motivation for any social dropout is identity. The search for a viable identity produces any number of effects in youngsters and "cop-outs" is one of these effects. There is a current feeling among today's young people that there is little in mass society with which to identify. Current standards, to them, are meaningful only in terms of getting a job. Appearance, class, school grades, athletic ability, and ambition represent success in establishment terms, but postadolescents want something more. They want respect, and they want to be credited with the ability to choose their own frame of reference and be held responsible for their own mistakes. The mass society is reticent about giving its respect to this group primarily because adults notice in it a deviation from their own set of standards. It is this lack of respect that many dropouts are rebelling against and running away from. They take the negative course from that of their parents, aligning themselves with marijuana and alcohol. Sex is openly discussed and experimented with among young people rather than treated as a "hang-up," as it is among older people. Above all, youth is concerned with the realistic and moral issues rather than the romantic and material issues of their parents. When they find no tolerance for their views among those in authority, there is bound to be a reaction.

Value confusion

Emerging adulthood appears to be a critical period in alcohol and drug usage. Most of today's youthful alcohol users are from middle class or upper middle class homes, usually have higher-than-average intelligence, and have some degree of affluence. They are free from worry about providing for themselves; they are well fed, clothed, housed, and educated. What motivates them to imbibe? Is it peer pressure, desire for adventure, lack of value certainty, a search for something better, or what?

As adolescents cast a judicious view at the cultural environment and its values, they see that gain is the gross national product, without all people having access to its rewards. A man is landed on the moon, but the earthly environment continues to deteriorate with its air too foul for breathing, its aquatic life dying, and man drowning in the midst of junked used cars and tin cans. They see cheating, lying, stealing, adultery, and even premeditated murder conditionally and situationally identified and approved, while honesty, fidelity, and virtue are situationally disapproved.

In adolescents' attempt to realize the "adult pattern of life" they are highly affected by their interaction with their cultural environment. From a mass of diversified societal and cultural interaction they must develop a set of moral values that they perceive to be acceptable to themselves and to their society. Often confused, upset, and frustrated by the unpredictable and contradictory morality of their cultural environment, youths seek immediate relief and escape from a futile situation. They may become aggressive, and they strike out at an unfair, unhappy world filled with nothing but despair and failure for them. They may avoid or postpone the responsibilities of a threatening adulthood by withdrawing into an aura of drugs or alcohol. Many young people neither strike out nor seek to escape the world. They work out a moral code by which they can live in peaceful coexistence with society, in spite of its shortcomings.

Youth culture

The mentifacts and artifacts of a particular time in history reflect the cultural taste of the bulk of society at that moment. Acceptance of these modes of thought and objects, including fashion paraphernalia, makes one part of the majority in society. Occasionally a group, consciously or unconsciously, seeks to advance its own thoughts, fashions, and objects. This movement becomes a counterculture, which appeals to youth who are

seeking recognition or wish to express their resentment or rejection of society's cultural interests. How long should a point of view last? How long should people continue to wear certain clothing styles? Change in taste and styles must come. Individuals on the move are those kinds of beings. They must have variety; they must seek improvement to satisfy their need for self-assertion and for achievement. Youth seeks to promote change through their fads and fashions. At the very least, even if they are not promoting change, they are encouraging styles of thought and living that are unique to their age group.

It was the mass media of television, radio, newspapers, and magazines that woke up the youth of America and united them into a highly important part of the culture. Ever since that September evening in 1956, when Elvis Presley appeared on nationwide television with the bottom half of the television screen masked so that his pelvic movements could not be seen, society has awakened to the realization that youth was a force on the move and had to be reckoned with. His tight pants and his hip gyrations were objected to by many parents, but his songs and style of dance started to rock and roll the very foundations of the values system that parents supposed would always be acceptable for their children.[15]

In the Western countries like the United States the arts and humanities are the means by which youth can create a new communal sense of taste. This is the type of approval that youth prefers, rather than going through a process of psychosocial maturing.[16] To find alternatives to mass society values in music young musicians constantly reevaluate and adjust their style to what might be termed the *avant-garde*. One of the reasons that the Beatles managed to maintain their long-time high standing in the young music world, for example, is because their style changed almost drastically from album to album. Their early records consisted almost exclusively of simple melodies in 4/4 time, easy to dance to, and designed to coincide with the introduction of the current dance rage. They popularized hard rock music. As drug cultures among young people expanded, the Beatles reflected the trend in their lyrics: "Lucy in the Sky With Diamonds" stand-

Free to be, to be me,
   Not you, not like, not them.
Free to know, to be known,
   Without facade, without demand.
Free to hear, to be heard,
   Not to gainsay, not to demean.
Free to have, to behave,
   To seek, to search, to find.
Free to love, to be loved,
   To touch, to taste, to feel.
Free to be, to become,
   To think, to trust, to do.
Free to accept, to be accepted,
   Because you are, because I am.

Wallace D. LaBenne
Free

ing for L.S.D. They were quick to add sitar music to their repertoire when Ravi Shankar appeared on the scene from India. Finally, when the wave of nostalgia hit the youngsters, old-time honky-tonk turned up in the Beatles' "When I'm Six-ty-four" and "Rocky Raccoon." The group quickly anticipated the trend and acted on it.

Music, important to the postadolescent because a certain area of it belongs exclusively to his age group, is a medium of intense involvement for him. It yields escape from his detached life. This is particularly true of psychedelic and electronic music.

Soul music reveals youth's disaffection for the affluent way of life. Many middle-class youngsters believe that there is no soul in their own economic strata. There is a spontaneity, depth of feeling, and vibrancy in soul music that was unknown in the tunes of the 1950s, and it is underscored by intense, highly dramatic performances of these numbers. Soul music originates in the part of society where ideals and character can express themselves without being molded by the mass society, such as among minorities and in ghettos. Its blues lyrics and somewhat repetitious melodies challenge establishment notions about such things as male-female roles, marriage, and steady jobs.

Indian music also negates middle-class values and embraces Eastern (as opposed to Western) thought. It offers the most coherent complete alternative to the mode of thinking dictated by the mass society. Indian music is traditional rather than technical, introspective rather than demonstrative. Its acceptance among young people has led to an acceptance and following of the philosophy and religious ideals of the East.

With time the young person expects more excellence in the music designed for his generation. The 18- to 21-year-old will look at a development in rock music, such as "Bubble Gum Music," with the same disdain that he would reserve for the music of the late 1950s.[17] Today's rock music is broken down into hard rock, progressive rock, jazz rock, country rock, punk rock, disco music, and other genre. Rock, jazz, country, folk music, and the big band sounds are often heard in the popular band groups of college-aged people.

Youth's contribution to the field of art has not been as highly productive as their contribution to music. Except for the contributions made by the serious art student, the art form peculiar to youth is the poster. Photography has come into its own with today's postadolescent, partly because of his insistence on reality and partly because of a flagrant desire to exhibit shocking life styles to a disapproving establishment. One senses a bold defiance among the youngsters who throw these posters in the face of the previous generation, to whom certain subjects are verboten. Gimmicks also attract youthful art fanciers, often reflecting the pop-art approach of the Campbell soup can.[18]

Fashion is the one area of culture most affected by the postadolescent. No matter whom the clothes are for, the accent is on youth: It is fashionable to be young! This attitude is reflected in most department stores, who give their moderately priced departments names like "The Casual Look" or "Youth Circle." These are designed to entice the older woman. The same philosophy applies to advertising. The older woman is virtually nonexistent in department-store clothing advertisements, even though the older woman has more money to spend. Youth affects style for the whole society. One gets the feeling that "anything goes" in fashion. Clothes for men, previously a rather conservative area, have become an area of concentration for designers. Oldsters respond to youth worship where fashion is concerned. However, there is some movement back to conservation and executive styles in suits, especially among businessmen. There is no question but that the youth culture in music, art, and fashions has influenced the living styles of all generations of the day.

Youth and government

There are many postadolescents taking an active interest in politics today, and nearly all of them are characterized by a deep concern with the moral and psychological implications of the political process. As in many other areas, they seek honesty in politics—genuine noncorruption must be evident on the human side of a candidate, and his convictions must not be altered when political aspirations step in. In general, youth views the government as seemingly compromising, existing more for personal gain and the furthering of personal ends than to better serve the interests of the American people. Young people are extremely idealistic in their views on government, and when attacking its institutions as they so often do, they come armed with stringent moral principles that may not be strayed from.

A distrust for mass society is supported by an intrinsic emotional dislike for the conformity it demands. This reaction generally leads the post-adolescent against specific institutions like bureaucratic education and outmoded churches because these bulwarks against the onslaught of change seem the most imposing.

Implicit in the term *liberal* is the essence of the goals set by young people for *their* adult society. They want freedom assured to them and their contemporaries—freedom to conduct individual life styles in any manner of choosing, freedom to decide moral as opposed to immoral issues in government, freedom to change what is unjust in law, freedom to enter or refuse induction into the military, and many more specific freedoms. They are asking for their dissenting voices to be considered by society as constructive rather than subversive in nature, and they ask only to be respected rather than ridiculed.

A FINAL WORD

Alfred North Whitehead[19] made an interesting observation relative to the need of the generations to get together. He writes to the effect that youth is imaginative, and if his imagination can be strengthened by discipline, this energy of imagination can be preserved for life. The tragedy of the world, as he sees it, is that those who are imaginative have slight experience and those who are experienced have feeble imaginations. Fools act on imagination without knowledge; penchants act on knowledge without imagination. The task of the university, says Whitehead, is to weld together imagination and experience. One must go to those older to learn the past; but one must go to youth to learn the future because they are the only ones native to the new technological age.

In every age, every generation, youth takes bold steps toward adulthood. The style and the clamor of those steps change from period to period. The activism and the apathy of the past decade will give way to a new look. No one knows what the future holds, but the underlying universal principles pertaining to the movement of emerging adulthood state that youth will make itself known.

STUDY GUIDE

1. Read the beginning section of this chapter, which is our point of view. Do you agree or disagree? Support your position.
2. The developmental tasks as presented in this chapter are not as objectively and precisely presented as in other chapters. Try to list them by identifying the specific task.
3. What is the intellectual competency level of most 18- to 20-year-olds?
4. The section on "commentary on moral uncertainty" takes a rather conservative view on morals and morality. Read the next section on "religious uncertainty." In your opinion are the positions overstated or distorted? You recognize, we hope, that you are at liberty to take issue with personal views that are not supported directly by research. In your judgment, what would be a suitable moral climate for society today? Compare your judgment with Kohlberg's findings on the stages of moral development.
5. In a description of the fashions and themes of the day, such as in the section on "youth and society," there is the possibility that the fashions, themes, and words will have changed after the book has been in print for a few years. The youth culture is particularly subject to change. View this entire section from a historical perspective. How do you see youth and society today?

REFERENCES

1. Keniston, K. *Youth and dissent.* Harcourt Brace Jovanovich, Inc. 1971.
2. Interview of James A. Michener. What's good about today's youth. *U.S. News and World Report,* December 10, 1973.
3. Special Section on Religion. A portrait of religious America. *U.S. News and World Report,* April 11, 1977.
4. Ornstein, R. *The psychology of consciousness.* New York: Viking Press, 1973.

5. Welford, A. T. *Skill and age: an experimental approach*. New York: Oxford University Press, 1951.
6. Pildes, W. F. Youth: society's hope for love. *Theory into Practice,* 1969, **8,** 121.
7. Ohlsen, M. M. Dissident students. *Contemporary Education,* 1971, **42,** 157.
8. Kelly, D. H., & Pink, W. T. Status origins, youth rebellion, and delinquency: a reexamination of the class issue. *Journal of Youth and Adolescence,* 1975, **4,** 339-347.
9. Bienvenu, M. J. Kids want more religion. *America,* 1969, October 4, 252.
10. Kohlberg, L. Moral stages and moralization: the cognitive-developmental approach. In T. Lickona (Ed.), *Moral development and behavior: theory, research and social issues.* New York: Holt, Rinehart, & Winston, 1976.
11. Yankelovich, D., & Clark, R. College and noncollege youth values. *Change,* 1974, **6**(7), 45-46.
12. Special Section. A new generation: where is it heading? *U.S. News and World Report,* September, 6, 1976.
13. Yankelovich, D. *The new morality, a profile of American youth in the 70's.* New York: McGraw-Hill Book Co., 1974.
14. The new morality. Poll by Yankelovich, Skelly, and White. *TIME,* November 21, 1977.
15. Zalaznich, S. Youthquakes in pop culture. *Fortune,* January, 1969, 85.
16. Arastelk, R. The rebirth of youth in the age of cultural change. *Acta Paedopsychiatry (Basel),* 1969, **36,** 322-345.
17. Horowitz, I. L. Rock in the rocks, or bubblegum anybody? *Psychology Today,* January, 1971, 59.
18. Canady, J. The revolution that couldn't in a show that doesn't. *New York Times,* section D, June 27, 1971, 23.
19. Whitehead, A. N. *Aims of education.* New York: Macmillan Co., 1957.

MY WEDDING DAY The hour was late, but falling asleep seemed to be an impossible task. Although my body desperately wished for sleep, my mind refused to submit to this condition. My thoughts seemed to run the entire spectrum of emotions. An anxious thought would be followed by a happy one, which in turn would be followed by one of fear. The reason for this turmoil was that in seven more hours I was to be married!

Since sleep still seemed to be impossible, I began to dwell on these thoughts. First, I attempted to speculate as to what marriage was really like. I tried to imagine what the honeymoon would be like; how it would be to come home from work to a wife; whether we would be able to have children. These were only a few of my thoughts as I mentally tried to encompass the life span of a marriage.

Next my thoughts turned to ones of anxiety. "Was I really ready to get married?" was the foremost one. I began to question myself in relation to this thought. Would I be able to make the transition from being a bachelor to being a married man; could I cope with the responsibilities inherent in marriage; would I resent the loss of my so-called "freedom" that I had heard other married men speak about so often? These were some of the thoughts that raced through my troubled mind. It was with these thoughts that I finally fell asleep.

Again I was awakened. Although I felt as if I had only slept for a few minutes, a glance at my watch showed that three hours had passed. My first thought was "Only four more hours until I'm married!"

I decided to go with my brother and eat breakfast. I thought that having something to do and having someone to talk with would ease the tension that I was starting to feel. However, this proved to be an erroneous assumption on my part. I had little appetite for food and all conversation invariably returned to the subject of my marriage. My brother's attempts to assure me that all men had these last-minute thoughts did little toward alleviating the nervousness that I was feeling. There seemed to be a direct relationship between the passage of time and the intensity of this feeling of nervousness. The closer it came to the hour of eleven, the more nervous I felt!

We returned to my apartment and I started to dress. As I put on my tux, my thoughts took a new and somewhat strange twist. I began to wonder why I had selected this particular woman to be my mate for life. I had dated other girls but had never really considered marriage with any of them. What quality or qualities did this woman possess that made her so different from other women I had known? What was so special about her that I was wanting to change my entire life pattern? She certainly was physically attractive, was interesting to talk with, had a pleasant personality, and was fun to be with. However, I had known other girls who had these same qualities, and I didn't marry any of them. I continued to think along these lines but, try as I did, I couldn't arrive at a concrete solution. My thought process was interrupted by the sound of my brother's voice as he announced it was almost time to leave for the church.

Now I was standing in the sacristy of the chapel. It was now ten minutes before eleven o'clock and the nervousness which began at breakfast had reached a new height. The best man's attempts to ease my tension with some humorous remarks about marriage met with no success. I was again dwelling on the same thoughts that had plagued me since early this morning.

The music started. We left the sacristy and I walked to the center of the chapel. My bride-to-be was walking down the aisle with her father. As I watched her approach, I felt as if a great weight had been lifted from my shoulders. All of the doubts, fears, tensions, and nervousness disappeared. They were replaced by a feeling of happiness and confidence. She arrived at the place where I was standing. I looked at her and she took my arm; as we approached the altar, I had one thought in my mind. I now knew why I had selected this woman to be my wife. I loved her.

After the turbulent stage of late adolescence, the developing individual is faced with yet another major task—that of competent, satisfactory integration into adult society and culture. The challenges and responsibilities that must be met and accepted are varied, and the possible hindrance to satisfactory adjustment and development are many. The time has come to be independent, as well as interdependent. The point in time when people become adults cannot be designated in years, but rather as that point when they begin to assume the responsibilities of adulthood and take on the role of adults. For most people this time will be in the early twenties.

One fourth of an individual's life is spent growing up. Three fourths of a person's life is spent in adulthood, growing older. Should we not have more concern than we do with the nature of adulthood and how to enter it, as well as leave it, gracefully and with hope?

EARLY ADULTHOOD

Early adulthood, or the period from approximately 20 to 35 or 40 years of age, is a busy and exciting time for most people. In the more complex societies of the world, it is the "expansion of growing phase" of adulthood. It is that time of life when adults invest enormous amounts of energy in their work, striving for promotions, positions, and raises. They are also extending their social contacts, widening their circle of friends, and seeking to become part of organized social entities. They marry, establish homes, and have children. There is forward movement in watching and helping the children grow. A home, a car, a color television set, and a stereo layout become part of the dimensions of a higher standard of living. For early adults who are striving to get ahead the road stretches into an indefinite future, a goal beyond dreams. The developing period of adulthood is an ever-growing, ever-expanding time of life. It is beautiful but hectic!

Developmental tasks

Early adults find themselves confronted with the role of adults, which includes that of being workers, consumers, social beings, citizens, taxpayers, and either family persons with children or single persons who choose to pursue a career. They are the ones who must now and for the rest of their life make decisions, rather than having them made for them. In addition, they are confronted with a number of life-style changes and new experiences. It is in the course of coping with these experiences that people are likely to undergo changes in their personalities. No longer children, early adults learn to tolerate some frustration and aggravation. They are expected to use some logical reasoning and insight in making decisions. The requirements of the adult role not only contribute to changes of personality and modes of adjustment but also to the need for an updated value-judgment system. Up to the age of 30 years it is common for both men and women to be underdeveloped in some areas of behavior and

Early adulthood is a time for career development. For most people, vocational interests mature and occupational preferences emerge.

judgment, whereas at the same time showing considerable maturity in other areas. With new experiences and new expectations by others, however, a more even development on a more mature level begins to take place.

The social and economic roles of early adulthood are so familiar and clearly defined that few early adults have any doubt as to what the expectations of society are. These expectations, indicated as developmental tasks, are (1) selecting a mate, (2) learning to live with a marriage partner, (3) starting a family, (4) rearing children, (5) managing a home, (6) getting started in an occupation, (7) taking on civic responsibility, and (8) finding a congenial social group.[1] Successful achievement of these tasks will do much to bring about a more satisfying middle and late adulthood. Whether or not the ultimate future is in clear focus for early adults, they are planting the seeds that will bear the crops for harvest in their later years.

Personal independence

"To me, independence and responsibility for a male just out of college or just turning twenty-one means getting out from under parental control and influence and moving into the world of freedom and self-reliance." This opinion typifies the early adult's view of independence and responsibility. Independence is usually demonstrated by early adults moving out of the parents' home and into an apartment to live on their own. They hope to prove to their parents and to themselves that they can accept and handle the responsibilities of living away from home. As our friend said, "I'm supporting myself and, in a sense, going through a dry run for the later responsibilities of marriage and a family." Early adults are formulating goals and probing new areas. This is opposed to their earlier years of waiting until they "grew up" to achieve any goals in life. Now it is time for them to be what they are to be.

The task of becoming independent and responsible entails attaining emotional independence, social independence, and economic independence. Emotional independence is the most important, yet the most difficult to achieve. The need is to progress from emotional dependence on parents, or others, to relative autonomy while

still being able to maintain close emotional ties. The need is to reach a point where, although individuals have extremely personal feelings for those close to themselves, they are still able to be emotionally independent enough so that they are not unduly influenced by the emotional responses of despair, displeasure, or disappointment of others around them.

To be self-reliant rather than self-sufficient is the answer. Self-sufficient people draw a circle around themselves and say, "I don't need anybody else—I can take care of my needs." Actually, they are often afraid to let anyone into their bubble for fear of being hurt. Insufficient people say, "I need everybody's love, attention, and support." These people need all kinds of help. Self-reliant people say, "I can stand on my own two feet, emotionally, but I'm willing to share my feelings with others and let them become part of me." The key to emotional independence is the ability to receive, share, and give love, to be interdependent, without becoming overwhelmed and emotionally dominated. The capacity to love someone other than oneself is an integral factor in adult emotional independence. The self-reliant person is such an individual.

Social independence comes more readily because young adults have been working in this direction ever since they were early adolescents. Of course, social independence carries with it responsibilities in civic, political, occupational, educational, religious, social, and community affairs. The essence of social independence is not a "cop-out" or denial of social responses; it is not a matter of "doing my own thing"; rather, it is an element of social trust and of self-direction in social thought and decision.

The element of social trust entails the extent to which others (society) can count on the individual to make an effort to contribute to the well-being of others by being socially responsible. As someone in our group of young adults said, "I should be able to count on you to drive on your side of the road, to stop at stop signs when I have the right of way, to pay your share of the taxes for our common welfare, and to trust you to control those primitive impulses of yours that would permit you to strike out at me and to steal and to cheat. In return, you should be able to trust me to do my best to act in accordance to those principles that would enable us to live together amicably.''

Self-direction implies being free from group domination in establishing or determining a social pattern of living and of thought. Adolescence is a time when the desire for social acceptance is so great that whatever the group says is what the adolescents do or think. At some point individuals must separate themselves from the social and emotional domination of others: "to be my own person." Individuals may subscribe to the views of a group, political, religious, or social in nature, but within that allegiance they should still be able to be selective in the social views, ideals, values, and behaviors that they will follow.

Economic independence demands an acceptance of financial responsibility, self-support, and support of family. Knowing the value of money and how to spend it wisely and learning to limit desires to ability to pay are equally important. To be constantly in debt shows poor management and economic immaturity.

Economic independence involves several measures to ensure financial success. First, early adults should have at least one marketable or saleable vocational skill that they can offer an employer in return for a job that will pay enough to provide for basic needs. Second, there should be some type of career plan involving specific training, apprenticeship, or schooling that can lay a foundation for future training and experience. Third, some money management knowledge is needed in terms of budget making, clothing management, household expenditures, and repair costs. Fourth, some knowledge of credit buying, interest rates, and life insurance would be desirable. Economic independence is more than having a job and being on one's own—it includes the whole concept of economics and money management. It begins with decisions that adolescents make when they decide what courses or programs they want to take in school, what interest areas they develop, and what attitudes they adopt toward work.

Career development

Almost all adults devote a major part of their activity and interest to the occupation in which they earn their living. A successful vocational adjustment is therefore a strong integrative factor in the lives of most men and women. Success in a job not only ensures one's economic existence but provides many other satisfactions as well. In the American culture a person's occupation and achievements in it are major determiners of social status and self-esteem. Emotional needs for approval, preeminence, and security are satisfied by a good vocational adjustment.

Career development in adulthood includes establishment and maintenance of a career and adjustments throughout the years while in the vocation. The individual must first find a place in the occupational world. Successful establishment may involve mobility as much as security and stability in an occupation. Adult vocational identity is largely a function of career movement within occupations and work organizations, although the individual may progress within the same organization.[2]

Many women pursue dual careers of homemaker and of an occupational role outside the home.[3] Few would quarrel with the observation that women have a fundamental biological difference from men, manifested in the ability to conceive, bear, and nurse offspring. Woman's role has been traditionally organized around the children and the support of the effort of the family's breadwinner. Neither the biological nor social role of the homemaker is as static as some advocates would have us believe. Women now have an option in childbearing. Fathers are much more involved in child rearing than previously. The feminist-suffragette movement of the nineteenth century and the acceptance of women into the work force in World War II have set in motion challenges to the stereotyped social role for women that, paired with the changes in social expectations for men, may ultimately dispel the stereotype roles. Women, free from social pressures, can decide to remain single and to devote themselves to careers of their choosing. Some women prefer to be part of a dual-career family —married, husband and wife both involved in their careers and, perhaps, also having children.

A large part of a young person's time and energy during young adulthood is spent getting started in an occupation. In the early years of one's working life there is much changing of jobs. The skilled and professional workers, however, after spending several years of searching tend to settle into a particular occupation and remain until retirement. In contrast the less skilled workers continue to switch employment and employers for most of their working years. Truck drivers and construction workers sometimes show employment in ten to twenty different jobs before retirement.

Professionals, such as chemists, accountants, teachers, and others, rate the nature of their work as the single greatest source of satisfaction.[4] Industrial workers with less schooling indicate that working in an area of genuine interest is an important factor in job satisfaction. However, they emphasize job security and pay rates as conditions that play the most important part in job satisfaction.

Phases of adulthood

Freud, Spock, and Piaget have charted almost every inch of childhood. Erik Erikson presented a convincing map of adolescence and touched on adulthood. Yet in most cases the charting of life cycles generally stopped near the age of 21, as if there were no further changes or development in adulthood. Or perhaps the changes and directions were so numerous that it was deemed impossible to plot out the periods of adulthood. Researchers are now sharing an interest in charting adult life cycles.

One of the simpler, yet meaningful, chartings of developmental periods over the life course was done by Levinson, et al.[5] Using the traditional stages of development, Levinson also makes special note of "entering," "transition," and "culmination" periods. For example, the early adult period is listed as ages 17 to 22 years, early adult transition; 22 to 28 years, entering the adult world; 28 to 33 years, transition; and 33 to 40 years, settling down. The middle adult era starts with a midlife transition period between 40 and 45 years of age; 45 to 50 years, entering middle adulthood; 50 to 55, transition; and 55 to 60, culmination of middle adulthood. At 60, the late adult era begins, with the late adult transition period being 60 to 65. From 65, 70, and on, late adulthood is in evidence. The implication is that no period begins and ends abruptly.

Klemme believes that failure to resolve the young adulthood to middle age helps explain the high rate of alcoholism, depressing suicide, divorce, and similar problems that occur during this period. The transition from young adulthood to mature adulthood is equal in difficulty to any other period of transition in the growth and development of people. A "midlife crisis" occurs in some people. According to Klemme,[6] this crisis is a feeling that what one is doing no longer seems important or fulfilling. A failure to make the transition smoothly can begin a long process of personal frustration and failure. A woman may feel this negative mood with her job or when the children are grown and no longer need her. A meaning in work or a sense of newfound purpose in life is needed. The periods involved are ages 21 to 35, stage of achieving mastery and material gain; 35 to 60, stage of self-mastering and personal satisfaction; and 60 or so until death, becoming concerned with altruistic causes and social issues.

A more subtle approach by Gould, Levinson, and Vaillant[7] adds new dimensions to the topography of post-adolescent life. Briefly, the main features are: ages 16 to 22, leaving the family, where youthful fantasies about adulthood give way to realities; ages 23 to 28, reaching out for personal identity, developing an ability to respond to intimacy, and seeking to master the world; ages 29 to 34, a period of questions, questions, questions. There is a crisis about the age of 30 where life begins to look more painful and difficult; there is a decline socially, vocationally, and maritally that must resolve itself by age 34. A midlife explosion occurs between ages 35 and 43. Midlifers wonder if there is time to change in order to become one's own person and to still make it big in one's career. Between 44 and 50 there is a settling down, a stable period; more attention is paid to old values and to friends and less to making money. After 50, a mellowing sets in, marked by a softening of feelings and relationships. There seems to be an implication in these views of threatening 30s and mellowing 50s, with the 40s being a make-or-break period in terms of reaching goals set in early adulthood.

MATURITY AND THE EARLY ADULT

To understand what adult maturity is it is better to think in terms of principles that reflect the nature of maturity rather than to consider a list of specific forms of behavior. One could not possibly cover all the types of ''mature behavior'' that exist. The first principle is that mature adults have developed a system of internal and external behavior controls that are acceptable on the adult level. Ever since these individuals were early adolescents, they have been trying to learn how to control their emotions and behavior so they would be acceptable to society at large. As adults, they should have reached this goal.

The second principle is that mature individuals have developed a value-judgment system that will enable them to live acceptably within a social group. This value-judgment system is a personal philosophy of what is important or unimportant, good or evil, desirable or undesirable. It enables individuals to make choices and decisions that are in keeping with what they consider to be their individuality and their personal well-being. At the same time their value-judgment pattern should permit them to live within a social pattern. They may not necessarily live as others do, but at least they are not offensive to the point that they are rejected.

Traits of maturity

Mature individuals have perspective. Their behavior is based on a good balance of intellectual insights and some emotions and imagination. They learn to live with problems they recognize as unsolvable and work to find a solution for those that can be solved. They are open to suggestion but are not overly influenced by others. They learn to profit not only by their own experience but also from the experience of others.

They have some knowledge of social life, love and marriage, and the requirements for living in a society. They take responsibility for their own welfare, do not expect others to make decisions for them, and are willing to work for what they want. Mature adults live partly by intelligent compromise, but at the same time they respect their own individuality. Along with this they accept authority to the point that they know that the first attempt to improve a situation should be through rational discussion.

Mature individuals also take responsibility for their own behavior. They do not blame their background for mistakes they make or use it as an excuse for a shortcoming. They do not evade responsibility or put the blame on someone else.

Mature adults realize the relation of personal gain to personal effort. They are able to endure present discomfort for future gain and satisfaction. Their behavior is based on principles. They do things because they consider them as values and not because someone forces them to do so. Maturity refers to a person's ability and motivation to accept adult rights and obligations in a variety of adult role relationships. Adult responsibility entails attempting to deal with all contingencies as sincerely as possible.

Individuals in this age group, because of the recency of their exposure to the demands and expectations of a formalized learning environment, are probably more receptive to learning than any other age group. However, young adults, especially those who are married, are plagued by numerous distractions that may constitute barriers to the learning process. Some of these are adjusting to marriage, getting ahead on the job, rearing a family, buying a home, and the like. The degree to which these tasks constitute barriers in the educational process depends on the maturity of the learner.

Heath[8] did a study on maturity that compared definitions of maturity as written by experts and by nonexperts. Definitions of maturity from the writings of thirty-five expert psychologists were collected. These definitions were based on rich and intimate experiences with a wide range of persons or on the results of diffuse and general empirical observations. Forty-three nonexpert college male youths were asked to select the most mature person they knew and in 5 to 10 minutes describe that person's most central characteristics. A content analysis was made of both sets of definitions.

Without any pretension of having exhausted available expert definitions or of having used the most rigorous of empirical procedures, the most striking result of the study was the essential similarity of the traits selected both by nonexperts (in 5 to 10 minutes of reflection) and by experts (after years of reflection). Both groups of judges agreed on eight of the thirteen trait categories. In both cases the mature persons emerge as judiciously realistic individuals with a reflective

Association needs are met by affiliation with others who share the same interests. Recreational and leisure time activities provide opportunities for social contacts.

Harold Geyer

sense of values and an underlying meaning to their life that they maintain with integrity. However, they are not closed to new experience but are open to continued growth. Such persons can adapt to others and can tolerate and control most of the tensions of living. They have a basic human warmth or compassion and respect for their fellow man. The experts add that they are integrated, basically accepting of themselves, self-reliant, capable of tender, loving relationships, and creative. The nonexperts say mature persons have wide interests, are happily married, have close family ties, are generous, empathic, and sensitive to others.

Hierarchy of basic values

Man has values. He tries to reach for his total potentiality. Animals, pretty much, have a "horizontal development." Once they have established their systems for survival and response, they seem to be limited in growth of value insight. Some animals, such as our pet cat Paddy, do seem to have some humanlike qualities, but on examination their value system is greatly restricted in scope and depth. Man, however, is capable of "vertical development." Not only does he learn survival values but he also learns human values and spiritual values.

Maslow's hierarchy of basic needs[9] can be translated readily into a hierarchy of basic values. The level of values and needs closest to survival are the physiological needs of food, water, sex, and other biological needs. Security needs represent a step-up in values, as manifested in the economic needs of man to make money and collect material possessions. Money-hungry people may live most of their lives on this level. Some animals also collect materials, in terms of food, to last them over the winter months. Recreation or play needs are a step-up in the ladder of values. To have some fun and to partake in leisure-time activities it is necessary to re-create the body and spirit (Table 13-1).

It is more fun to play with someone, however, so people move up to a category more closely resembling human needs. Belonging to a group, having friends, and being part of an organization have association values. Some people stress these values more than any others. But people also talk about reputation and "being well thought of" so that on a higher level there are character values, which go beyond the individual's need to just be part of a group. A man could live a whole lifetime on the character value level, and when he died, people could say. "He was a good man." Yet he may not have made the most of his potential as a human being. There is a higher category of values on the intrinsic, abstract level.

This same man could have made more use of his intellect in a search for truth, intellectual values, curiosity, or seeking just for the sake of learning. Even beyond that are the values of creativity and material beauty. Things that have been created by the hands and minds of man are precious, and so are the things of nature that have been created by wondrous ways. The highest intrinsic level to which man can aspire is the total being or spiritual level—the level of self-actualization wherein man gives of himself in devotion

Table 13-1. Hierarchy of basic needs and values in pursuit of self-realization*

Highest	Spiritual needs and values	Devotion to ideal beyond the self
"Others"	Association needs and values Intellectual needs and values	Beauty, creativeness, nature Understanding, knowledge, curiosity
"We"	Character needs and values Association needs and values	Respect, self-esteem, independence Friends, belongingness, love
"I"	Recreational needs and values Economic needs and values	Pleasure, leisure time Material possessions, comfort
Lowest	Physiological needs and values	Food, drink, sex, security

*Based on data from Maslow, A. H. *Toward a psychology of being* (2nd ed.). New York: Van Nostrand Reinhold Co., 1968.

to an ideal beyond himself. On this level personal, material needs are transcended for the common welfare. The self-actualized man, the mature person, according to Maslow,[10] has a realistic orientation, is accepting of self, has spontaneity, is task oriented, has a sense of privacy, independence, appreciativeness, and spirituality, has a sense of identity with mankind, a feeling of intimacy with loved ones, democratic values, philosophical humor, creativeness, and some nonconformity.

All the needs and values on the hierarchy are important; at times some are more important than others. Certainly if a man is starving, his physiological needs must be met. What is crucial, however, all things being equal, is which category or which values does the individual tend to emphasize as his prime motivator of behavior? Does he emphasize the survival values, the social values, or the intrinsic values? What he stresses will determine his basic philosophy of life and his level of maturity in terms of potential as a human being.

To keep a proper perspective on life there are four things that people ought to do at least once a year. They should visit a museum to see what the creative mind of man has been able to produce throughout the years and to note that modern man does not have a claim to an intellect which is superior to that of ancient man. Cro-Magnon man was also an intellectual giant. Modern men should use their creative powers just as the cavemen did. Second, they should attend a wedding to see and feel the excitement of a couple getting together, prayerfully, for a lifetime together to create a home and a family unit and to raise children. Third, they should go to a hospital to visit some sick friends to see the frailty of man and his body—to be reminded that the physical housing of humans is perishable and destructible and that the individual must take care of it. Finally, they should attend a funeral, at least once a year, to be reminded that this life is limited, that there is an end. This will reinforce a person's awareness that physical things die but that intrinsic, spiritual things continue to live even after the physical death. A proper perspective on life is needed to encourage human beings to seek the better parts of this earthly existence.

GETTING MARRIED

Vast social changes have been taking place in American and Western society. The change from the rural to urban society, the economic emancipation of women, the increased secularization of social life, the resulting decline in religious sanctions, the individual approach to mate selection and marital expectations have all had their impact on the nature of family life. It is axiomatic that whenever social systems of any type go through change, instability of some type will result. Many professionals see the current crisis in family life as one phase in the process of social change. The alleged current family and marriage crises are viewed as stemming from the fact that whereas the traditional basis of family has apparently been weakened, a new basis for family living has not yet fully emerged. In the meanwhile, young couples will continue to fall in love, some will marry and some will not, and children will be conceived in either case. Some couples will be happy with their situation; others will not.

The why and wherefore of marriage

Mating is an inborn drive in man, but marriage is a formal institution. One of the considerations in instituting the custom of marriage was probably the desire to enjoy the sex drive as fully as possible with a minimum of hazards and anxieties. The natural sexual impulses of man and the aim of procreation needed to be satisfied, and yet some responsible control over it was also necessary. The man and the woman involved had to be protected, in a way, and security needed to be provided. Historically, general promiscuity has been abandoned in all types of societies in favor of the stability and security of family life.

More important, family living affords a means for the nurture and care of the young child. Two parents are important for the proper rearing of the human infant because he remains helpless for a much longer period than do the offspring of animals. Experience indicates that the emotional needs for growth and development of the child, as well as his physical needs, are best fulfilled by two parents through the stability afforded by the institution of marriage.

Every age had its share of common-law marriages, trial marriages, cohabitation or "people just living together because there's no hard, fast commitment that way.'' Yet the interesting observation is that as long as there has been recorded history, regardless of the sophistication or the simplicity of the society, the family was always the basic biological and social unit, and with it there was some aspect of the marriage institu-tion. Society can absorb a goodly number of couples who ''live together for as long as we love each other, even without the benefit of a piece of paper indicating marriage.'' However, when the number of marriageless couples reaches a saturation point, the political fiber of society's structure will alter. Not only will the element of sta-

Heterosexual interaction is a prime focal point of early adulthood. A socially active individual may choose to remain single or to get married.

Harold Geyer

bility deteriorate but so will the pattern of record keeping, on which so much of current, complex societies depend. Obtaining a marriage license is a systematic method by which government can keep track of the status of its adults and give legal sanction to the union.

Reasons for marriage. Over 95% of all Americans will be married at least once before they die. The reasons why people marry are many—love, economic security, desire for a home and children, emotional security, parents' wishes, escape from loneliness or from a parental home situation, money, companionship, sexual attraction, protection, notoriety, social position and prestige, gratitude, pity, spite, adventure, and common interests.[11] The law indirectly plays a part in marriage. The individual is not forced by law to marry, but to enjoy certain rights and privileges he must do so.

A socially induced reason for marriage is conformity. The single person finds himself different because the majority are married. A married couple may tend to play matchmaker for the individual still single by arranging dates or even inviting two "singles" for dinner. The individual in this way may be pressured into marriage.

The individual may marry for satisfaction of ego needs. To be wanted more than anyone else and to be of value to the other person are important needs for some people. Ego satisfaction plays an important role throughout the individual's entire life, and marriage is one way of achieving this. In general, marriage provides for security, recognition, response, and new experiences. These factors are basic to the emotional needs of human beings.

Marriage and college. Until World War II marriage was generally delayed until education was completed. Before World War II many colleges and universities actually expelled students who married while in school, but with the return in the late 1940s of tens of thousands of veterans who attended schools all over the United States on the GI Bill, the married student ceased to be a statistical rarity. Indeed low-rent housing units for him and his family were quickly provided by the hundreds on campuses. The schools also tried to provide part-time jobs for student husbands and wives. Today one in five undergraduates attend-

ing American colleges is married and living with his spouse (United States Bureau of the Census, 1973), and more than half of the graduate students are married.[12]

Perhaps the central reason for this large percentage of student marriage is the increasing stress associated with the contemporary American mass society. Among the present generation of young people (more than one half of the population is under 25 years) the need to belong, which translated means the need for emotional support and security, for companionship, for love, and for a paired relation, has become more pressing and significant in the context of an impersonal and materialist society. Marriage is the primary institution in our society that can reliably and satisfactorily fulfill this need. Cohabitation, however, seems to be practiced in increasing numbers in many college communities. There are some disadvantages to marrying while attending school. The husband, for example, who both works and attends classes knows that if he falls behind on his job, he may be fired; if he does not keep up his grades, he may flunk out for the rest of his life. On the other hand, if his wife works to support him and any children they may have, he may feel guilty or ashamed at not fulfilling what he considers to be the traditional breadwinning role of the husband. At the same time the working wife may resent the time her student husband devotes in the evenings and on weekends to his studies and may regret that she, too, cannot experience the social and intellectual stimulation of student life.

Cohabitation practices also have their limitations. The impact in this case is not so much economic inasmuch as both members generally contribute to their mutual support. The sting comes in social and emotional matters. Regardless of the rationale given by the couple for living together—such as a sense of personal freedom, honesty and openness in a relationship, rejection of marriage for the time being, and sexual equality—strong emotional attachments usually develop and the couples move into a deep level of intimacy on all fronts, not just the sexual front.[13] The need for personal commitments frequently appears and, if not honored, jealousy and possessiveness may enter the picture. Marriage at

When your cup is full,
Spill some wine into the wind;
For in a thousand songs,
It will return to you.

And when your cup is empty,
Just lift it up and sing;
And it will fill itself slowly
With the wine that someone spills,
Into the wind.

Author Unknown

some future time is usually planned, but in many cases it never materializes.[14]

Meaning of love

Love is more than just the physical, sexual aspect in marriage, yet a definitive meaning of love is a difficult item to come by, since each source that speaks of love has its own definition. However, one definition which seems to have widespread appeal is that taken from the New Testament of the Bible, I Corinthians 13:4-8, which reads, "Love is patient, it is kind; love does not envy, it is not pretentious nor puffed up; love is not ambitious, nor is it self-seeking; love is not provoked; thinks no evil and does not rejoice over wickedness, but rejoices with the truth; it bears with all things, believes all things, hopes all things, and endures all things. Love never fails, whereas prophecies will disappear, and tongues will cease, and knowledge will be destroyed." From this definition comes the meaning of love that lasts through times of frustration and achievement, sadness and joy, youth and maturity.

Love, then, is a quality that defies exact definition but can mend strained relationships and reestablish lines of communication between the marriage partners when they have been cut off. In her study of fifty-two married couples over a ten-year period beginning in undergraduate years, Rachel Cox[15] found that, except for a very few, the strength and satisfaction of the marriage tie increased as the years went by. She asked her subjects to grade various aspects of love as listed on a rating scale. In analyzing the answers, she found that a hopeful, supportive, and essentially uncritical love characterized thirty-three of the fifty-two marriages. In eighteen marriages love was such that the spouses were more objective about the flaws in the other spouse and in their marriage. Love was found to be a needed element in exploring the reaches of another personality and redefining one's own emerging self in relation to the expectations and needs of that other personality.

People "fall in love" for different reasons. Some fall in love for physical reasons—for physical attraction and sexual response. Others fall in love for social reasons—"It is the thing to do."

Among some adolescents, "You're nobody unless you've got a boyfriend (girlfriend) and going steady." An older man, having finished time in the Armed Forces or returning to college from a job, often finds himself quickly married simply because he was heard to express the idea that "Well, I'm older now; it's time for me to settle down." Some people fall in love for emotional reasons. It is a tremendous feeling to have "someone who understands me" or to think "she needs me." To want and to be wanted, and to have emotional needs satisfied is truly a good feeling but hardly enough of a basis for a lifetime relationship.

There is infatuation, artificial love, romantic love, and mature love. Infatuation is exciting and tingling, but it is shallow because the individual is responding to what he or she is getting out of the relationship. "It's real love—she loves *me*!" Artificial love stems from motives, often not even associated with love. Some individuals marry to escape from an unhappy parental relationship or home or from intense feelings of loneliness. Some marry so that they can find meaning in life by living through the accomplishments of their marital partner. Others marry for possessions, a change of scenery, the opportunity to travel to a distant place, or for money. These reasons for marrying are often based on artificial love.

Romantic love is storybook love. "Love means never having to say you're sorry." This kind of love carries with it immature beliefs such as the idea of the one and only, love at first sight, and the thought that love can solve all problems. Romantic love has its place. Some people experience this type of love several times in their lives before marrying. It can serve as a binding or cementing force to help a young couple through their first months, when adjustments are being made toward a more mature outlook on married life.[11]

Mature love emerges out of human interaction. It comes about through the process of adjustment and readjustment of the personalities of two people who have a great regard for each other as total personalities and have a desire to do all that they can to make the other person's life meaningful and happy. An individual who is ready for marriage (1) likes the one who is loved, (2) is not merely in love with the idea of love, and (3) is emotionally mature to the point of surviving an adjustment period while still maintaining a high regard for the other person.

Love, like a diamond, has many sides or facets to it to make it sparkle. If you experience only one or two facets of the diamond, you may miss a serious flaw in one of its other sides. You could be purchasing a worthless diamond. The same is true with love. You must look at all the different aspects of love before you can be sure you have a good love. Unlike a diamond, however, love can grow if it does not have any serious defects.

Accepting a marriage partner

Young adults are expected by their society to be able to love a person of the opposite sex and to choose a partner with whom they will live out their life. Studies of marriage for the past generation have tended to emphasize reasons for mate selection as the principal basis for explaining happy or unhappy outcomes. However, explaining what John sees in Mary or why they chose to marry each other can be complex indeed. Their reasons for selecting their mate will vary greatly. In any society, however, there are factors that generally affect and "partially" explain who marries whom. Certainly laws, religion, age, class, and race are factors that influence the choice of mates.

There are several influential reasons and theories why certain people come together. First, considerable study has centered around the propinquity theory as a major factor in mate choice. Propinquity means nearness or in close proximity. People who usually meet each other in some form of close association, such as at work, school, neighborhood, church, or leisure-time activity tend to gravitate together because of familiarity. A positive reaction to this association can become very meaningful. A second theory is related to the "ideal mate" concept, with traits and characteristics they would like to see in their marriage partner. "She's everything I've ever wanted." A person with this approach can usually make a list of the qualities they desire in a husband or wife. This theory is close to the value theory, which holds that each person possesses a

value system that consciously or unconsciously guides them in their mate selection.[16]

The theory of complementary needs states that people are attracted to others who have the characteristics they have always wished they had themselves or who can help them to be the person that they need and want to be. Wish fulfillment is the motive for marriage. In people with deep psychological needs opposites do tend to attract, thus complementing the self.

A more widely recognized theory of why certain persons are chosen as marriage partners is the homogamy theory. In general, couples respond readily to each other if they have similar economic, racial, and social characteristics. Even the divorced and widowed tend to marry their kind.

The last theory is that of compatibility, which in all of its forms does much to bring couples together. Couples who can enjoy a variety of activities together and can communicate, understand, and accept each other because they share a common feeling or philosophy respond to each other deeply. They are compatible. It might be desirable to have complementary emotional needs patterns so that a couple can support and strengthen each other, but it would be just as important to have a supplementary or a common interest pattern in some aspects of their lives so that they can share wonderful experiences together. Love is a useful criterion in choosing a marriage partner. However, a more thorough, mutual understanding of the individuals involved is needed to discover the cause-and-effect relationships of why they chose each other.

Predictors of marital happiness

Although love is needed in marriage, it is not the sole requirement. Studies have been made to determine the ingredients of a successful marriage. The studies take on a specific pertinence in view of the increased divorce rate in society today. Unfortunately, there are so many variables involved and the personalities of individuals are so varied that it is difficult to make predictions for individual couples. However, suggestions related to success can be made for the group as a whole (Table 13-2).

One of the most comprehensive studies in the

Table 13-2. Factors in marital happiness*

	Favorable	Unfavorable		Favorable	Unfavorable
Premarital factors			7. Reason for marriage		
1. Happiness of parents' marriage (high)	X		a. Love	X	
			b. Loneliness		X
a. Parents divorced		X	c. Escape from one's own family		X
b. Parent or parents deceased		X	d. Common interests	X	
2. Personal happiness in childhood	X		**Postmarital factors**		
3. Ease of premarital contact with the opposite sex	X		1. Attitudes		
			a. Husband more dominant		X
4. Mild, but firm discipline by parents	X		b. Pair equalitarian	X	
5. Lack of conflict with parents	X		c. Wife more dominant		X
6. Courtship			d. Jealous of spouse		X
			e. Feels superior to spouse		X
a. Acquainted under one year		X	f. Feels more intelligent than spouse		X
b. Acquainted over one year	X		2. Good relationships with in-laws	X	
c. Approval of parents	X		3. Not living with in-laws	X	
d. Similarity of age	X		4. Community of interest	X	
e. Satisfaction with affection of other	X		5. Desire for children	X	

*Based on data from Kirkpatrick, C. *The family as process and institution.* New York: The Ronald Press Co., Copyright 1955, pp. 346-354, 599-617.

field of marriage was conducted by Stanford psychologist L. M. Terman[17] and his associates. In their project they tested and interviewed several thousand subjects and followed their progress. From the analysis of their data some surprising conclusions were drawn. It was found that their most important predictor of a happy marriage was the happiness of the parents in their marriage. Other factors were happiness during childhood and firm and consistent discipline during childhood.

In another area Terman found that adequacy of sex instruction, the amount of "petting" before marriage, the use of contraceptives, varieties and types of sexual techniques, and differences between how often intercourse is desired and the actual number of times it occurs had little or no relationship to marital happiness. Terman deter-

mined that marital happiness was more dependent as a whole on family background than on sexual factors. He concluded that "a large proportion of incompatible marriages are so because of a predisposition to unhappiness in one or the other spouse." The key is the type of attitude toward life and marriage that each partner has. An embittered pessimistic one has a poor prognosis.

Barry[18] did a review on factors related to a successful marriage. Some of the predictors of happiness in marriage that he found were (1) possession of positive personality traits such as an optimistic temperament, emotional balance, and sympathetic attitude, (2) similarity of cultural backgrounds, (3) a socially responsive personality, (4) a harmonious family environment, (5) compatible religious observations, (6) satisfying

Working couples who cooperate and share the responsibilities of household tasks ease the stress of daily living.

Image, Inc.

occupation and working conditions, (7) a love relationship growing out of companionship rather than infatuation, and (8) a wholesome growth of attitudes toward sex relations. In general, the most important factors are the social environment within the marriage, the personality factors of the people involved, and the patterns and processes of family interaction. The success factors are always relative to the values held by the individuals and the society to which they respond.

Ultimately, the success of a marriage depends on the capacity of the man and woman to make it successful. This capacity involves personal values, personality traits, social characteristics, and ability to adapt, adjust, and change. The key factors are self-insight, self-acceptance, awareness of the needs of one's partner, and the ability to cope, understand, and accept. Expectations are also crucial, since they give the individuals a point of view that will affect their behavior. In additon, consider these detrimental factors to happiness: intense personal problems, incongruity of main personality traits, inabilty to meet growing obligations, and poor outlook on life. They all reflect some inadequacy in personality maturity.

It is important that the couple learn communicative as well as interpersonal social skills. How do you get along with others, living in a highly personal, close, intimate relationship? The skills required for prolonged, close living are somewhat different from those required for neighborly, occasional social contacts. The success of a marriage will depend largely on the psychological, emotional, and social readiness of the couple, individually and as a pair, to meet the demands of married living.

In addition, covert as well as overt personality and social characteristics are important. A predisposition to unhappiness or pessimism in one or both spouses can lead to unhappiness. No one appreciates or likes to live with a "Gloomy Gus." An optimistic point of view on life in general is desirable. It is interesting to know that all couples, happy and unhappy, have about the same number of grievances and problems in daily living. It turns out that the unhappy couples are the ones who are bothered by them more; they complain longer and more bitterly.

It would also be helpful socially if the couple enjoy some leisure-time activities together and hold some values in common. It is important for the husband and wife to be friends and companions to each other as well as lovers. Companionship has been singled out as being the primary basis for marital satisfaction.[19] It encompasses love, esteem, acceptance, insight, and enjoyment of the other individual, receiving as well as giving. It focuses primarily on the affectional relationship of a man and a woman, a husband and a wife.

BEING MARRIED

Getting married may seem like the biggest job to be done, especially to the person who has not found a marriage partner as yet. However, being married also requires an effort. There is an adjustment period to go through in which two people learn to live as a couple. Then there is the never-ending task of working with the problems, decisions, and unexpected circumstances that always seem to occur. Do not despair. Life is made up of changes, challenges, and choices. That is what it is all about. Meeting these situations individually and as a couple is what makes life interesting and exciting if you let yourself see it that way.

Developmental tasks of newlyweds

Marriage is a developmental process, and the conditions of the marriage are modified in time as people change and adjust to life's situations. A marriage keeps changing as each partner changes, and a successful marriage comes about through its potential for continued development and adaptation. Adjustment and attainment of the developmental tasks in early married life will do much to bring about desirable adult development and to lay the groundwork for success and happiness in marriage.

Very early in marriage the couple will need to (1) learn to live as a couple instead of singles, (2) work toward integrating their personality traits and styles of living, (3) achieve a satisfying sexual relationship and understanding, (4) become aware of acceptance of the realities of married life, and (5) evolve a marriage development plan that will bring to the couple their desired short-

Harold Geyer

Consumerism is a family matter. Today's markets make it necessary for all members of the family to be knowledgeable about products, shopping patterns, and buying skills.

term and long-term goals in life. Some of the developmental tasks to be accomplished before the first child is born are (1) developing competency in decision making, (2) getting and spending the family income, (3) learning to accept and communicate each other's feelings, (4) developing an attitudinal, as well as material, readiness for parenthood, (5) learning social skills and increasing socialization as a couple instead of singles, (6) developing a pattern of cooperation and understanding that permits them to overcome adjustment problems with less friction, and (7) working out routine schedules and chore tasks around the house.[20]

To accommodate one's mate it sometimes is necessary to change some pet habits and develop new ways of doing things. Although one should not expect to "make people over" after marriage, both partners should be reasonable and considerate. Certainly no expectations of major change should be anticipated. The girl who says, "but I know he will not want to do that after we're married" may well be fooling herself and doing wishful thinking. Even simple behavior patterns and habits can be problems that require adjustment—how late one is used to staying up at night, whether one likes to shower in the morning or evening, being accustomed to eating at 5:30 instead of 6:30 P.M., sleeping with a window open, finding it hard to give up the personal privacy of a bathroom, learning how to accept relatives who are overwhelming.

Personal adjustment

The marriage relationship may have either a positive or a destructive influence on the psychological well-being of the husband or wife. It involves many of the most crucial adjustments a person will ever have to make. Each partner brings to marriage the equipment of motives, attitudes, and preferred modes of adjustment that have been learned through previous experiences.

The two personalities are brought into an intimate and pervasive contact that has unusual potentialities for working out emotional responses. Some adjustment problems, such as those of school or employment, can be relieved temporarily by evading or ignoring them, but the adjustments of marriage are less escapable. For a successful outcome the personalities of the partners in marriage must be complementary and harmonious at the outset or sufficiently flexible to make new adjustments without undue anxiety or hostility.

If a couple can make the following adjustments, their marriage can be happy, successful, and fun. First, marriage requires a continuous process of adjustment by both members. Second, the couple must have an understanding and acceptance of each other as persons. Third, the couple must be aware of problems and solve

them together. Fourth, the couple must learn to accept the insolvable problems. Fifth, the couple must have a desire for success in marriage. Sixth, marriage is not a fifty-fifty situation but, rather, a situation where the one member may give more in a certain aspect than the other. Seventh, it is the interaction of psychological, interpersonal, social, sexual, and financial aspects that makes the marriage a success.

The constructive influence of marriage includes factors other than stable home life and sexual adjustment, although the importance of these primary satisfactions must not be minimized. The well-adjusted husband and wife provide a kind of continuous psychotherapy for one another. This close and confidential relationship aids each partner to gain insight into his or her attitudes and to feel the strength of a united effort against difficulties.

Sex in marriage

The function of sex in marriage is an integral part of the concept of marital oneness. It is so defined by society and culture. Religion and customs can influence the sexual attitudes of married couples. In recent years, however, psychologists, marriage experts, and other social scientists have broadened the definition of normal sexual intercourse to include acts that the couple themselves freely and willingly perform in the love-making ritual. One husband and wife may believe particular precopulatory tactile, visual, oral, and other activity a vital necessity. Another pair may regard as desirable anything but direct intromission.[21]

The specific drives, attitudes, and outlooks of the married couple determine the nature, frequency, and attitude toward their particular sexual activities. Generally, it is important that the marriage partners understand each other's levels of sexual arousal, length of orgasm, sensitivity to tactile stimuli, and other facets leading up to and following intercourse.

The problem of sexual adjustment usually occurs during the early months of marriage. During this time, sexual relations will need to be followed with considerable care if the couple is to arrive at a fully satisfactory relationship. One should recognize that sexual satisfaction does not necessarily have to include consistently reaching orgasm. Intercourse does not have to take place each time there is sexual play. The point of view of both partners will determine the nature of sexual satisfaction for themselves.

Sex in marriage provides a sense of mutual gratification between marriage partners. In fact it has been shown that far from becoming bored with the same sexual partner, in the great majority of marriages that have endured, the couple discovered that the exclusive mutuality of their married love was accompanied by increasing capacity to give and receive. Sex is a form of communication, probably the most intimate, in which two people express a oneness of mind and feeling.

Marital problems

Marital conflicts are not necessarily undesirable or harmful to a marriage if they do not involve attacks on the self-worth of the marriage partner. Conflicts can be healthy in exposing areas of dissatisfaction and can lead to their eventual resolution. An overriding need to make the marriage work is essential when a conflict occurs. If there is no attempt at making a marriage function successfully under some stress or conflict, any conflict, however mild, will only serve to drive apart the partners of an already shaky marriage relationship.

The dynamics of conflict need to be understood. How does a person react under stress or frustration? Things being equal, people are likely to externalize their feelings by finding fault with others when the stresses and tensions that they normally carry become too burdensome. This reaction is frequent among men who work in competitive jobs where there is an emphasis to produce. When the husband returns home, he is irritable and anxious. The family suffers a great deal until the stress is relieved. As far as the wife is concerned, the social and career roles, as well as the husband's expectations of her, may create stress and result in externalization in the form of exaggerated behavior.

Another dynamic of conflict takes the form of concealed discord. In this case the partners suppress their true feelings toward each other; they express them by frustrating the other partner or by dropping subtle remarks designed to hurt the other person. If the conflict is not resolved, tension can build up over a period of time and suddenly explode when one of the partners can no longer contain it. Unresolved conflicts usually have a chronic effect on the marriage and may emerge as sexual unresponsiveness.

Conflict between two people may also be expressed by forms of resistance that make it difficult for the couple to resolve their differences. One form of resistance is a reluctance to admit that a marital problem exists; another form is a lack of communication between partners. Without communication all types of distortions and imagined grievances can occur. Occasionally, a partner will not communicate to avoid hostility and argument, or perhaps he will hold communication in abeyance to be used strategically at the opportune time. Other dimensions of conflict include (1) dealing with symptoms rather than causes, (2) substituting superficial problems for the real problems, (3) generalizing a problem so that only the surface but none of the nitty-gritty details are recognized, and (4) intellectualizing the problem on a cognitive level to the point that the underlying feelings, which are highly important in conflicts, are ignored.

The areas from which marital problems can arise are numerous, and the problems themselves are complex (Table 13-3). The most often used term to describe an inability to get along is *incompatibility,* but it is only a general term that does not specify the conditions under which marital conflicts arise. Incompatibility, for example, may arise because the ethnic, religious, or cultural backgrounds of the couple are different; thus there may be differences with respect to attitudes, values, and what each partner may wish to achieve in life and marriage. Some conflicts arise simply because people do not know how to handle stress. Sometimes conflicts are intensified because neither partner has learned skills for dealing with conflicts. As a result, it is usually "the problem" that gets the blame and not the individual's personality which is inadequately prepared for dealing with problems.

What do most married couples quarrel about? What problems lead to separations and divorce? A University of Pennsylvania research team

Table 13-3. Analysis of 1,412 help-request letters addressed to the American
Association of Marriage Counselors*

Category	Husband (%)	Wife (%)	Total (%)
Affectional relations	11.5	31.0	27.6
Spouse cold, unaffectionate			
Spouse is in love with another			
Has no love feelings for spouse			
Spouse is not in love with me			
Spouse attracted to others, flirts			
Excessive, "insane" jealousy			
Sexual relations	42.1	20.6	24.4
Sexual relations "unsatisfactory"			
Orgasm inability; frigidity, impotence			
Sex deprivation; insufficient coitus			
Spouse wants "unnatural" sex relations			
Personality relations	23.4	17.2	18.3
Spouse domineering, selfish			
Own "poor" personality, instability			
Clash of personalities; incompatible			
Spouse's violent temper tantrums			
Spouse withdrawn, moody, "neurotic"			
Spouse quarrelsome, bickering, nagging			
Spouse irresponsible, undependable			
Intercultural relations	11.5	11.4	11.4
In-law relations troublesome			
Religion and religious behavior			
Deviant behavior	7.5	8.7	8.5
Heavy drinking, alcoholism of mate			
Own heavy drinking or alcoholism			
Spouse's "loose" sex behavior			
Own illicit sex behavior			
Compulsive gambling			
Role tasks–responsibilities	0.0	6.0	4.9
Disagreement over "who should do what"			
Spouse's failure to meet material needs			
Situational conditions	4.0	3.4	3.5
Financial difficulties, income lack			
Physical illness, spouse or self			
Parental-role relations	0.0	1.7	1.4
Conflict on child discipline			
Parent-child conflict			

*From De Burger, J. E. Marital problems, helpseeking, and emotional orientation as revealed in help-seeking letters. *Journal of Marriage and the Family,* 1967, **29,** 712-721.

interviewed 300 couples, 200 of whom had once sought marital advice.[22] Husbands and wives, questioned separately, reported that the following problems bothered them most frequently: (1) money, (2) household management, (3) personality clashes, (4) sex, (5) sharing household jobs, (6) children, (7) leisure-time activities, (8) the husband's mother, (9) personal habits, (10) jealousy, (11) husband's occupation, and (12) the wife's mother. Infidelity ranked seventeenth on the list.

Many persons come to physicians with marital problems, even though they are not marital counselors. Herndon and Nash[23] reported the following problems mentioned in physicians' offices. Men ranked their marital problems as follows: (1) sex, (2) money, (3) too much or too little affection, (4) inability to discuss problems with wife, (5) in-laws, (6) failure of wife to express appreciation, (7) inability of wife to conceive, and (8) wife's fear of pregnancy. Women brought up problems related to (1) sex, (2) fear of pregnancy, (3) too much or too little affection, (4) money, (5) inability to discuss problems with husband, (6) failure of the husband to express appreciation, (7) inability to conceive, and (8) in-laws. For both men and women half of the first six most-mentioned problems had to do with appreciation and communication.

How important is sex in a marriage? It all depends upon whether you are male or female. Clifford Adams[24] at Pennsylvania State University ranks the importance of sex second with men and sixth with women. After studying 6,000 couples Adams reports that men rank the various ingredients of marriage in the following order: (1) companionship, (2) sex, (3) love-affection, (4) home and family, (5) encouraging helpmate, and (6) security. Women listed (1) love-affection, (2) security, (3) companionship, (4) home and family, (5) community acceptance, and (6) sex. Again social and emotional responses ranked high. Marriages founded on sexual attraction usually have a flimsy foundation on which to build.

We would like to make one last point concerning marital problems. Numerous studies will show that sex and money are most frequently mentioned by couples as their major problems.

Experts have long known that these factors may simply be the outer manifestations of more crucial, deeper, underlying conflicts. There is a real need to "get to the root of the problem." Money problems are easy to pick on because so many people simply do not have enough money for everything they want to do. And how can two people feel free to have sexual intercourse with each other when underneath they are heartsick about the problems they are having with their marriage? It is difficult to have a satisfactory sexual relationship with someone who is causing you to have personal problems.

Crises in marriage

A crisis exists when the family faces a complicated state of affairs for which there is no available solution; for example, loss of income, infidelity, bereavement, and divorce. These crises may permanently disable the family involved, especially if the surviving members are incapable of absorbing the duties of the individuals handicapped by the crisis. On the other hand, the family may be drawn closer together by the threat to their cohesion and may emerge from the crisis stronger than ever.

Loss of income. After the depression of 1929-1936 research found that many afflicted families surprisingly absorbed the shock of poverty without demoralization or great personal disorganization. The disorganization that did occur culminated when the family accepted the fact that it could not function by its old buying and living pattern. A period of emotional stress followed the loss of income, but it usually terminated with an adjustment to the situation; otherwise evidence of pathological reactions resulted.

A crisis, because it sweeps away the customary ways of living, tends to expose the resources or deficiencies of the family. The families studied who had refused to face issues in earlier family crises were found to have evaded facing the changes in family life brought about by sudden poverty. This crisis did not seem to cause new reactions, but it did seem to exaggerate family traits previously exhibited. For example, the occasional drinker began to drink excessively; the happy family became more unified and loyal.[25]

Infidelity. It is hard to know if infidelity is a

cause or an effect in a crisis. Many men and women turn to another person when they have been deeply hurt by their partner. The Hunt[26] report states that one fourth of the married (not divorced) wives and one half of the husbands studied had at least one extramarital affair during their marriage. For women the incidence between the ages of 18 and 24 years was three times higher than a generation ago. The percentage of women over 30 involved in extramarital affairs also increased sharply.

A husband's infidelity may be an attempt to prove his manliness; it may be a revolt against his conscience; or it may possibly be a method of solving misunderstood impulses originating during childhood. His other woman may be a sanctuary from an overprotective wife or a means of ''getting back'' at his wife. In the Kinsey study[27] among 221 cases of infidelity by wives in which the husbands knew of the affair, only 42% created any serious difficulty in the marriage; 58% of the husbands seemed able to tolerate and forgive their wives' infidelity, and wives were even more tolerant of their husbands' infidelity.

Bereavement. Prolonged illness and/or death of a member of a family is both a financial and emotional difficulty. A closely knit family will have more security on which to lean, and they will be more readily able to overcome the crises than the family without close ties.

Two things happen to a member of the family when another member dies: (1) he senses that the circle is broken and that the family is threatened, (2) he senses that a part of himself as a person has been lost. The first reaction is a sense of disbelief and then numbness, which helps to ease the shock.

The routines of the funeral help the family to accept the idea of death, but afterward there is no professional help. This is the most difficult period. Families are supposed to adjust quickly and then carry on in a normal manner. Our personal experiences are that children generally do not manifest a change in their school work patterns until about the third month after the death. Then there is a lowering of grades and sometimes a start of behavior problems.

Divorce. The impression created by the mass media, and professionals as well, is that divorce rates are astronomical and that the family unit, as it was traditionally known, is deteriorating rapidly. It would be very important to put these matters into a clear perspective. Some quick answers: Yes, the divorce rate is higher than it used to be; no-fault divorce laws do make it easier to get divorces. No, the family unit is not deteriorating because of the divorce rate nor because of alternative styles of living.

The divorce figures generally given are those that compare the number of divorces in one year with the number of marriages in the year. That's like mixing oranges and apples to get an average. We're dealing with two different sets of people. It's a misleading way to use statistics. In the first place, the comparison is between people getting divorces who may have been married 3 months, 3 years, or 30 years or more, and individuals getting married during one year's time. A better approach is to look at what happens to marriages over a period of time. Glick[28] did such a study on the lifetime marriage and divorce experience in 50,000 homes. Of the married women now in their late 20s or early 30s, the study showed that 71% to 75% of these married women *stayed* married. (A big difference from the idea that one in two or three marriages ends in divorce.) A second factor to consider is that four out of every five divorced persons get married again. Of these, only 2% will be divorced twice and married three times. Beyond that, there is less than one fourth of 1% divorcing and remarrying. By far the highest incidence of divorce is found in the below 25 age group—three times the overall average. Wives under 20 are involved in almost half of all the divorces recorded yearly. The reason most often given for the divorces is a shortage of money because of a lack of preparation for the job of supporting a family.

Kieren and associates[29] found that girls who marry before they are 18 years old are nearly three times more likely to be divorced than the girls who marry when they are 22 to 24 years old. Why are early marriages generally less stable than later marriages? No one knows for sure, but there are several possible interpretations. Early marriages may simply reflect the socioeconomic pressure of this group. Also, chronologically immature people are likely to be emotionally immature and, in consequence, make unsound mate selections. Often early marriage curtails the husband's education; thus there would be greater economic pressures in early marriages than in later marriages. If the husband does continue his education while his wife works, he may "outgrow" her. Finally, in many young marriages the wife was pregnant before marriage; premarital pregnancy is correlated with a relatively high divorce rate.

The current estimates based on numbers of marriages and divorces reported by the various states indicate that about one out of every four marriages is terminated by divorce or annulment compared to one out of eight marriages in 1922 and one out of twelve in 1900. In addition to this high rate of divorce 3% of all marriages are terminated by "true separation," that is, those couples with legal decrees of separation, those living apart with the intention of obtaining a divorce, and those permanently or temporarily separated because of marital discord. Finally, numerous studies agree that about 15% to 20% of all married couples can be classified as unhappy cohabi-

tants—those whose marriage is considered extremely unhappy, both by the couple themselves and by their friends (Fig. 13-1).

The pregnancy

Among man's basic instincts is the procreation of the species. Starting a family is one of the developmental tasks of early adulthood. The nature of the task is to have a first child successfully (Fig. 13-2). As for the psychological task of starting a family, Havighurst[30] raises the questions of acceptance or rejection of the pregnancy on the part of the woman, confidence in the physician, worry over possible failure to have a normal baby, desire for sexual relations during pregnancy, the uncertainty of breast feeding, and the matter of the reactions of relatives and friends to the pregnancy.

Probably the most crucial task is that of acceptance or rejection on the part of the mother. If she is scared or disgusted at the thought of pregnancy, the task will be difficult for her. The husband's attitude toward the baby must also be considered. An attitude of rejection on his part

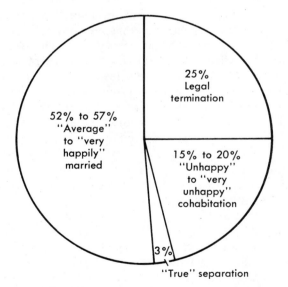

Fig. 13-1. Total incidence of marriage failure. (From Saxton, L. *The individual, marriage, and the family* [2nd ed.]. Copyright 1968, 1972, by Wadsworth Publishing Co., Inc. Belmont, Calif. Reprinted by permission of the publisher.)

Fig. 13-2. The fertility rate in the United States for a 12 month period ending July, 1973, declined 7% compared to the previous year. Rate of natural increase was 5.9 persons per 1,000 population compared to 6.9 persons for the previous 12 months. Marriage rate in the same period was up 1.4% with 2.2 million marriages; divorce rate was up 9% with 884,000 divorces. (Redrawn from National Center for Health Statistics. *Monthly Vital Statistics Report,* Sept., 1973, **22,** No. 7.)

can have almost as serious an effect on the woman and the family as if the woman had rejected the pregnancy.

Next in order of importance is confidence in the physician. To some extent he will have both lives in his hands during the period of birth. The woman's confidence in her physician can cure many lingering doubts she may have about her pregnancy.

Some women experience little desire for sexual intercourse during pregnancy, whereas others have increased sexual desire. The adjustment of the husband's sexual behavior is important.

There can be a deep sense of pride in being pregnant since the mother "makes" the baby. The sense of pride, however, also fills her with concern about the many possible "things that could go wrong." While fathers pace up and

Motherhood can be very demanding when so much has to be done, but love and care of the infant come first.

"THE TWO OF US"

Donna and I had been engaged about half a year when we decided to live together for a week. We left for college a week early during the summer before my senior year.

We moved into my apartment on a Saturday morning, so we actually had nine days until classes started. The first day was set aside to get everything in some sort of order and to do general cleaning. Our thoughts seemed to be centered on the idea of how wonderful it would be if we were married and this was our first apartment together.

The freedom we had enjoyed the three previous years at college seemed so much sweeter after a summer of being at home under "parental guidance." We were filled with the excitement of returning to this freedom, and especially so because we returned with each other.

During our stay together, we realized how much we didn't know about each other—spiritually, emotionally, physically, and socially. For example, we quickly learned that each other's early morning grumpiness was short-lived and, in a way, humorous. I began to understand why a girl has to start getting ready for a date an hour before her date. Donna in turn was amazed at how I could get ready in the span of five minutes.

Helping each other with everyday routine such as vacuuming and cooking was so much more enjoyable than ever before. Washing the car and shopping also took on added meaning since it was for and by us.

We found our ideas on sex, and the human body in general, to be different. We both felt sex was an expression of love and should be given and received as such. This view had not been Donna's original outlook, but through sincere talks and my openness she gradually took on my viewpoint. I come from an extremely uninhibited family. My parents had literature for us children on birth and conception and would answer any of our questions honestly. We were taught that there was nothing sinful about the human body. It was not an uncommon event to see one another nude while dressing or going to or from the bathroom. We would often skinny-dip in the pool before going to bed.

Donna's background was very inhibited, and her sexual knowledge came entirely from a sex education class and her peers. Her parents viewed sex as dirty and sinful and they never talked to her about it.

Our first sexual relations were enjoyable even though she was scared. She thought it was wonderful because we viewed sex as a shared expression of love. We now feel that the best and only way to deal with sex is openly and honestly.

Through our experiences we learned many things, but perhaps the most important thing was that love is sharing—total sharing of mind, body, and soul into a beautiful relationship.

down hospital floors waiting for the baby to be born, the mother is afraid of miscarriage, neonatal death, or a deformed baby.

The question of breast feeding can be answered with a sterilized bottle and enriched milk. Many women in past decades preferred not to nurse the child. There seems to be a general trend back toward breast feeding.

Finally, the reaction of friends and relatives should be considered. The in-laws especially may express adverse opinions about the entire idea of having a baby or of what to do with him after he is born. This seems to be the least tenuous task.

Once the child is born, the family life revolves around the newborn child for some time. During this period the parents have to adjust to new demands placed on their time and energy. One young couple said, "The baby can be quite demanding of attention and help; often at times it is a real sacrifice to stop whatever you're doing and tend to his needs." The early years of childhood are day-to-day happenings in which the child slowly develops physically, emotionally, socially, morally, and mentally.

CHOICE TO STAY SINGLE

Not everyone wants to be married. The U.S. Census Bureau reports that from 1970 to 1975 the number of adults aged 25 to 34 who had never married increased by 50%; the number of unmarried women aged 20 to 24 increased from 28% in 1970 to 40% in 1975. Among 20- to 35-year-olds, one in four was single.[31]

The social pressure to get married is not as strong as it used to be. The unmarried young adult has more freedom to leave home, to change jobs, and to travel. The poor prognosis for teenage marriages and the frightening cries of divorce rate traumas cause many young people to wait before making a permanent commitment. Career opportunities for women have increased and many are choosing to enter the job market before, or instead of, considering marriage. There is a freedom of choice that did not exist before without questions and pressures to get married.

Marriage is still part of the picture of the future, however. Of the men still unmarried at 30 years of age, 75% will ultimately marry; of the girls still unmarried at 30 years, 55% will marry before 50

years of age.[32] Of those still unmarried at 35 years, half the men and about one third of the women will marry. By 40 years of age the ratio of men getting married is one in four and for women it is one in six.

By 30 most women who are still unmarried are building up economic independence, an investment in work, and a viable value system. There are a number of sources of personal and social satisfaction in areas other than marriage and family. It is important to recognize that if the woman's first choice was to get married, she must not build a dissatisfaction around her life. A careful evaluation of her assets can lead to a rewarding life in spite of her initial wishes.

Living-together-arrangements (LTA) or cohabitation has an appeal for some people because of the simplicity of the arrangement—you just move in together. In the United States unmarried couples living together make up 1% of the population. In Sweden, 12% of couples living together are unwed. The idea is not as new as some mass media would suggest. There have always been "common-law marriages." Communes and multiple marriages were tried in the 1870s. The free-love and trial marriage movements were well publicized in the 1920s. Sociologists indicate that there is no solid research to support the notion that a significant, meaningful trend toward new marital or nonmarital living arrangements exists. Open marriages, swinging couples or mate swapping, group marriages, and communal living are relatively rare in the United States.[33] Nowadays women do not want to put up with marital situations that they find unsatisfactory and that they cannot fix.

Of all the new approaches to adulthood, "singlehood," when the individual chooses to remain unmarried and unencumbered, is the one new style of life and living that is most rapidly emerging in Western societies and seems to be the most acceptable to those who wish to remain single.

STUDY GUIDE

1. What is meant by "the developing years" or "the age of expansion"?
2. Review the developmental tasks of early adulthood. How many of these tasks are

you in the process of achieving, have achieved, or will be starting to achieve soon?

3. Personal independence implies emotional independence, social independence, and economic independence. How are these forms of independence interrelated? How do they aid and abet, or possibly interfere with, career development?

4. What are the "whys and wherefores" of marriage? In print and in the news media descriptions have currently appeared about "communal living" with the concept of shared partners, about unmarried couples living together without the confining demands of marital ties, about clubs and apartments for "singles." Several authors suggest that "marriage is on the way out." What do you think? Do you agree or disagree?

5. What is love?

6. What appears to be the central ingredient for a successful, happy marriage? "It all boils down to . . ."

7. Several studies are cited as predictors of marital happiness. Make a composite list of these predictors and compare it to Table 13-2.

8. Review the developmental tasks of a newly married couple.

9. Marital problems are often adjustment problems. Different kinds of adjustment need to be made at different stages of a marriage. Can you think of changes in life-style or life patterns that may necessitate a change and an adjustment of the couple in their thinking and behavior toward each other?

10. The section describing the unmarried adult is not intended to suggest that unmarried adults represent a deviant type of behavior. Unmarried adults do constitute a minority, however, in a marriage-oriented society. With the median age of marriage getting slightly higher (older) and with the current emphasis on "singles" cultures and living, how do you view the unmarried adult in today's society? How do you see this person ten years from now? Twenty years from now?

11. What constitutes maturity of adults?

12. What do you consider to be your main emphasis, philosophically and pragmatically, in terms of the hierarchy of basic values presented in the last section?

13. What is it like to be an adult 21 to 30 years of age? What are the sociological, psychological, and physiological factors involved?

REFERENCES

1. Havighurst, R. *Developmental tasks and education* (3rd ed.). New York: David McKay Co., Inc., 1972.
2. Flaste, R. Career ambitions: keeping the options open. *The New York Times,* February 27, 1976, p. 15.
3. Wilson, S. R., & Wise, L. *The American citizen: 11 years after high school.* Palo Alto, Calif.: American Institutes for Research, 1975.
4. Bird, D. *The case against college.* New York: David McKay Co., Inc., 1975.
5. Levinson, D. J., Darrow, C. N., Klein, E. B., Levinson, M. H., & McKee, B. *The seasons of a man's life.* New York: Alfred Knopf, 1978.
6. Klemme, H. L. as reported in Rausberger, B. Three phases of adulthood: transitions termed as difficult as adolescences. *The New York Times,* July 11, 1971, p. 32.
7. From, New light on adult life cycles. Time. In White, S. *Human development in today's world.* Boston: Educational Associates of Little, Brown & Co., 1976.
8. Heath, D. *Explorations of maturity.* New York: Appleton-Century-Crofts, 1965.
9. Maslow, A. H. *Toward a psychology of being.* New York: Van Nostrand, 1962.
10. Maslow, A. H. *Farther reaches of human nature.* Esalen Institute Book-Publishing Program. New York: Viking Press, 1971.
11. Bowman, H. A. Marriage for moderns (6th ed.). New York: McGraw-Hill Book Co., 1970.
12. U.S. Bureau of Census Current Population Reports Series P20. No. 303. *Social and economic characteristics of students,* October 1975. Washington, D.C.: U.S. Government Printing Office, 1976.
13. Thoman, G. Living together unmarried: a study of thirty couples at the University of Texas. *The Humanity,* 1974, March/April, 15-18.
14. Macklin, E. A third cohabit at Cornell. *New York Times,* December 23, 1973.
15. Cox, R. *Youth into maturity.* New York: Mental Health Materials Center, 1970.
16. Landis, P. *Making the most out of marriage.* New York: Appleton-Century-Crofts, 1965.
17. Terman, L. M. *Psychological factors in mental*

happiness. New York: McGraw-Hill Book Co., 1938.

18. Barry, W. A. Marriage research and conflict: an integrative review. *Psychological Bulletin,* 1970, **73**(1), 41-45.

19. Hawkins, J. L. Associations between companionship, hostility, and marital satisfaction. *Journal of Marriage and the Family* 1970, **17,** 282.

20. Kenkel, W. F. *The family in perspective.* New York: Appleton-Century-Crofts, 1966.

21. Hass, K. *Understanding adjustment and behavior.* Englewood Cliffs, N.J.: Prentice-Hall, Inc., 1970.

22. Problems of marriage. *Parade,* November 6, 1966, p. 28.

23. Herndon, C. N., & Nash, E. M. Premarriage and marriage counseling: a study of North Carolina physicians. *Journal of the American Medical Association,* 1962, **180,** 395-401.

24. Sense of values *Parade,* November 2, 1969, p. 12.

25. Covan, R. S., & Ranck, K. H. *The family and the depression.* Chicago: University of Chicago Press, 1958.

26. Hunt, M. *Sexual behavior in the 70's.* New York: Dell Books, 1974.

27. Kinsey, A. C. et al. *Sexual behavior in the human female.* Philadelphia: W. B. Saunders Co., 1953.

28. Glick, P. (quoting census figures). In Velie, L. The myth of the vanishing family. *Reader's Digest,* February, 1973.

29. Kieren, D., Henton, J., & Marotz, R. *Hers and his.* Hinsdale, Ill.: Dryden Press, 1975.

30. Havighurst. *op. cit.* 78pp.

31. Census Report on Marriages and Divorce. Washington, D.C.: U.S. Census Bureau, March, 1976.

32. Adams, M. The single woman in today's society: a reappraisal. *American Journal of Orthopsychiatry,* 1971, **41**(5), 776-786.

33. Constantine, L., & Constantine, J. M. The group marriage. In M. E. Losswell, & T. E. Losswell (Eds.), *Love, marriage and family. A developmental approach.* Glenview, Ill.: Scott Foresman, 1973.

Middle adulthood

The years of stability

Some years ago, during my undergraduate years in college, I read a book entitled, *The Best Is Yet to Come*. I don't recall the author or much that was written other than, as each stage of life was described, the author developed the theme that when an individual was in a certain stage in life, even though he was contented and happy, the best was yet to come. I remember that in the later stages of life the author believed that then and then only did the individual realize real contentment as he evaluated his life and looked toward death, believing that the best was yet to come. Young at the time, in my early twenties, I remember thinking, "Well, that's his opinion."

Today, on the other side of 40, I am inclined to think that perhaps the author knew what he was talking about. Does life begin at 40? Well, it depends on what you mean concerning "life."

If you mean that physical life begins at 40 years, we all know that isn't so. By that age, after having lived over 45 years—days and nights—physical being is definitely not beginning. Oh, no, physical suffering would be more like it! If you have had a healthy body, prepare for aches and pains of a general nature to creep into your being. Chronic illnesses may emerge at this time so that yearly check-ups begin to make sense. Believe me, even the faithful eyes that have always seen everything and never failed begin to sting, water, and even blur everything together. Needles can no longer be threaded. Help is obviously needed.

On the other hand, when you are on the other side of 40, you have begun to accept your limitations. A certain amount of rest is needed so you see that you get it—not because some health book tells you but because you know you have to have it. You also follow a sensible diet because you now know that you alone will suffer the consequences if you don't. It is easier to do the right thing after you are 40 years old. You accept and understand what must be and go on from there.

You don't become so upset over the trivial things of life. By the age of 40 years you have experienced enough really important incidents of life so that energy is not wasted on the unimportant. What once seemed likely to be "the end of the world" is no longer viewed disproportionately. Little things are left to take care of themselves, and activities and problems are kept in their proper place.

When you are young, you have so many dreams and ideals. When you are over 40 years old, you now know that some of these dreams will never come true. Rich? Probably you will never be rich in material things, only in the things that make your life what you want it to be. You no longer plan to conquer or improve the world. You no longer expect the impossible from yourself or from those you love. What a relief! Now you can settle down to do the kind of thing you can do well and be satisfied with the doing of it. Gone is frustration. Now you can be satisfied. Now you can realize self-fulfillment in many facets of life.

If you are a parent, by this time your children are well on their way to adulthood. How nice it is not to wash diapers, observe schedules, and pick up after messy children! How proud you can be of your children and their accomplishments. How great it is to discuss interesting affairs of the world with them. If you are so fortunate as to be the mother of sons, how delightful it is to be "spoiled" by these fast-growing men. I love every minute of it!

Married couples who are over 40 years old have found the person they most want to be married to. Long ago they gave up trying to change the other member in their marriage. They accept him, limitations, behavior lackings, and all, and are thankful for them. So what if your husband is not the greatest lover of the century! After all, you are no prize package yourself. Positive attributes are appreciated, and negative aspects are either forgotten or overlooked. It is so nice to love and be loved just as one is. Gone are the role playing, games, and lack of communication that characterize a new marriage. Understanding and insight have taken over, and it is marvelous!

The sad part of being on the other side of 40 years is that you begin losing some of your loved ones, especially those parents whom you have loved for so long. Sitting through my own dear mother's funeral and listening to the preacher expound on some of the familiar and beautiful passages from the Bible: "I am the Way and the Life . . . The Lord is my Shepherd," I was suddenly overwhelmed with the feeling that this is what life is all about. Life does go on! Life does have meaning! Wonderful!

When you are over 40, you don't have to keep up with the Joneses any more. In fact, who cares about the Joneses? Let them have or do what pleases them, and we'll find our own satisfaction. How free it is to relax with those of your choosing, those you really enjoy being with, and to no longer worry what others will think.

Being on the other side of 40 is nice careerwise, too. By now you hope that you have developed some common sense and learned some valuable lessons from experience which will enable you to do a better job. Some of us have reached our goals or see them in sight. Some of our dreams have been fulfilled.

Intellectually, it is pleasant to know a little bit about a lot of things. It is also good to realize that even though you can't know everything—ever—you can know where to find out what you don't know. This calms down nervous feelings of inferiority. By 40 years of age you know that others are just like you. No one is ever perfect. There is a lot of congenial give-and-take and little pretense at this time.

At 40, or on the other side, you can look at the world, love it; look at yourself, accept it; and feel that it's a great thing to be alive after all. Life is meaningful and fulfilling, and the best is yet to come!

Forty?
Contented, fulfilled,
Facing the future confidently,
  Enjoying the present.
The other side is best.

The developmental trend has come to that point in time known as "middle age" or as our Pennsylvania Dutch friends say, "Ve get too soon oldt, und too late schmart." They also say, "Throw the horse over the fence some hay," which does not make much sense. But, then, to many people middle age does not make much sense, yet somehow the message gets across. However, we are not here to condemn middle age. We wish to present it in its proper perspective and place in the total life span. It can be a beautiful time of life because it ushers in the years of stability and freedom. The age of anxiety is over.

Early adulthood comprises the "developing years"—that period when all growth movement is vertical, upward and forward. The expansion phase of adulthood is a fast-moving period in which the young adult strives to achieve mastery over the external world, seeking material gain and approval of others. Sooner or later in each life there comes a time when the expansion phase tapers off. When and how this time occurs varies. It may come when the man finds himself looking over his life situation and saying, "You know, if I can just maintain what I now have and am for the rest of my working days, I would be happy." To maintain the status quo, to just keep pace, to live and let live because life is satisfying at that point is to have arrived at the years of stability, where life will be on a more even keel. Now is the time when a person can turn his interests inward to achieve self-satisfaction and self-mastery. Activities that offer personal satisfaction can now be most important. The children are out of school, many of them are married, and the mother and father now have more time for each other and their own interests.

THE AGE LEVEL

As with most age levels, it is difficult to cite an age at which middle adulthood begins and ends. When one reads the literature, it is interesting to note that as the life span of man lengthens into the upper seventies, the ages cited for different adult levels are shifted upward. Three and four decades ago middle adulthood, or midlife, was indicated as starting at the age of 35 years, and in some cases at 30 years, and extending to 45 and 50 years of age. More recent writings equate the early 40s as the beginning of middle age and continuing to the early 60s. There is more agreement on the circumstances that surround these years than on the actual age range itself. Middle age is generalized as the period between the time when the traditional roles of child rearing and becoming established as a provider have been completed and full retirement. The intervening period is one of more personal freedom, less economic stress, greater availability of leisure time, and fewer demands for material growth.

Developmental tasks

The connotation of the years of stability and freedom can be grasped more clearly by examining the developmental tasks of middle adulthood. The tasks are more intrinsic in nature; they relate to interpersonal roles as well as intrapersonal development, and for the first time many of them stress the "comforts" of life.[1]

Relating to spouse. This is a time for the renewal and full development of the wife-husband relationship. It is a time of cutting through the thick overlay of habits of child-centered days and of nurturing a deep and abiding intimacy as a couple. This renewed awareness of the initial relationship in the marriage partnership will lead to rich and satisfying interaction between husband and wife. The couple will find encouragement, support, and reassurance from each other. There will be the time and desire to do things as a couple again and to find each other after years of struggling with the physical, financial, and emotional strain of parenthood.

The joint responsibility that seems to be most difficult for couples at this time is the finding of each other as individuals again and of redefining or modifying their roles as husband and wife. The ability to meet each other's needs emotionally and sexually at this time is a goal to which the middle-aged couple must address itself if this drawing together is to become a reality. The man and woman need to reassure and fully accept one another as they are at this moment if their individual identity is to be recognized and, with that, their identity as a couple. Learning to share feelings and satisfactions and to recognize and appreciate each other as individuals who have desires, aspirations, and disappointments will lead to a fuller life for both partners.

Grown children. The "mature" mother responds to the tasks of middle adulthood with the serenity born of a knowledge of "selfhood" that has been nurtured over the years. Her children are free to develop as persons without her being emotionally dependent on them. She feels no threat in sharing the affection of her offspring as their circle of social contacts grows. Standing by to assist their children practically or in an emotionally supportive way is a positive task of the mother and father at this stage in life.

At this time in life the task of intergenerational adjustment comes to the fore as well. The new in-law and grandparent roles are now part of the middle-aged adult's emotional scope. The way in which each member accepts these new roles, whether enthusiastically or reluctantly, will determine in some measure his contentment at this time. Fragmentation of the whole family unit may result, with its ensuing loneliness and heartache if this task is not successfully met. Middle-aged

couples must rise to the occasion and realize the enrichment that these relationships can bring to their lives.

Leisure time. Development of creativity that has perhaps lain dormant during the child-rearing phase can be a highly satisfying task of the woman or man at this point in life. This may take the form of career pursual or resumption, of an active part in civic, social, or religious organizations, and of exploring new hobbies and areas of talent and skill. The satisfactory use of leisure will be a source of contentment and bring feelings of self-worth to the woman of this age group. The use of leisure time is the task that befuddles the male born and brought up in the utilitarian framework of American culture. This task is a "natural" for those who have learned the art of the "minivacation" and the joy of the long weekend, but to many serious, competitive business and professional men this poses a great challenge.

Social responsibility. Mature social and civic responsibility is a goal toward which the middle-aged adult must grow. This includes the understanding of one's civic responsibilities and how one can fit into the broad scheme of civic and social betterment of the world. As a rule, at this time the man and the woman have the time and vision to make their mature judgment a source of community, national, and international contribution.

Aging parents. The middle-aged adult also faces the task of developing a wholesome relationship with aging parents. Being aware of their interests and needs without allowing dominance or undue dependence to creep in requires much maturity and compassion. The adult of this age must stand as a bridge between the younger generation and the aging parent, allowing each to understand and value the other.

Physical changes. The middle-aged woman must come to terms with the changes in her physical being. Menopause must be viewed as a normal functional change rather than a threat to youth and desirability. Distress at signs of changes in hair, skin, and energy output tends to rob the woman of the ability to face the task at hand—that of "relishing the bloom and peace of maturity as a woman."

Economic standards. Creation and mainte-

These are the thankful things in our lives:
   . . . things that make memories of yesterday
   . . . things that make life worth living today
   . . . things that make for peace and love and hope
in each tomorrow.

Meriem Kaluger

nance of a pleasant home occupies the adult at this stage, meaning the enrichment of the existing home for nine out of ten couples to meet the needs and long unrealized desires of the couple. For the other small percentage of couples this may mean moving to an apartment and giving up what is considered a burdensome house and yard.

Learning to hit a balance between spending money for personal gratification and putting aside funds for future security is another challenge for the family unit. Many couples find great joy in "living it up" without neglecting their future security needs now that their children have been successfully launched. Conversely, some cannot free themselves of their former frugal habits and cannot strike a healthy balance between having some fun and salting away every available cent for the proverbial rainy day.

There is an important lesson to be learned in middle age—that all that any of us really has is the moment we are now living. The time has come to be prudent about how much stress should continue to be placed on "saving for a rainy day." The world of economics is different today. Life is also short, and there are no guarantees. Now is the time to enjoy, the time to fulfill dreams.

The youth cult threat: a commentary

For some not entirely clear reason the United States has developed a thought form that places great stress on the desirability of being young, looking young, and feeling young. The emphasis on youth has been overwhelming—so much so that youth fashions dictate mature adult fashions; youth foods dictate the eating and drinking styles of many middle-aged persons; and social pronouncements by youth have been influential in dictating the degree and type of value acceptance by the older generation. The overabundance of "youth-a-mania" has done much to confuse the self-concept image and identity of middle adulthood.

As a group, the middle-age group seems to feel a need for a prestige role in American society. The age group of 40 to 60 years comprises about one fifth of the population, yet it is this group that occupies the seats of power, foots the bills, and makes decisions that affect the other four fifths of the people. It is the "in-charge generation." Nevertheless, this age group needs to feel that its role as the generation in command is approved by those around them, rather than to feel defensive or self-conscious. Their chief antagonist is the youth cult in the United States.

The self-concept of the middle-aged person is further fragmented by the humorists, who enjoy capitalizing on a reluctance of many people to release their hold on youth and its often-glorified advantages. We saw a cartoon recently in which a man is saying to his wife, who is hiding under the bed, "But, Ethel, everyone has to become 40 some day!" Most oldsters forget how they dreaded becoming 30 years old. And how many people refer to middle age as "fifteen years older than I am"? Humorist Peg Bracken[2] notes the period as "not quite twilight, and certainly not bedtime! Call it the cocktail hour, the happy hour, or high tea if you prefer." She refers to contemporaries who resist the aging process as victims of the "Peter Pan syndrome: everyone else is supposed to grow older but me."

Age needs to be put into its proper perspective without the undue distortions caused by the beating advertising drums from Madison Avenue. It is not that 40 years is so awfully old, it is just that being 20 years old is so awfully young! How much has a 20-year-old really lived and experienced of life? If we are speaking of people who went to college, they actually have spent almost all their life "going to school." Is this living? Think of what people do in the second twenty years of their life as compared to the first twenty years. It is in that second twenty-year period that life is lived, loved, lost, laughed at, regained, reconstituted, enhanced! Change is an inevitable aspect of life. The man of 40 years is different in many ways from the youth of 20. The 40-year-old man anticipates change and knows how to bring about desired changes. By this age life has meaning based on having been lived, not on the expectations of what will be. The 40s are the old age of youth; the 50s are the youth of old age.

Probably most people associate getting older with a loss of the physical attractiveness of youth. But ask the question, "At what age does a woman reach her highest peak of physical attractiveness?'' Pick an age, any age from one to a hundred. Would you believe that the majority of people are their most attractive in their late thirties and early forties? It is at the age of 38 years that average adults reach their peak of total development. That could be hard to believe if you are in your early twenties, but it is true. There is an essence of beauty and attractiveness that can only come with age. Call it a mellowness, if you wish. It is an inner glow that manifests itself outwardly in beauty. It takes time to mature. For physical beauty we would choose women in their late 30s; for excitement and exuberance in living, the 20s; for volatileness, the teens; for simplicity of life and faith, the little child; for charm, graciousness, and sincerity, old age. On the college campus it is always interesting to visit the various five-year reunion classes on alumni day. Invariably, the most attractive women and men are in the twentieth year reunion class. They know how to dress, how to communicate, and how to be attractive. Each class, however, has its own aura of attractiveness about it, each in its own way.

A final word on attractiveness. Each age level has its own criteria for attractiveness. The important thing for the individual is to learn how to be attractive to people of his or her own age level, not to those who are twenty years younger (or older) than themselves. It is important for adults, women especially, to keep up with changing fashions for their age levels, particularly hair styles. What looked good on the individual in college may continue to be attractive for another five years or so, but at some point a change in clothing or hair style may be needed. Some men were still sporting their GI haircuts twenty-five years after World War II ended. How sad. Will the straight, stringy, long hair on the college girls of the late 1960s and early 1970s still look good on them when they are 40 years old? Straight, long hair gives some girls that ''intellectual, unwashed look.'' What will it look like on them twenty years later?

THE MIDDLE YEARS

The period of life called middle adulthood is a relatively new period of development in American lives. People in the United States have been living longer, and there are many more people. Medical science and technology have increased rapidly, especially since a flight has been made into space. New industrial techniques are used that prevent people from draining themselves during their younger years. Early retirement ages are in effect in many businesses, and for the first time people are living long enough and healthily enough to enjoy retirement.

Since middle age is such a recent phenomenon, there are few guidelines and criteria for living available for this age level. Precedent and tradition are noticeably absent. Psychologists and other researchers are just beginning to turn their attention to middle-aged development. Most studies have focused on either the very young or the very old. According to *Science News* (July 29, 1978), there has been a major increase in the number of research projects relating to this middle adulthood group who create and manage society for the rest of the population.

Developmental changes during the middle adult years occur slowly, since this period represents a long ''plateau'' in the life span. Furthermore, there is an overlapping of ages at both ends of middle adulthood when some adults are manifesting the changes and characteristics of an earlier or later developmental stage. The point is that changes will take place—sooner in some people and later in others. We must discuss these changes, but some judgment must be used in applying the characteristics too rigidly to ages. It is important to consider the characteristics and changes in the total developmental perspective of the individual. Seen in that manner, changes that seem pessimistic when viewed in isolation lose some of their harshness when seen in the total framework of developmental age.

Physical characteristics

Generally speaking, the human body is still functioning at almost peak efficiency as a person enters the phase of life that has been labeled the middle years. There are few characteristics to distinguish the ''middle adult'' from the young adult at the onset of this developmental stage. However, as this phase progresses, gradual changes can be identified as being peculiar to this time of life. It can be stated, however, that bar-

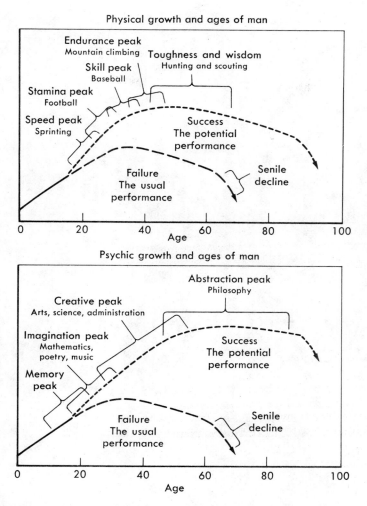

Fig. 14-1. Potential and actual performance. The upper lines indicate the physical and psychological potentials of normal people with peak periods for various activities; the lower lines indicate how most people fail to measure up. (Modified from Still, J. W. *Man's potential and his performance*. Copyright 1957 by the New York Times Co. Printed by permission.)

ring disease, physical vigor can be expected to be retained during the middle adult years (Fig. 14-1, upper chart). Most of the characteristics listed in the next paragraphs pertain to the individual closer to 50 or 55 than to 40 years of age.

Most readily identifiable are the slight and gradual changes beginning to take place in physical appearance that have a tendency to "sneak up" on the individual. One day the "fortyish" adult becomes aware of a few gray hairs beginning to appear. The all-discerning mirror reflects an image of small creases or lines (optimistically referred to as laugh lines rather than wrinkles!). Skin may become dry and begin to show signs of loss of elasticity. There is a redistribution of fatty tissue in both males and females at this time, regardless of lack of change in diet or exercise patterns.

Motor and energy. Energy is no longer something that can be expended endlessly. There is a

The peak of total development is attained about the age of 38 years. A large measure of that physical strength and body tone can be maintained by regular exercise and a good diet.

Harold Geyer

longer period needed to recoup strength after strenuous and extended activity. Few middle-aged adults can work long hours and pursue a taxing and unabated social life without feeling the need of slowing down. Minor illnesses such as the common cold seem to hang on longer, and there is a decided increase in the length of time necessary to recover from more serious ailments.

Physical fitness has become a middle-aged obsession, especially among men. There are more and more men of this group jogging, running, and working out in gymnasiums. Medical science approves of their physical activities. Some men go to great lengths to convince themselves and others that their bodies are still in good condition. However, they find that after a day of hard physical exercise it takes longer to get the weariness out of their joints and muscles. Activities that improve cardiovascular function are more healthful than muscle-building ones. Middle-aged women are also more conscious of health and fitness, but they show more concern

Table 14-1. Functional capacity of men at various age levels compared to 100% capacity of an average 30-year-old man*

Physiological characteristic	Age					
	30	40	50	60	70	80
Nerve conduction velocity	100%	100%	96%	93%	91%	87%
Basic metabolic rate	100	98	95	92	86	83
Body water content	100	98	94	90	87	81
Work rate	100	94	87	80	74	
Cardiac output (at rest)	100	93	83	58	70	
Filtration rate of kidney	100	98	90	82	77	59
Maximum breathing capacity (voluntary)	100	92	78	61	50	41

*Modified from Shock, N. W. *The psychology of aging.* Copyright 1962 by Scientific American, Inc.

with the physical well-being of their husbands than with their own. Women are involved in jogging, stretching exercises, and aerobic dancing. Women tend to be healthier.

A person employed as a laborer will realize soon after his fiftieth birthday that he does not have the vigor that he had formerly. However, his muscles are still as strong. When a person reaches middle age, he is best at tasks that require endurance rather than quick bursts of energy. The middle-aged person must learn his new limitations.

It is a fact that bodies do undergo changes at about the time of middle age. The skeletal muscles increase in bulk until the age of 50 years, but they stay on a plateau until they begin to degenerate at the age of 60 years. Gross motor coordination depends on these muscles, and therefore the peak is at an earlier age. It has been found that the smooth muscles change little with age. Therefore the vital organs can, in reality, be kept healthy until death.

Sense organs. The sense organs of middle-aged people undergo change at an amazing rate of uniformity among individuals. The sense organs are the means by which people keep in contact with the external world. Thus any change in the development of the senses affects people not only in physical but also in psychological ways.

One of the most noticeable changes is in the eyes. Many people feel the shock of realizing that they have hit middle age when they are required to wear bifocals or reading glasses. One of the

most common occurrences at approximately 45 years of age is presbyopia, a condition characterized by the reduction in the elasticity of the crystalline lens of the eye that has progressed to the point where the lens can no longer change its curvature sufficiently to allow accommodation for near points of vision. This is the reason why older people start to hold their reading material at arm's length until they are fitted for glasses with convex lenses. Many ophthalmologists are now finding this condition initially at the age of 50 years instead of 45 years. Man's sensory ability level appears to be improving.

The ears also undergo change during middle life. This sensory change especially brings a need for emotional adjustment to the individual, since it is this change that can affect the individual's relations with others. Beginning with middle age there is a gradual deterioration and hardening of the auditory cells and nerves. Thus almost everyone experiences some degree of loss of auditory acuity. The most common hearing difficulty is identified with age and is not pathological in origin. This is presbycusis, which is the loss of hearing for tones of higher frequency. This decline begins in early adulthood and becomes greater as age increases. There are significant sex differences in auditory sensitivity between men and women of all ages. There are no differences between the sexes up to the middle ranges of frequency, 2,048 cycles, but above this point women of all ages are able to hear much better than men. Deafness for voice-range tones or lower usually does not occur until about the age of 60 years. Most individuals can adjust to these changes unconsciously, but when hearing loss interferes with work or participation in normal activities, a hearing aid of some type is needed.

State of change. It is pragmatic to consider that most problems peculiar to aging start at about 40 to 45 years of age, the approximate median of life. There is a general slowing down of metabolism in the early forties, causing a weight gain and its undesirable effects on the other systems of the body. There may be signs of diabetes, and the incidence of kidney and gall stones increases. General decrease in the elasticity of the lungs is evident around 45 years of age; chronic bronchitis may develop slowly. The loss of elasticity and changes in appearance and structure of the lining coats of the arteries that can lead to many cardiovascular conditions is an acknowledged fact for people past the age of 45 years. The body systems should be periodically checked as the middle years begin so that physiological vigor can be maintained throughout the middle adult years. It is completely possible for a person to remain in a condition of sound health throughout this time period, despite the general slowing down process (Table 14-1).

It is of interest to note that scientists working with the space program consider the age of 38 years to be the peak year of adult development. The adult of this age can be more mentally alert, physically sound, and emotionally stable than at any other age. Neil Armstrong, first man to step on the moon, was 38 years old. The ages of the moon astronauts ranged from 36 years to Alan Shepard's 45 years. The look of youth may not be present, but the stamp of maturity is indelible.

Social characteristics

Socially speaking, it can be said that middle age is the time when there is an expansion of horizons through friendships, business contacts, and acquaintances made in the community. This is the stage of development in which the individual enjoys the highest social status in adult society.

Active club and organization membership is at its peak during these years. Adults who never before had time become productive and enthusiastic members of the groups that have goals akin to their own. Some aspects of a man's social contacts will be business or professionally related because career advancement still plays a role in his social life. However, there is now time to become involved socially in things that really matter to him as an individual. Wilensky's study[3] demonstrates that there is a positive relationship between amount of social participation in formal associations and job satisfaction. Furthermore, this general curve reflects the number of workers who are satisfied on their jobs. There is a sharp drop in formal participation in the early twenties, especially among hard-pressed married couples; there is a climb to a peak in the middle years, a slight drop off, and then a sag in the sixties.

The family-centered woman will now find that her social life can be "other directed" and can take on a more creative aspect rather than simply being an extension of her mother role. Cultivation of new friends and enjoyment of friends of long standing are often a pleasant aspect of life now. Visiting friends without an eye to the clock and the tyranny of what to have for dinner or what time to pick the children up can be a rewarding social aspect for the woman whose family is now fairly independent. Church-related social life with its often-attendant social service aspect may become more significant. Pressures of time and finances that did not allow for this activity previously are possibly the reason for this increased involvement. The way in which people adjust to changes in their social life depends on the way in which they have adjusted to the physical and emotional changes that are occurring.

Middle-aged individuals find themselves with more freedom from responsibility and the job; this in turn leaves them often with more money to spend and more leisure time. Some people use this leisure time as an extension of interests, broadening their scope with enrichment and fulfillment in new activities. But many people engage in activities that do not offer a worthwhile return, and others drift into boredom and dissatisfaction. The manner in which people conduct themselves in middle age depends on the way they have conducted their whole life. Table 14-2 indicates opinions concerning characteristics and behavior.

Table 14-2. Consensus among middle-class, middle-aged people regarding the appropriate time for various characteristics and behavior*

Characteristics or behavior	Age range designated as appropriate or expected	Percent who agree on the age range	
		Men (N=30)	Women (N=43)
Best age for a man to marry	20-25	80	90
Best age for a woman to marry	19-24	85	90
When most people should become grandparents	45-50	84	70
Best age for most people to finish school and go to work	20-22	86	82
When most men should be settled on a career	24-26	74	64
When most men hold their top jobs	45-50	71	58
When most people should be ready to retire	60-65	83	86
A young man	18-22	84	83
A middle-aged man	40-50	86	75
An old man	65-75	75	57
A young woman	18-24	89	88
A middle-aged woman	40-50	87	77
An old woman	60-75	83	87
When a man has the most responsibilities	35-50	79	75
When a man accomplishes most	40-50	82	71
The prime of life for a man	35-50	86	80
When a woman has the most responsibilities	25-40	93	91
When a woman accomplishes most	30-45	94	92
A good-looking woman	20-35	92	82

*Adapted from Neugarten, B., Moore, J. W., & Lowe, J. C. Age norms, age constraints, and adult socialization. *The American Journal of Sociology,* 1965, **70**, 710-717.

A major period of adjustment in this time of life is a loss of status in physical and social prowess. Educated people of the middle class reach this time of life later than others because in getting their education they put off having children until later; therefore they are older when the children leave the home.

However, these same people started at the beginning of their marriage to build status. They view status as wealth, a professional or business career, a home, a boat, two cars, lovely children, tennis and golf trophies—the list can be endless. These are status symbols that one can and often does lose in middle life. Forced retirement or younger men in the office can replace the middle-aged man or lessen his authority. The children marry and move out, and often the home is then too big for the couple. Generally, the older person's physical being eliminates the role of an athlete, therefore no more trophies or awards.

This shows the importance of building up good interpersonal relationships throughout life. Making friends by being thoughtful, kind, and generous is the kind of status that cannot be taken away during middle life. The college athlete who helped and respected his teammates will be remembered long after he made the winning touchdown. The people from the big house with the swimming pool who were kind and helpful to their neighbors will be remembered even after the big house and pool are gone. The best insurance for an emotionally rich and satisfying old age is to build a vast store of interests that are varied and not dependent on the conditions that old age automatically removes and to work with people

Middle age can be a time for fun. Social contacts are usually well established and interaction comes easy.

in such a way that the individual keeps their respect and his own self-respect.

Stability of personality traits

Personality traits are relatively fixed by the time a person reaches middle adulthood. The adult personality is a product of the interaction of biological forces, life space, and the individual's own ego organization. These forces reach a culmination by middle age, and changes do not come readily. Since the adult has had much practice over the years in learning role behavior, this role behavior becomes an attitudinal and perceptive set that is not easily modified. Most people persevere in habits, opinions, and attitudes; that is,

they become deeply ingrained in their personality. They will resist, as a rule, any change that tends to threaten their practices and precepts.[4]

For some reason many people still like to believe that they can change their personal orientation at will. Some harbor a thought that a new life awaits persons who will only change their way of thinking, believing, or feeling. This can be accomplished, but *only* by the intervention of experiences that happen to be appropriate to the needs and physical capacities of the persons involved. Change comes about because of a learning experience. Old habits have to be unlearned. People do not change automatically. Interaction with an outside agency or event or series of

Jack Corn/Image, Inc.

Personality traits, attitudes, and values become stabilized with age. Like-minded individuals are willing to band together to pursue economic and political gain.

events is necessary to accomplish change and, unless such interaction is meaningful, little discernible change may result.

Most people in the middle adult years have settled down and become ethnocentric in their personal adaptations. There are some people who are more flexible and open to change. Exposure to continuing education, diversified experiences, and an open society, make possible expectations for personality growth and accomplishment in the middle adult years.

A series of large-scale investigations of the so-cial and psychological aspects of middle age and aging was carried out over a ten-year period under the sponsorship of The Committee on Human Development of the University of Chicago.[5] Cross-sectional data gathered on more than 700 men and women, ages 40 to 70 years, revealed seven psychological attributes or characteristics that were related to overall adjustment and mental health of the middle-aged person. These characteristics include the following:

1. Cathectic or emotional flexibility, the capacity to shift emotional investments from

one person to another and from one activity to another.

2. Mental flexibility, the capacity to use experience and prior mental sets as provisional guides rather than as fixed, inflexible rules in the solution of new problems.

3. Ego differentiation, the capacity to pursue and to enjoy a varied set of major activities in life and not to rely entirely on one or two life roles.

4. Body transcendence, the capacity to feel whole and happy because of one's social and mental powers and to avoid preoccupation with health, physique, and bodily comfort.

5. Ego transcendence, the capacity to engage in a direct, gratifying manner with the people and events of daily life with a strong concern for the well-being of others and not with self-centered desires.

6. Body satisfaction, the degree of satisfaction one subjectively feels with one's body.

7. Sexual integration, the capacity to mesh one's sexual desires with other aspects of life, among them affection for the sex partner and an integration of sexual and other motivations in social relationships.

Personality adjustment in the middle years appears to be related to the individual's capacity to properly utilize these seven characteristics. Emotional flexibility is needed because middle age is a period when parents die, children leave home, and the individual's circle of friends begins to be broken by death. He needs to be able to reinvest his emotions in others and to redefine existing relationships. Mental flexibility is needed in middle age to be able to work out a set of answers to life. The impact of retirement can be lessened by a good capacity for ego differentiation, permitting the individual to take up new roles. Body transcendence, ego transcendence, and body satisfaction are needed to be able to move beyond the self so that one's interests can lie in others rather than self. Sexual integration becomes necessary because of the "change of life" that occurs in middle age. There is no question that the transition from young adulthood to middle adulthood is equal in difficulty to any other period of transition in the growth and development of people.

Emotional crises of middle age

There are three significant crises that come to many during middle adulthood—children leaving the home, middle-age affairs, and identity crises.

Children leaving the home. One of the major events in a person's life, which brings the realization that an individual is in middle age, is the time when the children leave the home. Most children become fully independent on graduation from college or on their marriage. This can be a time of happiness and reward, or it can be a time of heartbreak and disillusionment.

Too often during parenthood the adult, especially the mother, will focus all of her attention on the children, sometimes at the expense of ignoring her spouse. Most adults do not even realize that they are doing this, and thus it is a traumatic occasion when the last child leaves the home. The husband and wife will really see each other for the first time in twenty or twenty-five years. All too often they are shocked by what they see. They have changed gradually, but the change is not noticed until this time. The only bond between them, the children, is no longer there. Many people at this stage believe that their life is over; there is nothing more to be done so they will wait for old age and eventually death. Some parents take a different approach by encouraging continued dependency of their children by making mother's house too readily available and father's pocketbook too easily opened.

The couples who manage this period gracefully are those who have kept their interest and love for each other alive and also have common interests and hobbies. Therefore, when they find themselves alone again, they can enjoy each other and often view it as a second honeymoon. Many find that at this time they can afford to travel and take up activities that they missed when they were young and struggling. These are the people who believe that the spouse's needs take precedence over those of the children. This not only leads to a happier middle age for the parents but can help to prevent the development of self-centered children.

Middle-aged affairs. In recent years there has been a sharp rise in divorces between middle-aged couples. Many people are shocked to find friends who have been married for twenty-five or thirty years and who seemed to have had a good

When the children leave home, there is time for the husband and wife to relate more to each other and to enjoy activities they found difficult to pursue in the past.

David Strickler

"REJECTION— AND DEJECTION"

Two people have been married for fourteen and a half years. As half of that marriage, I had expected to be a part of the relationship until one of us died. We shared many things—numerous friends, the creation of two children, the stillborn birth of another, the adoption of a third, many and varied sexual experiences, camping vacations in many areas, three different homes, ideas, books, and many other things. Now I wonder if maybe there wasn't a lack of inner sharing and feeling of these things that I thought were so meaningful to both of us; otherwise why would a split occur and a parting of the ways seem necessary?

There was a feeling of utter desolation within me when I realized that someone I still loved had rejected me. I can't sleep at night, and in my nightmares I continually ask: Why? How could I have avoided this? What is wrong with me that I am rejected so? I examine and look at things that have happened during recent years, and many of them I see in a different light. I wonder why I was so naive about some things that seem so obvious now. Or maybe I now understand words that were spoken long ago in a new way. For example, I asked: "Do you love me?" and got the answer: "I'm committed to you." Why didn't I see through that half-hearted reply?

First and foremost, I realize how little I knew and understood about him, even though I supposedly lived very close to him. I know, even more now, how we are all truly islands unto ourselves when it comes to knowing what goes on within our minds. Some people apparently seem to prefer to maintain more of that "island-ness" than others. Why do some people not want to share what is going on inside? Are they afraid of what other people will see and know about them or don't they know how to share themselves? Who can understand and comprehend the mind?

I know that more than anything else I dread the aloneness that is at hand. I wonder about my attractiveness and whether I have the courage to try to build a new relationship. Am I even capable of a satisfying relationship with another human being, especially if that being is male? I know that I don't want to go to bed alone for the next twenty, thirty, or forty years that I might have yet to live. I know that I want to have someone with whom to share ideas, love, laughter, sex, problems, and all that makes up life. Can I ever trust myself to someone again? I ask: "Will someone want me or does my having been rejected mean that I'm not much to be desired?" If someone else never comes along, can I live alone happily? Looking at my marriage through new eyes, I realize that in its present state it could never be very fulfilling and, as much as it pains me to see it end, I somehow know that it may very well be for the good. No matter how I look at it, the pain is excruciating; unless one has experienced it, I doubt that another can understand.

I can't quite put the puzzle together, but somehow I know that some of what is being said in the women's liberation movement has some logic. Women should have their own identity. What they are should not depend completely on their husbands. Women should not be raised to all fit into one mold type—that of wife and mother. New ways of dealing with marriage have to be tried. What and where are the answers?

He is gone, and he has even refused to communicate with me, so I am completely in the dark and very much alone. My heart aches, my stomach churns, and I wonder each day how I can ever continue to live without falling apart. I watch people around me laugh and carry on life's simplest tasks with contentment and I wonder if ever again I will be able to live as happily.

marriage, suddenly get divorced. Much of this drifting apart is because the partners have lost touch with each other during parenthood and no longer have a common bond.

Some middle-aged adults suddenly find themselves trapped by their lives and their marriage. They try to recapture some of their youth and experience the "good life" before they are too far over the hill. This feeling of entrapment usually hits women in their middle forties and men in their late forties. Some people in middle age suffer through an identity crisis, and sometimes they lose sight of their values temporarily by engaging in extramarital affairs. These affairs often do not depend on what the husband or wife is like—in fact, many of these people still love their spouse deeply. Yet they jeopardize their marriage, their business prestige, and their relations with friends by seeking "the romance of a bygone era."

Sometimes the spouse never learns of the extramarital affair. Some, when they do learn, forgive and forget—but too often it leads to divorce after many years of marriage.

Identity crisis. With rapid technology and social changes and with today's emphasis on youth, many of today's middle-aged adults are faced with the question of their position in society. They are in a period of extreme internal and external pressures. They become uncertain of values; some feel bored, restless, dissatisfied, self-involved, and hemmed in by society.

Middle-aged people are suddenly faced with the shortness of life. They can choose to handle it in two ways, either to start new resolutions and activities or to begin the long, slow decline.

Either way, the persons' self-concept is challenged, especially their physical image. They ask themselves, "Am I really young at heart, or do I have one foot in the grave?" Many psychologists see similar traits between adolescence and middle age, such as the sexual change, identity crisis, and uncertainty of the role expected of them.

The ways of handling this crisis are as varied as the individuals themselves. Some indulge in hypochondria; others try to act like their college children; many find new interests and hobbies; and still others find a change in jobs, careers, or houses. A poll of this age group reveals that middle-aged adults do not really want to be young again and have to suffer through the struggling of the young. They believe that they have done their work and now deserve the freedom to enjoy it.[6]

When people reach this age, they enjoy the freedom of expressing themselves unselfconsciously. They do not depend on peer acceptance. Most adults realize that they will not impress their peers or their juniors by being false so they are usually honest. They can indulge in their whims and be a little eccentric without offending anyone. Possibly the greatest pleasure of middle age is the acceptance of one's limitations without surrender, the right to relax without giving in. Life *can* begin at 40 years for the one who has learned to give up inhibitions brought on by false social and personal values.

Mental characteristics

Contrary to popular belief, mental functions, if used, are at a peak in middle age. Cerebral capacities deteriorate slowly and only begin to weaken at the age of 70 years. Many cultures, in fact, look to their middle-aged population for wisdom and judgment. Studies now reveal that a person's general intellectual capacity is as great in middle age as it was when the person was younger (Fig. 14-1, lower chart).

Adults who have used their minds actively and productively throughout their years will have a highly refined ability to use these powers through the middle years and later perhaps. Adults who have "completed" their education with the last formal class attended will be subject to a more rapid rate of deterioration of these powers. Since the growth of the mind is a product of many outside factors, it is possible for the adult to grow intellectually through involvement in subjects and activities other than those of an academic nature.

However, most middle-aged people do not make full use of their intellectual power; they cling to the old idea that "You can't teach an old dog new tricks." To most it is a convenient excuse to not make use of their capabilities. Many older people find that they have trouble learning new ideas and techniques, but these

Mental alertness and involvement are necessary to maintain a high level of intellectual responsiveness. There is time to develop interests and hobbies that contribute to overall well-being.

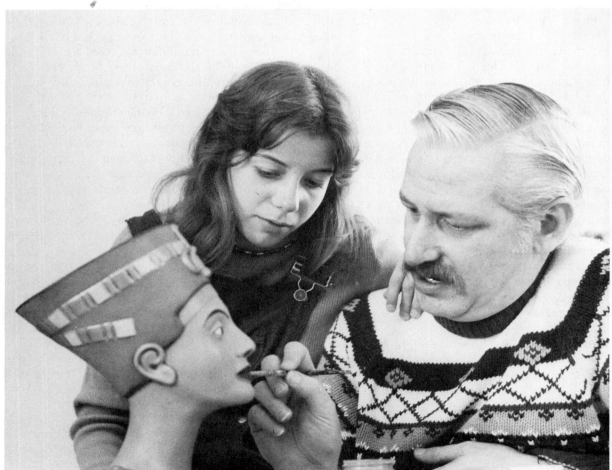

David Strickler

people have not lost their recall or their ability to learn. They have merely become "rusty," or they refuse to change their life patterns to allow for study time and work.

When adults enroll in a class, it often takes them a few weeks to adjust to the demands of learning; they have trouble remembering what they have heard or read. Unfortunately, many people get discouraged or quit at this time, but those who stay with it soon reach a high level of proficiency. People at the age of 45 years learn at nearly the same rate and in the same manner as they did at 25 years. The only difference is that they emphasize accuracy rather than speed as they get older.

Lehman[7] provided information regarding the sciences, medicine, philosophy, arts, practical invention, and other areas. He found that within fields of endeavor the maximum production rate for quality work occurred during the age decade of 35 to 45 years. The rate of creative production did not decline rapidly after the peak years, however. It was gradual at most ages—more gradual for lesser quality products than for higher quality products. Lehman's study showed that creativity varied within different fields of endeavor. For instance, in the study of philosophy the peak age of quality production was from age 60 to 64 years; the highest quality productions in science occurred from 35 to 40 years; for athletes it was 29 years; for soldiers and explorers it was 47 years; for historians, judges, and naturalists it was 54 years; and the overall peak was at 38 years of age. The use of fine motor coordination improves gradually to the early fifties, and mental and spiritual insights increase to about the age of 65 years. However, top speed is at about the age of 30 years, and top energy usage is at about the age of 35 to 38 years.

Botwinick[8] makes the following observations concerning the maintenance of decline of various mental abilities: (1) a gradual decline in all types of measureable ability sets in after the age of 30 years but does not become significant until well after 50 years; (2) sensory and perceptual abilities decline most and earliest—about the age of 50; (3) motor abilities hold up well until late middle age, but there is a chance in the methods by which the tasks are done; (4) decline in learning ability varies with the type of material to be learned; and (5) there are wide individual differences so that in any age group some persons are superior to the average for groups much younger.

Vocational status

The peak of vocational success for men comes during middle age, in the forties and early fifties. After the age of 35 years men are more stable in their jobs and are skilled to avoid acts that cause accidents. Between the ages of 30 and 34 years men show stable employment of 40%, upward mobility of 33%, and downward mobility of 3%.[9]

Most people reach their peak of income in the 40- to 45-year age bracket. There are fewer accidents by the older worker than by the younger worker, and the older worker has less absenteeism from work. It is at this time that men attain their greatest power and prestige in the business world. For both men and women it can be a time of great accomplishments in their lives.

It would seem that man's vocational adjustment problems are over, but for some people middle age brings new complications. Dissatisfaction with the present job, instability, restlessness, and loss of child-rearing responsibilities prompt many men to make a vocational change at this time of life. However, most of these "vocational change" seekers are individuals who have never really fulfilled their vocational desires and goals. They soon find out that such a change is almost impossible and impracticable, unless the job change is closely related to their present position. Soon the desire to change jobs diminishes and is replaced by a desire to remain in the same occupation until retirement.

The vocational adjustment problem of middle age is as serious for women today as for men, if not more so. At present more than one-half the women between the ages of 35 and 55 years are in the labor force.[10]

Many reasons can be cited for the overflow of middle-aged women desiring work outside the home. The various labor-saving devices permit them to care for their home in much less time than in the past. Earlier marriages, earlier childbearing, and smaller families ready the middle-aged woman for employment outside the home. The increase in cost of living and the desire for a

David Strickler

Career patterns are fairly well developed and a high level of occupational skills is attained. This is an age of vocational competency.

better standard of living demand more money than the husband can bring home, thus the wife is willing to take a job to have some of the finer things in life.

Without question the opportunity for women to earn money outside the home is security in itself. If the time were to arise that she would need to be self-supporting (through divorce or death of the husband), she could carry on with much less frustration.

As the latter years of middle age bring retirement into focus, it is conceivable that retirement benefits from both husband's and wife's company retirement plan, in addition to Social Security

benefits, will make the "golden years" most enjoyable.

The social and civil rights movements have brought about a major change in the economic circumstances of at least part of the black community. There is a definite emerging black middle class that is larger than ever before. The national effort to give blacks a more equitable share of the nation's good and benefits has had results—uneven, but undeniable. Increasingly, blacks are seen in offices of corporations and banks, in classrooms of colleges, in officers clubs, affluent suburbs, and in tourist areas. To be black and qualified is a very valuable commodity. For the most part, tokenism has diminished, although many young blacks find it difficult to be convinced of that fact. As middle-class blacks have prospered, a gap has opened between them and the black underclass that remains fixed in poverty and despair.

Statistics are an inadequate way to demonstrate middle class status. After all, to be middle class is a matter of income, education, life-style, attitude, and that indefinable sense of well-being—being a useful, functioning part of society. For some individuals, black, white, or brown, different levels of income would bring about this condition. Some would live very comfortably on $10,000 to $12,000 a year. Others would not make it on $30,000 to $40,000 a year.[11]

The rise of the black middle class is suggested by a variety of statistics. Comparing 1965 to 1974, there are 30% more blacks making over $10,000 a year and 12% more making over $15,000. In the North and West, in 1971, a black husband and wife unit earned 93% of comparable white income. College enrollment of blacks doubled between 1967 and 1972; 18% of blacks, compared to 26% of whites, attend college. Professional and technical positions for blacks have increased by 128%. The number of black managers, officials, and proprietors has doubled. The implications are that, as this trend continues, the socioeconomic composition of the middle-aged, middle-class population of the near future will change to more equalitarian levels.

THE CHANGE OF LIFE

In the middle years a change occurs for men and women. Climacteric (andropause), the change of life in men, and menopause, the change of life in women, are the cause of much anxiety in the minds of both sexes. The concerns and fears of the change of life are without scientific reason. Every period of life, from childhood to old age, has its joys and trials. This change of life is no different; it has its compensations and can become an era of great fulfillment leading to years of happiness and serenity.

What is it?

At a certain time in middle adulthood the body will undergo certain physical changes that are associated with the gradual inability of certain glands to secrete the hormones that they provided earlier. The word *menopause,* used to designate the change-of-life period in women, comes from the Greek words "month" and "cessation." It refers to that time in a woman's life when there is a pause in the menses, a cessation of the monthly reproductive function. The word *climacteric* comes from two Greek words meaning "rung of a ladder" and "a critical time." In popular usage it is applied to a change in men, although the word *andropause* would be more appropriate to indicate the change in men. The term *change of life* for both men and women denotes the leaving of one phase of life and the beginning of a new one.

Symptoms of menopause begin with major hormonal shifts that take place in the woman between the ages of 40 and 55 years. Out of 903 cases investigated in 1967 the average age at which there was a complete cessation of menses was 49.2 years.[12] Only 3.5% of the cases occurred before the age of 40 years; 20% occurred between 40 and 44 years; 44% occurred between 45 and 49 years; 30% occurred between 50 and 54 years; and only 1.5% occurred at the ages of 55, 56, or 57 years. It usually takes two to four years for menopause to be completed. There is some indication of a hereditary pattern for the onset of menopause. All things being equal, daughters generally begin and end menopause in the same manner and at the same age as their mothers.

Symptoms of menopause

During menopause, there is a reduction of action of the ovaries, affecting other glands and producing symptoms that can be disturbing to a woman. In about 75% of women menopausal disturbances are either absent or minor. Only about 25% of women need medical therapy.[13]

Menopause starts with a change in a woman's menstrual pattern. One of the following four things will happen: (1) there will be a general slowing down of flow of blood without irregularity; (2) there will be an irregularity of timing with skipped periods; (3) there will be an irregularity of timing and an irregularity in the amount of flow; or (4) there will be an abrupt cessation of menstruation. The usual pattern is skipped periods, with the periods coming farther apart until there may be only one period in six months.

Inside the woman's body certain changes take place. The ovaries become smaller; no longer do they secrete ova regularly as before. The fallopian tubes, having no more eggs to transport, also become smaller and shorter. The uterus hardens and shrinks. The vagina shortens and loses some of its elasticity. The urine is even different in its hormonal content. The internal changes all concern the reproductive system because there is no longer a need for this function.[14]

There are other internal physical symptoms that have nothing to do with the reproductive system. The spleen and lymphatic glands decrease in size. There is an increased tendency to constipation due to the changes in the wall of the intestine. There may be urinary incontinence.

The symptoms noticed most by women are the external physical ones. There are many symptoms, however, and not all will occur in every woman. Some women will experience one or two symptoms; some women will experience the symptoms for several years, some for several months, and some not at all.

One of the most common and most talked-about symptoms is the hot flushes, sometimes called hot flashes. Most symptoms, including the hot flush, involve the nervous system and the blood. During a hot flush, the body becomes warm and there is excessive perspiration followed by chilliness. These hot flushes may involve only the face and neck, or they may extend over the whole body. They occur frequently during the months when periods are missed. They usually stop after the menses stop completely. They are never fatal, but they are probably the most annoying of all the symptoms. They usually last only a minute or so and can be controlled by medication.

There are many other symptoms. The breasts eventually become smaller and flabby. The body contour changes, and there is often a tendency to become obese. This may be checked by a careful diet. However, some women get progressively thinner. The hair on scalp and external genitalia becomes thinner. The labia may lose their firmness and become flabby. Muscles, especially of the upper arms and legs, may lose their elasticity and strength. Itchiness, particularly after bathing, may occur. Insomnia occurs frequently, and headaches are common. Certain male characteristics may appear, such as hair growth at the corners of the mouth or the upper lip. This can be helped by prescribed hormones. These symptoms are the ones that occur most frequently.

Hormonal deficiency, causing many of the physical and psychological symptoms of menopause, has been greatly reduced in the past several years by the use of estrogen replacement therapy. However, hormonal therapy helps only those complaints that are related directly or indirectly to hormonal deficiency. A woman who has reached menopause may have other reasons to feel the depression and general psychological upset that can be part of her life at this time.

In addition to the various physical symptoms there are also psychological ones, but, again, not every woman experiences psychological symptoms. Usually if a woman is well adjusted mentally and emotionally before menopause, she will have no problems. However, if a woman has been poorly adjusted or unhappy, she may have mental problems during menopause (Table 14-3).

Psychologically, the cessation of menstruation for some women is a state of anxiety that is related to the woman's concept of herself as a human being. Some women, since they no longer can bear children, believe that they are losing their usefulness. This symbolizes aging to some, and they become emotionally upset about it. This loss of reproductive power may even be equated with castration and connected to the castration complex.[15] Many women become saddened because they see themselves aging in a youth-oriented society.

What happens to the woman who will not let herself get old? She will become especially interested in youth and their ideas. She will try to think like them and dress like them. She will want to be admired and loved by many young men. She will begin to wonder if her old husband is really worth hanging onto. She may be laying the groundwork for marital unhappiness.

Some women believe that with the menopause comes the end of their attractiveness, thus the end of their sex life. Their children are grown and

Table 14-3. Women's attitudes and views toward menopause*

	Percent		Percent
The worst thing about middle age		The worst thing about menopause	
Losing your husband	52	Not knowing what to expect	26
Getting older	18	The discomfort and pain	19
Cancer	16	Sign of getting older	17
Children leaving home	9	Loss of enjoyment in sexual relations	4
Menopause	4	Not being able to have more children	4
Change in sexual feelings and behavior	1	None of these	30
What I dislike most about being middle-aged		How menopause affects a woman's appearance	
Getting older	35	Negative changes	50
Lack of energy	21	No effect	43
Poor health or illness	15	Positive changes	1
Feeling useless	2	No response	6
None of these	27	How menopause affects a woman's physical and emotional health	
The best thing about the menopause		Negative changes	32
Not having to worry about getting pregnant	30	No effect	58
		Positive change or improvement	10
Not having to bother with menstruation	44	How menopause affects a woman's sexual relations	
Better relationship with husband	11	Sexual relations become more important	18
Greater enjoyment of sex life	3		
None of these	12	No effect	65
		Sexual relations become less important	17

*Modified from Neugarten, B. *Vita Humana*, 1963, **6,** 140-151.

married. They no longer feel needed. They no longer use their leisure time advantageously. They just worry. What happens to these women who cannot adjust? Some women drink to solve their problems. Some seek out "loving" men. Some avoid a social life of any kind—they isolate themselves. Some women cry all the time and are usually depressed.

The larger majority of women do not have these psychological problems because their lives have been filled with usefulness, happiness, charm, self-appreciation, and accomplishment. They have been emphasizing values and interests in life that can be pursued with vigor at any age.

When is menopause over? This is an interesting question. No one knows exactly when ovulation will end for any woman. She may not have a period for five or six months and then another may occur. Most authorities agree that meno-

pause has been completed if there has been no menstrual period for one year. With the end of ovulation also usually comes the end of the physical symptoms. If they do not end, they are caused by something other than menopause.

Middle-aged pregnancy is uncommon as women approach menopause. The "change-of-life" baby is a possibility but not the usual occurrence for the woman who begins noticing changes in the menstrual cycle. One study indicated that, in general, pregnancy after 47 years of age is highly unlikely; another study stated that pregnancy in women over 50 years of age is "extremely rare."[16] During the time of irregular periods, it is difficult to know when ovulation takes place. Conception would be possible, but the whole combination of events would be unexpected and unlikely. When middle-aged pregnancy becomes a reality, particularly if the child is the first conceived, there is a greater tendency for longer labor due to the loss of elasticity of the cervix and vagina. There is a higher risk of the over 40-year-old mother producing a child with some defect. The rate of mongolism in the off-spring of younger mothers is one in 600, whereas the rate of mongolism in the offspring of older mothers rises to one in every fifty births. Spontaneous abortions are frequent in women who become pregnant after the age of 40 years. Some doctors who believe that menopause is over when there is no menstrual period for twelve months still suggest that some type of birth control be continued for another twelve months.

What about men?

There is really no such thing as a "male change" in the literal sense of the word. There is no physical change in the male comparable to the change in the female. Some emotional changes occur in men around middle age, but these can be attributed to progressive aging and to diminishing sexual desire.[17] The main change is in the man's thinking patterns and self-image. This is not the result of hormonal deficiency—androgen levels decline very slowly. The reproductive function does not end, and sperm manufacture continues with no sudden change until old age. Fertility is not interfered with even when sperm production slows. Fatherhood is possible until extremely late in life. Possible loss of sex drive and potency is more a matter of the mind than a set of physical facts.

Psychologically, there are two facts that may suggest a kind of male climacteric. First, some men have almost neurotic reactions to middle age. They do not want to be old, and like some women they try to look and act very young. Some even shed their wives and marry women ten or twenty years younger. Second, some men have depressive reactions, but they occur about ten or fifteen years later in men than in women, around the ages of 55 to 65 years. These are probably due to fatigue, retirement, boredom, financial problems, or fear of sexual impotency.

However, in about one of every 100 men there is a period of changing years in which their reproductive powers suddenly end. When this happens, it is due to primary testicular failure. The discomforts of this disease are similar to the symptoms of menopause in women. The cure is slow and expensive because it is an illness and does not occur naturally like menopause.[18]

Sex in middle age

The years between the ages of 20 and 30 are ones in which sexual capacity and drives are greatest. However, with the aging process and physiological changes the male experiences a gradual decline in sexual behavior at about his fifty-fifth year. It is at this stage in some men that sexual pleasures leave the desirous state, and sex serves only as an outlet. This can best be illustrated by the male who seeks youthful sex partners to regain his self-esteem and shelter his declining virility. Hunt[19] reports that at 60 years of age only 5% of males in his study were inactive sexually. By the age of 70 years nearly 30% were inactive, but 70% were active. There is usually little decrease in sexual interest, but there may be a decrease in sexual activities due to pressures or psychological attitudes (Fig. 14-2).

Decline in female sexual interest and activity usually begins earlier than in the male. It is a time of extreme sensitivity to her environment, irritability, and physical changes. She is aware of these changes. Her ovaries cease to produce ova, and her appearance begins to show the signs of age. The woman who is unable to cope with the problems this phase brings can resort to sexual preoccupation and seeking young men or can become emotionally upset over her new role in life.

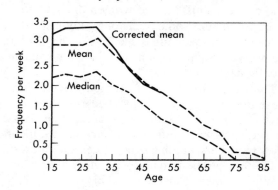

Fig. 14-2. Frequency of sexual outlet declines with age. (Modified from Kinsey, A. C., Pomeroy, W. B., & Martin, C. E. *Sexual behavior in the human male.* Philadelphia: W. B. Saunders Co., 1948.)

During the change, it is a good time for a woman to take stock of her sexual self and to ascertain if she has really reached the pinnacle of marital bliss with her husband. It must be emphasized that women who have always enjoyed marital relations to the fullest may expect to continue to do so; those who have never achieved sexual fulfillment now have an opportunity to "try again."

There is one condition that will prevent a woman from having sexual pleasure during or after menopause; it may even cause severe pain. This is dyspareunia, or painful intercourse. During and after menopause (and in some women approaching this time of life), an insufficient quantity of female sex hormone (estrogen) causes the lining of the vagina to thin out and become raw and painful to the touch. The administration of estrogen by injection, by mouth, and/or by suppositories in the vagina will thicken the epithelium lining of the vagina and repair the damage.[20]

The extent and degree of waning sex energy in middle-aged men and women vary with the individual's state of mind and physical fitness. The so-called change of life tends to intensify existing body disorders and permit others to occur. More often than not a woman's mental and emotional disturbance over menopause does more harm than the process itself. Anxiety has been proved to be the prime danger to the well-being of a man or woman during this period.

STUDY GUIDE

1. What is it like to be an adult 31 to 45 years of age? What are the sociological, psychological, and physiological factors involved?
2. What is meant by "the years of stability" or "the maintenance years"?
3. Review the developmental tasks of middle adulthood. They will need to be derived from the section with that title. Do the tasks appear to you to be more philosophical in nature?
4. What's so bad about becoming 40 years old? What's so great about it?
5. What physical changes occur during middle adulthood?
6. There are seven psychological characteristics in the middle years of adulthood that are related to overall adjustment. What are these attributes, and how do they contribute to good mental health?
7. Are adults of middle age capable of doing good reasoning and thinking? Are they beginning to lose or deteriorate in mental abilities?
8. What happens to cause menopause? Why does it happen? How does it show itself? What understanding is needed by the woman involved and by those associated with her?
9. Should sex activities decline after the ages of 45 or 50 years because a couple may no longer be capable of reproducing? What seems to be the key to continued sex?
10. What is it like to be an adult 46 to 59 years of age? What are the sociological, psychological, and physiological factors involved?

REFERENCES

1. Havighurst, R. J. Human development (2nd ed.). New York: David McKay Co., 1972.
2. Bracken, P.: Middle age: for adults only. *Reader's Digest,* 1969, **95,** 86.
3. Wilensky, H. L. Orderly careers and social participation. In H. J. Peters, & J. C. Hausen. Vocational guidance and career development. New York: Macmillan Co., 1968.
4. Neugarten, B. L. Personality and aging. In J. E. Berren, & K. W. Schaie (Eds.), *Handbook of the psychology of aging.* New York: Van Nostrand Reinhold Co., Chap. 26, 1977.
5. Neugarten, B. L., & Datan, N. The middle years. In S. Arieti (Ed.), *American handbook of psychiatry.* New York: Basic Books, Publishers, Inc., 1974.
6. Lynes, R. A cool cheer for middle-aged. *Look* 1967, **31,** 46.
7. Lehman, H. C. The most creative years of engineers and other technologists. *Journal of Genetic Psychology,* 1966, **108,** 263-277.
8. Botwinick, J. Intellectual abilities. In J. E. Berren, & K. W. Schaie (Eds.), *Handbook of the psychology of aging.* New York: Van Nostrand Reinhold Co., Chap. 24, 1977.
9. Birren, J. E. *The psychology of aging.* Englewood Cliffs, N.J.: Prentice Hall, Inc., 1964.
10. Sheppard, H. L. Work and retirement. In R. H. Binstock, & E. Shanos. *Handbook of aging and the social sciences.* New York: Van Nostrand Reinhold Co., 1976.

11. America's rising black middle class. *Times,* June 17, 1974, 19-28.

12. Olds, S. Menopause: something to look forward to? *Today's Health,* May, 1970, p. 48.

13. Kirby, I. J. Hormone replacement therapy for postmenopausal symptoms, Lancet, 1973, **2,** 103.

14. Smith, A. *The body.* New York: Walker and Co., 1968.

15. Chapman, D. J. *The feminine mind and body.* New York: Citadel Press, Inc., 1968.

16. Bardick, J. *The psychology of women.* New York: Harper & Row, Publishers, 1971.

17. Beard, R. J. The menopause. *British Journal of Hospital Medicine,* 1975, **12,** 631-637.

18. Kimmel, D. C. *Adulthood and aging.* New York: John Wiley & Sons, Inc., 1974.

19. Hunt, M. *Sexual behavior in the 70's.* New York: Dell, 1974.

20. Goldstein, B. *Human sexuality.* New York: McGraw-Hill Book Co., 1976.

MY OLD AGE IS GETTING TO ME

Old age can become very frustrating and depressing when one increasingly realizes a growing dependence on others accompanied by a feeling of failure in oneself. I am eighty-five years old, and I have observed a gradual decline in my physical and mental alertness over the past few years. This age reminds me greatly of the young child who needs someone to guide his actions and make his decisions. To me it seems like a sad and difficult period of life.

At the age of eighty, just five short years ago, I lived a very full, patterned, and contented life. My wife and I were both in good health, owned our home, and were able to care for ourselves. I enjoyed gardening in my double lot of ground while my wife busied herself cooking delicious foods and cleaning house. We passed the evenings watching television and reading the newspaper. We had daily visits from our three children and their families who lived in the same community. Yes, life was pleasant then, with few upsets in the routine.

Two years later my beloved wife died suddenly, and that pleasant way of living came to an abrupt end. Henceforth, life was rather lonely in that big house, even though friends and family visited regularly and tried to brighten each day. Oh, there were still things to do: garden to tend, furnace to fire, and house to clean; but somehow life was empty. The children bought me a little house dog, and he became my main concern and constant companion. Here was someone who needed me and shared my day from sunrise to sunset. Summer days became enjoyable with gardening in the morning, a nice nap with my pup curled at my feet through the afternoon, and a relaxing evening on the back porch under the stars. Winter days found me more restless since I could not get outside. The children were wonderful to me, always visiting, cooking my meals, doing my laundry, and helping in countless other ways. I had life better than many at my age. Then, one by one, my old friends died off, leaving me more and more alone. But my dog and I carried on.

Gradually, almost unnoticed by me, I became a little less responsible. A few times I forgot to turn down the furnace thermostat before retiring for the night, and then I misplaced my phone bill once or twice. My memory grew shorter and I misplaced things continually. They tell me I asked the same questions five or six times within an hour, and still I couldn't recall the answer. Yes, I was going downhill, but never would I leave my home; it was my life.

Then one day I did a foolish thing but it was very important at the time. I was eighty-four and, as always, the spring housecleaning had to be done. There was a hired lady to help, but washing windows was no job for a woman. That had always been my department, and this year was no exception. We began upstairs and although I had been warned not to do the windows this year, I positively could not surrender my duties! Well, you can picture the rest. I climbed out on the porch roof and two minutes later was on the cement floor below, unable to move. It was a miracle that my injuries were light—a few broken ribs and a concussion. A few weeks in the hospital and I would be as good as new, or so I thought.

I demanded to go back home, but the family seemed to have full say now and I soon found myself in an old folks home. I've been here now for several months and I suppose you'd say I've adjusted well. I can't walk on my own any more, but I have a walker and a wheelchair to help me get around. The aches and pains are more prominent these days, and I get so bored with myself. Neither television nor the newspaper is of any interest to me. People keep trying to interest me in something, but my mind can't concentrate on any one thing for longer than a few minutes. That is, unless it is something that worries me. For instance, some days all I want to talk about is getting new pants or needing socks. About every five minutes I bring it up again, even though others keep trying to change the subject.

The other people at this home are so irritating. I declare they're always stealing my clothes, although my family insists I just misplace them. But they can't fool me; they're stealing them! When I get new things, I hide them under my pillow or behind the dresser. You just can't trust these folks at their old age.

My family is rather disgusting these days. They never agree with me and always try to change my mind. They tell me my bedroom is on the first floor, but I've gone upstairs to bed all my life, and I want to go upstairs to my room. Why can't they understand these facts?

I guess I can put up with this kind of life until spring, but then I'm going to get a trailer and live alone again. I could do everything I used to do if I were in my own home. I'll get my dog back from the farm where he is now, and we'll have a good life together again. I'll put the trailer on my son's lot, have a little garden to tend, and have a back porch to sit on during those nice summer evenings. All those friends will come to visit again and life will be nice.

Early adulthood was the period of the developing years, a time when expansion was taking place in all phases of life. At some point in time enough growth, development, and accumulation had taken place so that individuals became content to maintain their position and status in life, not pushing for any further major gain. The years of stability and status quo were ushered in. There comes a time, however, when more change has taken place chronologically and physically, so that the individual finds himself in a drastically different role and status of life, as compared to that of the younger population. This time usually occurs at retirement.

From the time of retirement on, individuals are in the age of recompense, the bitter-sweet years.

David Strickler

Old age has its young years and its old years. The early retirement years can be enjoyable, fruitful years.

This is a period when the major tasks of adulthood have either been completed or set aside, and a new role, that of older members of society, is assumed. How gracefully, how happily, how effectively the new role is lived will depend on the capability of the individuals to be graceful, happy, and effective. Their past life will determine how smoothly or awkwardly they move into this new stage and how well they can adapt to it. Recompense means a return for something done, suffered, or given. It is a compensation, in kind, for past efforts and services rendered. The age of recompense is the time when people reap the rewards of the kind of life they lived in earlier years. Bitter-sweet implies that some moments will be pleasant and others will be displeasing.

THE AGE LEVEL

Old age is the last major segment of the life span, within which there exists a variety of patterns of well-being and aging. Individual differences are probably greater at this time than at any other age. Not all older people are "old," and certainly they are not all senile. Most will be highly capable in many ways for many years. Yet a characteristic of the age level is that as age increases, there comes a regression, a decrease in effective functioning of the various bodily systems. Physical and mental decline occur with considerable individual differences, but 60 to 65 years is usually set as the dividing line between middle and old age. Gerontologists have attempted to deal with this unreliable concept of "oldness" after 65 years by dividing old age into

Table 15-1. Physiological age and life-span differences*

Reversible		Permanent	
Comparison	**Years**	**Comparison**	**Years**
Country vs. city dwelling	+5	Females vs. males	+3
Married status vs. single, widowed, divorced	+5	Familial constitutions‡	
		2 grandparents lived to age 80 years	+2
Overweight		4 grandparents lived to age 80 years	+4
25% overweight group	−3.6	Mother lived to age 90 years	+3
35% overweight group	−4.3	Father lived to age 90 years	+4.4
45% overweight group	−6.6	Both mother and father lived to age 90 years	+7.4
55% overweight group	−11.4		
67% overweight group	−15.1	Mother lived to age 80 years	+1.5
Or: an average effect of 1% overweight	−0.17	Father lived to age 80 years	+2.2
		Both mother and father lived to age 80 years	+3.7
Smoking		Mother died at 60 years	−0.7
1 package cigarettes per day	−7	Father died at 60 years	−1.1
2 packages cigarettes per day	−12	Both mother and father died at age 60 years	−1.8
Atherosclerosis			
Fat metabolism		Recession of childhood and infectious disease over past century in Western countries	+15
In 25th percentile of population having "ideal" lipoprotein concentrations	+10		
Having average lipoprotein concentrations	0	Life Insurance *Impairment Study*	
		Rheumatic heart disease evidenced by:	
In 25th percentile of population having elevated lipoproteins	−7	Heart murmur	−11
		Heart murmur + tonsillitis	−18
In 5th percentile of population having highest elevation of lipoproteins	−15†	Heart murmur + streptococcal infection	−13
		Rapid pulse	−3.5
		Phlebitis	−3.5
Diabetes		Varicose veins	−0.2
Uncontrolled, before insulin, 1900	−35	Epilepsy	−20.0
		Skull fracture	−2.9
Controlled with insulin		Tuberculosis	−1.8
1920 Joslin Clinic record	−20	Nephrectomy	−2.0
1940 Joslin Clinic record	−15	Trace of albumin in urine	−5.0
1950 Joslin Clinic record	−10	Moderate albumin in urine	−13.5

*From Jones, H. B. The relation of human health to age, place, and timing. In Birren, J. E., Imus, H. F. & Windle, W. F. *The process of aging in the nervous system.* Springfield, Ill.: Charles C Thomas, Publisher, 1959, p. 354.
†This 70% difference in distribution of lipoproteins, between 25% vs. 5% highest, is equivalent to a total of 25 years in relative displacement of physiological age.
‡As measured in 1900. These effects may be measurably less now, as environment is changing to produce greater differences between parents and progeny.

two groups: early old age, 65 to 74 years, and advanced old age, 75 years and above.

Physical age is a poor measure in determining the beginning of old age because there are many differences among individuals as to when aging actually begins. In most cases men and women of today, because of better living conditions and better medical care, do not show physical and mental characteristics of decline until the mid-sixties or even early seventies.

As people grow older, they may have less strength, vigor, and speed of reaction, but they learn to compensate for this change. For example, an older person's reactions may slow down and cause him to be accident prone when driving, but he compensates for this by driving more slowly and not driving when road conditions are dangerous. This period of old age when the decline is slow and gradual and when compensations can be made for the declines is known as *senescence*. Senescence means to grow old and to show the characteristics of old age. Depending on the degree of mental and physical decline, the person may become senescent in the late fifties or not until the late sixties. When the person has a more or less complete physical breakdown, mental disorganization, and/or loss of mental faculties, this is known as *senility*. In senility the person becomes careless, absent-minded, eccentric, socially withdrawn, and poorly adjusted. This may occur early, or it may never occur. Most people become senescent rather than senile.

A variety of factors that can produce individual differences in regard to the length of the life span are shown in Table 15-1. Some of these factors are reversible and can be changed to enhance or worsen the chances of extended life. Other factors are permanent and cannot be changed. For example, being 67% overweight may shorten a life span by 15 years. However, losing weight and being only 25% overweight adds 11.4 years to the life span, although this overweight still shortens life by 3.6 years. It is possible to lose weight and increase the number of years of life. On the other hand, being born a female implies that chances are she will live 3 years longer than a male born on the same day. This characteristic is permanent and cannot be changed.

Gerontology and geriatrics

The word *gerontology* refers to the scientific study of the aging process of life from a physiological, pathological, psychological, sociological, and economic point of view.

Geriatric, in the singular form, pertains to the aged or their characteristic tribulations (geriatric problems). For example, the "tea and toast geriatric" is an aged person who is too enfeebled or unable to shop adequately for food or to cook a meal. As a result, this person subsists on a diet of tea and toast or milk and cereal.

Geriatrics, in plural form, is the medical specialty of gerontology in which physiological and pathological changes of the aging human system are studied and treated. Much study and attention are also paid to "the aging process," that is, how aging takes place. The problems of the aged are one thing, the process of aging is another.

There are several factors that account for most of the interest and development of gerontology and geriatrics in recent years. A major factor is the decline of the death rate in Western societies. In 1860 only 2.7% (860,000 people) of the American people were over 65 years of age. By 1950 the percentage had risen to 7.6% and by 1980 there will be 12.1% (22 million people) in that age group. Since the life expectancy of people 65 years of age and over is now nearly thirteen additional years, the problems of older people can be of major consequence for both sexes, but for women especially. The ratio of women to men changes from 120 women per 100 men for ages 65 to 69 years to more than 160 women for every 100 men at the age of 85 years and over. Women should be taught how to be widows.

A second underlying factor for recent interest in gerontology is the vast array of problems that confront the aged. Many problems are brought on by a new adult role, problems of living and living arrangements, and changes that affect the well-being and life-style of the individual.

A third factor for increased interest is that many individuals are not prepared or educated for old age. Oftentimes retirement is unplanned. People who have worked hard all their lives suddenly reach compulsory retirement age and find nothing but a void in their lives. They are unable to cope with their leisure time.

Patricia and William Oriol

The large increase in the number of the elderly has given special impetus to the field of gerontology to study problems of housing, nursing care, social activities, and political and economic status. (From Butler, R. N., & Lewis, M. *Aging and mental health* (2nd ed.). St. Louis: The C. V. Mosby Co., 1977.)

A fourth factor in the growth of interest in gerontology and geriatrics has been the enactment of legislation on behalf of older people, including the Social Security Act, old age assistance, Medicare, and laws passed to prohibit discrimination against older workers.

A fifth factor is the long-festering dissatisfaction with almshouses, "poor farms," and homes for the aged as institutional forms of rehabilitation and terminal care. Newer forms, such as outpatient geriatric clinics, have been created. Seeing the state mental hospitals overcrowded with geriatric patients who no longer needed institutional care but who did require some form of rehabilitation before being placed in the community, the legislature of Pennsylvania established the South Mountain Geriatric Center to provide this service. They seek to rehabilitate the elderly to independent self-help care and then place them in foster homes.

The impressive increase in the number and variety of clubs and fraternal organizations by and for the aged is a sixth factor for new interest in geriatrics. Golden Age Clubs, American Association of Retired Persons, and similar "senior citizens" organizations are principally social and seek to overcome the detrimental by-products of isolation in old age. The Gray Panthers and other political pressure groups seek to influence all kinds of legislative action. All of these groups provide a measure of group therapy that helps to meet some of the needs of the aged.

The seventh factor is the evolving awareness of the traditional professions who have an interest in the problems of the elderly. More and more professional organizations of medicine, psychology, social science, nursing, and housing have formed committees and divisions to deal with the problems and needs of the aged.

Finally, gerontology and geriatrics have increased their activities in research. Systematic exploration into the aging process and its problems is now being conducted in every conceivable discipline. Two of the major areas of current research are aging and the diseases of old age. There are still a great many unanswered questions in this area, however. For example, some of the pressing questions include: What are the factors that influence the rate of aging? What potentials and capacities do older people possess? What methods are most appropriate in the care of the senile aged person?

Stereotyping and negativism

The aged were not always, as they are today, a significant proportion of the population. Wars, famines, injuries, diseases, and inadequate health knowledge and care contributed to a relatively brief life span up to the twentieth century. Life expectancy in 1900 was only 48 years.[1] However, since the time of recorded Biblical history, there have been expressions of interest and efforts on behalf of the elderly in the community. Gold and Kaufman[2] traced the development of institutional care for the elderly. They cite the Talmud and the Old Testament (Ruth IV, v. 5) as stressing the obligation "to provide for the support and comfort of the old." The earliest shelters for the aged were tents, but they did reflect one of the ideals of mankind: to care for those who cannot care for themselves. There is concern for the aged today, but along with that concern have emerged some stereotypes of old age that are mainly negative in nature.

As Butler and Lewis[3] state: "Few people in the United States can think of old age as a time of potential health and growth." In a way, the negative view of old age is an aspect of Western civilization; it is not found in Oriental thinking. The difference appears to be based on how life is viewed. Oriental philosophy emphasizes ancestral worship and places death within the process of human experience. Death is part of the full spectrum of life. The older person sees himself as approaching a point in time where he is to be revered. As a man in India said to us when we commented on frailties that age brings to a person, "But, old is gold!" We remember the aggressiveness, almost to the point of rudeness, of a young Japanese woman at a buffet dinner in a restaurant in Manila as she gathered food on a a plate. Our friend said, "Don't be upset or shocked by her behavior. The food is not for her; it is for her aged mother." We remember a sing-sing in a village on the Sepik River in New Guinea being held in honor of a very old man. His people wanted a party for him while he was still alive; they said it would please him immensely if we took his picture.

In Western societies the emphasis is on youth, on individuality, and on productivity. Death is considered beyond the living self and not acceptable. Death is something to be avoided rather than a logical and necessary aspect of life. As such, anything that implies "getting old" or "beginning to fail" is an affront to the individual and rejected because of the inference that the self is no longer in control. It is the worst thing that could happen to a person. We even joke and half-heartedly rationalize about it when we say: "Well, getting old isn't too bad when you consider the only alternative." Getting old is often used by the aged as an excuse not to do some things that they enjoyed formerly.

The negative image of old age is promoted, perhaps unconsciously, in several ways. There is no doubt that the emphasis on youth, young fashions, "new" ideas, and talk of the future world of the twenty-first century reinforces notions concerning old age. Expressions such as "being over the hill"; "They say life begins at forty—but nobody says what it begins. . . "; and that subduing realization, "They're saying I have to retire" are common. Scientific studies and medical science contribute to negative stereotyping by reporting debilitating characteristics of the elderly, but neglecting to mention that most studies are done on institutionalized persons whose physical and mental decline was primarily responsible for their being there in the first place. Literature written about the "age of decline," "the failing years," and "the waning time of life" does nothing to dispel the negative view of old age. Even physicians contribute to this idea when they say "Well, you'd better face it, you're getting older. Your problem is one of age." The truth of the matter is that nobody dies of "old age." They die of a heart condition, a disorder of the circulatory system, a cancerous development, or some other cause. They do not die because they are 69, 75, or 82 years of age. Of course, there are those who would say that biological deterioration brought on by age creates a state of susceptibility to disease and this susceptibility limits the length of life. This statement, however, is an overgeneralization and not true for all aged persons.

Life changes and attitudes

It is important not to place undue stress on changes that occur in an aged person. Changes occur at all stages of life. It is true that, because of some changes, older persons cannot do what they could do at an earlier age, but should this fact be the controlling element in determining how life should be considered and lived? The essential ingredient for having a happy old age is not the desire for longevity or the avoidance of change but the determination of how to improve the quality of life at that point in time, regardless of the physical condition of that phase of life. The quality of life emanates from within the self; it cannot be imposed from the outside by someone else. Outside factors and forces can make it easier for an individual to evolve a better quality of life through attitudes, thoughts, and feelings, but "it's what's inside" that counts. We have seen very miserable, mean, unhappy persons living in the finest of homes and receiving the best of care and love; we have seen accepting, gracious, loving, believing individuals living in the most unfortunate of circumstances.

What makes the difference between the complainer and the accepting individual? Their attitudes, faith, and consideration for others make the difference. Lest you get the wrong idea, this task is easier said than done. It is simplistic to say: "Change your attitudes and you change everything." Circumstances can be very overwhelming and detrimental, making coping behavior difficult to attain. In some cases, the older person may simply not know how to deal with

frustration and change. It is not easy to change patterns of thoughts, values, and dispositions. Studies by Riegel and Riegel[4] and Chown[5] in England found that old people hold to their views more tenaciously than others do. What is important is for others not to be too hard on older persons when they act cranky, crotchety, and hard-to-live-with. After all, change works both ways. Life circumstances are changed for the elderly, but they are also changed for those taking care of them. Why should the old be the only persons who are expected to readjust so they can better cope with circumstances? Should not the same principle apply to the younger persons who are taking care of them?

It is important to consult research studies to see what they might contribute to an understanding of attitudes of the aged toward aging and toward life in general. From the beginning, let us point out that the results of the research are inconclusive and limited. Apparently, according to statements of the researchers themselves, the proper form of research methodology and the proper control of variables have not been developed. For example, Kogan and Shelton[6] showed that most people in the United States held negative views toward aging, but that the old themselves were slightly less negative about old age than were the young. It may be that generalized negative attitudes concerning old people may indirectly affect certain individuals who, in turn, feel that they must also respond negatively to older people, thus reinforcing negative views toward aging. In addition, older persons, anticipating the feelings of young people, play the ascribed role or at least remain quiet in order to achieve acceptance and ward off rejection. Kogan and Shelton[6] also found that older people were more acquiescent on attitude questionnaires than young people were, leaving erroneous impressions.

Cameron[7] found that when ranking age decades for happiness, freedom from worry, and ambition, all age groups (including the old) put adulthood first, followed by childhood, middle age, and lastly, old age. There was general agreement that old age was the least desired period of life. In spite of these findings, research in the area of self-image showed about as many studies indicating that old people had positive views of themselves as there were studies indicating the opposite. Research of self-image, attitudes toward life in general, and morale seem to indicate that these attitudes were less affected by age than by some concomitant of aging, such as ill-health, low socioeconomic status, isolation, inactivity, and institutionalization. It is possible that improvement in the life conditions of the elderly would lead to a reduction of negative views held by the aged concerning themselves.

Changes and personal losses

Consider some of the changes and personal losses that are age-related. Pastalan and Carson[8] trace age level changes. Between the ages of 50 and 65, children leave the household, if they have not already done so, and the elders begin to consider retirement and its implications. At 65 to 75 years of age, there is a decline in income due to retirement from a job, a loss of younger friends, possibly of a spouse, and some changes in body image. During the period of 75 to 85 years there is an increased loss of sensory activity, health, strength, and independence. At 85 years plus, there is serious loss of health and independence.

Table 15-2, adapted from the National Center for Housing Management resource book,[9] gives a more detailed presentation of age-related environmental changes and personal loss.

Hurlock[10] writes of the conditions responsible for changes in old age. She mentions health status, social status, economic status, marital status, living conditions, educational level, and the sex of the individual. Changes in health and energy bring about an increased interest in sedentary pursuits and a decrease in activities requiring strength. As physical limitations such as poor eyesight or physical frailty develop, the individual tends to prefer activities that can be enjoyed in the home rather than going out into crowds and public places that requires more effort and care. Social status usually reflects the range of interests that a person has developed. Generally, the higher the social group with which an individual has associated, the wider the range of interests. Some of these interests, such as playing bridge or attending concerts and lectures, can carry over into old age.

Reduced income after retirement may force an individual to give up many interests that were appealing to him and force a concentration on

Table 15-2. Age-related environmental changes and personal losses*

50-65	65-75	75-85	85+
Loss of relationship to younger friends and acquaintances of children; loss of neighborhood role to schools and youth; home too large, but mortgage payments are low and equity high	Loss in relation to work environment, loss of mobility due to lessened income; dissolving of professional work associations and friendships; move to apartment, smaller home, or struggle with increased maintenance costs of larger home	Loss of ability to drive independently, must rely on bus or relatives and friends; connections with community, church associations slowly severed; move to more supportive housing, such as apartments with meals and maid service; maintenance costs for single-family house unmanageable	Losses of ability to navigate in the environment, loss of strong connection with outside neighborhood; dependence on supportive services; move to supportive environment necessary, such as nursing home, home for the aged, or siblings' home

*Adapted from *Managing housing and services for the elderly.* Washington: The National Center for Housing Management, Inc., 1977.

ones that he can afford. This is especially true of older people in low socioeconomic groups. Occasionally, we hear some individuals complain of people living in poor economic circumstances who have a large colored television set or some so-called luxury item much better than they have in their own homes. They point to this circumstance and say that the money could have been better spent. Yet they fail to realize that the TV set (or whatever) may be the only means of commercial entertainment that poor families, young or old, have. Others may go to the movies, go golfing or bowling, or go on trips, but the elderly and poor cannot afford such luxuries in abundance.

Marital status also determines what a person can do. When both spouses are living, their life-style and living arrangements are usually determined by their interests, economic status, and health. Single men and women find that frequently they have to make some changes in their pattern of living because one person cannot do, or does not enjoy doing, what two persons could do, such as being invited to parties and gatherings that are usually frequented by couples.

Living conditions also are responsible for changes in life. A home for the aged frequently has planned activities; living by oneself or in the home of a married child can limit opportunities for recreation. Poor or failing health or transportation problems can prevent participation in community-sponsored events. Usually, however, the more educational interests that a person has, the more intellectual activities, such as reading, working crossword puzzles, or watching game shows on television, can be enjoyed. Women tend to have more interests in old age than men because they usually have broader interests throughout adulthood. Men, by contrast, tend to limit their interests to sports or puttering around the house. Both of these activities must be curtailed to the spectator level as energy and strength diminish. Men who are retired often find it difficult to develop new interests to occupy their time.

Changes abound. The best remedy is to cultivate interests earlier in life that can be pursued in old age in a more sedentary setting. In addition, it is important to develop an attitude that not only

recognizes and accepts change but also encourages the individual to find positive, adaptable ways to deal with changes—and even to bring about desired changes. Since an individual is confronted with changes throughout life, it seems reasonable to consider learning how to confront, control, and adapt to changes in living and in physical being rather early in life, or certainly by early adulthood.

Developmental tasks

Old age is no different from other age levels when it comes to having special adaptations that need to be made and special tasks to be achieved if the individual wishes to live effectively, happily, and confidently on that age level. The only difference is that the developmental tasks of old age are the final or ultimate ones in life and revolve about the conditions of life in that time period. The person must accept the concept and the fact of retirement. Furthermore, he must adjust to living on Social Security and/or small retirement income. Both of these tasks will require a change in personal attitudes and concepts. Learning how to live in retirement and how to occupy leisure time so that life is pleasant will require some thought. Some people manage this problem by establishing contact with organizations for retirees and sharing with others of the same age group whatever benefits the organizations can offer. The elderly couple will also have to become closer companions to each other and learn how to intermesh their lives without getting on each other's nerves.

It will be necessary for the individual to reevaluate his self-concept and personal identity in light of the new role he plays in life. A workable, personal philosophy of life, including a view about death and eternity, will probably be evolved. A major task will be to accept physical changes and their limitations by learning to conserve strength and resources when necessary. Other specific developmental tasks include finding satisfactory housing on retirement income, maintaining interest in people outside the family, maintaining some degree of family ties with children and grandchildren, taking care of elderly relatives, being able to cope with bereavement and widowhood, and continuing to meet social

A developmental task of old age is to adjust to the changes that occur in life and in living. Companionship and something to look forward to each day are essential to personal well-being.

David Strickler

and civic responsibilities by being involved in society and its affairs.

Perhaps three of the most significant adjustive tasks in later life are adaptation to loss, identity or life review, and remaining active in order to retain function. Common losses include loss of spouse; loss of social relationship, especially of work associates and others still active in economic and community activities; decline in income: decrease in mobility; decline in physical vigor; and loss of opportunities for recognition and achievement. The task is to replace the losses with new relationships, new roles, or retraining of lost capacities.[11]

Clinicians have long recognized that most older persons engage in an evaluation review of their lives, reflecting on their accomplishments and failures, their satisfactions and disappointments, seeking to integrate or evaluate the diverse elements of their lives so that they can come to a reasonably positive or acceptable view of their life's worth. According to Butler and Lewis,[12] failure to accomplish this task may result in overt psychopathology in the aged. The third task, remaining active in order to retain function, is concerned with maintenance of physical activity, of social interaction, of intellectual and emotional stimulation, and of self-care capacity. Studies of successfully aging individuals by Pfeiffer at the Duke University Center for the Aging[13] indicate that such persons characteristically maintain regular, vigorous, and stimulating activities.

DEVELOPMENTAL AGING

As with all age levels, later adulthood has characteristics that are peculiar to it. Many changes take place in old age and if the types and numbers of these changes are carefully considered, they will be found to be no greater or more drastic than those of other age levels.

Factors influencing aging

Everyone ages. Genetic and prenatal influences set the stage for the aging sequence. Postnatal environmental factors, such as economic, social, and demographic conditions, act to modify this biological sequence. According to Wilson,[14] the rate of psychological aging is directly related to how well an individual will accept change. The acceptance or rejection of aging is an ingredient in psychological aging.

Most theories of aging are presented from a biological point of view; however, some do come from a sociological, environmental, or psychological perspective. An increasingly popular view is that of interactionism, which seeks to combine the various theoretical approaches and permits the consideration of multiple-causation factors of aging. Fig. 15-1 (Baltes and Willis[15]) shows the various types of views; it seeks to show the interaction of biological, psychological, and environmental theories that are related to aging. Individual differences, long-term processes of change, ontogenic and evolutionary (adaptive) influences, and change systems are also recognized as factors influencing aging.

Although the aging process is gradual, it is sometimes speeded up, starting during adolescence and increasing with the advent of disease. A person with a severe handicap will often age much faster and earlier than a person who is not handicapped. Even with the so-called "normal" person there is always a difference in the rate of aging due to the combined forces of biological, psychological, and sociological factors.

Many people do not realize that environmental factors play a large part in aging. Environmental factors include the people and attitudes that surround the individual. Activity tends to slow down the aging process, but insecurity, lack of someone to talk to, and a strange environment may speed up the aging process.[16]

Throughout life the body is exposed to a procession of accidents, illnesses, and stress, such as a bout of pneumonia, a broken leg, a severe burn, or a period of great psychological stress. The cumulative effect of such "biological insults" may well hasten aging. Ionizing radiation is cumulative and even in the smallest doses decreases the life-span. Radiation may be accumulated from medical and dental x-ray treatment, cosmic rays, and even the luminous dial of a wristwatch.[17]

Malnutrition is a major contributor to physical deterioration. An older person oftentimes "loses his appetite" and will not eat much. His diet may not be adequate, since he may not be eating the proper foods or not be eating enough of them. Poor eating habits may accelerate aging. In some people the connective tissue becomes increasingly hard and impervious, and this may interfere with the distribution of nutrients and the disposal of wastes.

Genetic inheritance definitely plays a role. People with long-lived parents have a somewhat greater life expectancy than people with short-lived parents. One theory supports the view that there is a certain length of time, genetically determined, in which the body has to function. A timing device within the organism causes tissues and organ systems to break down at specific times.

Functional activity of the cells seems to be all-important to the aging process. Cells sometimes make errors when they reproduce. This leads to an accumulation of mutant cells that are unable to

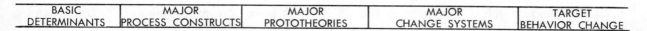

BASIC DETERMINANTS	MAJOR PROCESS CONSTRUCTS	MAJOR PROTOTHEORIES	MAJOR CHANGE SYSTEMS	TARGET BEHAVIOR CHANGE

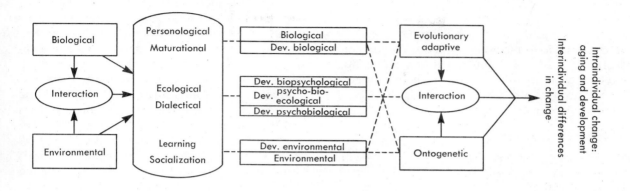

Time-ordered sequences and processes ⟶

Fig. 15-1. Illustration of major variables, processes, and theoretical orientations in the explication of psychological aging and development (interactive, reciprocal, and feedback influence patterns can be conceived at all levels of analysis). (From Baltes, P. B., & Willis, S. L. Toward psychological theories of aging development. In J. E. Birren & K. W. Schaie [Eds.]. *Handbook of the psychology of aging.* New York: Van Nostrand Reinhold Co., 1977.)

survive or cells that may become malignant. Occasionally, aberrations in cells activate the immune mechanism, which in turn reacts against these cells and seeks to destroy them. Ordinarily, the immune mechanism only reacts against bacteria and viruses. One theory states that poisonous by-products arise from the activity of the body, depositing metabolic "clinkers," which eventually block the transporting of nutrients within the cells.

Nature apparently has a built-in mechanism or factors that promote aging. Growing old is part of the natural developmental process. Biological aging is marked by a lowering metabolic rate, which slows down energy exchange. This in turn makes general health more precarious. Almost all bodily systems deteriorate in both their functional and structural efficiency. Structural decline occurs in the blood vessels, heart, and circulatory system in general. The capacity of the lungs at the age of 60 years is only half of that at 30 years. Therefore

less oxygen gets into the system and fewer nutrients and fluids are circulated throughout the body, permitting degenerative diseases and illnesses to occur and exist with a diminished capacity of bodily resources to overcome them.

In summary, the physical condition of the aging person depends on his (1) psychological temperament, (2) manner of living, (3) hereditary constitution, and (4) factors in the environment. Hereditary constitution plays the major role as a cause of physical change. Within a family group, the rate of aging shows a high correlation for the different family members. Secondary causes that have significant influences on the rate of physical decline include faulty diet, malnutrition, gluttony, emotional stresses, overwork, passivity, infections, drug or alcohol intoxications, traumas, and endocrine disorders. Environmental conditions such as heat and cold also influence the rate of aging.

Shock[18] supports these ideas by saying that the

evidence from research strongly implies that (1) there is a genetic program that sets the upper limits of the life span in a species, (2) there are some familial characteristics that influence differences in the life span among individuals, and (3) the expression of the genetic program can be altered by environmental (social and psychological) factors. Readers interested in a summation of biological theories of aging should consult Chapter 5 by Nathan Shock in the *Handbook of the Psychology of Aging.*

Physical characteristics in old age

It is true that physical changes do occur with aging and that they are generally in the direction of degeneration. Individual differences are so great, however, that no two individuals of the same age are necessarily at the same state of deterioration. Within the same person there are also variations in the rates of aging of different structures. Different parts of the body resist aging more than others, and the various abilities fade at different rates.

Appearance. Some age changes such as wrinkles, graying hair, stooping shoulders, reduced agility and speed of motion, decrease in strength, decrease in the steadiness of the hands and legs, and more difficulty in moving about are obvious in the aging individual. Some changes such as thinning hair and varicose veins can be upsetting to those who find it difficult to adjust to changes in physical appearance.

Wrinkling of the skin is caused by the loss of elastic tissue and the fatty layer. The skin does not snap back as readily when stretched. If you pinch the skin on the back of an older person's hand, you will see how it has lost much of its elasticity. The skin also has increased sensitivity to changes in temperature. Since automatic regulation of bodily functions no longer takes place as promptly as previously, older persons often "feel the cold more." The sense of touch also declines with age because there is a general drying, wrinkling, and toughening of the skin.

Sensory acuity. During the period of senescence, the sensory functions seem to be one of the first areas of the body to deteriorate. Hearing begins to decline about the age of 65 years. First affected in hearing is the ability to hear very

high tones, and as time goes on the level of auditory acuity becomes progressively lower.

There is also a decline in the individual's vision as he grows older—few people over 60 years of age see well without glasses. This decline is usually caused by deterioration of the cornea, lens, iris, retina, and optic nerve. Color perception and the power of the eye to adjust to different levels of light and dark are reduced. There is a gradual loss of orbital fat so that eventually the eyes appear sunken, the blink reflex is slower, and the eyelids hang loosely because of poorer muscle tone. However, writers in the *Handbook of the Psychology of Aging*[19] (Chapters 20 to 23) cite a number of research studies questioning the common belief, as suggested by earlier research, that individuals lose some sensory acuity, especially in touch, smell, and taste, as they get older. It appears that the state of health, previous living style, and sex differences influence the degree and type of deterioration that takes place.

By 1980, approximately 13% of the 24 million people who are 65 years or over will show advanced signs of presbycusis, an impairment of hearing in older people.[20] Fig. 15-2 illustrates the average amount of hearing loss that occurs in men and women of different ages. Women appear to retain more of their hearing capability than do men. Note that for men over 70 years, sound frequencies over 2,000 hertz are heard at a 30-decibel loss or more. Normal hearing is considered to be at 25 decibels or less.

The level of illumination required for various tasks differs according to the type of task and details involved. Special consideration must be given to planning a visual environment for the elderly so that sufficient light is available for the different activities in which they engage. As Guth[21] has shown, the level of illumination required for various tasks is greater for the elderly than for younger persons. It is recommended that greater freedom for individual control of lighting be available in areas where various tasks are performed. Fozard and Thomas[22] suggest that visual environments be designed for the average older eye rather than for the average young eye.

Cataracts are generally a concern to older persons. However, the Duke University study by Anderson and Palmore[23] shows that the incidence

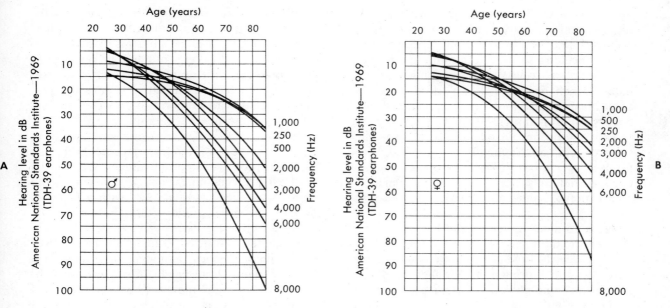

Fig. 15-2. A, Spoor's (1967) composite presbycusis curves for men, modified to conform to ANSI-1969 standard. **B,** Spoor's (1967) composite presbycusis curves for women, modified to conform to ANSI-1969 standard. (From Lebo, C. P., & Reddell, R. C. *Laryngoscope*, 1972, 1403.)

of senescent cataracts in persons over 65 is not high. The initial incidence was 9%, 18%, and 36%, respectively, for participants in their 60s, 70s, and 80s. After 10 years, the incidence increased by only 3% in the group initially in their 70s and not at all in the youngest group.

A cataract is an opacity of the lens that impairs vision. The consequences of a cataract for visual functioning depend on its location. The most common cataract is associated with excessive nuclear sclerosis, a hardening of cell tissues in the nucleus of the lens. Prior to any onset of cataracts, the hardening of the lens may increase the refractive power of the eye, improving myopia and making people believe that their near-point vision has improved. If the cataract is located in the anterior cortex, the front or outer layer of the lens, then acquired hyperopia, or far-point vision, may occur. Double vision may result if the degrees of opacity between the cortex and the nucleus are sufficiently large. Generally, cataracts are surgically removed and a substitute lens supplied. The use of contact lenses is then desirable.[24]

The senses of taste and smell are said to be reduced in functional capability during advancing years. However, studies by Hermel, Schönwetter, and Samueloff[25] on taste, and Rovee, Cohen, and Shlapack[26] on smell, report, as do a number of other studies, that reduced sensitivity to taste and smell are related more to health, illness, and sex differences than to age. It was also thought at one time that because there is a decrease of 36% in the number of taste buds in an older person as compared to younger individuals, these buds would not be as keen as they were at a younger age. Research by Beidler[27] indicates that taste buds are seldom damaged permanently and have the power of regeneration. Moulton[28] suggests that replacement and regeneration may also be possible in the case of the sense of smell. The older person who becomes easily upset about certain things associated with the senses, such as the taste of food, may be reflecting a poor health condition rather than a deterioration of sense organs due to aging.

Voice. Vocal changes are partly caused by the hardening and decreasing elasticity of the laryngeal cartilages. The voice becomes more highly pitched, and in advanced old age it becomes less powerful and is restricted in range. Singing and public speaking show deterioration earlier than do normal speaking voices in younger individuals. Speech becomes slower, and pauses become longer and more frequent; slurring often occurs due to pathological changes in the brain.

Vocal strain and vocal fatigue, the so-called "tired voice," are frequently encountered. Vocal misuse may interfere with the communication process and may lead to the development of nodes, polyps, and contact ulcers on the vocal folds.[29]

Teeth. In adult life teeth may cause pain and discomfort; the gums recede, and the teeth become yellowish. Loss of teeth or changes in their appearance may bring home the fact that the individual is aging physically. Having to resort to dentures often means that, at least temporarily, the person cannot eat or sleep as well, which may cause dismay and embarrassment. A person's disposition can be affected greatly. Changes in the jaws and face associated with old age are primarily consequences of reduction in size, and many of the facial evidences of old age may be prevented by proper care or replacement of teeth.

Homeostasis. There is some evidence that homeostasis is less efficient in older people. If stabilizing mechanisms become sluggish, the physiological adaptability of the individual is reduced. Wounds heal more slowly. It takes longer for the breathing and heart rate to return to normal. Heat losses are less quickly restored. Sleep habits may undergo a change. The thyroid gland is smaller, resulting in a lower rate of basal metabolism. The pancreas loses some of its ability to produce the enzymes that are used in sugar and protein metabolism. Most glands function at close to normal rates all through life.

Nervous system. There are some structural changes in the nervous system and brain that occur as the person ages. Although there is little functional change in the nerves, the nerve tissue will be gradually replaced by fibrous cells. There will be a slower reaction and reflex time. The folds of the brain become less prominent, possibly resulting in decreased circulation of blood within the brain. There might be a decrease in the total number of cells, but the brain functions normally unless its blood supply is blocked, even briefly. The cortical area of the brain responsible for organizing the total perceptual processes often experiences degenerative changes. A person afflicted with cerebral arteriosclerosis will show some atrophy of brain tissue.

Skeletal. The skeleton gives shape and firmness to the body, provides attachments for the muscles, protects important organs such as the brain, heart, and lungs, and together with the striated muscles provides man with a leverage system for pushing and lifting. Full stature is reached by the late teens or early twenties. Afterward there is little or no change in the length of the individual bones, although there may be a slight loss in overall height in old age, brought about by atrophy of the discs between the spinal vertebrae.[30] As age progresses, the chemical composition of the bone changes; the bones become less dense and more brittle. This increases the risk of breakage late in life. Movement of the joints becomes stiffer and more restricted, the incidence of diseases affecting these parts of the body increases with age, and the skeleton may suffer from cumulative effects of damage and disease.

In our contacts with the aged we have noticed an increase in this stiffness as the individuals begin to withdraw from activity. It therefore seems reasonable to follow the advice so often given—that you do as little as possible for them so that they will be forced to exercise their joints and keep them functioning for a longer time. As soon as someone begins to assist some elderly persons, they stop doing things for themselves and become dependent on others.

Muscular. The functional capacities of a 30-year-old man and a 75-year-old man are compared in Table 15-3. After the age of 30 years there is a gradual and small reduction in the speed and power of muscular contractions and a decreased capacity for sustained muscular effort due to biochemical changes in the protein molecules of the fibers. Muscles begin to lose their strength in the middle years. After about the age of 50 years the number of active muscle fibers steadily decreases, and eventually the typical di-

Table 15-3. Functional capacity of an average 75-year-old man compared to 100% functional capacity of a 30-year-old man*

Physical characteristic	Comparative percentage
Nerve conduction velocity	90
Body weight for males	88
Basal metabolic rate	84
Body water content	82
Blood flow to brain	80
Maximum work rate	70
Cardiac output (at rest)	70
Glomerular filtration rate	69
Number of nerve trunk fibers	63
Brain weight	56
Number of glomeruli in kidney	56
Vital capacity	56
Hand grip	55
Maximum ventilation volume (during exercise)	53
Kidney plasma flow	50
Maximum breathing capacity (voluntary)	43
Maximum oxygen uptake (during exercise)	40
Number of taste buds	36
Speed of return to equilibrium of blood acidity	17
Also:	
Less adrenal and gonadal activity	
Slower speed of response	
Some memory loss	

*From Shock, N. W. *The physiology of aging.* Copyright 1962 by Scientific American, Inc. All rights reserved.

minished appearance of the older person occurs. The involuntary smooth muscles that operate under the autonomic nervous system are affected only slightly, as compared to the other structures. They appear to function without difficulty even until late senescence. The ligaments, however, do tend to contract and harden, causing the familiar hunched-over body position.

Digestive. The digestive system also seems to alter with age; in fact, complaints about the digestive system are among the most common of all the complaints of the aged. There is a reduction in the amount of saliva, gastric juices, and enzyme action, thus upsetting the digestion pro-

cess. Because the digestive system is highly sensitive to emotional disturbances, anxieties and worries that accompany old age will play an important part in bringing about stomach deterioration.

Heart. Of all the organs in man's body, the heart and the blood vessels are the ones in which aging produces the most detrimental changes. Most of the other organs, such as the lungs, kidneys, and brain, would probably last for 150 years if they were assured an adequate blood supply. The heart and arteries are the weakest link in the chain of life.[31]

Aging affects the heart in several ways. The muscles in the heart tend to become stringy and dried out with the passage of time. Deposits of a brown pigment within the cells of the heart tend to restrict the passage of blood and impede the absorption of oxygen through its walls. The heart shrinks in size during the normal course of aging, and the fat in the heart increases. The valves of the heart lose their elasticity, and deposits of calcium and cholesterol may further decrease their efficiency. The heart of an older person pumps 70% as much blood as that of a young man. These changes in themselves are not necessarily dangerous, provided the heart is treated with the respect it deserves and not subjected to the stress of physical effort more appropriate to the young.

In later life many heart diseases involve the coronary artery, which has a tendency to harden and narrow and may become partially blocked. It is the site of many heart attacks brought on by increased physical effort or emotional stress. Hardening of the coronary artery may also be responsible for increased blood pressure, reducing the flow of blood to most parts of the body. Poor circulation of blood, whatever the cause, may result in trouble or breakdown of the kidneys and other organs. Poor circulation to the brain causes many personality deviations in older persons.

Respiration. Another effect of aging is the reduction of respiratory efficiency. There is a decrease of oxygen utilization due to a decrease in the size of the lungs in senescence. Some functioning air sac membrane is replaced by fibrous tissue, interfering with the exchange of gases within the lungs. According to Leaf,[32] maximum

There are major individual differences in the rate at which physical aging and muscular changes take place. Only the changes that take place in oneself are considered personally; the others are accepted philosophically.

David Strickler

lung capacity in old age is 56%, and breathing capacity is 43%. Moderate exercise is ideal for keeping oxygen intake and blood flow at their level of highest potential, thus slowing down the aging and deterioration process.

Summary. According to Wolff,[33] the ten most common physical characteristics of biological aging are (1) an increase in connective tissue, (2) the disappearance of cellular elements in the central nervous system, (3) the loss of elastic properties in the connective tissue, (4) a reduction in the number of normally functioning cells, (5) an increase in fatty tissue, (6) a decrease in the utilization of oxygen, (7) a decrease in the volume of air expired by the lungs, (8) an overall decrease in muscular strength, and (9) a decrease in the excretion of hormones, especially by the sex and adrenal glands.

These changes in the body do not necessarily mean that the healthy aged person cannot function within normal limits. It does mean that there is less resistance to physical stress and less ability to recuperate. There is no single change that is of supreme major importance. It is the accumulation of changes that will be meaningful.

Sexuality

There is a substantial body of research literature that indicates that both sexual interest and behavior gradually decline among healthy aging individuals.[34,35] However, there are many misconceptions about the nature and extent of the decline in interest and in activity. In addition, most people believe that biological aging is basically responsible for diminishing interest and activity. To a degree, this belief is true, but it is not true to the magnitude that this idea is being expressed. It is becoming increasingly apparent in the research that a significant proportion of this decline is not due to physical incapacities but is attributed to social, cultural, and psychological factors that adversely affect the expression of sexual drives and desires. Specifically, some of these factors are related to the powerful influence of attitudes and misconceptions regarding sex in the later years of life; the lack of privacy in many living arrangements that the elderly have to share; the loss of a spouse, thus the loss of a sexual partner; feelings of guilt or moral trans-

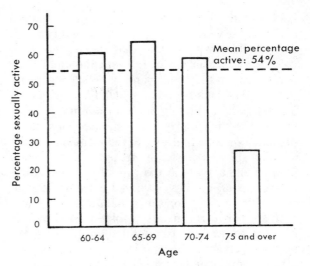

Fig. 15-3. There is a decline in sexual activity with advancing age. (Adapted from Newman, G., & Nichols, C. R. Sexual activities and attitudes in older persons. In E. B. Palmore [Ed.]. *Normal aging.* Durham, N. C.: Duke University Press, 1970. pp. 277-281. Used by permission.)

gressions for any number of unwarranted reasons; and feelings of anxiety, depression, or hostility. According to Butler and Lewis,[36] the fear of death due to a heart attack or stroke deters some individuals from engaging in excitable sexual activity. Studies show that there is a greater interest and desire for sexual activity in old age than is generally assumed by both oldsters and younger people. It must also be stated, however, that because of some of the reasons listed above, there is usually more interest than there is sexual activity. Pfeiffer[37] found that both healthy males and females are capable of sexual activity, including intercourse, well into the seventh decade. Fig. 15-3 shows the percentage of sexually active individuals for different age levels above 60. Between 60 and 75, about 50% of the persons in this major study indicated some degree of sexual involvement. After the age of 75, the percentage who were sexually active declined sharply.

The three most significant studies of geriatric sexual behavior have been made by Kinsey et al.,[38] Duke's Center for the Study of the Aging,[39] and Masters and Johnson.[40-42] In each, the findings clearly show that men and women in general good health are physiologically able to have a satisfying sex life well into their 70s and beyond. The studies also indicate that those who were most active sexually during youth and middle age usually retain their vigor and interest longer into old age. The Duke studies, which have been conducted on a continuing basis for twenty years or more, are particularly interesting because they present evidence that 15% of the men and women studied showed a steady rising rate of sexual interest and activity as they got older. The nature of the sexual activity involved either participation with a partner or self-stimulation.

In regard to the needs of older persons, one matter that is all too frequently overlooked is the need for privacy. This is true in congregate living arrangements, such as homes for the aged, nursing homes, family care homes, or living-in with relatives or children. The right to privacy is an important social right that should not be curtailed just because care facilities did not consider the matter of privacy when the plans were made for construction.[43]

By the same token, the right to private behavior should not be abrogated, whether that behavior is related to expressions of sexual interest or not. Sexuality is reflected in many forms and has several purposes. The primary function of sex is the creation of new life so that the species may be propagated. Beyond that, another sig-

nificant function of sex is the expression of love, by means of intimate communication, between two people who are very fond of each other. Sexuality need not involve coitus in order to provide an intimate relationship of love. There is a rewarding, emotional exchange of shared joy in the comforting warmth of physical nearness, the positive response to being touched by someone who cares, and the stimulating pleasure of close companionship. Do not those who are older need an expression of love as much as anyone else? Older people should not be denied the opportunity to find, to experience, and to express the closeness that says, ''I care about you.''

HEALTH MAINTENANCE

Physical and psychological well-being are matters of great social and personal concern. Health and illness affect an individual's performance of basic personal tasks of daily living and of expected economic and social roles. As Shanas and Maddox[44] state it, health is a key personal resource for any individual because performance of social roles in economic, family, and community organizations requires individuals who can function competently.

Perceived health status and aging

In a Southern California study of 1,269 black, Mexican-American and Anglo respondents,

Table 15-4. Perceived health status by ethnicity*

	Percent who consider their health to be poor or very poor (ethnicity)		
	Black (n: 413)	Mexican-American (n: 449)	Anglo (n: 407)
Ages: 45-54	13.8	16.9	1.7
55-64	15.2	20.8	9.1
65-75	27.0	23.2	4.0

*From Bengtson, V. L., Kasschau, P. L., & Ragan, P. K. The impact of social structure on aging individuals. In J. E. Birren & K. W. Schaie (Eds.). *Handbook of the psychology of aging.* New York: Van Nostrand Reinhold Co., 1977.

Table 15-5. Average remaining years of life at ages 40, 50, and 65, by sex and race: United States, 1975*

Sex and race	Average remaining years of life		
	At age 40	At age 50	At age 65
White			
Men	33.0	24.3	13.7
Women	39.4	30.3	18.1
All others			
Men	29.8	22.4	13.7
Women	36.2	27.5	17.5

*From U.S. National Center for Health Statistics. Life tables and acturial tables; and vital statistics of the United States Annual. In *Statistical Abstracts,* 1977.

Bengtson, Cuellar and Ragan[45] asked about self-perceived and functional health status of the participants. Table 15-4 indicates the perceived health status by ethnicity and age. At age 45 to 54, almost 17% of the Mexican-Americans considered their health to be poor, almost 14% of the blacks considered their health poor, but only about 2% of the Anglos considered that they had poor health. The figures jumped to 23% Chicano, 27% black, and 4% Anglo by 65 to 75 years of age. The percent that considered themselves elderly also varied widely. Before age 57 to 59, none of the groups who considered themselves as being "old" exceeded 15% of their respective groups. At 63 to 65, about 48% of the Mexican-Americans, 33% of the blacks, and only 8% of the Anglos thought of themselves as being elderly. Between the ages of 69 to 71, the figures changed respectively to 61%, 55%, and 39%. Of the three groups, however, at the age of 69 to 71, blacks had the greatest expectation of living 10 or more years (62%). Only 28% of the Mexican-Americans and the Anglos had the same expectation.

In the United States individuals who were 45

Perceived health status and involvement in activities are highly correlated. The more the elderly are involved in activities, the more likely it is that their health status will be positive in nature.

David Strickler

years of age in 1968 (that is, persons born in 1923) had already lived as long as the average person born in 1900 could have expected to live. Yet, the 45-year-old male in 1968 still had 26.8 years of life remaining and the female had 32.5 years. Even so, the average life expectancy for males in the United States ranked eighteenth among nations of the world. Sweden ranked first in male life expectancy with 71.6 years. Females in Netherlands ranked first with a 75.9 year life expectancy, while women in the United States ranked eleventh. Table 15-5 presents the average remaining years of life at ages 45, 65, and 75 by sex and color. Whites have a longer life expectancy than all other colors up to age 75, and women have a longer life expectancy than men. Of interest are the age categories used by the U.S. National Health Survey reports. They speak of the *young old* as being 45 to 64, the *old* as 65-74, and the *old old* as 75 and over.

There appears to be an upper age limit for human beings. The life span of anyone who reached the age of 65 years since 1900 has not been increased much. People are not living to be 200 years old, in spite of medical advances. Scientists have pretty much given up the idea of increasing man's life span in older age and are now concentrating on making the latter years of life a time that has less debilitating disease and a higher quality of enjoyment and comfort.

Stress and health changes

Changes in a person's life produce a stress situation. Holmes and Rahe[46] have shown that any major change in daily living, in either a pleasant or unpleasant way, produces a greater susceptibility to disease. This reaction holds true regardless of educational level, wealth, intellectual skills, or social class of the individual. Older people are particularly affected by the close relationship between stress and illnesses, although not all researchers in gerontology agree on the degree of the relationship. The speculation is that in old age fewer conditions would be required to produce health changes, particularly if the physiological being is already weakened by disease. An existing illness or a relatively passive social pattern may result in an accentuated reaction to a given life change event in old age.

Six of the thirteen most stressful life changes characteristic of later life are: death of a spouse, death of a close family member, personal injury or illness, retirement, change in the health of a family member, and sex difficulties. Holmes and Rahe evaluate the impact of life changes empirically and determine a "life crisis unit" or total score. The higher the score, the greater the likelihood of developing an illness in a reasonably short time, such as three to six months. This reaction is especially true if the life change is accompanied by depression and much anxiety.

Diet and nutrition

Any advice to the elderly concerning the maintenance of good health consistently includes suggestions for an adequate diet. Increasingly, evidence points to the necessity for the aged to be vitally concerned about their eating habits. The report of the White House Conference on Aging[47] indicates that individuals in 53% of the households containing people over 60 years of age had generally inadequate diets. Of concern, especially in recent years, has been the diet and its relationship to cardiac problems. As a result, physicians have almost always put their older patients on low-fat, high-protein diets. An interesting observation is made by volunteers of the Meals on Wheels program that brings at least one warm meal per day to an elderly person. The volunteers often note a distinct improvement in the physical appearance and health of the individuals who receive a regular, balanced meal.

Older people have the tendency to neglect their diets for a variety of reasons. Sadly, this neglect can frequently be traced to inadequate incomes. As a consequence, these people eat inexpensive foods that invariably are of the high-calorie, low-protein variety. Many times food is packaged in too large a quantity for one or two persons to use in a reasonable amount of time. Another common reason why people often do not receive adequate food is the preparation necessary for a nourishing, well-balanced meal. Often the person sees no real reason to go to a lot of "fuss" for just himself or perhaps one other person. As a result, shortcuts are taken and an inadequate diet results.

Another danger concerning the diet is that often elderly people have a tendency to overeat.

They do not seem to realize that their caloric requirements are probably decreasing as the years pass, and the excess calories they consume simply turn into fat. This, then, becomes one more factor in the eventual deterioration of health. Physicians will frequently prescribe light exercise for their elderly patients. The exercise or activity is beneficial physically and also mentally because it helps the older person to avoid the "illness of idleness."

Sleep

Many elderly persons complain of a variety of sleep disturbances. These include difficulty in falling asleep, insomnia, early awakening, falling asleep while watching television, restless sleep, not enough sleep, frequent awakening during the night, and feeling tired or exhausted after having had a good night's sleep. Relatives worry about the older person sleeping too much, falling asleep while company is present, or taking catnaps too often during the day, resulting in not being able to sleep at night. What is a normal sleep pattern for the elderly?

It is important to be aware of stereotype fallacies concerning sleep in old age and to differentiate between changes in sleep patterns that are part of normal aging and those sleep disturbances that indicate physical or emotional distress. How much sleep does an older person need? It is doubtful that any elderly person in reasonably good health requires any more sleep than was required in middle adulthood. Although some researchers say that people need less sleep as they grow older, it is probably more correct to say that sleep patterns tend to change as a result of illness, anxiety, depression, or simply the need for more exercise and activity during the day. Early morning awakenings are common among those who are inactive and go to bed early, those who catnap too much, and those who have physical discomfort, such as arthritic pains or poor circulation, that builds up during long periods of rest. Older people who suffer from illnesses and degenerative diseases may need more sleep, not less. According to Tiller,[48] sleep in these cases is a vital restorative.

Some important changes in patterns of sleep do take place in elderly persons. Kahn and Fisher[49] and others have found that deep sleep (stage 4 of sleep) virtually disappears. The elderly require a somewhat longer period to fall asleep, their sleep is lighter, and they have more frequent awakenings. Of greater importance is the fact that normal aging persons distribute their sleep somewhat differently during the 24-hour cycle. They generally have several catnaps of 15 to 60 minutes during the daylight hours.[50] Since this pattern is normal, caution should be used when considering regular use of sleeping medication to keep the person asleep for 8 hours throughout the night or in some other way disturbing the normal pattern of sleep developed in old age. People develop their own individual patterns of sleep according to their conditions and their needs.

Exercise and aging

Much has been written in recent years about the value of exercise in maintaining good health and in slowing down aging. An interesting study is being conducted by Herbert de Vries[51] of the University of Southern California's Gerontology Center on this topic. He and his team took a mobile laboratory designed for research in the physiology of exercise and aging to a retirement community in Laguna Hills, California. Over 125 older men volunteered to work out in his program. Statistics indicated dramatic improvement in physical conditioning of the subjects who followed a program of modified Royal Canadian Air Force calisthenics, jogging, walking, a static stretching routine, and swimming. For the group, maximum oxygen increased 9.2% and oxygen pulse (a measure of cardiovascular function) improved 8.4%. Oxygen intake appears to be the key to endurance fitness.

De Vries found that age-related losses in functional capacity of the individual were due to (1) the true aging process, (2) a functional decline resulting from loss in physical fitness, which Kraus and Raab[52] called the "hypokinetic disease," and (3) incipient, undiagnosed degenerative disease processes. The loss in vigor by older people is the result of well-documented losses in aerobic (intake of oxygen) capacity, which, in turn, lessens physical working strength. The significance of aerobic capacity and lessened working performance is suggested by "bedrest"

David Strickler

Exercises that improve cardiovascular functions help maintain better body tone and retard the aging process. Adult size tricycles have many personal, social, and healthful uses.

studies where, in a matter of weeks, young, well-conditioned individuals approximate long-term aging effects. With proper exercise programs, these young people could regain their functional working capacities. De Vries learned that both middle-aged and older healthy men and women are relatively as trainable as are young people. The training effect on older people is demonstrable in the cardiovascular and respiratory systems, in the musculature, and in decreased percentage of body fat, lowered blood pressure, and the ability to achieve neuromuscular relaxation.

In general, improvement from training varies directly with the type of exercise involved, the intensity of the exercise, and inversely with the pretraining aerobic capacity. Brief walking may suffice for poorly conditioned elderly males (age 60 to 79). Later, a jog-walk regimen can be initiated under proper medical supervision. Exercises for older people should maximize the rhythmic activity of large muscle masses and minimize isometric (static) contraction and extensive use of small muscle masses. The natural activities of walking, jogging, running, and swimming are best suited to this purpose.

Table 15-6. Suicide rates (per 100,000) in the U.S. for 1975 by age, sex, and race*

Age range	White males	White females	Non-white males	Non-white females
5-14	0.8	0.2	0.1	0.2
15-24	19.6	4.9	14.4	3.9
25-34	24.4	8.9	24.6	6.5
35-44	24.5	12.6	16.0	4.9
45-54	29.7	13.8	12.8	4.5
55-64	32.1	11.7	11.5	4.1
65 plus	39.4	8.5	11.8	3.0

*From *Vital Statistics of the United States. 1975 (Vol. II). Mortality, Part A.* Rockville, Maryland: U.S. Public Health Service, 1977.

Illness and causes of death

Because of lower resistance to disease and of diminished organic and systemic functional capacities, 86% of very old people have chronic health problems of one kind or another.[53] They visit the doctor more frequently than the young do, go to the hospital more often and stay there longer, and spend more days each year sick at home. Older people complain chiefly of ill-defined discomfort, rheumatism, some form of arthritis, and digestive problems. Despite these complaints, 81% of older adults move around on their own and only 5% live in institutions.

It is interesting that the five more common categories of causes of death are the same for those between the ages of 45 and 64 as for those above age 65. The percentage distribution varies, however. Cardiovascular diseases are the cause of 39% of the deaths of the middle-age group but cause 50% of the deaths in those over 65. Cancer is responsible for more deaths in the 45 to 64 age group than in the older group (24% to 15%). Hypertension causes more deaths in the over 65 groups (15% to 7%). Respiratory diseases are nearly the same—5% in the 45 to 64 and 6% in the older group. Accidents are responsible for 5% of the deaths in the 45 to 64 age group but only 2% of the over 65 group. These figures are from Smith and Bierman.[54]

The suicide rates in the United States show a different picture for males and females and for age groups. Table 15-6 reveals that the suicide rate among the elderly was more than triple that of the younger population. Of the elderly group, there were substantially more suicides among white males than among all the other categories, white and nonwhite combined.

Accidents and safety

Older people have a disproportionate share of accidents that cause bodily injury or death. This is especially true for accidents that occur in the home. They also have an extremely high accident rate on the highway when the total number of miles driven is taken into consideration. According to Lang,[55] persons 65 years of age and older made up 9% of the total population but accounted for 28% of all accidental deaths and 20% of all accidents causing bodily injury.

An analysis of accidents by young and old persons found that those that increased in frequency with age could be explained by slowness in getting out of the way of hazards or recovering balance, whereas those that became less frequent with age were attributable to carelessness and taking undue risks. Automobile accidents among older drivers seem to be due to slowness and a tendency to confusion, whereas those characteristic of younger drivers are due to various kinds of recklessness. Similar causes seem to lie behind the traffic violations characteristic of older and younger drivers.[56]

It has been found that safety devices, especially those that help the older person maintain balance, have contributed significantly to their physical and mental well-being. In addition, care should be taken to remove all accident "traps" that may cause the elderly to fall, such as loose carpets. A small amount of concern on the part of the family and neighbors of the elderly person may save him from dangers he does not realize exist and to which he is therefore extremely susceptible.

AGING AND COGNITIVE ABILITIES

As Arenberg and Robertson-Tchabo state in their chapter in the book, *Handbook of the Psychology of Aging*,[57] "If the adage, 'You can't teach an old dog new tricks,' was not buried in the previous handbook (by Birren), the research reported since then should complete the interment.'' It is important to note that mental decline associated with old age may not be as great as was previously supposed. Researchers in the field are beginning to recognize the inadequacy of research studies of the past and are designing better research instruments. Many earlier studies were done with institutionalized elderly, which could hardly be considered a typical or normal sample of the aged population. Current studies are finding that individual differences in learning and cognitive abilities are substantially influenced by such factors as intellectual level, educational status, physical condition, stimulating environment, and possibly, even the number of years left before death. The research in the area has narrowed from the use of gross variables, which covered too much territory, to more judicious specifics.[58]

Individual differences and cognition

It has been observed by lay people as well as researchers that, in general, the more that an individual involves himself in stimulating learning and thinking situations and the more he uses his mind and memory, the better and longer he will be able to learn, think, and remember. This notion has been substantiated by Eisdorfer and Lawton[59] who concluded, after a review of studies made of intellectual changes in the aged, that those who continue to work or to interact with intellectually stimulating environments as they reach old age, have more normal brain functioning and do better on intelligence tests than those who are inactive or unoccupied. We have noticed this intellectual enhancement in elderly persons who, when in their late 70s and 80s, wrote papers for presentation to our Historical Society and to the Tuesday Club. Old people who watch and enjoy television game programs that involve some form of cognitive or informative involvement, such as Hollywood Squares, also appear to be mentally alert and interested in community and national affairs.

The amount of formal education (and in some cases, informal education) also appears to be instrumental in reducing the amount of decline in intellectual functional ability in the elderly. Birren and Morrison,[60] for example, reported a higher correlation between intelligence test scores and education level than between these scores and age. The same type of emphasis has been given to the role of education by other researchers, including Granick and Friedman[61] who found that performance in a variety of intellectual tasks was modified by the level of education of the individuals in these studies. The age variable accounts for only about 25% of the variance in IQ test scores.

It would be misleading to say that there is no decline in intellectual functioning as age progresses. There is some decline but not as much nor as quickly as some may think. The classic study by Schaie,[62] where he gave the Primary Mental Ability Test to 500 people—50 in each of ten 5-year intervals—showed no appreciable decline in intellectual functions between the ages of 20 and 50 years. Peak performance was attained in the 31 to 35 age group. But, it was not until after the age of 60 that the scores were lower by more than one standard deviation. In a longitudinal study, Owens[63] found that those individuals with higher intellectual levels experienced relatively less decline in mental efficiency than those of lower levels. Studies of the gifted also reveal that for these individuals mental decline sets in much later than is generally surmised.

Mental changes

If intelligence is considered in terms of performances that require the use of long-term memory and the use of acquired skills, there appears to be an insignificant decline in intellectual ability until after the age of 60 or 65 in healthy persons. In fact, acquired skills or ''crystallized'' functions (those that involve language skills and the use of long-established habits) reveal some increase in performance, a late peak, and high stability or slow decline. Often, the value of experience and knowledge are ignored when the intellectual competence of older persons is being evaluated. If one defines intelligence in terms of a set of behaviors that reflect rapid responding and competency with problem-solving ability with an emphasis on visual-motor skills, older persons do not do as well as younger ones.[64] It may be that these skills are not as important to the elderly adult as they are to the younger person. However, when time constraints are relaxed, elderly adults improve in performance. It is wise to remember, nevertheless, that older adults must still function in a world where rapid response and problem-solving ability are important.

Learning. Studies indicate that the ability to learn is approximately the same at the age of 80 years as it is at 12 years. If the aged want to learn, they can. Learning may be slower, but it can be accomplished. The Duke University Center for Study of Aging and Human Development[65] has exhaustively tested the learning ability of the aged. The researchers conclude that the aged can learn, but more slowly than the young. They state that the older person's goal is more to avoid failure than to gain success. However, certain changes in the brain can make a difference in thinking along the "flexibility-rigidity" continuum. The person becomes more rigid and less capable of doing the problem-solving reasoning that requires a broad dimension of thought.

An elderly person attacks a problem differently than a younger person, tending to refer back to his own previous experience in his attempt to solve problems. If this approach is appropriate, he can cope effectively with the situation; but if it is inappropriate, the older person often misunderstands the problem and makes frequent mistakes because of his misconceptions and misinterpretations. He adopts a literal instead of a hypothetical approach to solving problems with logical implications.

In training situations the older person seems to be more involved and shows more care and greater concentration than a younger person. In working to minimize the risk of error, the older person usually sacrifices speed to stress accuracy. There is a slowing down of mental action and sensorimotor speed due to delay within the central nervous system. The slower performance of the elderly on many tasks is not necessarily due to a loss of capacity for the task but, rather, is caused by insufficient time for the slowed cerebral processes to be completed.[66]

Mental alertness. Lack of mental alertness is common in many older people. "I just can't remember anything. I am becoming so forgetful," said one elderly person. There are two major reasons for this forgetfulness. First, it may be or-

ganically caused by a deterioration of the arteries, commonly called hardening of the arteries. When blood flow is impaired, the brain ceases to receive the nourishment necessary for effective functioning of cognitive processes. The other reason is an apparent loss of interest in current events. Often older people take refuge in their memories of previous undertakings in which they were successful.

Another significant factor is the fact that older persons often have less to do in their everyday world. There are few major events or changes that take place and, as a result, there is a great deal of "sameness" to each day. Consequently, one day flows into the next one without anything significant to differentiate them. There is very little worth remembering. Reminiscence of the past is more attractive. It is remembered. The immediate, dull affairs of the present time are not. It is no wonder that the most noticeable symptoms of mental decline in old age are the deterioration of memory for recent events and the gradual loss of power of attention. Of course there can be other contributing causes besides "sameness."

Test performance. In spite of the fact that an older person may score lower on intelligence tests than before, the ability to learn declines slowly in senescence. Age changes in the ability to learn are small under most circumstances. When differences do appear, they do not seem to be readily attributed to a change in the capacity to learn but rather to a change in the processes of perception, set, attention, motivation, and physiological state of the organism, including that of disease states.[67]

Perceptual accuracy shows a decline in the older person and is due to the decline of the peripheral sense organs. The motor skills deteriorate next, followed by intellectual functions. The elderly person is not as efficient intellectually as he was in earlier years.

During senescence, however, not all aspects of intellectual functioning decline at the same rate. In most cases the person's intelligent use of vocabulary and the recall of general information are not affected until the later years of senile decline. Verbal skills seem to deteriorate more slowly than mathematical skills. Judgment and imagina-

Recipe For Contentment

Health enough to make work a pleasure.
Wealth enough to support your needs.
Strength to battle with difficulties and
   overcome them.
Grace enough to confess your sins and forsake
   them.
Patience enough to toil until some good is
   accomplished.
Charity enough to see some good in your
   neighbor.
Faith enough to make real the things of God.
Hope enough to remove all anxious fear
   concerning the future.

Goethe

tion generally do not decline as rapidly as memory and attention. Little is known about the difference between men and women in the way the intelligence is affected by aging. Existing evidence suggests that the age changes are the same for both sexes.

In a twelve-year study conducted by the National Institute of Health and the Philadelphia Geriatric Center[68] with regard to the correlation between intelligence and longevity, it was found that the subjects who lived longest functioned at a higher intellectual level than those who died before the study was completed. Of the original forty-seven volunteers, twenty-three survived until the end of the study (1968), with an average age of 81 years at that time. Intelligence tests used were the Wechsler Adult Intelligence Scale (WAIS) and the Raven Progressive Matrices Test. The researchers found "no significant decline" on the test performances and actually saw "significant increases in ability" for the vocabulary and picture arrangement subtests of the WAIS. Therefore, for these forty-seven men, survival seemed to be associated with retention of intellectual vigor and capabilities.

Keeping active apparently is of vital importance not only for one's physiological well-being but also for helping to retain intellectual capabilities. The word *active* applies both to mental activity and to physical activity through a regular fitness routine.

Terminal drop. Retrospective analyses of test results suggest that certain test performance levels or changes in these levels over a period of time may be related to the closeness to death of the aged individual. The implication is that those elderly subjects who succumb to death before the others tend to be the ones who had the lowest test scores. This phenomenon is called terminal drop. The concept of *terminal drop* is defined as a decline in test performance some few years prior to death, due perhaps to physiological deterioration or damage. In other words, age decline in test results is generally to be found in those test takers who are in the process of dying. The others, with longer lives to live, show little or no age decline. At the moment, these observations are still speculative.

The twelve-year study mentioned in the previous section is often cited in survival discussions because the elderly subjects who were involved in the study had extraordinarily good health. Five years after the initial testing, the survivors showed better scores in verbal information skills than those who subsequently died. The subjects were tested a third time and again there was a difference in the results. Blum, Clark, and Jarvick[69] found a correlation between the decline on three tests of cognitive functioning and mortality, although they were careful to say that the decline was not a predictor of mortality. These three tests are Digit Symbol, Similarities, and Vocabulary. Over a period of ten years, an annual decrement rate of at least 2% on Digit Symbol, 10% on Similarities, or any decline on the Vocabulary test was associated with death resulting during the following five years. Prospective studies are needed to confirm these results.

STUDY GUIDE

1. What is it like to be an adult of 60 to 75 years of age? What are the sociological, psychological, and physiological factors involved?
2. What is meant by the "age of recompense"?
3. Why have gerontology and geriatrics become such significant areas for research in recent years?
4. Review the developmental tasks of later adulthood. Can you see these tasks being pursued by your parents, your grandparents, or other older adults whom you know?
5. Make a list of sayings, quotations, or expressions that people state concerning the aged. How many of these are negative in nature? How many tend to stereotype the elderly? In what ways can these ideas hurt the young as well as the old?
6. Think of elderly white persons. Think of elderly black persons. Think of elderly Spanish-speaking persons. Think of elderly Italians. Think of all the different ethnic elderly groups that you can recall. How do these groups differ? How are they the same? Are they more alike or different? How and why?
7. Who would you enjoy being with more, a young old person, an old young person, an

old old person? What difference would there be?

8. What appears to be a central cause of physical changes that begin to take place in later adulthood? Note that old age spans a number of years, and the beginning years of old age are not like the later years.
9. How healthy are most older people? Do they get enough sleep, enough to eat, and enough exercise?
10. What can you do now to slow down the aging process in your body?
11. Which intellectual traits seem to hold and not deteriorate in older persons and which ones do not hold?
12. What do old people have to talk about? Consider that their days are pretty much the same, one day flowing into the next, with nothing in particular standing out. What is there to remember from the present?
13. Do you find it offensive or disgusting to think that people over 65 may have sexual interests? What would be a reasonable point of view on this question of sexuality and the aged?
14. Do you want to live a long life? How long? Why? Do you have any reservations such as "only if . . ."?

REFERENCES

1. Eisdorfer, C., & Lawton, M. P. *The psychology of adult development and aging.* Washington, D.C.: American Psychological Association, 1973, p. 529.
2. Gold, J. G., & Kaufman, S. M. Development of care of elderly: tracing the history of institutional facilities. *Gerontologist,* 1970, **10,** 262-274.
3. Butler, R. N., & Lewis, M. J. *Aging and mental health* (2nd ed.). St. Louis: The C. V. Mosby Co., 1977.
4. Riegel, K. F., & Riegel, R. A. A study of changes of attitudes and interests during later years of life. *Vita Humana,* 1960, **3,** 177-206.
5. Chown, S. H. The effects of age on the relationship between different types of rigidity. *Bulletin of the British Psychological Association,* 1961, **44,** A 12 (Abstract).
6. Kogan, N., & Shelton, F. Images of "old people" and "people in general" in an older sample. *Journal of Genetic Psychology,* 1962, **100,** 3-21.
7. Cameron, P. The generation gap: beliefs about stability of life. *Journal of Gerontology,* 1971, **26,** 81.
8. Pastalan, L., & Carson, D. *Spatial behavior of older people.* Ann Arbor: University of Michigan Press, 1970, p. 98.
9. National Center for Housing Management. *The one-site housing managers resource book: housing for elderly.* Washington, D.C.: The National Center for Housing Management, Inc., 1974.
10. Hurlock, E. B. *Development psychology* (3rd ed.). New York: McGraw-Hill Book Co., 1975, p. 31.
11. Pfeiffer, E. Psychopathology and social pathology. In J. E. Birren, & K. W. Schaie (Eds.), *Handbook of the psychology of aging.* New York: Van Nostrand Reinhold Co., 1977, Chap. 27.
12. Butler, R. N. & Lewis, M. J. *Op. cit.*
13. Pfeiffer, E. *Successful aging.* Durham, North Carolina: Duke University Center for the Study of Aging and Human Development, 1974.
14. Wilson, D. L. The programmed theory of aging. In M. Rockstein (Ed.), *Theoretical aspects of aging.* New York: Academic Press, 1974, pp. 11-22.
15. Baltes, P. B., & Willis, S. L. Toward psychological theories of aging and development. In J. E. Birren, & K. W. Schaie (Eds.), *Handbook of the psychology of aging.* New York: Van Nostrand Reinhold Co., 1977, Chap. 7.
16. Cottrell, F. A young science looks at aging. *Business Week,* August 26, 1967, p. 118.
17. Boehm, G. A. W. The search for ways to keep youthful. *Fortune,* March, 1965, **71,** 139.
18. Shock, N. W. Biological theories of aging. In J. E. Birren, & K. W. Schaie (Eds.), *Handbook of the psychology of aging.* New York: Van Nostrand Reinhold Co., 1977, Chap. 5.
19. Birren, J. E., & Schaie, K. W. *Handbook of the psychology of aging.* New York: Van Nostrand Reinhold Co., 1977, Chap. 20-23.
20. U.S. Department of Health, Education and Welfare. *Human communications and its disorders.* Bethesda, Maryland: U.S. Government Printing Office, 1969.
21. Guth, S. K. Effects of age on visibility. *American Journal of Optometry,* 1957, **34,** 463-477.
22. Fozard, J. J., & Thomas, J. C. *Why aging engineering psychologists should get interested in aging.* Presented at American Psychological Association, Montreal, Ontario, Canada, August, 1973.
23. Anderson, B., & Palmore, E. Longitudinal evaluation of ocular function. In E. Palmore (Ed.), *Normal aging.* Durham, North Carolina: Duke University, 1974, pp. 24-32.

24. Paton, D., & Craig, J. A. Cataracts: development, diagnosis, management. *CIBA Clinical Symposia,* **26**(3), 1-32 (no date).

25. Hermel, J., Schönwetter, S., & Samueloff, S. Taste sensation identification and age in man. *Journal of Oral Medicine,* 1970, **25,** 39-42.

26. Rovee, C. K., Cohen, R. Y., & Shlapack, W. Life span stability in olfactory sensitivity. *Developmental Psychology,* 1975, **11,** 311-318.

27. Beidler, L. M. Comparison of gustatory receptors, olfactory receptors, and free nerve endings. In *Cold Spring Harbor Symposia on Quantitative Biology,* 1965, **30,** 191-200.

28. Moulton, D. G. Cell renewal in the olfactory epithelium of the mouse. *Annuals New York Academy of Science,* 1974, **237,** 52-61.

29. Cooper, M. Voice problems of the geriatric patient. *Geriatrics,* 1970, **25,** 107-110.

30. Weg, R. B. The changing physiology of aging. *American Journal of Occupational Therapy,* 1973, **27,** 213-217.

31. Deropp, R. S. *Man against aging.* New York: St. Martin's Press, Inc., 1960, p. 186.

32. Leaf, A. Getting old, *Scientific American,* 1973, **229,** 45-52.

33. Wolff, K. *The biological, sociological, and psychological aspects of aging.* Springfield, Ill.: Charles C Thomas, Publisher, 1959, p. 7.

34. Kinsey, A. C., Pomeroy, W. B., & Martin, C. R. *Sexual behavior in the human male.* Philadelphia: W. B. Saunders Co., 1948.

35. Masters, W. H., & Johnson, V. E. *Human sexual response.* Boston: Little Brown & Co., 1966.

36. Butler, R. N., & Lewis, M. J. *Op. cit.*

37. Pfeiffer, E. *Sexuality in the aging individual.* Paper presented as part of the Symposium on Sexuality in the Aging Individual at the 31st Annual Meeting of the American Geriatric Society, Toronto, Canada, 1974.

38. Kinsey, A. C., Pomeroy, W. B., & Martin, C. R. *Op. cit.*

39. Pfeiffer, E. *Op. cit.*

40. Masters, W. H., & Johnson, V. E. *Op. cit.*

41. Masters, W. H., & Johnson, V. E. *Human sexual inadequacy.* London: J & A Churchill, Ltd., 1970.

42. Masters, W. H., & Johnson, V. E. Human sexual response: the aging female and the aging male. In B. L. Neugarten (Ed.), *Middle age and aging: a reader in social psychology.* Chicago: University of Chicago Press, 1968, 269-279.

43. Butler, R. N., & Lewis, M. *Sex after sixty. A guide for men and women for their later years.* New York: Harper & Row, Publishers, 1976.

44. Shanas, E., & Maddox, G. Aging, health and the organization of health resources. In R. H. Binstock, & E. Shanas (Eds.), *Handbook of aging and the social sciences.* New York: Van Nostrand Reinhold Co., 1976, Chap. 33.

45. Bengtson, V. L., Cuellar, J. B., & Ragan, P. K. Contrasts and similarities in attitudes toward death by race, age, social class and sex. *Journal of Gerontology,* 1977, **32,** 204-216.

46. Holmes, T. H., & Rahe, R. H. The social readjustment scale. *Journal Psychosomatic Research,* 1967, **11,** 213-218.

47. Federal Council on Aging. *White House Conference on Aging chart book.* Washington, D.C.: U.S. Government Printing Office, 1961, p. 60.

48. Tiller, P. H., Jr. Bedrest, sleep and symptoms. Study of older persons. *Annals of International Medicine,* 1964, **61,** 98-105.

49. Kahn, E., & Fisher, C. The sleep characteristics of the normal aged male. *Journal of Nervous Mental Disorders,* 1968, **148,** 477-494.

50. Pfeiffer, E. *Op. cit.*

51. De Vries, H. A. Physiology of exercise and aging. In D. S. Woodruff, & J. E. Birren (Eds.), *Aging: scientific perspectives and social issues.* New York: D. Van Nostrand Co., 1975, Chap. 12.

52. Kraus, H., & Raab, W. *Hypokinetic disease.* Springfield, Ill.: Charles C Thomas, Publisher, 1961.

53. Weg, R. B. The aging and the aged in contemporary society. *Journal of Physical Therapy,* 1973, **53,** 749-756.

54. Smith, D. W., & Bierman, E. L. (Eds.), *The biologic ages of man.* Philadelphia: W. B. Saunders Co., 1973.

55. Lang, G. (Ed.), *Old age in America.* New York: H. W. Wilson Co., 1961, p. 53.

56. Road Traffic Board of South Australia. *The points demerit scheme as an indication of declining skill with age,* 1972.

57. Arenberg, E. A., & Robertson-Tchabo, E. A. Learning and aging. In J. E. Birren & K. W. Schaie (Eds.), *Handbook of the Psychology of Aging.* New York: Van Nostrand Reinhold Co., 1977, Chap. 18.

58. Schaie, K. W., Labouvie, G. V., & Buech, B. V. Generational and cohort-specific differences in adult cognitive functioning: a fourteen-year study of independent samples. *Developmental Psychology,* 1973, **9,** 151-161.

59. Eisdorfer, C., & Lawton, M. P. *The psychology of adult development and aging,* Washington, D.C.: American Psychological Association, 1973.

60. Birren, J. E., & Morrison, D. F. Analysis of the WAIS subtests in relation to age and education, *Journal of Gerontology,* 1961, **16,** 363-369.

61. Granick, S., & Friedman, A. S. Educational experience and maintenance of intellectual functioning by the aged: an overview. In L. F. Jarvik, C. Eisdorfer, & J. E. Blum (Eds.), *Intellectual functioning in adults.* New York: Springer, 1973, pp. 59-64.

62. Schaie, K. W. Cross-sectional methods in the study of psychological aspects of aging. *Journal of Gerontology,* 1959, **14,** 208-215.

63. Owens, W. A. Age and mental abilities: a longitudinal study. In D. C. Charles, & W. R. Looft (Eds.), *Readings in psychological development through life.* New York: Holt, Rhinehart & Winston, 1973, pp. 243-254.

64. Elias, M. F., Elias, P. K., Elias, J. W. *Basic processes in adult developmental psychology.* St. Louis: The C. V. Mosby Company, 1977, Chap. 4.

65. Wilkie, F., & Eisdorfer, C. *Intellectual changes: a 15-year follow-up of the Duke sample.* Unpublished manuscript read at the 26th Annual Meeting of the Gerontological Society, Miami, Florida, 1973.

66. Spirduso, W. W. Reaction and movement time as a function of age and physical activity level. *Journal of Gerontology,* 1975, **30,** 435-440.

67. Botwinick, J. *Aging and behavior.* New York: Springer, 1973.

68. Birren, J. E., Butler, R. N., Greenhouse, S. W., Sokoloff, L., & Yarrow, M. R. *Human aging.* Public Health Pub. No. 986, Washington, D.C.: Government Printing Office, 1968.

69. Blum, J. E., Clark, E. T., & Jarvick, L. F. The New York State Psychiatric Institute study of aging twins. In L. F. Jarvick, C. Eisdorfer, & J. E. Blum (Eds.), *Intellectual functioning in adults.* New York: Springer, 1973, pp. 13-19.

Later adulthood

Social and personal

I am of the opinion that many people in our society today consider an individual in the later phases of life as a person who has lived his life fully, grown old gracefully, and is now biding his time here on earth. They feel these individuals should be content with being given a comfortable place in which to live, food to eat, and their monthly retirement or welfare checks to buy their necessities. Many people fail to see the tremendous adjustment these older individuals have to make and how totally alone they are in a world that offers so much to the younger generations.

Aunt Byrd was ninety-five on June 13 of this year, which definitely places her in a later phase of life. Upon meeting her, everyone will invariably say: "Isn't she marvelous for her age?" and I agree. Just to be ninety-five is an accomplishment in itself!

Aging, in the physical or biological aspect, can be seen quite readily, but Aunt Byrd still possesses many characteristics that enable her to get along in this world. She is almost deaf but, through the use of a hearing aid, she can function quite adequately. Her eyesight is very good; she reads two newspapers daily and *Time* and *Newsweek* each week. She has difficulty walking and must constantly use a cane to aid her. This presents a mobility problem; therefore, she can never go far from home. Her sense of taste is deficient, because she complains of never being able to tell whether things are too salty or too sweet.

Her biological or physical aging is not as great as it would be for most ninety-five-year-old individuals, due to the fact that her diet has always been and still is quite adequate and substantial. She eats everything, even at this age. Also, she had not suffered from any major illnesses for the past thirty years; she has always led a very healthy life. She was a nurse at one time.

Since her ability to move about is curtailed but she still has the desire to get about, she has taken quite a number of spills in her adventures. She has bruised herself quite badly at times but still has not learned her lesson. She feels she is being a burden by asking others to get things for her and wants to get these things for herself. It is difficult for her to accept the fact that she must now depend on others to do even simple things for her.

In memory ability, Aunt Byrd has declined greatly in some aspects. She can vividly remember days of long ago and can relate them in detail, but she can't remember such things as where she placed her pocketbook or what happened to her the previous day. I think she realizes that she is declining in cognitive ability because she admits her memory isn't as good as it used to be. This must be a difficult adjustment to make as she was always very alert and interested in world events and affairs.

She is interested in politics and is staunch, even stubborn, in her beliefs. She follows the role: "I have always been a _____ and I will always remain so." Her stubborn trait shows in other aspects of her personality as well as in her politics. Of course, in her younger days, she was remarkably well known in her family for stubbornness. This aspect of her personality has remained even where others have declined.

Social adjustment has probably been the most difficult for Aunt Byrd. Her husband passed away thirty years ago, and she has no children of her own. She lives with her nephew and his family. All her friends have passed away, and she really has no one to communicate with or reminisce about old times. Every chance she gets, she likes to talk about how things used to be when she was young. She wants desperately to talk with someone but only about her time. She can't communicate about the "now" or present age.

Her chief source of interest is television. She sits for hours watching the television and enjoys this medium thoroughly. The only other interest she has is reading.

As I think about the social aspect of adjustment in old age, I can't help but feel sorry for people at this stage of life. They are so very much alone because of their lack of communication with the younger generation. Aunt Byrd is content, though, to be considered a part of the family with whom she lives. They help reduce some of her needs for companionship. It would be of such great help to elderly people if others could realize this difficult adjustment to loneliness and the desire to relate to someone.

Perhaps Aunt Byrd's greatest strength is in her spiritual and religious commitments. She has much faith and her beliefs are strong. It very well may be that her life has been so full and rewarding because of her beliefs and her tenacity in following them. No doubt her faith has helped her through her period of adjustment.

I have always wondered how she compares life of now to life as it was during her childhood. She has seen so many changes in her lifetime that it must be both rewarding and yet bewildering. I envy her the fact that she has seen and experienced so much in her lifetime. Imagine living in an age that started before the invention of the automobile and eventually saw man walking on the moon. It is no wonder she regrets that we all couldn't have lived "back then." Perhaps if I had lived back then, I would feel the same way.

The process of aging and old age itself have become major topics of discussion, research, and speculation in recent years. One of the reasons for such activity is that more and more people are reaching old age. Approximately 4,000 Americans have their sixty-fifth birthday every day, and 10% of the population is over the age of 65 years. Western society has never experienced such a large percentage of its population living in retirement. The social, economic, and medical implications of this increased aged population are tremendous. Problems never before encountered are now facing a society that must not only learn how to live with a sizable number of its members in retirement but also how to incorporate this older segment of the population into the mainstream of life. For the most part the aged are people who still have vigor and vitality for life. To isolate and segregate them will only serve to force them into becoming "old" before their time.

DEMOGRAPHY OF OLD AGE

Who are the elderly, how many are there, and where do they live? The answers to these questions have all sorts of social, political, and economic ramifications. For example, Ragan and Dowd[1] point out that the growth in the number of older persons, in conjunction with such matters as inflation, increases in health care costs, and decreased value of pension dollars, has caused the elderly to identify themselves as a group, seeking to promote political actions favorable to their needs and status. Prominent among these groups are the American Association of Retired Persons (AARP) and the Gray Panthers, an aggressive political action group. Another area of concern is the sky-rocketing cost of old age insurance payments to Social Security recipients. The number of people eligible for payments has far exceeded the estimate envisioned when the Social Security Act was passed in 1937. There is concern, not only in the United States of America, but in most countries of the world that have some form of old age pension, that the system may become bankrupt and not be able to pay those who are eligible for Social Security allotments.

According to United Nations calculations, of the total of 3.6 billion persons on the globe in

Table 16-1. Population and older persons of world by eight United Nations regions, 1970 and projected to 2000 (medium variant)*

World and region	Total population				Persons 65 and over			
	Number (000,000's)		Percent distribution		Number (000,000's)		Percent distribution	
	1970	2000	1970	2000	1970	2000	1970	2000
World	3,632	6,515	100.0	100.0	190	396	100.0	100.0
East Asia	930	1,424	25.6	21.9	40	99	21.0	24.9
South Asia	1,126	2,354	31.0	36.1	36	99	18.8	24.9
Europe	462	568	12.7	8.7	52	71	27.1	17.8
U.S.S.R.	243	330	6.7	5.1	19	39	9.9	9.8
Africa	344	818	9.5	12.6	10	27	5.5	6.8
Northern America	228	333	6.3	5.1	22	31	11.6	7.8
Latin America	283	652	7.8	10.0	10	29	5.5	7.3
Oceania	19	35	0.5	0.5	1	3	0.6	0.8

*From Total Population, from United Nations, *World and Regional Population Prospects: Addendum, World Population Prospects Beyond the Year 2000*, p. 13; Persons 65 and over, from same for year 2000; for year 1970, estimated from United Nations, *The World Population Situation in 1970*, pp. 46-50.

To be old need not mean to be alone or to not enjoy life. Facilities must be provided, however, where the elderly can gather for various activities.

1970, approximately 190 million were 65 years of age or older. The rate of increase of this age group will average about 2.5% per year until the year 2000. By that year the number of persons over 65 in the world is expected to double. Table 16-1 shows the estimated changes in population between 1970 and 2000. Note that developing regions of the world are expected to have a higher percentage of older people as the years go on. It is reasoned that their prior higher fertility rate and a rapidly declining mortality rate for persons of all ages due to better health care will account for the increased number of older people in these regions.

As far as the United States of America is concerned, the older population has grown from 3.1 million in 1900 to almost 20.2 million in 1970. Of the total older population in 1970, 14.6 million or 73% lived in urban areas, the majority of whom lived in heavily urbanized areas in central cities. Only 4.3 million old people lived in the suburbs. This disproportionate distribution of older people in the central city makes problems of congestion, transportation, housing, crime, and living costs of paramount importance to those interested in the health and well-being of older persons.[2] Table 16-2 shows the ten leading states with popula-

tions of age 65 or older. California, New York, Pennsylvania, and Florida account for nearly one third of the older population of the United States. These states also have the largest total populations, so the figures are not unexpected. However, note the states that have the greatest percentage of increase since 1960. Due to a widespread migration of retired persons to the South and the sun belt, Florida's percentage of people over 65 has increased 78.9%; Texas, 33.1%; and California 30.9%. Although Arizona is not listed as one of the top ten states with the number of people over 65, it did increase its aged population by 79.0%; that represented only 71,000 additional people, however. More and more people are living to increasingly older ages. In 1900, 3.1% were over 65, in 1940, it was 9.0%, in 1960, 16.6%, and in 1980 it is estimated to be 24.5% of the population.[3]

The ratio of females to males by age levels is interesting. Cutler and Harootyan[4] constructed age-sex population pyramids for the years 1900, 1940, and 1970, as shown in Fig. 16-1. A look at the pyramids shows how the age population has changed during this century. As fertility and mortality rates changed from the beginning of the century, so have the age and sex composition.

Table 16-2. Population age 65 and over: ten leading states in the United States: 1976*

Rank	State	Number	Percent increase 1960-1970	Percent of state total in 1970
1	California	2,121,000	30.9	9.9
2	New York	2,068,000	16.2	11.4
3	Pennsylvania	1,404,000	12.7	11.8
4	Florida	1,383,000	78.9	16.4
5	Texas	1,193,000	33.1	9.6
6	Illinois	1,171,000	12.2	10.4
7	Ohio	1,089,000	11.2	10.2
8	Michigan	834,000	18.0	9.2
9	New Jersey	787,000	24.4	10.7
10	Massachusetts	682,000	11.3	11.1
	United States	22,934,000	21.0	10.7

*Adapted from United States Bureau of the Census. *Census of Population: 1970, General Population Characteristics* (Washington, D.C.: United States Government Printing Office) Final Report, PC (1)-B1, Tables 59 and 62; Census of Population Report, Series P-25, No. 646 (Washington, D.C.: United States Printing Office), 1977.

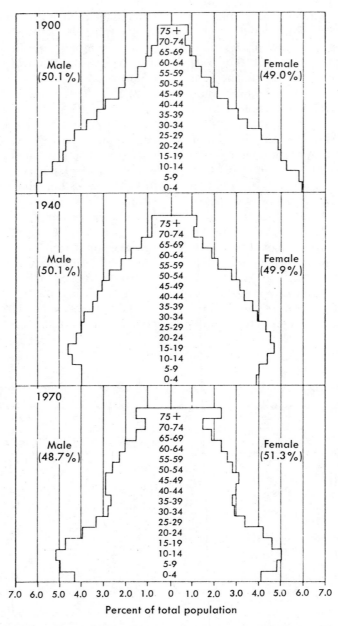

Fig. 16-1. Age-sex population pyramids for the United States: 1900, 1940, 1970. (United States Bureau of the Census. *Census of Population: Characteristics of the Population,* 1940, 1970.)

Table 16-3. Number of females per 100 males by age in 1976*

Age in years	Females per 100 males
Under 14	96.2
14 to 24	98.5
25 to 44	103.4
45 to 64	108.2
65 and over	131.8
Total U.S.	105.2

*Data from Current Population Reports, Series P-25, No. 643. In *Statistical abstracts,* U. S. Bureau of the Census, Washington, D.C.: United States Government Printing Office, 1977.

A clearer representation of the ratio of females to males is seen in Table 16-3. In the United States in 1976 there were 105.2 females per 100 males in the total population. More boy babies were born than girls and boys outnumbered girls until age 18. Then a shift occurred so that by age 25 males only outnumbered females by 1.5 persons. After that age, the number of females exceeded the number of males. After the age of 65, there were 131.8 females for every 100 males.

The distribution of older persons by marital status shows the reason for the difference in the percentage of the sexes. In the census figures for 1974, 52.4% of the women over 65 were widowed, while only 14.4% of the men were. Life expectancy makes a difference. Related figures show that 78.9% of the men over 65 and 38.7% of the women over 65 were married, while only 2.2% of the men and 2.6% of the women were divorced. Only 4.6% of the men and 6.3% of the women never married.[5]

Black people in the United States have a shorter life expectancy than whites. Although black people comprise more than 10% of the total population, they make up only 8% of the older age group. The number of black elderly has risen from 1.2 million in 1960 to 1.6 million in 1970. They now constitute 7.8% of the total black population. Black elderly women outlive black men to an increasing degree. Black females make up 56.7% of the total black aged population. In 1970, there were 131.0 black females over 65 for every 100 black males.

PSYCHOLOGICAL CHANGES

The study of psychological and personality changes in the aged is both perplexing and difficult. The state of the art is such that very little is known about how to measure psychological characteristics and changes. Even less is known about the dimensions, attributes, and variances that make up personality dynamics and traits. So, it is a matter of groping in the dark, coming up with a tidbit here and a tidbit there, but not being certain of what you really have or are dealing with. Nevertheless, it is important to make a start and, inconclusive and unsubstantiated as it may be, it is a beginning at evolving a scientific concept of the parameters of personality. In reference to the aged, it is important to know about the psychological changes that are taking place because, for most, it is a period of stress and change, and the strength and adaptability of the entire personality structure and its well-being are being tested.

Challenges to the ego

Older people need tangible relationships and experiences that will bolster their waning ego and provide them with evidence that will help them to sustain their identity.[6] Psychological changes in senescence are a result of a developmental process in which the psychological phenomena may be morbid at one moment and adaptive at another. Older people face a variety of stresses, comparable to those of combat soldiers in a struggle to protect themselves. The soldiers' personal inclinations for preservation often run counter to what the cultural milieu expects of them. However, soldiers still receive some support from their culture. Older people, however, receive little or no support from society in their struggle for ego survival. This is because society, as a whole, is poorly informed as to what is appropriate behavior for older individuals and what to do to help them.

The essential task of the ego is to enable the individual to adapt to the outside world and to cope with the progressive losses of aging, such as loss of physical capacities, loss of modes for release of basic drives, losses in a culture oriented to the future and to youth, and some loss of social attractiveness. Changes in ego, as the result of aging, lead old people to seek new sources of gratification to shore up their declining self-esteem. They are essentially seeking the love, respect, and gratification that they have difficulty in acquiring from other people. These needs are intensified at a time when their availability is diminished.

Role changes and depression

As the person changes intellectually and physically, so will personality change as well. Elderly people who are in contact with reality can easily see that younger people are taking a place in the world that their generation formerly occupied. They also realize that they are now dependent on the younger person, whereas the younger person was once dependent on them. As their sensory acuity deteriorates, their effective contacts with the outside world are reduced. Many of their friends are suffering with old age diseases or are dead, and thus the older persons find themselves lonely, isolated, and preoccupied with themselves and with small matters that may not even involve them.

Neugarten and Gutmann[7] found that, regardless of their social class, older men and women, as compared to middle-aged individuals, see themselves as reversing their roles in family authority. Many people over 65 years of age *think* of an older man as being submissive, whereas they *think* of the older woman as being dominant and an authority figure. The *behavior* of some older men and women also appears to undergo a change that is consistent with this reversed image of sex roles. Of course, the degree to which these changes occur is a matter of individual characteristics of the couple. Often there is simply a matter of sharing more in decision making, with the woman taking the initiative in carrying out the decision. There are some cases where the woman, in a quiet, subtle way, is the acknowledged authority figure and decision maker. The man will not take the initiative or make a decision unless "Mother" approves the action. "What do you think, Mother; shall we buy this one?"

In terms of perceived self-concept, there are differences between the generations. Ahammer and Baltes[8] found that middle-aged adults were more concerned about achievement than were young adults and the elderly. Both the early and late adult groups were more concerned with affiliation. All three groups wanted to be providing for themselves and to be autonomous. The early and middle-aged adult groups, however, saw the elderly as being more nurturing and less independent than the older adults actually wanted to be. Also, the self-concept of older people differed between (1) what they desired for themselves and (2) what they actually had of themselves, as changes in health and social roles made them less independent. Older people also tend to cling to views they have had of themselves. As Atchley[9] points out, older people continue to think of themselves as the skilled workman or the professional they had been, or as someone who always "walked five blocks downtown, twice a day," with the assumption they should still be able to do as they did before. The same kind of processes that help preserve an older person's self-concept also help him maintain a sense of self-esteem.

The older person is usually a lonely person. Most people 65 years or older are divorced, single, or widowed. Individuals who have been single throughout life will not experience as much loneliness because they have been accustomed to it, but people who were married early in life and enjoyed love, devotion, and constant companionship throughout their earlier life will have a different reaction. If a loved one is lost, this results in a sense of loneliness that seems unbearable, and the years ahead seem full of nothing but emptiness, unless of course the person can grasp reality and adjust to it. In later years, even in cases when both spouses are alive, an elderly person will show a certain amount of depression and moodiness.

The psychological aspect of depression is sadly a part of the life of many elderly people. Concerned with themselves, depressed people lack suitable judgment of their own self-worth. Depression in old age may be evident by feelings of uselessness, of loneliness, of being a burden, of hopelessness, and too often, of being unneeded.

Depression is often accompanied by regressive behavior; it also shows somatic symptoms of fatigue, loss of appetite and weight, constipation, insomnia, and dryness of the mouth. This is an extremely important point to remember because many so-called losses of health could be due to the individual's state of depression.

Changes in personality

For many years the Committee on Human Development at the University of Chicago (also known as the Chicago group) studied questions related to personality changes associated with chronological age in the latter part of life. These studies were known as the Kansas City Studies of Adult Life because the field work was carried out in Kansas City. A series of investigations of the social and psychological aspects of middle age and aging, involving over 700 men and women, were carried out for over 15 years. This work has resulted in a sociopsychological theory of aging (the disengagement theory) and has laid the groundwork for a number of studies regarding personality changes by other investigators.

Bernice L. Neugarten,[10] one of the Chicago group, did a series of studies related to inner-life processes. She focused on the individual's perception of and styles of coping with the inner world of experiences. She found that 40-year-olds saw the environment as a place of rewarding boldness and risk-taking and saw themselves as being capable of meeting the opportunities of the outer world. Sixty-year-olds saw the environment as complex and dangerous and the self as conforming to outer-world demands. As a person grew older, different modes of dealing with impulse life became obvious. Preoccupation with the inner life became greater; the concentration of emotional energy toward persons and objects in the outer world seemed to decrease; the readiness to attribute activity and affect to persons in the environment was reduced; and, in general, there was a movement away from outer-world to inner-world orientation.[11] These decreases began in the late 40s and 50s.

Differences between the sexes appear with age. Aging men seem to move from active involvement with the world to more introversive, passive, and self-centered positions. Women, however, move in the opposite direction, from passive mastery to active involvement, become more domineering and aggressive. According to Chiriboga and Lowenthal,[12] men appear to cope with the environment in increasingly abstract and cognitive ways while women cope in increasingly affective and expressive terms.[13] In both sexes, however, older people move toward more eccentric, self-preoccupied behavior. They seek to be more in charge of controlling and satisfying their personal needs.

There is no general decrease in competency of performance of adult social skills nor any decline of social interaction until the mid 60s or early 70s. It is true that as people get older they may give up various role responsibilities with relative ease and remain highly content with life. Some show a drop in life satisfaction as they experience a drop in social interaction, but others who had been content with a low level of activity in younger years tend to remain content in later years with a small amount of social participation. Neugarten, Havighurst, and Tobin[14] refer to eight different patterns of aging that they observed emerging in a group of 70- to 79-year-olds. They named these categories of behavior patterns as the Reorganizers, the Focused, the Disengaged, the Holding-on, the Constricted, the Succorance-seeking, the Apathetic, and the Disorganized. The implication of all of these studies on personality changes is that individual differences do abound in old age, even though there are some general characteristics or patterns of old age that are different from those exhibited at a younger age.

Disengagement theory

There have been two theories that have speculated on the reasons as to why people curtail their activities as they get old. The earlier view might be called the "activity theory" or "social needs theory." This point of view implies that older people have essentially the same psychological and social needs as do middle-aged people, except for needs brought on by changes in physiological makeup and health. As a person gets older, society withdraws or pulls away from that person, causing decreased social interaction. The older person does not want this to happen but society backs off, regardless. The efforts of the older people should be to stay active and try to resist the shrinkage of their social world.

The disengagement theory states that there is decreased social interaction, but that both society and the aging person withdraw. There is a mutual involvement in lessening the degree of interaction. The older people no longer desire the deeper emotional involvement in activities and relationships that they had in middle age. Cumming and Henry,[15] who first set forth the disengagement theory, also believed that as older persons were able to disengage themselves from outer world social interaction, they would have a better sense of psychological well-being. The studies of the Chicago group found that this last assumption was not necessarily so and that great diversity in individual differences existed. At the same time that they found a positive correlation between engagement and life satisfaction, they also found that the relationship was not consistent.

Neugarten, et al.[16] concluded that personality organization or personality type was the pivotal factor in predicting which individuals would age successfully. She and her associates also found that the ability to adapt to biological and social changes was paramount in determining the degree of life satisfaction. Aging is not a leveler of individual differences. Psychological disengagement seems to precede social disengagement. Havighurst, et al.[17] found that there is an overall positive relationship between social engagement and life satisfaction, with personality types playing a central role in producing diverse patterns of adjustment. Both personality factors and sociocultural settings are important. It is in the process of adaptation that personality is the key element. There is evidence now that voluntary disengagement is not harmful to morale, but that forced disengagement, whether due to poor health, forced retirement, disability, widowhood, or low income, affects both social interaction and morale.[18] In terms of morale, readiness for disengagement is more significant than age, sex, or current social interaction.

RETIREMENT

Few issues in recent years have raised the ire and interest of older persons more than have issues relating to retirement. There are those who want early retirement so they may spend some leisure years in relatively good health, still capable of getting around. They would reject plans to force continued work. There are those who vigorously oppose mandatory or compulsory retirement on the grounds that they are not ready to retire and feel that they are being discriminated against just because of their age. There is a third group known as the "double-dippers" who get involved in several retirement systems. They work long enough under one system to qualify for a pension, then leave that job and go to work elsewhere under a different retirement plan, thus qualifying for two or maybe three pension plans before they retire. For example, a person may retire with a state and/or federal pension, a military retirement, a railroad or industrial pension, and, in addition, still receive Social Security payments. Needless to say, double-dippers receiving more than one pension from funds paid for by taxpayers are being criticized but what they are doing is currently legal.

The age of 65 years has been established in American society as the usual retirement age. This age was chosen by the United States Congress on the basis of actuarial charts and concepts of longevity of the mid 1930s. Little did the planners realize that longevity would increase so much in the next forty years. The age of 65 is no longer the harbinger of old age. Table 16-4 presents retirement age and other related data for countries of the Organization for Economic Cooperation and Development.[19]

Retirement shock

Perhaps the most important immediate result of retirement is what some have chosen to call "retirement shock." This condition may further be identified as a period of great personal crisis and turmoil, not unlike that which individuals face during late adolescence or early adulthood when they are faced with the responsibility of finding a meaningful field of endeavor. More frequently, it is the prospect of retirement rather than retirement itself that leads to a morbid state of mind. This "shock" or feeling of estrangement manifests itself in many ways. Doubts about one's future usefulness, financial worries be-

Table 16-4. Pension systems in OECD countries, by normal age of retirement, qualifications for early retirement, reduced payments for early retirement, by requirement for retirement, and by increments paid for deferment of normal retirement*

Country	Normal age for retirement		Early retirement qualifications				Early retirement, less pay	Substantial requirement to retire	Increments if retirement deferred
	Male	Female	Work 35-40 years	Unemp. 1 year	Tiring work	Long illness			
Austria	65	60	x	x		x		x	
Belgium	65	60					5 yrs	x	
Canada†	65	65						†	
Denmark	67	62				x			
France	60	60							x
West Germany	65	65		x					
Greece	62	57			x		2 yrs	x	
Iceland	67	67							x
Ireland	70	70							
Italy	60	55	x		x				x
Japan	60	55						x	
Luxembourg	65	65	x						
Netherlands	65	65							
Norway	70	70							
Portugal	65	65						x	
Spain	65	65			x			x	
Sweden	67	67					4 yrs		x
Switzerland	65	63							
Turkey	60	55				x		x	x
United Kingdom	65	60						x	x
United States	65	65					3 yrs	x	x

*Adapted from Hyden, S. *Flexible retirement provisions in public pension systems in organization for economic cooperation and development flexibility in retirement age.* Paris: The organization, 1971, pp. 21-37.
†In Canada the universal pension program does not require retirement, but the social insurance program does require substantial retirement.

cause of reduced income, and the emptiness felt because of the lack of social intercourse are only a few ramifications of the retirement shock phenomenon.

Everyone must have some feeling of apprehension concerning their future usefulness to society. Satisfactions once derived from a job well done are now removed from the immediate experience and can now only be used as the material for reflection. This would seem to be especially true for persons engaged in helping or service occupations, where much or all of the persons' time was spent helping other people. Occupations such as teaching, the ministry, medicine, and social work would seem to fall into this category. On the other hand, an industrial-type occupation, where workers are a small part of an assembly-line process, would give them little opportunity to see the results of their labor, and therefore little personal satisfaction would result. In this respect perhaps the shock of retirement is not as great for the person who is engaged in an industrial type of occupation.

As Fillenbaum[20] points out, people deeply involved in their work continue to work as long as they possibly can. Table 16-5 shows, by occupations, the percentage of men, ages 58-63, who continued to be in the work force. Black men in

Table 16-5. 1969 labor force participation of men 58-63, by occupation*

Occupation of longest job	Percent in labor force
Professional	90
Farmer	88
Manager	87
Clerical	83
Sales	89
Craftsmen	84
Operative	79
Service	79
Farm laborer	76
Nonfarm laborer	73

*From Schwab, K. Early labor force withdrawal of men: participants and nonparticipants aged 58-63. *Social Security Bulletin,* August, 1974.

Western societies are more typically employed in less desirable occupations, from a health, educational, economic, or socially acceptable point of view. Such factors provide much of the explanation for the greater decline in labor force participation rates of black men 45-64 by the time they are older, in contrast to their white cohorts.[21]

Financial matters preoccupy many people of postretirement age. It is possible that this is the most realistic concern of old age. After being financially independent for forty-five or fifty years most elderly people dread the possibility of not being able to support themselves. As a result, they have a tendency to become rather parsimonious with their financial resources. We know of several persons who went into great depth trying to figure out how they were going to live on their retirement income. Every penny was counted. Fixed expenditures were figured out. Often the person would say things like, "I have to stop subscribing to the newspaper," or "I'll have to give up smoking." It should be emphasized, however, that for many old people retirement incomes are inadequate for current prices, and becoming miserly is an economic necessity. On the other hand, it is also true that less income is needed in retirement. Income needs decrease by 40% to 60% because of the decrease in employment-related activities, social activities, and even clothing and eating needs.[22]

The theory of disengagement states that one of the elements of aging is a decreased amount of social interaction between the elderly and their former social life space. In this regard, retirement represents perhaps the most important occurrence in the process of disengagement. Often the workers' associates constitute the bulk of their social acquaintances. The severance of the associations with the people with whom they work may also mean a corresponding loss in more general social activity. Here, then, is another source of shock to which retirees need to adjust.

Mandatory vs. voluntary retirement

As more and more is being learned about the specific problems of retirement, increased attention is being focused on the problem of forced retirement. Researchers are finding that many of the problems associated with retirement are the results of individual differences and the state of "readiness" for the transition.[23] Some of the country's largest employers are split "down the middle" on whether or not retirement should be compulsory at the age of 65 years.

Those who support compulsory retirement argue their position with the following point of view: It is the fairest way and avoids giving workers the stigma of being "washed up" while someone else the same age is kept on; it is a painless way of getting rid of those who have outlived their usefulness; finally, compulsory retirement opens promotion opportunities for younger people.

Those who are opposed to compulsory retirement but in favor of discretionary retirement insist the following: It is necessary to keep people of great value for longer than the age of 65 years; the valuable people will fall into the hands of the competition if released; some people will be forced into unhappy idleness. W. Ferguson Anderson,[24] University of Glasgow Department of Medicine, maintains that in the age group of 60 to 80 years is an "immense potential of knowledge, skill and experience." It would be the ultimate in wastefulness to retire all people because they are 65 years old.

Each of the preceding arguments has some merit, but perhaps the ideal situation would be to treat each worker as an individual instead of adhering to all-inclusive policies that will benefit some and adversely affect others. Employers need to reexamine their present policies and come up with plans that will most benefit the employees in their own situations.

When people retire voluntarily, presumably they do so because they believe that they will be happier in retirement than continuing as a member of the labor force. Granted they may be dissatisfied with their job or have some motive other than the primary motive of entering into a better way of life with retirement. In any case, if the decision to retire is theirs, the chances are that they enter retirement without the feeling of having outlived their usefulness to society that so often accompanies compulsory retirement.

A most obvious and prevalent form of discrimination of old persons is the fixing of a chronological age at which it is compulsory to abandon their jobs, or above which employers will not hire them. This practice clearly applies a classification that is irrelevant to the efficiency of given individuals, to the need for their services, or to their own needs. Workers who are told that their employment is being terminated involuntarily on age alone may suffer an affront to their personal dignity and status. They enter retirement with a resentment toward the society that forced them into it. Instead of enjoying retirement, they will tend to brood over the injustice done to them.

The question of mandatory vs. voluntary retirement is being resolved to some extent. The Congress of the United States has revised its thinking on mandatory retirement at age 65 and is changing the age to 70. Economic in addition to political reasons have brought about a change. Economically, the burden on the Old Age Insurance Plan will be lessened because fewer people will opt to retire at 65. The other side of the coin, however, is that older people will not be moving out of the job market to make room for younger people who need to work. Politically, the main reason for changing the mandatory retirement age is that discrimination by virtue of age was an untenable position in the eyes of many people.

Advent of retirement

Whether or not a person wishes to retire, the time does eventually come. Ideally, retirement should come gradually, with a tapering off of job activity. Some company executives, if they happen to be owners or part owners of the company, are able to do this. Professional people are often able to slow down and move out gradually. But most people cannot do this; therefore, it would seem advisable to begin making retirement plans long before the time actually arrives—to anticipate and overcome as many of the problems of retirement as possible.

Individuals should prepare themselves for retirement in the same way that they would prepare themselves for any other undertaking. Planning should start in a practical and positive way while workers are still on the job. They should cultivate a wholesome attitude toward retirement. It is vitally important that they look at retirement from the forward-looking position of "retiring to" rather than "retiring from." In this way retirees will possess the optimism and adaptability necessary to cope with the various problems they will almost certainly have to face.

In preparing themselves, it should be remembered that security in retirement is a balance of three things: physical security—reasonably good health to be able to do the things they really want to do; activity security—a program and the opportunity for satisfying and rewarding accomplishments; financial security—having sufficient money to make it possible to achieve these goals. Of the three, activity security usually receives the least consideration during the planning, yet it is extremely important.

Osborn[25] states that much of the physical and mental ill health of old men can be traced to their retirement. There is no easy solution to the problem of enforced leisure in retirement, but many forward-looking attempts are being made to meet the difficulties. These include courses in preparation for retirement, in which workers approaching retirement are given an understanding of the financial, social, and psychological changes that they can anticipate and are advised about how to make constructive use of their leisure. Some firms encourage retired workers to return to the factory and offer them part-time employment in a special workshop. In some areas local authorities and voluntary groups provide workshops and craft centers where the skills of the retired worker can still be used.

Ewald W. Busse,[26] Director of The Center for

Retirement provides time to renew old skills and interests. Everyone should have some type of activity, not necessarily a hobby, that they can pursue as they get older.

Harold Geyer

"TO RETIRE GRACEFULLY"

My dad had been employed by a communications company as an electronic engineer, a well-paying position that he held for his entire working career until his retirement. He found his work a constant challenge and was very happy at it.

He was always a great perfectionist and would not settle for anything unless it was correctly done. He was creative and spent much of his leisure time working out problems, making things for his work, and seeing if he could improve anything and everything in any way possible. Actually, it might be said that he did not permit himself to have any leisure time to relax.

To quote him, "Television was the biggest piece of trash ever invented." He thought that it kept people from expanding their knowledge to a useful degree. He also had little use for anyone who wasted his time and money "boozing it up" in the local tavern or puffing away on a cigarette. As he once said, "There is not enough time in life to throw it around carelessly." He was definitely a man geared to work—almost like a machine that never wanted to quit. But, he was 64 years of age.

As retirement time grew nearer, Dad became uneasy. He started to wonder what he would do with himself. He wrote down a list of his many hobbies and interests that might occupy his time after retirement. He also started making lists of engineering companies that would hire an "old man" to work for them. He discussed moving to a farm for the sole purpose of raising hogs and experimenting with breeding. There were other ideas that passed through his mind, but they all seemed to be in hopes of finding a way out of being forced into retirement.

An outsider looking at Dad would most likely think that he was a calm man—a man who would have no difficulty adjusting to his retirement. It appeared that his financial standing would enable him to maintain his family and home and his interests would enable him to occupy his mind successfully. All of these things were true; however, it did not seem quite so easy to Dad at this time.

The expected day of retirement arrived. To quote him, "One minute I am a useful working citizen, contributing to the welfare of my country, and the next minute I am no longer of any use to anyone." It was a discouraging thought for a man of his nature.

During the first couple of weeks in retirement, he found himself sitting around watching television, the "trash box" that he despised so much, and taking the dogs for their morning walk. He would trail around after mother, watching every move she made, seeing if he could be of help. However, he found that he was only getting in the way of her daily household chores. He started taking naps in the afternoon just as if he had become an old man at the precise time that his retirement went into effect. It was sad to see all of his talent and enthusiasm for life being wasted.

He had grown accustomed to feeling sorry for himself until months after his retirement, when he received a phone call from an engineering associate. He wanted to employ him on a part-time basis. Of course, Dad accepted immediately. He had received his chance to become useful again. This new job required him to work for a period of ninety days, with the option of continuing in another area at the end of that period.

The first job that he completed for his new company was acceptable. However, during the ninety days he found that there were many young men who were working successfully in engineering and could soon be doing the identical job that he had been doing. He also found that he was not used to keeping up with the fast pace that was common in such a company. He realized that he was not as young as he wished. He also found that he enjoyed having leisure time when he desired it, and consequently he decided that it was not so bad to be retired after all. After realizing all of this he turned the second job offer down. He had finally made his own choice to accept retirement gracefully and, I might add, graciously.

At this point in life he was a changed man, but actually he had not changed at all. It seems likely that he would have made his adjustment to retirement sooner or later without the assistance of his acquaintance and the part-time job; however, I do believe that this opportunity helped to speed him on his way to successful adjustment. He now had a feeling of self-worth that had been temporarily discarded but was fortunately restored.

the Study of Aging and Human Development at Duke University Medical Center, Durham, North Carolina, urges a "social career" for the retired person. Young persons have student careers, adults have economic careers, and if older persons have social careers, it will provide them with an orderly work pattern as well as the concomitant personal recognition and respect in their community. This corresponds with the point of view that states that health in old age is improved through mental and physical activity. The elderly can and should make valuable contributions to society.

SOCIAL LIFE CHANGES
Social aspects

One of the most important things an older person must do is to keep active. An old proverb says: "It is difficult to remain at peace in idleness." A life of doing nothing will only lead to increased emptiness. Work, to some degree, should continue.

George Burns, the noted comedian, appearing on a TV talk show at the age of 84, gave this advice, "Get up every morning about 8:00 or so and do something. Plan any kind of activity that will get you out of bed. Go some place, if you can. If you can't, have someone come to your house to play bridge, talk, or relax." At this age, Burns was making films after having been on the sidelines for a while.

Men and women should start some of the projects that they have put off for so long. Reading, travel, visits to art museums, and developing new talents are all important in old age. Although it is important for people to keep active and alert, they must also know when to stop, even if they are just taking a walk.

Social contacts

As people develop, they become part of a social unit. They are members of a family, and they have friends who add satisfaction and joy to their life. The social life of old people is narrowed

Social contacts for the elderly are important. Community centers and similar projects can provide a variety of social outlets that can put meaning into life at old age.

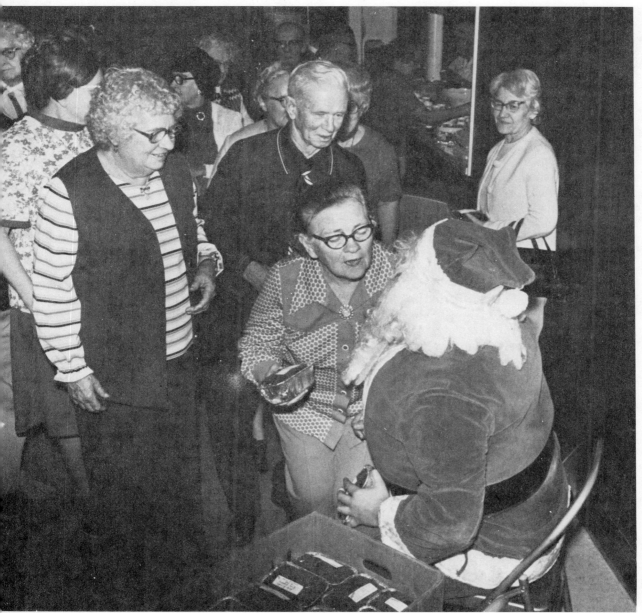

Harold Geyer

increasingly by the loss of work associates, the death of relatives, friends, and spouse, and poor health, which restricts their participation in social activities. There are three types of social relationships that are affected by aging: close personal friendships, such as husband and wife, siblings, and friends from childhood days; friendship cliques made up of couples banded together in a social crowd when they were younger; and formal groups or clubs. Once broken, these social relationships are rarely replaced in old age. Also, as the elderly person's interest in self increases, interest in other people decreases. Married people are socially more active in old age than are those who are single or widowed, and those from upper socioeconomic groups are more socially active than those from lower socioeconomic groups.

Many communities are trying to meet the social needs of the aged by starting social clubs for them with activities planned to fit into their interests and capacities. Those who take advantage of any opportunities they have for social participation and who make an effort to retain old friendships or establish new ones not only make a better adjustment to old age than do those who are socially inactive but find old age a far happier period of life than they had anticipated when they were younger. As is true at every age, the social needs of individuals at that period of their life must be met to their satisfaction if they want to be happy.

Frequently, a retired couple will decide that their present home is too large to take care of, so they decide to sell their home and move to a more convenient size dwelling. Sometimes a home is sold to move from a neighborhood that has deteriorated with time. The neighborhood has changed so much that the couple no longer feels comfortable or at ease in it. The choice of where to move is usually made in terms of (1) moving near one of the children, (2) moving to the "sun belt" area or to a better climate, or (3) moving to a retirement village or home.

Moving always requires adjustments. If the move is to the sun belt area or a retirement village, it may entail the purchase or rental of a house, a condominium, an apartment, or a mobile home, often in an area inhabited primarily by older people. New adjustments to living quarters and social contacts are needed.[27] The couple must learn to live in a new town (or neighborhood), in a new climate, and among new people. They are usually far from old friends, children, and grandchildren. Some people can make the adjustments without any problems. Others yearn for "back home" and often feel they made a mistake in moving. Still others find it depressing or nonstimulating to be cut off from younger people. Occasionally some are disappointed at the class or caliber of people who live in their new location. "They're not the kind of people I feel comfortable with; our values are so different." However, the fact that so many people do adjust to such a change in life-style indicates that changes can be made and that they can be happy. The best advice is not to make decisions too quickly nor without a thorough investigation of the new dwelling site. The social, climatic, housing, medical, cultural, and political (including taxation) situations should be studied.

Family

For elderly persons their family makes up the nucleus of their social life. The older they become, the more they must rely on their family for companionship. Their friends have either died or are physically unable to do things with them. They cannot keep pace with younger friends and, as a result, no longer consider themselves welcome members of a younger group. Thus older persons must limit their social contacts to family members or to individuals their own age. This means generally a group of intimate friends, some of whom have been friends since childhood or young adulthood days. One advantage of living in a social institution, a retirement home or village, is that it provides the great advantage of opportunities for social contacts with contemporaries. Elderly persons' contemporaries have interests, problems, and physical traits in common with theirs. However, many elderly people resist making this adjustment and, as a result, cut themselves off from social contacts.

The aged and their children. The aged often have definite opinions concerning their relationships with their children. In a study at Cornell University by Streib[28] 84% of the parents of adult children believed that the children should visit often; 82% wanted the children to write often. Many of the feelings that older individuals experience are vicarious ones. Because of this, they feel a deep need to keep in close touch with their children and to continue to share their experiences. At the same time the grandparents do not want to interfere in their children's lives.

The aged think that their children should be expected to "help some" in financial assistance but "not a great deal." Many of the children, however, want the parents to apply for old age assistance, even though the children themselves could help.

Most aging parents consider their relationship with their children to be satisfactory. They have reached some kind of mutual agreement and know how each stands. They have a list of acceptable responses from their children that are usually met. Many elderly individuals, when surveyed, present a picture entirely different from that usually thought of in connection with the elderly. Instead of a lonely person sitting around in a rocking chair, Streib found a group of people who were useful both to themselves and society with a wide range of interests that many younger people do not have.

The degree of satisfaction that elderly persons find in their relationships with their sons and daughters depends, to a large degree, on the extent to which both parents and children can communicate in a pleasant, friendly way with each other. The ease and clarity of communication depends, in part, on the attitudes that both groups have toward each other and toward their age levels in general. It also depends somewhat on the willingness of the son-in-law or daughter-in-law to be respective and responsive. Some parents cannot shift their attitudes or perspectives toward their children to match their adult age (usually in middle adulthood or later) and the needs of these grown-up children and their family groups. Some elderly have to remain as the dominant authority figure until their dying day, no matter how totally dependent they are on their children and regardless of how competent the children may be. On the other hand, the children may resent the lack of recognition of their competency by their parent(s). This same disregard

for changing levels of development, changing values, and changing life-styles may also filter down to the grandchildren and great-grandchildren. Fortunate is the family that can respect each other's individuality and values and accept differences as they exist for the different age levels.

Probably the time of greatest conflict between aged parents and their children is at retirement. One should remember that retirement at the age of 65 years means that the "children" are probably about 45, 40, or 35 years old—at the peak of adulthood. The retiring couple are having their problems adjusting their thoughts and attitudes to the idea of retirement. They are uncertain and indecisive. They worry out loud about their concerns and try to reason out their problems from all angles. They may come up with "logical" answers, but they never seem to do anything about them. They are on a merry-go-round with their concerns and do not know how to get off. The children always seem to see things more clearly, "It's so obvious," and they are quick to give them opinions. "You should move out of this big house into a smaller place, maybe an apartment, where you won't have as much housekeeping to do." "You should move here (or there) . . ." for any number of reasons that make sense to the children. Yet the old couple are reluctant to act. It becomes most exasperating to their children.

This would be the moment for the children to step back and examine what is happening. Their parents are at a point in life where they are contemplating major changes and moves. On the one hand the move seems so sensible, yet on the other hand the "feel" is not quite right, thus the hesitancy. It should be recognized that not all good decisions can be based on cold, hard facts alone. People are not machines. They are warm-blooded human beings with feelings, sentimental attachments, and maybe even fears. Children must keep in mind that just because their parents of retirement age find it hard to make decisions about where to live and what to do, this is no indication that their parents have become enfeebled and have lost their powers of intellectual reasoning and judgment. The parents should be allowed to move at their own pace. It is surprising how, in spite of all the concerns, they work things out. Children should not interfere unless asked specifically to do so. Even then, they should not be upset if their advice is not taken. The final decision should rest with the parents.

William T. Swaim, Jr.,[29] a former administrator of Presbyterian Homes of Central Pennsylvania, has written much on the aged and their lives. He gives some tips in *What Shall We Do With Granny?*

1. Let Granny do what she wants to do, even if it kills her. She is not as vulnerable as you think.
2. Do not expect perfection.
3. Make due allowance for any words or actions that may be caused by cerebral changes.
4. Treat Granny as a person. Let her make her own decisions. Respect her interests and needs.
5. Be demonstrative. Shake hands, hug her, kiss her.
6. Learn to listen long and smile even if you've heard it all before.
7. Do everything possible to build up her ego.
8. Impart information, tell her why, if you must change her mind or wishes.
9. Do not ruin your own health and happiness to minister to her nursing needs if they are beyond your capabilities.
10. Encourage Granny to remain employed as long as possible.
11. If Granny desires to remarry, remember "It is not good that man should be alone."
12. Move heaven and earth to keep Granny living with her own furniture and amid familiar scenes and faces as long as possible.
13. Do not force three-generation living which may deny Granny privacy, quiet and independence.
14. Make it easy and delightful for Granny to share chores.
15. Let her go to a home for the aging if that is her desire.
16. Welcome old age. Let your study of Granny's personality remind you to grow older graciously.
17. Have respect for Granny's age. Nurses should not call elderly patients by their first names.

Burr[30] did an interesting study showing the degree of satisfaction that parents had with their children at different stages of married life. The findings are indicated in Fig. 16-2. Not surprisingly, there is much parental satisfaction with young children. But, as the children get into school and become teenagers, there is decreasing satisfaction. Satisfaction with their children as adults is quite good, only to diminish somewhat after retirement. Women always show more interest and are more absorbed in the lives of their children and grandchildren than men.

Among American old people, 85% live an hour or less from a child. Twenty-eight percent live with a middle-aged child, usually a daughter. About 10% to 20% have no relatives or family living near them.[31]

Marital adjustment. According to the research of Stinnett, Carter and Montgomery,[32] most older people feel that their marriages have been very satisfactory, that their lives are calmer now that their children are grown, and that they have a new freedom to do as they please. This is as true for husbands as for wives. There may be worries about how fast the money is going, disagreements about moving, disagreements over relationships with children, and health problems, but, all-in-all, a married couple who have reached the later adulthood years together will probably be able to handle the stress engendered. Often the most significant transition point in later marital life is the husband's retirement. With thoughtful consideration and planning, the stress of this time can also be minimized.

Generally, marriages that were good to begin with will continue to be good. But, marriages that were unhappy in their earlier years do not seem to get better unless major improvements are made in attitudes, respect, and acceptance of one another. It appears that the more the relationship meets each other's needs for love, fulfillment, respect, recognition, communicaiton, and meaning in life, while downplaying negative or weak aspects of an individual's personality or behavior, the happier the marriage is in later years. Happy older people generally say that companionship and being able to express true feelings to each other are the most rewarding aspects of their relationship. With time, mutual leisure time

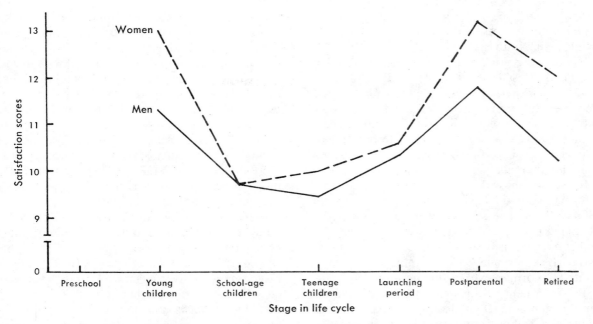

Fig. 16-2. Parents' satisfaction with their children at different stages of their married life. (Adapted from Burr, W. R. *Journal of Marriage and the Family,* 1970, **32,** 29-37. Used by permission.)

interests can or should be developed, drawing the partners closer together. Problems and crises also have the potential of pulling a couple together in a common bond to face the adversity.

When a spouse dies

According to the U.S. Bureau of Census,[33] 25% of the women aged 60 to 64 are currently widows but only 6% of the men are widowers. Half of the women aged 70 to 74 are widows, while 85% of the women aged 85 and older are widows. Of the men 85 years of age and over only half are widowers.

Adjustment to the death of a spouse is especially difficult in old age because at this age all adjustments are increasingly difficult to make.[34] The widow usually has a decreased income necessitating giving up interests and certain social contacts, possibly moving to smaller quarters or going to live with a child or in an institution. The widower may not have as serious an economic problem, but he will miss the care of a wife who provided him with companionship, cared for his

needs, and managed the home. Men are more reluctant to enter a home for the aged or move in with their children, so they frequently remarry in order to overcome loneliness and dependency problems. A number of older people find it impossible to deal with widowhood. It is not uncommon for an older widowed person to die soon after the spouse's death. Some commit suicide. According to Bernado[35] the suicide rate among older widowed people is among the highest of all groups.

The Harvard Bereavement Study,[36] although dealing with middle-aged individuals who lost their spouses, gives some indication of the bereavement and recovery process after a death. The immediate impact of bereavement was somewhat the same for both men and women in the sense of being overwhelmed, having shock and anguish, and feeling that there were no limits to their suffering. The newly bereaved woman felt numb and seemed as if she could not move or she cried as if she could never stop. She reported a sense of abandonment, of being left alone. The husband who became a widower had the same feelings but he reported a sense of dismemberment, as if "both my arms were cut off."

There were some differences encountered if the death was anticipated rather than sudden. One in five experienced a completely unexpected bereavement, by accident or a sudden coronary thrombosis, for example. Another 20% knew their husband was not in good health but did not expect death. The other 60% had known for some time that their spouses were seriously ill. Only in a few cases, however, did the women use this information as the basis for making plans for life as a widow. The women who anticipated the death felt pained and desolate when the death did come, but they also were better able to pull themselves together and to more quickly regain a relatively normal level of functioning.

Bewilderment and despair often continued after the first impact of death was experienced. Many physical symptoms appeared and lingered for weeks. Sleep disturbances were common and distressful. The widowers were more likely to be uncomfortable with direct emotional expression of their distress. They seemed to require more rational justification for their thoughts and feelings. Although less troubled by anger, as were the women, they did have difficulty with guilt about not doing as much as they could have to show their love or help her out. Leave-taking ceremonies, as the funeral and memorial service, served the purpose of establishing the fact of death as an emotional reality for both the widowed person and the community. However, for widows the funeral was more of a milestone, whereas for many widowers it was a necessary involvement. The men were more concerned with how to manage in the months to come.[37]

The type of emotional recovery and social recovery from the impact of mental bereavement appeared to be related to the suddenness of the death, to the preparation for death, and to the quality of the marital relationship. Men seemed to make a quicker adjustment. Actually their recovery was more social in nature than it was emotional. The widower who had not sought out female companionship a year after his wife's death was much more likely than the widow to feel lonely and depressed. Parkes[38] found that poor recovery by both men and women occurred if the death was sudden as in cases of accidents or heart attacks. Poor recovery usually means being socially withdrawn or still preoccupied with the details of the death slightly more than a year after a death. Those who were most disturbed a few weeks after the death usually were the ones who continued to be disturbed a year or so later. The quality of the marital relationship also seemed related to the rapidity of recovery. Recovery was more difficult where there were mixed or ill feelings toward one another or where there was a clinging, dependency relationship.

In recovery, the widowed person must develop a new social identity and learn to relate to other people differently, especially people of the opposite sex.[39] It is a time of learning to live alone. Friends and relatives mean well but they can only do so much. After a while they drift back into their life patterns and find it difficult to be as attentive to the bereaved as they would like to be. There is a need for social adjustment for both the bereaved and his friends and family. In the final analysis, sooner or later, the widowed person will have to reach out to others for social interaction. If it is offensive to their sense of values to be with the opposite sex, then at least they should reach out to contact members of their own sex.

Remarriage

According to Butler and Lewis,[40] despite the fact that women over 65 years of age outnumber men by 3 million, there are more than twice the number of men remarrying as there are women of that age group who remarry. Several factors play a part in this phenomenon. To begin with, if every elderly single man were to get remarried, or even married for the first time, there would still not be enough men for all the available women. Second, there seems to be an unfortunate cultural bias about elderly widows getting remarried, especially if they remarry "too soon" after their spouses die. The bias seems to rationalize itself around the idea that "I have too much respect for my late husband to ever let anyone replace him in my love life." Right or wrong, for better or for worse, such ideas do keep some individuals, both men and women, from getting remarried. Occasionally the individual involved does not hold too strongly to the idea, but the important (significant) people left in the widowed person's life have that view and the widowed individual is hesitant to go against the bias of the group.

The third factor restricting or inhibiting the remarriage of the elderly is, again, a cultural bias in terms of how long a person should wait before getting remarried. It appears that it is socially more acceptable for a widower to remarry after about a year's time than it is for a widow. Widowers rarely wait more than a year or so before remarrying. McKain[41] found that widows are more likely to take their time, usually about seven years. McKain also found that over half of the older people who remarry have known their new spouses for a long time before being widowed. In many cases they have known these individuals for most of their lives, were already related by marriage, were childhood sweethearts, or were simply old friends or neighbors. Considering the companionship, joy, and comfort that two people can bring to each other when they share a common life space or home, and considering the relatively short number of surviving years that remain, it seems somewhat cruel to have a criterion based on ''what others think'' to prohibit, postpone, or delay a marriage of two elderly persons capable of contributing to a meaningful relationship. McKain, again, found that most couples who marry late in life have highly successful marriages.[41] The decision of remarriage or not should be left primarily to the couple rather than to the consent and approval of others, such as the children. However, it is true that each group of concerned and involved individuals must work out their own decisions.

There is an emergence of alternatives to marriage on the part of some of the elderly. The usual alternative is simply living together without the benefit of a legal recording of the marriage. We do not know to what an extent such a living arrangement would, under the differing laws of the various states, eventually constitute a ''common law'' marriage, with all the legal rights pertaining thereto. The major reason for this type of a living-in arrangement is mostly financial. One or the other of the spouses would lose a source of income, such as income from a trust, a pension fund of the deceased spouse, or Social Security

benefits. The reduction in income for the couple could make it difficult to live comfortably or adequately on the income of just one spouse. At this writing, there is some effort being made in Congress to permit widows to retain Social Security benefits, based on their deceased or divorced husband's earnings, even if they do remarry. Another alternative life-style is a form of communal living where several older people, sometimes including married couples, group together to share living expenses and living quarters. We are not aware of any research done on these living arrangements. They do not exist in sufficiently large numbers so that they can provide adequate research data. We do believe that eventually some type of acceptable arrangements should be made to care for the lonely, the impoverished, and the ailing elderly.

Growing old and being single

Some individuals grow old and have been single for all or most of their lives. Sometimes the choice to be single was deliberately made and in other instances the decision was one of happenstance or circumstances. The reason for remaining single is not the issue. The question is how these people do as elderly individuals. It is true that single elderly individuals do not live as long as married individuals, but that statistical bit of information does nothing to indicate the level of life satisfaction. The research concerning being single and old is meager. The results of observational studies done in clinical and institutional settings suggest that single men and women who have reached a stage of competent, independent living in younger years develop attitudes, interests, and involvement in activities that tend to decrease their need for close family relationships. Such persons sometimes develop a vicarious response of closeness to others through the families of their relatives, close friends, or even pets. Doing work with social agencies or volunteer work in group or individual care services sometimes provides satisfaction. Others find precious contentment in moments of solitude, in worship, or church activity.

To grow to be a happy, nice, little old woman or a nice old man, you must start early in life to give, to share, and to respond to the needs and the well-being of others. Happiness can only be had if it is shared with others; sorrow is something that can be engaged in by yourself. Married or single, the principle is the same.

Leisure activity

Gordon, Gaitz, and Scott,[42] in a rather large study that they call the Houston Study of Leisure Across the Life Span, conducted structured interviews with 1,441 persons stratified according to sex and ethnicity (Anglo, black, and Mexican-American) to learn something about their leisure activities, value preferences, social attitudes, and mental health. The results were tabulated across life-cycle stages representing five age groups. These groups were Group 1, ages 20 to 29, the young adults; Group 2, ages 30 to 44, early maturity; Group 3, ages 45 to 64, full maturity;

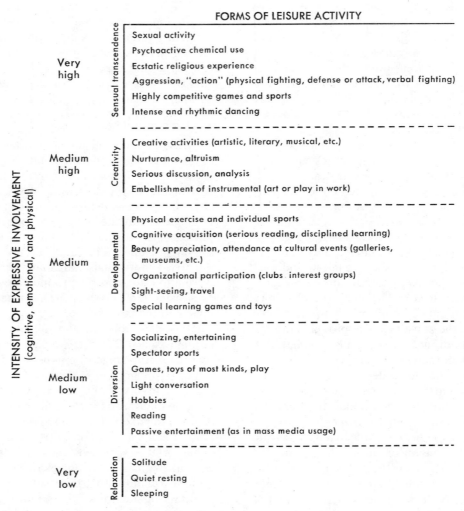

Fig. 16-3. Qualitatively varying forms of leisure activity (expressive primacy in personal activity) according to intensity of expressive involvement. (From Gordon, C., Gaitz, C. M., & Scott, S. Leisure and lives: personal expressivity across the life span. In R. J. Binstock & E. Shanas. *Handbook of aging and the social sciences.* New York: Van Nostrand Reinhold Co., 1977, p. 314.)

Group 4, ages 65 to 74, old age; and, Group 5, ages 75 to 94, very old age.

One of the interesting outcomes of the study was a categorization of leisure activities, which is presented in Fig. 16-3. The five categories of activities were qualitatively designated to represent activities of varying intensity of expressive personal involvement.

The significance of Fig. 16-3 is that it identifies a variety of activities in which adults of all ages can participate in varying degrees of intensity.

The researchers in the Houston study found that the older the respondent, the lower the level of total general leisure activity. Whereas approximately 55% of the men and women in the 45 to 64 age group had high participation in leisure activities, only 34% of the females and 37% of the males in the 65 to 74 age group had high participation. These figures dropped to 21% for females and 26% for males in the 75 and over age group. The results were not unexpected. What was unexpected, to some degree, was the lower frequency of participation by individuals over 65 in such activities as dancing and drinking (10% and 31%), movies (28% and 32%), sports and exercise (24% and 26%), outdoor activities (22% and 37%), travel (36% and 37%), reading (both 30%)

Table 16-6. Within-dwelling-unit behaviors, day prior to interview*

Behavior	Percent engaged in behavior	Median hours spent by all engaged
Eating, cooking	99	2.5
Personal care	97	1.0
Television	70	3.0
Housework	67	2.0
Reading	61	1.0
Napping, idleness	56	2.0
Radio, records	17	1.5
Handiwork	15	2.0
Entertaining	9	2.5
Writing	8	1.5
Crafts, collections	1	2.0

*From Beyer, G., & Woods, M. E. *Living and activity patterns of the aged.* Ithaca, N.Y.: Cornell University Center for Housing and Environmental Studies, 1963, p. 9.

and cultural production (58% and 38%). The female participation percentage is given first. Activities that compared favorably in degree of participation scores as compared to younger age groups were TV viewing, discussion, spectator sports, cultural consumption, entertaining, membership in clubs, and home embellishment. The older age group participated more than younger groups in solitary activities and cooking.

Table 16-6 indicates the types of within-dwelling behavior that older persons participated in during the day. Almost all engaged in eating and cooking and personal care.[43] Television, housework, reading, and napping occupied much of the day's time. Few participated in crafts, collections, writing, or entertaining. Table 16-6 gives a better picture of what older people usually do with their time than does the Houston Study, which examines how often older people do some activities as compared to younger age groups.

HOUSING AND LIVING ARRANGEMENTS
Housing

A place in which to live poses yet another problem. Most older people prefer to live in their own dwellings. The next acceptable arrangement would be to live with someone of the same sex. Most widows think that it would not be wise to live with married sons or daughters. Living with relatives often causes overcrowding, annoying situations caused by small children, and tense situations with the children. In today's society, however, family belongingness, in many cases, is being replaced by community belongingness, which is making individuals less dependent on their families.

There are a few main prerequisites of good housing for older people. Housing should provide as much independence and privacy as possible, while still being near other older people and proper medical facilities. Older people need greater warmth and freedom from drafts and often other types of controls such as air pollution and humidity controls. Proper illumination is also important because the eyes of older people are slower to adjust to changes in light; therefore each room that they use should have the same intensity of light. Noise level is a problem that many people do not realize. Older people, es-

The "sun belt" is an attraction for retirees. Suitable housing is usually found, the weather is generally good, and many activities are available.

pecially those with a vision problem, become most annoyed and tense when there is too much silence because they depend on their hearing for sensory input. As older people gradually lose their hearing, they must adjust sound volume to a higher level.

Table 16-7 from Hurlock[44] very nicely summarizes the physical and psychological needs in living arrangements. The older an individual gets, the more frail his body strength becomes. Equilibrium and balance also deteriorate and, as a result, everything possible should be done in living accommodations to prevent accidents that in-

volve falling. In many cases the mind of the individual is still very alert even though the body is weak. The story is told of Oliver Wendell Holmes, the famous jurist, who, although in his 80s, was out taking a walk. An acquaintance met him and asked, ''How is Oliver Wendell Holmes today?'' The reply was, ''Oliver Wendell Holmes is very well, thank you, but the housing of his body is slowly deteriorating and falling apart.'' The mind was clear but the physical organism was not what it used to be. Faith Baldwin, the writer, when she was 80, said something to the effect that she wished people would stop telling

There are a variety of homes for the elderly. Some only provide living accommodations, some contribute minimal care, and others are nursing centers for special skills care.

David Strickler

Table 16-7. Physical and psychological needs in living arrangements*

Physical needs

The house temperature should be comparatively even from floor to ceiling because poor circulation makes the elderly person especially sensitive to chilling.

The elderly person needs large windows to ensure plenty of light because of the gradual impairment of his vision.

Provisions should be made for the safety of the elderly person. He should have to climb few steps, and floors should be unwaxed.

There should be adequate space for indoor and outdoor recreation, a condition best met in multiple housing developments or homes for the aged.

Noise should be controlled, especially during the night. This can be done by locating the elderly person's sleeping quarters in a quiet part of the house.

The elderly person should have laborsaving devices, especially for cooking and cleaning.

The living quarters should be on one floor to avoid possible falls on steps.

Psychological needs

The elderly person should have at least one small room of his own so that he can have an opportunity for privacy. The living arrangements should include space for sedentary recreations, such as reading and television watching.

There should be provision for storage of cherished possessions.

The elderly person should live close to stores and community organizations so that he can be independent in his activities, and he should also be near relatives and friends so that frequent contacts are possible.

*From Hurlock, E. B. *Developmental psychology* (4th ed.). New York: McGraw-Hill Book Co., 1975, p. 353.

her how well she looked for her age and that she should not complain about her age but be glad that she got to live so long. Her response was that those comments didn't make her feel any better because, although she was in her right mind, she was not enjoying life simply because "I hurt."[45] The point is that in living arrangements it is important to consider psychological needs as well as physical needs, as indicated in Table 16-7.

At present a popular notion is that the best way to spend one's retirement years is to move into the "sunshine belt." The results are by no means conclusive, but many "transplanted" people find little or no real satisfaction in moving away. What many of them need most is the friendship and concern of family and close friends. Moving away generally results in serious feelings of loneliness for these people. Coping with an unfamiliar environment just adds one more complication to an already complicated problem for some people.

On the other hand, a new environment for some people is definitely beneficial. A "retirement community" or a temporary "Florida-for-the-winter" type of venture may be just the po-

tion some people need to regain vitality and interest in life; but it is not for everybody.

The proceedings of the 1971 White House Conference on Aging[46] raises the question, "What does housing mean to the elderly?" Their answer, "Aside from his spouse, housing is probably the single most important element in the life of an older person." On the research side there is clear documentation that housing can have a decisive impact upon the life-style and well-being of older persons.[47] The type of housing that an elderly person may have frequently depends on family setup and attitudes, health conditions, economic status, and personal desire. Patterns of living arrangements that are common are presented in Table 16-8. The types of arrangements are a married couple living alone; a person living alone in his own home; two or more members of the same generation living together in a nonmarital relationship (brothers, sisters, friends of the same sex, friends of different sexes); a widow or widower living with children, grandchildren, or relatives; and an elderly person living in a home for the aged, a nursing home, a club or hotel, or an institution. The table shows that 79% of the

Table 16-8. Percent of elderly men and women in various living arrangements, 1970*

Living arrangement	Men	Women
Family	79	59
Head of household	71	10
Wife is head of household	x	33
Other relative is head of household	8	16
Alone or with nonrelative	17	37
Head of household	14	35
Living with a nonrelative	3	2
Institution	4	4

*Courtesy: Population Reference Bureau, Inc., 1975, p. 16: Taken from Administration on Aging. *Facts and figures on older persons,* No. 5 (Washington, D.C. Department of Health, Education and Welfare Pub. [OHD] 74-20005) pp. 4-6.

men and 59% of the women lived with family-related persons. The tendency is for the old to maintain independent households. Only 4% were living in an institutional setting. The types of housing are home-owned; apartments, usually in older buildings; rooms, boarding houses, and hotels, generally used by old men; mobile home parks; vacant dormitories, usually on college campuses, for housing the elderly; intermediate housing, such as nursing homes, for those not requiring institutional care; institutions for the aged; and residential villages or large building units especially developed for retired people.

Group housing units tend to be either relatively affluent retirement communities designed for people who can afford more luxurious living environments or low-cost public-supported facilities for the elderly. Since 60% of the elderly live in metropolitan areas, most public-supported housing units are found in larger cities. The inner city is apt to house predominantly ethnic minority groups and the frailest of the old from the ethnic majority.[47] However, the rural old, especially if black, have the worst housing and living arrangements. The rural poor are among the most impoverished segment of the oldest population and are among the least healthy of the elderly groups. Other groups at special risk are the black elderly, about 70% of whom live in pover-

ty[48]; Mexican-American and Spanish-speaking (mostly Puerto Rican) elderly; Asian-American, especially elderly residents of America's Chinatowns; Jewish slum dwellers, who tend to be less mobile and less socially active; widows; and the poorly educated and multiply deprived. A great deal of study must be conducted before a satisfactory solution can be found for housing the elderly of all geographic, economic, and ethnic groups in satisfactory housing arrangements.

DYING AND DEATH

In considering dying and death the matter of individual differences once again is important. Some people truly seem to be unconcerned. They "trust in the Lord" and have faith that, no matter how they die, after death (in Heaven) they will not only be reunited with loved ones who have "gone before" but will see God "face to face." Others regard this view as scientifically and intellectually unrealistic, and they matter-of-factly (and without fear) insist that the only life human beings have is here on earth. Certain individuals, probably those who have seen loved ones suffer in their last days, state that they are not afraid of death itself but are afraid of the event of dying. Still others, who may not fear the act of dying, have a fear of the cessation of life. They dread the thought of nothingness, of ceasing to exist, of being in everlasting, dreamless sleep.

Concerns of death

Death is a difficult concept for young adults to comprehend. They think of death occasionally but do not linger on the thought. They can appreciate traumatic deaths, brought on by accidents, but deaths due to illness or organic failures seem to be something that happens only to "older people." In middle adulthood the notion of death comes closer to home. Few adults in their forties or fifties will not have experienced the death of at least one of their parents. Forty-year-old people also begin to read in the papers about someone not many years older than themselves who died; at 50 years they are surprised at how many people their age and younger have died. In late adulthood they are greatly concerned to realize how many friends and associates are dying, and this notion may become phobic. The first thing many older adults read in the newspaper is the obituary column. We recall an elderly person telling us, "You know, of all the charter members of the church, there are only five of us left." Later, "Now there are only two of us left." Finally, "I am the only surviving member that helped found this church." This kind of a realization must have some emotional impact on the individual. The interesting thing is that in spite of these thoughts, most older people continue to make the most of their days as best they can.

Lieberman[49] found that death as a salient theme only occurs frequently when the aged individual is within close proximity to death, not throughout all of old age. Elderly people living in a stable environment approach death as if they had made peace with many issues, including death. These people do not have a denial or avoidance attitude toward death. On the other hand, persons living in unstable settings regard death as a disruption. They view the approach of death more anxiously and have not formulated any personal philosophy to deal with it. His data suggest that death is not a prime issue of the very aged.

Several authorities have found that the dying elderly are not afraid of dying and death. Cicely Saunders[50] of St. Joseph's Hospice in London (a lodging for the terminally ill), although acknowledging the fact that every case is different, insists that most deaths come quietly and peacefully. When other terminally ill patients see this occurring to those about them, they become relieved of their own anxieties and are able to discuss death openly and without fear. Saunders believes that (1) the patient should not be in pain—it should always be controlled, (2) the physician and others should be ready to discuss dying and death when the patient wishes it, (3) the patient must always be aware of "personal, caring contact," and (4) when death comes, it should be with dignity, and the patient should not be alone.

Kastenbaum and Weisman,[51] reporting on the psychological autopsies of 100 cases, indicated that the commonly held assumption that old people lose contact with reality when they are dying is a fallacy. The behavior and conversation of most of these persons seemed to be influenced by the recognition of impending death and by an attitude of acceptance or readiness. Kastenbaum defines the psychological autopsy as an interdisciplinary effort to reconstruct the preterminal and terminal phases of a recently deceased patient.

The experience of dying

Undoubtedly, as more and more people live longer lives, researchers will continue to try to learn more about dying and death and what can be done to make the final phase of life less fearsome and more natural. Elisabeth Kubler-Ross,[52] whose seminars on death at the University of Chicago have attracted much attention, expresses the view that the terminally ill can teach people much about the anxieties, fears, and hopes in the last stages of life. In her seminars dying patients are interviewed, and their responses and needs are noted and evaluated. She states unequivocally that a patient who is terminally ill should be told that he is seriously ill. He should then be given hope immediately by being told of all the treatment possibilities. The patient is given straightforward answers if he asks for specifics. However, he is not told that he is dying or that he is terminally ill; he is told that everything humanly possible will be done to help him. No judgment should be given as to the length of time until death.

Kubler-Ross believes that dying patients go through five stages or ways of responding to the prospect of death and the miseries of dying. A person varies as to the rate at which he goes through these stages. Some people do not make it all the way through all five stages, or may move back and forth through the stages. Denial is the first response to the bad news. It is usually a period of anxiety or of shock and, frequently, is a temporary defense. The second stage is one of anger. "Why me?" Rage and resentment are expressed in many directions and toward many people, including close family. The middle or third stage is that of bargaining. He seeks to make some kind of a deal with fate. "Just let me live long enough to see my daughter get married." Depression and grief characterize the fourth stage as the person experiences a feeling of hopelessness, increasing weakness, or physical deterioration. The symptoms are too obvious to ignore. Finally, the stage of acceptance, representing the end of the struggle. Acceptance is not necessarily a happy or blissful state, but it is a time when recognition of the end is accepted without anger.

Kastenbaum[53] has some friendly reservations about the Kubler-Ross stage theory of dying. He points out that knowing the five stages is not the equivalent of knowing what the dying process is all about. More significantly, the stage theory is just a theory, he says, and it must not be used as objective truths to determine what should or should not be done with a dying patient. Kastenbaum believes that more evidence is needed to demonstrate the existence of the stages and of movement through the stages. He does praise Kubler-Ross for her work and believes it is a good basis on which to build a more comprehensive understanding of the nature of death and dying. He believes that Kubler-Ross's work has helped to bring the topic of death out of the "conspiracy of silence" and into the open, to the benefit of all concerned—especially to students of medicine, theology, sociology, and psychology.

What is it like to die?

There is increasing interest in the phenomenon referred to as life after death or a "personal glimpse at the other side." Raymond A. Moody, Jr., M.D.[54] in his medical experience observed over 150 cases of survival after "bodily death," people who were resuscitated after being pronounced clinically dead, people who came very close to physical death in the course of accidents, severe injury, or illness, and people who, as they died, told of their experience to others. Moody noted that the experiences of dying of these individuals had a striking similarity in their accounts.

There were a number of elements that recurred again and again, not in the same words or form but at least the same in principle. In general, the most common element in the near death experience was (1) linguistic difficulty in describing what happened to them. Words were inadequate to describe what was experienced. Other elements were: (2) the effect of hearing the news of being pronounced dead, or nearly so, when the others did not know the person could hear; (3) a pleasant feeling of peace and quiet during the early stages of their near-death experience, often reported by people saved at the last moment from drowning; (4) in many cases, various auditory sensations, such as buzzing noises or music were noted; (5) often in concurrence with the noise was a sensation of being pulled very rapidly through a dark space of some kind, such as a dark tunnel, a void, or an enclosure.

Another element was (6) an out-of-body experience, wherein the person found himself looking down at his own physical body while others were trying to help him. This phenomenon was reported by many individuals. Quite a few told of (7) becoming aware of the presence of spiritual beings trying to help them or, in the case of a few, telling them that their time had not come to die yet and to go back. One of the most incredible common elements, certainly one that had a profound effect on the individual, was (8) an encounter with a white or clear light that became very bright. Not one person who experienced this phenomenon expressed any doubt that it was a personal being of light. Often with the light there was a nonjudgmental probing effect that resulted in (9) a panoramic review of one's life. The review frequently occurred after the presence of the light.

A few persons described (10) a border or a limit of some kind, a line beyond which there would be no return to life. After encountering this depth in the near-death experience, (11) the person did come back, although a number said "I never wanted to leave" or "I am not ready to cross over." After the return there was (12) no doubt of the reality of the experience and its importance, (13) an effect on the lives involved, usually a change to more subtle, quiet form, and (14) new views of death, usually containing no fear of death. There were a number of (15) corroborations of the feelings experienced by those who had near-death experiences. These corroborations were usually of the sort experienced in elements 2 and 6 where people were involved in "telling the news" or "working on the patient" while the patient was having an out-of-body experience. The words spoken and the activities committed were remembered by those involved.

"The day will bring some lovely thing,"
I say it over each new dawn:
"Some gay, adventurous thing to hold
Against my heart when it is gone."
And so I rise and go to meet
The day with wings upon my feet.

I come upon it unaware—
Some sudden beauty without name:
A snatch of song—a breath of pine—
A poem lit with golden flame;
High tangled bird notes—keenly thinned—
Like flying color on the wind.

No day has ever failed me quite—
Before the grayest day is done,
I come upon some misty bloom
Or a late line of crimson sun.
Each night I pause—remembering
Some gay, adventurous lovely thing.

Author Unknown

Is this what dying is like? Of course it is difficult to say. But people involved in near-death experiences seldom, if ever, are skeptical of the existence of life after death. They also seem to have less fear of death.

Coming to terms with death

Not everyone can come to terms with death as did Abraham Maslow. He had just finished an important piece of work when he suffered a near-fatal heart attack, and in discussing it afterward he stated that since he had really "spent" himself and had done the best he could do, it would have been a good time to die—a "good ending." He believed that his life after that was a bonus, and everything—flowers, babies, friendships, the very act of living—became more beautiful; he had a "much-intensified sense of miracles." Maslow,[55] who was President of the American Psychological Association in 1968, stated in the last tape recording that he made just before his death: "If you're reconciled with death or even if you are pretty well assured that you will have a good death, a dignified one, then every single moment of every single day is transformed because the pervasive undercurrent—the fear of death—is removed."

Religion ties the individual in to past, present, and future. Through understanding, growth, and participation the healthy aging person can attain a stature, intellectually and spiritually, that can bring fulfillment in the evening of life. Research shows that elderly persons increase in favorable attitudes toward religion as they grow older. Belief that there is an afterlife is held by two thirds of those who are 65 years old and by 100% of those at the age of 90 years.[56] As a person's age increases past 65 years, listening to church services over the radio also increases. More blacks attend church and participate in church-related activities than do the white elderly.[57] Attending church and reading the Bible weekly increases up to the age of 80 years, declining somewhat thereafter. This decline is not due to lack of interest but to the decline of physical powers, which limit mobility and amount of reading. As a person grows older, there is an increase in the feelings of security afforded by religion, especially among women.[58] Death can be considered the final stage of growth.

STUDY GUIDE

1. Who are the elderly, how many are there, and where do they live?
2. Discuss the social, economic, emotional, and physical implications of having so many more elderly women living than men.
3. Is there an identity problem in old age? What role changes and self-concept changes take place?
4. What is the disengagement theory? Do you believe it holds true for most elderly?
5. The advent of retirement has been a traumatic experience for many people. How much should be done for the person approaching retirement to help him (her or them) to make a satisfactory transition? How much should they do for themselves? Is the age of 20 years too early to do some planning for retirement? At what age would you begin —25, 30, 40, 45, 50 years?
6. Should there be a mandatory retirement age? If there is one, would you consider it a discriminatory practice?
7. Housing is a problem for many elderly people. What alternatives are available for the varying tastes, needs, or economic capabilities?
8. What social changes can be anticipated for those over 75 years of age? Should they be involved in social tasks? What about social relationships between the elderly and their children?
9. A discussion concerning death is distasteful to some people, yet death touches everyone in one way or another. What does the research state concerning the aged, their views on death, and the advent of death?
10. How would you teach a spouse to be a widow (widower)? What should each one learn and know?
11. What is it like to be over 75 years of age? What are the sociological, psychological, and physiological factors involved?

REFERENCES

1. Ragan, P. K., & Dowd, J. J. The emerging political consciousness of the aged: a generation interpretation. *Journal of Social Issues,* 1974, **30,** 137-158.
2. Cutler, N. E., & Harootyan, R. A. Demography

of the aged. In D. S. Woodruff & J. E. Birren (Eds.), *Aging: scientific perspectives and social issues*. New York: Van Nostrand Co., 1975, 31-69.

3. *Increase in the older population of the United States, 1900-2000*. U.S. Bureau of Census, Current population reports, Series P-25, No. 390, 1974.

4. Cutler, N. E., & Harootyan, *op. cit.*

5. *Facts about older Americans*. U.S. Department of Health, Education and Welfare, DHEW Pub. No. (OHD) 75-20006, 1975.

6. Weiss, R. Changes in the ego as the result of aging, *Geriatric Focus*, 1964, **3**, 1.

7. Neugarten, B. L., & Gutmann, D. L. Age-sex roles and personality in middle age: a thematic apperception study. In B. L. Neugarten (Ed.), *Middle age and aging: a reader in social psychology*. Chicago: University of Chicago Press, 1968, pp. 58-71.

8. Ahammer, I. M., & Baltes, P. B. Objective versus perceived age differences in personality: how do adolescents, adults, and older people view themselves and each other? *Journal of Gerontology*, 1972, **27**, 46-51.

9. Atchley, R. C. *The social forces in later life: an introduction to social gerontology*. Belmont, Calif.: Wadsworth Publishing Co., 1972.

10. Neugarten, B. L. Personality and the aging process. *Gerontologist*, 1972, **12**(1), 9-15.

11. Neugarten, B. L. Personality changes in late life: a developmental perspective. In C. Eisorfer & M. P. Lawton (Eds.), *The psychology of adult development and aging*. Washington, D.C.: American Psychological Association, 1973, 319-321.

12. Chiriboga, D., & Lowenthal, M. F. Psychological correlates of perceived well-being. *Proceedings of the 79th Annual Convention of the American Psychological Association*, 1971, **6**, 603-604.

13. Neugarten, B. L. Personality and aging. In J. E. Birren & K. W. Schaie (Eds.), *Handbook of the psychology of aging*. New York: Van Nostrand Reinhold Co., 1977, Chap. 26.

14. Neugarten, B. L., Havighurst, R. J., & Tobin, S. S. Personality and patterns of aging. In B. L. Neugarten (Ed.), *Middle age and aging*. Chicago: University of Chicago Press, 1968, 173-177.

15. Cumming, E., & Henry, W. E. *Growing old*. New York: Basic Books Publishers, Inc., 1961.

16. Neugarten, B. L., Havighurst, R. J., & Tobin, S. S., *op. cit.*

17. Havighurst, R. J., Munnichs, J. M. A., Neugarten, B. L., & Thomas, H. *Adjustment to retirement*. Assen, Netherlands: van Gorcum, 1969.

18. Tallmer, M., & Kutner, B. Disengagement and the stresses of aging. *Journal of Gerontology*, 1969, **24**, 70-75.

19. Hyden, S. Flexible retirement provisions in public pension systems. In Organisation for Economic Cooperation and Development. *Flexibility in retirement age*. Paris: The Organisation, 1971, 21-37.

20. Fillenbaum, G. The working retired. *Journal of Gerontology*, 1971, **25**, 82-89.

21. Sheppard, H. L. Work and retirement. In R. H. Binstock & E. Shanas (Eds.), *Handbook of aging and the social sciences*. New York: Van Nostrand Reinhold Co., 1976, Chap. 12.

22. Irelan, L. M., & Bond, K. Retirees of the 1970s. In C. S. Kart & B. B. Manard (Eds.), *Aging in America: readings in gerontology*. New York: Alfred Publishing Co., 1976, 231-251.

23. Streib, G. F., & Schneider, C. J. *Retirement in American society: impact and process*. Ithaca: Cornell University Press, 1971.

24. Anderson, W. F. Potentials of the elderly. In H. Alpert (Ed.), World scientists analyze aging. *Harvest Years*, 1969, **9**, 33.

25. Osborn, R. W. Social and economic factors in reported chronic morbidity. *Journal of Gerontology*, 1971, **26**, 217-223.

26. Busse, E. W. Viewpoint. *Geriatrics*, 1969, **24**, 42-44.

27. Brand, F., & Smith, R. Life adjustment and relocation of the elderly. *Journal of Gerontology*, 1974, **29**, 336-340.

28. Streib, G. F. The older person in a family context. In C. Tibbitts (Ed.), *Handbook of social gerontology*. Chicago: University of Chicago Press, 1960, 478-485.

29. Swaim, W. T., Jr. *What shall we do with Granny?* Dillsburg, Pa.: Presbyterian Homes of Central Pennsylvania, undated.

30. Burr, W. R. Satisfaction with various aspects of marriage over the life cycle: a random middle-class sample. *Journal of Marriage and Family*, 1970, **32**, 29-37.

31. Riley, M. W., & Foner, A. *Aging and society* (Vol. 1). *An inventory of research findings*. New York: Russell Sage Foundation, 1968.

32. Stinnett, N., Carter, L. M., & Montgomery, J. E. Older persons' perceptions of their marriage. *Journal of Marriage and Family*, 1972, **34**, 665-670.

33. U.S. Bureau of Census, 1970 Census of Popula-

tion. *Subject reports: marital status*. Washington, D.C.: U.S. Government Printing Office, 1972.

34. Hurlock, E. *Developmental psychology* (4th ed.). New York: McGraw-Hill Book Co., 1975.

35. Bernardo, F. Widowhood status in the United States: perspective on a neglected aspect of the family life-cycle. In M. E. Lasswell & T. E. Lasswell (Eds.), *Love, marriage, family: a developmental approach*. Glenview, Ill.: Scott Foresman, 1973, 458-464.

36. Glick, I. O., Weiss, R. S., & Parkes, C. M. *The first year of bereavement*. New York: Wiley-Interscience, 1974.

37. Kastenbaum, R. J. *Death, society and human experience*. St. Louis: The C. V. Mosby Co., 1977.

38. Parkes, C. M. *Bereavement*. New York: International Universities Press, 1972.

39. Kimmell, D. *Adulthood and aging*. New York: John Wiley & Sons, Inc., 1974.

40. Butler, R. N., & Lewis, M. J. *Aging and mental health: positive psychosocial approaches*. St. Louis: The C. V. Mosby Co., 1973.

41. McKain, W. A new look at older marriages. *The Family Coordinator*, 1972, **21**, 61-69.

42. Gordon, G., Gaitz, C. M., & Scott, S. Leisure and lives: personal expressivity across the life span. In R. H. Binstock & E. Shanas (Eds.), *Handbook of aging and the social sciences*. New York: Van Nostrand, 1976, Chap. 13.

43. Beyer, G., & Woods, M. E. *Living and activity patterns of the aged*. Ithaca, N.Y.: Cornell University Center for Environmental Studies, 1963.

44. Hurlock, E. B. *Developmental psychology* (4th ed.). New York: McGraw-Hill Book Co., 1975, p. 353.

45. Baldwin, F. My crabbed age. *Today's Health*, 1976, **53**(3), 18.

46. Proceeding of the 1971 White House conference on aging. *Toward a national policy on aging*. No-

vember 28-December 2, 1971, Washington, D.C.: U.S. Government Printing Office, 1973.

47. Carp, F. M. Housing and living environments of older people. In R. H. Binstock & E. Shanas (Eds.), *Handbook of aging and the social sciences*. New York: Van Nostrand Reinhold Co., 1976, Chap. 10.

48. Jackson, H. C. National caucus on the black aged; a progress report. *Aging and Human Development*, 1971, **3**, 226-231.

49. Lieberman, I. Social setting determines attitudes of aged to death. *Geriatric Focus*, 1967 **6**(1), 1-6.

50. Saunders, C. St. Christopher's Hospice. In E. S. Shneidman (Ed.), *Death: current perspectives*. Palo Alto, Calif: Mayfield Publishing Co., 1976.

51. Weisman, A. D., & Kastenbaum, R. The psychological autopsy: a study of the terminal phase of life. *Community Mental Health Journal Monograph*, New York: Behavioral Publications, Inc., 1968.

52. Kubler-Ross, E. *On death and dying*. New York: Macmillan, Inc., 1969.

53. Kastenbaum, R. J. *Death, society and human experience*. St. Louis: The C. V. Mosby Co., 1977.

54. Moody, R. A., Jr. *Life after life: the investigation of survival of bodily death*. New York: Bantam Books, 1975.

55. Maslow, A. Editorial. *Psychology Today*, 1969, **24**, 26-34.

56. Cavan, R. S., Burgess, E. W., Havighurst, R. J., & Goldhamer, H. *Personality adjustment in old age*. Chicago: Science Research Associates, 1949, p. 58.

57. Hirsch, G., Kent, D. P., & Silverman, S. L. *Homogeneity and heterogeneity among low income Negro and White aged*. Paper presented at the Annual Gerontological Society Meetings, Denver, Colorado, 1968.

58. Britton, J. H., & Britton, J. O. *Personality changes in aging*. New York: Springer, 1972.

Glossary

A

aberration A general term for any deviation from the normal or typical.

accommodation The tendency to change one's schema or operations or to make new ones to include new objects or experiences enabling a higher level of thinking. Term is used by Piaget in his theory on cognitive development. See also **assimilation.**

achievement quotient (AQ) The ratio between a person's scores in scholastic performance and the standard.

ACTH Adrenocorticotrophic hormone produced by the pituitary gland to stimulate corticoid production in stress situations.

action-instrument In the two-word stage of language development, the indication of knowledge of the use of instruments, as in ''cut knife.''

action-location In the two-word stage of language development, the expression of the location of an action, as in ''sit chair.''

action-recipient In the two-word stage of language development, the indication of who is to benefit from an action, as in ''cookie me.''

actualization-fulfillment theory The version of the fulfillment theory of personality, holding that the personality force is in the form of an inherited blueprint determining the person's special abilities. Term *self-actualization* was used by Maslow.

actualizing tendency The potential for the fullest development that, under appropriate circumstances, will occur.

acuity The ability to see objects clearly and to resolve detail.

adaptation A key principle in ethological theories, referring to the way that behavior changes or develops to meet environmental demands and to insure survival and reproduction.

addition According to Flavell, a sequence in intellectual development in which the later-emerging skill is added to the earlier one and supplements but does not replace it. An example is the addition of counting ability to one's knowledge of number concepts.

adjustment Processes and behaviors that satisfy a person's internal needs and enable the person to cope effectively with environmental, social, and cultural demands.

adjustment, emotional A state of emotional maturity proper to the age of a person and marked by a relatively stable and moderate emotional reactivity to affect- and mood-eliciting stimuli.

adjustment, social Reaction patterns toward others conducive to harmonious relationships within family and other reference groups.

adolescence The developmental period beginning with the onset of major pubertal changes and continuing until adult maturity.

adrenals A pair of ductless or internal secretion glands attached to the kidneys and secreting epinephrine and cortin, important in emergency and stress situations.

adult A postadolescent person whose growth is completed in most aspects of development and who is capable of satisfactory reality testing and adjustment to self and environment.

adulthood The stage of the human life cycle that begins when the individual achieves biological and psychological maturity and ends with the gradual onset of old age.

affect A vital feeling, mood, or emotion characterized by specific physiological (psychophysical) changes and states.

afterbirth The placenta, its attached membranes, and the rest of the umbilical cord, delivered in the final stages of labor.

age, mental (MA) The level of development in intelligence, particularly, is the age level at which the child has the attained capacity to function intellectually. The term should be obtained from the results of a mental test.

age norm The average for a given age as revealed by sample group performances at this age.

agent, action, and object In the two-word stage of language development, the expression of an agent's action on an object, using only two of the components of the thought, as in "Daddy ball" for "Daddy throw ball."

aggression Feeling and behavior of anger or hostility.

aggressiveness Verbal or physical behavior that is inappropriate or harms someone.

aging The continuous developmental process beginning with conception and ending with death during which organic structures and functions of an immature organism first grow and mature, then decline and deteriorate.

alienation A feeling of estrangement from and hostility toward society or familiar persons, based in part on a discrepancy between expectations and promises and in part on the actual experience of the role one is playing.

alleles Pairs of genes on corresponding chromosomes that affect the same traits. When the two alleles are identical, a person is said to be homozygous for that trait. When the alleles carry differing instructions, he is said to be heterozygous for that trait.

allergy Heightened sensitivity to pollen or any other foreign substance, causing respiratory, skin, or gastrointestinal irritation, including swelling. Hay fever and hives are frequent allergic conditions.

altruism Deep unselfish concern for others, often expressed in helping them or in charitable activities.

ambivalence Internal tendency to be pulled (usually psychologically) in opposite directions, for example, acceptance-rejection, love-hate, participation-withdrawal.

amnesia Defensive forgetting caused by a strong conflict or inability to face a certain event or experience, with subsequent repression.

amniocentesis A means of detecting fetal abnormality by the insertion of a hollow needle through the maternal abdomen and the drawing out of a sample of amniotic fluid on which chromosomal analyses can be performed.

amnion The translucent sac in which the developing prenatal organism lies.

amniotic fluid The fluid in the amnion in which the developing prenatal organism is suspended; it protects the organism from external pressure.

anal stage In psychoanalytic theory the second stage of psychosexual development, during which the child's interest centers on anal activities such as those related to toilet training. See also **genital stage; oral stage; phallic stage.**

androgens Male sex hormones, produced primarily by the testes.

androgynous The capability of expressing both masculine and feminine behaviors and attitudes, depend-

ing on their appropriateness to the particular situation.

anencephaly The lack of a brain at birth.

anesthesia Lack of psychophysical response to sensory stimuli; unawareness of pain.

anlage An original basis for or a disposition toward a specific developmental trend or factor.

anoxia A severe deficiency in the supply of oxygen to the tissues, especially the brain, causing damage to their structural integrity.

anterior pituitary gland The front part of the pituitary gland, an endocrine gland situated at the base of the brain. The anterior pituitary produces hormones that regulate growth and other hormones that regulate the functions of the other endocrine glands.

anxiety A feeling of uneasiness or distress that arises when a person is torn by inner conflict because of incompatible motives, or when he feels apprehension over a possible threat to himself.

anxiety neurotic Distress and helplessness due to ego damage or weakness, accompanied by an expectation of danger or misfortune.

Apgar score Developed by Apgar and James in 1962, a much-used and practical scoring system for assessing, on a scale from 0 to 2, appearance, heart rate, reflex irritability, activity, muscle tone, and respiratory effort in newborns. The totaled score may vary from 0 to 10 (10 being best).

aphasia The loss or impairment of the ability to use speech resulting from lesions in the brain.

apperception A mental process of interpreting and assimilating a new experience or behavior in the experimental background (apperceptive schema).

aptitude The potential ability to perform certain tasks or functions effectively in certain situations if given proper training or opportunity to develop skill or learning.

arthritis Inflammation or deformation of one or several joints, accompanied by pain, stiffness, and swelling, often chronic.

aspiration, level of The intensity of striving for achievement, or the standard by which a person judges his own activity in reference to expected end results.

assertiveness Verbal or physical behavior that is appropriate and that injures no one.

assimilation The incorporation of new objects and experiences into a structure or schemata in the mind to be used later in problem-solving situations. See also **accommodation.**

asymmetrical One side of the physique, object, or figure lacks similarity or correspondence with the other side.

asynchrony The maturation of different body parts at different rates. This disproportion becomes most pronounced during puberty.

atrophy Progressive decline of a part, its decrease in size, or possible degeneration.

attachment The primary social bond that develops between an infant and its caretaker.

attention The focusing of perception on a certain stimulus while ignoring others. Needed for learning to take place.

attitude An acquired persistent tendency to feel, think, or act in a certain way.

attribution In the two-word stage of language development, the modifying of nouns with attributes, as in "red truck."

autism A schizophrenic syndrome characterized by absorption in fantasy to the exclusion of interest in reality and in others.

autistic Self-centered; with perception, feeling, and thinking unduly controlled by personal needs, desires, and preferences at the expense of sensitivity to others or to situational demands.

autogenous Self-originated, as distinguished from what is initiated by outside stimuli and learning.

autonomy A feeling of self-control and self-determination. According to Erikson's theory of psychosocial development, this feeling develops around the ages of 2 to 4 and manifests itself in the child's increasing demands to determine his own behavior.

axillary hair Underarm hair.

B

babbling Speech patterns found in infants, comprising repetitious sequences of alternating consonants and vowels, such as "ba ba ba ba." They may be a form of motor practice that facilitates later speech development.

basal metabolism The rate of energy required to maintain the body's functioning while resting.

behavior Any kind of reaction, including complex patterns of feeling, perceiving, thinking, and willing, in response to internal or external, tangible or intangible stimuli.

behavior modification An approach to changing behavior that involves a wide variety of techniques based on learning principles such as conditionng and reinforcement.

behavioral sciences Those disciplines that study the various aspects of human living. Psychology, sociology, and social anthropology are considered to be the major behavioral sciences. However, the evolution of the interdisciplinary approach to the study of behavior has introduced certain aspects of history, economics, political science, physiology, zoology, and physics into the field of the behavioral sciences.

behaviorism The school of psychology holding that the proper object of study in psychology is behavior alone, without reference to consciousness. Behavior theorists are particularly interested in learning mechanisms.

binocular disparity The incongruent views the two eyes receive because of their different positions in space.

binocular fusion The integration of the two different views of the eyes.

birth injury Temporary or possibly permanent injury to the infant that occurs during the birth process. Many disabilities are attributed to brain damage occurring as a result of birth injury.

blastocyst The cluster of cells that begins to differentiate itself into distinct parts during the germinal period of prenatal development.

blastula The cluster of cells that make up the prenatal organism in the first few days after conception.

body ideal The body type defined by one's culture as ideally attractive and sex appropriate.

body stalk During the germinal period of prenatal development, the structure that differentiates to become the embryonic disc and the umbilical cord.

breech delivery A birth in which the baby's buttocks appear first, then the legs, and finally the head.

C

canalization The temporary deviation from and subsequent return to a child's normal growth curve.

carcinogenic Capable of eliciting cancer.

catharsis The relief of feelings, particularly negative ones, through talking, playing, drawing, or painting; it is a technique used in psychology and psychiatry.

cathexis Attachment of affects and drives to their goal objects; direction of psychic energy into a particular outlet.

central nervous system (CNS) The brain and spinal cord.

cephalocaudal development The progression of physical and motor development from head to foot. For example, a baby's head develops and grows before the torso, arms, and legs.

cerebral dominance Refers to the fact that one cerebral hemisphere is dominant over the other in the control of body movements, as in handedness.

cervix The narrow canal connecting the vagina and the uterus.

cesarean section A surgical operation through the walls of the abdomen and uterus for the purpose of delivering a child.

character The acquired ability to act and conduct oneself in accordance with a personal code of principles based on a scale of values, and facility in doing so.

child A person between infancy and puberty.

childhood The period of development between infancy and puberty (or adolescence).

chorion The protective and nutrient cover of the amnion, which contains the developing organism in the womb.

chorionic villi Capillaries that link the developing umbilical veins and arteries of an embryo with the uterine wall; they eventually become part of the placenta along with the surrounding maternal tissues.

chromosome The minute, threadlike body within the nucleus of the cell that carries many DNAs, RNAs, proteins, and genes and transmits hereditary traits.

chronological age (CA) Age in calendar years.

cirrhosis Replacement of regular tissue, especially of the liver, by fibrous tissue—a frequent liver disease of alcoholics.

classical conditioning An experimental method in which a conditioned stimulus is paired with an unconditioned stimulus to condition a particular response.

climacteric The period marking the end of the time at which women can conceive, and for men the time at which there is a significant decline in sexual virility. The term *menopause* is generally used for women instead of *climacteric*.

clinical study A study consisting of in-depth interviews and observations. It can be controlled or can be varied for each subject.

cognition The process of gaining knowledge about the world through sensing, perceiving, using symbols, and reasoning; the actual knowledge that an individual has about the world. Knowing the world through the use of one's perceptual and conceptual abilities.

cognitive development The development of a logical method of looking at the world, utilizing one's perceptual and conceptual powers.

cognitive processes The operations or routines that the mind performs including the encoding of information, the storage and retrieval of information in memory, the generation of hypotheses, their evaluation according to criteria, and inductive and deductive reasoning.

cognitive theorists Theorists such as Jean Piaget and Jerome Bruner who describe intellectual development and Roger Brown who describes early language behavior. They see children's thinking as different but no less effective than that of adults.

cohorts The members of a certain age group; a group of people of the same age.

coitus Sexual intercourse.

compensation A defense mechanism in which the individual works especially hard to avoid defeat or failure (direct compensation) or turns to another area of endeavor to allay anxiety (indirect compensation).

concept A type of symbol that represents a set of common attributes among a group of other symbols or images.

conception The merging of the spermatozoon and ovum in human fertilization, which signals the beginning of life.

conceptualization The process of concept formation in which various items are grouped into units on the basis of commensurable characteristics.

concrete operational stage The stage of cognitive development that occurs from about 7 to 12 years of age and during which the child develops the operations of conservation, class inclusion, and serialization. This stage begins when children understand new kinds of logical operations involving reversible transformations of concrete objects and events.

conditioned reflex In classical conditioning, one of two kinds of reflexes in which the reflex is one that comes to be elicited by a previously neutral stimulus.

conditioning A mode of training whereby reinforcement (reward or punishment) is used to elicit desired (rewarded) responses.

conduct That part of a person's behavior, including insufficiencies and reverses, which is guided by ethical, moral, or ideological standards.

confabulation An attempt to fill in the gaps of memory without awareness of the falsification involved.

conflict An intrapsychic state of tension or indecision due to contrary desires, ungratified needs, or incompatible plans of action; such tension may also exist between conscious and unconscious choices.

congenital Referring to characteristics and defects acquired during the period of gestation and persisting after birth as distinguished from heredity.

connective tissue Fibers that lie between cells of the body.

consciousness Cognizance of the immediate environment plus the ability to utilize encoding, memory, and logic at will.

conservation The realization that one aspect of something (for example, quantity) remains the same, while another aspect is changed (for example, shape, position). Used by Piaget. For example, rearranging a row of objects does not affect their number.

constitution The organization of organic, functional,

and psychosocial elements within the developing person that largely determines his or her condition.

continuous reinforcement In operant conditioning, a schedule in which each correct response is reinforced.

contraception The prevention of pregnancy by artificial means.

control The intentional modification of any condition of an investigation. These modifications may include the selection of subjects for study, the experiences they have in the study, and the possible responses that they can give to that experience.

control group A group used for comparison with an experimental group with the exception that the independent variable is not applied to the control group.

conventional stage A stage of moral development in which the individual strives to maintain the expectations of his family, group, or nation, regardless of the consequences. See also **postconventional stage; preconventional stage.**

convergence The mechanism by which the slightly different images of an object seen by each eye come together to form a single image.

conversion As used in the present work, transformation of anxiety and energies elicited by a conflict into somatic symptoms.

cooperative (reciprocal) play Play in which the children begin to adjust their behavior to the activities and desires of their peers.

correlation The relationship between two variables as measured by the correlation coefficient.

correlation coefficient A statistical index for measuring correspondence in changes occurring in two variables. Perfect correspondence is $+1.00$; no correspondence is 0.00; perfect correspondence in opposite directions is -1.00.

critical periods Specific times in development during which a child is best able to learn a specific lesson; also, in fetal development, crucial times at which various specific physical features and organs develop; detrimental environmental influences during those periods can adversely affect organic development.

cross-sectional studies Studies that compare different age groups at some specific point in time.

culture The man-made aspects of human environment —customs, beliefs, institutions, modes of living— including the attitudes and beliefs held, and acted on, by a specific group of people about aspects of living that they consider important.

D

daydreaming A form of withdrawal from unpleasant or frustrating reality into the realm of fantasy and reverie, frequently of a pleasant, wish-gratifying type.

DDT Acutely poisonous pesticide. If ingested by man it produces heightened excitability, muscular tremors, and motor seizures; deadly in larger amounts.

defense mechanism Any habitual response pattern that is spontaneously used to protect oneself from threats, conflicts, anxiety, frustration, and other conditions that a person cannot tolerate or cope with directly.

dependence The desire or need for supporting relationships with other persons. See also **independence.**

detachment The infant's desire to try out new experiences and to expand his competence. Developing in the second year, it coexists and interacts with the attachment system.

development, level of A period in a person's life marked by specific clusters of traits, interests, and attitudes and by a similarity in interests and concerns to other persons in that period of life.

developmental-level approach In psychology, the approach in which the total personality of the person is considered at each phase of life.

developmental psychology A division of psychology that investigates the growth, maturation, and aging processes of the human organism and personality, as well as cognitive, social, and other functions, throughout the span of life.

developmental task A specific learning problem that arises at a particular stage of life and that individuals must accomplish to meet the demands of their culture. Developmental tasks vary with one's age and persist as objectives throughout life. The nature of the developmental task is such that one learning is related to, merges into, and forms the basis for the next learning.

differentiation The process by means of which structure, function, or forms of behavior become more complex or specialized; the change from homogeneity to heterogeneity.

dimension A coherent group of processes having a particular denominator—for example, intelligence, emotion, and language dimensions of personality.

dimensional approach In psychology, the approach in which a specific aspect or area of personality is considered throughout various phases of life.

disequilibrium According to Piaget, disequilibrium exists whenever the mind is confronted with inconsistencies or gaps in knowledge and a change is needed from one level of understanding to another to attain a more clearly delineated structure of knowledge; for example, movement is toward a state of relative equilibrium of cognitive structures.

disjunctive concept A concept in which a member of a category may possess some, but need not possess all, of several different attributes to be included in the category.

displacement The ability to communicate information about objects, people, and events in another place or another time; one of three formal properties of language.

dizygotic (DZ) twins Twins who develop from two separate eggs; fraternal twins. See also **monozygotic (MZ) twins.**

DNA Deoxyribonucleic acid molecule, containing the genetic code—"the molecule of life." Each cell in its nucleus contains DNAs arranged in the form of a double helix.

dominant gene A gene whose hereditary characteristics always prevail.

Down's syndrome A congenital physical condition associated with mental retardation, characterized by thick, fissured tongue, flat face, and slanted eyes. Formerly called Mongolism.

drive The tension and arousal produced by an ungratified need and directed toward a chosen object or end.

dynamic Refers to forces and potent influences that are capable of producing changes within the organism or personality.

dysfunction Disturbance or impairment of the functional capacity of an organ or system, including mental abilities.

dyadic As used in the present work, pertaining to active relationships between two persons, for example, mother and child, father and son.

E

ecological The approach to studying development that takes into account the limiting and determining effects of the physical and social environment.

ectoderm The outermost cell layer in the embryo from which structures of the nervous system and skin are developed.

EEG Electroencephalogram or electroencephalograph. A graphic record of the electric activity of the brain obtained by placing electrodes on the skull.

egg cell See **ovum.**

ego The conscious core of personality that exercises control demanded by the superego and directs drives and impulses of the id in accordance with the demands of reality; guides a person's realistic coping behavior and mediates the eternal conflicts between

what one wants to do (id) and what one must or must not do (superego).

ego identity According to Erik Erikson, a clear and continuing sense of who one is and what one's goals are.

egocentrism In cognitive development, the tendency of individuals to think that others see things from the same point of view and that they also experience their own behavior, thought, and feelings in relation to these things.

embryo The form of prenatal life from the second to the eighth week. The period of the embryo follows the germinal period and is succeeded by that of the fetus.

embryology The study of the development of the individual from conception to birth.

embryonic disc During the germinal period, the part of the prenatal organism that will eventually become the embryo.

emotion A conscious state of experience, characterized by feeling or excitement that is accompanied and frequently preceded by specific physiological changes and frequently resulting in excitation of the organism to action. Emotions are the physiological forms that result from one's estimate of the harmful or beneficial effects of stimuli.

emotional dependence Dependence on others, which has as its aim the obtaining of their comfort and nurturance.

empathy The emotional linkage that characterizes relationships between individuals; the ability to sense the feelings of others.

encoding The transformation of external stimuli into internal signals that stimulate behavior appropriate to them. In the perceptual process it is the point wherein the message or meaning is translated into behavior that is deemed an appropriate response to the stimuli.

endocrine glands The ductless glands of internal secretion, such as the pituitary, thyroid, and adrenals, that secrete hormones into the bloodstream or lymph system.

endoderm The innermost of the three cell layers of the embryo from which most of the visceral organs and the digestive tract are developed.

endowment Capacity for development, physical or mental, conditioned by heredity and constitution.

envy A distressful feeling aroused by the observation that another person possesses what one desires to have.

epigenesis Appearance of new phenomena not present at previous stages in an organism's development from fertilized egg to adult maturity.

epistemology The branch of philosophy that is concerned with discovering the nature of knowledge and knowing.

equilibration The most general developmental principle in Piaget's theory, which states that an organism always tends toward biological and psychological balance and that development is a progressive approximation to an ideal state of equilibrium that it never fully achieves.

estrogens Female sex hormones, produced primarily in the ovaries.

estrous cycle The periodic waxing and waning of sexual desire and receptivity, with accompanying physiological changes, in the female animal.

ethical relativity The doctrine stating that different cultures or groups hold different fundamental moral values and that these values cannot themselves be judged as more or less adequate or more or less moral.

ethics Moral values and ideals. See also **morality.**

etiology The investigation of origins, causes, and factors contributing to a trait, attitude, or disease.

euphoria An intense, subjective sensation of vigor, well-being, and happiness that may exist despite some problem or disability.

existentialism The philosophy that man forms his own nature in the course of his life, with man's situation in the universe seen as purposeless or irrational.

expectancy Anticipation of a given stimulus determined by one's previous experiences with related stimuli. Deviation from expectancy is a factor in selective attention.

experiential freedom According to Carl Rogers, the subjective sense that one is free to choose among alternative courses of action in defining one's life.

experimentation A type of study designed to control the arrangement and manipulation of conditions in order to systematically observe particular phenomena.

expression The second component of a baby's sucking, during which the nipple is pressed against the roof of the mouth with the tongue applying heavy pressure at the front of the mouth and then progressively moving toward the rear.

extended family The family that consists of three generations—children, parents, grandparents, and even aunts and uncles—under the same roof. See also **nuclear family.**

extinguish To gradually eliminate a response by withholding reinforcement.

extrovert A type of personality whose thoughts, feelings, and interests are directed chiefly toward persons, social affairs, and other external phenomena.

eye-hand coordination The ability to coordinate vision with motor activities so that one can accurately reach for and grasp objects.

F

fallopian tube Either of the tubes that carries the ovum from the ovaries to the uterus.

fantasy A function of imagination marked by engagement in vicarious experiences and hallucinatory actions; reveries, daydreaming.

fertilization The union of an egg cell with a spermatozoon.

fetus The prenatal human organism from approximately eight weeks after conception to birth. See also **embryo.**

field study A study of naturally occurring behavior in which the researcher controls only some aspects of the situation.

fixation The persistence of infantile, childish, pubertal, or adolescent response patterns, habits, and modes of adjustment throughout successive phases of development.

formal operational stage According to Jean Piaget, the fourth stage of thought, which begins at about 12 years of age, is the time the individual begins to engage in thinking that is characterized by the ability to consider what is possible, as well as what is. It is the period during which logical thinking begins and is the final step toward abstract thinking and conceptualization. See also **concrete operational stage; preoperational stage; sensorimotor stage.**

formal rules Statements of relations between units or classes that are always true and specifiable, such as the rules of mathematics.

fraternal twins See **dizygotic (DZ) twins.**

frustration The experience of distress induced by failures and by thwarting of attempts to gratify one's needs or ambitions.

fully functioning person Carl Rogers' term for an individual characterized by openness to experience, existential living, organismic trusting, experiential freedom, and creativity.

G

G-factor The common root of intellectual behavior that runs through the functioning of those specific subabilities identified by various authorities. G-factor is not general intelligence but the pervasive element in all types of intelligence.

galvanic skin response (GSR) A change in the electrical resistance of the skin.

gamete A mature reproductive cell; an egg or a sperm.

genes The microscopic elements carried by the chromosomes. They contain the codes that produce inherited physical traits and behavioral dispositions.

genetic epistemology The developmental study of what is known and how it comes to be known; most closely associated with Piaget's theory.

genetic psychology The branch of psychology that studies the human organism and its functions in terms of their origin and early course of development.

genetics The branch of biology concerned with the transmission of hereditary characteristics.

genital organs The male and female sex organs.

genital stage In psychoanalytic theory the final stage of psychosexual development, during which heterosexual interests are dominant. This stage begins in adolescence and lasts throughout adulthood. See also **anal stage; oral stage; phallic stage.**

genome All the genes found in a haploid set of chromosomes.

genotype The characteristics of an organism that are inherited and that can be transmitted to offspring; also, the traits or characteristics common to a biological group. See also **phenotype.**

geriatrics The medical study and care of aging persons.

germinal period The first stage of prenatal development. It is roughly the first two weeks after conception, during which time the developing individual is primarily engaged in cell division. See also **embryo; fetus.**

gerontology The study of the improvement of the life habits of aging persons; the psychology and sociology of aging.

gestation period The amount of time the prenatal organism spends in the uterus; the total period of prenatal development calculated from the beginning of the mother's last menstruation (280 days, 40 weeks, or 9 calendar months).

gestational age The age of the fetus calculated from the date of conception.

gonadotrophic hormones Secretions of the anterior pituitary that stimulate activity in the gonads.

gonads The sex glands; the ovaries in females and the testes in males.

gonococcus The bacterium that produces gonorrhea.

gonorrhea A venereal disease.

grammar The structural principles of a language; syntax.

grasping reflex The tendency during the first few weeks of life for an infant to clutch any small object placed in his hand.

group, reference The group a person belongs to or is interested in belonging to, for example, peer groups, usually with a molding influence on the individual.

growth Strictly speaking, the addition of height and weight through simple physical accretion; sometimes used interchangeably with development, which includes the foregoing but also embraces the improvement of function.

guidance Refers to a variety of methods, such as advising, counseling, testing, and use of special instruction and corrective teaching, by means of which a person may be helped to find and engage in activities that will yield satisfaction and further adjustment.

guilt A negative feeling that stems from deviation from one's own internalized moral standards.

H

habit An acquired or learned pattern of behavior, relatively simple and regularly used with facility, which leads to a tendency to use such acts rather than other behavior.

habituation The process of becoming accustomed to a particular set of circumstances or to a particular stimulus, resulting in decreased awareness.

handedness The tendency to use either the right or the left hand predominantly.

hedonism A psychological or philosophical system of motivation explaining all behavior and conduct in terms of seeking pleasure and avoiding pain.

heredity The totality of characteristics biologically transmitted from parents and ancestors to the offspring at conception.

heritability An estimate, based on a sample of individuals, of the relative contribution of genetics to a given trait or behavior.

heterogeneous A term used to describe any group of individuals or items that show great differences in reference to some significant criterion or standard.

heterosexual Emotionally and sexually centered on the opposite sex; seeking and finding erotic gratification with a person of the other sex.

heterozygous The condition in which cells contain different genes for the same trait. The dominant gene will determine the appearance of the trait.

homeostasis The tendency to preserve a stable or constant internal state, despite fluctuations of bodily conditions and external stimulations. Cannon's term for the relative constancy—for example, in temperature, blood pressure, and pulse rate—that the body must maintain to function properly.

hominids Members of several extinct species of the primate order from which man is descended.

homogeneous A term used to describe any group of individuals or items that show great similarity or low variability in the qualities or traits considered.

homosexual Centered on the same sex; marked by a

tendency to find sexual and erotic gratification with a person of the same sex.

homozygous The condition in which cells have matching genes for a trait.

hormone A specific chemical substance produced by an endocrine gland, which brings about certain somatic and functional changes within the organism.

hostile aggression Behavior that aims at hurting another person.

hypothesis A tentative interpretation of a complex set of phenomena or data on the basis of supportive facts or findings.

I

id According to Freud, that part of the personality consisting of primitive instincts toward sexuality and aggression; an aspect of personality in which all unconscious impulses reside. The id seeks immediate gratification regardless of the consequences but is held in check by the superego. See also **ego; superego.**

ideal A standard approaching some level of perfection, usually unattainable in practice.

identical twins See **monozygotic (MZ) twins.**

identification The process by which a person takes over the features of another person whom he admires and incorporates them into his own personality.

identification (language) In the two-word stage of language development, the verbal extension of a simple pointing response, as in "See doggy."

identity A sense of one's self; sense of sameness despite growth, aging, and environmental change.

imitation The principle and the processes by which an individual copies or reproduces what has been observed.

implanted Attached; after floating freely for several days, the fertilized ovum becomes implanted in the uterine wall.

imprinting The alteration of an apparently instinctive behavior that occurs at a certain, extremely early critical period of development; for example, ducklings from an incubator will follow a man or dog as though they were following a mother duck, and form a strong, long-lasting social attachment to the surrogate.

impulsivity Uncontrolled action; acting without first thinking.

inclusion According to Flavell, a sequence in intellectual development in which the earlier item becomes incorporated as an integral part of the later item. An example is the inclusion of children's early naming skills into all later language development.

incubation A period in assimilation and the problem-solving process during which certain presented ideas gain in motivational strength and begin to condition a part of behavior, especially during childhood.

independence Self-reliance.

independent variable The variable that is controlled by the experimenter to determine its effect on the dependent variable.

individuation Differentiation of behavior into more distinct and less dependent parts or features.

induced abortion The premature removal of the fetus by deliberate interference.

infancy The stage of human development lasting from birth until the organism is able to exist independently of its mother, capable of feeding itself, of walking, and of talking, usually until the age of 2 years.

infantile Pertaining to the lowest level of postnatal maturity; mode of behavior or adjustment resembling the infant level.

inferiority attitude or complex An emotionally conditioned and frequently unconscious attitude with reference to one's organism, self, or personality, characterized by serious lack of self-reliance and notions of inadequacy in many situations.

informal rules Statements of imperfect relations between two or more units or classes. See also **formal rules.**

inhibition Prevention of the starting of a process or behavior by inner control despite the presence of the eliciting stimulus.

innate Existing before birth and accounting for a particular trait or characteristic.

instinct Unlearned, biologically based behavior.

instrumental aggression Behavior that aims at retrieving or acquiring an object, territory, or privilege.

instrumental conditioning See **operant conditioning.**

instrumental dependence Dependence that involves seeking assistance as a means of accomplishing some task or activity.

integration (hierarchic) The developmental trend of combining simple, differentiated skills into more complex skills.

intelligence The ability to conceptualize effectively and to grasp relationships; also, according to Jean Piaget, the coordination of operations.

intelligence quotient The index or rate of mental development. The ratio of mental to chronological age as expressed in the formula: Mental age divided by chronological age, times 100, equals IQ. IQ must be regarded as an indication rather than a measure, since different tests yield different results and performance fluctuates.

internalization The incorporation of beliefs, attitudes, and ideas into the personality so that they become part of one's makeup.

interval reinforcement In operant conditioning, the schedule of the partial reinforcement in which a person is reinforced for his first correct response after a specified period of time has passed.

introjection A basal (crude) form of identification in which a person assimilates simple behavior patterns of other persons.

introvert Orientation inward toward the self rather than toward association with others.

J

juvenile Pertaining to an older child or adolescent.

K

kibbutz An Israeli collective farm or settlement.

kinship Blood relationship between two or more persons; usually includes marriage and adoption ties.

Klinefelter's syndrome A congenital physical condition in men that occurs when the individual has two X chromosomes and one Y chromosome. The symptoms include sterility, small testes, small femalelike breasts, and usually mental retardation.

knee-jerk reflex See **patellar reflex.**

kwashiorkor The severe, often fatal, disease caused by prolonged protein deficiency.

L

lability In psychology the tendency to shift erratically from one emotional state to another. See also **stability.**

language An abstract system of word meanings and syntactic structures that facilitates communication.

lanugo A fine, wooly fuzz that appears briefly on the fetus in the later months of development; the fine hair appearing on parts of some newborns' bodies that may remain several weeks before disappearing.

latency period In psychoanalytic theory a stage in psychosexual development that appears between the phallic and genital stages and during which sexual drives become temporarily dormant; usually begins about the age of 4 or 5 years and lasts until adolescence.

lateralization The developmental process in which one hemisphere of the brain becomes dominant.

learning A relatively permanent modification of behavior resulting from experience.

level of significance In the T test expression of the confidence with which a null hypothesis can be rejected, usually expressed as a decimal fraction. If the desired result could occur by chance one in twenty times, the level of significance is .05.

libido According to Freud, a basic psychological energy inherent in every individual; this energy supplies the sexual drive, whose goal is to obtain pleasure.

life cycle The total time from birth to death, divided into a number of stages and phases and emphasizing recurrence of certain important events.

life expectancy The number of years, based on a statistical average, that a person is expected to live in a given culture.

life-style The particular and unique pattern of living that characterizes the individual. It is a product of one's capacities, abilities, social milieu, family experiences, and the values one holds.

location In the two-word stage of language development, the signaling of the location of an object with such words as "here" and "there."

locus of control The perceived location of the control over an individual's life. It can be internal, as when one believes he controls his own life, or it can be external, as when one believes his life is controlled by forces outside himself.

longitudinal study A study technique in which the same individual is examined over a long period or over a complete developmental stage.

love In the general sense an intense emotional response involving a feeling of affection toward a person or persons. According to John B. Watson, it, along with fear and rage, is one of the inherent or primary emotions.

M

marijuana (also spelled **marihuana**) A product derived from *Cannabis sativa* containing tetrahydrocannabinol (THC), which has sedative-hypnotic effects and induces the experience of a "high" and some release of tension.

maternal deprivation Disturbance of the mother-infant relationship in which the infant is rejected or abandoned, thus disrupting the usual physical and emotional mother-infant bonds.

matrix A framework or enclosure that gives form, meaning, or perspective to what lies within it.

maturation Developmental changes manifested in physiological functioning primarily due to heredity and constitution; organismic developments leading to further behavioral differentiation.

maturity The state of maximal function and integration of a single factor or a total person; also applied to age-related adequacy of development and performance.

median The measure of central tendency that has half of the cases above it and half below it; the fiftieth percentile.

mediating mechanisms Mechanisms assumed to intervene between a stimulus situation and a response and to explain the resulting behavior.

mediation According to Flavell, a sequence of intellectual development in which an earlier-developed item serves as a bridge to a later one. An example is the necessity of knowing how to count before one can understand that five coins remain the same no matter how they are arranged.

meiosis The process of cell division in which the daughter cells receive half the normal number of chromosomes, thus becoming gametes.

memory The mental activity or reliving past events. It can be considered as having two functions: the storage of experience for a period of time and the revival of that information at a later time.

menarche The first occurrence of menstruation.

Mendelian ratio The proportion of dominant to recessive phenotypes.

menopause The stage in a woman's life when menstruation ceases, usually in the late forties or early fifties.

menstrual age The age of a prenatal organism calculated from the first day of its mother's last menstrual period.

menstruation The cyclic discharge of blood and discarded uterine material that occurs in sexually mature females monthly from puberty to menopause, except during pregnancy.

mental age The knowledge of concepts or the ability to perform tasks appropriate to a certain chronological age as determined by specific tests. Mental age is thus a unit of mental measurement that, like IQ, is a relative measure. A child of any age whose tested performance equals that of an average 8-year-old is said to have a mental age of 96 months (8 × 12 months).

mental conflict See **conflict.**

mental hygiene The art and science of mental health; application of the principles and measures necessary for its preservation and promotion.

mental retardation A condition of mental deficiency, usually defined as being below 75 in IQ.

mentifact The ideas, customs, values, cultural heritage, and knowledge of a society.

mesoderm The middle of the three fundamental layers of the embryo that forms a basis for the development of bone, muscle structure, alimentary canal, and various digestive glands.

metabolism The physicochemical changes within the body for supplying, repairing, and building up (anabolism) and for breaking down and removing (catabolism).

method A logical and systematic way of studying a subject.

miscarriage The spontaneous expulsion from the uterus of a fetus less than twenty-eight weeks old.

modeling A principle and a process by which an individual learns by observing the behavior of others.

modification According to Flavell, a sequence in intellectual development in which the later-emerging behavior represents a differentiation or a generalization of a more stable form of an earlier skill. An example is children's coming to realize that quantities do not change if only certain perceptual properties do.

mongolism See **Down's syndrome.**

monozygotic (MZ) twins Twins who develop from the same fertilized ovum; identical twins. See also **dizygotic (DZ) twins.**

moral conduct A form of complex behavior involving three aspects: reasoning, feeling, and action.

moral development The nature and course of development of an individual's moral thoughts, feelings, and actions.

moral judgments Judgments as to the rightness or wrongness of actions.

morality A sense of what is right and wrong.

mores Social norms of behavior invested with great moral importance. They involve matters of health, sex, religion, property, and other activities that are deemed important.

Moro response The newborn infant's involuntary response to having his head fall backward—he stretches his arms outward and brings them together over his chest in a grasp gesture. A reflex that is most easily elicited during the infant's first three months of life.

morpheme A combination of phonemes that makes up a meaningful unit of a language.

mother fixation Deep identification with the mother to the virtual exclusion of other females as models or idols.

motivation A general term referring to factors within an organism that arouse and maintain behaviors directed toward satisfying some need or drive or toward accomplishing a goal.

motive Any factor that stimulates or contributes to a conscious effort toward a goal.

motor skill Any skill, such as walking or riding a bicycle, that requires muscular coordination.

mutagenic Altering the genetic structure of cells, which results in the production of new forms.

mutation Any change of a gene, usually from one allele to another.

myelin sheath A white fatty covering on many neural fibers that serves to channel impulses along fibers and to reduce the random spread of impulses across neurons.

myelinization The process by which neural fibers acquire a sheath of myelin.

N

naturalistic observation A form of study in which there is observation of behavior without any interference from the investigator.

nature The genetic-biological determinants used to explain developmental changes.

need Any physicochemical imbalance within the organism due to a lack of particular nutrients that arouses tension and drives. By analogy, psychological and personality needs are recognized. Primary or genetically determined needs and derived needs (generated by the operation of primary needs) are usually distinguished.

negation In the two-word stage of language development, the use of a negative construction to contradict or to avoid a misunderstanding.

negative pressure The first component of a baby's sucking. A vacuum is produced by closing the oral cavity in the back of the mouth, sealing the lips around the object to be sucked, and lowering the jaws.

negative reinforcement In operant conditioning the termination of an aversive stimulus as the result of a response. See also **positive reinforcement.**

negativism A primary mode of expressing one's own will by persistent refusal to respond to suggestions from parental and authority figures.

neonate A newborn infant.

neuromuscular Pertaining to both nerve and muscle, their structure and functions.

neurosis A mental disorder that prevents the victim from dealing effectively with reality; it is characterized by anxiety and partial impairment of functioning.

neurotic Mentally and emotionally disturbed; characterized by recurrent symptoms often caused by unconscious conflicts.

nonexistence In the two-word stage of language development, the expression of object disappearance or cessation of activity, as in ''all-gone ball.''

norm An outline that describes the development of an important attribute or skill and the approximate ages at which it appears in the average child.

normative Based on averages, standards, values, or norms.

novelty A possible factor in selective attention, involving a different or unique aspect of a stimulus.

nuclear family The family, rather typical in the United States, that consists of only parents and children. See also **extended family.**

nurture The impact of environmental factors on child growth and development. Nurture is usually contrasted with nature in describing development.

O

object identity In cognitive development, the understanding that an object remains the same even though it may undergo various transformations.

object permanence In cognitive development, the ability to recognize the continuing existence of an object that is no longer visible or audible. It is achieved at about eleven months by the majority of infants.

oedipal conflict According to Freud, a conflict that appears during the phallic stage. It consists of sexual attraction to the parent of the opposite sex and hostility toward the parent of the same sex.

ontogenesis Origin and development of an individual organism and its functions from conception to death. See also **phylogenesis.**

openness to experience According to Carl Rogers, the state in which every stimulus from the organism or the external environment is freely relayed through the individual without distortion by defenses.

operant conditioning A type of conditioning in which an organism's responses change as a result of the application of reinforcement or reward. It is based on the principle that organisms tend to engage in behavior that succeeds in producing desirable outcomes. Associated with B. F. Skinner, it is also called instrumental conditioning.

operation According to Jean Piaget, the mental action one performs in adapting to the environment.

oral stage In psychoanalytic theory the first stage of psychosexual development. In this stage gratification centers around the mouth and oral activities. See also **anal stage; genital stage; phallic stage.**

organismic age The average of all basic measures of a person's development at a particular time, such as carpal development, dental development, height, weight, and lung capacity. Often it includes achievement and educational, mental, and social age.

orgasm A period of intense physical and emotional sensation usually resulting from stimulation of the sexual organs, as in sexual intercourse, and generally followed in the male by the ejaculation of semen.

orienting reflex (OR) The initial response to any novel situation, maximizing its stimulus value.

orthogenesis Theory that the germ plasm is gradually modified by its own internal conditions and that the organism (and personality) has a sequential and specific, species-related course of development unless blocked.

ovaries The female reproductive organs in which egg cells or ova are produced.

overextension A generalization in the apparent meaning of a word so that it includes a number of dissimilar objects or events.

overregularization A kind of temporary error in language development in which the apparent attempt is to simplify or to make language more regular than it actually is. In English, this is likely to be shown when a child overregularizes the past tense of verbs ("breaked") and the plural forms of nouns ("foots").

ovum The female reproductive cell, sometimes called the egg; produced by one of two ovaries; the plural of ovum is ova.

P

parallel play The side-by-side play of two or more children with some independence of action yet heightened interest because of each other's presence.

parasocial speech In a young child, talking to one's self. This behavior, thought to be social in origin, occurs most frequently when others are listening or when the child encounters difficulties.

partial reinforcement In operant conditioning, the reinforcement of a selected response on an interval or ratio schedule.

parturition The act of bringing forth the young; delivery of the baby.

patellar reflex The involuntary response that occurs when the patellar tendon is tapped, commonly known as the knee-jerk reflex.

patterns of behavior Organized ways of behaving in certain situations.

peer Any individual of about one's same level of development and therefore equal for play or any other mode of association.

peer group The group of persons who constitute one's associates, usually of the same age and social status.

penis The male copulatory organ.

percentile The rank of a given measure in a theoretical group of 100. High rank is indicated by 99, meaning that the individual exceeds 99 out of 100 subjects in the measure concerned; middle average would be 50.

percept The unit of immediate knowledge of what one perceives.

perception The awareness of one's environment obtained through interpreting sensory data.

perfection-fulfillment theory The version of the fulfillment theory of personality maintaining that the personality force that takes the form of internalized but culturally universal ideals of what is good and meaningful in life. See also **personality, fulfillment theory of.**

perfectionism The tendency to demand frequently of oneself or others a maximal quality of achievement, without proper consideration of limiting factors.

personality An individual's characteristic pattern of behavior and thought, including an accordant self-concept and a set of traits consistent over time.

personality, fulfillment theory of The theory maintaining that maturity lies in the full expression of one psychological force, lying within the individual. See also **actualization-fulfillment theory; perfection-fulfillment theory.**

phallic stage In psychoanalytic theory the third stage of psychosexual development, during which gratification centers on the sex organs. The Oedipal conflict also manifests itself during this stage. See also **anal stage; genital stage; oral stage.**

phase (in development) A concept that indicates that development is continuous across the life span; the divisions are culturally determined.

phenotype The observable features of a person, including genetic traits and characteristics. See also **genotype.**

phenylketonuria (PKU) An error of metabolism caused by a recessive gene that gives rise to a deficiency in a certain enzyme. It can cause mental retardation if it is not caught in time. The inherited inability to metabolize phenylalanine a component of some foods. It occurs when the two recessive genes for PKU are paired.

phyletic Pertaining to species.

phyletic scale A line of descent from the lowest to the highest living species.

phylogenesis Evolution of traits and features common to a species or race; rehearsal of the prehistory of man. See also **ontogenesis.**

placebo An inert preparation often used as a control in experiments.

placenta The organ that forms in the uterine lining and through which the developing prenatal organism receives nourishment and discharges waste.

placing A reflex movement, which is most easily elicited during the first three months of an infant's life, consisting of a baby's lifting his foot onto a surface.

polygenic Indicates that several genes have an equal and cumulative effect in producing a trait.

positive reinforcement In operant conditioning the presentation of a rewarding consequence contingent on the desired response. See also **negative reinforcement.**

possession In the two-word stage of language development, the expression of ownership, as in "Daddy coat."

postconventional stage A stage of moral development in which the individual defines moral values and principles in relation to their validity and application rather than in relation to the dictates of society or of any particular group. It is characterized by self-chosen ethical principles that are comprehensive, universal, and consistent. See also **conventional stage; preconventional stage.**

postpartum Immediately after birth; the first week of life.

practice play Play in which the infant finds pleasure and satisfaction in repeating what he already knows.

precausal A kind of thinking in which a child maintains that some events are either completely or partly caused by psychological, subjective factors. An example is a child's ideas about the origins of dreams.

preconventional stage A stage of moral development in which the child responds to cultural rules and labels of good and bad only in terms of the physical or hedonistic consequences of obeying or disobeying the rules. See also **conventional stage; postconventional stage.**

premoral level The level of moral reasoning in which value is placed in physical acts and needs, not in persons or social standards.

prenatal Before birth; the stage of human development lasting from conception to birth.

preoperational stage According to Jean Piaget, the stage in a child's development occurring from 18 months to 7 years of age, during which he begins to encounter reality on the representational level. A subperiod of the representational period, which begins when children start to record experiences symbolically; involves the use of language to record experiences, and involves the appearance of the ability to think in terms of classes, numbers, and relationships. See also **concrete operational stage; formal operational stage; sensorimotor stage.**

principled level The level of moral reasoning in which value resides in self-chosen principles and standards that have a universal logical validity and can therefore be shared.

problem solving Thinking directed toward the goal of solving a problem.

productivity The ability to combine individual words into an unlimited number of sentences; one of the three formal properties of language.

projection A type of defense mechanism characterized by the tendency to blame others or external circumstances for one's own shortcomings or failures. May attribute to others his own qualities and traits, usually undesirable ones, such as hostility or dishonesty.

proximodistal development The progressive growth of the body parts in a center-to-periphery direction. See also **cephalocaudal development.** For example, a baby learns to control the movements of his shoulders before he can direct his arms or fingers.

psychoanalysis A method of psychotherapy developed by Sigmund Freud. Psychoanalysis has been subsequently extended to include the theoretical foundations of Jung, Adler, Rank, Sullivan, Horney, and their followers. It emphasizes the techniques of free association and transference and seeks to give the patient insight into his unconscious conflicts and motives.

psychoanalytic theory The basis of the school of psychology that emphasizes the development of emotions and their influence on behavior. It postulates a theory of the development and the structure of personality.

psychological growth Personality change; the increasing of inner differentiation and integration, the acquisition of autonomy and flexibility, and the development of new capacities for self-determination.

psychosexual development In Freudian theory, the sequence of stages through which the child passes, each characterized by the different erogenous zones from which the primary pleasure of the stage is derived. See also **anal stage; genital stage; oral stage; phallic stage.**

psychosis Severe mental disorder.

psychosomatic Pertaining to the effects of psychological and emotional stress on health and pathology; indicating that a phenomenon is both psychic and bodily.

psychotherapy The various techniques for the systematic application of psychological principles in the treatment of mental or emotional disturbance or disorder.

pubertal Pertaining to anything related to the developmental period of puberty.

puberty The period of life during which an individual's reproductive organs become functional and secondary sexual characteristics appear; the period characterized by rapid somatic growth and the assumption of adult traits or features.

pubescent Pertaining to an individual in the early part of puberty or to anyone who exhibits significant characteristics of that period of maturation.

pubic hair Hair that appears in the genital area during adolescence.

Q

questions In the two-word stage of language development, the transformation of all sentence types into questions by the use of rising intonation or question words, as in "Where ball?"

quickening The first fetal movements that a mother can readily perceive.

R

race An aggregate of persons who share a set of genetically transmitted and physically identifiable characteristics.

rage An emotional response involving intense anger and feelings of hostility. According to John B. Watson, it, along with fear and love, is one of the inherent or primary emotions.

rapid eye movement (REM) A type of eye movement that occurs during a certain period of sleep and that is accompanied by changes in respiratory, muscle, and brain-wave activity.

rationalization To rationalize; a dynamism of self-defense whereby a person justifies his activities or conduct by giving rational and acceptable, but usually untrue, reasons; the opposite of rational thought.

ratio reinforcement In operant conditioning, the partial reinforcement schedule in which a person is reinforced only after he has responded correctly a certain number of times.

reaction formation A defense mechanism involving the replacement in consciousness of an anxiety-inducing impulse or feeling by its opposite.

reaction range The limits set by genetic conditions on an individual's possible behavior.

reaction time The interval of time that elapses between the instant a stimulus is presented and the individual's reaction to it.

readiness The combination of growth development and experience that prepares an individual to acquire a skill or understanding with facility.

readiness, principle of Refers to the neurological and psychological disposition to attend to and assimilate a category of stimuli to which sensitivity and learning responses were previously lacking.

recall The form of remembering in which previously learned material is reproduced with a minimum of cues. See also **recognition.**

recessive gene A gene whose hereditary characteristics will not prevail when paired with a dominant gene.

recognition The form of remembering in which the previously learned material is merely recognized as such without actually being recalled. See also **recall.**

recurrence In the two-word stage of language development, the indication of the presence, absence, or repetition of things and actions, as in "book again."

reductionism A general point of view that holds that complex phenomena can be understood and explained by breaking them into simpler components.

reference groups The groups that affect in substantial measure the individual's personal goals and behavior. The groups to which he belongs and wants to belong.

reflex An unlearned or naturally occurring reaction to a stimulus.

regression Returning, because of frustrating experiences, to an earlier and less mature level of behavior and personality functioning than that previously achieved.

reinforcement In operant conditioning, the presentation or withdrawal of an event following a response, which increases or decreases the likelihood of that response occurring again.

releasing stimuli Those events that regularly evoke certain behavior in all members of a species; a key concept in ethological theories.

reliability The dependability and consistency of a measure, observation, or finding.

replication In studies, the attempt to repeat the essential features of an investigation and its findings.

representational level The level of cognitive development at which the child begins to use symbols as well as images.

representational skills Those cognitive skills or ways in which an individual represents and constructs an understanding of his world and the people, objects, and events in it.

representational stage A stage in Piaget's theory of cognitive development that begins with the preoperational and ends with the concrete-operational period.

repression In psychoanalytic theory the defense mechanism of forcefully rejecting unpleasant memories or impulses from conscious awareness.

resistance Opposition offered by a child or adolescent to the suggestions, orders, or regulations of the parents.

respiratory distress syndrome The lung condition (formerly called hyaline disease of the lungs) in which the fetus is unable to maintain necessary surfactin levels and dies.

retrolental fibroplasia Condition in which an opaque fibrous membrane develops on the posterior surface of the lens; occurs chiefly in premature infants subjected to high oxygen concentration.

reversibility The mental operation or understanding, according to Piaget's theory of cognitive development, in which one can think of a transformation that would reverse a sequence of events or restore the original condition.

Rh factor An agglutinizing factor present in the blood of most humans; when introduced into blood lacking the factor, antibodies form. Such a situation occurs when an organism with Rh-positive blood inherited from its father resides within a mother whose blood is Rh negative. A first-born child is rarely affected, but subsequent children may require transfusions.

ribonucleic acid (RNA) RNA molecules playing the role of a messenger or transfer agent for vital DNA functions by lining up amino acids in ribosomes to form proteins according to a particular sequence.

rickets The condition caused by a calcium deficiency during infancy and childhood and characterized by the softening and malformation of the bones.

role See **sex roles; social role.**

role conflict The situation in which a person is expected to play two or more roles that he cannot integrate into his self-system.

role taking The ability to take the role or point of view of another person; a requirement in cognitive and other forms of development.

rooting reflex A reflex that is most easily elicited during the baby's first two weeks of life, consisting of the baby turning his head in the direction of any object that gently stimulates the corner of his mouth; the newborn infant's involuntary movement of his mouth toward any source of stimulation in the mouth area.

rote learning Memorization in which the task is to commit the various components of the material to memory with little or no understanding, requiring only the ability to later reproduce what has been learned in the exact form in which it was presented.

rubella German measles. Rubella in a pregnant woman can cause damage to the developing child if she contracts it during the first three months of pregnancy.

S

schedules of reinforcement In operant conditioning, the timetables for reinforcing behavior; they have different effects on the rate of responding.

schemes Piaget's term for action patterns that are built up and coordinated throughout the course of cognitive development. In the infant, they are like concepts without words. Throughout development, such schemes are presumed to be involved in the acquisition and structuring of knowledge.

schizophrenia A form of psychosis in which the patient becomes withdrawn and apathetic. Hallucinations and delusions are common.

sebaceous Fatty, oily; sebaceous glands secrete oily matter for lubricating hair and skin.

secondary sex characteristics Physical characteristics that appear in humans around the age of puberty and that are sex differentiated but not necessary for sexual reproduction. Such characteristics include breast development and the appearance of pubic hair in girls and the appearance of facial and pubic hair, enlargement of the penis, and deepening of the voice in boys.

self-actualization According to Abraham Maslow, the need to develop one's true nature and fulfill one's potentialities; the human tendency to realize one's full potential in work and love. It develops after the basic needs of food, security, and esteem are met.

self-concept The individual's awareness of and identification with his or her organism, cognitive powers, and modes of conduct and performance, accompanied by specific attitudes toward them.

self-demand feeding A feeding schedule in which a baby is fed according to when he is hungry, not according to a schedule designed by others.

self-direction Independent selection of goals and of the proper means and actions to attain them.

self-esteem The amount and quality of the regard that a person has toward himself.

self-realization The lifelong process of unhampered development marked by self-direction and responses in terms of one's capabilities or potentialities.

self-regulation The regulation of one's own conduct.

semanticity The learning of the meaning of words, and the process of communicating meaning. One of the three formal properties of language.

semen The fluid produced by the male testes that contains the spermatozoa.

senescence The period of old age.

senility Significant loss of physical and cognitive functions in old age or preceding it.

sensation A necessary aspect for cognitive development involving the reception, through the various sense organs, of stimulation from the external world.

sensitive periods Periods of development during which an organism is most likely to be susceptible to a particular influence.

sensorimotor reflexes The basic reflex repertoire with which the infant is born—the Moro response, rooting reflex, patellar reflex, and so on.

sensorimotor stage According to Jean Piaget, the stage in a child's cognitive development during which he is essentially involved in perfecting his contact with the objects that surround him. It generally occurs from birth to 2 years of age. It is characterized by the development of sensory and motor functions and by the infant's coming to know the world as a result of interacting with and affecting it. See also **concrete operational stage; formal operational stage; preoperational stage.**

sentiment An affective and cognitive disposition to react in a certain way toward a particular value, object, or person.

separation anxiety The distinctly negative reaction of an infant to separation and his attempts to regain contact with his attachment figure.

sequence (in development) A concept used to explain the relationship among developmental changes in behavior, indicating that some behaviors precede others in a meaningfully related way.

sex roles Patterns of behavior deemed appropriate to each sex by society.

sex-role stereotypes Simplified fixed concepts about the behaviors and traits typical of each sex.

sex typing The learning of behavior patterns appropriate to the sex of the person, for example, acquisition of masculine behavior traits for a boy.

shame A negative feeling response that is a reaction to the disapproval of others.

sibling One of two or more offspring of the same parents; a brother or sister.

sickle cell anemia A form of anemia (a blood condition) in which abnormal red blood corpuscles of crescent shape are present.

skeletal age A measure of the maturity of the skeleton, determined by the degree of ossification of bone structures.

skelic index The index that measures the ratio of lower limb length to sitting height.

small-for-dates The condition in which a baby is underweight for his gestational age.

social age Age measured in terms of an individual's social habits relative to society's expectations.

social class A social stratum or category differentiated from other such strata on the basis of such economic considerations as wealth, occupation, and property ownership. See also **socioeconomic class.**

social deprivation The lack of economic, educational, and cultural opportunities.

social role A set of expectations or evaluative standards associated with an individual or a position.

social-learning theory A set of concepts and principles from behavior learning theory, frequently used in describing and explaining personality characteristics and social behavior.

socialization A progressive development in relating and integrating oneself with others, especially parents, peers, and groups; the process of psychologically growing into a society, in which an individual acquires the behaviors, attitudes, values, and roles expected of him.

socioeconomic class A grouping of people on a predetermined scale of prestige according to their social and economic status. Such status is based on many factors, including nature of occupation, kind of income, moral values, family genealogy, social relationships, area of residence, and education. See also **social class.**

sociogram A graphic representation of social preferences within a group; a mapping of preferences and rejections in social behavior.

sociometric analysis A method for charting how often a child is chosen by his peers as a preferred friend or companion.

sociometry The graphical or columnar representation of interpersonal attractions or avoidances in group situations. The study of reactions and avoidances between individual members of a social group. The study of interpersonal relationships—person to person, person to group, and group to group—pursued through tabulations or the plotting of lines of attraction, indifference, or dislike.

somatic Pertaining to the body or organism.

sperm The male germ cell, or spermatozoon, containing chromosomes, DNA, RNA, protein, and other substances.

spermatozoon A single sperm cell.

spontaneous abortion The expulsion, from the uterus, of a fetus older than twenty-eight weeks.

standard deviation A statistical technique for expressing the extent of variation of a group of scores from the mean. It is a distance on a curve of probability, of which the first unit in both directions from the mean includes 68.3% of the total group of scores. About 99.7% of the scores are within three standard deviations in each direction from the mean.

stage (in development) A concept used to explain the orderly relationship among developmental changes in behavior and indicating that the organization of behavior is qualitatively different from one stage to the next.

startle response A reaction to stimuli in infants outwardly characterized by eye widening, jaw dropping, cooing, squealing, or crying and inwardly characterized by changes in heart rate, respiration, and galvanic skin potential.

stepping A reflex movement, which is most easily elicited during the infant's first two weeks of life, that consists of straightening the legs out at the knees and hip, as if to stand, when the infant is held with his feet touching a surface.

stimulus Any form of environmental energy capable of affecting the organism.

stimulus generalization A process or phenomenon in which a response learned in reaction to one stimulus can be elicited by separate but similar stimuli.

strain The condition within a system or organ exposed to stress, for example, overactivity or deprivation.

stranger anxiety The negative response and withdrawal that occurs in reaction to strangers, usually developing a month or two after specific attachments begin.

sublimation A dynamism of self-defense whereby the energies of a basic, socially unacceptable drive are redirected into a higher and socially more acceptable plane of expression. The altering, in socially acceptable ways, of forbidden impulses. According to Freud, it is one of the processes important in the development of rational behavior.

substitution According to Flavell, a sequence in intellectual development in which the later-emerging item replaces the earlier one completely or almost completely. An example is children's recognition of the true nature of their dreams.

successive approximations In operant conditioning, a procedure in which behaviors that resemble more and more closely the final desired response are reinforced.

superego A psychoanalytic term that refers to the part of the personality structure that is built up by early parent-child relationships and helps the ego to enforce the control of primitive instinctual urges of the id; later functions as a moral force; analogous to an early form of conscience. An aspect of personality, in Freud's theory, defined as the conscience.

surfactin The liquid that coats the air sacs of the lungs and permits them to transmit oxygen from the air to the blood.

surrogate mother Someone or something that takes the place of a mother in an organism's life.

symbolic play Play that becomes more symbolic and complex as the ability to imagine and pretend develops.

syphilis A venereal disease due to systemic infection with treponema pallidum.

T

temperament The general nature, behavioral style, or characteristic mood of the individual; usually thought to have a physical or constitutional basis.

tension A state of acute need, deprivation, fear, apprehension, and so on that keeps an organism or certain organs in a state of intensified activity, for example, adrenal glands.

teratogenic Capable of causing organic malformation.

term (prenatal development) The gestational age of 266 days from conception. Formerly, babies born before term were considered premature.

terminal illness A disease that results in death.

testes The male reproductive organs in which spermatozoa are manufactured; testicles.

thalidomide A drug once used by women during pregnancy to assuage morning sickness; it caused birth defects in the limbs of children.

theory (developmental) A set of logically related statements about the nature of development that help psychologists understand, predict, and explain human behavior.

thinking The active process of conceptualization, involving integrating percepts, grasping relationships, and asking further questions.

thumb opposition The ability to oppose the thumb to the fingers and to bring the fingertips in contact with the ball of the thumb.

thyroxine A hormone produced by the thyroid gland; it regulates metabolism.

toddler The child between the ages of about 15 and 30 months.

totalism Defined by Erikson as an organization of one's self-concept that has rigid, absolute, and arbitrary boundaries.

toxemia Blood poisoning. The presence of poisonous or infective matters in the bloodstream.

tracking The act of following an object with one's eye.

trait A distinctive and enduring characteristic of a person or his behavior.

transfer A process or phenomenon in which the learning of one task results in improvement of learning or performance in another related, but different, task.

transitivity A concept that requires the joining together of two or more instances of an abstract relation; for example, if A is larger than B and B is larger than C, then A is larger than C.

trauma Any somatic or psychological damage to the individual, including stressful and terrifying experiences.

trimester A period of approximately three months; often used in discussing pregnancy.

Turner's syndrome A congenital physical condition resulting from the individual's having only one X chromosome and no Y chromosomes. The afflicted individual looks like an immature female and is characterized by a lack of reproductive organs, abnormal shortness, and mental retardation.

U

umbilical cord The cord that connects the prenatal organism with the placenta. The embryo receives nourishment from the blood that is supplied by the arteries within the cord that connects the placenta and the fetus.

unconditioned reflex In classical conditioning, one of

two kinds of reflexes; it is inborn and occurs naturally to a stimulus.

unconscious The area of motivational structure and thought process of which the person is not directly aware.

unconscious impulses In Freud's theory, those irrational impulses that reside in the id and that the individual is unaware of.

uniformism A concept indicating immersion into the peer group and the acceptance of its norms as infallible and regulatory.

universal principles Moral propositions that are the end point of an unchanging ethical developmental sequence. They are of an absolute nature as opposed to beliefs or standards developed or determined by a reasoning approach to morality.

uterus The female organ in which the prenatal organism develops and is nourished prior to birth.

V

vagina The female genital canal (passage) extending from the uterus to the vulva. It is a copulatory organ.

valence In gestalt psychology, a term referring to the subjective appraisal of an object or situation in the life space, by virtue of which the object is sought (positive valence) or avoided (negative valence). The term was introduced by K. Lewin.

value The worth or excellence found in a qualitative appraisal of an object by reliance on emotional and rational standards of the individual or of selected reference groups.

variability Variations due to individual differences as well as other sources of influence.

variables Those factors in an investigation that can vary in quantity or magnitude, or in some qualitative aspect, and that may or may not affect the results of the investigation.

vernix The white greasy material that covers and lubricates the newborn for passage through the birth canal.

vernix caseosa A sebaceous deposit covering the fetus due to secretions of skin glands.

viability Capability for maintaining life. A fetus is viable after twenty-eight weeks, since it can then usually be kept alive if born prematurely.

visual accommodation The ability to alternate focus for objects at different distances.

vital capacity The air-holding capacity of the lungs.

vital capacity age (VA) Relationship between lung capacity and age.

W

Wechsler Adult Intelligence Scale A widely used individual intelligence test.

weltanschauung A configuration of attitudes and views toward all dimensions of reality, both material and metaphysical; key tenets of a philosophy of life.

Wetzel grid A graphical representation of the longitudinal development of an individual in height and weight, devised by N. C. Wetzel. Rather than making interpersonal comparisons, as on height-weight charts, the grid takes into account variations in basic body build.

womb See **uterus**.

X

X chromosome A chromosome that, when paired with another X chromosome, programs a gamete to develop as a female.

Y

Y chromosome A chromosome that determines an individual will be male.

yolk sac A nonfunctional sac that forms during the germinal period of human prenatal development.

youth A stage of the human life cycle experienced by persons who are psychologically and physically mature but who are not sociologically mature, in that they have not made any commitments to career or family. This stage intervenes between adolescence and adulthood.

Z

zygote A new individual formed by the union of male and female gametes; the resultant globule of cells during the first phase of prenatal development after conception and lasting approximately two weeks.

REFERENCES

Developmental psychology today. Del Mar, Calif: CRM Books, 1971.

English, H. B., & English, A. C. *A comprehensive dictionary of psychological and psychoanalytical terms.* New York: David McKay Co., Inc., 1958.

Hinsie, L. E., & Campbell, R. J. *Psychiatric dictionary* (3rd ed.). New York: Oxford University Press, Inc., 1960.

Taber, C. W. *Taber's cyclopedic medical dictionary* (11th ed.). Philadelphia: F. A. Davis Co., 1970.

Author index

Subject index

Visual-motor organization and perception, fine, 183-185
Vitamin D, 154
Vocabulary; *see also* Speech
  adolescence and, 327
  childhood and
    early, 182-183
    late, 262-263
    middle, 226
  later adulthood and, 449, 451
Vocalization; *see also* Speech
  development of, 136-137
  reflexive, 136
Vocations; *see* Careers
Voice
  aging and, 438
  changes in, 281-282
Volume concepts, 222
Voluntary nerves, 30
Vowel sounds, 136

W

WAIS; *see* Wechsler Adult Intelligence Scale
Walking, 124-125
  sequence of, 114
Walking reflex, 111
Watermelon theory, 24, 25
Wechsler Adult Intelligence Scale, 451
Weight
  adolescence and, 309-311
  of adults, 279, 310, 348
  childhood and
    early, 167
    late, 247, 248
    middle, 209
  concepts of, 222
  of newborn, 105
    low, 91-93
    maternal smoking and, 89

Weight—cont'd.
  pregnancy and, 85
Weight-shift balance, 131, 180
Well-being, physical and emotional, 8-10
Wetting, 152
Wharton's jelly, 64
Widows and widowers, 462, 475-476
  as parents, 234
Wisdom teeth, 311
Withdrawal mechanisms, 283
Women; *see also* Sex
  menopause and, 417-421
  singlehood and, 393
  working, 370, 415-416
Work, production rates for quality, 415; *see also* Careers
Work ethics, 359
Working mothers, 236
World, conception of, 221
Worries
  adolescence and, 329
  late childhood and, 267
  middle age and, 418-421
Wrist bones, 248
Wrong and right; *see* Moral development

X

X cell, 57

Y

Y cell, 57
Yolk sac, 61, 63
Youth; *see* Adolescence; Adulthood, emerging
Youth culture, 361-363, 401-402
Youth market, 337-339

Z

Zygote, 61-62

1. family

1 mon stares

2 mon attend to care giver

3 mon attend to a noise or movt

4 mon like

5 mon may attend father/sibling

7 mon - peek-a-boo
doubt strangers

8 mon more aggressive

10 mon dont like to be alone

1-6 weeks reflexive

6-7 week babbling cooing

6-7 months lalling & imperfect imitation

7-8 repeat sounds. na-na

9-10 mons.

echolalia

10-12 mon true speech

12-18 mon use true speech

18 mon 10 words

2 years 50 words

1 mon
excitement
distress

2 mon
delight

3-6 mon
anger
fear
disgust

18 mon fear of strangers discrimination